CCH INCORPORATED
4025 West Peterson Ave.
Chicago, IL 60646-6085

W9-DCB-654

TAX ★★★ 2000

Order your copies TODAY!

Get the
most complete
resources available

BY PHONE:
Call 1 800 248 3248
Priority Code: GCY1047

BY FAX:
1 800 224 8299

For the latest news on tax legislation developments, please visit the CCH Tax Website at tax.cch.com

NO POSTAGE
NECESSARY
IF MAILED
IN THE
UNITED STATES

BUSINESS REPLY MAIL
FIRST-CLASS MAIL   PERMIT #57   CHICAGO, ILLINOIS

POSTAGE WILL BE PAID BY ADDRESSEE

CCH INCORPORATED
PO BOX 5490
CHICAGO IL   60680-9808

Get expert analysis of the 2000 Tax Legislation and other new developments.
Order today and put these references to work for you!

Tax Legislation 2000: Law, Explanation and Analysis
This indispensable reference includes practical guidance, planning strategies and hands-on advice on the 2000 tax legislation changes. Provides full text coverage of added, amended or repealed Code sections with controlling committee reports. CCH's expert analysis clarifies complicated tax provisions contained in the 2000 tax legislation, and provides sound advice on how various taxpayer groups and situations are affected. The law is arranged in Code section order, using italicized type for each changed section, so you can quickly see the specific changes to the law. *Prices: 1-4 copies, $37.50 ea., 5-9, $34.00 ea., 10-24, $30.00 ea., 25-49, $27.00 ea. Est. pub.: Jan. 2001, about 250 pages, 6" x 9".* **Book #: 04780101**

ADDITIONAL TAX RESOURCES:

CCH Analysis of Top Tax Issues for 2001 — Return Preparation and Planning Guide
Identifies the top tax developments for 2000, analyzing each development within the context of the applicable business and personal transactions that may be affected. Also examines the impact on tax return preparation for the April 15, 2001 deadline. *Prices: 1-4 copies, $45.00 ea., 5-9, $40.00 ea., 10-24, $36.00 ea., 25-49, $33.00 ea. Est. pub.: Jan. 2001, about 400 pages, 6" x 9".* **Book #: 04972101**

Income Tax Regulations—As of January 1, 2001
The full, official text of Treasury Department interpretation of the Internal Revenue Code in six comprehensive volumes. *Prices: 1-4 sets, $109.00 ea., 5-9, $99.00 ea., 10-24, $91.00 ea., 25-49, $84.00 ea. Est. pub.: March 2001, about 11,650 pages in six volumes, 6 1/4" x 9 1/8".* **Book #: 04953101**

2001 U.S. Master Tax Guide®—84th Edition
The leading guide in the industry! Reflects all pertinent federal tax law changes, to date of publication, and provides fast, reliable answers to questions affecting personal and business income taxes. *Prices: 1-4 copies, $49.50 ea., 5-9, $45.50 ea., 10-24, $41.50 ea., 25-49, $37.50 ea. Pub.: Nov. 2000, 720 pages, 5 7/8" x 9".* **Book #: 05951101**

Earn CPE credit online! Visit the CCH LearningCenter at http://tax.cch.com/learningcenter

Qty.	Standing Order	Item
_____	❏	*Tax 2000: Law, Explanation and Analysis (04780101)*
_____	❏	*CCH Analysis of Top Tax Issues for 2001 (04972101)*
_____	❏	*Income Tax Regulations (04953101)*
_____	❏	*2001 U.S. Master Tax Guide (05951101)*

Yes! Please place my order today!

BILLING INFORMATION

Charge my ❏ VISA   ❏ AMEX   ❏ MasterCard

Card # _____ Exp. Date _____

Signature _____
(required to process order)

BY PHONE:
Call 1 800 248 3248
Priority Code: GCY1047

SHIPPING INFORMATION

Ship via (check one):   ❏ UPS or ground parcel   ❏ First Class

BY FAX:
1 800 224 8299

Name & Title _____

Firm _____

Address _____

City _____ State _____ ZIP _____

CCH Account # _____

Phone # _____

Applicable shipping, handling and sales/use tax will be added to each order.
Prices quoted apply only in the U.S. and are subject to change.

MP210001-GCY1047

2000
Tax Legislation

Law,
Explanation
and Analysis

Tax Provisions of:

**FSC Repeal and Extraterritorial
Income Exclusion Act of 2000**

Installment Tax Correction Act of 2000

**Community Renewal Tax Relief Act of 2000,
Including Technical Corrections**

CCH INCORPORATED
Chicago

This publication is designed to provide accurate and authoritative information in regard to the subject matter covered. It is sold with the understanding that the publisher is not engaged in rendering legal, accounting, or other professional service. If legal advice or other expert assistance is required, the services of a competent professional person should be sought.

ISBN 0-8080-0586-3

©2001, **CCH** INCORPORATED

4025 W. Peterson Ave.
Chicago, IL 60646-6085
1 800 248 3248
http://www.cch.com

No claim is made to original government works; however, within this Product or Publication, the following are subject to CCH's copyright: (1) the gathering, compilation, and arrangement of such government materials; (2) the magnetic translation and digital conversion of data, if applicable; (3) the historical, statutory and other notes and references; and (4) the commentary and other materials.

All Rights Reserved
Printed in the United States of America

106th Congress Ends with Triple Play
for Tax Professionals

With a long partisan budget battle between the White House and Congress which at times threatened to "go into extra innings" and a hotly contested presidential election, it seemed highly unlikely that any new tax legislation would emerge in 2000. Yet, despite this highly charged political environment, Democrats and Republicans were able to put aside their differences, and "late in the bottom of the ninth" of the 106th Congress, enact two interesting pieces of tax legislation in the closing weeks of 2000. This came on the heals of a much awaited repeal of the Internal Revenue Code's foreign sales corporation provisions, which was enacted a few weeks earlier.

On December 21, 2000, President Clinton signed into law the Consolidated Appropriations Act, 2001 (P.L. 106-554), which includes the Community Renewal Tax Relief Act of 2000. Contained within this Act are a number of tax-related provisions—most notably several community renewal measures designed to spur investment in low and moderate-income, rural and urban communities. In addition, this Act includes an extension of tax-favored Medical Savings Accounts, several administrative and procedural provisions, and technical corrections of prior laws.

The following week, on December 28, the Installment Tax Correction Act of 2000 (P.L. 106-573) was also signed into law by President Clinton. This Act repeals controversial aspects of the Ticket to Work and Work Incentives Improvement Act of 1999 (P.L. 106-170), which disallowed use of the installment method of accounting for accrual-method taxpayers. Both the House and Senate passed this measure unanimously.

In this volume, CCH is providing tax professionals with a single integrated law and explanatory reference that addresses this late session legislation. In addition, we have included complete coverage of the FSC Repeal and Extraterritorial Income Exclusion Act of 2000 (P.L. 106-519), which was signed into law by President Clinton on November 15, 2000. Taken as a whole, this work represents the most comprehensive and timely analysis available of the over 60 new tax provisions that were passed in the final days of the 106th Congress.

Mark Hevrdejs

Executive Editor

Federal and State Tax Group

January 2001

OUTSIDE CONTRIBUTORS

Ben G. Baldwin
Baldwin Financial Systems, Inc.
Northbrook, Illinois

Neal J. Block
Baker & McKenzie
Chicago, Illinois

Prof. Karen V. Kole
Valpariso University, School of Law
Valpariso, Indiana

Charles R. Levun
Levun Goodman & Cohen
Northbrook, Illinois

Vincent J. O'Brien
Vincent J. O'Brien, CPA, P.C.
Lynbrook, New York

CCH EDITORIAL STAFF

Karen Heslop, J.D.
Project Coordinator

Washington News Division

Jeff Carlson
Paula Cruickshank
Larry Holbrook
Catherine Hubbard

Rosalyn Johns
Joyce Mutcherson-Ridley
Cynthia A. Zirkle, C.P.A.

Analysis

Mark A. Luscombe, J.D., LL.M., C.P.A.

George G. Jones, J.D., LL.M.

Explanations

Karin Old, J.D.

Ray G. Suelzer, Jr., J.D., LL.M.
Coordinating Editors

Maureen C. Bornstein, J.D.
Anne E. Bowker, J.D.
Mildred Carter, J.D.
Tom Cody, J.D., LL.M., M.B.A.
Laurel Gershon, J.D., LL.M.
Bruno L. Graziano, J.D., M.S.A.
Thomas H. Kabaker, J.D.
Mary Krackenberger, J.D.
Laura M. Lowe, J.D.
Michael A. Luster, J.D., LL.M.
Tracy Gaspardo Mortenson, J.D., C.P.A.

John J. Mueller, J.D., LL.M.
Jean T. Nakamoto, J.D.
Jerome Nestor, J.D., C.P.A., M.B.A.
Karen A. Notaro, J.D., LL.M.
Marie T. O'Donnell, J.D., C.P.A.
David E. Origenes, J.D.
Lawrence A. Perlman, J.D., LL.M., C.P.A.
John W. Roth, Jr., J.D., LL.M.
Carolyn M. Schiess, J.D.
Marcia Richards Suelzer, J.D.
Kenneth L. Swanson, J.D., LL.M.

Internal Revenue Code

Karen J. Elsner, C.P.A.
Coordinating Editor

Kathleen M. Higgins
Anita Nagelis, J.D.

Warren L. Rosenbloom
Christine C. Wyllie

Committee Reports

Sheri Miller, J.D.

Dawn Wagner, J.D.
Coordinating Editors

Ellen Mitchell

Catherine Olson

Effective Dates

Katherine Baransky, J.D.
Coordinating Editor

Richard Waldinger, J.D.

Production

Mary Ellen Guth

Diana Roozeboom
Production Coordinators

Holly J. Porter
Jennifer Schencker
Sandy Silverman

Eileen Slivka
Monika Stefan

Editorial Assistants

Tara Fenske
Coordinator

Rebecca Little

David Turpin

Electronic Release Development

David Schuster
Coordinator

Doug Bretschneider
Kay Harris, J.D.

Molly Munson
Christopher Zwirek

How to Use

¶ 1

CCH's *2000 Tax Legislation: Law, Explanation and Analysis* provides you with CCH explanations and analysis of the FSC Repeal and Extraterritorial Income Exclusion Act of 2000 (P.L. 106-519), the Community Renewal Tax Relief Act of 2000 (P.L. 106-554) and the Installment Tax Correction Act of 2000 (P.L. 106-573). In conjunction with CCH editors, practitioners and academics have infused the explanations in this text with practical guidance and planning strategies, and warn of latent pitfalls contained in these new legislative packages. Included in this text are the provisions of the Internal Revenue Code, as amended, added or repealed by the new laws, and the relevant controlling Committee Reports.

Here is a guide to the numerous features provided in this text:

CCH EXPLANATIONS

CCH-prepared explanations of the FSC Repeal and Extraterritorial Income Exclusion Act of 2000, the Community Renewal Tax Relief Act of 2000 and the Installment Tax Correction Act of 2000 are arranged according to subject matter for ease of use. The material is also flagged as either "FSC Repeal," "Community Renewal Tax Relief," "Technical Correction," or "Installment Tax Correction Act" provision. Each explanation includes a discussion of background or prior law that helps to put into perspective the corrections and changes introduced by the various new tax acts.

Incorporated throughout the explanations is expert commentary provided by practitioners and academics. This commentary highlights planning opportunities and strategies engendered by the new laws and identifies how to avoid pitfalls and hazards in the legislative language.

Each explanation chapter is preceded by a chapter table of contents listing the chapter contents. A detailed table of contents for the entire explanation portion of the LAW, EXPLANATION AND ANALYSIS text is also included for easy identification of subject matter.

Each individually numbered explanation paragraph ends with the applicable effective date of the provision discussed. The effective date is preceded by a ★ symbol for easy reference.

The explanation paragraphs are followed by boldface amendment captions which (1) identify the Act Section of the applicable Act and the Code Section added, amended, or repealed and (2) provide cross references to the law and to the reproduced controlling Committee Reports. *The CCH explanations begin at ¶ 105.*

INDEX. Because the topical or subject matter approach to new legislation is usually the easiest to navigate, you may also access the material in the CCH explanations through the extensive Index. The Index begins at *page 371*. The Index is also available on the electronic version of this publication.

AMENDED CODE PROVISIONS

CCH has reflected the changes to the Internal Revenue Code made by the FSC Repeal and Extraterritorial Income Exclusion Act of 2000, the Community Renewal Tax Relief Act of 2000 and the Installment Tax Correction Act of 2000 in the "Law Added, Amended or Repealed" provisions. Deleted Code material or the text of the Code provision prior to amendment appears in the Amendment Notes following each reconstructed Code provision. *Any changed or added portion is set out in italics.*

The applicable effective date for each Amendment Note is set out in boldface type. Preceding each set of amendment notes, CCH provides references to (1) the corresponding controlling Committee Reports and (2) the CCH explanation related to that amended, added, or repealed Code provision. Subscribers to the electronic product can link to the related explanation or Committee Report material using these references. *The text of the Code begins at ¶ 5001.*

NON-CODE PROVISIONS

The sections of the Community Renewal Tax Relief Act of 2000 that do *not* amend the Internal Revenue Code appear in full text in Act Section order following the "Law Added, Amended or Repealed" section of the text. Included is the text of Act Sections that amend prior tax acts, such as the Tax and Trade Extension Act of 1999 (P.L. 106-170), the IRS Restructuring and Reform Act of 1998 (P.L. 105-206), Taxpayer Relief Act of 1997 (P.L. 105-34) and the Balanced Budget Act of 1997 (P.L. 105-33). *The text of these provisions appears in Act Section order beginning at ¶ 7001.*

COMMITTEE REPORTS

The Controlling Committee Reports officially explain the intent of Congress regarding the provisions in the FSC Repeal and Extraterritorial Income Exclusion Act of 2000 (P.L. 106-519) and the Community Renewal Tax Relief Act of 2000 (P.L. 106-554). There were no Committee Reports for the Installment Tax Correction Act of 2000 as this measure was passed as introduced under a suspension of the rules. At the end of the Committee Report text, CCH provides a caption line that includes references to the corresponding explanation and Code provisions. Subscribers to the electronic version can link from these references to the corresponding material. *These Controlling Committee Reports appear in Act Section order beginning at ¶ 10,001.*

EFFECTIVE DATES

A table listing the major effective dates provides you with a reference bridge between Code Sections and Act Sections and indicates the retroactive or prospective nature of the laws explained. *These effective date tables begin at ¶ 20,001.*

SPECIAL FINDING DEVICES

A table cross-referencing Code Sections to the CCH explanations is included *(see ¶ 25,001)*. Other tables include Code Sections added, amended, or repealed *(see ¶ 25,005)*, provisions of other acts that were amended *(see ¶ 25,010)*, Act Sections not amending Internal Revenue Code Sections *(see ¶ 25,015)*, and Act Sections amending Code Sections *(see ¶ 25,020)*, so that you can immediately determine whether a provision in which you are interested is affected. In addition, a listing of clerical amendments and the Code sections they impact is provided *(see ¶ 30,050)*.

A detailed table of contents for the entire LAW, EXPLANATION AND ANALYSIS text is also included for easy identification of subject matter.

¶ 1

11

Table of Contents

Detailed Table of Contents

CHAPTER 1. COMMUNITY RENEWAL

CHAPTER 2. BUSINESS AND INVESTMENT

CHAPTER 3. PROCEDURE AND ADMINISTRATION

CHAPTER 4. SPECIAL BUSINESS ENTITIES

Chapter 1

Community Renewal

RENEWAL COMMUNITIES

Designation and Treatment of Renewal Communities

¶ 105

Background

Since 1994, areas in economically depressed sections of the country have been designated as empowerment zones (Code Sec. 1391). A number of tax incentives are available to taxpayers who operate businesses in these areas. The tax breaks include a wage-based employment credit that motivates employers to hire disadvantaged workers and youth living in the community, increased section 179 deductions to boost investment in assets used in the targeted areas, and tax-exempt bond financing benefits (Code Secs. 1394, 1396 and 1397A). Other areas have been designated as enterprise communities but receive more limited tax incentives than the empowerment zones.

The empowerment zones were selected from areas nominated by local and state governments. Applications for designation as an empowerment zone had to demonstrate that the nominated area satisfied eligibility criteria, had to include a strategic plan, and had to provide other information (Code Sec. 1391(e) and (f)). Some of the eligibility criteria that were evaluated in selecting the empowerment zones include the nominated area's population, general economic distress, size, and poverty rate (Code Sec. 1392(a)).

The current empowerment zones were designated in stages. The zones designated in each stage were selected based on different criteria, have different periods of applicability, and receive somewhat different tax benefits. In Round I, the Secretary of Housing and Urban Development (HUD) designated six urban empowerment zones and the Secretary of Agriculture designated three rural empowerment zones, effective December 21, 1994. Sixty-five urban and 30 rural enterprise

Background

communities were also designated. Two additional urban empowerment zones were later designated that are considered Round I empowerment zones but are effective January 1, 2000 (Code Sec. 1391(b)).

For the Round II designations effective December 31, 1998, the Secretary of HUD designated 15 additional urban empowerment zones and the Secretary of Agriculture designated five more rural empowerment zones (Code Sec. 1391(g)(1)). These Round II empowerment zones were selected under different eligibility criteria than the Round I empowerment zones and are not entitled to the empowerment zone employment credit (Code Secs. 1391(g)(3) and 1396(e)).

Designations of empowerment zones and enterprise communities will generally remain in effect until the end of the 10th calendar year beginning on or after the date of designation. However, the designation may end earlier on the termination date provided by the state and local governments in their nomination or on the date the Secretary of HUD or Agriculture revokes the designation (Code Sec. 1391(d)(1)).

Community Renewal Tax Relief Act Impact

Renewal communities mimic enterprise zones.—Up to 40 new areas called "renewal communities" will be designated to receive tax breaks similar to the present empowerment zones (see ¶ 107–¶ 125). As in the case of empowerment zones, the criteria for selection as a renewal community include high rates of poverty and unemployment in the area. The selection of renewal communities will be handled primarily by the Secretaries of Housing and Urban Development (HUD) and Agriculture with input from other government officials (Code Sec. 1400E, as added by the Community Renewal Tax Relief Act of 2000).

Renewal community defined. Obtaining status as a renewal community is a two-step process. First, the area must be nominated for designation as a renewal community by one or more local governments and the state or states in which it is located (Code Sec. 1400E(a)(1)(A), as added by the 2000 Act). A local government is any county, city, town, township, parish, village, or other general purpose political subdivision of a state, and any combination of those political subdivisions that is recognized by the Secretary of HUD (Code Sec. 1400E(f)(2), as added by the 2000 Act). If the nominated area is on an Indian reservation, then the reservation governing body is treated as both the state and local governments for the area (Code Sec. 1400E(a)(5), as added by the 2000 Act).

Second, the nominated area must be designated as a renewal community by the Secretary of HUD. In making the decision, the HUD Secretary must consult with the Secretaries of Agriculture, Commerce, Labor, and Treasury, the Director of the Office of Management and Budget (OMB), and the Administrator of the Small Business Administration (SBA). If the area is on an Indian reservation, the Secretary of the Interior must also be included in the consultation (Code Sec. 1400E(a)(1)(B), as added by the 2000 Act).

Number of designated areas. A maximum of 40 nominated areas may be designated by the Secretary of HUD as renewal communities. At least 12 of these must be in rural areas. A rural area is defined as an area that meets one of the following three criteria:

¶ 105

(1) it is within a local government jurisdiction or jurisdictions with a population of less than 50,000;

(2) it is outside a metropolitan statistical area, as defined by the Secretary of Commerce (Code Sec. 143(k)(2)(B)); or

(3) it is determined to be a rural area by the Secretary of HUD, after consulting with the Secretary of Commerce (Code Sec. 1400E(a)(2), as added by the 2000 Act).

Administrative procedures. To start the process of determining the renewal communities, the Secretary of HUD is directed to publish regulations by April 21, 2001 (within four months after the date of enactment, December 21, 2000). These regulations must describe the nomination procedures, limits on the size and population of a renewal community, and the method for evaluating the nominated areas (Code Sec. 1400E(a)(4)(A), as added by the 2000 Act). The regulations must provide the manner and form for submitting a nomination and the information that must be included (Code Sec. 1400E(a)(4)(C)(ii), as added by the 2000 Act). In developing the regulations, the Secretary of HUD must consult with the Secretaries of Agriculture, Commerce, Labor, and Treasury, the Director of the OMB, the Administrator of the SBA, and, with respect to areas on an Indian reservation, the Secretary of the Interior (Code Sec. 1400E(a)(4)(A), as added by the 2000 Act).

Comment. States and local governments will have a limited amount of time to nominate renewal communities after the publication of administrative procedures since the Secretary of HUD is required to complete the renewal community designations by December 31, 2001.

In order for a nominated area to be eligible for designation as a renewal community, the local governments and the states in which the nominated area is located must have the authority to nominate the area, to make commitments to provide assistance to the area, and to provide assurances that their commitments will be met. The local governments and the states in which the nominated area is located must follow the forthcoming regulatory procedures for nominating the area (Code Sec. 1400E(a)(4)(C)(i) and (ii) and (d), as added by the 2000 Act). If more than one government nominates an area, all of the governments are subject to the requirements for renewal communities that are imposed on such governments (Code Sec. 1400E(f)(1), as added by the 2000 Act).

Comment. The Secretary of HUD will not designate a nominated area as a renewal community unless it is determined that the information provided by the nominating governments is reasonably accurate (Code Sec. 1400E(a)(4)(C)(iii), as added by the 2000 Act).

Time limitations. Following the nomination process, the Secretary of HUD has only until December 31, 2001, to designate the renewal communities. The first day on which a designation can be made is the first day of the first month after the month in which the regulations describing the nominating and selection procedures are issued (Code Sec. 1400E(a)(4)(B), as added by the 2000 Act).

Eligibility requirements. A nominated area may be designated as a renewal community only if it exhibits certain characteristics related to geographic area and population and economic distress. As to geographic area, the area must be within the jurisdiction of one or more local governments and have a continuous boundary. As to population, the area must have a maximum population of not more than 200,000. The area must have a minimum population of at least 4,000 if any portion of the area is located within a metropolitan statistical area defined by the

Secretary of Commerce (Code Sec. 143(k)(2)(B)) that has a population of 50,000 or more, or at least 1,000 in any other case. An area that is entirely within an Indian reservation does not have to meet the population requirements (Code Sec. 1400E(c)(2), as added by the 2000 Act).

A nominated area meets the requirement related to economic distress if the state and local governments in which the area is located certify in writing that:

     (1) the area is one of pervasive poverty, unemployment, and general distress;

     (2) the unemployment rate in the area is at least 1½ times the national unemployment rate;

     (3) the poverty rate for each population census tract within the nominated area is at least 20 percent; and

     (4) for urban areas, at least 70 percent of the households in the area have incomes below 80 percent of the median income of households within the local government's jurisdiction (Code Sec. 1400E(c)(3), as added by the 2000 Act).

Prior to accepting the state and local governments' certification, the Secretary of HUD must conduct any review of the data supporting the certification as he deems appropriate (Code Sec. 1400E(c)(3), as added by the 2000 Act).

If an area is not tracted for population census tracts, the equivalent county divisions, as defined by the Bureau of the Census for defining poverty areas, are used to determine the poverty rates (Code Sec. 1400E(f)(3), as added by the 2000 Act; Code Sec. 1392(b)(4)). The population and poverty rates shall be determined through the 1990 census data (Code Sec. 1400E(f)(4), as added by the 2000 Act).

Other factors that the Secretary of HUD will consider in designating renewal communities include the extent of crime in the area and whether the area has census tracts identified in the May 12, 1998, report of the General Accounting Office (GAO) as economically distressed areas (Code Sec. 1400E(c)(4)(A), as added by the 2000 Act). Also, instead of considering the poverty criteria for one of the designated rural areas, the Secretary may take into account any outmigration from the area (Code Sec. 1400E(c)(4)(B), as added by the 2000 Act).

State and local participation. Before the Secretary of HUD will designate a nominated area as a renewal community, the Secretary must receive commitments from the local government and state in which the nominated area is located. The state and local government must agree in writing that they will follow a course of action to reduce burdens on employers and employees in the area and will take steps to promote economic growth (Code Sec. 1400E(d)(1), as added by the 2000 Act).

The state and local governments' course of action must be stated in a written document that is signed by the state or local government and by neighborhood organizations and that indicates a partnership between the government and the community-based organizations. Each signing party must make a commitment to reach specific, measurable goals, actions, and timetables (Code Sec. 1400E(d)(2)(A), as added by the 2000 Act).

The course of action must include at least four of the following steps for the renewal community:

     (1) a reduction of tax rates or fees in the community;

(2) an increase in the level of efficiency of local services in the community;

(3) crime prevention or reduction strategies for the community;

(4) actions to reduce, remove, simplify, or streamline governmental requirements in the community;

(5) involvement in the renewal program by private entities, organizations, neighborhood organizations, and community groups, particularly those in the community, including a commitment from the private entities to provide jobs, job training, and technical and financial assistance;

(6) gifts or sales at below fair market value of surplus real property in the renewal community to neighborhood organizations, community development corporations (CDCs) or private companies (Code Sec. 1400E(d)(2)(A), as added by the 2000 Act).

In evaluating the course of action, the Secretary of HUD will take into account the past efforts of the state or local government in reducing the burdens on employers and employees in the area (Code Sec. 1400E(d)(2)(B), as added by the 2000 Act).

In addition to defining a course of action, the state and local government must take steps to promote economic growth in the renewal community. The state and local government in which the nominated area is located must certify in writing that they have repealed or reduced or will not enforce or will reduce at least four of the following government restrictions:

(1) licensing of occupations that do not ordinarily require a professional degree;

(2) zoning of home-based businesses that do not create a public nuisance;

(3) permits for street vendors that do not create a public nuisance;

(4) zoning laws that impede the formation of schools or child care centers;

(5) franchises or other restrictions on competition for businesses providing public services, including taxicabs, jitneys, cable television, or trash hauling (Code Sec. 1400E(d)(3), as added by the 2000 Act).

Selection criteria. The areas designated as renewal communities are those nominated areas that have the highest average ranking in the categories of unemployment rate (unemployment rate in the area is at least 1½ times the national unemployment rate); poverty rate (poverty rate for each population census tract within the nominated area is at least 20 percent); and low income levels (for urban areas, at least 70 percent of the households in the area have incomes below 80 percent of the median income of households within the local government's jurisdiction) (Code Sec. 1400E(a)(3)(A) and (c)(3)(B), (C) and (D), as added by the 2000 Act).

Caution. Despite having the highest rankings of unemployment, poverty and low income levels, an area will not be designated as a renewal community if the state and local governments' course of action (see above) for reducing burdens on employers and employees in the area and promoting economic growth is inadequate (Code Sec. 1400E(a)(3)(B), as added by the 2000 Act).

Comment. Existing empowerment zones and enterprise communities have an advantage over other areas for designation as a renewal community. If existing empowerment zones or enterprise communities meet the requirements for a renewal community and are nominated, the Act specifically grants them preference for the first 20 renewal community designations (Code Sec. 1400E(a)(3)(C), as added by the 2000 Act).

Length of designation. The designation of an area as a renewal community will be effective from January 1, 2002, to December 31, 2009. This period can be shortened if an earlier termination date is designated by the state and local governments in their nomination or if the Secretary of HUD revokes the designation (Code Sec. 1400E(b)(1), as added by the 2000 Act). If the designation of area as a renewal community terminates before December 31, 2009, the day after the date of such termination is used in place of January 1, 2010, as the date by which qualified community assets must be acquired in order to qualify for the zero-percent capital gains rate (see ¶ 107) and the date by which qualified renewal property must be acquired in order to qualify for increased section 179 expensing (see ¶ 120) (Code Sec. 1400E(b)(3), as added by the 2000 Act).

Comment. If an existing empowerment zone or enterprise community is designated as a renewal community, the empowerment zone or enterprise community designation ends on the date that the renewal community designation takes effect (Code Sec. 1400E(e), as added by the 2000 Act).

Grounds for revoking designation. The Secretary of HUD can revoke an area's designation as a renewal community on two grounds. A designation can be revoked if the Secretary of HUD determines that the state or local government in which the area is located has modified the boundaries of the area. A designation also can be revoked if it is determined that the state or local government is not complying with or is not making progress in achieving its commitments to provide certain assistance to the area, such as tax reduction, crime prevention, increased local services, etc. (Code Sec. 1400E(b)(2) and (d), as added by the 2000 Act).

Audit report. The U.S. Comptroller General must conduct audits and submit reports to Congress on the renewal community program and the empowerment zone and enterprise community program and their effect on poverty, unemployment, and economic growth within the designated areas. The reports must be submitted by January 31, 2004, January 31, 2007, and January 31, 2010 (Act Sec. 101(c) of the 2000 Act).

PRACTICAL ANALYSIS. Professor Karen V. Kole of Valparaiso University, School of Law, notes that under Act Sec. 101, 40 new "renewal" communities will be designated to receive tax breaks similar to the current empowerment zones. The Secretary of HUD will select the communities, and the Secretary must consult with four other departments, including the OMB and the SBA. In Professor Kole's opinion, this is an extremely burdensome bureaucratic requirement that seemingly provides safeguards from all angles of government which will be difficult to comply with by the December 31, 2001, deadline. This does not even take into account the necessary involvement of state and local governments in the process.

Moreover, HUD must publish regulations for the process of determining renewal communities by April 21, 2001, four months after the date of enactment. The volume of work to be accomplished by various independently managed departments by these tight dead-

lines becomes even more unmanageable when coupled with the fact that following the nomination process, the Secretary of HUD only has until December 31, 2001, to designate the renewal communities. In addition to all this, the state and local governments must submit written commitments as to the various obligations that they will take on to reach specific, measurable goals, actions and timetables. If this involvement at the front-end is not itself overwhelming, the U.S. Comptroller General must conduct audits and submit reports on the renewal community program and its affect on poverty, unemployment and economic growth within the designated areas.

★ *Effective date.* No specific effective date is provided by the Act. The provision is, therefore, considered effective on December 21, 2000, the date of enactment.

Act Sec. 101(a) of the Community Renewal Tax Relief Act of 2000, adding Code Sec. 1400E; Act Sec. 101(c); Act Sec. 101(d). Law at ¶ 5800 and ¶ 7060. Committee Report at ¶ 10,135.

Renewal Community Capital Gain

¶ 107

Background

Parts of the District of Columbia are treated as an empowerment zone, called the District of Columbia Enterprise Zone (DC Zone) (Code Sec. 1400). As with all designated empowerment zones, special tax incentives are provided for the DC Zone in order to attract businesses to the area. One tax break for DC Zone businesses is an exclusion from income for qualified capital gain from the sale or exchange of a DC Zone asset held for more than five years (Code Sec. 1400B). DC Zone assets include DC Zone business stock, DC Zone partnership interests and DC Zone business property (Code Sec. 1400B(b)).

Community Renewal Tax Relief Act Impact

Exclusion for renewal community capital gain.—Beginning in 2002, a zero-percent capital gains rate will apply to qualified capital gain from the sale of qualified renewal community assets held for more than five years. Thus, qualified capital gain from the sale or exchange of corporate and partnership interests in a renewal community business and tangible property used in a renewal community business will be excluded from income if the interest or property is held for more than five years (Code Sec. 1400F, as added by the Community Renewal Tax Relief Act of 2000).

Qualified capital gain. Qualified capital gain is any gain recognized on the sale of a capital asset or property used in the trade or business under Code Sec. 1231(b) (for example, depreciable property and real property used in the business and not held for sale to customers) (Code Sec. 1400F(c)(1), as added by the 2000 Act). Qualified gain does not include gain attributable to periods before January 1, 2002, or after December 31, 2014 (Code Sec. 1400F(c)(2), as added by the 2000 Act).

Comment. Although qualified gain attributable to periods after December 31, 2014, is not eligible for the zero capital gains rate, qualified renewal community assets held for more than five years do not have to be sold on that date to receive some benefit. If a qualified renewal community asset is held past December 31, 2014, then gain attributable to the period from the date of the asset's acquisition to December 31, 2014, receives the zero capital gains rate and gain attributable to the period after December 31, 2014, is taxed under the regular capital gain rules.

Exclusions from qualified capital gain. Rules similar to the rules in Code Sec. 1400B(e)(3), (4) and (5) for DC Zone property will apply to exclude certain types of gain from qualified capital gain (Code Sec. 1400F(c)(3), as added by the 2000 Act). Thus, qualified capital gain does not include gain attributable to real property or an intangible asset that is not an integral part of a renewal community business (Code Sec. 1400B(e)(4); Code Sec. 1400F(c)(3), as added by the 2000 Act). Also, gain that would be treated as ordinary income under the Code Sec. 1245 or Code Sec. 1250 depreciation recapture provisions, if Code Sec. 1250 applied to all depreciation rather than the additional depreciation, is not treated as qualified capital gain (Code Sec. 1400B(e)(3); Code Sec. 1400F(c)(3), as added by the 2000 Act).

In addition, gain from related party transactions is also ineligible for the zero-percent capital gains rate. This rule applies to gain attributable, directly or indirectly, in whole or in part, to a transaction with a related party (Code Sec. 1400B(e)(5); Code Sec. 1400F(c)(3), as added by the 2000 Act). Some of the persons treated as related parties include:

• family members,

• a corporation and an individual who owns more than 50 percent in value of the corporation either directly or indirectly,

• two corporations that are members of the same controlled group,

• a partnership and a person owning more than a 50-percent capital or profits interest in the partnership,

• two partnerships in which the same persons own more than 50 percent of the capital or profits interests either directly or indirectly,

• a corporation and a partnership in which the same persons own more than 50 percent in value of the corporation and more than 50 percent of the capital or profits interests in the partnership,

• two S corporations in which the same persons own more than 50 percent in value of each corporation,

• an S corporation and a C corporation in which the same persons own more than 50 percent in value of each corporation,

• a grantor and a fiduciary of a trust, and

• a fiduciary and a beneficiary of a trust (Code Secs. 267(b) and 707(b)(1)).

Qualified community assets. The tax-free capital gain treatment applies to qualified community assets, which include:

(1) qualified community stock,

(2) qualified community partnership interests, and

(3) qualified community business property (Code Sec. 1400F(b)(1), as added by the 2000 Act).

Qualified community stock. Qualified community stock is stock in a domestic corporation that is a renewal community business. The stock must be acquired at original issue for cash after December 31, 2001, and before January 1, 2010. The corporation must qualify as a renewal community business at the time the stock was issued and during substantially all of the taxpayer's holding period for the stock. New corporations must have been organized for the purpose of being a renewal community business (Code Sec. 1400F(b)(2), as added by the 2000 Act).

A redemption rule similar to the rule of Code Sec. 1202(c)(3) will apply (Code Sec. 1400F(b)(2)(B), as added by the 2000 Act). Thus, stock acquired by the taxpayer may not be treated as qualified community stock if the corporation redeemed stock from the taxpayer or a person related to the taxpayer within two years before or after the stock was issued or if the corporation engaged in significant redemptions of its stock within one year before or after the stock was issued. This includes redemptions of stock through related corporations (Code Secs. 1202(c)(3)(C) and 304(a)).

Qualified community partnership interests. A qualified community partnership interest is any capital or profits interest in a domestic partnership that is a renewal community business. The interest must be acquired from the partnership for cash after December 31, 2001, and before January 1, 2010. The partnership must qualify as a renewal community business at the time the interest was acquired and during substantially all of the taxpayer's holding period for the interest. New partnerships must have been organized for the purpose of being a renewal community business (Code Sec. 1400F(b)(3), as added by the 2000 Act).

A redemption rule similar to the rule of Code Sec. 1202(c)(3) will apply (Code Sec. 1400F(b)(2)(B) and (3), as added by the 2000 Act). Thus, it appears that a partnership interest acquired by the taxpayer may not be treated as a qualified community partnership interest if the partnership acquired an interest from the taxpayer or a person related to the taxpayer within two years before or after the partnership interest was issued or if the partnership engaged in significant acquisitions of its interests within one year before or after the partnership interest was issued. Presumably, this would include acquisitions of interests through related entities (Code Secs. 1202(c)(3)(C) and 304(a)).

Qualified community business property. Qualified community business property is tangible property used in a renewal community business and purchased after December 31, 2001, and before January 1, 2010. The original use of the property in the renewal community must begin with the taxpayer. Further, during substantially all of the taxpayer's holding period for the property, substantially all of the use of the property must be in the taxpayer's renewal community business (Code Sec. 1400F(b)(4)(A), as added by the 2000 Act).

Tangible property that the taxpayer has substantially improved before January 1, 2010, and the land on which the property is located can be treated as if it were purchased by the taxpayer and its original use in the renewal community began with the taxpayer. Property is substantially improved if, during any 24-month period beginning after December 31, 2001, additions to the property's basis exceed the greater of the property's adjusted basis at the beginning of such 24-month period, or $5,000 (Code Sec. 1400B(b)(4)(B)(ii); Code Sec. 1400F(b)(4)(B), as added by the 2000 Act).

Renewal community business. A renewal community business is any entity or proprietorship that would be a qualified business entity or qualified proprietorship under the definition of an enterprise zone business if references to renewal communities were substituted for references to empowerment zones (Code Sec. 1400G, as added by the 2000 Act; Code Sec. 1397C, as redesignated by the 2000 Act). This definition generally requires that the entity or proprietorship derive at least half of its income from the active conduct of a business in the renewal community, that it use a substantial portion of its property in the community or in the active conduct of the business, that a portion of its employees live in the community and perform a substantial portion of their services in the community, and that not more than a minimal amount of its property is attributable to collectibles or certain financial property (Code Sec. 1397C(b), (c) and (e), as redesignated by the 2000 Act).

Comment. Termination of the renewal community designation will not, by itself, result in property failing to be treated as a qualified community asset for purposes of the zero-percent capital gains rate (Code Sec. 1400B(b)(5); Code Sec. 1400F(d), as added by the 2000 Act). However, even though the property may continue to be treated as a qualified community asset, any gain attributable to the period after December 31, 2014, will be ineligible for the exclusion (Code Sec. 1400F(c)(2), as added by the 2000 Act; Conference Committee Report).

Subsequent purchasers. Property will continue to be a qualified community asset if sold or transferred to a subsequent purchaser, provided that the property continues to represent an interest or tangible property used in a renewal community business (Conference Committee Report). Qualified community business property continues to be qualified community business property in the hands of a subsequent purchaser if, during substantially all of the subsequent purchaser's holding period, substantially all of the use of the property is in a renewal community business. Qualified community business stock or qualified community partnership interests continue to be qualified in the hands of a subsequent purchaser, if, at the time of original acquisition and during substantially all of the subsequent purchaser's holding period, the corporation or partnership was a renewal community business (Code Sec. 1400B(b)(6); Code Sec. 1400F(d), as added by the 2000 Act).

Five-year safe harbor. If property or an ownership interest ceases to be a qualified community asset after the five-year period beginning on the date the taxpayer acquired the property because the property is no longer used in a renewal community business or because the corporation or partnership no longer qualifies as a renewal community business, that property continues to be treated as a qualified community asset. However, the amount of gain eligible for the zero-percent capital gain rate upon the sale or exchange of the property cannot exceed the amount that would be qualified capital gain had the property been sold on the date the property ceased to be a qualified community asset (Code Sec. 1400B(b)(7); Code Sec. 1400F(d), as added by the 2000 Act).

With respect to the sale or exchange of an interest in a partnership or stock in an S corporation that is a renewal community business during substantially all of the period the taxpayer held the interest or stock, the amount of qualified capital gain is determined without regard to (1) gain attributable to real property or an intangible asset that is not an integral part of a renewal community business and (2) gain attributable to periods before January 1, 2002, or after December 31, 2014 (Code Sec. 1400F(d), as added by the 2000 Act, Code Sec. 1400B(g)).

Other applicable rules. Rules similar to those of Code Sec. 1202(g), relating to the treatment of pass-through entities; Code Sec. 1202(h), relating to certain tax-free and other transfers; Code Sec. 1202(i)(2), relating to the treatment of certain contributions to capital; and Code Sec. 1202(j), relating to the treatment of certain short positions, apply for purposes of the zero-percent capital gains rates provisions (Code Sec. 1400F(d), as added by the 2000 Act; Code Sec. 1400B(f)). Thus, a zero-percent capital gains rate may apply to gain from qualified community assets held by a pass-through entity and passed through to the entity's owner or to gain from qualified community assets acquired through gift or inheritance.

Caution. Gain from the sale of qualified community assets may not be eligible for the zero-percent capital gains rate if the taxpayer or a related person holds an offsetting short position with respect to the assets (Code Sec. 1400F(d), as added by the 2000 Act; Code Secs. 1400B(f) and 1202(j)).

PRACTICAL ANALYSIS. Professor Karen V. Kole of Valparaiso University, School of Law, observes that one of the primary tax benefits offered by the community renewal legislation is relief from taxation of qualified capital gain from the sale of qualified renewal assets held for more than five years. The rules governing what constitutes qualified capital gain, the recapture provisions and the timing requirements, however, are quite burdensome and will increase recordkeeping requirements for taxpayers claiming this benefit.

Regulations. The IRS has been instructed to issue regulations that are appropriate to carry out the purpose of the capital gain rules for renewal community property. The regulations may include ways to prevent taxpayers from avoiding the purpose of these capital gain rules (Code Sec. 1400F(e), as added by the 2000 Act).

★ *Effective date.* No specific effective date is provided by the Act. The provision is, therefore, considered effective on December 21, 2000, the date of enactment.

Act Sec. 101(a) of the Community Renewal Tax Relief Act of 2000, adding Code Sec. 1400F and Code Sec. 1400G. Law at ¶ 5810 and ¶ 5820. Committee Report at ¶ 10,137.

Renewal Community Employment Credit

¶ 110

Background

Employers doing business in certain empowerment zones are entitled to a tax credit for qualified wages paid to employees who work and live in the zones (Code Sec. 1396). For 2000, the empowerment zone employment credit is equal to 20 percent of the first $15,000 of qualified wages paid to full-time or part-time employees (Code Sec. 1396(b) and (c)). The employee must live in the empowerment zone and must perform substantially all of his work in the zone in the employer's trade or business (Code Sec. 1396(d)).

The current empowerment zones were designated in stages. A total of 11 empowerment zones were ultimately designated in Round I (Code Sec. 1391(b)(2)). Businesses in the Round I empowerment zones can qualify for the 20-percent employment credit in 2000 with a phaseout of the credit in subsequent years. Businesses in the special empowerment zone in the District of Columbia (DC Zone) can qualify for the 20-percent employment credit with no phaseout (Code Sec. 1400(d)(2)).

Background

An additional 20 empowerment zones were designated in Round II (Code Sec. 1391(g)(1)). These Round II empowerment zones were selected under different eligibility criteria than the Round I empowerment zones and are not entitled to the empowerment zone employment credit (Code Secs. 1391(g)(3) and 1396(e)).

Community Renewal Tax Relief Act Impact

Fifteen-percent employment credit.—Employers doing business in renewal communities will be entitled to a tax credit for qualified wages paid to employees who work and live in the renewal communities (Code Sec. 1400H, as added by the Community Renewal Tax Relief Act of 2000). With a few differences, the renewal communities will be treated as empowerment zones for purposes of the employment credit (Code Sec. 1400H(a), as added by the 2000 Act; Code Sec. 1396). The renewal community employment credit will be equal to 15 percent of the first $10,000 of qualified wages paid to full-time or part-time employees (Code Sec. 1400H(b), as added by the 2000 Act; Code Sec. 1396(b) and (c)).

Comment. Since the designation of an area as a renewal community will generally be effective during the period that begins on January 1, 2002, and ends on December 31, 2009 (Code Sec. 1400E(b)(1), as added by the 2000 Act), the renewal community employment credit will first be available for wages paid in 2002.

Aside from a lower amount of the credit, the rules for claiming the credit for empowerment zone employees will apply to renewal community employees (Code Sec. 1400H(a), as added by the 2000 Act; Code Sec. 1396). See ¶ 140. Thus, the employees must have a principal place of residence in the renewal community and must perform substantially all of their work in the community in the employer's trade or business (Code Sec. 1396(d)(1)). Also, the credit may be denied for certain employees, such as five-percent owners of the business, persons who are employed less than 90 days, employees of large farming businesses, and individuals employed in gambling and other specified businesses (Code Sec. 1396(d)(2)).

Example. Steve Jones and Amanda Smith live in a designated renewal community and are employed in the community by Z Corp. For 2002, Jones receives a salary of $8,000 and Smith receives a salary of $25,000. Z Corp.'s renewal community employment credit for Jones is $1,200 (15% of $8,000 of wages) and for Smith is limited to $1,500 (15% of the first $10,000 of wages).

PRACTICAL ANALYSIS. Professor Karen V. Kole of Valparaiso University, School of Law, notes that the statutory time frame for the selection process is extremely short, December 31, 2001, and qualification hurdles are extremely high (i.e., the mechanical complexity of many of the provisions and the mandatory involvement of various governmental departments besides the IRS and the lack of clear guidance as to standards to be applied). Professor Kole believes the goals of these provisions of the Act are worthy, but that the complexity and compliance aspects of the community renewal provisions are so vast, that many attorneys, not only tax attorneys, will be kept busy for a long time.

¶ 110

Professor Kole also notes that Act Sec. 101(a) provides for a relatively straightforward tax credit for qualified wages paid to employees who live and work in renewal communities. However, while the technical requirements calculating the credit are relatively simple, policing who is an employee and ensuring that employees actually reside in the renewal community may present problems.

★ *Effective date.* No specific effective date is provided by the Act. The provision is, therefore, considered effective on December 21, 2000, the date of enactment.

Act Sec. 101(a) of the Community Renewal Tax Relief Act of 2000, adding Code Sec. 1400H. Law at ¶ 5830. Committee Report at ¶ 10,138.

Commercial Revitalization Deduction for Renewal Communities

¶ 115

Background

Taxpayers can recover the cost of many kinds of property used in their trade or business or held for the production of income through depreciation deductions (Code Sec. 167). Machinery, buildings, cars and other property that have useful lives that extend beyond the year in which they were placed in service and that deteriorate or wear out over time can be depreciated. In general, depreciation deductions for property placed in service after 1986 are determined under the modified accelerated cost recovery system (MACRS). Under MACRS, property is assigned a class and a recovery period. Nonresidential real property has a recovery period of 39 years (Code Sec. 168(c) and (e)(2)(B)) and is depreciated under the straight-line method using a mid-month convention (Code Sec. 168(b)(3) and (d)(2)).

Taxpayers who substantially rehabilitate certain buildings may claim a rehabilitation credit for a percentage of their costs (Code Sec. 47). The rehabilitation credit is part of the investment credit (Code Sec. 46). Generally, this credit can be claimed for 10 percent of qualified rehabilitation expenditures incurred with respect to buildings that were originally placed in service before 1936 (Code Sec. 47(a)(1) and (c)(1)(B)) and 20 percent of qualified rehabilitation expenditures incurred with respect to certified historic structures (Code Sec. 47(a)(2) and (c)(3)).

Community Renewal Tax Relief Act Impact

Deduction for revitalization expenditures.—Taxpayers who construct or rehabilitate nonresidential buildings in renewal communities will be able to claim a commercial revitalization deduction for qualified revitalization expenditures instead of claiming depreciation deductions. The taxpayer can either deduct one-half of the qualified revitalization expenditures that are chargeable to the capital account of a qualified building in the tax year in which it is placed in service or deduct all of the qualified revitalization expenditures ratably over the 120-month period beginning with the month in which the building is placed in service (Code Sec. 1400I(a), as added by the Community Renewal Tax Relief Act of 2000). The deduction will not apply to any building placed in service after December 31, 2009 (Code Sec. 1400I(g), as added by the 2000 Act).

Election. A taxpayer can elect the form of the revitalization deduction—either an immediate deduction equal to one-half of the qualified revitalization expenditures for the tax year in which the building is placed in service or a deduction for all of the qualified revitalization expenditures taken over a 120-month period that begins when the building is placed in service (Code Sec. 1400I(a), as added by the 2000 Act).

Qualified revitalization building. A qualified revitalization building is a building plus its structural components that are placed in service in a renewal community. The original use of the building must begin with the taxpayer or the building must be substantially rehabilitated by the taxpayer and placed in service after rehabilitation (Code Sec. 1400I(b)(1), as added by the 2000 Act). Thus, both new buildings and old rehabilitated buildings can qualify. In general, a building is substantially rehabilitated if the qualified rehabilitation expenditures for a 24-month period selected by the taxpayer and ending in the tax year exceed the greater of the adjusted basis of the building and its structural components, or $5,000 (Code Sec. 47(c)(1)(C)). A substantial rehabilitation is treated as a separate building for purpose of the deduction (Code Sec. 1400I(f)(3), as added by the 2000 Act).

Caution. Since the original use of the building must begin with the taxpayer, existing commercial buildings in renewal communities cannot be purchased in hopes of claiming the commercial revitalization deduction unless the taxpayer intends to rehabilitate the property.

Planning Note. Deducting all of the qualified revitalization expenditures over a 120-month period is generally better than the regular depreciation deduction under MACRS because the cost of the building is recovered over a shorter period of time. The alternative of deducting only half of the qualified revitalization expenditures immediately in the tax year in which the building is placed in service may also be beneficial if the business has sufficient income for that year against which to claim the deduction. Otherwise, the taxpayer may have to carry back or carry forward unused net operating losses.

Qualified revitalization expenditures. Qualified revitalization expenditures are amounts chargeable to a capital account for depreciable nonresidential real property and Code Sec. 1250 property that is functionally related and subordinate to the nonresidential real property (Code Sec. 1400I(b)(2)(A), as added by the 2000 Act).

If the taxpayer is rehabilitating an existing building, its acquisition cost is treated as a qualified revitalization expenditure only to the extent that it does not exceed 30 percent of the aggregate qualified revitalization expenditures for the building, excluding the acquisition cost (Code Sec. 1400I(b)(2)(B)(i), as added by the 2000 Act).

Qualified revitalization expenditures do not include amounts that the taxpayer may take into account in computing any credits, unless the taxpayer elects to take the amount into account only for purposes of the commercial revitalization deduction (Code Sec. 1400I(b)(2)(B)(i), as added by the 2000 Act). For example, costs that could be used to compute the rehabilitation credit (Code Sec. 47) cannot be included in qualified revitalization expenditures unless the taxpayer elects to use them only for that purpose.

Commercial revitalization expenditure amount. The amount that may be treated as qualified revitalization expenditures for a building cannot exceed the lesser of $10,000,000 or the amount allocated to the building by the commercial revitalization agency for the state in which the building is located (Code Sec. 1400I(c), as added by the 2000 Act). A commercial revitalization agency is any agency authorized by the state to carry out these rules (Code Sec. 1400I(d)(3), as added by the 2000 Act).

The authorized commercial revitalization agency is limited in the amount of commercial revitalization expenditures that it may allocate. The total amount of commercial revitalization expenditures that the agency can allocate is the state commercial revitalization expenditure ceiling for the calendar year (Code Sec. 1400I(d)(1) and (3), as added by the 2000 Act). The state commercial revitalization expenditure ceiling is $12,000,000 for each renewal community in the state per calendar year after 2001 and before 2010 and $0 thereafter (Code Sec. 1400I(d)(2), as added by the 2000 Act). Allocations are made at the same time and in the same manner as they are for purposes of the low-income housing credit (Code Sec. 1400I(d)(4), as added by the 2000 Act; Code Sec. 42(h)(1) and (7)).

Allocation plan. State commercial revitalization agencies are required to develop a plan for allocating commercial revitalization expenditures. The plan must be approved by the governmental unit of which the agency is a part. If the commercial revitalization expenditure amount for a building is not allocated according to an approved qualified allocation plan, the commercial revitalization expenditure amount is treated as zero (Code Sec. 1400I(e)(1)(A), as added by the 2000 Act). The commercial revitalization expenditure amount for a building is also treated as zero unless the agency notifies the chief executive officer of the local jurisdiction where the building is located of the allocation and provides the officer with a reasonable opportunity to comment on the allocation (Code Sec. 1400I(e)(1)(B), as added by the 2000 Act).

A qualified allocation plan must set forth the selection criteria to be used to determine the priorities of the commercial revitalization agency that are appropriate to local conditions. The plan must also consider the degree to which a project contributes to the implementation of a strategic plan that is devised for a renewal community through a citizen participation process, the amount of any increase in permanent, full-time employment by reason of any project, and the active involvement of residents and nonprofit groups within the renewal community. Finally, the plan must provide a procedure that the commercial revitalization agency or its agent will follow in monitoring compliance with the rules for the revitalization deduction (Code Sec. 1400I(e)(2), as added by the 2000 Act).

Special rules. No depreciation is allowed for amounts claimed as the commercial revitalization deduction (Code Sec. 1400I(f)(1), as added by the 2000 Act). Thus, if the taxpayer elects the immediate deduction of one-half of the qualified revitalization expenditures, then no depreciation deduction that would otherwise be allowed on one-half of the expenditures can be claimed. If the taxpayer elects the 120-month ratable deduction of all of the qualified revitalization expenditures, then no depreciation deduction that would otherwise be allowed on all of the expenditures can be claimed.

The adjusted basis of the property is reduced by the amount of the commercial revitalization deduction (Code Sec. 1400I(f)(2), as added by the 2000 Act; Code Sec. 1016). The commercial revitalization deduction is treated as a depreciation deduction in applying the depreciation recapture rules of Code Sec. 1250.

The commercial revitalization deduction is allowed in computing a taxpayer's alternative minimum taxable income (AMTI) (Code Sec. 1400I(f)(4), as added by the 2000 Act).

Exception from passive loss rules. The commercial revitalization deduction is treated in the same manner as the low-income housing credit in applying the passive loss rules. Generally, up to $25,000 of passive activity losses from rental real estate activities can be applied by an individual against nonpassive income if the individual actively participates in the rental real estate activity. However, the rehabilitation credit, low-income housing credit, and the commercial revitalization deduction are allowed under the $25,000 rule regardless of whether the taxpayer actively participates in the rental real estate activity that generates the credit or deduction (Code Sec. 469(i)(6)(B), as amended by the 2000 Act).

The $25,000 amount is phased out by 50 percent of the amount by which the taxpayer's adjusted gross income (AGI) exceeds $100,000 (Code Sec. 469(i)(3)(A)). However, the phaseout does not apply to the portion of the individual's passive activity loss that is attributable to the commercial revitalization deduction (Code Sec. 469(i)(3)(C), as added by the 2000 Act).

Comment. The phaseout also does not apply to the portion of the individual's passive activity credit that is attributable to the low-income housing credit (Code Sec 469(i)(3)(D), as redesignated by the 2000 Act). If any portion of the individual's passive activity credit is attributable to the rehabilitation credit, then the $25,000 amount is phased out by 50 percent of the amount by which the taxpayer's AGI exceeds $200,000 (Code Sec. 469(i)(3)(B)).

If the special phaseout rules for the commercial revitalization deduction, low-income housing credit, or rehabilitation credit apply, then the remaining portion of the $25,000 amount is applied in the following order:

(1) to the portion of the passive activity loss to which the commercial revitalization deduction does not apply;

(2) to the portion of the passive activity credit to which the rehabilitation credit or the low-income housing credit does not apply;

(3) to the portion of such credit to which the rehabilitation credit applies;

(4) to the portion of such loss to which the commercial revitalization deduction applies; and

(5) to the portion of such credit to which the low-income housing credit applies (Code Sec. 469(i)(3)(E), as redesignated and amended by the 2000 Act).

★ *Effective date.* No specific effective date is provided by the Act. The provision is, therefore, considered effective on December 21, 2000, the date of enactment.

Act Sec. 101(a) of the Community Renewal Tax Relief Act of 2000, adding Code Sec. 1400I; Act Sec. 101(b)(1), redesignating former Code Sec. 469(i)(3)(C), (D) and (E) as (D), (E) and (F), respectively, and adding new Code Sec. 469(i)(3)(C); Act Sec. 101(b)(2), amending Code Sec. 469(i)(3)(E), as redesignated; Act Sec. 101(b)(3), amending Code Sec. 469(i)(6)(B) and adding Code Sec. 469(i)(6)(B)(iii). Law at ¶ 5340 and ¶ 5840. Committee Report at ¶ 10,139.

¶ 115

Increased Expensing Under Section 179 for Renewal Property

¶ 120

Background _____

Taxpayers may elect to deduct the cost of certain tangible depreciable property used in a trade or business in the year in which it was placed in service, rather than capitalizing the cost and claiming depreciation deductions over time (Code Sec. 179). The deductible amount is limited to a maximum of $20,000 for tax years beginning in 2000, $24,000 for tax years beginning in 2001 and 2002, and $25,000 for tax years beginning in 2003 and thereafter (Code Sec. 179(b)). The maximum deductible amount is reduced on a dollar-for-dollar basis by the amount by which the cost of section 179 property that is placed in service during the tax year exceeds $200,000 (Code Sec. 179(b)(2)).

Qualified enterprise zone businesses are entitled to an increased section 179 deduction for the cost of qualified zone property used in an empowerment zone and placed in service during the tax year (Code Sec. 1397A). The maximum deductible amount is increased by the lower of $20,000 or the cost of section 179 property that is qualified zone property and placed in service during the tax year (Code Sec. 1397A(a)(1)). However, the maximum deductible amount is reduced by the amount by which 50 percent of the cost of section 179 property that is qualified zone property and placed in service during the tax year exceeds $200,000 (Code Sec. 1397A(a)(2)).

Community Renewal Tax Relief Act Impact

Section 179 expensing increased for renewal community property.— Renewal communities will be treated as empowerment zones with respect to the increased section 179 first-year expensing allowed for certain depreciable business property. Renewal community businesses will be treated as enterprise zone businesses and qualified renewal property will be treated as qualified zone property for this purpose (Code Sec. 1400J(a), as added by the Community Renewal Tax Relief Act of 2000; Code Sec. 1397A, as amended by the 2000 Act).

Thus, renewal community businesses can elect to deduct the cost of section 179 property that is qualified renewal property and placed in service during the year up to a higher maximum amount of $59,000 for tax years beginning in 2002 and $60,000 for tax years beginning in 2003 and thereafter (Code Sec. 1397A(a)(1), as amended by the 2000 Act; Code Sec. 179(b)(1)). The property must be used in the renewal community.

The higher expensing limitation for tax years beginning after 2001 reflects:

(1) the regular section 179 maximum deductible amount of $24,000 for tax years beginning in 2002 and $25,000 for tax years beginning in 2003 and thereafter, plus

(2) an additional amount of $35,000 or, if lower, the cost of section 179 property that is qualified renewal property placed in service during the year (Code Sec. 1397A(a), as amended by the 2000 Act).

Example. RC Corp. purchases and places a machine in service in a designated renewal community in 2002. The machine is section 179 property that is qualified renewal property and has a cost of $30,000. Since the increased dollar limitation for qualified renewal property applies, the entire cost is deductible under Code Sec. 179 in 2002. If the machine was not qualified renewal property, only $24,000 of the cost would be deductible in 2002 due to the regular Code Sec. 179 dollar limitation.

The current rule that reduces the expensing limitation by the amount by which: (1) 50 percent of the cost of section 179 property that is qualified zone property and placed in service during the year, exceeds (2) $200,000 still applies (Code Sec. 1397A(a)(2)). Thus, if the cost of section 179 property that is qualified renewal property and placed in service in a tax year beginning in 2002 equals or exceeds $518,000, no section 179 deduction is available.

Qualified renewal property. Qualified renewal property is depreciable property under Code Sec. 168 (or property to which Code Sec. 168 would apply but for Code Sec. 179):

(1) that was purchased by the taxpayer after December 31, 2001, and before January 1, 2010;

(2) whose original use in the renewal community began with the taxpayer; and

(3) substantially all of the use of which is in the renewal community and is in the active conduct of a qualified business by the taxpayer in the renewal community (Code Sec. 1400J(b)(1), as added by the 2000 Act; Code Sec. 1397D(a)(1), as redesignated by the 2000 Act).

The special rules for substantial renovations and sale-leasebacks of qualified empowerment zone property (Code Sec. 1397D(a)(2) and (b), as redesignated by the 2000 Act) apply when defining qualified renewal property (Code Sec. 1400J(b)(2), as added by the 2000 Act). Under the sale-leaseback rule, if property is sold and leased back by the taxpayer within three months after the date the property was originally placed in service, the earliest that it can be treated as originally placed in service is the date on which the property is used under the leaseback (Code Sec. 1397D(b), as redesignated by the 2000 Act).

Under the rule for substantial renovations, property that is substantially renovated by the taxpayer will be treated as if it were purchased by the taxpayer and its original use in the renewal community began with the taxpayer. Property is substantially renovated if, during any 24-month period beginning after the date on which the renewal community designation took effect, additions to the property's basis exceed the greater of the property's adjusted basis at the beginning of such 24-month period, or $5,000 (Code Sec. 1397D(a)(2), as redesignated by the 2000 Act).

Planning Note. Although buildings are not eligible for the section 179 deduction (Code Sec. 179(d)(1)), taxpayers may be able to claim a commercial revitalization deduction for constructing or rehabilitating nonresidential buildings in renewal communities (see ¶ 115). Either one-half of the qualified revitalization expenditures that are chargeable to the capital account of a qualified building is deductible in the tax year in which it is placed in service or all of the qualified revitalization expenditures are deductible ratably over the 120-month period beginning with the month in which the building is placed in service (Code Sec. 1400I(a), as added by the 2000 Act).

★ *Effective date.* The provision increasing the additional Code Sec. 179 expensing allowance to $35,000 for enterprise zone businesses is effective for tax years beginning after December 31, 2001 (Act Sec. 114(c) of the Community Renewal Tax Relief Act of 2000). No specific effective date is provided by the Act

¶ 120

for the provision to increase the expensing allowance for renewal community property. The provision is, therefore, considered effective on December 21, 2000, the date of enactment.

Act Sec. 101(a) of the Community Renewal Tax Relief Act of 2000, adding Code Sec. 1400J; Act Sec. 114(a), amending Code Sec. 1397A(a)(1); Act Sec. 114(c). Law at ¶ 5720 and ¶ 5850. Committee Report at ¶ 10,140 and ¶ 10,148.

Work Opportunity Credit for Youth in Renewal Communities

¶ 125

Background

Employers are entitled to a tax credit as an incentive to hire individuals from targeted groups that have high rates of unemployment or difficulty finding work (Code Sec. 51). Two of the eight targeted groups are high-risk youth who live in an empowerment zone or enterprise community and qualified summer youth employees who live in an empowerment zone or enterprise community (Code Sec. 51(d)(5) and (7)). The other targeted groups include qualified needy individuals with minor children, veterans, ex-felons, individuals with a physical or mental disability, food stamp recipients, and individuals receiving supplemental security income benefits (Code Sec. 51(d)(2) through (9)).

The work opportunity credit is equal to 40 percent of up to $6,000 of qualified first-year wages paid to members of the targeted groups (Code Sec. 51(a) and (b)). For qualified summer youth employees, a maximum of $3,000 of wages is taken into account for the credit (Code Sec. 51(d)(7)(B)(ii)). Only amounts paid or incurred with respect to an individual who begins work before January 1, 2002, can qualify for the credit (Code Sec. 51(c)(4)). In addition, the worker must perform at least 400 hours of services in order for the employer to receive the full amount of the credit. No credit is allowed if the worker provides less than 120 hours of services (Code Sec. 51(i)(3)).

Community Renewal Tax Relief Act Impact

Work opportunity credit for renewal community youth.—Employers will be entitled to a work opportunity credit for hiring high-risk youth and summer youth employees who live in renewal communities and begin work after December 31, 2001 (Code Sec. 51(d)(5) and (7), as amended by the Community Renewal Tax Relief Act of 2000; Act Sec. 102(d) of the 2000 Act). In addition to living in the renewal community, the high-risk youth and summer youth employees must satisfy age and other requirements in order for the employer to claim the credit.

Comment. The work opportunity credit is currently available for employers that hire high-risk youth and summer youth employees who live in empowerment zones and enterprise communities (Code Sec. 51(d)(5) and (7)).

The work opportunity credit is equal to 40 percent of up to $6,000 of qualified first-year wages paid to high-risk youth employees (Code Sec. 51(a) and (b)). Qualified first-year wages are wages paid for services provided during the one-year period that begins on the day the high-risk youth begins work for the employer. For summer youth employees, a maximum of $3,000 of qualified wages can be taken into account (Code Sec. 51(b)(3) and (d)(7)(B)(ii)). Qualified wages of summer youth employees are wages paid for services provided during any 90-day summer period between May 1 and September 15 (Code Sec. 51(d)(7)(B)(i)).

Caution. The work opportunity credit is currently scheduled to terminate with respect to wages paid or incurred with respect to individuals who begin work after December 31, 2001 (Code Sec. 51(c)(4)(B)). Since the work opportunity credit for renewal communities would only apply to youth who begin work after that date, an extension of the general termination date is necessary before the credit can be claimed for renewal community youth.

High-risk youth. An employee qualifies as a high-risk youth if the individual is certified by the designated local agency as being at least age 18 but younger than age 25 on the hiring date and as living within the renewal community, empowerment zone or enterprise community (Code Sec. 51(d)(5)(A), as amended by the 2000 Act). Qualified wages do not include amounts paid for services performed while the youth's principal place of abode is outside the renewal community, empowerment zone or enterprise community (Code Sec. 51(d)(5)(B), as amended by the 2000 Act). Thus, the high-risk youth must continue to live in the renewal community, empowerment zone or enterprise community during the employment period covered by the credit.

Summer youth employees. A qualified summer youth employee is an individual who works for the employer between May 1 and September 15. The youth must be certified by the designated local agency as being at least age 16 but younger than age 18 on the hiring date or May 1 of the calendar year, if later, and as living within the renewal community, empowerment zone or enterprise community (Code Sec. 51(d)(7)(A), as amended by the 2000 Act). The summer-employed youth cannot have been an employee of the employer during any period before the 90-day summer employment period.

As with high-risk youth, qualified wages of summer youth do not include amounts paid for services performed while the youth's principal place of abode is outside the renewal community, empowerment zone or enterprise community (Code Sec. 51(d)(7)(C)). Thus, summer youth employees must continue to live in the renewal community, empowerment zone or enterprise community during the employment period covered by the credit.

Caution. Wages taken into account in computing the work opportunity credit may not also be taken into account in computing the renewal community employment credit (see ¶ 110) or the empowerment zone employment credit (see ¶ 140) (Code Sec. 1400H(a), as added by the 2000 Act; Code Sec. 1396(c)(3)).

★ *Effective date.* The amendments apply to individuals who begin work for the employer after December 31, 2001 (Act Sec. 102(d) of the Community Renewal Tax Relief Act of 2000).

Act Sec. 102(a) of the Community Renewal Tax Relief Act of 2000, amending Code Sec. 51(d)(5)(A)(ii) and (B); Act Sec. 102(b), amending Code Sec. 51(d)(7)(A)(iv); Act Sec. 102(c), amending Code Sec. 51(d)(5)(B) and (7)(C); Act Sec. 102(d). Law at ¶ 5090. Committee Report at ¶ 10,141.

¶ **125**

EMPOWERMENT ZONES

Authority to Designate New Empowerment Zones

¶ 130

Background _____

Since 1994, areas in economically depressed sections of the country have been designated as empowerment zones (Code Sec. 1391). A number of tax incentives are available to taxpayers who operate businesses in these areas. The tax breaks include a wage-based employment credit that motivates employers to hire workers living in the community, increased section 179 deductions to boost investment in assets used in the targeted areas, and tax-exempt bond financing benefits (Code Secs. 1394, 1396 and 1397A). Other areas have been designated as enterprise communities but receive more limited tax incentives than the empowerment zones.

The empowerment zones were selected from areas nominated by local and state governments. Applications for designation as an empowerment zone had to demonstrate that the nominated area satisfied eligibility criteria, had to include a strategic plan, and had to provide other information (Code Sec. 1391(e) and (f)). Some of the eligibility criteria that were evaluated in selecting the empowerment zones include the nominated area's population, general economic distress, size, and poverty rate (Code Sec. 1392(a)).

The current empowerment zones were designated in stages. The zones designated in each stage were selected based on different criteria, have different periods of applicability, and receive somewhat different tax benefits. In Round I, the Secretary of Housing and Urban Development (HUD) designated six urban empowerment zones and the Secretary of Agriculture designated three rural empowerment zones, effective December 21, 1994. Sixty-five urban and 30 rural enterprise communities were also designated. Two additional urban empowerment zones were later designated that are considered Round I empowerment zones but are effective January 1, 2000 (Code Sec. 1391(b)).

For the Round II designations effective December 31, 1998, the Secretary of HUD designated 15 additional urban empowerment zones and the Secretary of Agriculture designated five more rural empowerment zones (Code Sec. 1391(g)(1)). These Round II empowerment zones were selected under different eligibility criteria than the Round I empowerment zones and are not entitled to the empowerment zone employment credit (Code Secs. 1391(g)(3) and 1396(e)).

Designations of empowerment zones and enterprise communities will generally remain in effect until the end of the 10th calendar year beginning on or after the date of designation. However, the designation may end earlier on the termination date provided by the state and local governments in their nomination or on the date the Secretary of HUD or Agriculture revokes the designation (Code Sec. 1391(d)(1)).

Community Renewal Tax Relief Act Impact

Nine new empowerment zones.—An additional nine new empowerment zones entitled to special tax benefits may be designated by the appropriate authorities, primarily the Secretaries of Housing and Urban Development (HUD) and Agriculture. Not more than seven of the empowerment zones can be designated in urban areas and not more than two can be designated in rural areas (Code Sec. 1391(h)(1), as added by the Community Renewal Tax Relief Act of 2000).

Comment. The new designations will bring the total number of empowerment zones to 40—11 zones designated in Round I, 20 zones designated in Round II, and nine new zones to be designated in Round III. After the Round III designations, the breakdown of the empowerment zones will be 30 urban and 10 rural empowerment zones.

Eligibility criteria. The nine new empowerment zones will be selected under the less restrictive eligibility criteria (Code Sec. 1391(g)(3)) that were applied to the 20 empowerment zones designated in Round II of the selection process (Code Sec. 1391(h)(3), as added by the 2000 Act). Thus, the new Round III empowerment zones will be subject to a poverty rate requirement and a size limitation, but the aggregate population limitation for urban empowerment zones will not be applied. In addition, previously designated enterprise communities and Indian reservations may be nominated for designation as a Round III empowerment zone (Code Sec. 1391(g)(3)).

Under the poverty rate requirement, each population census tract within the nominated area must have a poverty rate of not less than 20 percent, and the poverty rate for at least 90 percent of the population census tracts within a nominated area must not be less than 25 percent. Special rules apply to sites in a nominated area that may be developed for commercial or industrial purposes, small population census tracts with a population of less than 2,000, and rural areas (Code Sec. 1391(g)(3)(A)).

Generally, under the size limitation, a nominated urban area cannot exceed 20 square miles and must be located within no more than two contiguous states, and a nominated rural area cannot exceed 1,000 square miles and must be located within no more than three contiguous states. The nominated area generally must have a continuous boundary. Special rules apply to rural areas and areas that include a central business district (Code Secs. 1391(g)(3)(B) and 1392(a)(3)).

Coordination with renewal communities. Up to 40 new areas called "renewal communities" will be designated that will receive tax breaks similar to empowerment zones (see ¶ 105). The designation of an area as an empowerment zone or an enterprise community shall cease to be in effect as of the date that the designation of any portion of such area as a renewal community takes effect (Code Sec. 1400E(e), as added by the Act). If an area loses its designation as an empowerment zone because any part of the area has been designated as a renewal community, then the number of areas that may be designated as empowerment zones in Round III will be increased on a one-for-one basis. Each of these additional Round III empowerment zones will have the same urban or rural character as the area it replaces (Code Sec. 1391(h)(4), as added by the 2000 Act).

Comment. Businesses in the Round III empowerment zones will be eligible for the same tax incentives that are available to the Round I and Round II empowerment zones, namely, a 20-percent employment credit, increased section 179 expensing, and the more generous tax-exempt financing benefits available to the Round II empowerment zones (Conference Committee Report).

Time limitations. The Round III empowerment zone designations will be made after December 21, 2000, and before January 1, 2002. The designations made in this selection round generally will remain in effect from January 1, 2002, to December 31, 2009 (Code Sec. 1391(h)(2), as added by the 2000 Act). However, the designation may end earlier on the termination date provided by the state and local governments in their nomination or on the date the Secretary of HUD or Agriculture revokes the designation (Code Sec. 1391(h)(2), as added by the 2000 Act; Code Sec. 1391(d)(1)(B) and (C)).

Comment. The new law also extends the expiration date of Round I and II empowerment zones to December 31, 2009. See ¶ 135.

★ *Effective date.* No specific effective date is provided by the Act. The provision is, therefore, considered effective on December 21, 2000, the date of enactment.

Act Sec. 111 of the Community Renewal Tax Relief Act of 2000, adding Code Sec. 1391(h). Law at ¶ 5690. Committee Report at ¶ 10,145.

Extension of Empowerment Zones Through 2009

¶ 135

Background

Designations of empowerment zones and enterprise communities will generally remain in effect until the end of the 10th calendar year beginning on or after the date of designation (Code Sec. 1391(d)). Designations of these areas took place in stages and, thus, have different periods of applicability.

In Round I, the Secretaries of Housing and Urban Development (HUD) and Agriculture designated 65 urban and 30 rural enterprise communities, effective December 21, 1994. In addition, the Secretary of HUD designated parts of the following cities as urban empowerment zones: Atlanta, GA; Baltimore, MD; Chicago, IL; Detroit, MI; New York City, NY; and Philadelphia, PA/Camden, NJ. The Secretary of Agriculture also designated the following rural empowerment zones: the Kentucky Highlands; Mid-Delta, Mississippi; and Rio Grande Valley, Texas. Additional Round I urban empowerment zone designations effective January 1, 2000, include parts of the following cities: Cleveland, OH; and Los Angeles, CA (Code Sec. 1391(b); IRS Publication 954, "Tax Incentives for Empowerment Zones and Other Distressed Communities" (Rev. Feb. 1999)).

For the Round II designations effective December 31, 1998, the Secretary of HUD designated parts of the following cities as urban empowerment zones: Boston, MA; Cincinnati, OH; Columbia/Sumter, SC; Columbus, OH; Cumberland County, NJ; El Paso, TX; Gary/East Chicago, IN; Huntington, WV/Ironton, OH; Knoxville/Knox County, TN; Miami/Miami-Dade County, FL; Minneapolis, MN; New Haven, CT; Norfolk/Portsmouth, VA; Santa Ana, CA; and St. Louis, MO/East St. Louis, IL. The Secretary of Agriculture also designated the following rural empowerment zones: Desert Communities Empowerment Zone, California; Steele-Griggs County Empowerment Zone, North Dakota; Oglala Sioux Tribe Empowerment Zone, South Dakota; Southernmost Illinois Delta Empowerment Zone, Illinois; and Southwest Georgia United Empowerment Zone, Georgia (Code Sec. 1391(g); IRS Publication 954, "Tax Incentives for Empowerment Zones and Other Distressed Communities" (Rev. Feb. 1999)).

Community Renewal Tax Relief Act Impact

Designations extended for some empowerment zones.—Designations of areas as empowerment zones are scheduled to remain in effect through December 31, 2009 (Code Sec. 1391(d)(1)(A), as amended by the Community Renewal Tax

Relief Act of 2000). Thus, the Round I empowerment zones effective December 21, 1994, the Round I empowerment zones effective January 1, 2000, and the Round II empowerment zones effective December 31, 1998, are now all scheduled to expire at the same time. However, the designation of an empowerment zone can end on the termination date designated by the state and local governments in their nomination of the empowerment zone or on the date that the designation is revoked if those dates are earlier (Code Sec. 1391(d)(1)(B) and (C)).

Comment. The Round I empowerment zones effective December 21, 1994, that were previously scheduled to expire under the 10th-calendar-year rule on December 31, 2004, receive a five-year extension. The Round I empowerment zones effective January 1, 2000, that were already scheduled to expire under the 10th-calendar-year rule on December 31, 2009, do not receive an extension. The Round II empowerment zones effective December 31, 1998, that were previously scheduled to expire under the 10th-calendar-year rule on December 31, 2008, receive a one-year extension.

Comment. The nine new empowerment zones that will be designated in Round III (see ¶ 130) will be in effect for eight years from January 1, 2002 through December 31, 2009 (Code Sec. 1391(h)(2), as added by the 2000 Act).

Enterprise communities. In the case of an enterprise community, the designation period will continue to be determined under the 10th-calendar-year rule. Under the 10th-calendar-year rule, designations of enterprise communities will expire on the close of the 10th calendar year beginning on or after the date of designation (Code Sec. 1391(d)(1)(A), as amended by the 2000 Act). Thus, the 65 urban and 30 rural enterprise communities designated in Round I and effective December 21, 1994, will expire on December 31, 2004. As under existing law, the designation of an enterprise community can end earlier on the termination date designated by the state and local governments in their nomination of the enterprise community or on the date that the designation is revoked (Code Sec. 1391(d)(1)(B) and (C)).

Comment. Effective January 1, 1998, parts of Washington, D.C. were designated as an empowerment zone. This treatment was to remain in effect until the end of 2002. However, the new law extends D.C. empowerment zone status through 2003. See ¶ 170.

★ *Effective date.* No specific effective date is provided by the Act. The provision is, therefore, considered effective on December 21, 2000, the date of enactment.

Act Sec. 112 of the Community Renewal Tax Relief Act of 2000, amending Code Sec. 1391(d)(1)(A). **Law at ¶ 5690. Committee Report at ¶ 10,146.**

20-Percent Employment Credit for All Empowerment Zones

¶ 140

Background

Employers doing business in certain empowerment zones are entitled to a tax credit for qualified wages paid to employees who work and live in the zones (Code Sec. 1396). For 2000, the empowerment zone employment credit is equal to 20 percent of the first $15,000 of qualified wages paid to full-time or part-time employees (Code Sec. 1396(b) and (c)). The employee must live in the empower-

Background

ment zone and must perform substantially all of his work in the zone in the employer's trade or business (Code Sec. 1396(d)).

The current empowerment zones were designated in stages. Initially, six urban empowerment zones and three rural empowerment zones were designated in Round I, effective December 21, 1994. For these Round I empowerment zones, the credit percentage of 20 percent decreases after 2001 (Code Sec. 1396(b)(1)). The employment credit for the special empowerment zone in the District of Columbia (DC Zone) remains at a rate of 20 percent through 2002 (Code Sec. 1400(d)(2)). For the two additional urban empowerment zones that are considered Round I empowerment zones but are effective January 1, 2000 (Code Sec. 1391(b)(2)), the credit percentage decreases after 2004 (Code Sec. 1396(b)(2)).

In Round II, an additional 15 urban empowerment zones and five rural empowerment zones were designated effective December 31, 1998 (Code Sec. 1391(g)(1)). These Round II empowerment zones are not entitled to the empowerment zone employment credit (Code Secs. 1391(g)(3) and 1396(e)).

Community Renewal Tax Relief Act Impact

All empowerment zones receive employment credit.—Employers doing business in any of the designated empowerment zones will be entitled to the employment credit for qualified wages paid after 2001 to employees who work and live in the zones (Code Sec. 1396, as amended by the Community Renewal Tax Relief Act of 2000). Thus, the employment credit will be available for employers in the empowerment zones designated in Round II and the nine new empowerment zones that will be designated in Round III (see ¶ 130), as well as the zones that were designated in Round I.

Planning Note. Employers located in the 20 Round II empowerment zones that went into effect December 31, 1998 (see ¶ 135), and are currently denied the credit (Code Sec. 1396(e), prior to repeal by the 2000 Act) will be able to take the credit for qualified wages paid after 2001. Thus, employers looking to expand their businesses or hire new employees may want to start recruiting residents of the Round II empowerment zones late this year for employment in 2002.

The empowerment zone employment credit is equal to 20 percent of the first $15,000 of qualified wages paid to full-time or part-time employees (Code Sec. 1396(b) and (c)). The credit percentage will not be phased out in future years (Code Sec. 1396(b), as amended by the 2000 Act). Thus, the credit percentage will remain at 20 percent for the entire period for which the empowerment zone designations are in effect, which is through December 31, 2009 (Code Sec. 1391(d)(1)(A), as amended by the Community Renewal Tax Relief Act of 2000). See ¶ 135.

Comment. Employers in the empowerment zone in the District of Columbia (DC Zone) are entitled to the full 20-percent employment credit with no phaseout under both the old and new law. The credit is available during the period that the DC Zone designation is in effect, which has been extended through 2003 (Code Sec. 1400(f), as amended by the 2000 Act). See ¶ 170.

The employee for whom the credit is claimed must have a principal place of residence in the empowerment zone and must perform substantially all of his work in the zone in the employer's trade or business (Code Sec. 1396(d)(1)). The credit may be denied for certain employees, such as five-percent owners of the business, persons who are employed less than 90 days, employees of large farming businesses, and individuals employed in gambling and other specified businesses (Code Sec. 1396(d)(2)).

★ *Effective date.* The amendments apply to wages paid or incurred after December 31, 2001 (Act Sec. 113(d) of the Community Renewal Tax Relief Act of 2000).

Act Sec. 113(a) of the Community Renewal Tax Relief Act of 2000, amending Code Sec. 1396(b); Act Sec. 113(b), striking Code Sec. 1396(e); Act Sec. 113(c), amending Code Sec. 1400(d); Act Sec. 113(d). Law at ¶ 5710 and ¶ 5760. Committee Report at ¶ 10,147.

Increased Expensing Under Section 179

¶ 145

Background ————————————————————————————————

Taxpayers may elect to deduct the cost of certain tangible depreciable property used in a trade or business in the year in which it was placed in service, rather than capitalizing the cost and claiming depreciation deductions over time (Code Sec. 179). The deductible amount is limited to a maximum of $20,000 for tax years beginning in 2000, $24,000 for tax years beginning in 2001 and 2002, and $25,000 for tax years beginning in 2003 and thereafter (Code Sec. 179(b)). The maximum deductible amount is reduced on a dollar-for-dollar basis by the amount by which the cost of section 179 property that is placed in service during the tax year exceeds $200,000 (Code Sec. 179(b)(2)).

Qualified enterprise zone businesses are entitled to an increased section 179 deduction for the cost of qualified zone property used in an empowerment zone and placed in service during the tax year (Code Sec. 1397A). The maximum deductible amount is increased by the lower of $20,000 or the cost of section 179 property that is qualified zone property and placed in service during the tax year (Code Sec. 1397A(a)(1)). However, the maximum deductible amount is reduced by the amount by which 50 percent of the cost of section 179 property that is qualified zone property and placed in service during the tax year exceeds $200,000 (Code Sec. 1397A(a)(2)).

For purposes of the section 179 deduction, qualified zone property does not include property where substantially all of its use is in certain developable sites (Code Sec. 1397A(c)). These developable sites are noncontiguous parcels in a nominated area that may be developed for commercial or industrial purposes and the aggregate area of which does not exceed 2,000 acres (Code Sec. 1391(g)(3)(A)(iii)).

Community Renewal Tax Relief Act Impact

Section 179 expensing increased for zone property.—Enterprise zone businesses can elect to deduct the cost of section 179 property that is qualified zone property and placed in service during the year up to a higher maximum amount of $59,000 for tax years beginning in 2002 and $60,000 for tax years beginning in 2003 and thereafter (Code Sec. 1397A(a)(1), as amended by the Community Renewal Tax Relief Act of 2000; Code Sec. 179(b)(1)). The property must be used in the empowerment zone.

The higher expensing limitation for tax years beginning after 2001 reflects:

(1) the regular section 179 maximum deductible amount of $24,000 for tax years beginning in 2002 and $25,000 for tax years beginning in 2003 and thereafter, plus

(2) an additional amount of $35,000 or, if lower, the cost of section 179 property that is qualified zone property placed in service during the year (Code Sec. 1397A(a), as amended by the 2000 Act).

The current rule that reduces the expensing limitation by the excess of: (1) 50 percent of the cost of section 179 property that is qualified zone property and placed in service during the year, over (2) $200,000 still applies (Code Sec. 1397A(a)(2)). Thus, if the cost of section 179 property that is qualified zone property and placed in service in a tax year beginning in 2002 equals or exceeds $518,000, no section 179 deduction is available.

Example. EZ Corp. places a machine in service in an empowerment zone in 2002. The machine is section 179 property that is qualified zone property and has a cost of $64,000. Under the dollar limitation, only $59,000 of the cost is deductible under Code Sec. 179 in 2002. If EZ Corp. had placed other equipment in service in 2002 with a cost of $450,000, then only $2,000 of the cost of the machine would be deductible under Code Sec. 179. One-half of the total cost of all section 179 property that is qualified zone property (($64,000 + $450,000) × $\frac{1}{2}$ = $257,000) over $200,000 is $57,000. The expensing limitation of $59,000 has to be reduced by $57,000, leaving a maximum deduction of $2,000.

Qualified zone property is depreciable property under Code Sec. 168 (or property to which Code Sec. 168 would apply but for Code Sec. 179):

(1) that was purchased by the taxpayer after the date on which the designation of the empowerment zone took effect;

(2) whose original use in the empowerment zone began with the taxpayer; and

(3) substantially all of the use of which is in the empowerment zone and is in the active conduct of a qualified business by the taxpayer in the zone (Code Sec. 1397D(a)(1), as redesignated by the 2000 Act).

Caution. Qualified zone property is not eligible for the increased Code Sec. 179 expense deduction unless the property is also "section 179 property" as defined in Code Sec. 179(d)(1). Thus, while buildings can be categorized as qualified zone property, they would not be eligible for the Code Sec. 179 expense deduction because section 179 property is defined to include only tangible section 1245 (personal) property (Code Sec. 179(d)(1)).

Developable sites. The prior restriction on the categorization of property as qualified zone property where substantially all of its use is in certain developable sites has been lifted (Code Sec. 1397A(c), prior to being stricken by the 2000 Act). The developable sites are an exception to the poverty rate requirement for noncontiguous parcels in a nominated area that may be developed for commercial or industrial purposes and the aggregate area of which does not exceed 2,000 acres (Code Sec. 1391(g)(3)(A)(iii)).

★ *Effective date.* The amendments apply to tax years beginning after December 31, 2001 (Act Sec. 114(c) of the Community Renewal Tax Relief Act of 2000).

Act Sec. 114(a) of the Community Renewal Tax Relief Act of 2000, amending Code Sec. 1397A(a)(1)(A); Act Sec. 114(b), striking Code Sec. 1397A(c); Act Sec. 114(c). Law at ¶ 5720. Committee Report at ¶ 10,148.

Higher Limits on Tax-Exempt Zone Facility Bonds

¶ 150

Background _____

The Omnibus Budget Reconciliation Act of 1993 (P.L. 103-66) authorized the designation of nine empowerment zones (Round I empowerment zones) to provide tax incentives for businesses to locate within targeted areas designated by the Secretaries of HUD and Agriculture. The Taxpayer Relief Act of 1997 (P.L. 105-34) authorized the designation of two additional Round I urban empowerment zones (Code Sec. 1391(b)(2)). The 1997 Act also authorized the designation of 20 additional empowerment zones (Round II empowerment zones) (Code Sec. 1391(g)). Code Sec. 1394 authorizes the issuance of tax-exempt enterprise zone facility bonds. Businesses in the Round II empowerment zones are eligible for more generous tax-exempt financing benefits than those available in the Round I empowerment zones (Code Sec. 1394(f)). Specifically, the tax-exempt financing benefits for the Round II empowerment zones are not subject to the State private activity bond volume caps (but are subject to separate per-zone volume limitations). Also, the per-business size limitations that apply to the Round I empowerment zones and enterprise communities (*i.e.,* $3 million for each qualified enterprise zone business with a maximum of $20 million for each principal user for all zones and communities) (Code Sec. 1394(c)) do not apply to qualifying bonds issued for Round II empowerment zones.

Community Renewal Tax Relief Act Impact

Round II benefits extended to Round I zones.—Businesses located in Round I empowerment zones (other than the DC Enterprise Zone) are eligible for the more generous tax-exempt bond rules that apply to Round II empowerment zones, with respect to bonds issued after December 31, 2001 (Code Sec. 1394(f), as amended by the Community Renewal Tax Relief Act of 2000). Thus, with respect to bonds issued after December 31, 2001, the tax-exempt financing benefits for both Round I and Round II empowerment zones are not subject to the State private activity bond volume caps of Code Sec. 146 (but are subject to separate per-zone volume limitations of Code Sec. 1394(f)(2)(B)). Furthermore, such bonds are not subject to the per-business size limitations of Code Sec. 1394(c) (*i.e.,* $3 million for each qualified enterprise zone business with a maximum of $20 million for each principal user for all zones and communities).

Bonds that have been issued by businesses in Round I zones before January 1, 2002, are not taken into account in applying the limitation on the amount of new empowerment zone facility bonds that can be issued under the Act (Conference Committee Report).

Comment. The Act also authorizes the designation of nine additional empowerment zones ("Round III zones") by January 1, 2002. See ¶ 130. The enhanced tax-exempt financing benefits available to Round I and II zones are also available to Round III zones.

★ *Effective date.* The amendments apply to obligations issued after December 31, 2001 (Act Sec. 115(b) of the Community Renewal Tax Relief Act of 2000).

Act Sec. 115(a) of the Community Renewal Tax Relief Act of 2000, amending Code Sec. 1394(f)(3); Act Sec. 115(b). Law at ¶ 5700. Committee Report at ¶ 10,149.

Gain Rollover on Empowerment Zone Investments

¶ 155

Background

In general, gain or loss is recognized on any sale, exchange, or other disposition of property. A noncorporate taxpayer may elect to roll over, without current payment of tax, any capital gain realized upon the sale of qualified small business stock held for more than six months where the taxpayer uses the proceeds to purchase other qualified small business stock within 60 days of the sale of the original stock (Code Sec. 1045). Through such an election, the recognition of the gain realized is deferred until the replacement stock is sold by reducing the basis of the replacement stock. Under Code Sec. 1202, prior to amendment by the Community Renewal Tax Relief Act, a 50-percent gain exclusion applies to the sale of small business stock that is held for more than five years. The 50-percent exclusion is increased to 60 percent in the case of qualified small business stock in an empowerment zone business that is acquired after December 21, 2000 (Code Sec. 1202, as amended by the Community Renewal Tax Relief Act of 2000). See ¶ 160.

Community Renewal Tax Relief Act Impact

Empowerment zone asset gain rollover.—A taxpayer can elect to roll over, or defer the recognition of, capital gain realized from the sale or exchange of any qualified empowerment zone asset purchased after December 21, 2000, and held for more than one year ("original zone asset") where the taxpayer uses the proceeds to purchase other qualifying empowerment zone assets in the *same* zone ("replacement zone asset") within 60 days of the sale of the original empowerment zone asset (Code Sec. 1397B, as added by the Community Renewal Tax Relief Act of 2000).

Generally, a "qualified empowerment zone asset" is an asset that would be a qualified community asset if the empowerment zone were a renewal community (and the asset is acquired after December 21, 2000) (Code Sec. 1397B(b)(1)(A), as added by the 2000 Act).

Caution. Gain that is treated as ordinary income is not eligible for rollover treatment (Code Sec. 1397B(b)(2), as added by the 2000 Act). Thus, for example, rollover treatment does not apply to the extent that gain is recaptured as ordinary income under the depreciation recapture rules. Also ineligible is gain that is attributable to real property or an intangible asset that is not an integral part of an enterprise zone business.

The holding period of the replacement zone asset includes the holding period of the original zone asset, except that the replacement asset must actually be held for more than one year to qualify for another tax-free rollover (Code Sec. 1397B(b)(5), as added by the 2000 Act).

The recognition of the rollover gain is deferred until the sale of the replacement asset by reducing the basis of the replacement asset by the amount of the realized gain which is not recognized (Code Sec. 1397B(b)(4), as added by the 2000 Act). If more than one replacement asset is acquired, the basis of the replacement assets are reduced in the order in which the replacement assets are acquired. If the replacement asset is qualified small business stock, then this basis reduction rule does not apply for purposes of determining the amount of gain eligible for purposes of the partial gain exclusion that applies to the sale of small business stock under Code Sec. 1202 (Code Sec. 1397B(b)(4), as added by the 2000 Act).

> **Example.** Anita Gonzalez operates a business within an empowerment zone. She purchases a building on March 1, 2001 for $10,000. Assume that she uses the asset as an integral part of the empowerment zone business and sells the building more than one year later for $50,000. She then purchases another business building for use in the same empowerment zone for $100,000 within 60 days of the sale. Assume further that she claimed $1,000 in depreciation on the first building (none of which is subject to recapture), so that her adjusted basis in the building is $9,000 ($10,000 − $1,000). The $41,000 gain ($50,000 − $9,000 adjusted basis) is not recognized and the basis of the replacement building for purposes of determining gain or loss is reduced by $41,000 to $59,000 ($100,000 − $41,000).

Comment. According to the Conference Committee Report to the Community Renewal Tax Relief Act, if the replacement zone asset is qualified small business stock (as defined in Code Sec. 1202), the partial gain exclusion provided by Code Sec. 1202 for such stock would not apply to gain accrued on the original zone asset. Code Sec. 1045 provides rules for the rollover of gain on qualified small business stock to other small business stock.

Comment. The Act authorizes the designation of 40 "renewal communities" which are eligible for special tax benefits (Code Sec. 1400E, as added by the 2000 Act). These are in addition to the current law empowerment zones and enterprise zones. See ¶ 105 and following.

Code Sec. 1400F covers renewal community capital gain and provides a 100-percent capital gain exclusion upon the sale of qualified community assets held for more than five years. A qualified community asset is defined in new Code Sec. 1400F. The term generally includes any qualified community stock (original issue stock of a domestic corporation that operates a renewal community business), any qualified community partnership interest (an interest in a partnership acquired from a partnership that operates a renewal community business), and any qualified community business property (business property used in a renewal community business). See ¶ 107 for additional details regarding these definitions.

Caution. Assets in the DC Enterprise Zone are not eligible for the tax-free rollover treatment (Code Sec. 1397B(b)(1)(B), as added by the 2000 Act). However, a qualifying DC Zone asset held for more than five years is eligible for a 100-percent capital gains exclusion under other rules (Code Sec. 1400B).

¶ 155

★ *Effective date.* The amendments apply to qualified empowerment zone assets acquired after December 21, 2000 (Act Sec. 116(c) of the Community Renewal Tax Relief Act).

Act Sec. 116 of the Community Renewal Tax Relief Act of 2000, redesignating former Code Secs. 1397B and 1397C as Code Secs. 1397C and 1397D, respectively, and adding Code Sec. 1397B; Act Sec. 116(b)(1), amending Code Sec. 1016(a)(23); Act Sec. 116(b)(2), amending Code Sec. 1223(15); Act Sec. 116(c). Law at ¶5580, ¶5630 and ¶5730. Committee Report at ¶10,150.

Increased Exclusion of Gain on Sale of Empowerment Zone Stock

¶160

Background

Subject to limitations, a noncorporate taxpayer may exclude 50 percent of the gain from the sale of qualifying small business stock held more than five years (Code Sec. 1202). The portion of the capital gain included in income is subject to a maximum regular tax rate of 28 percent (Code Sec. 1(h)). Furthermore, a maximum of 42 percent of the *excluded* gain is a minimum tax preference (Code Sec. 57(a)(7)).

Community Renewal Tax Relief Act Impact

Increased exclusion for empowerment zone stock sales.—The exclusion of gain from the sale or exchange of qualified small business stock is increased to 60 percent in the case of the sale or exchange of certain empowerment zone stock (Code Sec. 1202(a), as amended by the Community Renewal Tax Relief Act of 2000). Thus, 60 percent of the gain from the sale of qualified small business stock is not recognized if:

(1) the stock is acquired after December 21, 2000;

(2) the stock is in a corporation that is a qualified business entity during substantially all of the taxpayer's holding period for such stock; and

(3) the stock is held for more than five years.

A "qualified business entity" means a corporation that satisfies the requirements of a qualifying business under the empowerment zone rules during substantially all of the taxpayer's holding period. The most important of these requirements are that the corporation conduct all its businesses within an empowerment zone, that it derive at least 50 percent of its total gross income from such businesses, and that at least 35 percent of its employees are residents of an empowerment zone (Code Sec. 1397C(b), as redesignated by the 2000 Act).

Caution. This increased exclusion does not apply to gain attributable to periods after December 31, 2014 (Code Sec. 1202(a)(2)(C), as amended by the 2000 Act). Also, this increased exclusion does not apply to stock in a DC Enterprise Zone, since the DC Enterprise Zone is not treated as an empowerment zone (Code Sec. 1202(a)(2)(D), as amended by the 2000 Act). However, a different statutory rule provides a 100-percent exclusion for qualified capital gain from the sale of any DC Zone asset, including DC Zone business stock, held for more than five years (Code Sec. 1400B).

If a corporation ceases to be a qualifying business after the five-year holding period for the stock has ended, the exclusion only applies to the gain that accrued up to the point that the corporation ceased to be a qualifying business (Code Sec. 1202(a)(2)(B), as amended by the 2000 Act).

Comment. The portion of the capital gain that is included in income is still subject to a maximum regular tax rate of 28 percent (Code Sec. 1(h)(8), as amended by the 2000 Act). Forty-two percent (28 percent, in the case of stock with a holding period that begins after December 31, 2000) of the *excluded* gain continues to be a minimum tax preference (Code Sec. 57(a)(7)).

★ *Effective date.* The amendments apply to stock acquired after December 21, 2000 (Act Sec. 117(c) of the Community Renewal Tax Relief Act of 2000).

Act Sec. 117(a) of the Community Renewal Tax Relief Act of 2000, amending Code Sec. 1202(a); Act Sec. 117(b), amending Code Sec. 1(h)(8) and 1202; Act Sec. 117(c). Law at ¶ 5001 and ¶ 5620. Committee Report at ¶ 10,155.

DISTRICT OF COLUMBIA

Extension of D.C. Homebuyer Credit

¶ 165

Background

First-time homebuyers of a principal residence in the District of Columbia are allowed a credit of up to $5,000 of the purchase price of the residence. The maximum amount of the credit is $2,500 each for married taxpayers filing separate returns (Code Sec. 1400C(a) and (e)(1)(A)). To qualify for the credit, the D.C. residence must have been purchased after August 4, 1997, and before January 1, 2002 (Code Sec. 1400C(i)). If the D.C. residence is newly constructed by the taxpayer, the date that the taxpayer first occupies the residence is treated as the purchase date (Code Sec. 1400C(e)(2)(B)). Eligible taxpayers file Form 8859, District of Columbia First-Time Homebuyer Credit, with their Form 1040 to claim the credit.

There are a number of restrictions and limitations on the use of the D.C. homebuyer credit. Since the credit is targeted for first-time homebuyers, neither the individual nor the individual's spouse may have held a present ownership interest in a principal residence in the District of Columbia during the one-year period that ends on the purchase date of the residence for which the credit is claimed (Code Sec. 1400C(c)(1)). Also, an individual cannot claim the credit more than once (Code Sec. 1400C(c)(2)). The credit is phased out for joint filers with modified adjusted gross income (AGI) between $110,000 and $130,000 and for other individuals with modified AGI between $70,000 and $90,000 (Code Sec. 1400C(b)). Although the credit is treated as a nonrefundable personal credit, any part of the credit that is not used due to the limitation on nonrefundable personal credits may be carried over to the next tax year (Code Sec. 1400C(d) and (g)).

Community Renewal Tax Relief Act Impact

D.C. homebuyer credit extended.—The credit for first-time homebuyers of a principal residence in the District of Columbia has been extended for two years. The credit of up to $5,000 of the purchase price of the residence, or $2,500 each for married taxpayers filing separate returns, now applies to property purchased after August 4, 1997, and before January 1, 2004 (Code Sec. 1400C(i), as amended by the Community Renewal Tax Relief Act of 2000).

★ *Effective date.* No specific effective date is provided by the Act. The provision is, therefore, considered effective on December 21, 2000, the date of enactment.

Act Sec. 163 of the Community Renewal Tax Relief Act of 2000, amending Code Sec. 1400C(i). Law at ¶ 5790. Committee Report at ¶ 10,220.

Extension of DC Zone

¶ 170

Background———————————————————————————————————————

Parts of the District of Columbia are treated as an empowerment zone, called the District of Columbia Enterprise Zone (DC Zone) (Code Sec. 1400). The designation of the area as the DC Zone is scheduled to end on December 31, 2002 (Code Sec. 1400(f)).

As with the other empowerment zones, special tax incentives are provided for the DC Zone in order to attract businesses to the area. One tax break for DC Zone businesses is an exclusion from income for qualified capital gain from the sale or exchange of a DC Zone asset held for more than five years (Code Sec. 1400B). The DC Zone asset must be acquired before January 1, 2003, and the gain cannot be attributable to periods before January 1, 1998, or after December 31, 2007 (Code Sec. 1400B(b) and (e)(2)).

The DC Zone also receives special tax-exempt financing incentives that apply to bonds issued from January 1, 1998, through December 31, 2002 (Code Sec. 1400A). Generally, the limit on the amount of bonds that can be allocated to a particular DC Zone business in the DC Zone is higher than the amount that can be allocated to a particular enterprise zone business in an empowerment zone or enterprise community (Code Sec. 1400A; Code Sec. 1394(c)).

Community Renewal Tax Relief Act Impact

DC Zone extended one year.—The designation of parts of the District of Columbia as the District of Columbia Enterprise Zone (DC Zone) and the tax benefits for the DC Zone have been extended for one year (Code Secs. 1400(f), 1400A(b) and 1400B, as amended by the Community Renewal Tax Relief Act of 2000). Thus, the designation of the DC Zone is now scheduled to end on December 31, 2003 (Code Sec. 1400(f), as amended by the 2000 Act).

The zero-percent capital gains rate for qualified capital gain from the sale or exchange of a DC Zone asset held for more than five years has also been extended by one year (Code Sec. 1400B, as amended by the 2000 Act). To qualify, DC Zone assets, including DC Zone business stock, DC Zone partnership interests and DC Zone business property, now must be acquired before January 1, 2004 (Code Sec. 1400B(b), as amended by the 2000 Act). Qualified capital gain cannot include gain attributable to periods before January 1, 1998, or after December 31, 2008 (Code Sec. 1400B(e)(2), as amended by the 2000 Act).

The DC Zone also receives a one-year extension of the special tax-exempt financing incentives. Thus, this incentive now applies to bonds issued from January 1, 1998, through December 31, 2003 (Code Sec. 1400A(b), as amended by the 2000 Act).

★ *Effective date.* No specific effective date is provided by the Act. The provision is, therefore, considered effective on December 21, 2000, the date of enactment.

Act Sec. 164(a) of the Community Renewal Tax Relief Act of 2000, amending Code Secs. 1400(f) and 1400A(b); Act Sec. 164(b), amending Code Sec. 1400B. Law at ¶ 5760, ¶ 5770, and ¶ 5780. Committee Report at ¶ 10,225.

_____

Chapter 2

Business and Investment

ACCOUNTING

Reinstate Installment Method for Accrual Basis Taxpayers

¶ 205

Background _____

Installment sales of personal or real property by nonaccrual method nondealers are reported under the installment method unless a taxpayer elects out (Code Sec. 453). The installment method permits the reporting of gain from qualified installment sales as payments are received rather than in the year of sale.

Section 536(a) of the Ticket to Work and Work Incentives Improvement Act of 1999 (P.L. 106-170) generally repealed the installment method of accounting for accrual basis taxpayers for sales and dispositions on or after December 17, 1999. The installment method had allowed an accrual basis taxpayer to defer taxes on gain from a sale of property until the taxpayer actually received payment. Small businesses have said the repeal caused them hardship when they tried to sell their business by accelerating the payment of taxes or by lowering the amount offered by potential buyers, according to a House Ways and Means Committee release.

Many groups, including the American Institute of Certified Public Accountants (AICPA), urged Congress to fix the problem. Citing numerous complaints from members whose clients have had trouble selling their businesses, David A. Lifson, chair of the AICPA Tax Executive Committee, said at a congressional hearing, "Many negotiated transactions for the sale of all or part of a taxpayer's business have recently fallen apart." The Independent Insurance Agents of America, Inc., claims that for small business owners seeking to sell their businesses, the ban drove down the price by five to 20 percent.

Installment Tax Correction Act Impact

Ban on installment method repealed.—The prohibition on the use of the installment method for dispositions of property that would otherwise be reported by a taxpayer using an accrual method of accounting is repealed, retroactive to the date the prohibition was enacted. (Code Sec. 453, as amended by the Installment Tax Correction Act of 2000.) The Internal Revenue Code will be applied and administered as if the ban had not been enacted (Act Sec. 2(b) of the 2000 Act.)

Comment. The installment method pledge rule (Code Sec. 453A(d)), in which proceeds of indebtedness secured by a pledge of an applicable installment obligation are treated as a deemed payment on the pledged obligation, is not affected by this provision (the pledge rule was modified by Act Sec. 536(b) of the 1999 Act (P.L. 106-170)).

PRACTICAL ANALYSIS. Charles R. Levun, of Levun, Goodman & Cohen, Northbrook, Ill., comments that practitioners should especially note that the ability of accrual method taxpayers to utilize the installment method of reporting was reinstated as of the effective date of its original repeal (December 17, 1999). Consequently, for instance, a calendar year accrual method taxpayer that sold its business between December 17, 1999, and December 31, 1999, and could not report the transaction on the installment method by reason of the repeal of Code Sec. 453(a) for accrual method taxpayers, might consider filing an amended return to take advantage of the accrual method of reporting for such transaction.

Mr. Levun also observes that, in response to the repeal of Code Sec. 453(a) for accrual method taxpayers, the IRS released Rev. Proc. 2000-22, I.R.B. 2000-20, 108, which permitted certain "smaller" taxpayers to opt out of the accrual method of accounting, but that there has been no guidance yet as to whether a taxpayer that took advantage of this Rev. Proc. will be allowed to retroactively revoke its election to be subject to the accrual method of accounting.

★ *Effective date.* The provision is effective for sales or other dispositions on or after December 17, 1999 (Act Sec. 2(a) of the Installment Tax Correction Act of 2000).

Act Sec. 2(a) of the Installment Tax Correction Act of 2000, repealing Act Sec. 536(a) of the Ticket to Work and Work Incentives Improvement Act of 1999 (P.L. 106-170) (Code Sec. 453(a), (d), (i) and (k) were amended by Act Sec. 536(a)) (thus, these amendments are removed from the Code); Act Sec. 2(b). Law at ¶ 5330. Committee Report at ¶ 10,375.

Original Issue Discount

¶ 210

*Background*_____

The rules for recognizing original issue discount (OID) income on debt instruments were expanded by the Deficit Reduction Act of 1984 (P.L. 98-369). The 1984 Act created an exception from the definition of "debt instrument" for certain annuity contracts to which Code Sec. 72 applies that are issued by an insurance company subject to tax under Code Secs. 801 through 848 (Subchapter L) (Code Sec. 1275(a)(1)(B)(ii)). An exception from the definition of "debt instrument" was also provided for annuity contracts that depend in whole or substantial part on the life expectancy of one or more persons (Code Sec. 1275(a)(1)(B)(i)). These "life annuities," sometimes referred to as "private annuities" are, thus, excluded from the OID rules.

Technical Corrections Impact

Clarification of existing OID rules.—A technical correction clarifies that an annuity contract, otherwise meeting the applicable OID requirements, is exempt from the OID provisions if it is issued by a tax-exempt 501(c) organization that would be taxed as an insurance company were it not tax-exempt (Code Sec. 1275(a)(1)(B)(ii), as amended by the Community Renewal Tax Relief Act of 2000).

Example. A tax-exempt fraternal beneficiary society issues an annuity contract for which there is no consideration other than cash. This annuity falls within the insurance company exception of Code Sec. 1275(a)(1)(B)(ii).

The Conference Report to the 2000 Act clarifies that charitable gift annuities, as defined in Code Sec. 501(m), fall within the life annuity exception of Code Sec. 1275(a)(1)(B)(i) because these annuities depend in whole or in substantial part on the life expectancy of one or more individuals.

★ *Effective date.* This provision is effective for tax years ending after July 18, 1984 (Act Sec. 318(c)(2) of the Community Renewal Tax Relief Act of 2000; Act Sec. 41(a) of the Tax Reform Act of 1984).

Act Sec. 318(c)(1) of the Commmunity Renewal Tax Relief Act of 2000, amending Code Sec. 1275(a)(1)(B)(ii); Act Sec. 318(c)(2). Law at ¶ 5670. Committee Report at ¶ 10,345.

Straight-line Depreciation Under AMT

¶ 215

*Background*_____

Depreciation claimed as a deduction for regular tax purposes is an item of tax adjustment to the extent that it exceeds the depreciation allowable for alternative minimum tax (AMT) purposes. For property placed in service after December 31, 1998, there is no AMT adjustment required for property that is depreciated for regular tax purposes under the straight-line method or for personal property depreciated using the 150-percent declining balance method. This is because AMT depreciation for this property is calculated using the regular tax recovery periods and (1) the straight-line method in the case of property subject to the straight-line method under regular tax, or (2) the 150-percent declining balance method where

Background————————————————————————————————————

the straight-line method does not apply (Code Sec. 56(a)(1)(A), as amended by the Taxpayer Relief Act of 1997 (P.L. 105-34)). Property for which no AMT adjustment is required includes section 1250 residential rental property and nonresidential real property because this property is required to be depreciated under the straight-line method for regular tax purposes (Code Sec. 168(b)(3)). The treatment of section 1250 property, other than residential rental property or nonresidential real property, where accelerated depreciation for regular tax purposes is allowed (*e.g.*, the 150-percent declining balance method or the 200-percent declining balance method) is uncertain. Although prior to amendment by the 1997 Act, it was clear that such section 1250 property placed in service before January 1, 1999, had to be depreciated using the straight-line method under the AMT, it is arguable that changes made by that Act inadvertently allow accelerated depreciation on such property placed in service after December 31, 1998, under the AMT.

Technical Corrections Impact

AMT depreciation for section 1250 property.—A technical correction clarifies that *all* section 1250 real property, not just residential rental and nonresidential real property, placed in service after 1998 must be depreciated using the straight-line method of depreciation for AMT purposes. Thus, if an item of section 1250 property is depreciated using an accelerated method for regular tax purposes (*i.e.*, the 150-percent declining balance method or the 200-percent declining balance method), then an AMT adjustment is required (Code Sec. 56(a)(1)(A)(ii), as amended by the Community Renewal Tax Relief Act of 2000 (P.L. 106-554)).

Comment. Nonresidential real property must be depreciated under MACRS and the AMT using the straight-line method. The term "nonresidential real property" includes any section 1250 property that is not residential rental property and has a class life of at least 27.5 years. Thus, section 1250 property may be eligible for the accelerated depreciation methods under regular tax MACRS only if the class life is less than 27.5 years. Section 1250 property is defined in Code Sec. 1250 as any real property (other than property described in Code Sec. 1245(a)(3)) that is depreciable (Code Sec. 1250(c)).

Example. An item of section 1250 property costing $20,000 is placed in service in 2000. Assume that the property is considered 7-year property. Thus, the 200-percent declining balance method applies for regular tax purposes. Assuming further that the half-year convention is used, regular tax depreciation in 2000 is $2,858 ($20,000 × 14.29%). The technical correction clarifies that the AMT depreciation must be calculated using the straight-line method and a seven-year recovery period. AMT depreciation is $1,428 ($20,000 × 7.14%). The AMT adjustment is $1,430 ($2,858 − $1,428).

Planning Note. Since the provision is retroactive, taxpayers who failed to use the straight-line method to depreciate section 1250 property for AMT purposes may need to file amended returns.

★ *Effective date.* The provision is effective on August 5, 1997 (Act Sec. 314(g) of the Community Renewal Tax Relief Act of 2000; Act Sec. 402(a), of the

¶ 215

Taxpayer Relief Act of 1997 (P.L. 105-34)). Note, however, that the provision actually only impacts property placed in service after December 31, 1998.

Act Sec. 314(d) of the Community Renewal Tax Relief Act of 2000, amending Code Sec. 56(a)(1)(A)(ii); Act Sec. 314(g). Law at ¶ 5100. Committee Report at ¶ 10,325.

DEDUCTIONS

Corporate Donations of Computer Technology

¶ 220

Background ——————————————————————————

Generally, a corporation's charitable contribution deduction is limited to 10 percent of taxable income (with modifications) (Code Sec. 170(b)(2)). However, certain corporate contributions qualify for preferred treatment. In tax years beginning after December 31, 1997, an "augmented charitable deduction" is available to C corporations that contribute computer technology and/or equipment to educational organizations (Code Sec. 170(e)(6)) or tax-exempt charitable entities organized primarily for the purpose of supporting elementary and secondary education. Qualification for the augmented charitable deduction permits a greater deduction than is generally allowed in typical situations, such as the contribution of short-term gain property, inventory, or other ordinary income property, in which the deduction is normally limited to the basis of the donated property.

As with contributions of inventory for care of the ill, needy or infants and contributions of research property (Code Sec. 170(e)(3) and (4)), the augmented charitable deduction is equal to the corporate donor's basis in the donated property plus one-half of the ordinary income that would have been realized if the property had been sold. However, the deduction cannot exceed twice the corporation's basis in the property.

Qualified gifts of computer technology and equipment include contributions of computer software, computer or peripheral equipment, and fiber optic cable related to computer use that are to be used within the U.S. for educational purposes in any grade K through 12 (Code Sec. 170(e)(6)(E)). The donated property must fit productively into the educational plans of the school.

An eligible donee for these purposes is:

(1) an educational organization that normally maintains a regular faculty and curriculum and has a regularly enrolled body of pupils in attendance at the place where its educational activities are regularly conducted;

(2) a Code Sec. 501(c)(3) entity that is organized primarily for purposes of supporting elementary and secondary education; and

(3) a private foundation that within 30 days after receipt of the contribution contributes the property to an eligible donee, as described in (1) and (2) above, and notifies the donor of the contribution (Code Sec. 170(e)(6)(B) and Code Sec. 170(e)(6)(C)).

Qualified contributions are limited to gifts made no later than two years after the date the taxpayer acquired or substantially completed the construction of the donated property. The original use of the property must be by the donor or the donee (accordingly, a manufacturer is not eligible for the benefits of the special deduction). The donee may not transfer the donated property for money, services, or other property, except for shipping, transfer, and installation costs (Code Sec. 170(e)(6)(B)). Only donations made by C corporations can qualify for the enhanced credit; S corporations, personal holding companies, and service organizations are not eligible donors (Code Sec. 170(e)(6)(E)(ii)).

Sunset of provision. This augmented charitable deduction for contributions of computer technology and/or equipment to schools is scheduled to terminate for contributions made during any tax year beginning after December 31, 2000 (Code Sec. 170(e)(6)(F)).

Community Renewal Tax Relief Act Impact

Limits on charitable contributions of computers by C corporations expanded.—There are four basic modifications made to the provisions for enhanced charitable contribution deductions for donations of computer technology by C corporations. They are as follows:

(1) The restriction requiring the contribution to be made no later than two years after the date on which the donor acquired (or substantially completed construction on) the property has been relaxed to three years (Code Sec. 170(e)(6)(B)(ii), as amended by the Community Renewal Tax Relief Act of 2000).

(2) The definition of eligible donees for these purposes has been expanded to include public libraries (as defined in section 213(2)(A) of the Library Services and Technology Act (20 U.S.C. § 9122(2)(A)) (Code Sec. 170(e)(6)(B)(i), as amended by the 2000 Act).

(3) A person that constructs equipment that is required from the original user and then donates the equipment within three years after its construction was substantially completed qualifies for the reduction (Code Sec. 170(e)(6)(D), as amended by the 2000 Act).

(4) The termination date for the period in which donations may qualify for augmented charitable deduction treatment has been extended from contributions made during tax years beginning after December 31, 2000 to contributions made during tax years beginning after December 31, 2003 (Code Sec. 170(e)(6)(F), as amended by the 2000 Act).

Comment. The prior rule which limited donations to equipment that was no more than two years old was deemed overly restrictive. Most computers have a business life cycle of approximately three years. Thus, many businesses were reluctant to make donations.

Example. On January 3, 2001, Flotsam Inc., a C corporation, donates computer equipment which it purchased new on March 1, 1998, to a public library in the United States. At the time of the contribution, the equipment has a fair market value of $100,000 and an adjusted basis of $30,000. The contribution of eligible property that is less than three years old to a qualified donee qualifies the donor for an enhanced charitable deduction, which is calculated under Code Sec. 170(e)(3) as follows: to the donor's basis, $30,000, is added one-half of the gain that would have been realized if the property had been sold at its fair market value, $35,000 ($100,000 − $30,000 ÷ 2), for a total of $65,000 ($30,000 + $35,000). However, since this amount exceeds twice the donor's basis in the contributed property, $60,000 ($30,000 × 2), the enhanced charitable deduction is limited to $60,000.

Regulatory authority. The Secretary of the Treasury is given the authority to issue regulations describing the minimum functionality and educational suitability requirements that any computer technology must meet in order for the donation to qualify for the charitable contribution deduction under Code Sec. 170 (Code Sec. 170(e)(6)(B)(viii), as amended by the 2000 Act).

Comment. Although many proponents of the special deduction for computer technology equipment wanted to extend the deduction to donations by original manufacturers, the Act only extends the deduction to manufacturers that reacquire equipment from the original user and then donate the property within three years after its manufacture (Code Sec. 170(e)(6)(D), as amended by the 2000 Act).

The Conference Report indicates that the IRS should issue guidance in determining the retail value of equipment donated by a reacquirer in situations where the actual number of retail sales of that type of equipment is small in relation to the equipment donated.

★ *Effective date.* This provision is effective for contributions made after December 31, 2000 (Act Sec. 165(f) of the Community Renewal Tax Relief Act of 2000), and prior to January 1, 2004 (Code Sec. 170(e)(6)(F); Act Sec. 165(c)).

Act Sec. 165(a), (b) and (c) of the Community Renewal Tax Relief Act of 2000, amending Code Sec. 170(e)(6); Act Sec. 165(d), adding new Code Sec. 170(e)(6)(B)(viii); Act Sec. 165(e), redesignating Code Secs. 170(e)(6)(D), (E) and (F) as Code Secs. 170(e)(6)(E), (F) and (G), and adding new Code Sec. 170(e)(6)(D); Act Sec. 165(f). Law at ¶ 5190. Committee Report at ¶ 10,230.

Environmental Remediation Costs

¶ 225

Background ————————————————————————————

A taxpayer can elect to currently deduct certain environmental cleanup costs for both regular and alternative minimum tax purposes (Code Sec. 198, as added by the Taxpayer Relief Act of 1997 (P.L. 105-34)). The expenditure must be incurred in connection with the abatement or control of hazardous substances at a qualified contaminated site. The provision is somewhat limited in that it only applies to qualifying costs related to the cleanup of hazardous substances located on sites within a "targeted area."

A qualified cleanup cost (also referred to as a qualified environmental remediation expenditure or QER expenditure) eligible for current deduction under Code Sec. 198 is an expenditure:

(1) otherwise chargeable to a capital account; and

(2) paid or incurred in connection with the abatement or control of hazardous substances at a "qualified contaminated site" (Code Sec. 198(b)(1)).

Qualified contaminated site. The term "qualified contaminated site" refers to any area:

(1) that is held by the taxpayer for use in a trade or business, for the production of income, or as a stock in trade or inventory;

(2) that is within a "targeted area"; and

(3) at or on which there has been a release (or threat of release) or disposal of any hazardous substance (Code Sec. 198(c)(1)(A)).

In order to satisfy requirements (2) and (3) above (*i.e.*, targeted area and hazardous substance), the taxpayer must obtain a statement that the requirements are met from the environmental agency of the state where the subject area is located. The chief executive officer of a state may consult with the Administrator of the Environmental Protection Agency (EPA) and designate the appropriate state environmental agency. If the chief officer of the state has not designated the appropriate state agency, the EPA will designate the appropriate state agency (Code Sec. 198(c)(1)(B) and (C)).

Targeted area defined. In order to qualify for the cleanup election, the contaminated site must be in a targeted area. The term "targeted area" is defined as:

(1) any population census tract with a poverty rate of at least 20 percent;

(2) a population census tract with a population of less than 2,000 if more than 75 percent of the tract is zoned for commercial or industrial use, and the tract is contiguous to one or more other population census tracts that have a poverty rate of at least 20 percent;

(3) any empowerment zone or enterprise community (and any supplemental zone designated on December 21, 1994); and

(4) any site announced before February 1, 1997, as being part of the brownfields pilot project of the EPA (Code Sec. 198(c)(2)(A)).

A targeted area does not include any site on, or proposed to be on, the National Priorities List (NPL). The NPL is a list of contaminated sites that is issued by the President and revised at least on a yearly basis (Code Sec. 198(c)(2)(B)).

The 20 additional empowerment zones, authorized by the Taxpayer Relief Act of 1997 (P.L. 105-34), as well as the D.C. Enterprise Zone, are "targeted areas" for purposes of the Code Sec. 198 environmental cleanup rules.

The term "hazardous substance" is defined by reference to the definition contained in Section 101(14) of the Comprehensive Environmental Response, Compensation, and Liability Act of 1980 (CERCLA) and any substance which is designated as a hazardous substance under section 102 of that Act (Code Sec. 198(d)(1)). The term hazardous substance does not include any substance with respect to which a removal or remediation action is not permitted under Section 104 of CERCLA by reason of Section 104(a)(3) (Code Sec. 198(d)(2)). Section 104(a)(3) of CERCLA relates to asbestos and similar substances within buildings, certain natural substances (*e.g.*, radon) and other substances released into drinking water due to deterioration through ordinary use.

The election is not available for expenses paid or incurred after December 31, 2001 (Code Sec. 198(h), as amended by the Tax Relief Extension Act of 1999 (P.L. 106-170)).

Community Renewal Tax Relief Act Impact

Extension and expansion of environmental remediation expensing.— The election is extended two years and is now available for eligible expenses paid or incurred before January 1, 2004 (Code Sec. 198(h), as amended by the Community Renewal Tax Relief Act of 2000).

The 2000 Act eliminates the requirement that a qualified contaminated site be within a targeted area, thereby, significantly expanding the availability of the deduction.

After the elimination of the targeted area requirement, a qualified contaminated site is defined as any area (1) that is held by the taxpayer for use in a trade or business, for the production of income, or as stock in trade or inventory and (2) at or on which there has been a release (or threat of release) or disposal of any hazardous substance (Code Sec. 198(c)(1), as amended by the 2000 Act).

As under current law, to meet the requirement set out in (2), the taxpayer must receive a statement from the state environmental agency certifying that the requirement is met. Also, as under current law, a qualified contaminated site does not include any site on, or proposed to be on, the National Priorities List under Section 105(a)(8)(B) of the Comprehensive Environmental Response, Compensation, and Liability Act of 1980.

Comment. The general tax law principle regarding expensing versus capitalization of expenditures continues to apply to environmental remediation efforts not specifically covered under Code Sec. 198. Thus, depending upon the specific situation, these costs may need to be capitalized.

★ *Effective date.* These provisions are effective for expenditures paid or incurred after December 21, 2000 (Act Sec. 162(c) of the Community Renewal Tax Relief Act of 2000).

Act Sec. 162(a) of the Community Renewal Tax Relief Act of 2000, amending Code Sec. 198(c); Act Sec. 162(b), amending Code Sec. 198(h); Act Sec. 162(c). Law at ¶ 5210. Committee Report at ¶ 10,215.

Worthless Securities of Affiliated Corporations

¶ 230

Background

The loss deduction for worthless securities of an affiliated corporation is treated as an ordinary loss (Code Sec. 165(g)(3)). The test for affiliation set out in Code Sec. 165 does not match the definition of "affiliated group" contained in Code Sec. 1504(a)(2). Code Sec. 1504(a)(2) was changed as part of the Deficit Reduction Act of 1984 to a vote and value test, but the definition in Code Sec. 165(g)(3) was not changed to conform to that definition.

Technical Corrections Impact

Definition of "affiliated group."—The definition of "affiliated group" is changed to reflect the 1984 changes by referencing to the definition of "affiliated group" in Code Sec. 1504(a)(2) (Code Sec. 165(g)(3)(A), as amended by the Community Renewal Tax Relief Act of 2000). Thus, under this technical correction, a corporation is part of an affiliated group if the parent owns at least 80 percent of the total voting power of the stock and the owned stock has a value equal to at least 80 percent of the total value of the stock of such corporation.

★ *Effective date.* This provision is effective for tax years beginning after December 31, 1984 (Act Sec. 318(b)(3) of the Community Renewal Tax Relief Act of 2000; Act Sec. 60(a) of the Deficit Reduction Act of 1984 (P.L. 98-369)).

Act Sec. 318(b)(1) of the Community Renewal Tax Relief Act of 2000, amending Code Sec. 165(g)(3)(A); Act Sec. 318(b)(2), amending Code Sec. 165(g)(3); Act Sec. 318(b)(3). Law at ¶ 5180. Committee Report at ¶ 10,345.

CREDITS

New Markets Tax Credit

¶ 235

Background ————————————————————————

The Tax Code offers few incentives to taxpayers to either invest in, or make loans to, small businesses located in low-income communities. One indirect opportunity is offered to those who invest in small business investment companies licensed by the Small Business Administration for making loans to, or investing in, small businesses owned by persons who are socially or economically disadvantaged (Code Sec. 1044).

Community Renewal Tax Relief Act Impact

New markets tax credit.—A new tax credit is created to spur investment in low-income or economically disadvantaged areas—the new markets tax credit. The new markets tax credit (part of the general business credit) is five percent of a qualified equity investment in a qualified community development entity (CDE) as of the original issue date (Code Sec. 45D(a), as added by the Community Renewal Tax Relief Act of 2000). The five-percent rate is for the first three allowance dates and increases to six percent for each of the four remaining allowance dates. The allowance dates are the initial offering date and the first six anniversary dates of the initial offering date.

Comment. The total credit is, therefore, 39 percent and is claimed over seven annual allowance dates.

Qualified entity investment. A qualified equity investment is the cost of any stock in a corporation or any capital interest in a partnership that is a qualified CDE, if:

(1) the investment is acquired on the original issue date solely in exchange for cash,

(2) substantially all of the cash is used to make qualified low-income community investments, and

(3) the investment is designated by the qualified CDE for new markets credit purposes (Code Sec. 45D(b), as added by the 2000 Act).

A safe harbor is available with respect to item (2) if at least 85 percent of the aggregate assets of the qualified CDE is properly invested (Code Sec. 45D(b)(3), as added by the 2000 Act). Further, with respect to item (1), the investments will maintain their characterization for subsequent purchasers, allowing the credit to continue to be claimed (Code Sec. 45D(b)(4), as added by the 2000 Act).

Community development entity. A qualified community development entity is any domestic corporation or partnership:

> (1) whose primary mission is serving or providing investment capital for low-income communities or persons,

> (2) that maintains accountability to residents of low-income communities through representation on any governing or advisory boards of the entity, and

> (3) is certified by the Secretary of the Treasury as an eligible CDE.

These requirements are met by any specialized small business investment companies as defined in Code Sec. 1044(c)(3) and any community development financial institution as defined by Section 103 of the Community Development Banking and Financial Institution Act of 1994 (12 U.S.C. §4702) (Code Sec. 45D(c), as added by the 2000 Act).

Low-income housing community. A low-income community is any population census tract that:

> (1) has a poverty rate of at least 20 percent, or

> (2) if not located within a metropolitan area, the median family income does not exceed 80 percent of the statewide median family income, or

> (3) if located within a metropolitan area, the median family income does not exceed 80 percent of the greater of the statewide median family income or the metropolitan area median family income.

For possessions of the United States, the possession-wide median income is to be used to make the above determination instead of statewide median income (Code Sec. 45D(e), as added by the 2000 Act).

The Secretary of the Treasury is given the authorization to qualify target areas within a census tract that might not meet the above requirements as long as:

> (1) the boundary of the area is continuous,

> (2) the area would satisfy either the poverty rate or median income requirements if it were a census tract, and

> (3) there is inadequate access to investment capital in the area.

Low-income community investment. A qualified low-income community investment is:

> (1) any capital or equity investment in, or loan to, any qualified active low-income community business,

> (2) the purchase from another CDE of any loan made by the CDE which is a qualified low-income community investment,

> (3) financial counseling or other services specified in regulations by the Secretary to businesses located in, and residents of, low-income communities, and

> (4) any equity investment in, or loan to, any qualified CDE (Code Sec. 45D(d)(1), as added by the 2000 Act).

With respect to item (1), a qualified active low-income community business is defined to be any corporation, nonprofit corporation, or partnership which for the tax year:

(1) has at least 50 percent of its total gross income derived from the active conduct of a qualified business within any low-income community,

(2) uses a substantial portion of its tangible property within any low-income community,

(3) has a substantial portion of the services of its employees performed in any low-income community,

(4) has less than five percent of the average of its aggregate unadjusted bases attributable to collectibles, unless the collectibles are held primarily for sale in the ordinary course of business, and

(5) has less than five percent of the average of the aggregate unadjusted bases of its property attributable to nonqualified financial property as defined under Code Sec. 1397C(e) (as redesignated under Act Sec. 116 of the 2000 Act) (Code Sec. 45D(d)(2)(A), as added by the 2000 Act).

Proprietorships and a portion of a business also qualify if they would meet the requirements above had they been separately incorporated (Code Sec. 45D(d)(2)(B) and (C), as added by the 2000 Act). A qualified business (see item (1), above) is defined by reference to Code Sec. 1397C(d) (as redesignated under Act Sec. 116 of the 2000 Act), except that rental of improved commercial real estate will qualify as a business despite the character of its tenants (and the restrictions on the rental of personal tangible property contained in Code Sec. 1397C(d)(3) is not applicable) (Code Sec. 45D(d)(3), as added by the 2000 Act).

Limitations. There are national limitations on the amount of investments to be used to claim the new markets tax credit (Code Sec. 45D(f), as added by the 2000 Act). The amount gradually increases from $1 billion in 2001 to $3.5 billion in 2006 and 2007. The Secretary of the Treasury is authorized to allocate the amounts to qualified CDEs, giving priority to CDEs that have a record of successfully providing capital or technical assistance to disadvantaged businesses or communities, or those that intend to satisfy the requirements of investing substantially all of the cash from the equity offering in low-income community investments in one or more business that are unrelated to the majority equity interest.

To ensure these investments benefit businesses located in low-income communities, accountability requirements must be met (Code Sec. 45D(c)(1)(B), as added by the 2000 Act). Also, if the allocation given to the CDE is not used within five years of the issue date, then the CDE loses the unused balance of the allocation and the Secretary is authorized to reissue the remaining allocation (Code Sec. 45D(b)(1), as added by the 2000 Act). Additionally, if the yearly limitation is not totally allocated, the balance is carried over and added to the next year's limitation amount until the entire limitation amount is allocated. No amount can be carried beyond the year 2014 (Code Sec. 45D(f)(3), as added by the 2000 Act).

Recapture. If, during the seven years from the original issue date of the qualified equity investment in a qualified CDE, a recapture event occurs with respect to the investment, then the new markets tax credit must be recaptured (Code Sec. 45D(g), as added by the 2000 Act). Recapture events occur when:

(1) the entity ceases to qualify as a CDE,

(2) the proceeds cease to be used as required, or

(3) there is a redemption of the investment by the entity.

The recaptured credit will increase the tax for the year in an amount equal to the amount of credits claimed plus interest for the resulting underpayment. The interest will not be deductible, nor may any other credits be taken against the addition to tax caused by the credit recapture.

Caution. The recapture penalty is severe. Although only the credits claimed (*i.e.* those credits for which the taxpayer received a tax benefit) are recaptured, the underpayment interest begins to accrue from the due date of the return without extensions for each year the credits were claimed. Additionally, the interest may not be deducted as a reasonable and necessary business deduction. Finally, the recapture amount is treated as an increase in the tax after the regular tax liability and the alternative minimum tax liability are determined.

Basis reduction. The basis of any qualified equity investment is reduced by the amount of the new markets tax credit taken with respect to that investment. This basis reduction will not apply for purposes of Code Secs. 1202, 1400B and 1400F (as added by Act Sec. 101 of the 2000 Act) (Code Sec. 45D(h), as added by the 2000 Act).

Interaction with general business credit. As part of the general business credit, the new markets tax credit is subject to the limitations of Code Sec. 38 and the carryover rules of Code Sec. 39. However, the credit may not be carried back to tax years before January 1, 2001. If any unused new markets tax credit carryover remains at the end of the carryforward period, then under Code Sec. 196, it may be claimed in the following year. If a recapture event occurs, all carryovers will be adjusted accordingly (Code Secs. 38(b), 39(d) and 196(c), as amended by the 2000 Act).

Additional guidance. The Secretary of the Treasury is authorized to prescribe regulations for this section that:

(1) limit the amount of credit for investments which are directly or indirectly subsidized by other federal tax benefits, such as the low-income housing credit or the exclusion of interest on state and local bonds,

(2) prevent abuses of this section,

(3) provide guidance to determine if the investment requirements are met,

(4) impose appropriate reporting requirements, and

(5) apply this provision to newly formed entities (Code Sec. 45D(i), as added by the 2000 Act).

Further, the Secretary is instructed to issue guidance on (a) how entities apply for an allocation under this section, (b) the competitive procedure through which the allocations are made, and (c) the actions the Secretary will take to ensure the allocations are made to the appropriate entities, within 120 days of enactment of this Act (Act Sec. 121(f) of the 2000 Act).

Additionally, the Comptroller General of the United States is instructed to present no later than the 31st of January 2004, 2007 and 2010 a report on its audit of the new markets tax credit program (Act Sec. 121(g) of the 2000 Act).

¶ 235

★ *Effective date.* These provisions apply to investments made after December 31, 2000 (Act Sec. 121(e) of the Community Renewal Tax Relief Act of 2000).

Act Sec. 121(a) of the Community Renewal Tax Relief Act of 2000, adding Code Sec. 45D; Act Sec. 121(b), amending Code Secs. 38(b) and 39(d); Act Sec. 121(c), amending Code Sec. 196(c); Act Sec. 121(d), amending the table of sections for subpart D of Part IV of subchapter A of chapter 1; Act Sec. 121(e). Law at ¶ 5030, ¶ 5040, ¶ 5080, ¶ 5200, and ¶ 7065. Committee Report at ¶ 10,165.

Low-Income Housing Credit

¶ 240

Background————————————————————————————

A nonrefundable income tax credit may be claimed by the owner of newly constructed or substantially rehabilitated rental housing that is occupied by tenants with gross incomes below specified levels. The maximum amount of credit that may be claimed is 70 percent of total qualified expenditures made to construct or rehabilitate the housing and this amount must be claimed over a 10-year period. If the housing is federally subsidized, or is an existing low-income unit, this percentage may be reduced to as low as 30 percent.

In order to compute the applicable credit, an owner of qualified low-income housing must multiply the appropriate credit percentage (determined by the type of project) by the qualified basis allocable to low-income units in each building. The amount of qualified basis is a function of the number of low-income housing units per building versus the total number of residential units per building, or the relative square footage of each.

The total dollar amount of low-income housing credit that may be claimed by all taxpayers is limited on a state-by-state basis. Taxpayers may not claim a credit with respect to a qualified low-income housing project in excess of the housing credit dollar amount allocated to them by an appropriate state or local agency.

Each state is authorized to annually allocate a total dollar value of credits based on the state's aggregate population. This amount is known as the "housing credit ceiling." Currently, states' housing credit ceiling is equal to $1.25 per resident. In addition, the total amount of the annual ceiling includes the following amounts: (1) any unused credit ceiling from the prior year, (2) any credit ceiling returned in the calendar year and (3) any amount of the national pool allocated to the state by the Treasury Department. The national pool consists of states' unused housing credit carryovers.

A state's use of its allocated credit is subject to an ordering rule known as the "stacking rule." The present law stacking rule provides that a state is treated as first using its annual allocation of $1.25 per resident and any returns in the calendar year. Second, the state is treated as using its unused credits carried forward from the preceding year's credit ceiling. And, lastly, the state is treated as using any applicable allocations from the national pool.

Each state is required to develop a plan for allocating low-income housing credits and such plan must include certain allocation criteria including: (1) project location, (2) housing needs characteristics, (3) project characteristics, (4) sponsor characteristics, (5) participation of local tax-exempt organizations, (6) tenant populations with special needs and (7) public housing waiting lists. In addition, the states' plan must give allocation preference to housing projects that serve low-income tenants and those which are obligated to serve qualified tenants for the longest period of time.

Generally, a taxpayer must obtain its allocation from the state not later than the close of the calendar year in which the building is placed in service in order to qualify for the credit. Exceptions are provided for certain binding commitments or increases in qualified basis. An additional exception is provided for buildings not yet placed in service when a taxpayer has expended an amount equal to 10 percent or more of the taxpayer's reasonably expected basis in the building by the end of the calendar year in which the allocation is received and certain other requirements are met. These exceptions are colloquially referred to as the "placed in service" exceptions.

Certain buildings located in high cost areas, such as in qualified census tracts and difficult development areas, are eligible for an enhanced low-income housing credit. The enhancement increases the eligible basis for such buildings to 130 percent of the otherwise qualified basis. Under the enhanced credit, therefore, the 70-percent and 30-percent credit are increased to a 91-percent and 39-percent credit, respectfully. For these purposes, a qualified census tract is an area designated by the Secretary of Housing and Urban Development in which 50 percent or more of the households have an income that is less that 60 percent of the area median gross income for the year. The enhancement does not apply, however, to federally subsidized buildings or to buildings that receive assistance under the HOME investment partnership program.

Community Renewal Tax Relief Act Impact

Expansion of the low-income housing credit.—In an effort to spur the development of affordable housing in urban neighborhoods, Congress has attempted to increase the availability of low-income housing credits and broaden the requirements for qualification. To further this intent, it has raised state credit ceilings, revised criteria for credit allocation, required comprehensive market studies, modified rules relating to qualified basis computation, expanded the definition of placed in service and reordered the historic stacking rule.

State ceiling on low-income housing credit. As a major step towards increasing credit availability, each state's per capita housing credit cap has been raised from $1.25 to $1.50 per resident in 2001 and to $1.75 per resident in 2002. In addition, smaller states will be awarded a minimum of $2 million of annual credit cap in 2001 and 2002 (Code Sec. 42(h)(3)(C), as amended by the Community Renewal Tax Relief Act of 2000). These amounts, the $1.75 per capita cap and the $2 million small state cap, will be indexed for inflation beginning in 2003. The 2000 Act also provides for rounding of these indexed amounts (Code Sec. 42(h)(3)(H), as added by the 2000 Act).

Comment. Historically, the per capita credit limitation had not been increased by Congress since the introduction of the low-income housing credit in 1986. According to the National Association of Home Builders (NAHB), a strong proponent of the housing provisions contained in the 2000 Act, the credit acts as "a cornerstone of revitalization in low income communities." The NAHB estimates

¶ 240

that approximately 70,000 jobs, $2.3 billion in wages and $1.2 billion in taxes can be attributed to the effectiveness and efficiency of the low-income housing credit.

Criteria for allocating housing credits among projects. The Community Renewal Tax Relief Act of 2000 amends the criteria that must be included in a state's qualified allocation plan. States no longer have to take into account the participation of local tax-exempt organizations, but instead must consider tenant populations of individuals with children and projects intended for eventual tenant ownership (Code Sec. 42(m)(1)(C), as amended by the 2000 Act). The 2000 Act also provides that in connection with considering sponsor characteristics, a state must consider whether the project involves the use of existing housing as part of a community revitalization plan. In addition, states must now give preference in allocating housing credit amounts to projects located in qualified census tracts that contribute to a concerted community revitalization plan (Code Sec. 42(m)(1)(B), as amended by the 2000 Act).

Responsibilities of housing credit agencies. In order to gauge the need for assistance and to assure funds are properly appropriated, Congress included a provision requiring a comprehensive market study, to be conducted by a disinterested third party, of the housing needs of the low-income individuals in the area to be served by the project in question. Such study is to be conducted at the developer's expense, and a written explanation must be made available to the general public for any allocation not made in accordance with the established priorities and selection criteria of the applicable housing credit agency (Code Sec. 42(m)(1)(A), as amended by the 2000 Act). The 2000 Act also requires site inspections by the housing credit agency to monitor compliance with habitability standards applicable to the project (Code Sec. 42(m)(1)(B), as amended by the 2000 Act).

Basis of building eligible for credit. Three changes have been made to the rules relating to the determination of qualified basis for low-income housing. First, the definition of census tract for the purposes of qualification for the enhanced credit is expanded to include areas with a poverty rate of 25 percent or greater (Code Sec. 42(d)(5)(C)(ii)(I), as amended by the 2000 Act). Second, qualification for the enhanced credit is extended to any portion of a building used as a community service facility (not to exceed 10 percent of the total eligible basis in the building). A community service facility, by definition, caters primarily to individuals whose income is 60 percent or less of area median income (Code Sec. 42(d)(4)(D), as added by the 2000 Act). Lastly, when determining whether a building is federally subsidized for purposes of calculating the applicable credit percentage, assistance received under the Native American Housing Assistance and Self-Determination Act of 1996 shall be disregarded (Code Sec. 42(i)(2), as amended by the 2000 Act). As a result, such buildings will not be subject to the credit limitations applicable to federally subsidized buildings.

Comment. Historically, assistance received under the HOME investment partnership program can be disregarded when computing the applicable low-income housing credit percentage as long as 40 percent of the residential units in the building in question are occupied by individuals earning less than 50 percent of area median gross income. The HOME program was created by the Cranston-Gonzales National Affordable Housing Act of 1990. The 2000 Act extends this exception to funds received under the Native American Housing Assistance and Self-Determination Act, which established a separate Indian housing and community development block grant.

¶ 240

Expenditure exception to placed in service requirement. A building that receives an allocation from its State in the second half of the calendar year can now qualify for the placed in service exception if the taxpayer expends an amount equal to 10 percent or more of the taxpayer's reasonably expected basis in the building within six months of receiving the state allocation (Code Sec. 42(h)(1)(E)(ii), as amended by the 2000 Act). It is now irrelevant whether this six-month period extends beyond the end of the calendar year.

Example. By December 31, 2002, John L. Developer reasonably expects to have a $1,000,000 basis in Building A, which he is constructing as housing for low-income families. On September 15, 2001, he receives an allocation of low-income housing credit from State B. By December 31, 2001, Developer's qualified expenditures on Building A total $60,000. By February 3, 2002, however, Developer's qualified expenditures on Building A total $110,000.

Prior to the Community Renewal Tax Relief Act of 2000, Building A would not qualify for the placed in service exception, and thus would not qualify for the low-income housing credit, because qualified expenditures made by the calendar year end of 2001 did not total more than 10% of Developer's reasonably expected basis in Building A as of the close of 2002. Currently, however, Building A would be eligible for the credit because expenditures totaling 10% or more were made within six months of receiving the allocation from State B.

Stacking rule. The stacking rule has been modified so that each state would first use its allocation of the unused housing credit ceiling from the preceding calendar year, then use its unused credit from the current year's allocation (including any credits returned to the State) and then, lastly, use any national pool allocations (Code Sec. 42(h)(3)(D)(ii), as amended by the 2000 Act).

★ *Effective date.* The provisions are generally effective for housing credit amounts allocated after December 31, 2000, and for buildings placed in service after such date with respect to projects that receive financing with proceeds of tax-exempt bonds subject to the private activity bond volume limit that are issued after such date (Act Sec. 137 of the Community Renewal Tax Relief Act of 2000). The increase in the per capita cap amount is effective for calendar years beginning after 2000 (Act Sec. 131(d) of the 2000 Act).

Act Sec. 131 of the Community Renewal Tax Relief Act of 2000, amending Code Sec. 42(h)(3); Act Sec. 132, amending Code Sec. 42(m)(1); Act Sec. 133, amending Code Sec. 42(m)(1); Act Sec. 134(a), amending Code Sec. 42(d)(4); Act Sec. 134(b), amending Code Sec. 42(i)(2)(E); Act Sec. 135(a), amending Code Sec. 42(h); Act Sec. 135(b), amending Code Sec. 42(d)(5)(C)(ii)(I); Act Sec. 136, amending Code Sec. 42(h)(3); Act Sec. 137. Law at ¶ 5050. Committee Reports at ¶ 10,175, ¶ 10,180, ¶ 10,185, ¶ 10,190, ¶ 10,195, and ¶ 10,200.

Work Opportunity Tax Credit

¶ 245

Background _____

Generally, an employer who hires an individual from one or more of eight targeted groups may claim a work opportunity tax credit (WOTC) equal to a percentage of the first-year wages paid to the worker (Code Sec. 51). One of the

Background

target groups is comprised of "qualified IV-A recipients." The Small Business Job Protection Act of 1996 (P.L. 104-188) amended Code Sec. 51(d) to define a qualified IV-A recipient as an individual who is certified as a member of a family receiving assistance under a state plan approved under Part A of Title IV of the Social Security Act "relating to assistance for needy families with minor children" (Aid to Families with Dependent Children (AFCD)) and any successor of such program.

Subsequent to enactment of P.L. 104-188, Congress reformed the welfare system through enactment of the Personal Responsibility and Work Opportunity Reconciliation Act of 1996 (P.L. 104-193). This Act replaced the Aid to Families with Dependent Children (AFDC) in Part A of Title IV with the Temporary Assistance for Needy Families (TANF) program. Thus, the reference to AFDC in the work opportunity credit became obsolete.

Technical Corrections Impact

Reference to former AFDC deleted.—A retroactive technical correction deletes the reference to the AFDC program to reflect the replacement of the AFDC program by the Temporary Assistance to Needy Families (TANF) program. In addition, the requirement that a State plan must be *approved* under part A of title IV of the Social Security Act is changed to provide that the State plan must be *funded* under part A of Title IV. This change reflects the operation of the TANF program. (Code Sec. 51(d)(2), as amended by the Community Renewal Tax Relief Act of 2000).

★ *Effective date.* The technical correction applies to individuals who began working for an employer after September 30, 1996 (Act Sec. 316(e) of the Community Renewal Tax Relief Act of 2000; Act Sec. 1201(b) of the Small Business Job Protection Act of 1996 (P.L. 104-188)).

Act Sec. 316(a) of the Community Renewal Tax Relief Act of 2000, amending Code Sec. 51(d)(2)(B); Act Sec. 316(e). Law at ¶ 5090. Committee Report at ¶ 10,335.

Enhanced Oil Recovery Credit

¶ 250

Background

Code Sec. 43 provides the owner of an operating mineral interest with an enhanced oil recovery (EOR) credit that is a component of the general business credit. Specifically, the enhanced oil recovery credit is equal to 15 percent of the qualified costs attributable to qualified EOR projects for the tax year (Code Sec. 43(a)). If the credit is claimed, the taxpayer must reduce the amount otherwise deductible or required to be capitalized by the amount of the credit.

A qualified EOR project is a certified domestic project involving a qualified tertiary recovery method where the first injection of liquid, gas or other matter occurs after 1990. There must be a reasonable expectation that the amount of crude oil ultimately recovered will be more than an insignificant increase (Code Sec. 43(c)(2)).

Background

Qualified EOR costs must be paid or incurred in connection with a qualified EOR project. Qualified EOR costs include the following: (1) amounts paid or incurred for tangible property that is an integral part of a qualified EOR project and is depreciable or amortizable, (2) intangible drilling and development costs that the taxpayer can elect to deduct under Code Sec. 263(c), and (3) qualified tertiary injectant expenses that are deductible under Code Sec. 193 (Code Sec. 43(c)(1)).

Technical Corrections Impact

Deductibility of tertiary injectant expenses.—A technical correction clarifies that a qualified enhanced oil recovery (EOR) cost includes any qualified tertiary injectant expense, as defined in Code Sec. 193(b), that is paid or incurred in connection with a qualified EOR project and that is deductible for the tax year under any Code section (Code Sec. 43(c)(1)(C), as amended by the Community Renewal Tax Relief Act of 2000 (P.L. 106-554)). The requirement that the tertiary injectant expense must be deductible under Code Sec. 193 has been removed.

Comment. The former reference to deductibility under Code Sec. 193 implicitly excluded costs that are nondeductible under Code Sec. 193(c), which prohibits deduction of costs that the taxpayer elected to deduct under Code Sec. 263(c) or that are deductible under another Code section.

★ *Effective date.* This provision is effective for costs paid or incurred with respect to EOR projects begun or significantly expanded in tax years beginning after December 31, 1990 (Act Sec. 317(b) of the Community Renewal Tax Relief Act of 2000; Act Sec. 11511(d) of the Revenue Reconciliation Act of 1990 (P.L. 101-508)).

Act Sec. 317(a) of the Community Renewal Tax Relief Act of 2000, amending Code Sec. 43(c)(1)(C); Act Sec. 317(b). Law at ¶ 5060. Committee Report at ¶ 10,340.

Coordination of Research and Puerto Rico Economic Activity Credits

¶ 255

Background

A qualified domestic corporation may claim the Puerto Rico economic activity credit for the portion of the U.S. tax it pays that is attributable to income from the active conduct of a trade or business in Puerto Rico or the sale or exchange of substantially all of the assets used by the corporation in the active conduct of a trade or business within Puerto Rico (Code Sec. 30A). In general, the credit may not exceed the sum of specified amounts, including a corporation's qualifying wage and fringe benefit expenses for the tax year and a specified portion of its depreciation deduction. The Ticket to Work and Work Incentives Improvement Act of 1999 (P.L. 106-170) (the "1999 Act") amended Code Sec. 41 to allow the credit for increasing research activities to be claimed with respect to research conducted in Puerto Rico and U.S. possessions (Code Sec. 41(d)(4)(F), as amended by the 1999 Act). The amount of the research credit is determined, in part, with reference to the amount of wages paid to employees conducting qualified research activities (Code Sec. 41(b)). Code Sec. 280C is designed to prevent taxpayer's from "double-

Background

dipping" by claiming deductions and credits with respect to the same expenditures. The anti-double-dipping provision relating to the research credit is provided in Code Sec. 280C(c)(1). Amendments made to this section by the 1999 Act are construed by some taxpayers as requiring reduction of the amount of wages on which the Puerto Rico credit is based by the amount of the research credit claimed, rather than by the amount of wages on which the research credit is based.

Technical Corrections Impact

Wages used in computing Puerto Rico economic credit are not research expenditures.—The Community Renewal and Tax Relief Act of 2000 (P.L. 106-554) includes a separate anti-double-dipping rule that specifically provides that any wages or other expenses taken into account in determining the amount of the Puerto Rico economic activity credit may not be taken into account in determining the amount of the research credit under Code Sec. 41 (Code Sec. 30A(f), as added by the Community Renewal Tax Relief Act of 2000).

Amendments to Code Sec. 280C(c)(1) also eliminate the changes made to that section by the 1999 Act. Thus, Code Sec. 280C(c)(1) now provides, as prior to the 1999 Act, that qualified research expenses or basic research expenses that are otherwise deductible must first be reduced by the amount of the research credit claimed (Code Sec. 280C(c)(1), as amended by the 2000 Act).

Caution. A corporation that filed a tax return in which wages taken into account in computing the Puerto Rico credit were reduced by the amount of the research credit claimed will need to file an amended return.

★ *Effective date.* The provision applies to amounts paid or incurred after June 30, 1999 (Act Sec. 311(d) of the Community Renewal Tax Relief Act of 2000; Act Sec. 502(c)(3) of the Ticket to Work and Work Incentives Improvement Act of 1999).

Act Sec. 311(a)(1) of the Community Renewal Tax Relief Act of 2000, amending Code Sec. 280C(c)(1); Act Sec. 311(a)(2), redesignating Code Sec. 30A(f) and (g), as Code Sec. 30A(g) and (h), respectively, and adding Code Sec. 30A(f); Act Sec. 311(d). Law at ¶5020 and ¶5250. Committee Report at ¶10,310.

SALES AND EXCHANGES

Securities Futures Contracts

¶260

Background

Gain or loss from the sale of stock, like other property, is generally recognized at the time of disposition, unless a specific nonrecognition provision applies. Special rules apply to Section 1256 contracts, dealers in securities (mark-to-market method permitted (Code Sec. 475), short sales (Code Sec. 1233), wash sales (Code Sec. 1091), and straddles (Code Sec. 1092).

In characterizing gain or loss from Code Sec. 1256 contracts, defined as regulated futures contracts, certain foreign currency contracts, nonequity options,

Background

and dealer equity options, the "mark-to-market" rule applies. Under this rule, each contract is treated as if it were sold (and repurchased) for its fair market value on the last business day of the year. Gains or losses on the sale of each Code Sec. 1256 contract are treated as if 40 percent of the gain or loss is short-term capital gain. The remaining gain or loss is long-term capital gain. Hedging transactions are not marked to market and do not qualify for this 40/60 capital gain treatment.

Dealers in securities must compute securities income under the mark-to-market method (Code Sec. 475). Gains and losses are considered ordinary, not capital. Traders in securities and dealers in commodities may elect to use this accounting method (and treat gain or loss as ordinary). For purposes of Code Sec. 475, Code Sec. 1256 contracts are not securities.

Depending on the circumstances surrounding the sale of capital assets, other rules may apply. For example, the wash sale rule disallows certain losses from the disposition of stock and securities if substantially identical stock or securities (or an option or contract for such stock or security) are acquired within the 30-day period before or after the sale date. Commodities futures are not considered stock or securities for purposes of the wash sale rule. The short sale rules (Code Sec. 1233), which apply to situations where borrowed property is sold but the sale is closed by payment to the seller of substantially similar property, generally treat gain as short-term capital gain.

A futures contract on individual stock is a single stock futures contract that is priced much like a stock index futures contract. The Commodity Futures Modernization Act of 2000 (P.L. 106-544) removed a long-standing ban in the United States on trading futures on single stocks. The tax treatment of single stock futures was originally included in the Commodity Futures Modernization Act of 2000. However, these provisions do not appear in that legislation but are instead included in the Community Renewal Tax Relief Act of 2000 (P.L. 106-554).

Community Renewal Tax Relief Act Impact

Gain and loss treatment for securities futures contracts.—The 2000 Act generally treats gain or loss on a "securities futures contract" as a gain or loss from the sale or exchange of property that has the same character as the property to which the contract relates has in the hands of the taxpayer (or would have in the hands of the taxpayer if acquired by the taxpayer) (Code Sec. 1234B(a)(1), as added by the 2000 Act). Thus, if the underlying security is a capital asset, the gain or loss on the sale or exchange of a securities futures contract will be treated as the sale or exchange of a capital asset.

Special rules apply to "dealer securities futures contracts," as explained below.

A security futures contract is defined by reference to the Securities and Exchange Act of 1934, which was amended by the Commodity Futures Modernization Act of 2000 to include single-stock futures (Code Sec. 1234B(c), as added by the 2000 Act). In general, section 3(a)(55)(A) of the 1934 Act provides that a securities futures contract means a contract of sale for future delivery of a single security or a narrow-based security index.

¶ 260

Planning note. According to the Wall Street Journal (12/19/00), the nation's two largest exchanges, the Chicago Board Options Exchange and the American Stock Exchange, will consider listing single stock contracts. However, that source notes that these products may not be widely available for another year.

Contracts that are inventory, hedging transactions, and ordinary income derived from a contract. The rule described in the first paragraph does not apply to securities futures contracts which are not capital assets because they are property described in Code Sec. 1221(a)(1), relating to the exception from capital asset treatment for inventory, or Code Sec. 1221(a)(7), relating to the exception from capital asset treatment for clearly identified hedging transactions (Code Sec. 1234B(a)(2)(A), as added by the 2000 Act). Also excepted is any income derived in connection with a contract which would be treated as ordinary income without regard to the securities futures contract provisions (Code Sec. 1234B(a)(2)(B), as added by the 2000 Act). Capital gain treatment will not apply to these securities futures contracts.

Capital gain or loss on securities futures contract to sell property is short-term capital gain or loss. Any capital gain or loss on the sale of a securities futures contract to sell property is treated as short-term gain or loss (Code Sec. 1234B(b), as added by the 2000 Act). In effect, as pointed out by the Conference Committee, a securities futures contract to sell property is treated as equivalent to a short sale of the underlying property. This rule does not apply to a loss that is treated as a long-term capital loss from a straddle under the regulations for Code Sec. 1092(b) or under IRS regulations for this new provision (*i.e.*, regulations under new Code Sec. 1234B).

Treatment of securities futures contracts under short sale rules. For purposes of the short sale rules of Code Sec. 1233, a securities futures contract to *acquire* property will be treated in a manner similar to the property itself (Code Sec. 1233(e)(2)(D), as added by the 2000 Act). The effect of this, as stated by the Conference Committee Report, is that the short sale rules described in Code Sec. 1233(b) will be applicable to the holding of a securities futures contract to acquire property and the short sale of property which is substantially identical to the property under the contract.

Comment. As explained above, a securities futures contract to *sell* property is treated in a manner similar to a short sale of property, and capital gain or loss resulting from such a sale is short-term capital gain or loss.

Under the Act, a securities futures contract is not treated as a futures contract with respect to commodities (Code Sec. 1234B(d), as added by the 2000 Act). Consequently, the short sale rule described in Code Sec. 1233(e)(2)(B), which provides that commodity futures are not substantially identical if they call for delivery in different months, will not apply to a securities futures contract.

Securities futures contracts held by nondealers ineligible for section 1256 contract treatment. Securities futures contracts (or options on such contracts) are *not* considered Code Sec. 1256 contracts (Code Sec. 1256(b)(5), as added by the 2000 Act). Therefore, the mark-to-market rule and the 60/40 capital gain/loss treatment provided for section 1256 contracts is not applicable to securities futures transactions. However, an exception applies to "dealer" securities futures contracts, as described below. According to the Conference Report, gain or loss on a securities futures contract that is not a section 1256 contract will be treated as a security for purposes of Code Sec. 475. This means traders in securities futures contracts that are not section 1256 contracts could elect to have Code Sec. 475 apply.

¶ 260

Terminations. Gain or loss arising upon the cancellation, lapse, expiration, or other termination of a securities futures contracts which is a capital asset in the hands of a taxpayer is treated as gain or loss from the sale of a capital asset (Code Sec. 1234A(3), as added by the 2000 Act).

Corporate transactions in securities futures contracts with respect to its own stock. No gain or loss is recognized by a corporation with respect to a securities futures contract to buy or sell its stock (Code Sec. 1032(a), as amended by the 2000 Act).

Wash sale rule applicable. In general, loss deductions are disallowed where they result from wash sales of stock or securities. A wash sale occurs if stock or securities are sold at a loss and the seller acquires substantially identical stock or securities (or an option or contract to acquire such property) 30 days before or after the sale (Code Sec. 1091). Under the 2000 Act, the wash sale rule will apply to a contract or option to acquire or sell stock or securities solely by reason of the fact that the contract or option is, or could be, settled in cash or property other than the stock or securities (Code Sec. 1091(f), as added by the 2000 Act). Thus, according to the Conference Committee Report, the acquisition of a securities futures contract to acquire corporate stock within the 30-day period prescribed under the wash-sale rule could trigger the wash sale rule, and disallow the loss on the sale, even if the contract is settled for cash.

Straddle rules. The straddle rules of Code Sec. 1092 are intended to prevent the deferral of income and conversion of ordinary income and short-term capital gain into long-term capital gain on straddle transactions. In the case of straddles that are not part of the mark-to-market system under Code Sec. 1256, this is achieved by deferring losses on unidentified straddles (Code Sec. 1092(a)(1)) and by requiring losses on identified straddles to be reported when the offsetting position is closed (Code Sec. 1092(a)(2)). A straddle is defined as offsetting positions with respect to personal property. The definition of the term "personal property" (any personal property of a type that is actively traded) has been expanded by the Act to include a securities futures contract (Code Sec. 1092(d)(3)(B)(i), as amended by the 2000 Act).

Comment. The Conference Committee, by way of illustration, indicates that the straddle rules apply where a taxpayer holds a long-term position in actively traded stock that is a capital asset and enters into a securities futures contract to sell substantially identical stock at a time when the stock has not appreciated in value (so that the constructive sale rules of Code Sec. 1059 do not apply). As a result, any loss on closing the securities futures contract will be a long-term capital loss pursuant to the principals of the short sale rules (Code Sec. 1233(d)) which are applied under Code Sec. 1092 regulations (Reg. § 1.1092(b)-2T(b)) to straddles.

Regulations authorized. Regulations are authorized to provide further guidance on the treatment of securities futures contracts (Code Sec. 1234B(e), as added by the 2000 Act).

Exception: dealer securities futures contracts are Code Sec. 1256 contracts. Dealer securities futures contracts are treated as Code Sec. 1256 contracts (Code Sec. 1256(b)(5), as added by the 2000 Act).

A dealer securities contract is a securities futures contract (or any option on such a contract) entered into by a dealer (or in the case of an option, purchased or granted by a dealer) in the normal course of his or her activity of dealing in such contracts or options and traded on a qualified board of trade or exchange (Code Sec. 1256(g)(9)(A) and 1256(g)(9)(C), as added by the 2000 Act). A person will be treated as a dealer if the Secretary of the Treasury determines that the person performs, with respect to such contracts or options, functions that are similar to an equity options dealer (Code Sec. 1256(g)(9)(B), as added by the 2000 Act; Code Sec. 1256(f)(4), as amended by the 2000 Act). The determination of who is a dealer in securities futures options is to be made no later than July 1, 2001 (Act Sec. 401(g)(4) of the 2000 Act).

Comment. The Conference Committee Report indicates that a class of traders in securities futures contracts (and options) may be considered dealers if relevant factors, including providing market liquidity for such contracts (and options), indicate that the market functions of the traders is comparable to that of equity options dealers even though such traders do not have the same market-making obligations as market makers or specialists in equity options.

As in the case of equity options, gains and losses allocated to a limited partner or limited entrepreneur with respect to a dealer securities contract is treated as short-term capital gain or loss (Code Sec. 1256(f)(4), as amended by the 2000 Act).

Treatment as dealer equity options. Under current law, a section 1256 contract is defined to include "dealer equity options," (Code Sec. 1256(b)(4), (g)(4), and (g)(6)). Only options dealers are eligible for section 1256 treatment with respect to equity options. The 2000 Act amends the mark-to-market provisions of Code Sec. 1256 so that dealer securities futures contracts are treated as dealer equity options (Code Sec. 1256(g)(6) as amended by the 2000 Act). Equity options are, accordingly, redefined to include (in addition to options to buy or sell stock) any option the value of which is determined by reference to any narrow-based security index as defined under section 3(a)(55) of the Securities and Exchange Act. The term "equity" option includes an option on a group of stocks only if the group meets the requirements for a narrow-based security index (Code Sec. 1256(g)(6), as amended by the 2000 Act).

Comment. Listed options that are not "equity options" are considered nonequity options to which Code Sec. 1256 applies for all taxpayers. Options relating to broad-based groups of stocks and broad-based stock indexes will continue to be treated as nonequity options under Code Sec. 1256, according to the Conference Committee Report.

Definition of contract markets. A contract market, for purposes of the Internal Revenue Code, is defined to include any designation by the Commodity Futures Trading Commission that could not have been made under the law before December 21, 2000, the date of the enactment of the Commodity Futures Modernization Act of 2000, except to the extent provided by regulations (Code Sec. 7701(m), as added by the 2000 Act).

Comment. The Commodities Futures Modernization Act designates certain new contract markets. These new contract markets will be considered contract markets for purposes of applying provisions of the Code which make reference to contract markets.

¶ 260

★ *Effective date.* The provisions are effective on December 21, 2000 (Act Sec. 401(j) of the Community Renewal Tax Relief Act of 2000).

Act Sec. 401(a) of the Community Renewal Tax Relief Act of 2000, adding Code Sec. 1234B; Act Sec. 401(b), amending Code Sec. 1234A; Act Sec. 401(c), amending Code Sec. 1032(a); Act Sec. 401(d), adding Code Sec. 1091(f); Act Sec. 401(e), amending Code Sec. 1092(d)(3)(B)(i); Act Sec. 401(f), amending Code Sec. 1233(e)(2); Act Sec. 401(g), amending Code Sec. 1256; Act Sec. 401(h), adding new Code Sec. 1223(16); Act Sec. 401(i), adding new Code Sec. 7701(m); Act Sec. 401(j). Law at ¶ 5590, ¶ 5600, ¶ 5610, ¶ 5630, ¶ 5635, ¶ 5640, ¶ 5650, ¶ 5660, and ¶ 6210. Committee Report at ¶ 10,355.

Liability Assumptions by Controlled Corporations

¶ 265

Background

Generally, no gain or loss is recognized if one or more persons transfer property to a corporation, other than an investment company, solely in exchange for its stock if immediately after the transfer those persons are in control of the corporation (Code Sec. 351(a)). However, a transferor recognizes gain to the extent it receives money or other property (boot) as part of the exchange (Code Sec. 351(b)).

The assumption of liabilities by the controlled corporation generally is not treated as boot received by the transferor (Code Sec. 357(a)). However if the liabilities assumed, or to which property transferred is subject, exceed the transferor's basis in the property, then, to the extent of the excess, the assumption is a gain from the sale or exchange of a capital asset (depending on the type of asset that was transferred) (Code Sec. 357(c)). Further if it can be shown that "the principal purpose" of the assumption is tax avoidance on the exchange or is a *non-bona fide* business purpose, the assumption of liabilities is treated as boot (Code Sec. 357(b)).

Where, as part of the consideration to the taxpayer, another party to the exchange assumes a liability of the taxpayer or acquires from the taxpayer property subject to a liability, such assumption or acquisition (in the amount of the liability) is treated as money received in the exchange, but only for the purpose of determining the basis of the property received in the exchange. The transferor's basis in the stock of the controlled corporation is the same as the basis of the property contributed to the controlled corporation, increased by the amount of any gain (or dividend) recognized by the transferor on the exchange and reduced by the amount of any money or property received, and by the amount of any loss recognized by the transferor (Code Sec. 358).

An exception to the general treatment of assumptions of liabilities applies to assumptions of liabilities that would give rise to a deduction, provided the incurrence of such liabilities did not result in the creation or increase of basis of any property (Code Sec. 357(c)(3)(B)). The assumption of such liabilities is not treated as money received by the transferor in determining whether the transferor has gain on the exchange. Similarly, the transferor's basis in the stock of the controlled corporation is not reduced by the assumption of such liabilities. The IRS has ruled that the assumption by an accrual basis corporation of certain contingent liabilities is covered by this exception (Rev. Rul. 95-74, 1995-2 C.B. 36).

Impact of Community Renewal Tax Relief Act of 2000

Prevention of duplication of loss through assumption of liabilities giving rise to a deduction.—If the basis of stock received by a transferor as part of a tax-free exchange with a controlled corporation exceeds the fair market value of the stock, then the basis of the stock received is reduced by the amount of any liability that is assumed in exchange for such stock and that did not otherwise reduce the transferor's basis of the stock by reason of the assumption. The basis of the stock received is not reduced below fair market value. For this purpose the amount of the liability is determined as of the date of the exchange. (Code Sec. 358(h), as added by the Community Renewal Tax Relief Act of 2000.)

Comment. This provision does not change the tax treatment with respect to the transferee corporation.

Example (1). Maureen Griffith transfers assets with an adjusted basis and fair market value of $8,000 to her wholly-owned corporation. The corporation assumes $2,000 of contingent liabilities, the payment of which would give rise to a deduction. The value of the stock received by the transferor is $6,000. Under Code Sec. 358(h), as added by the 2000 Act, the basis of the stock would be reduced to $6,000 (a reduction equal to the amount of the liability).

Comment. Under prior law, the basis of the stock in the example would be $8,000.

Definition of liability. For purposes of this provision, the term "liability" includes any fixed or contingent obligation to make payment, without regard to whether such obligation or potential obligation is otherwise taken into account under any other provision of the Code (Code Sec. 358(h)(3), as added by the 2000 Act). The determination whether a liability has been assumed is made in accordance with the provisions of Code. Sec. 357(d)(1) (as amended by the 2000 Act). Under that provision a recourse liability is treated as assumed if, based on all the facts and circumstances, the transferee has agreed to and is expected to satisfy such liability (or portion thereof), whether or not the transferor has been relieved of the liability (Code. Sec. 357(d)(1)(A)).

Example (2). Sid Frink transfers property and a liability, on which he is personally liable, to SF corporation. SF does not formally assume Frink's recourse obligation but agrees and is expected to indemnify Frink with respect to all of the obligation. The amount of the obligation is treated as assumed for purposes of this provision, even though Frink has not been personally relieved of the liability.

A nonrecourse liability is generally treated as assumed by the transferee of any asset subject to the liability (Code. Sec. 357(d)(1)(B)); however, Code Sec. 357(d)(2) contains certain exceptions.

Exceptions to applicability. Except as provided by the IRS, these provisions do not apply to any liability:

(1) if the trade or business with which the liability is associated is transferred to the person assuming the liability (the corporation) as part of the exchange (Code Sec. 358(h)(2)(A), as added by the 2000 Act), or

(2) if substantially all the assets with which the liability is associated are transferred to the person assuming the liability (corporation) as part of the exchange (Code Sec. 358(h)(2)(B), as added by the 2000 Act).

Example (3). Assume the same facts as Example 1, except Griffith transferred all of the assets used in a trade or business. Then the basis reduction rules would not apply, and she would have a basis of $8,000 in the stock.

Caution. The Conference Committee Report notes that these exceptions are intended to obviate the need for valuation or basis reduction in such cases. However, the exceptions are *not* intended to apply to situations involving the selective transfer of assets that may bear some relationship to the liability but that do not represent the full scope of the trade or business (or substantially all the assets) with which the liability is associated.

Partnerships and S corporations. For transactions involving partnerships the IRS is directed to prescribe regulations providing appropriate adjustments to prevent the acceleration or duplication of losses through the assumption of—or transfer of assets subject to—liabilities in transactions involving partnerships. For this purpose the term "liability" includes any fixed or contingent obligation to make payment (as defined in Code Sec. 358(h)(3)). With regard to S corporations, the IRS may also provide appropriate adjustments instead of the otherwise applicable basis reduction rules. (Act Sec. 709(c).)

Comment. The Act requires the IRS to issue regulations regarding partnerships, but only permits such regulations for S corporations.

★ *Effective date.* These provisions generally apply to assumptions of liability after October 18, 1999 (Act Sec. 309(d) of the Community Renewal Tax Relief Act of 2000). However, Act Sec. 309(c), which prescribes comparable rules for partnerships and S corporations, applies to assumptions of liability after October 18, 1999, or such later date as may be prescribed in regulations.

Act Sec. 309(a) of the Community Renewal Tax Relief Act of 2000, adding Code Sec. 358(h); Act Sec. 309(b), amending Code Sec. 357(d)(1); Act Sec. 309(c); Act Sec. 309(d). Law at ¶5260 and ¶5270. Committee Report at ¶10,295.

Sales of Section 1250 Property by Charitable Remainder Trust

¶270

Background _____

The character of a charitable remainder trust's (CRT) income is determined at the time the income is realized by the trust. The income beneficiary of a CRT includes the capital gain of the trust in income when the capital gain is distributed to the beneficiary, regardless of the year the income was realized by the trust. In 1997, Code Sec. 1(h) was amended to provide three different rates for capital gains realized at different times during 1997. As clarified by Notice 98-20, 1998-1 CB 776, long-term capital gain taken into account by a CRT falls into three groups: (1) the 28-percent group, (2) the 25-percent group, and (3) the 20-percent group. Long-term capital gain taken into account by a CRT from January 1 to May 6, 1997, was treated as falling under the 28-percent group.

A new Code provision (Code Sec. 1(h)(13)(A)), added by the Tax and Trade Relief Extension Act of 1998 (P.L. 105-277), changed the classification of a CRT's capital gain property taken into account during 1997 from the 28-percent group to the 25-percent group or the 20-percent group. To reflect this change, the IRS issued Notice 99-17, I.R.B. 1999-14, 6, in which it outlined which capital gains taken into account in 1997 would fall under the 25-percent group. Long-term capital gain that was taken into account during 1997 and that was distributed after 1997 fell under the 25-percent group if:

> (1) it was from property held more than 12 months, but not more than 18 months;

> (2) it was properly taken into account for the portion of the tax year after July 28, 1997, and before January 1, 1998, and

> (3) it otherwise satisfied the requirements for unrecaptured Code Sec. 1250 gain under Code Sec. 1(h)(7).

Technical Corrections Impact

Rates for 1997 capital gains.—A charitable remainder trust's long-term capital gain from Code Sec. 1250 property which is attributable to depreciation is taxed at 25 percent rather than 28 percent if the gain: (1) was from property held more than 12 months, but not more than 18 months, (2) was from property sold after July 28, 1997, and before January 1, 1998, and (3) was distributed after December 31, 1997. Any remaining long-term capital gains fall within the 20-percent group. This law change codifies the IRS policy set forth in IRS Notice 99-17, I.R.B. 1999-14, 6.

Comment. As directed by Notice 99-17, to reflect this change in the law, charitable remainder trusts should remove from the 28-percent group any long-term capital gains, other than collectibles gain, properly taken into account during 1997 that were not distributed in the 1997 tax year, and place those long-term capital gains in either the 25-percent group or the 20-percent group, as appropriate.

★ *Effective date.* This provision is effective for tax years ending after May 6, 1997 (Act Sec. 312(c) of the Community Renewal Tax Relief Act of 2000; Act Sec. 4003(b) of the Tax and Trade Relief Extension Act of 1998; Act Sec. 311 of the Taxpayer Relief Act of 1997 (P.L. 105-34)).

Act Sec. 312(b) of the Community Renewal Tax Relief Act of 2000, amending Act Sec. 4003(b) of the Tax and Trade Relief Extension Act of 1998 (P.L. 105-277); Act Sec. 312(c). Law at ¶ 7175. Committee Report at ¶ 10,315.

¶ 270

Capital Gains Election

¶ 275

Background

In order for a taxpayer in a greater than 15-percent tax bracket to take advantage of the lower than 18-percent capital gains rate that applies to property held for more than five years, the property must be acquired after December 31, 2000. Noncorporate taxpayers may make a special election to treat certain assets held on January 1, 2001, as sold and reacquired on the same day (deemed sale-and-repurchase election). This allows assets acquired before January 1, 2001, to qualify for the five-year holding period. The election applies to readily tradable stock and any other capital asset or property used in the taxpayer's trade or business, as defined by Code Sec. 1231(b). In general, the asset is treated as if it were sold and reacquired on January 1, 2001, at its fair market value and income tax is due from the gain on the sale. In the case of readily tradable stock not sold before January 1, 2001, the stock is treated as sold and reacquired on January 2, 2001, for an amount equal to the stock's January 2, 2001, closing market price. Loss on the sale is not recognized. Once the election is made, it is irrevocable (Act Sec. 311(e) of the Taxpayer Relief Act of 1997 (P.L. 105-34)).

Technical Corrections Impact

Election for assets held on January 1, 2001.—The deemed sale-and-repurchase election will not apply to an asset disposed of in a recognition transaction before the close of the one-year period beginning on the date the asset would have been treated as sold under the election (Act Sec. 311(e)(3) of the Taxpayer Relief Act of 1997, as amended by the Community Renewal Tax Relief Act of 2000 (P.L. 106-554)). As result, the asset will not qualify as five-year property for purposes of the lower 18-percent capital gains rate. In addition, the Conference Report indicates that for purposes of applying the Code Sec. 1091 wash sale rules, the deemed sale and repurchase of the asset subject to the election is not taken into account.

Example. Max Brand, a 28-percent tax bracket calendar-year taxpayer, purchases 10 shares of stock in Binnacle, Inc. in 1994 for $1,000. He still owns the shares on January 1, 2001, and their fair market value is $10,000. Brand could elect to treat stock as sold and repurchased on January 2, 2001, if he pays tax on the $9,000 of accrued gain. However, the election will not apply if he sells the stock during 2001.

Election. Procedures for making the election are contained in the 2000 Instructions to Form 4797, Sales of Business Property (Also Involuntary Conversions and Recapture Amounts Under Sections 179 and 280F(b)(2)). The instructions provide that the election is to be made on the tax return for the tax year that includes the date of the deemed sale. A taxpayer may make the election by the due date of the return, including extensions. If the return was timely filed without making the election, the election can be made by filing an amended return within six months of the due date of the return, excluding extensions. The instruction procedures provided in 2000 Form 4797 apply to fiscal-year taxpayers and state that calendar-year taxpayers will make the election on their 2001 return.

Planning Note. Taxpayers may decide to make the deemed sale-and-repurchase election in order to generate a capital gain that would offset capital losses from other assets, without requiring an actual disposition of the asset to which the election relates. Planning opportunities that involve generating short-term capital losses by selling within one year of the deemed disposition date are effectively eliminated by this technical correction. However, the election still enables the spreading of gain between two separate tax years if the actual sale is made in a tax year that does not include the deemed disposition date (January 1 or 2, 2000) and the sale is more than one year after that date.

★ *Effective date.* The provision applies to tax years ending after May 6, 1997 (Act Sec. 314(g) of the Community Renewal Tax Relief Act of 2000; Act Sec. 311(d) of the Taxpayer Relief Act of 1997 (P. L. 105-34)).

Act Sec. 314(c) of the Community Renewal Tax Relief Act of 2000, amending Act Sec. 311(e)(3) of the Taxpayer Relief Act of 1997 (P.L. 105-34); Act Sec. 314(g). Law at ¶ 7180. Committee Report at ¶ 10,325.

Losses from Section 1256 Contracts

¶ 280

Background _____

Regulated futures contracts, foreign currency contracts, nonequity options and dealer equity options are all governed by Code Sec. 1256. Although individuals normally cannot carry back a capital loss to past tax years, loss carrybacks from Code Sec. 1256 contracts are permitted to individuals by the Code's capital loss carryback and carryover rules (Code Sec. 1212(c), added by the Economic Recovery Act of 1981 (P.L. 97-34)), which apply to taxpayers other than corporations. However, Code Sec. 6411(a), which sets out the rules governing the application for an adjustment of a prior year's tax, refers to Code Sec. 1212(a)(1), which has no provision for applying the capital loss carryback rules to individuals.

Technical Corrections Impact

Loss carrybacks allowed.—The deduction of capital loss carrybacks for Code Sec. 1256 contracts is specifically provided for individuals by adding a reference to Code Sec. 1212(c) in the tentative carryback and refund adjustments provisions (Code Sec. 6411(a), as amended by the Community Renewal Tax Relief Act of 2000 (P.L. 106-554)).

★ *Effective date.* This provision is effective for property acquired or positions established after June 23, 1981 (Act Sec. 318(d)(2) of the Community Renewal Tax Relief Act of 2000; Act Sec. 504 of the Economic Recovery Tax Act of 1981 (P.L. 97-34)).

Act Sec. 318(d)(1) of the Community Renewal Tax Relief Act of 2000, amending Code Sec. 6411(a); Act Sec. 318(d)(2). Law at ¶ 6090. Committee Report at ¶ 10,345.

TAX-EXEMPT BONDS

Private Activity Bonds

¶ 285

*Background*_____

Interest on bonds issued by state and local governments is tax-exempt if the proceeds are used to finance activities paid for and conducted by the governmental unit. However, interest on state and local bonds generally is not tax-exempt if the proceeds are used to finance activities paid for and carried out by private persons (private activity bonds), unless those activities are among those specifically categorized as qualified bonds (Code Sec. 141(e)). Qualified bonds include exempt facilities bonds, qualified mortgage bonds, qualified veteran's mortgage bonds, qualified small issue bonds, qualified student loan bonds, qualified redevelopment bonds and qualified 501(c)(3) bonds.

Under current law (Code Sec. 146(d)(1)-(2)), the volume of tax-exempt private activity bonds that may be issued by states and local governments for most of these qualified purposes is limited by unified state-wide volume limits. The volume limits do not apply to qualified 501(c)(3) bonds, certain exempt-facility bonds (*e.g.* for airports, docks, and wharves), certain refunding bonds (other than advance refunding bonds), certain governmentally owned—but privately operated—solid waste disposal facilities, and certain high-speed rail facilities. The volume limits also do not apply to certain other types of tax-exempt private activity bonds that are subject to other volume limits, such as qualified veterans' mortgage bonds and certain empowerment zone bonds.

An increase in the volume limitation of tax-exempt private bonds is being phased-in ratably from 1999 through 2007. Through calendar year 2002, the annual state volume limits for tax-exempt private activity bonds are $50 per resident of the state or $150 million, whichever is greater. The volume limits will then increase by $5 per state resident and $15 million per year, beginning in the calendar year 2003. The phase-in will be complete at $75 per resident or $225 million, whichever is greater, beginning in calendar year 2007.

Community Renewal Tax Relief Act Impact

Increase in volume limits.—The Act will accelerate the increase in annual state volume limits of tax-exempt private bonds beginning in 2001, when the state ceiling will be the greater of $62.50 per state resident or $187.5 million. Beginning in 2002, the volume limit will increase to $75 per resident of each state or $225 million, whichever is greater (Code Sec. 146(d)(1), as amended by the Community Renewal Tax Relief Act of 2000).

The $75 per resident and $225 million state limit will be indexed for inflation beginning in calendar year 2003, using the cost-of-living adjustment determined under Code Sec. 1(f)(3) for such calendar year, with calendar year 2001 as the base year. Any increase that is not a multiple of $5 is to be rounded to the nearest multiple of $5 (Code Sec. 146(d)(2), as amended by the 2000 Act).

Comment. When the state volume limitation was established by the Tax Reform Act of 1986 (P.L. 99-514), the amount was set at the greater of $75 per capita or $250 million. Anticipating the sunset of the authority to issue mortgage revenue bonds and small-issue industrial development bonds, the amount was reduced to the current level for calendar years beginning after 1988. Instead, both bond provisions were made permanent, rather than being eliminated. However, there was no corresponding increase in the volume limitation until the delayed, phased-in increase was enacted by the Tax and Trade Relief Extension Act of 1998 (P.L. 105-277). Moreover, during the period in which the current volume limitation has been in place, inflation has reduced the real dollar value of the limitation amount by roughly fifty percent. This increase will enable state and local government to better meet the increasing demand for qualified private activity bonds.

★ *Effective date.* The provision is effective for calendar years after 2000 (Act Sec. 161(b) of the Community Renewal Tax Relief Act of 2000).

Act Sec. 161(a) of the Community Renewal Tax Relief Act of 2000, amending Code Sec. 146(d)(1)-(2); Act Sec. 161(b). Law at ¶ 5160. Committee Report at ¶ 10,210.

EMPLOYMENT TAXES

Treatment of Tribal Governments Under FUTA

¶ 290

Background

The Federal Unemployment Tax Act imposes a tax on employers who employ one or more persons on at least one day in each of 20 weeks during the current or preceding calendar year, or who pay wages of at least $1,500 ($20,000 for agricultural labor or $1,100 for domestic labor) in a calendar quarter in the current or preceding calendar year (Code Sec. 3306(a)). This federal unemployment tax (FUTA) is based on the first $7,000 of wages (as defined under Code Sec. 3306(b)) paid during the calendar year to each employee and is currently 6.2 percent (Code Sec. 3301). Certain employers, however, are granted a 5.4 percent credit, leaving the effective FUTA tax rate at 0.8 percent (Code Sec. 3302).

Both non-profit organizations, within the meaning of Code Sec. 501(c)(3), and state and local governments are currently entitled to forego the payment of FUTA taxes and instead elect to reimburse the unemployment compensation system for the unemployment benefits actually paid to their former employees (Code Sec. 3306(c)(7) and (8) and Code Sec. 3309). Indian tribes do not have such an option.

Community Renewal Tax Relief Act Impact

Indian Tribes May Elect Out of FUTA.—An Indian tribe will be treated like a non-profit organization or state or local government for FUTA purposes. Services provided by employees to Indian tribes, therefore, will not fall within the FUTA definition of employment, and Indian tribes will not be required to pay FUTA taxes (Code Sec. 3306(c)(7), as amended by the Community Renewal Tax Relief Act of 2000, and Code Sec. 3309(a), as amended by the 2000 Act).

Election. In lieu of the payment of FUTA taxes, Indian tribes will be entitled to elect to reimburse the unemployment compensation system for benefits actually paid to former employees (Code Sec. 3309(a), as amended by the 2000 Act). A tribe will be able to make separate elections for itself and any subdivision, subsidiary or business enterprise wholly owned by the Indian tribe (Code Sec. 3309(d), as added by the 2000 Act).

¶ 290

In addition, the Act provides that if an Indian tribe elects to avail itself of the reimbursement method, state law may require it to post a payment bond or to take other reasonable measures which would assure that payments in lieu of contributions will be made. If, after having been notified of any delinquency, an electing Indian tribe fails to make required contributions within 90 days, then service for the tribe shall not be excepted from the definition of employment, *i.e.*, the customary payment of FUTA taxes will be mandated until such delinquency is corrected (Code Sec. 3309(d), as added by the 2000 Act).

For purposes of the treatment of tribal governments under FUTA, the definition of an Indian tribe will be the same as the definition provided in Section 4(e) of the Indian Self-Determination and Education Assistance Act (P.L. 93-368) and includes any subdivision, subsidiary, or business enterprise that is wholly owned by the tribe (Code Sec. 3306(u), as added by the 2000 Act).

Comment. The Indian Self-Determination and Education Assistance Act, passed in 1975, authorized Indian tribes to contract for direct participation of tribal members in governmental programs impacting the Indian people. It defines an Indian tribe as "any Indian tribe, band, nation or other organized group or community, including any Alaska Native village or regional or village corporation as defined in or established pursuant to the Alaska Native Claims Settlement Act, which is recognized as eligible for the special programs and services provided by the United States to Indians because of their status as Indians."

★ *Effective date.* This provision is generally effective with respect to services performed beginning on or after December 21, 2000, the date of enactment. Under a transition rule, service performed in the employ of an Indian tribe is not treated as employment for FUTA purposes if: (1) it is service performed before December 21, 2000, and with respect to which FUTA tax has not been paid, and (2) such Indian tribe reimburses a state unemployment fund for unemployment benefits paid for service attributable to such tribe for such period (Act Sec. 166(e) of the 2000 Act).

Act Sec. 166(a) of the Community Renewal Tax Relief Act of 2000, amending Code Sec. 3306(c)(7); Act Sec. 166(b), amending Code Sec. 3309(a)(2) and 3309(b); Act Sec. 166(c), adding Code Sec. 3309(d); Act Sec. 166(d), adding Code Sec. 3306(u); Act Sec. 166(e). Law at ¶ 5890 and ¶ 5900. Committee Report at ¶ 10,235.

EXCISE TAXES

Tobacco Tax Corrections

¶ 293

Background _____

The Balanced Budget Act of 1997 (P.L. 105-33) increased the excise tax on tobacco products and extended the tax to "roll-your-own" tobacco (Act Sec. 9302 of the Balanced Budget Act of 1997 (P.L. 105-33)). The rate increases were made effective in two phases: January 1, 2000, and January 1, 2002. A floor stocks tax is imposed on these products at the time of the rate increases. However, the 1997 amendment provides that the person liable for the tax is the person holding *cigarettes* on the date of the tax increases. Other changes provided that the tax on cigarette papers applies, regardless of the number of papers in the book. Civil penalties are also imposed on persons who sell, reland or receive tobacco products in a jurisdiction of the United States that are labeled or shipped for exportation.

The Harmonized Tariff Schedule of the United States (HTS) was enacted by the Omnibus Trade and Competitiveness Act of 1988 (P.L. 100-418), effective January 1, 1989. Under the HTS, import and export schedules are based on international nomenclature, but rates of duties are set by the contracting parties. In specific circumstances, Chapter 98 of the HTS allows duty free entry or partial duty-free entry of goods otherwise subject to duty. Special duty treatment might apply, for example, to goods reimported after having been exported from the United States or goods brought back to the United States by a U.S. resident for personal use.

Technical Corrections Impact

Tobacco excise taxes.—A technical correction clarifies that the floor stocks tax applies to cigarettes, rather than to all tobacco products. Prior to the clarification, the provision could be read to impose the floor stocks tax on all tobacco products, while imposing liability only on the person holding cigarettes on the date of the tax increases (Act Sec. 9302(j)(1) of the Balanced Budget Act of 1997, as amended by the Community Renewal Tax Relief Act of 2000 (P.L. 106-554)).

Cigarette papers. An additional clarification eliminates the definition of cigarette papers as taxable books or sets of papers (Code Sec. 5702(f), as stricken by the 2000 Act, and Code Sec. 5702(g), as amended and redesignated by the 2000 Act). The excise tax on cigarette papers is imposed regardless of whether the papers are in a book.

Civil penalties. The civil penalties under Code Sec. 5761(c) will not apply to a person who relands or receives tobacco products in an amount allowed under Chapter 98 of the Harmonized Tariff Schedule (HTS) of the United States. Chapter 98 of the HTS may provide duty or partial duty-free entry in to the United States under special circumstances. For instance, a U.S. resident returning from abroad may import no more than 200 cigarettes or 100 cigars for personal use. To be relieved of the penalties, the person must voluntarily relinquish any excess product. Amounts relanded or received for personal use must also be in amounts allowed under the HTS (Code Sec. 5761(c), as amended by the 2000 Act).

★ *Effective date.* The provisions are generally effective for articles removed from the factory or from internal revenue bond under Code Sec. 5704, or released from customs custody after December 31, 1999 (Act Sec. 315(b) of the Community Renewal Tax Relief Act of 2000; Act Sec. 9302(i)(1) of the Balanced Budget Act of 1997 (P.L. 105-33); Code Sec. 5702(k)).

Act Sec. 315(a)(1) of the Community Renewal Tax Relief Act of 2000, amending Act Sec. 9302(j)(1) of the Balanced Budget Act of 1997 (P.L. 105-33); Act Sec. 315(a)(2)(A), amending Code Sec. 5702(h); Act Sec. 315(a)(2)(B), striking Code Sec. 5702(f) and redesignating Code Sec. 5702(g) through (p) as Code Sec. 5702(f) through (o), respectively; Act Sec. 315(a)(3), amending Code Sec. 5761(c); Act Sec. 315(b). Law at ¶ 5960, ¶ 5970, and ¶ 7185. Committee Report at ¶ 10,330.

Highway Trust Fund

¶ 295

Background _____

The 1990 Revenue Reconciliation Act (P.L. 101-508) increased the tax rate on fuels made from ethanol and, in connection with that increase, directed that the amount of fuel excise taxes described in Code Secs. 4041 and 4081 that would otherwise be deposited from the general fund to the Highway Trust Fund should be reduced by an amount equivalent to the increased tax on ethanol fuels (Code Sec. 9503(b)(5), as added by the 1990 Act). Thus, the tax increase was left in the general fund. The tax increase was eliminated in 1993; however, the provision requiring reduction of the fuel taxes transferred to the Highway Trust Fund was not repealed. As a result, the amount of fuel taxes being deposited in the Highway Trust Fund continues to be reduced by an amount that is equal to the additional tax that would have been collected if the increased rate was still in effect.

Technical Corrections Impact

Highway Trust Fund transfer reduction eliminated.—The provision requiring the reduction of fuel excise tax transfers to the Highway Trust Fund by the amount of the repealed ethanol fuels tax increase is stricken (Code Sec. 9503(b)(5), stricken by the Community Renewal Tax Relief Act of 2000).

Comment. The Conference Committee Report accompanying the 2000 Act specifically notes that no retroactive adjustments are to be made to the Highway Trust Fund.

★ *Effective date.* This provision is effective for taxes received after December 21, 2000 (Act Sec. 318(e)(2) of the Community Renewal Tax Relief Act of 2000).

Act Sec. 318(e)(1) of the Community Renewal Tax Relief Act of 2000, striking Code Sec. 9503(b)(5) and redesignating Code Sec. 9503(b)(6) as Code Sec. 9503(b)(5); Act Sec. 318(e)(2). Law at ¶ 6260. Committee Report at ¶ 10,345.

Vaccine Trust Fund

¶ 297

Background _____

The Vaccine Injury Compensation Trust Fund is funded with amounts paid from a tax imposed on any taxable vaccine sold by a manufacturer, producer or importer (Code Sec. 4131). Expenditures from the fund are permitted only for vaccine-related injury or death. The payment of compensation is governed by subtitle 2 of title XXI of the Public Health Service Act, as in effect on December 31, 1999.

Technical Corrections Impact

Trust fund provisions extended.—The reference to December 31, 1999, is stricken and the reference is changed to October 18, 2000 (Code Sec. 9510(c)(1)(A), as amended by the Community Renewal Tax Relief Act of 2000).

Comment. The Vaccine Injury Compensation Trust Fund provisions have been extended several times in the past.

★ *Effective date.* No specific effective date is provided by the Act. The provision is, therefore, considered effective on December 21, 2000, the date of enactment.

Act Sec. 318(f) of the Community Renewal Tax Relief Act of 2000, amending Code Sec. 9510(c)(1)(A). Law at ¶6270. Committee Report at ¶10,345.

Chapter 3

Procedure and Administration

IRS DISCLOSURE AND CONFIDENTIALITY

Confidentiality of Agreements

¶ 305

Background _____

Tax returns and tax return information are confidential and, except as authorized by the Internal Revenue Code, cannot be disclosed by officers and employees of the United States or of any state or local agency administering specified federal programs (Code Sec. 6103). Other persons who disclose returns or return information do not violate the disclosure rules in the Code, although other laws may prevent disclosure. A return includes any tax or information return, declaration of estimated tax, or claim for refund that is required or allowed by the Code. Return information includes any information on a return, whether a return is being or will be investigated or audited, and any other data collected by the IRS concerning a return or the existence of any tax liability.

Background ⎯⎯⎯⎯⎯⎯⎯⎯⎯⎯⎯⎯⎯⎯⎯⎯⎯⎯⎯⎯⎯⎯⎯⎯⎯⎯⎯⎯⎯⎯⎯

The Freedom of Information Act (FOIA) (5 U.S.C. § 552) generally allows the public access to information held by government agencies. However, tax return information is specifically exempted by the statute (Exemption 3, FOIA).

The FOIA generally allows the public access to information held by government agencies, with a number of significant exceptions. One such exception is for material that is exempted by a statute that requires no discretion on what material must be withheld from the public or establishes particular criteria for withholding or refers to particular types of material to be withheld. All courts that have considered the issue have held that Code Sec. 6103, which governs disclosure of tax return information, is within Exception 3 and that materials protected from disclosure under Code Sec. 6103 are exempt from disclosure under the FOIA.

Written determinations and background file documents relating to written determinations are generally open to public inspection (Code Sec. 6110(a)). A written determination is a ruling, determination letter, technical advice memorandum, or Chief Counsel advice (Code Sec. 6110(b)). A written determination does not include an Advance Pricing Agreement (APA), any related background information, or any application for an APA. A ruling is a written statement by the IRS's National Office to a taxpayer that interprets and applies tax laws to a specific set of facts.

Suits brought under the FOIA have resulted in the disclosure of much IRS material, including the Internal Revenue Manual, letter rulings, general counsel's memoranda, technical advice memoranda, and actions on decisions. Other material disclosable by the FOIA include field service memoranda that are prepared by attorneys in the Office of Chief Counsel for field attorneys, revenue agents and appeals officers, except that information related to specific taxpayers must be deleted.

Treaties. U.S. treaties include provision for the exchange of information between treaty partners. Absent a treaty, no authority for exchange exists. Information is exchanged on request, automatically or spontaneously, to facilitate investigations. U.S. treaties generally include broad authority to exchange tax information between treaty partners. The U.S. model exchange of information article is applicable to information concerning nonresidents as well as residents (U.S. Model Treaty Art. 26(1) (September 20, 1996)). Under U.S. practice, information is exchanged:

　　　(1) upon request;

　　　(2) automatically, for example when information about one or more categories of income having their source in one contracting state and received in the other contracting state is transmitted systematically to the other state; and

　　　(3) spontaneously, for example in the case of a state having acquired, through certain investigations, information that it supposes to be of interest to the other state.

The U.S. Model Treaty provides that Article 26 applies to all taxes of every kind imposed by a contracting state. In general, disclosure of information that is received from such exchange of information between treaty partners is not allowed except to those authorities involved in the administration, assessment, collection, or enforcement of taxes to which the treat applies.

On October 2, 2000, the Treasury Office of Tax Policy sent to Congress the "Report to the Congress on the Scope and Use of Taxpayer Confidentiality and

Background _____

Disclosure Provisions, Volume I: Study of General Provisions." The report recommends that information reflected in returns and return information properly made a part of the public record not be protected under Code Sec. 6103. Other recommendations made by the report relate to amending or clarifying Code Sec. 6103 with respect to its interaction with other statutes, including the FOIA, and regarding disclosure issues with respect to IRS documents.

Community Renewal Tax Relief Act Impact

Agreements with foreign governments.—Agreements and information received under a tax convention are confidential and generally cannot be disclosed (Code Sec. 6105(a), as added by the Community Renewal Tax Relief Act of 2000). A tax convention is any income or gift and estate tax convention, or any other convention or bilateral agreement (including multilateral conventions and agreements and any agreement with a possession of the United States) providing for the avoidance of double taxation, the prevention of fiscal evasion, nondiscrimination with respect to taxes, the exchange of tax relevant information with the United States, or mutual assistance in tax matters (Code Sec. 6105(c)(2), as added by the 2000 Act).

Tax convention information includes any:

(1) agreement entered into with the competent authority of one or more foreign governments under a tax convention;

(2) application for relief under a tax convention;

(3) background information related to such an agreement or application;

(4) document implementing such an agreement; and

(5) any other information exchanged under a tax convention that is treated as confidential or secret under the tax convention (Code Sec. 6105(c)(1), as added by the 2000 Act).

Comment. It is the Conference Committee's intent that tax convention information include documents and any other information that reflects tax convention information, such as the association of a particular treaty partner with a specific issue or matter.

Disclosure permitted. However, tax convention information may be disclosed:

(1) to persons or authorities (including courts and administrative bodies) that are entitled to disclosure under a tax convention;

(2) to any generally applicable procedural rules regarding applications for relief under a tax convention (such as Rev. Proc. 96-13, 1996-1 CB 18);

(3) where the information does not relate to a particular taxpayer and, after consultation with each party to the tax convention, the Secretary of the Treasury determines that the disclosure would not impair tax administration (Code Sec. 6105(b), as added by the 2000 Act). According to the Conference Report, the "impairment of tax administration" includes, but is not limited to, the release of documents that would adversely affect the working relationship of treaty partners. Thus, unless otherwise provided, taxpayer-specific information could not be disclosed, even if it did not impair tax administration.

Example. An agreement between the competent authorities of Mexico and the United States regarding the maquiladora industry is an example of a general agreement that could be disclosed under this provision (see Internal Revenue News Release IR-INT-1999-13, October 29, 1999). The Mexican maquiladora industry is a production-sharing system between Mexico and foreign countries, mainly the United States, in which investors establish production facilities in Mexico, either as subsidiaries or as joint ventures with Mexican enterprises, to manufacture products at competitive prices.

Closing agreements treated as return information. The 2000 Act clarifies that return information includes closing agreements and other similar agreements. Code Sec. 7121 closing agreements, "any other similar" agreement, and any background information relating to such an agreement or request for such an agreement, are treated as confidential return information (Code Sec. 6103(b)(2)(d), as added by the 2000 Act). The Conference Agreement states that it is the conferee's intent that similar agreements include negotiated agreements that (1) are the result of an alternative dispute resolution or dispute avoidance process relating to the liability of any person under the Internal Revenue Code for any tax, penalty, interest, forfeiture, or other disposition or offense and (2) do not establish, set forth, or resolve the government's interpretation of the relevant tax law.

Comment. It is not the Conference Committee's intent to override the disclosure of tax-exempt organization closing agreements that may be authorized under Code Sec. 6104. Nor is it meant to preclude citation or repetition of the Code, regulations, or other published rulings.

Comment. However, it is the Committee's intent that pre-filing agreements are covered by the provision. Pre-filing agreements, under Notice 2000-12 (February 11, 2000), allow large businesses to request a review and resolution of specific issues relating to certain tax returns. In addition, the Committee does not intend that this provision be used as justification for avoiding public disclosure of determinations, such as technical advice memoranda or Chief Counsel advice that would be issued in a form that is subject to public inspection. Thus, technical advice memoranda or Chief Counsel advice would not be exempt from disclosure merely because the material is included in a background file for a closing agreement.

Example. An IRS revenue agent seeks technical advice in connection with a pre-filing agreement. It is the Committee's intent that the technical advice would remain subject to the Code Sec. 6110 public inspection requirements since the pre-filing agreement program involves only settled issues of law.

The Committee has directed the Secretary of the Treasury to make an annual report on the pre-filing agreement program available to the public. This requirement is for a five-year period, or the duration of the program, whichever is shorter. The first report, which will cover calendar year 2000, is to be issued by March 30, 2001.

Written determination exception. The 2000 Act clarifies that closing and similar agreements are not included within the definition of "written determination" subject to public disclosure under Code Sec. 6110 (Code Sec. 6110(b)(1), as amended by the 2000 Act). Thus, closing and similar agreements are not subject to public disclosure. These agreements are defined as return information under Code Sec. 6103 and are exempt from disclosure under the Exemption 3 of the FOIA.

Further, the requirements for public inspection of written determinations under Code Sec. 6110 would not apply to tax convention information (Code Sec.

6110(l)(1), as amended by the 2000 Act). However, the Conference Report clarifies that taxpayer-specific competent authority agreements not relating to a particular taxpayer and other tax convention information relating to such agreements could be disclosed under the FOIA if the disclosure would not impair tax administration.

★ *Effective date.* The provisions are effective on December 21, 2000, the date of enactment (Act Sec. 304(d) of the Community Renewal Tax Relief Act of 2000). Thus, the provisions apply to disclosures on or after December 21, 2000, and to all documents in existence on, or created after, such date.

Act Sec. 304(a) of the Community Renewal Tax Relief Act of 2000, amending Code Sec. 6103(b)(2); Act Sec. 304(b), adding Code Sec. 6105; Act Sec. 304(c), amending Code Sec. 6110(b)(1) and 6110(l)(1); Act Sec. 304(d). **Law at ¶ 6000, ¶ 6020, and ¶ 6030. Committee Report at ¶ 10,270, ¶ 10,271, and ¶ 10,272.**

Disclosure of Return Information to Congressional Budget Office

¶ 307

Background _____

Federal tax returns and return information are confidential and cannot be disclosed without penalty unless authorized by the Internal Revenue Code (Code Sec. 6103). Code Sec. 6103 authorizes certain agencies to receive tax returns and return information for statistical use and other specified purposes.

A "federal tax return" means any tax return, information return, declaration of estimated tax, or claim for refund filed on behalf of or with respect to any person (Code Sec. 6103(b)(1)).

"Return information" includes:

(1) the taxpayer's identity;

(2) the nature, source or amount of income, payments, receipts, deductions, net worth, exemptions, credits, assets, liabilities, and deficiencies;

(3) whether or not any taxpayer's return is, was, or will be the subject of an investigation;

(4) whether any data collected or prepared by the IRS is related to the determination of any possible deficiency, penalty, interest, fine, forfeiture, or similar imposition upon a taxpayer; and

(5) any part of an IRS written determination or background file document not open to public inspection (Code Sec. 6103(b)(2)).

At the close of each calendar year, the IRS is required to provide a written report that describes procedures and safeguards taken by specified recipients of return information to ensure the confidentiality of the return information to the Ways and Means Committee, Committee on Finance, and Joint Committee on Taxation (Code Sec. 6103(p)(5)). The Comptroller General is authorized to determine ("audit") the procedures and safeguards to determine whether they are adequate (Code Sec. 6103(p)(6)).

Community Renewal Tax Relief Act Impact

Authorization of return information disclosure to CBO.—The list of authorized agencies that may receive return information is expanded to include the Congressional Budget Office (CBO) (Code Sec. 6103(j)(6), as added by the Community Renewal Tax Relief Act of 2000 (P.L. 106-554)). Under the provision, return information may be provided to officers and employees of the CBO, upon written request by the Director of the CBO, for the purpose of developing and maintaining long-term models of social security and medicare programs.

Comment. This provision is intended to give the CBO access to two critical social security administration files necessary for the development of its long-term planning models: the Social Security Earnings Record and the Master Beneficiary Record. These files contain individual earnings data compiled from tax returns (Forms W-2) protected from disclosure as return information. However, the provision will allow the Secretary of Treasury to furnish other return information necessary for development of the models.

The Act also makes the CBO subject to the same series of safeguards prescribed by Code Sec. 6102(p) to protect the confidentiality of return information provided to other Federal agencies (Code Sec. 6103(p)(4), as amended by the 2000 Act).

The Act adds the CBO to the list of return information recipients for which the IRS must provide an annual written report to the Ways and Means Committee, Committee on Finance, and Joint Committee on Taxation describing the procedures and safeguards taken by those recipients to ensure the confidentiality of the return information (Code Sec. 6103(p)(5), as amended by the 2000 Act). The Act, also, makes the CBO subject to the Comptroller General's audit procedures (Code Sec. 6103(p)(6)(A), as amended by the 2000 Act).

The new law amends the Congressional Budget Act of 1974 (2 U.S.C. § 603) to require the CBO to provide the same level of confidentiality to data it obtains from other agencies (*e.g.*, the IRS) as that to which the agencies themselves are subject. Officials and employees of the CBO are made subject to the same statutory penalties for unauthorized disclosure as the employees of the agencies from which the CBO obtains data (Section 203(e) of 2 U.S.C. § 603, as added by the 2000 Act).

★ *Effective date.* No specific effective date is provided by the Act. The provision is, therefore, considered effective on December 21, 2000, the date of enactment.

Act Sec. 310(a) of the Community Renewal Tax Relief Act of 2000, adding Code Sec. 6103(j)(6) and amending Code Sec. 6103(p)(4), (5), and (6); Act Sec. 310(b), adding Section 203(e) to 2 U.S.C. § 603. Law at ¶ 6000 and ¶ 7165. Committee Report at ¶ 10,300.

Return Disclosures by Treasury Inspector General

¶ 310

Background _____

The Office of the Chief Inspector within the IRS was eliminated by the IRS Restructuring and Reform Act of 1998 (P.L. 105-206). A new independent office of oversight and inspection of the IRS was created—the Office of Treasury Inspector General for Tax Administration (TIGTA). The former Chief Inspector's responsibilities were assigned to TIGTA.

TIGTA personnel were charged with performing certain duties which required them to make investigative disclosures of return information. Nevertheless, under Code Sec. 6103(k)(6), only an internal revenue officer or employee was authorized to make investigative disclosures of return information to obtain information which was not otherwise reasonably available, with respect to the correct determination of tax, liability for tax, or the amount to be collected or with respect to the

*Background*_____

enforcement of any other provision of the Code. Thus, TIGTA personnel, who are Treasury personnel rather than IRS personnel, were prevented from making authorized investigative disclosures.

Technical Corrections Impact

Investigative disclosures of return information by Treasury Inspector General.—Personnel from the Office of Treasury Inspector General for Tax Administration (TIGTA) are permitted to make investigative disclosures of tax return information. Thus, under this technical correction, both IRS personnel and TIGTA personnel are now authorized to make investigative disclosures (Code Sec. 6103(k)(6), as amended by the Community Renewal Tax Relief Act of 2000).

★ *Effective date.* This provision is effective on July 22, 1998 (Act Sec. 313(f) of the Community Renewal Tax Relief Act of 2000; Act Sec. 1103 of the IRS Restructuring and Reform Act of 1998 (P.L. 105-206)).

Act Sec. 313(c) of the Community Renewal Tax Relief Act of 2000, amending Code Sec. 6103(k)(6); Act Sec. 313(f). Law at ¶ 6000. Committee Report at ¶ 10,320.

Public Inspection of Chief Counsel Advice

¶ 315

*Background*_____

Generally, the text of any written determination and any background file document relating to such written determination shall be open to public inspection as the IRS may prescribe by regulations (Code Sec. 6110(a)). The term "written determination" means a ruling, determination letter, or technical advice memorandum. The IRS Restructuring and Reform Act of 1998 expanded the disclosure rules, including the definition of "written determination," to encompass Chief Counsel advice (Code Secs. 6110(b)(1) and 6110(i), as amended by the IRS Restructuring and Reform Act of 1998 (P.L. 105-206)). Nonetheless, Chief Counsel advice was inadvertently left from the list of documents that the IRS is not required to disclose if the document relates to a pending civil fraud or criminal investigation, or a pending jeopardy or termination assessment.

Technical Corrections Impact

Nondisclosure of Chief Counsel advice.—Chief Counsel advice is now among the types of written determinations that are not required to be disclosed by the IRS when the advice involves any matter that is the subject of a civil fraud or criminal investigation, or jeopardy or termination assessment that is incomplete. Such Chief Counsel advice does not need to be disclosed until after any action relating to the investigation or assessment is completed (Code Sec. 6110(g)(5), as amended by the Community Renewal Tax Relief Act of 2000).

★ *Effective date.* This provision applies to any Chief Counsel advice issued more than 90 days after July 22, 1998 (Act Sec. 313(f) of the Community Renewal Tax Relief Act of 2000; Act Sec. 3509 of the IRS Restructuring and Reform Act of 1998 (P.L. 105-206)).

Act Sec. 313(e) of the Community Renewal Tax Relief Act of 2000, amending Code Sec. 6110(g)(5)(A); Act Sec. 313(f). Law at ¶ 6030. Committee Report at ¶ 10,320.

REPORTING AND NOTICE REQUIREMENTS

Periodic Federal Reporting Requirements to Continue Despite Sunset

¶ 320

*Background*_____

In an effort to thin out the clutter of reports coming into Capital Hill, Congress enacted the Federal Reports Elimination and Sunset Act of 1995 (P. L. 104-66) which eliminated many reporting requirements effective May 15, 2000. The Act applies to reports set out in a document called "Reports to be Made to Congress" (House Document 103-7), dated January 5, 1993, and issued by the Clerk of the House of Representatives. The list has been subject to changes since the 1995 Act was first passed.

Technical Correction Impact

Code provisions exempted from sunset.—Despite the general application of the sunset provisions, the following reports required by various Code provisions still must be filed with Congress (Act Sec. 301(15) of the Community Renewal Tax Relief Act of 2000).

(1) *Confidentiality of tax returns.* Every year, the Secretary of the Treasury must furnish a report which describes the procedures and safeguards established and used by various agencies, bodies, or commissions and the General Accounting Office for ensuring the confidentiality of returns and return information. The report must describe instances of deficiencies in, and failure to establish or use, such procedures (Code Sec. 6103(p)(5)).

(2) *IRS undercover operations.* The IRS must furnish an annual report specifying its undercover operations, including information on the number of such operations, the expenses for each operation and their results (Code Sec. 7608(c)(4)(B)).

(3) *IRS Oversight Board.* The Oversight Board must report annually to the president and to various named congressional committees on its operations. In addition, if the Board determines that the organization and operation of the IRS are not allowing it to carry out its mission, then it must report this to the House Ways and Means Committee and the Senate Finance Committee (Code Sec. 7802(f)(3)).

(4) *Joint Committee on Taxation.* The Joint Committee on Taxation may report from time to time to Congress on the results of its investigations and any recommendations it may have resulting from its investigations. Also, the Committee must report to Congress at least once in every two years on the overall state of the federal tax system. Other annual reports are required on how the IRS is fulfilling its functions, but this requirement is to expire at the end of 2003 (Code Sec. 8022(3)(B)).

(5) *Management of trust funds.* The Secretary of the Treasury must report to Congress annually on the financial condition and operations of each trust fund established under the Trust Fund Code (Code Secs. 9501 through 9510). The report also must cover the expected condition and operations of the trust funds for the next five years (Code Sec. 9602(a)).

Other related revenue law provisions. In addition to the above reports that must still be filed with Congress, the following non-Code provisions are also exempted from the sunset provision:

(1) the compilation by the Secretary of the Treasury and the Tax Court every two years, as required by Act Sec. 1552(c) of the Tax Reform Act of 1986 (P.L. 99-514), of its cases and the measures taken to efficiently bring these cases to a conclusion (Act Sec. 301(16)(A) of the 2000 Act);

(2) a report by the Secretary of the Treasury, as required by Act Sec. 231 of the Deficit Reduction Act of 1984 (P.L. 98-369), on the taxation of insurance companies and the effect of such taxation on growth of such companies (Act Sec. 301(16)(B) of the 2000 Act);

(3) the report by the Secretary of the Treasury, as required by Act Sec. 208 of the Tax Treatment Extension Act of 1977 (P.L. 95-615), on persons claiming the benefits of Code Secs. 911 and 912, their revenue effect, and the administration of these Code sections (Act Sec. 301(16)(C) of the 2000 Act);

(4) the annual report by the Railroad Retirement Board, as required under Act Sec. 7105 of the Technical and Miscellaneous Revenue Act of 1988 (P.L. 100-647), regarding the financial status of its unemployment insurance system with recommendation for financial changes (Act Sec. 301(16)(D) of the 2000 Act);

(5) the report by the Pension Benefit Guaranty Corporation, as required under Act Sec. 4008 of the Employee Retirement Income Security Act of 1974 (P.L. 93-406), setting forth its financial condition, administration, and the actuarial expectations for the next five years (Act Sec. 301(17) of the 2000 Act);

(6) the annual report by the Commissioner of Social Security and the Secretary of Labor under Act Sec. 426 of the Black Lung Benefits Revenue Act (P.L. 95-227) (Act Sec. 301(18) of the 2000 Act); and

(7) the audit reports of non-Federal entities receiving Federal award equal to or greater than $300,000 as required by Section 7502(g), of Title 31, of the United State Code (Act Sec. 301(19) of the 2000 Act).

★ *Effective date.* No specific effective date is provided by the Act. The provision is, therefore, considered effective on December 21, 2000, the date of enactment.

Act Sec. 301 of the Community Renewal Tax Relief Act of 2000, amending Section 3003(a)(1) of the Federal Reports Elimination and Sunset Act of 1995 (31 U.S.C. § 1113). Law at ¶ 7140. Committee Report at ¶ 10,255.

Extension of IRS Deadline for Providing Notices

¶ 325

Background ───

Provisions of the IRS Restructuring and Reform Act of 1998 (P.L. 105-206) imposed the following three notice requirements on the Internal Revenue Service:

First, the 1998 Act requires the IRS to provide any taxpayer with an installment agreement in effect an annual statement describing the taxpayer's beginning balance for the year, all payments made during the year, and the remaining balance at year's end. This requirement became effective on July 1, 2000 (Act Sec. 3506 of the 1998 Act).

Second, for notices issued, and penalties assessed, after December 31, 2000, the IRS must include on each required notice of penalty the name of the penalty, the Code section that authorizes the penalty, and the computation that results in the penalty shown on the notice (Code Sec. 6751(a)). "Penalty" includes any addition to tax or any additional amount (Code Sec. 6751(c)).

The Senate Committee Report to the 1998 Act expresses the congressional belief that taxpayers are entitled to an explanation of the penalties imposed upon them. This provision is intended to address the concern that penalties are often used as a bargaining chip by lower-level IRS employees who focus on collecting the maximum amount possible from taxpayers in order to satisfy any IRS collection-based performance goals. Presumably, there will be less artificial inflation of assessed penalties if prior supervisory approval and discernible computations are required.

Third, IRS notices that include interest that the IRS claims is owed to it by an individual must include a detailed computation of the interest charged and the Code section under which the interest is imposed. Interest computations and the applicable Code section must be included with notices issued after December 31, 2000 (Code Sec. 6631).

───

Community Renewal Tax Relief Act Impact

Deadlines extended for IRS to provide certain required notices.─ Substantial systems modifications, plus the programming concerns associated with the year 2000, have resulted in the inability of the IRS to comply with all of the notice requirements imposed upon it by the IRS Restructuring and Reform Act of 1998. Therefore, the deadlines for complying with the penalty, interest, and installment agreement notice requirements have been extended (Act Sec. 302 of Community Renewal Tax Relief Act of 2000).

First, the requirement that the IRS provide any taxpayer who has an installment agreement in effect with an annual statement, which became effective on July 1, 2000, has been amended so that the beginning effective date is now September 1, 2001 (Act Sec. 302(a) of the 2000 Act; Act Sec. 3506 of P.L. 105-206).

Comment. The notification requirements, while an improvement over past IRS procedure, do not require the IRS to explain why the penalty is assessed, the procedures for appealing, or possible grounds for abatement or waiver.

Second, the date on which the IRS must begin to include the following information on each required notice of penalty:

(1) the name of the penalty,

(2) the Code section that authorizes the penalty, and

(3) the computation that results in the penalty shown on the notice,

has been extended from January 1, 2001, to July 1, 2001 (Act Sec. 302(b)(1) of the 2000 Act). In addition, for any notice of penalty issued from July 1, 2001 through June 30, 2003, the IRS need only include in the notice a telephone number at which the taxpayer may request a copy of the assessment and the payment history with respect to that penalty. By including such telephone number, the IRS will be considered to be in compliance with the requirements of Code Sec. 6751(a) (Act Sec. 302(b)(2) of the 2000 Act).

Third, the date on which IRS notices, which include interest that the IRS claims is owed to it by an individual, must begin to include a detailed computation of the interest charged and the Code section under which the interest is imposed has been extended from January 1, 2001, to July 1, 2001 (Act Sec. 302(c)(1)). In addition, for any notice required under Code Sec. 6631 that is issued from July 1, 2001, through June 30, 2003, the IRS need only include in the notice a telephone number at which the taxpayer may request a copy of the taxpayer's payment history with respect to such interest amounts. By including such telephone number, the IRS will be considered to be in compliance with the requirements of Code Sec. 6631 (Act Sec. 302(c)(2) of the 2000 Act).

★ *Effective date.* No specific effective date is provided by the Act. The provision is, therefore, considered effective on December 21, 2000, the date of enactment.

Act Sec. 302(a) of the Community Renewal Tax Relief Act of 2000, amending Act Sec. 3506 of the IRS Restructuring and Reform Act of 1998 (P.L. 105-206); Act Sec. 302(b), amending Act Sec. 3306(c) of the 1998 Act; Act Sec. 302(c), amending Act Sec. 3308(c) of the 1998 Act. Law at ¶ 7145. Committee Report at ¶ 10,260.

Exempt Organizations Subject to Disclosure Requirements

¶ 330

Background _____

Tax-exempt organizations, including charitable trusts and private foundations, are required to allow public inspection of annual returns filed with the IRS for the three most recent tax years (Code Sec. 6104(d)(1) and Code Sec. 6104(d)(2)). However, it was not clear whether the public inspection requirement was to apply to nonexempt charitable trusts and nonexempt private foundations.

Technical Corrections Impact

Application of disclosure to nonexempts.—Code Sec. 6104(d) is amended to clarify that nonexempt charitable trusts (Code Sec. 6033(d)(1)) and nonexempt private foundations (Code Sec. 6033(d)(2)) are required to allow public inspection of their annual returns in the same manner as exempt charitable trusts and exempt private foundations (Act Sec. 312(a) of the Community Renewal Tax Relief Act of 2000).

Comment. In legislation passed earlier in 2000 dealing with the disclosure of political activities by Code Sec. 527 organizations (P.L. 106-230), the same provision (Code Sec. 6104(d)(6)) was erroneously added twice (Act Sec. 1(b)(4)(D) and Act Sec. 2(b)(3) of P.L. 106-230). Consequently, after passage of the above amendment there are now three provisions designated as Code Sec. 6104(d)(6). This oversight will ultimately necessitate further technical corrections.

★ *Effective date.* This provision is effective for requests made after June 8, 1999, which is 60 days after the issuance of regulations under Code Sec. 6104(d) (Act Sec. 312(c) of the Community Renewal Tax Relief Act of 2000; Act Sec. 1004(b)(3) of the Tax and Trade Relief Extension Act of 1998; Treasury Decision 8861, I.R.B. 2000-5, 441.)

Act Sec. 312(a) of the Community Renewal Tax Relief Act of 2000, amending Act Sec. 1004(b) of the Tax and Trade Relief Extension Act of 1998 and adding Code Sec. 6104(d)(6)[(8)]. Law at ¶ 6010. Committee Report at ¶ 10,315.

DEFICIENCY AND REFUND PROCEDURES
Clarifications to Innocent Spouse Relief

¶ 335

Background————————————————————————————————

Despite filing a joint return for a tax year, certain taxpayers ("innocent spouses") may elect to seek relief from liability for a deficiency (including interest and penalties) assessed with respect to the return. Under current law, the operative provision is Code Sec. 6015, as added by the IRS Restructuring and Reform Act of 1998, effective for tax liabilities arising after July 22, 1998, and any tax liability arising on or before July 22, 1998, but remaining unpaid as of such date.

A taxpayer may elect innocent spouse relief under Code Sec. 6015 in two ways: (1) under procedures applicable to all joint filers (Code Sec. 6015(b)); and (2) under procedures applicable to taxpayers who are no longer married, legally separated, or not living together for at least 12 months before the election (commonly known as the "separation-of-liability" election (Code Sec. 6015(c)). If a taxpayer does not qualify for relief under (1) or (2), the IRS is authorized to grant equitable relief (Code Sec. 6015(f)). Form 8857 is used to request all three types of relief and must generally be filed within two years of the commencement of collection activities.

Code Sec. 6015(b) relief is only available to the extent that a spouse did not know or had no reason to know that there was an understatement attributable to erroneous items of the other individual and it would be inequitable to make the spouse liable for the tax deficiency. Separation-of-liability relief involves no equitable considerations; however, the election does not apply to the extent that a spouse has actual knowledge of an erroneous item that caused the deficiency. Under the separation-of-liability procedures, the spouses are treated as if they filed separate returns. Items of income and deduction are allocated between the two spouses to determine their separate tax liabilities. If a taxpayer is denied innocent spouse relief under Code Sec. 6015(b) or (c), the taxpayer may petition the Tax Court for review of the IRS's determination. Further, IRS collection actions are restrained during the pendency of a Tax Court proceeding for redetermination.

Technical Corrections Impact

Clarifications to innocent spouse relief.—Technical corrections have clarified the proper timing for requesting innocent spouse relief and other innocent spouse relief provisions that were implemented by the IRS Restructuring and Reform Act of 1998 (P.L. 105-206).

Timing of election to request relief. A technical correction provides that the election to seek innocent spouse relief under the separation of liability procedures for a particular tax year may be made at any point after a deficiency has been asserted by the IRS for that tax year (Code Sec. 6015(c)(3)(B), as amended by the Community Renewal Tax Relief Act of 2000 (P.L. 106-554)). According to the Conference Committee Report, a deficiency is considered asserted by the IRS at the time the IRS states that additional taxes may be owed. This most commonly occurs during the Examination process. It is not required that an assessment be made, or that all administrative remedies be exhausted, in order for a taxpayer to request innocent spouse relief (Conference Committee Report).

Caution. The Conference Committee Report specifically states that this technical correction applies to both the separation-of-liability election (Code Sec. 6015(c)) and the general election for all joint filers (Code Sec. 6015(b)). However, the technical correction actually only amends the period described in Code Sec. 6015(c)(3)(B) for the separation-of-liability election. No change was made to the election period described for the general election in Code Sec. 6015(b)(1)(E). The Code does not provide a time-frame for requesting equitable relief under Code Sec. 6015(f). Form 8857, however, currently uses the same deadline that applies under Code Sec. 6015(b) and (c). Presumably, another technical correction will be enacted to rectify the error and a revised Form 8857 will be updated to change the election periods to conform to Congressional intent.

According to the Conference Report, the change is intended to clarify that the proper time for a taxpayer to raise and have the IRS evaluate a claim for innocent spouse relief is at the same time that the IRS is considering and asserting a deficiency. This method allows the taxpayer and the IRS to focus on the innocent spouse issue and other items that may cause a deficiency as well as permitting all issues, including the innocent spouse issue, to be resolved in a single administrative and judicial process.

Comment. No change is made to the present law rule that the innocent spouse claim must be asserted no later than two years after collection activities against the "innocent spouse" begins. Prior to this technical correction, some persons have interpreted the statute as prohibiting consideration of innocent spouse relief until after assessment.

Allowance of credits and refunds. A technical correction clarifies that the allowance of a credit or refund to an innocent spouse may be granted administratively (*i.e.*, by the IRS) or by any court with jurisdiction (Code Sec. 6015(g), as added by the 2000 Act). Prior to the technical correction, the placement of the provision describing the credit or refund rule within Code Sec. 6015(e) may have incorrectly suggested that credits and refunds were only available through the Tax Court (Code Sec. 6015(e)(3)(A), prior to amendment by the 2000 Act). The new law also clarifies that credits and refunds are not available if a taxpayer obtains relief under the separation-of-liabilities election (Code Sec. 6015(g)(3), as added by the 2000 Act).

Res judicata applies to final decisions of all courts. Current law treats any final decision of the Tax Court for the same tax year for which an innocent spouse election is made under Code Sec. 6015(b) or (c) as conclusive, except with respect to the qualification of the individual for innocent spouse relief (unless innocent spouse relief was also an issue before the court or the individual seeking relief participated meaningfully in the Tax Court proceeding) (Code Sec. 6015(e)(3)(B), prior to amendment by the 2000 Act). The new law clarifies that res judicata rule applies to a final decision of *any* court (Code Sec. 6015(g)(3), as added by the 2000 Act).

¶ 335

Non-exclusivity of Tax Court judicial remedy. A technical correction clarifies that the judicial procedures under Code Sec. 6015(e), with respect to Tax Court review of an IRS determination regarding the innocent spouse relief available to an individual, are not the exclusive avenues through which innocent spouse relief can be considered (Code Sec. 6015(e)(1)(A), as amended by the 2000 Act). The procedures were intended to be additional, non-exclusive avenues by which innocent spouse relief could be considered (Conference Committee Report).

Time for filing a petition for review with the Tax Court. A technical correction conforms the time period for seeking a redetermination of innocent spouse relief with the generally applicable 90-day time period for judicial review of a deficiency notice (Code Sec. 6015(e)(1)(A), as amended by the 2000 Act). Thus, the time period for seeking a redetermination of innocent spouse relief is 90 days *after* the date the IRS mails the taxpayer notice of its final determination with respect to innocent spouse relief. Conforming amendments are made to the period for which collection activities are prohibited and collection limitations suspended (Code Sec. 6015(e)(1)(B) and (e)(2), as amended by the 2000 Act).

Comment. Prior to the technical correction, the 90-day period for seeking a redetermination of innocent spouse relief began on the date of mailing. This meant that the period for seeking review of an innocent spouse determination was one day *shorter* than the time for seeking review of a deficiency notice. The clarification should eliminate confusion in applying the limitations period.

Caution. The effective date of this provision is December 21, 2000. Accordingly, taxpayers may not utilize this provision retroactively to revive any late-filed petitions filed by taxpayers who mistakenly thought that the deficiency and innocent spouse petition deadlines were identical.

Waiver of final determination upon agreement as to relief. A technical correction clarifies that a taxpayer and the IRS may enter into a written agreement regarding the taxpayer's tax liability with respect to a request for innocent spouse relief, thereby allowing the taxpayer's liability to be immediately adjusted as agreed and eliminating any need for a formal Notice of Determination (Code Sec. 6015(e)(5), as added by the 2000 Act). The written agreement must specify the details of the agreement as to the nature and extent of the innocent spouse relief granted. The clarification essentially provides a waiver of a formal notice under the innocent spouse provisions that is analogous to that which applies under the deficiency procedures at Code Sec. 6213(d) (Conference Committee Report).

Caution. If a waiver under new Code Sec. 6015(e)(5) is made, the running of the period of limitations under Code Sec. 6502 for collection of the assessment to which the petition for relief relates is suspended from the date the claim for relief was filed until 60 days after the waiver is filed with the IRS (Code Sec. 6015(e)(2), as amended by the 2000 Act).

Comment. A formal "Notice of Determination" contains a statement of the time period in which a petition for relief may be filed in the Tax Court and delays the final resolution of the request for innocent spouse relief until the expiration of the limitations period for filing for relief in the Tax Court. The clarification is intended to eliminate potential confusion to taxpayers caused by the issuance of a formal Notice of Determination in situations where the requested relief was fully granted, or where the taxpayer and the IRS agreed on the application of the innocent spouse provisions to the taxpayer's case. The provision should eliminate unnecessary filings with the Tax Court and potential delays in the closing of cases until the time for filing for relief with the Tax Court has expired.

★ *Effective date.* The provisions are effective on December 21, 2000, the date of enactment (Act Sec. 313(f) of the Community Renewal Tax Relief Act of 2000).

Act Sec. 313(a)(1) of the Community Renewal Tax Relief Act of 2000, amending Code Sec. 6015(c)(3)(B); Act Sec. 313(a)(2)(A), redesignating Code Sec. 6015(g) as Code Sec. 6015(h) and adding new Code Sec. 6015(g); Act Sec. 313(a)(2)(B), amending Code Sec. 6015(e)(3); Act Sec. 313(a)(3)(A)-(C), amending Code Sec. 6015(e)(1); Act Sec. 313(a)(3)(D)(i), adding Code Sec. 6015(e)(5); Act Sec. 313(a)(3)(D)(ii), amending Code Sec. 6015(e)(2); Act Sec. 313(f). Law at ¶ 5980. Committee Report at ¶ 10,320.

Tax Court Small Case Procedures

¶ 340

Background

Code Sec. 7463 provides special small case procedures for taxpayers to apply to disputes involving $50,000 or less, if the taxpayer chooses to utilize these procedures and the Tax Court concurs. Taxpayers are not required to use the small case procedures. The Tax Court will usually approve a taxpayer's request for small case treatment unless the case involves an issue that should be heard under the normal procedures. The Tax Court may order the small case procedures to be discontinued if (1) the amount in controversy will exceed $50,000 or (2) the orderly administration of justice requires a change in procedure.

Proceedings for small cases are informal. Thus, briefs and oral arguments are not required and strict rules of evidence are not applied. Although taxpayers may be represented by anyone admitted to practice before the Tax Court, taxpayers usually represent themselves in small tax cases. Decisions rendered under the small case procedures may not be cited as precedent in future cases and may not be appealed by the government or the taxpayer.

Technical Corrections Impact

Additional cases permitted on small case calendar.—A technical correction clarifies that the Tax Court's small case procedures, generally available to disputes involving $50,000 or less, are available for innocent spouse relief redeterminations under Code Sec. 6015(e) and disputes continuing from pre-levy administrative due process hearings under Code Sec. 6330(d)(1)(A) (Code Sec. 7463(f), as added by the Community Renewal Tax Relief Act of 2000 (P.L. 106-554)). Use of the small case procedure is optional to the taxpayer but must be approved by the Tax Court.

Comment. This clarification may increase the number of cases in the small case calendar, which may have significant precedential value. Accordingly, the conferees "anticipate" that the Tax Court will carefully consider (1) IRS objections to small case treatment based on significant precedential value or orderly administration of the tax laws and (2) the financial impact to the taxpayer, including additional legal fees and costs, of denying small case treatment (Conference Committee Report).

★ *Effective date.* The provision is effective on December 21, 2000, the date of enactment (Act Sec. 313(f) of the Community Renewal Tax Relief Act of 2000).

Act Sec. 313(b)(1) of the Community Renewal Tax Relief Act of 2000, adding Code Sec. 7463(f); Act Sec. 313(f). Law at ¶ 6180. Committee Report at ¶ 10,320.

Tax Court Authority to Enjoin Collection

¶ 345

Background ─────────────────────────────────

At least 30 days prior to a proposed levy, the IRS is required to provide written notification to a taxpayer of his right to request a hearing before the IRS Office of Appeals to challenge the levy action (Code Sec. 6330). The written notification is referred to as a pre-levy Collection Due Process Hearing Notice (CDP Notice). The hearing before Appeals is referred to as a pre-levy Collection Due Process hearing (CDP hearing). The determination of the IRS hearing officer is subject to judicial appeal. If the taxpayer requests the hearing, the statute of limitations is suspended for the lien or levy action that is the subject of the hearing. In addition, the limitations periods under Code Sec. 6502 (relating to collection after assessment), Code Sec. 6531 (relating to criminal prosecutions), and Code Sec. 6532 (relating to other suits) are suspended during the pendency of the hearing and any related appeals. The IRS may not levy on the taxpayer's property while the hearing is pending. If the underlying tax liability is at issue, collection activity is also suspended while a judicial appeal of the determination is pending (Code Sec. 6330(e)). Although the Tax Court and district courts have the authority to enjoin collection actions generally, prior to the amendment of Code Sec. 6330(e) by the Community Renewal Tax Relief Act of 2000 (P.L. 106-554), that authority did not explicitly extend to an improper levy action that occurred during the period when the levy action is statutorily suspended under the administrative due process provisions.

───

Technical Corrections Impact

Tax Court's authority to enjoin collection actions.—A technical correction clarifies that proper courts, including the Tax Court, have the authority to enjoin levy actions during the period that the levy action is required to be suspended under the pre-levy administrative due process hearing procedures (Code Sec. 6330(e)(1), as amended by the Community Renewal Tax Relief Act of 2000 (P.L. 106-554)). However, jurisdiction is not conferred to the Tax Court unless a timely appeal has been filed under Code Sec. 6330(d)(1) and then only with respect to the unpaid tax or proposed levy to which the appeal relates (Code Sec. 6330(e), as amended by the 2000 Act).

A conforming amendment provides that the explicit grant of authority to enjoin collection actions with respect to levy actions during pre-levy administrative due process procedures is applicable notwithstanding the provisions of Code Sec. 7421 (commonly referred to as the "Anti-Injunction Act") (Code Sec. 7421(a), as amended by the 2000 Act).

★ *Effective date.* The provisions are generally effective on December 21, 2000, the date of enactment (Act Sec. 313(f) of the Community Renewal Tax Relief Act of 2000).

Act Sec. 313(b)(2)(A) of the Community Renewal Tax Relief Act of 2000, amending Code Sec. 6330(e)(1); Act Sec. 313(b)(2)(B), amending Code Sec. 7421(a); Act Sec. 313(f). Law at ¶ 6060 and ¶ 6150. Committee Report at ¶ 10,320.

Tax Court Jurisdiction Over Employment Taxes

¶ 350

Background

In connection with an audit and actual controversy , Code Sec. 7436 gives the Tax Court jurisdiction to review the IRS's determination as to whether a service provider is an independent contractor or an employee for purposes of subtitle C (Employment Taxes and Collection of Income Tax) and whether section 530 of the Revenue Act of 1978 (P.L. 95-600) applies. In general, this safe-harbor allows independent contractor status if an employer consistently treated the worker and others in similar positions as independent contractors, filed federal tax returns on the basis of independent contractor status, and had a reasonable basis for independent contractor treatment. A redetermination of the Tax Court has the full force and effect of a Tax Court decision and is appealable to an Appellate Court. In *Henry Randolph Consulting,* 112 TC 1, Dec. 53,201, the Tax Court held that Code Sec. 7436 does not confer jurisdiction to determine the amount of employment tax liability under subtitle C.

Technical Corrections Impact

Tax Court given jurisdiction over amount of employment tax.—The Tax Court's jurisdiction to review Code Sec. 7436 employment tax issues is extended to include the determination of the proper amount of employment tax (Code Sec. 7436(a), as amended by the Community Renewal Tax Relief Act of 2000 (P.L. 106-554)).

Comment. The provision is beneficial to taxpayers because judicial review of employment tax liability can now also take place in the Tax Court on a prepayment basis, thus eliminating the need to file a suit for refund in a federal district court or the Court of Federal Claims. However, note that the provision does not give the Tax Court jurisdiction to consider the proper amount of employment tax due unless the IRS has also made a determination pursuant to an audit in which the employment tax status of workers are in controversy.

★ *Effective date.* The provision is effective on August 5, 1997 (Act Sec. 314(g) of the Community Renewal Tax Relief Act of 2000; Act Sec. 1454(c) of the Taxpayer Relief Act of 1997 (P.L. 105-34)).

Act Sec. 314(f) of the Community Renewal Tax Relief Act of 2000, amending Code Sec. 7436(a); Act Sec. 314(g). Law at ¶ 6170. Committee Report at ¶ 10,325.

Pre-Levy Due Process Hearings

¶ 355

Background

The IRS Restructuring and Reform Act of 1998 (P.L. 105-206) includes a provision that requires the IRS to notify a taxpayer at least thirty days prior to any levy that the taxpayer has a right to an impartial hearing before the property is seized (Code Sec. 6330, as added by P.L. 105-206). The hearing, which is referred to as a "pre-levy administrative due process hearing," is conducted by the IRS Office of Appeals. No levy may be made while this hearing is being conducted unless collection of the tax is in jeopardy (Code Sec. 6330(e) and (f)). Within thirty days after the determination of the Appeals Office, the taxpayer may appeal the

Background————————————————————————————————

determination to the Tax Court or, if the Tax Court does not have jurisdiction over the underlying tax liability, file an appeal to a United States District Court (Code Sec. 6330(d)). Collection activities are generally suspended during the pendancy of the appeal unless the IRS shows good cause for proceeding with the levy (Code Sec. 6330(e)). The statutory provision, however, is unclear as to whether a determination of the Tax Court is an appealable decision.

Technical Corrections Impact

Tax Court pre-levy administrative due process determination is an appealable decision.—The Act clarifies that the determination of the Tax Court (other than under the small case procedures) in a dispute concerning a pre-levy administrative due process hearing is a decision of the Tax Court and reviewable as such (Code Sec. 6330(d)(1), as amended by the Community Renewal Tax Relief Act of 2000 (P.L. 106-554).

★ *Effective date.* The provision applies to collection actions initiated after the date, which is 180 days after July 22, 1998 (Act Sec. 313(f) of the Community Renewal Tax Relief Act; Act Sec. 3401(d) of the IRS Restructuring and Reform Act of 1998).

Act Sec. 313(d) of the Community Renewal Tax Relief Act of 2000, amending Code Sec. 6330(d)(1); Act Sec. 313(f). Law at ¶ 6060. Committee Report at ¶ 10,320.

Deficiency Attributable to Nonrefundable Child Credit

¶ 360

Background————————————————————————————————

A taxpayer is allowed a child credit for each qualifying child under the age of 17 (Code Sec. 24). Although credits are generally either refundable or nonrefundable, the child credit is hybrid in nature. A portion of the credit may be treated as refundable if a taxpayer has three or more qualifying children and his social security taxes or one-half of his self-employment tax exceed any earned income tax credit that is claimed (Code Sec. 24(d)).

Refundable credits under the Code Sec. 32 earned income tax credit and the Code Sec. 34 credit for gasoline and special fuels are recovered through the deficiency determination by treating these credits as negative tax in the deficiency determination (Code Sec. 6211(b)(4)). Treating the refundable portion of a credit as a negative tax is the equivalent to adding it to the deficiency.

When the child credit was enacted by the Taxpayer Relief Act of 1997 (P.L. 105-34), however, Congress failed to amend the Code Sec. 6211 deficiency provisions to take into account the refundable portion of the child credit by treating it as a negative tax. (Nonrefundable credits, including the nonrefundable portion of the child credit, are recoverable under the deficiency procedures).

Expressed as a formula, the definition of a deficiency is: Correct Tax − (Tax Shown on Return + Prior Assessments − Rebates) (*M. Kurtzon,* 17 TC 1542, Dec. 18,854).

> **Example.** Joe Parent's income tax return shows a pre-credit $0 tax liability and a refundable $500 earned income tax credit. He receives a $500 refund from the IRS. Later, the IRS determines that Joe Parent's pre-credit

Background———————————————————————————————

income tax liability is $81 against which he can claim an earned income credit of $378. He should have received a $297 refund ($378 − $81). For purposes of the deficiency procedures, Joe's "correct tax" is ($81 − $378) or ($297). His "tax shown on the return" is ($0 − $500) or ($500). His deficiency is $203 (($297) correct tax − ($500) tax shown on return).

Technical Corrections Impact

Deficiency includes refundable portion of child credit.—A technical correction provides that the refundable portion of the child tax credit is treated as a negative tax in making a deficiency determination. Thus, the normal assessment procedures apply to both the refundable and nonrefundable portions of the child credit (Code Sec. 6211(b)(4), as amended by the Community Renewal Tax Relief Act of 2000 (P.L. 106-554)). The provision reverses the opposite conclusion that was reached in IRS Chief Counsel Memorandum 199948027.

> **Example.** Joe Parent files a tax return and claims an earned income tax credit of $489. Joe also claims a child credit for four qualifying children. The refundable portion of the child credit claimed is $396 and the nonrefundable portion of the child credit is $1,204. Assume that tax shown on Joe's return before credits is $1,204 so that the $1,204 nonrefundable portion of the child credit reduces his net tax to $0. The IRS subsequently determines that Joe is entitled to claim a child credit for only three qualifying children. Joe's pre-credit income tax remains at $1,204, but the nonrefundable portion of the child credit is reduced to $1,200. Four dollars of the earned income tax credit is used to reduce the remaining $4 of pre-credit tax liability. The remaining refundable portion of the earned income credit is reduced to $485 ($489 − $4). Joe's "correct income tax" for purposes of the deficiency procedures is, therefore, ($485) (the amount of the earned income credit refund). The "tax shown on the return" for purposes of the deficiency procedures is ($885), the sum of the incorrectly claimed $885 in refundable credits ($396 + $489). Joe's deficiency is $400 (($485) correct tax − ($885) tax shown on return).

Comment. Without this technical correction, the IRS was required to recover incorrectly claimed refundable child credits through voluntary repayment or by filing a civil suit under Code Sec. 7405 (Action for Recovery of Erroneous Refunds), within the two-year limitations period of Code Sec. 6532(b)).

★ *Effective date.* The provision applies to tax years beginning after December 31, 1997 (Act Sec. 314(g) of the Community Renewal Tax Relief Act of 2000; Act Sec. 101(e) of the Taxpayer Relief Act of 1997 (P.L. 105-34)).

Act Sec. 314(a) of the Community Renewal Tax Relief Act of 2000, amending Code Sec. 6211(b)(4); Act Sec. 314(g). Law at ¶ 6050. Committee Report at ¶ 10,325.

Extension of Limitations Period for Installment Agreements

¶ 365

Background———————————————————————————————

Generally, the IRS may not levy on a person's property or rights to property while that person has an installment agreement offer pending with the IRS. This prohibition extends for 30 days after the IRS rejects an installment agreement offer and while an appeal of the rejection is pending, provided the appeal is filed

Background _____

within 30 days of the rejection. Further, no levy may be made while an installment agreement is in effect. If the IRS terminates the installment agreement, no levy may be made for 30 days after the termination and during the pendency of any appeal of the termination, provided that the appeal is filed within 30 days of the termination (Code Sec. 6331(k)(2)).

The 10-year statute of limitations on collection under Code Sec. 6502 is suspended during the period the IRS is prohibited from making a levy or taking other collection measures against the liability that is subject to the installment agreement (Code Sec. 6331(k)(3)).

Technical Corrections Impact

Extension of limitations period for installment agreements.—A technical correction clarifies that the permissible extension of the period of limitations in the context of installment agreements is governed by the pertinent provisions of Code Sec. 6502 (Code Sec. 6331(k)(3), as amended by the Community Renewal Tax Relief Act of 2000 (P.L. 106-554)). This correction is intended to eliminate uncertainty as to whether the permissible limitations period with respect to installment agreements is governed by reference to an agreement of the parties pursuant to Code Sec. 6502 or by reference to the period of time during which the installment agreement is in effect pursuant to Code Sec. 6331(k)(3) and Code Sec. 6331(i)(5) (Conference Committee Report).

★ *Effective date.* The provision is effective on December 21, 2000, the date of enactment (Act Sec. 313(f) of the Community Renewal Tax Relief Act of 2000).

Act Sec. 313(b)(3) of the Community Renewal Tax Relief Act of 2000, amending Code Sec. 6331(k)(3); Act Sec. 313(f). Law at ¶ 6070. Committee Report at ¶ 10,320.

REFUNDS

Joint Committee Refund Review Increased to $2 Million

¶ 370

Background _____

Refunds that exceed $1 million are subject to review by the Joint Committee on Taxation (Code Sec. 6405(a)). Refunds of this size are not issued to a taxpayer until 30 days after the IRS submits a report on the refund to the Joint Committee in order to afford the Committee the opportunity to review the decision. The report must state the taxpayer's name, the amount of the refund or credit, a summary of the facts, and the IRS's decision on the matter. The large refund review applies to income, estate, gift, and certain excise taxes. Tentative refunds attributable to net operating loss carrybacks under Code Sec. 6411 that are in excess of $1 million are also subject to Joint Committee review, but may be issued prior to such review (Code Sec. 6405(b)). The IRS is required to submit its report to the Joint Committee after the correct amount of tax is determined.

Community Renewal Tax Relief Act Impact

Review of refunds in excess of $2,000,000.—The threshold above which refunds must be submitted to the Joint Committee on Taxation for review is increased from $1 million to $2 million (Code Secs. 6405(a) and (b), as amended by the Community Renewal Tax Relief Act of 2000). In addition, the Conference Committee Report indicates that the Joint Committee on Taxation will continue to exercise its existing statutory authority to conduct a program of expanded post-audit reviews of large deficiency cases and other select issues. The IRS is expected to fully cooperate in this expanded program.

Comment. The increased threshold should speed up the issuance of refunds for many taxpayers and free up valuable IRS and Joint Committee Staff resources. As a historical note, the threshold was increased from $100,000 to $200,000 in 1976. In 1990, it was increased to $1 million.

★ *Effective date.* The provision is effective on the date of enactment, December 21, 2000, except that such amendment does not apply with respect to any refund or credit with respect to a report that was made before December 21, 2000 (Act Sec. 305(b) of the Community Renewal Tax Relief Act of 2000).

Act Sec. 305(a) of the Community Renewal Tax Relief Act of 2000, amending Code Sec. 6405(a) and (b); Act Sec. 305(b). Law at ¶ 6080. Committee Report at ¶ 10,275.

INFLATION AND INTEREST RATE STANDARDS

Remove References to 52-Week Treasury Bills

¶ 375

Background————————————————————————

Recent efforts by Congress and the President to reduce budgetary expenditures and exercise fiscal restraint have resulted in current and projected Federal budget surpluses which, in turn, have reduced the need for the Treasury Department to issue certain kinds of securities. The Treasury Department has recently notified Congress that, because of more efficient debt management and increased predictability and liquidity in the financial markets, it is likely to cease issuing 52-week Treasury bills. In anticipation of this change, it is necessary to amend the Internal Revenue Code, as well as selected provisions of federal law, to remove references to 52-week Treasury bills and replace them with new references.

Under current law, the interest charge on the deferred tax liability of the shareholders of a Domestic International Sales Corporation (DISC) is determined by reference to the average investment yield on U.S. Treasury bills with maturities of 52 weeks (Code Sec. 995(f)(4)). Provisions of federal law relating to interest on certain unpaid criminal fines and penalties of more than $2,500 (18 U.S.C. § 3612(f)(2)(B)), interest on monetary judgments in civil cases recovered in federal district court and on a judgment against the United States affirmed by the Supreme Court (28 U.S.C. §§ 1961(a) and 2516(b)), and interest on compensation for certain takings of property (40 U.S.C. § 258e-1) also refer to 52-week Treasury bills rates as a benchmark for determining applicable interest rates.

Community Renewal Tax Relief Act Impact

References to 52-week U.S. Treasury bills replaced.—References to the average investment yield of U.S. Treasury bills with maturities of 52 weeks contained in Code Sec. 995(f)(4); 18 U.S.C. § 3612(f)(2)(B), 28 U.S.C. §§ 1961(a) and 2561(b); and 40 U.S.C. § 258e-1 have been deleted and replaced by references to the weekly average one-year constant maturity Treasury yield, as published by the Board of Governors of the Federal Reserve System, for the applicable period.

★ *Effective date.* No specific effective date is provided by the Act. The provision is, therefore, considered effective on December 21, 2000, the date of enactment.

Act Sec. 307(a) of the Community Renewal Tax Relief Act of 2000, amending 40 U.S.C. § 258e-1; Act Sec. 307(b), amending 18 U.S.C. § 3612(f)(2)(B); Act Sec. 307(c), amending Code Sec. 995(f)(4); Act Sec. 307(d), amending 28 U.S.C. § § 1961(a) and 2516(b). Law at ¶ 5560 and ¶ 7150. Committee Report at ¶ 10,285.

Use of Corrected Consumer Price Index

¶ 380

Background _____

The Bureau of Labor Statistics (BLS) announced on September 28, 2000, that a computational error in the quality adjustments of air conditioning figure (relating to the cost of housing) resulted in errors in the consumer price index (CPI) reported for certain months during the period January 1999 through August 2000. The errors caused the CPI to be understated in the affected months by 0.1 or 0.2 index points. Consistent with agency practice, the BLS reissued corrected figures for the months in the year in which the error was discovered (2000) but made no corrections for 1999.

Community Renewal Tax Relief Act Impact

2001 tax tables and other inflation-adjusted figures to reflect correct 1999 CPI.—The Act provides that in the case of tax years (and other periods) beginning after December 31, 2000, if any CPI, as defined in Code Sec. 1(f)(5), reflects the CPI computational error for 1999, the correct CPI is to be taken into account for purposes of the Code in the manner and to the extent that the Secretary of Treasury determines appropriate. Any tax tables for the year 2001 that were based on the incorrect CPI, however, must be corrected to reflect the correct CPI (Act Sec. 308(i) of the Community Renewal Tax Relief Act of 2000).

Comment. The tax tables (and certain other inflation-adjusted figures) are determined by reference to the average monthly CPI for the 12-month period that ends on August 31 of the preceding calendar year (Code Sec. 1(f)(3) and (4)). For example, the 2001 tax tables are determined by reference to the CPI issued for the months September 1999 through August 2000. Thus, without this legislation, the 2001 tax tables would be based on incorrect CPI figures issued during the period September 1999 through December 1999. The tax tables previously issued for 2000 are also affected by the CPI errors since they are based on the CPI reported for the months September 1998 through August 1999 and, therefore, reflect CPI errors for the months January 1999 through August 1999. The legislation, however, does not require the IRS to issue new 2000 tax tables or authorize it to correct any other inflation adjusted figures for the 2000 tax year that were affected by the 1999 CPI errors. Apparently, the administrative inconvenience involved at this point would outweigh any benefits that taxpayers would receive.

Rev. Proc. 2001-13, I.R.B., 2001-3, which was recently issued by the IRS, contains inflation-adjusted figures for the 2001 tax year. The procedure singles out figures affected by the incorrect 1999 CPI and provides inflation-adjustments based on both the incorrect CPI and the correct CPI. With the promulgation of this provision, taxpayers should rely on the figures based on the correct CPI. These figures are contained in Part I of Section 3 of the procedure and affect only the tax rate tables, the earned income credit, the aggregate amount of gifts received from foreign persons for purposes of determining whether an information return must be filed (Code Sec. 6039F), and the amount used to determine the validity of certain mechanic's liens under Code Sec. 6323(b)(7). The IRS is expected to announce formally that the Part I Section 3 figures apply.

The inflation-adjustment errors caused by the 1999 CPI error are very small and would probably go unnoticed by most taxpayers. For example, in the case of a married person filing jointly, the error first appears in the 2001 tax rate schedule in the $109,250 to $166,450 taxable income bracket. As corrected, this bracket is $109,250 to $166,500. In the case of the earned income credit, only taxpayers with one qualifying child are affected. The maximum corrected credit amount is $2,428; the uncorrected credit amount is $2,424. The Code Sec. 6039F information reporting threshold is $11,273 using the correct CPI and $11,271 using the incorrect CPI. Finally, the tax-lien exemption for a mechanic's lien with respect to repairs or improvements of residential property (Code Sec. 6323(b)(7)) applies to the extent such a lien does not exceed $5,490 using the corrected CPI and $5,480 using the incorrect CPI.

Federal benefit programs. The Act also requires federal agencies that administer benefit programs to compensate beneficiaries for payment shortfalls that may have resulted from the 1999 CPI errors for the year 2000 and later to the extent "practicable and feasible" (Act Sec. 308(a), (b), (c), and (e)). Any payments made to compensate for a shortfall in benefits will be disregarded for purposes of determining income under federal means-tested benefit programs, including Social Security (Act Sec. 308(d)). Affected programs include the old-age and survivors insurance program, the disability insurance program, and the supplemental security income program under the Social Security Act, as well as any other programs determined by the Director of the Office of Management and Budget (OMB) (Act Sec. 308(h); Conference Committee Report). The Director of the OMB must by April 1, 2001, issue a report to Congress regarding the compensation of benefit shortfalls (Act Sec. 308(g)).

No judicial review. The new law specifically prohibits any person from judicially challenging any action taken pursuant to this provision (Act Sec. 308(f)).

★ *Effective date.* No specific effective date is provided by the Act. The provision, therefore, is effective on December 21, 2000, the date of enactment.

Act Sec. 308 of the Community Renewal Tax Relief Act of 2000. Law at ¶ 7155. Committee Report at ¶ 10,290.

IRS UNDERCOVER OPERATIONS

Extension of Authority to Churn Undercover Funds

¶ 385

Background _____

The Anti-Drug Abuse Act of 1988 (P.L. 100-690) added Code Sec. 7608(c) to prescribe rules pertaining to IRS undercover operations. In general, Code Sec. 7608(c) authorizes the IRS to use funds recovered from an undercover operation to offset necessary and reasonable expenses incurred during the undercover operation. Without the churning authority granted in Code Sec. 7608(c), the IRS would have to deposit into the Treasury's general fund all income earned during the undercover operation and would have to pay all expenses out of appropriated funds. The current law authorizing the churning of funds expires on January 1, 2001.

Community Renewal Tax Relief Act Impact

Five-year extension of churning authority.—The new law extends the authority of the IRS to churn the income earned from undercover operations through December 31, 2005 (Code Sec. 7608(c)(6), as amended by the Community Renewal Tax Relief Act of 2000).

Comment. The churning provision has enabled the IRS to finance undercover criminal investigations into activities such as money laundering and the avoidance of fuel excise tax liability. The five-year offset period authorized by the Act will enable the IRS to finance multi-year undercover operations.

★ *Effective date.* No specific effective date is provided by the Act. The provision is, therefore, considered effective on the date of enactment, December 21, 2000.

Act Sec. 303 of the Community Renewal Tax Relief Act of 2000, amending Code Sec. 7608(c)(6). Law at ¶ 6200. Committee Report at ¶ 10,265.

DEDUCTIONS AND EXCLUSIONS

Tax Benefits for Missing Children

¶ 390

Background

Parents whose children are kidnapped face additional anguish every year when they complete their tax returns. As far as the parents are concerned, their children are alive. However, they are not allowed to take the various deductions, exemptions, and credits that they had taken in the past because, absent the child's presence in their home, they can not meet the Code's requirements, *e.g.*, that the taxpayer provide over one-half of the support in order to claim the child as a dependent (Code Sec. 151(c)) or that the child have the same principal living quarters as the taxpayer for more than one-half of the tax year for the earned income credit (Code Sec. 32(c)).

This situation received widespread attention when the IRS issued a Chief Counsel Advice Memorandum that ruled that parents were not allowed to claim a dependency exemption for a child kidnapped by a nonrelative for the tax years following the kidnapping because they did not meet the support test (CCA 200034029). The IRS subsequently revised its conclusions in CCA 200038059. In that memorandum, the IRS stated that the parents of a kidnapped child were presumed to have incurred sufficient expenses to satisfy the Code Sec. 152(a) support requirements, where no individual other than the parents had custody of the child or could claim a dependency exemption. Under these limited circumstances, the parents would not be required to establish that the expenses they incurred constituted over half of the total support that the child received from all sources that year and were entitled to claim a dependency exemption.

Despite the IRS's reversal of its position, the House unanimously passed H.R. 5117 (The Missing Children Tax Fairness Bill of 2000) to provide statutory authority allowing families of kidnapped children to continue to claim a dependency exemption, child credit and earned income tax credit, and to maintain their filing status in the years following the abduction. The measure was incorporated into H.R. 5542 (The Taxpayer Relief Act of 2000).

Community Renewal Tax Relief Act Impact

Dependency exemptions and other tax benefits for parents of kidnapped children.—A taxpayer's child who is presumed by law authorities to have been kidnapped by a nonrelative and who qualified as the taxpayer's dependent for the portion of the year prior to the kidnapping will be treated as the taxpayer's dependent for the following purposes:

(1) the dependency exemption allowed under Code Sec. 151;

(2) the child tax credit under Code Sec. 24; and

(3) the determination of eligibility for surviving spouse or head of household status under Code Sec. 2.

This entitlement applies to all tax years ending during the period that the child is kidnapped. (Code Sec. 151(c)(6)(A)-(B), as added by the Community Renewal Tax Relief Act of 2000).

Relief is provided also for parents who would otherwise be eligible for the earned income credit had their child not been kidnapped. A child who is presumed by law enforcement authorities to have been kidnapped by a nonrelative and who shared the taxpayer's principal place of abode for more than one-half of the portion of the year prior to the kidnapping will be treated as meeting the residence requirement of Code Sec. 32(c)(3)(A)(ii) for all the tax years ending during the period of the kidnapping (Code Sec. 151(c)(6)(C), as added by the 2000 Act).

This special treatment terminates with the first tax year beginning after the calendar year in which the child was determined to be dead or in which the child would have reached age 18, whichever occurs earlier (Code Sec. 151(c)(6)(D), as added by the 2000 Act).

Caution. This provision does not apply to children who are presumed to have been kidnapped by relatives. Thus, children kidnapped during and after divorce proceedings do not fall under the parameters of this law. Similarly, children who run away from home are not covered.

★ *Effective date.* The provision is effective for tax years ending after December 21, 2000 (Act Sec. 306(b) of the Community Renewal Tax Relief Act of 2000).

Act Sec. 306(a) of the Community Renewal Tax Relief Act of 2000, adding Code Sec. 151(c)(6); Act Sec. 306(b). Law at ¶5170. Committee Report at ¶10,280.

Chapter 4

Special Business Entities

INSURANCE COMPANIES

Modified Endowment Contracts

¶ 405

Background

The legislative history of Code Sec. 7702A(a), which defines the term "modified endowment contract," indicates that once a life insurance contract becomes a modified endowment contract (MEC), the MEC status cannot be eliminated by exchanging the MEC for another contract. However, Code Sec. 7702A(a)(2) conceivably could be read to permit a policyholder to exchange an MEC for a contract that does not fail the seven-pay test of Code Sec. 7702A(b) (which reduces the tax benefits if the endowment benefits are reduced during the first seven years of the contract), and then exchange the second contract for a third contract which would not literally have been received in exchange for a contract that failed to meet the seven-pay test.

A second loophole relates to exchanges of insurance contracts designed to circumvent the premium limitation. If a life insurance contract that is not a modified endowment contract is exchanged for a new life insurance contract, the seven-pay limit under the new contract must first be computed without reference to the premium paid using the cash surrender value of the old contract and then is reduced by one-seventh of the premium paid, taking into account the cash surrender value of the old contract.

> **Example.** Joanne Jones exchanges a life insurance contract with a cash surrender value of $14,000. The seven-pay premium on the new contract would have equalled $10,000 per year if she had not exchanged the old contract. Therefore, the seven-pay premium on the new contract equals $8,000 ($10,000 − ($14,000 ÷ 7)).

However, Code Sec. 7702A(c)(3)(A) arguably might be read to suggest that if, in the example above, the cash surrender value on the new contract was $0 in the first two years due to surrender charges, then the seven-pay premium might be $10,000, unintentionally permitting policyholders to engage in a series of "material changes" to circumvent the premium limitations in Code Sec. 7702A.

Technical Corrections Impact

Elimination of modified endowment contract status through certain contract exchanges prohibited.—A technical correction to Code Sec. 7702A(a)(2) prevents a taxpayer from avoiding modified endowment contract status by exchanging a modified endowment contract for a contract which does not fail the seven-pay test and then exchanging that contract for another contract (Code Sec. 7702A(a)(2), as amended by Act Sec. 318(a) of the Community Renewal Tax Relief Act of 2000).

Circumvention of premium limitations. A second technical correction prevents the circumvention of the premium limitations of Code Sec. 7702A by requiring that the cash surrender value of an "old" contract be taken into account in determining whether a new contract satisfies the seven-pay test (Code Sec. 7702A(c)(3) (Code Sec. 7702A(c)(3), as amended by the 2000 Act).

★ *Effective date.* These provisions are effective generally for contracts entered into or materially changed on or after June 21, 1988 (Act Sec. 318(a)(3) of the Community Renewal Tax Relief Act of 2000; Act Sec. 5012 of the Technical and Miscellaneous Revenue Act of 1988).

Act Sec. 318(a)(1) of the Community Renewal Tax Relief Act of 2000, amending Code Sec. 7702A(a)(2); Act Sec. 318(a)(2) amending Code Sec. 7702A(c)(3)(A)(ii); Act Sec. 318(a)(3). Law at ¶ 6220. Committee Report at ¶ 10,345.

PARTNERSHIPS

Basis Adjustments for Distributions of Controlled Corporation Assets

¶ 410

Background

If a member of an affiliated group of corporations that is eligible to file a consolidated return owns stock in a corporation that is not a member of the affiliated group (the issuing corporation), the ownership of the issuing corporation's stock is determined by including the stock owned by all the other members of the affiliated group (Reg. § 1.1502-34). This rule applies, among other instances, for purposes of applying the 80-percent voting and value test governing the recognition of gain or loss upon the liquidation of an affiliated corporation.

Technical Corrections Impact

Partnership distributions.—A technical correction provides that the affiliated group rules also apply for purposes of determining basis adjustments to assets of a controlled corporation received by the controlling corporation through a distribution from a partnership in which the controlling corporation is a partner (Act Sec. 311(c) of the Community Renewal Tax Relief Act of 2000). Specifically, the reference to Code Sec. 332(b)(1) in Reg. § 1.1502-34 is deemed to include a reference to Code Sec. 732(f).

Election. For a distribution made by a partnership in existence on July 14, 1999, the partner receiving the distribution must elect to have this provision apply on its federal income tax for the tax year in which the distribution occurs.

★ *Effective date.* In general, this provision is effective for distributions made after July 14, 1999. However, for partnerships in existence on July 14, 1999, the rule generally applies to distributions made after June 30, 2001. However, this provision does not apply to distributions made after December 17, 1999, and before July 1, 2001, unless the partner so elects (see "Election," above) (Act Sec. 311(d) of the Community Renewal Tax Relief Act of 2000; Act Sec. 538 of the Ticket to Work and Work Incentives Improvement Act of 1999 (P.L. 106-170)).

Act Sec. 311(c) of the Community Renewal Tax Relief Act of 2000; Act Sec. 311(d). Law at ¶ 7170. Committee Report at ¶ 10,310.

REAL ESTATE INVESTMENT TRUSTS

Exclusion from Redetermined Rents of Certain Subsidiary Amounts

¶ 415

Background

For tax years beginning after December 31, 2000, a 100-percent excise tax is imposed when a real estate investment trust (REIT) and a taxable REIT subsidiary engage in certain transactions that do not reflect arm's-length amounts. The tax covers three items: redetermined rents, redetermined deductions, and excess interest. Redetermined rents are rents that would need to be reduced under a Code Sec. 482 allocation to clearly reflect the income of the REIT and the taxable REIT subsidiary when the subsidiary provides services to a tenant of the REIT (Code Sec. 857(b)(7)).

Under one safe harbor, amounts received directly or indirectly by the REIT for certain tenant services will not be included in redetermined rents and will not be subject to the 100-percent excise tax. Such services include customary services and services provided through an independent contractor from whom the REIT does not derive or receive any income (Code Sec. 857(b)(7)(B)(ii) and Code Sec. 856(d)(7)(C)(i)). Customary services are those that are ordinarily provided to tenants of rental property, such as garbage collection or security services (Code Sec. 856(d)(1)(B); Reg. § 1.856-4(b)(1)).

Technical Corrections Impact

REIT excise tax safe harbor clarified.—A technical correction clarifies when one of the safe harbors for avoiding the 100-percent excise tax on redetermined rents of a real estate investment trust (REIT) applies. The safe harbor applies to amounts received directly or indirectly by a REIT:

(1) for customary tenant services provided by the taxable REIT subsidiary; and

(2) from a taxable REIT subsidiary that would be excluded from unrelated business taxable income (UBTI) as rents if received by a Code Sec. 511(a)(2) organization, which includes most tax-exempt organizations and state colleges and universities (Code Sec. 857(b)(7)(B)(ii), as amended by the Community Renewal Tax Relief Act of 2000; Code Sec. 856(d)(7)(C)(ii)).

Rents that are excluded from UBTI are all rents from real property and all rents from personal property leased with the real property, if the rents attributable to the personal property are an incidental amount of the total rents received or accrued under the lease. Rents attributable to personal property are incidental if they do not exceed 10 percent of the total rents from all of the leased property (Reg. § 1.512(b)-1(c)(2)(ii)). This determination is made at the time the personal property is placed in service (Code Sec. 512(b)(3)(A)).

Excess personal property rent and certain rents based on profits are not excluded from UBTI. There are excess personal property rents when more than 50 percent of the total rent received or accrued under the lease is attributable to personal property leased with the real property. Rents are also not excluded from UBTI if the determination of the amount of rent depends in whole or in part on the income or profits derived by any person from the property leased, other than an amount based on a fixed percentage of receipts or sales (Code Sec. 512(b)(3)(B); Reg. § 1.512(b)-1(c)(2)(iii)).

★ *Effective date.* The provision is effective for tax years beginning after December 31, 2000 (Act Sec. 311(d) of the Community Renewal Tax Relief Act of 2000; Act Sec. 545 of the Ticket to Work and Work Incentives Improvement Act of 1999 (P.L. 106-170)).

Act Sec. 311(b) of the Community Renewal Tax Relief Act of 2000, amending Code Sec. 857(b)(7)(B)(ii); Act Sec. 311(d). Law at ¶ 5420. Committee Report at ¶ 10,310.

SMALL BUSINESS TRUSTS

State and Local Government Permissible Beneficiaries

¶ 420

Background

An electing small business trust may be a shareholder in an S corporation. The electing small business trust provisions were enacted under the Small Business Job Protection Act of 1996 (P.L. 104-188) in order to broaden estate planning opportunities for S corporations by allowing trusts to be funded with S corporation stock. To qualify as an electing small business trust, all beneficiaries must be individuals or estates eligible to be S corporation shareholders, except that charitable organizations may hold contingent remainder interests (Code Sec. 1361(e)(1)(A)(i), as added by the Small Business Job Protection Act). Code Sec. 170(c)(1) state and local government organizations were not included as qualifying beneficiaries.

Technical Corrections Impact

Small business trust beneficiaries include state and local governments.—A technical correction clarifies that an electing small business trust may have a state or local government as a beneficiary *if* such organization holds a contingent interest and is not a potential current beneficiary (Code Sec. 1361(e)(1)(A)(i), as amended by the Community Renewal Tax Relief Act of 2000 (P.L. 106-554). Such restrictions do not apply to other charitable organizations.

★ *Effective date.* The provision is effective for tax years beginning after December 31, 1996 (Act. Sec. 316(e) of the Community Renewal Tax Relief Act of 2000; Act Sec. 1302 of the Small Business Job Protection Act of 1996 (P.L. 104-188)).

Act Sec. 316(b) of the Community Renewal Tax Relief Act of 2000, amending Code Sec. 1361(e)(1)(A)(i); Act Sec. 316(e). Law at ¶ 5680. Committee Report at ¶ 10,335.

Chapter 5

Foreign Sales Corporations

FSC REPEAL AND EXTRATERRITORIAL INCOME EXCLUSION

Overview of FSC Rules

¶ 505

Background

In 1984, the United States enacted a new export incentive scheme to provide tax benefits to certain qualifying foreign sales corporations (FSCs) (Code Secs. 921 through 927). The FSC provisions were enacted in response to objections from its trading partners that the favorable tax deferral treatment of Domestic International Sales Corporations (DISCs) constituted an export subsidy that violated U.S. commitments under the General Agreement on Tariffs and Trade (GATT). It is worth noting that the United States adopted the FSC provisions without ever conceding that the DISC provisions actually violated GATT.

A foreign sales corporation, defined under Code Sec. 922, is a corporation that: (1) is organized in a qualifying foreign jurisdiction or U.S. possession; (2) has a maximum of 25 shareholders; (3) has no outstanding preferred stock; (4) maintains an office in a qualifying foreign country where its permanent books of account are kept (and also keeps certain records in the United States); (5) has a board of directors, at least one member of which is not a U.S. resident; (6) is not a member of any controlled group of corporations of which a DISC is a member; and (7) has made an election to be treated as a FSC. In addition, the FSC must engage in certain export-related activities/economic processes outside of the United States.

The major tax benefits arising from the FSC provisions are that: (1) income from an eligible FSC is partially exempt from U.S. income tax since its exempt foreign trade income is treated as foreign-source income that is not effectively connected with the conduct of a U.S. trade or business; and (2) a U.S. corporation generally is not subject to U.S. income tax on dividends distributed from certain earnings of the FSC because the 100-percent dividends-received deduction applies.

In July 1998, the European Union requested that a World Trade Organization (WTO) Dispute Settlement Panel determine whether the FSC provisions were consistent with WTO rules, including the WTO Agreement on Subsidies and Countervailing Measures and the Agreement on Agriculture. On October 8, 1999, the Panel ruled that the FSC provisions did not comply with the United States' WTO obligations. The United States appealed the ruling but was unsuccessful. On

Background

February 24, 2000, the WTO Appellate Body affirmed the Panel's ruling and gave the United States until October 1, 2000 to implement the rulings.

On October 12, 2000, the WTO Dispute Settlement Body extended the October 1, 2000 deadline for implementation of the rulings until November 1, 2000 to allow time for Congress to pass legislation repealing the FSC provisions. Also on that date, the Dispute Settlement Body took note of a bilateral Understanding between the United States and the European Union on how to proceed if the parties disagreed about the proper implementation of the rulings and when retaliatory measures could be invoked.

Repeal of FSC Rules

¶ 510

The FSC Repeal and Extraterritorial Income Exclusion Act of 2000 (P.L. 106-519) repeals the law governing the taxation of foreign sales corporations (FSCs), contained in Code Secs. 921 through 927, generally effective for transactions after September 30, 2000. See ¶ 540 for exceptions and special rules on effective dates.

Act Sec. 2 of the FSC Repeal and Extraterritorial Income Exclusion Act of 2000, repealing Code Secs. 921-927; Act Sec. 5. Law at ¶ 5460, ¶ 5470, ¶ 5480, ¶ 5490, ¶ 5500, ¶ 5510, and ¶ 5520. Committee Report at ¶ 10,115.

Treatment of Extraterritorial Income

¶ 515

Exclusion of extraterritorial income.—The rules governing the taxation of FSCs are replaced with an exclusion from gross income for extraterritorial income that meets the requirements of "qualifying foreign trade income" (see ¶ 520). Extraterritorial income is income attributable to foreign trading gross receipts (¶ 525) (Code Sec. 114(d), as added by P.L. 106-519).

Qualifying foreign trade property (¶ 530) is the threshold for determining foreign trading gross receipts and ultimately qualifying foreign trade income. Qualifying foreign trade property, which generates foreign trading gross receipts, is generally defined as property held primarily for lease, sale or rental, in the ordinary course of business, for direct, lease, sale or rental *outside* of the United States. Foreign trading gross receipts are then used to calculate foreign trade income (¶ 525), which is the taxable income attributable to those receipts. Both foreign trading gross receipts and foreign trade income (and foreign sale and lease income, defined as an amount of foreign trade income (¶ 535)) are used to calculate qualifying foreign trade income, as described below.

Qualifying foreign trade income is defined as one of three comparable amounts that, if excluded from gross income, would result in the greatest reduction in the taxpayer's taxable income. The three amounts to compare in arriving at excludable foreign trade income are: (1) 30 percent of the "foreign sale and leasing income" derived by the taxpayer from the transaction; (2) 1.2 percent of the "foreign trading gross receipts" derived by the taxpayer from the transaction; or (3) 15 percent of the "foreign trade income" derived by the taxpayer from the transaction (Code Sec. 941(a)(1), as added by P.L. 106-519).

Comment. The new exclusion for extraterritorial income is similar to many European taxing systems which exclude income earned outside the taxing jurisdiction.

Deductions attributable to excluded extraterritorial income are not allowed (Code Sec. 114(c), as added by P.L. 106-519). Taxpayers are required to apportion and allocate deductions between excluded and nonexcluded foreign trade income. Also, no foreign tax credit will be allowed for any income taxes paid or accrued to any foreign country or U.S. possession (including taxes paid in lieu of tax) with respect to excluded extraterritorial income (Code Sec. 114(d), as added by P.L. 106-519; Code Sec. 903, as amended by P.L. 106-519). Also, foreign taxes paid or accrued with respect to qualifying foreign trade income may not be deducted (Code Sec. 275(a), as amended by P.L. 106-519). Special rules apply with respect to foreign withholding taxes where a foreign tax credit or deduction is denied (see ¶ 520).

Who is eligible for the exclusion. The extraterritorial income exclusion provisions apply in the same manner to individuals and corporations that are U.S. taxpayers. The exclusion will pass through to the owners of a partnership, S corporation, limited liability company or other pass-through entity (Conference Committee Report for P.L. 106-519). A foreign corporation may also be entitled to the exclusion if it makes the election to be treated as a domestic corporation (see ¶ 530).

Corporations that are members of a controlled group of corporations that has a domestic international sales corporation (DISC) as a member are not eligible for the exclusion (Code Sec. 943(f), as added by P.L. 106-519). "Controlled group of corporations" is defined in Code Sec. 927(d)(4), prior to repeal. The rules under Code Sec. 927(d) reference the consolidated return rules in Code Sec. 1563, but substitute a lower 50-percent control threshold.

Patrons of agricultural and horticultural cooperatives are also entitled to an exclusion for qualifying foreign trade income that is attributable to foreign trading gross receipts (see ¶ 520).

Comment. Under the former FSC regime, only domestic corporate shareholders could benefit from ownership in an FSC because the corporation could claim a 100-percent dividends received deduction under Code Sec. 245(c)(1)(A) for distributions received from the FSC. Noncorporate taxpayers were not entitled to the 100-percent dividends received deduction and so were fully taxed on dividends received from the FSC. Both corporate and noncorporate taxpayers can now benefit from the new exclusion for extraterritorial income.

Alternative minimum tax. The extraterritorial income exclusion applies for purposes of the individual and corporate alternative minimum tax (Code Sec. 56(g)(4)(B)(i), as amended by P.L. 106-519; Conference Committee Report for P.L. 106-519).

Prior regulations may govern temporarily. The taxpayer and the IRS may apply the principles of current regulations and other administrative guidance under Code Secs. 921 through 927, prior to repeal, to analogous concepts found in extraterritorial income exclusion law during a gap period that will exist prior to the issuance of new detailed administrative guidance (Conference Committee Report for P.L. 106-519).

¶ 515

Act Sec. 3(a) of the FSC Repeal and Extraterritorial Income Exclusion Act of 2000, adding Code Sec. 114; Act Sec. 3(b), adding Code Sec. 941 and Code Sec. 943; Act Sec. (4)(1), amending Code Sec. 56(g)(4)(B)(i); Act Sec. 4(2), amending Code Sec. 275(a); Act Sec. 4(4), amending Code Sec. 903; Act Sec. 5. Law at ¶ 5100, ¶ 5140, ¶ 5240, ¶ 5450, ¶ 5530, and ¶ 5550. Committee Report at ¶ 10,115.

Qualifying Foreign Trade Income

¶ 520

Qualifying foreign trade income.—The FSC Repeal Act provides an income exclusion for extraterritorial income that meets the requirements of "qualifying foreign trade income." Qualifying foreign trade income is defined with respect to any transaction as the amount of gross income which, if excluded, would result in a reduction in the taxpayer's taxable income equal to the greater of: (1) 30 percent of the "foreign sale and leasing income" derived by the taxpayer from the transaction; (2) 1.2 percent of the "foreign trading gross receipts" derived by the taxpayer from the transaction; or (3) 15 percent of the "foreign trade income" derived by the taxpayer from the transaction. The amount of qualifying foreign trade income that has been determined using 1.2 percent of the foreign trading gross receipts (option number 2) is limited to 200 percent of the qualifying foreign trade income that would result from using 15 percent of the foreign trade income (option number 3) (Code Sec. 941(a)(1), as added by P.L. 106-519). The term "foreign trade income" means, generally, the taxable income of the taxpayer attributable to the taxpayer's foreign trading gross receipts (Code Sec. 941(b)(1), as added by P.L. 106-519).

The calculations used in arriving at qualifying foreign trade income refer to a reduction in taxable income (a net income concept). Qualifying foreign trade income, on the other hand, is an exclusion from gross income. Therefore, after the taxpayer calculates the appropriate reduction in taxable income, that amount must then be "grossed up" to reflect related expenses in order to determine the amount of gross income that is excluded (Conference Committee Report for P.L. 106-519).

Planning Note. The IRS may issue regulations for marginal costing for taxpayers using the foreign trade income method in cases where a taxpayer seeks to establish or maintain a market for qualifying foreign trade property. Before administrative guidance is issued under the new rules, a taxpayer may apply principles similar to those found in Temporary Reg. § 1.925(b)-1T. In general, these rules provide that marginal costs include only direct costs (Conference Committee Report for P.L. 106-519).

Choosing among options for calculating qualifying foreign trade income. Although a taxpayer will generally choose to calculate qualifying foreign trade income using the method that results in the greatest tax savings, this is not required by the Code. A taxpayer is permitted to calculate its qualifying foreign trade income using any of the alternative methods stated in Code Sec. 941(a)(1) even though that method will not result in the greatest reduction in taxable income (Code Sec. 941(a)(2), as added by P.L. 106-519).

Transactions involving related parties. The rules for calculating qualifying foreign trade income are designed to prevent "double counting" of income from transactions between related parties. If the amount of foreign trade income (option 3) is calculated using a foreign transfer price from a related party, then the related party's qualifying foreign trade income for the transaction involving the same property is considered to be zero.

¶ 520

Example. A manufacturer and distributor of the same product are related. The manufacturer sells the product to the distributor at an arm's length price of $80, generating $30 of profit. The distributor in turn sells the item to an unrelated customer outside the United States for $100, generating $20 of profit. If the distributor chooses to calculate its qualifying foreign trade income on the basis of 1.2 percent of foreign trading gross receipts, including the $100 sale proceeds in its gross receipts, the manufacturer in turn will be treated as having zero qualifying foreign trade income from this transaction.

However, if the distributor chooses to calculate its qualifying foreign trade income on the basis of 15 percent of foreign trade income (*i.e.*, the $20 profit), then the manufacturer would also be eligible to calculate its qualifying foreign trade income based on 15 percent of its $30 profit. The total group foreign trade income of $50 is not double counted in this instance.

Persons are considered "related" if they are treated as a single employer under Code Sec. 52(a) or (b) (governing who is a single employer for purposes of the work opportunity credit) or under Code Sec. 414(m) or (o) (defining affiliated service groups for employee benefit purposes). Relationships determined under Code Sec. 52 do not take into account Code Sec. 1563(b), and thus the definition of related parties includes foreign corporations and other persons that would not otherwise be considered related.

The rules also prevent double counting of trade receipts under different options for calculating qualifying foreign trade income. For example, when using the foreign trading gross receipts method (option 2) to determine the amount of qualifying foreign trade income from a transaction, a taxpayer will be treated as having no qualifying foreign trade income (option 3) with respect to any transaction that involves the same property (Code Sec. 941(a)(3), as added by P.L. 106-519).

In determining whether a partner is a related person with respect to any other partner, a partner's interest in the partnership is not taken into account (Code Sec. 943(f)(2)(A), as added by P.L. 106-519).

Transaction defined. Qualifying foreign trade income is defined in the Code as an amount relating to a particular transaction. A "transaction" is (1) any sale, exchange, or other disposition; (2) any lease or rental; and (3) any furnishing of services (Code Sec. 943(b)(1), as added by P.L. 106-519).

It is possible for taxpayers to group related transactions in arriving at the excludable amount. A taxpayer is permitted to choose whether to calculate the amount of qualifying foreign trade income on a transaction-by-transaction basis or on an aggregate basis for groups of transactions (Code Sec. 943(b)(1), as added by P.L. 106-519). Groupings of transactions should be based on product lines or recognized industry or trade usage. Taxpayers will be given reasonable flexibility in identifying product lines or groups. A grouping will not be rejected merely because the grouped products fall within more than one of the two-digit Standard Industrial Classification codes (including industries as defined in the North American Industrial Classification System) (Conference Committee Report for P.L. 106-519).

Planning Note. The ability to group transactions instead of considering each transaction separately provides flexibility in meeting the requirements for excluding extraterritorial income. The IRS may issue regulations on grouping. Before new administrative guidance is issued, a taxpayer may apply principles similar to those found in the following regulations: (1) Reg. § 1.924(d)-1(c)(5) (grouping transactions for purposes of the foreign economic processes requirement and the sales activity test); (2) Reg. § 1.924(d)-1(e) (grouping transactions for purposes of the foreign economic processes requirement and the foreign direct costs test); and (3) Temporary Reg. § 1.925(a)-1T(c)(8) (grouping transactions for purposes of the FSC transfer pricing rules (Conference Committee Report for P.L. 106-519).

Trade income violating public policy. Qualifying foreign trade income will be reduced in the case of illegal bribes, kickbacks or other payments paid by or on behalf of the taxpayer, either directly or indirectly, to an official, employee, or agent-in-fact of a government. Additionally, qualifying foreign trade income will be reduced by the international boycott factor for operations in or related to a country associated in carrying out an international boycott, or participating or cooperating with an international boycott (Code Sec. 941(a)(5), as added by P.L. 106-519; Conference Committee Report for P.L. 106-519)).

Qualifying foreign trade income of partnerships. A partnership may allocate qualifying foreign trade income from certain shared partnerships to its partners. In general, if a partnership maintains a separate account for transactions involving foreign trading gross receipts with each partner, makes distributions to each partner based on the amounts in the separate account, and meets other requirements that the IRS may prescribe by regulations, then the partnership is permitted to allocate to each partner items of income, gain, loss, and deduction (including qualifying foreign trade income) from such transactions on the basis of the separate account (Code Sec. 943(f), as added by P.L. 106-519).

The special rules for partnership allocations under Code Sec. 943(f) are intended to apply in lieu of otherwise applicable partnership allocation rules (such as those in Code Sec. 704(b)), only with respect to allocations and distributions related to transactions between the partner and the shared partnership generating foreign trading gross receipts. For purposes of applying the special allocation rules, a partnership is a foreign or domestic entity that is considered to be a partnership for U.S. federal income tax purposes (Conference Committee Report for P.L. 106-519).

Cooperatives. The FSC Repeal Act also provides an income exclusion for certain distributions of qualifying foreign trade income by agricultural and horticultural cooperatives. The amount of any patronage dividends or per-unit retain allocations paid to a member of an agricultural or horticultural cooperative which is allocable to qualifying foreign trade income of the cooperative will be treated as qualifying foreign trade income of the member. Thus, the distributions are excludable from the member's gross income. This measure was viewed as necessary to avoid placing agricultural and horticultural producers that choose to market their products through cooperatives at a disadvantage when compared with those that market their products directly or through a pass-through entity like a partnership, limited liability company or S corporation (Code Sec. 943(g), as added by P.L. 106-519; Conference Committee Report for P.L. 106-519).

Deductions ordinarily allowable to cooperatives may not be allowable when the cooperative sells qualifying foreign trade property. In calculating the foreign trade income of a cooperative that is engaged in the marketing of agricultural and horticultural products, no deduction is allowed for patronage dividends, per-unit retain allocations or nonpatronage distributions (ordinarily excludable under Code Secs. 1382(b) and (c)) (Code Sec. 941(b)(2), as added by P.L. 106-519).

Treatment of withholding taxes. Foreign tax credits are disallowed for any income taxes paid or accrued on excluded extraterritorial income (¶ 515). In order

¶ 520

to ensure that taxpayers may continue to claim the foreign tax credit for taxes that are withheld by a foreign jurisdiction, the Code treats any taxes withheld as not having been paid or accrued with respect to qualifying foreign trade income. A withholding tax is any foreign tax that is imposed on a basis other than residence and that is otherwise a creditable foreign tax under Code Sec. 901 or Code Sec. 903 (Code Sec. 943(d), as added by P.L. 106-519). A similar rule applies in the case where foreign taxes paid or accrued with respect to qualifying trade income are disallowed as a deduction (¶ 515) (Code Sec. 275(a), as amended by P.L. 106-519).

This special rule for characterizing withholding taxes would also apply to any withholding tax that is creditable for U.S. foreign tax credit purposes under an applicable treaty. Such taxes would be similar to the gross-basis taxes described in Code Sec. 871 and Code Sec. 881.

The rule for characterizing withholding taxes does not apply if qualifying foreign trade income is determined based on 30 percent of foreign sale and leasing income. In that case, the foreign withholding taxes are treated as paid or accrued with respect to qualifying foreign trade income and will be creditable.

Act Sec. 3(b) of the FSC Repeal and Extraterritorial Income Exclusion Act of 2000, adding Code Sec. 941 and Code Sec. 943; Act Sec. 4(2), amending Code Sec. 275(a); Act Sec. 4(5), amending Code Sec. 999(c)(1); Act Sec. 5. Law at ¶ 5240, ¶ 5530, ¶ 5550 and ¶ 5570. Committee Report at ¶ 10,115.

Foreign Trading Gross Receipts

¶ 525

Foreign trading gross receipts.—In order to calculate qualifying foreign trade income, the amount of foreign trade income must first be determined. Foreign trade income is the taxable income attributable to foreign trading gross receipts (determined without regard to exclusion for "qualifying" foreign trade income, of course) (Code Sec. 942(a)(1), as added by P.L. 106-519). Foreign trading gross receipts are defined as the taxpayer's gross receipts which are: (1) derived from the sale, exchange, or other disposition of qualifying foreign trade property; (2) derived from the lease or rental of qualifying foreign trade property that was for use by the lessee outside of the United States; (3) for services which are related and subsidiary to any sale, exchange, or other disposition of qualifying foreign trade property (as described in (1) or (2) above); (4) for engineering or architectural services for construction projects located (or proposed for location) outside of the United States; or (5) for the performance of certain managerial services for a person other than a related person in connection with the production of foreign trading gross receipts (as described in (1), (2), or (3) above) (Code Sec. 942(a)(1), as added by P.L. 106-519).

Licensing income. Gross receipts from the lease or rental of qualifying foreign trade property (item (2) above) include receipts from the license of qualifying foreign trade property. This includes licensing of computer software for reproduction abroad, consistent with the policy adopted in the Taxpayer Relief Act of 1997 (P.L. 105-34) (Conference Committee Report for P.L. 106-519).

Managerial services income. There is a limitation on the use of gross receipts from the performance of managerial services in calculating foreign trading gross receipts. In order to be considered, at least 50 percent of the taxpayer's foreign trading gross receipts (exclusive of those for the managerial services) for the tax year must have been derived from activities noted in (1), (2) or (3) above (generally, sale and lease of foreign trade property or services related to the sale or lease of foreign trade property) (Code Sec. 942(a)(1), as added by P.L. 106-519).

Planning Note. Before new administrative rules are issued, principles under existing regulations that define foreign trading gross receipts apply. See, for example, Temporary Reg. § 1.924(a)-1T(a) (Conference Committee Report for P.L. 106-519).

Amounts excluded from foreign trading gross receipts. Foreign trading gross receipts do not include receipts from transactions that are (1) subsidized by a government, (2) for use in or by the U.S., or (3) electively excluded by the taxpayer.

Subsidized receipts are specifically excluded. The term "subsidized receipts" refers to receipts from a transaction that was accomplished by a subsidy granted by the government (or government instrumentality) of the country or possession where the property was manufactured, produced, grown, or extracted (Code Sec. 942(a)(2)(B), as added by P.L. 106-519).

Additionally, foreign trading gross receipts do not include gross receipts from a transaction where the qualifying foreign trade property or services are for ultimate use in the United States, or by the United States or any instrumentality thereof, and this use is required by law or regulation (Code Sec. 942(a)(2)(A), as added by P.L. 106-519).

A taxpayer that wants to increase its foreign tax credit also has the option to exclude certain receipts by election (Code Sec. 942(a)(3), as added by P.L. 106-519). A taxpayer who elects not to treat gross receipts as foreign trading gross receipts may then utilize any related foreign tax credits in lieu of the exclusion, as a means of avoiding double taxation. A taxpayer should demonstrate that it is making this election through its treatment of such items on its tax return for the tax year. Redeterminations as to whether the gross receipts from a transaction should be included in foreign trading gross receipts may be made as long as the three-year limitation period for filing refund claims (under Code Sec. 6511) had not expired (Conference Committee Report for P.L. 106-519).

An election to exclude certain gross receipts from foreign trading gross receipts under Code Sec. 942(a)(3) must be made separately by each partner with regard to any transaction for which the shared partnership maintains separate accounts for each partner (Code Sec. 943(f)(2), as added by P.L. 106-519).

Foreign economic processes. A taxpayer will be treated as having foreign trading gross receipts from a transaction only if certain economic processes took place outside of the United States (Code Sec. 942(b)(1), as added by P.L. 106-519).

The foreign economic processes requirement is met if the taxpayer (or any person acting under a contract with it) has participated outside of the United States in the solicitation (other than advertising), negotiation, or making of the contract relating to the transaction and has incurred a certain amount of foreign direct costs attributable to the transaction. In general, the taxpayer must have incurred foreign direct costs (see below) that are equal to or exceed 50 percent of the total direct costs that are attributable to the transaction. Alternatively, this requirement will be satisfied if, in at least two categories of direct costs, the foreign direct costs equal or exceed 85 percent of the total direct costs attributable to each category (Code Sec. 942(b)(2), as added by P.L. 106-519).

¶ 525

Total direct costs. The term "total direct costs" is defined as the total direct costs, with respect to any transaction, that were incurred by the taxpayer and attributable to activities relating to qualifying foreign trade property performed at any location by the taxpayer or any person acting under a contract with it (Code Sec. 942(b)(2)(C), as added by P.L. 106-519).

There are five categories of activities (costs) that are considered to relate to qualifying foreign trade property: (1) advertising and sales promotion; (2) processing customer orders and arranging for delivery; (3) transportation outside of the United States in connection with a delivery to a customer; (4) the determination and transmittal of a final invoice or statement of account or the receipt of payment; and (5) the assumption of credit risk (Code Sec. 942(b)(3), as added by P.L. 106-519).

The formula for satisfying the foreign economic processes requirement includes only those foreign direct costs incurred in the five specified activities. Costs incurred by related persons can be used to satisfy the requirement. Solely for the purpose of determining whether gross receipts are foreign trading gross receipts, the economic processes requirement is treated as satisfied with respect to a sales transaction if any related person has satisfied the foreign economic processes requirement in connection with another sales transaction involving the same qualifying foreign trade property (Code Sec. 942(b)(4), as added by P.L. 106-519).

Planning Note. Before new administrative rules are issued, principles under existing regulations that cover the foreign economic processes requirement, including the measurement of direct costs, apply. See, for example, Reg. § 1.924(d)-1 (Conference Committee Report for P.L. 106-519).

Exception where gross receipts under $5 million. An exception from the foreign economic processes requirement is provided in cases where the taxpayer's foreign trading gross receipts for that year do not exceed $5,000,000 (Code Sec. 942(c)(1), as added by P.L. 106-519). In determining whether this limit on foreign trading receipts has been exceeded, the receipts of related persons will be aggregated as prescribed in regulations (Code Sec. 942(c)(2), as added by P.L. 106-519). In the case of pass-through entities, the determination of whether the foreign trading gross receipts exceed $5,000,000 will be made at both the entity and the partner/shareholder level (Code Sec. 942(c)(3), as added by P.L. 106-519).

Act Sec. 3(b) of the FSC Repeal and Extraterritorial Income Exclusion Act of 2000, adding Code Sec. 942 and Code Sec. 943; Act Sec. 5. Law at ¶ 5540 and ¶ 5550. Committee Report at ¶ 10,115.

Qualifying Foreign Trade Property

¶ 530

Qualifying foreign trade property.—A transaction must generally include qualifying foreign trade property in order to generate foreign trading gross receipts. The term "qualifying foreign trade property" means property that is: (1) manufactured, produced, grown, or extracted (whether within or outside of the United States); (2) held primarily for sale, lease, or rental, in the ordinary course of trade or business for direct use, consumption, or disposition outside of the United States; and (3) not more than 50 percent of the fair market value of which is attributable to articles manufactured, produced, grown, or extracted outside of the United States and direct costs for labor performed outside of the United States (Code Sec. 943(a)(1), as added by P.L. 106-519).

Comment. Under the FSC regime, property was required to be manufactured in the United States. See Code Sec. 927(a), prior to repeal.

The fair market value of an imported article is its appraised value as determined under Sec. 402 of the Tariff Act of 1930 (19 U.S.C. § 1401(a)). Direct costs of labor performed outside of the United States do not include costs that would be treated as direct labor costs attributable to articles manufactured, produced, grown, or extracted outside of the United States (Code Sec. 943(a)(1), as added by P.L. 106-519).

Caution. Gross receipts from a transaction where the qualifying foreign trade property is for ultimate use in the United States do not constitute foreign trading gross receipts eligible for the exclusion (Conference Committee Report for P.L. 106-519).

Planning Note. Before new administrative rules are issued, principles under existing regulations that define the foreign use requirement apply. The rules provide guidance for taxpayers who do not want to run afoul of the foreign use requirement. For example, property that is located outside of the United States more than 50 percent of the time is considered to be used predominately outside of the United States (Temporary Reg. § 1.927(a)-1T(d)(4)(vi). See also Temporary Reg. § 1.927-1T(d)(4)(ii), (iii), (iv), and (v) (Conference Committee Report for P.L. 106-519).

U.S. taxation of foreign manufactured property. Property that is manufactured outside of the United States must be manufactured by: (1) a domestic corporation; (2) an individual who is a U.S. citizen or resident; (3) a foreign corporation that elects to be subject to U.S. taxation in the same manner as a U.S. corporation; or (4) a partnership or other pass-through entity whose partners or owners fall within categories (1), (2) or (3) (Code Sec. 943(a)(2), as added by P.L. 106-519).

Election to be taxed as domestic corporation. A foreign corporation may elect to be treated as a domestic corporation. In order to qualify, the foreign corporation must waive all benefits available to it under treaty and either: (1) manufacture, produce, grow, or extract property in the ordinary course of business or (2) substantially all of its gross receipts must be foreign trading gross receipts. Absent a waiver of treaty benefits, it is unclear whether the permanent establishment clause of a relevant tax treaty would override the electing corporation's treatment as a domestic corporation under Code Sec. 943 (Code Sec. 943(e), as added by P.L. 106-519; Conference Committee Report for P.L. 106-519).

The election must be made on original return. It will apply to the tax year when made and all subsequent tax years unless revoked by the taxpayer or terminated for failure to qualify. If a termination or revocation occurs, the corporation (and any successor corporation) will not be permitted to make another election to be taxed as a domestic corporation for five tax years beginning with the first tax year that begins after the termination or revocation. A foreign corporation that elects to be treated as a domestic corporation is not permitted to make an S corporation election (Code Sec. 943(e)(1), as added by P.L. 106-519).

Electing corporations are treated as transferring all of their assets in a deemed asset transfer under Code Sec. 367 that is treated as a reorganization under Code Sec. 354. The asset transfer is deemed to occur on the first day of the first tax year for which the election applies. The electing corporation is treated as transferring all of its assets to the domestic corporation in a reorganization under Code Sec. 368(a)(1)(F) and the U.S. taxpayer may be subject to tax on a deemed distribution to the extent provided in the Code Sec. 367(b) regulations (see Reg. § 1.367(b)-3 (Code Sec. 943(e)(4)(B), as added by P.L. 106-519). For special transition rules, see ¶ 540.

The IRS is granted authority to prescribe rules to ensure that foreign corporations that make this election pay their U.S. income taxes. The IRS is also granted authority to designate a certain class or classes of corporations as ineligible to make the election (Code Sec. 943(e)(4)(A) and (C), as added by P.L. 106-519).

Comment. The election is not limited to domestic owned foreign corporations. Additionally, the election is modeled after the Code Sec. 953(d) election that allows a controlled foreign corporation engaged in the insurance business to be treated as a U.S. foreign corporation. Notice 89-79, 1989-2 CB 392, contains guidance on making the Code Sec. 953(d) election (Conference Committee Report for P.L. 106-519).

Property manufactured in U.S. Regulations will provide for a foreign-source income limitation in the case of sales involving property that was manufactured in the United States (Code Sec. 943(c), as added by P.L. 106-519). This special source limitation does not apply when qualifying foreign trade income is determined using 30 percent of the foreign sale and leasing income from the transaction (Conference Committee Report for P.L. 106-519).

Property excluded from definition of foreign trade property. The following property is not considered qualifying foreign trade property: (1) property that was leased or rented by the taxpayer for use by a related person; (2) patents, inventions, models, designs, formulae, or processes (whether or not patented), copyrights (other than films, tapes, records, or similar reproductions, and other than computer software (whether or not patented) for commercial or home use), goodwill, trademarks, trade brands, franchises, or other like property; (3) oil or gas (or any primary product thereof); (4) products, the transfer of which is prohibited or curtailed to effectuate the policy set forth in Public Law 96-72; or (5) any unprocessed timber which is a softwood (Code Sec. 943(a)(3), as added by P.L. 106-519).

Property designated as in short supply by Executive Order is similarly excluded from the definition of qualifying foreign trade property (Code Sec. 943(a)(4), as added by P.L. 106-519).

Planning Note. Property may be excluded from qualifying foreign trade property because it is leased or rented to a related person. Until new administrative guidance is issued, similar principles found in Temporary Reg. § 1.927(a)-1T(f)(2)(i) apply. Under the regulation, an exception from the exclusion exists if the property leased to the related person is held for sublease, or is subleased, by the related person to an unrelated person. The property must then be used by the unrelated person predominately outside of the United States. Similarly, under the principles of Temporary Reg. § 1.927(a)-1T(g)(2)(iv), petrochemicals, medicinal products, insecticides and alcohols are not excluded as a primary product of oil or gas (Conference Committee Report for P.L. 106-519).

Computer software. Computer software that is licensed for reproduction outside of the United States is *not* excluded from the definition of qualifying foreign trade property. Computer software licensed for reproduction is considered to be property held primarily for sale, lease, or rental, consistent with the policy adopted in the Taxpayer Relief Act of 1997 (Conference Committee Report for P.L. 106-519).

Interest expense. Under Code Sec. 864(e)(3), for purposes of allocating and apportioning any deductible expense, tax-exempt assets are not taken into account. For purposes of allocating and apportioning any interest expense, there shall not be taken into account any qualifying foreign trade property as defined in Code Sec. 943(a) which is held by the taxpayer for lease or rental in the ordinary course of trade or business for use by the lessee outside of the United States (as defined in Code Sec. 943(b)(2)) (Code Sec. 864(e)(3), as amended by P.L. 106-519).

Act Sec. 3(b) of the FSC Repeal and Extraterritorial Income Exclusion Act of 2000, adding Code Sec. 943; Act Sec. 4(3), amending Code Sec. 864(e)(3); Act Sec. 5. Law at ¶ 5430 and ¶ 5550. Committee Report at ¶ 10,115.

Foreign Sale and Leasing Income

¶ 535

Foreign sale and leasing income.—The term "foreign sale and leasing income" means foreign trade income that is properly allocable to foreign economic process activities (as defined in Code Sec. 942(b)(2)(A)(i) or (3)). The activities must be performed by the taxpayer (or someone acting under a contract with the taxpayer) outside the United States. Alternatively, foreign sale and leasing income is foreign trade income derived by the taxpayer in connection with the lease or rental of qualifying foreign trade property for use by the lessee outside of the United States. Income received from the sale of a residual interest in leased qualifying foreign trade property is also considered foreign sale and leasing income (Code Sec. 941(c)(2), as added by P.L. 106-519).

Hypothetical arm's length transactions. Leased property that was manufactured, produced, grown, or extracted by the taxpayer or acquired by the taxpayer from a related person for a price that was not at arm's length (as determined under the rules of Code Sec. 482) is subject to a special limitation (Code Sec. 941(c), as added by P.L. 106-519). In these cases, the foreign sale and leasing income may not exceed the amount of foreign sale and leasing income that would have resulted had the taxpayer acquired the leased property through a hypothetical arm's length purchase and then engaged in the actual sale or lease of that property. For purposes of calculating the limit on foreign sale and leasing income, the manufacturer's basis and, therefore, depreciation would also be based on this hypothetical arm's length price (Conference Committee Report for P.L. 106-519).

> **Example.** A manufacturer leases qualifying foreign trade property that it manufactured. The foreign sale and leasing income derived from that lease may not exceed the amount of foreign sale and leasing income that the manufacturer would have earned from that lease if it had purchased the property for an arm's length price on the day that the manufacturer entered into the lease.

Income properly allocable to certain intangibles is excluded in determining foreign sale and leasing income under Code Sec. 941(c)(3). Further, only directly allocable expenses are taken into account in computing the amount of foreign trade income.

Act Sec. 3(b) of the FSC Repeal and Extraterritorial Income Exclusion Act of 2000, adding Code Sec. 941 and Code Sec. 942; Act Sec. 5. Law at ¶ 5530 and ¶ 5540. Committee Report at ¶ 10,115.

Effective Date and Transition Rules

¶ 540

Effective date and special rules.—With the exceptions and special rules noted below, the amendments made by the FSC Repeal and Extraterritorial Income Exclusion Act of 2000 apply to transactions after September 30, 2000 (Act Sec. 5(a) of P.L. 106-519).

No new FSCs and termination of inactive FSCs. No corporation may elect after September 30, 2000, to be a FSC, as defined by Code Sec. 922, prior to repeal. If a FSC has no foreign trade income, as defined in Code Sec. 923(b), prior to repeal, for any period of five consecutive tax years beginning after December 31, 2001, it will no longer be treated as a FSC for any tax year beginning after that period (Act Sec. 5(b) of P.L. 106-519).

Transition period for existing FSCs. The Act does not apply to certain transactions of a FSC in existence on September 30, 2000, and at all times thereafter. Specifically excepted is any transaction made in the ordinary course of the trade or business involving the FSC which occurs before January 1, 2002, or after December 31, 2001, pursuant to a binding contract in effect on September 30, 2000, and at all times thereafter. The binding contract must be between the FSC (or any related party as defined by Code Sec. 943(b)(3)) and an unrelated party. A binding contract includes a purchase option, renewal option, or replacement option that is included in the contract and that is enforceable against the seller or lessor (Act Sec. 5(c)(1) and (4) of P.L. 106-519).

Election to have the new law apply earlier. A taxpayer that is not subject to the new rules due to the transitional rules may elect to have the new rules apply to any transaction of a FSC or related party. The election is effective for the tax year in which the election is made and for all subsequent tax years. The election may be revoked only with the consent of the Secretary of the Treasury (Act Sec. 5(c)(2) of P.L. 106-519).

Old earnings and profits of certain corporations. A special transition rule applies to FSCs and certain controlled foreign corporations (CFCs) that are in existence on September 30, 2000 and that make the Code Sec. 943(e) election to be treated as a domestic corporation. Under the rule, the corporation's earnings and profits accumulated in tax years beginning before October 1, 2000 are *not* included in the shareholder's gross income as a result of the deemed asset transfer under Code Sec. 367 that occurs upon the election. In general, a foreign corporation that elects to be treated as a domestic is treated a transferring all of its assets to a domestic corporation in a reorganization to which Code Sec. 354 applies. Absent the transition rule, these earnings and profits may be included in the shareholder's gross income to the extent provided under the Code Sec. 367 regulations (¶ 530). However, the above rules do not apply to the earnings and profits acquired in a transaction after September 30, 2000, where the Code Sec. 381 rules governing carryovers in certain corporate acquisitions apply, unless the distributor or transferor corporation was a foreign corporation to which this earnings-and-profits rule applied immediately before the transaction (Act Sec. 5(c)(3)(A) of P.L. 106-519).

Rules similar to those that apply when a CFC engaged in the insurance business elects to be treated as a U.S. corporation determine whether pre-October 1, 2000 earnings and profits will, despite the transition rule, continue to be taken into account (Act Sec. 5(c)(3)(A)(ii) of P.L. 106-519). For example, under the CFC election rules, earnings and profits that would be subject to a transition rule will be taken into account if distributions are made from those earnings or for purposes of determining gain on the sale or exchange of foreign corporation stock under Code Sec. 1248 (Code Sec. 953(d)(4)(B)(ii), (iii), and (iv)). Guidance on the Code Sec. 953(d) election rules is contained in Notice 89-79, 1989-2 CB 392. Ordering rules similar to those found in Notice 89-79 can be used when distributions are made from the electing corporation (Committee Report for P.L. 106-519).

Existing FSCs. The transition rule relating to old earnings and profits applies to any CFC if: (1) the corporation is a FSC in existence on September 30, 2000; (2) the corporation may elect to be treated as a domestic corporation under Code Sec. 943(e)(2)(B) because substantially all of its gross receipts are foreign trading gross receipts; and (3) the corporation makes the election not later than its first tax year beginning after December 31, 2001 (Act Sec. 5(c)(3)(B) of P.L. 106-519).

Other corporations. Provided certain requirements are met, the transition rule relating to old earnings and profits applies to any CFC and the corporation shall be treated as an applicable foreign corporation for purposes of the Code Sec. 943(e) election. On September 30, 2000, the corporation must be in existence and wholly owned (directly or indirectly) by a domestic corporation determined without regard to the Code Sec. 943(e) election. The corporation must not have made an election to be treated as a FSC and must make the Code Sec. 943(e) election not later than its first tax year beginning after December 31, 2001. Additionally, certain income and activity tests must be satisfied for the three tax years preceding the first tax year of the Code Sec. 943(e) election. These tests require that (1) all of the gross income of the corporation is subpart F income (as defined in Code Sec. 952), including by reason of Code Sec. 954(b)(3)(B) (relating to the special rule for foreign base company income and insurance income in excess of 70 percent of gross income), and (2) in the ordinary course of the corporation's trade or business, the corporation regularly sold (or paid commissions) to a FSC which, on September 30, 2000, was a related person to the corporation. The above rules will cease to apply on the date that the domestic corporation's ownership of the CFC terminates (Act Sec. 5(c)(3)(C) of P.L. 106-519).

Special rules relating to leasing transactions. If foreign trade income in connection with the lease or rental of property described in Code Sec. 927(a)(1)(B), prior to repeal, is treated as exempt foreign trade income under Code Sec. 921(a), prior to repeal, the property is treated as property under Code Sec. 941(c)(1)(B) (foreign trade income derived in connection with the lease or rental of qualifying foreign trade property for use by the lessee outside of the United States) for purposes of applying Code Sec. 941(c)(2) (special rules for leased property) to any subsequent transaction involving the property (Act Sec. 5(d)(1) of P.L. 106-519).

Limitation on use of gross receipts method. If any person computed its foreign trade income from any transaction with respect to any property on the basis of a transfer price determined under a method described in Code Sec. 925(a)(1), prior to repeal, then the qualifying trade income under Code Sec. 941(a) of the person (or any related person) with respect to any other transaction involving the property shall be zero (Act Sec. 5(d)(2) of P.L. 106-519).

Act Sec. 5 of the FSC Repeal and Extraterritorial Income Exclusion Act of 2000. Committee Report at ¶ 10,115.

¶ 540

Computation of Qualifying Foreign Trade Income

¶ 545

Computation of qualifying foreign trade income, related expense disallowance and noncreditable foreign taxes.—The following example illustrates the basic computation of: (1) qualifying foreign trade income (QFTI) (Code Secs. 114 and 941-943), (2) related expenses that are disallowed (Code Sec. 114(c)), and (3) foreign taxes paid that are not creditable for foreign tax credit purposes (Code Sec. 114(d)).

The XYZ Corporation has both foreign trade income (FTI) and foreign sale and leasing income (FS&LI). The financial information for the XYZ corporation for the year is summarized in the table below. In the example, QFTP is Qualified Foreign Trade Property (Code Sec. 943(a)):

Income Statement	Total	Other Property	QFTP
(a) Gross receipts	$25,000	24,000	$1,000
(b) Cost of goods sold	17,000	16,400	600
(c) Gross income	$ 8,000	7,600	400
(d) Direct expenses	4,500	4,225	275
(e) Overhead expenses	500	475	25
(f) Net income	$ 3,000	2,900	$ 100
(g) Foreign taxes paid	$ 40		
(h) FS&LI—$35			

Computation of foreign trade income (FTI).—XYZ's foreign trade income equals $100, which is the $1,000 foreign trade gross receipts (Code Sec. 942) less related direct and overhead expenses, calculated as follows: ($1,000 − $600 − $275 − $25). The $25 is the amount of total overhead expense ($500) reasonably apportioned to foreign trading gross receipts ($500 × $400/$8,000) where apportionment by gross income is assumed to be a reasonable method of apportionment.

Computation of foreign sale and leasing income (FS&LI).—Of the $125 of foreign trade income ($400 − $275), $35 is foreign sale and leasing income. Note that only the direct expenses of $275 reduce the gross income from the sale of qualifying foreign trade property for purposes of this computation.

Computation of qualifying foreign trade income (QFTI).—QFTI is the greatest of three separate QFTI computational amounts. The three separate computational amounts are: (1) 1.2% of Foreign Trading Gross Receipts (FTGR); (2) 15% of Foreign Trade Income (FTI); and (3) 30% of Foreign Sale and Leasing Income (FS&LI). In the example, XYZ will be able to exclude $60 (15% of FTI), as computed below.

(1) Under the "1.2%" computation above, QFTI is $12 + $36 = $48, computed as follows: [(1.2% × $1,000) + ($300 × $12/$100)].

(2) Under the "15%" computation above, QFTI is $15 + $45 = $60, computed as follows: [(15% × $100) + ($300 × $15/$100)].

(3) Under the "30%" method, QFTI is $10.50 + $28.88 = $39.38, computed as follows: [(30% × $35) + ($275 × $10.50/$100)].

Gross-up for disallowed expenses. In each of the three computations above, the computation of QFTI includes the addition of an allocable portion of certain expenses, *e.g.*, $36 ($300 × $12/$100), $45 ($300 × $15/100), and $28.88 ($275 ×

10.50/$100). This "add back" is necessary because the statute defines QFTI as the amount of gross income that, if excluded, will result in a reduction of *taxable income* equal to the greatest of the three amounts computed above. Therefore, in order to calculate the amount that is excluded from gross income, taxable income must be determined and then "grossed up" for allocable expenses in order to arrive at the appropriate gross income figure.

Computation of disallowed expenses.—In connection with excluding $60 of gross income, certain expenses allocable to this income are not deductible for U.S. tax purposes. Thus, $45 ($300 × $60/$400) of expenses are disallowed, where $60 is the QFTI and $400 is the gross income from the sale of qualifying foreign trade property.

Computation of foreign tax credit.—For the XYZ Corporation, of the $40 foreign taxes paid to a foreign jurisdiction, $6 is not creditable for foreign tax credit purposes, computed as follows: ($40 × $60/$400), where $60 is the QFTI and $400 is the gross income from the sale of qualifying foreign trade property.

Conference Committee Report for the FSC Repeal and Extraterritorial Income Exclusion Act of 2000.

PRACTICAL ANALYSIS. Neal J. Block, of Baker & McKenzie, Chicago, Illinois, comments that the tax savings under the extra-territorial income exclusion, for most taxpayers, will be at least equal to the tax savings currently available under the FSC regime, which will be phased out for most taxpayers by the end of 2001. All the export and export-related transactions that gave rise to FSC benefits should give rise to at least the same benefits under the new regime.

In addition, S corporations, individuals, and partnerships that previously were unable to obtain FSC benefits will now be able to obtain the extraterritorial income exclusion benefit. Also, the benefit will also be available to a greater extent than the FSC regime for goods that are manufactured outside the United States, so long as not more than 50% of the value of the goods is attributable to articles manufactured and produced or grown outside the United States plus the direct costs of labor performed outside the United States.

The major difference from the FSC regime lies in the elimination of a separate legal entity to realize the tax savings. Under the new regime, an exporting corporation will simply exclude a portion of its qualifying income from U.S. taxation. Unlike the FSC benefit, this benefit is not subject to alternative minimum tax.

Left uncertain is whether this FSC replacement will pass muster with the World Trade Organization (WTO). The European Union announced that it intends to ask for a ruling that, similar to the FSC structure, the new regime constitutes an illegal export subsidy.

¶ 545

Chapter 6
IRAs, MSAs, and Qualified Plans

INDIVIDUAL RETIREMENT ACCOUNTS
IRA Contributions for Nonworking Spouse

¶605

Background

If a married couple files a joint return, each spouse may, in the great majority of cases, make deductible contributions to his or her IRA up to an applicable dollar limitation of $2,000 for the year 2000 (Code Sec. 219(b)(1)(A)). In the case where a taxpayer is an active participant in a qualified plan, the deduction is phased out for taxpayers with adjusted gross income (AGI) of $52,000 or more for 2000 (Code Sec. 219(g)(3)(B)(i)).

Under another restriction, the maximum IRA deduction is limited by the amount of the individual's earned income (Code Sec. 219(b)(1)(B)). However, in the case of a married couple, it is possible for a nonworking or lesser-earning spouse to make IRA contributions greater than the couple's combined earned income. In effect, a nonworking spouse may "borrow" his or her spouse's compensation for purposes of obtaining the maximum limitation (Code Sec. 219(c)). In such case, the spouse with the greater amount of includible compensation ("higher-paid" or "working" spouse) can make deductible contributions to an IRA of up to the lesser of:

(1) $2,000 (as phased out for active participants), or

(2) his or her includible compensation (Code Sec. 219(b)(1)).

The spouse with the lesser amount of includible compensation ("nonworking" or "lower-paid" spouse) can make deductible contributions to an IRA of up to the lesser of:

(1) $2,000 (as phased out for active participants), or

(2) the sum of:

(a) the includible compensation of the lower-paid spouse, and

(b) the includible compensation of the higher-paid spouse, reduced by: (i) the deduction allowed to the higher-paid spouse for IRA contributions, and (ii) the amount of any contribution on behalf of the higher-paid spouse to a Roth IRA (Code Sec. 219(c)(1)).

Technical Corrections Impact

Combined IRA contribution of spouses not to exceed combined earned income.—The earned income limitation on the maximum IRA deduction for a married person has been modified (Code Sec. 219(c)(1)(B)(ii), as amended by the Community Renewal Tax Relief Act of 2000). Contributions for the spouse with the lower income cannot exceed the combined earned income of the spouses. The deductible contribution by the lower-paid spouse to an IRA is now limited to the lesser of:

(1) $2,000 (as phased out for active participants), or

(2) the sum of:

(a) the includible compensation of the lower-paid spouse, and

(b) the includible compensation of the higher-paid spouse, reduced by: (i) the deduction allowed to the higher-paid spouse for IRA contributions, (ii) *the amount of any Code Sec. 408(o) designated nondeductible contribution on behalf of the higher-paid spouse;* and (iii) the amount of any contribution on behalf of the higher-paid spouse to a Roth IRA (Code Sec. 219(c)(1)(B)(ii)(II), as added by the 2000 Act).

Example. Grant and Holly are married and file a joint return. Both of them retire in the middle of January 2000. In 2000, Grant earned $1,000 and Holly earned $500. They are active participants in employer-sponsored retirement plans. For 2000, their AGI is $60,000. Because Grant's earned income is less than $2,000, his deduction, without application of the phaseout rules, is $1,000 (the lesser of his earned income or $2,000). After application of the income phaseout rules, his maximum deduction is $200. Grant makes a deductible contribution of $200 to his IRA. He may make a nondeductible contribution of $800 ($1,000 − 200) to the IRA.

Holly's maximum permitted deductible contribution to her IRA after the income phaseout is also $200. Her deduction as a lower-paid spouse is limited to the lesser of $200 or the sum of the includible compensation of the lower-paid spouse ($500) and the includible compensation of the higher-paid spouse ($1,000), reduced by: (i) the deduction allowed to the higher-paid spouse for IRA contributions ($200), (ii) the amount of the designated nondeductible contribution on behalf of the higher-paid spouse ($800), and (iii) the amount of any contribution on behalf of the higher-paid spouse to a Roth IRA ($0). Her nondeductible contribution is limited to $300 ($500 − $200). Thus, the total combined contribution of Holly and Grant is $1,500 ($1,000 + $500), which does not exceed their earned income (Conference Committee Report).

PRACTICAL ANALYSIS. Vincent O'Brien, President of Vincent J. O'Brien, CPA, PC, Lynbrook, N.Y., notes that a technical correction in the 2000 tax law closes an interesting but limited loophole that was created by the Small Business Job Protection Act of 1996 (P.L. 104-188). It only affects married couples whose combined earned income is less than $4,000, and it has no effect on those with higher earned income.

Under the 1996 Act, an individual who has no earned income may be allowed to make a contribution to an IRA if the individual's spouse has sufficient earned income. For example, if the spouse has earned income of more than $4,000, then both the individual and the spouse can each contribute up to $2,000 to an IRA. (The sum of contributions to both traditional and Roth IRAs is counted against this limit.)

Under the original provision in the 1996 Act, for a married couple, an individual's maximum IRA contribution was limited to the lesser of $2,000 or:

● the individual's earned income, plus

● the spouse's earned income minus any deductible contribution by the spouse to a traditional IRA and minus any contribution by the spouse to a Roth IRA. (Note: The rule does not specify that the spouse's nondeductible contributions to a traditional IRA be subtracted; this created the loophole.)

For example, assume that Spouse 1 has earned income of $1,000, and Spouse 2 has no earned income. In addition, assume that their income from all sources is below the phaseout levels for deductible contributions to a traditional IRA. Spouse 1 makes a $1,000 deductible contribution to a traditional IRA. Spouse 2 can make no IRA contribution for the year, since Spouse 1's contribution exhausts the couple's combined earned income.

If, however, Spouse 1 made a $1,000 nondeductible contribution to a traditional IRA, then Spouse 2's maximum IRA contribution remained $1,000. (The combined earned income was not reduced for Spouse 1's nondeductible contribution.) Thus, using this loophole, the sum of contributions made by the couple would be $2,000, which exceeds their combined earned income.

The 2000 law changes the formula so that Spouse 2's maximum contribution is now reduced by any contribution made by Spouse 1 to a traditional IRA (deductible or nondeductible) as well as any contribution made by Spouse 1 to a Roth IRA. Thus, under the new provision, if Spouse 1 makes a $1,000 nondeductible contribution to a traditional IRA, Spouse 2 can make no IRA contribution for the year.

Since this change is retroactively effective, any married couples who used this loophole in prior years should make corrective distributions from their IRAs to eliminate the excess contributions.

Reminder: Individuals should consider making contributions to Roth IRAs, if they are eligible, before making nondeductible contributions to traditional IRAs. For qualified withdrawals, earnings from a Roth IRA will not be included in income, while earnings included in a distribution from a traditional IRA will be included in income, even if the original contribution was not deducted.

★ *Effective date.* The provision is effective for tax years beginning after December 31, 1996 (Act Sec. 316(e) of the Community Renewal Tax Relief Act of 2000; Act Sec. 1427(a) of the Small Business Job Protection Act (P.L. 104-188)).

¶ 605

Act Sec. 316(d) of the Community Renewal Tax Relief Act of 2000, redesignating former Code Sec. 219(c)(1)(B)(ii)(II) as (III) and adding new Code Sec. 219(c)(1)(B)(ii)(II); Act Sec. 316(e). Law at ¶ 5220. Committee Report at ¶ 10,335.

Withholding Exemption for Roth IRA Distributions

¶ 610

Background

Withholding requirements are imposed on designated distributions from an employer deferred compensation plan, an individual retirement plan or a commercial annuity (Code Sec. 3405(d), Code Sec. 3405(e)(1)(A)). A designated distribution does not include distributions or payments where it is reasonable to believe that the amount will not be included in gross income. Distributions or payments from individual retirement accounts (IRAs) are treated as includible in gross income and are not excepted from withholding (Code Sec. 3405(e)(1)(B)).

Technical Corrections Impact

Roth IRAs excepted from withholding.—A technical correction clarifies that due to their tax-free nature, distributions from Roth IRAs are not treated as designated distributions for withholding purposes. Thus, payments or distributions from Roth IRAs are excepted from the withholding requirements imposed on regular IRAs (Code Sec. 3405(e)(1)(B), as amended by the Community Renewal Tax Relief Act of 2000 (P.L. 106-554)).

★ *Effective date.* The provision applies to tax years beginning after December 31, 1997 (Act Sec. 314(g) of the Community Renewal Tax Relief Act of 2000; Act Sec. 302(f) of the Taxpayer Relief Act of 1997 (P.L. 105-34)).

Act Sec. 314(b) of the Community Renewal Tax Relief Act of 2000, amending Code Sec. 3405(e)(1)(B); Act Sec. 314(g). Law at ¶ 5910. Committee Report at ¶ 10,325.

MEDICAL SAVINGS ACCOUNTS

Two-Year Extension and Name Redesignation

¶ 615

Background

Since 1997, employees of small businesses and self-employed individuals may establish medical savings accounts (MSAs) to pay for medical expenses, a concept similar to establishing an individual retirement account for retirement purposes (Code Sec. 220). Contributions to an MSA are deductible in determining adjusted gross income (Code Sec. 220(a)) and are excludable from gross income and wages for employment tax purposes if made by an employer (Code Sec. 220(f)). Earnings on amounts in an MSA are not currently taxable nor are distributions made for medical expenses. Distributions not made for medical expenses are taxable and may be subject to a 15-percent excise tax unless the distribution is made after age 65, death, or disability (Code Sec. 220(f)(2) and (4)).

An MSA is a tax-exempt trust or custodial account established to pay medical expenses in conjunction with a high deductible health plan.

Background———————————————————————

Participation in an MSA is conditioned upon coverage under a high deductible health plan (Code Sec. 220(c)(2)). A high deductible health plan is a health insurance plan that has the following deductibles and out-of-pocket limitations for 2000:

(1) For individual coverage: The minimum deductible is $1,550, the maximum deductible is $2,350, and the maximum out-of-pocket limitation is $3,100.

(2) For family coverage: The minimum deductible is $3,100, the maximum deductible is $4,650, and the maximum out-of-pocket limitation is $5,700 (Rev. Proc. 99-42, I.R.B. 1999-46, 568).

There is a 750,000 cap on the number of taxpayers who may benefit annually from an MSA contribution (Code Sec. 220(j)(2)). The cap does not apply for the 2000 year since the medical savings account provisions were to expire on December 31, 2000.

End of pilot project. After December 31, 2000, no new contributions may be made to MSAs except by or on behalf of individuals who previously had MSA contributions and employees who are employed by a participating employer. An employer is a participating employer if (1) the employer made any MSA contributions for any year to an MSA on behalf of employees or (2) at least 20 percent of the employees covered under a high deductible plan made MSA contributions of at least $100 in the year 2000 (Code Sec. 220(i)(4)).

Reporting by MSA trustees. MSA reporting requirements require trustees to provide, on an annual basis, MSA information to the IRS (Code Sec. 220(j)(4)). The IRS has developed three forms for this purpose: Form 1099-MSA, Distributions from an MSA or Medicare+ Choice MSA, used to report distributions from an MSA; Form 5498-MSA, MSA or Medicare+ Choice MSA Information, used to report contributions from an MSA; and Form 8851, Summary of Medical Savings Accounts, to report the number of MSAs established. No reporting is required in 2000, due to the expiration of the provision on December 31, 2000.

———————————————————————

Community Renewal Tax Relief Act Impact

Two-year extension and name redesignation.—The medical savings account provisions are extended through 2002. Thus, the "cut-off year" is calendar year 2002, unless the Secretary determines that the numerical limitation for 2001 has been exceeded (Code Sec. 220(i)(2), as amended by the Community Renewal Tax Relief Act of 2000). In the case of a cut-off year before 2002, an individual will not be treated as an eligible individual or an active MSA participant for any month of such year, or before the cut-off date, unless the individual is covered under a high deductible health plan (Code Sec. 220(i)(3)(B), as amended by the 2000 Act). The cap on the number of MSAs that may be established for 1999 and 2001 is 750,000 (600,000 in 1998) (Code Sec. 200(j)(2), as amended by the 2000 Act). The 750,000 cap does not apply for 2000 (Code Sec. 220(j)(2)(C), as added by the 2000 Act). Also, the reporting requirements for MSAs continue throughout the two-year extension, except that no reporting is required in 2000 (Code Sec. 220(j)(4), as amended by the 2000 Act).

Comment. Although the 2000 Act extends the MSA program through 2002, it does not change current law regarding the 2000 tax year. As under prior law, there is no cap and there are no reporting requirements for 2000.

Planning Note. New contributions may be made to an MSA after 2000, both by new participants, and by or on behalf of individuals who previously had made MSA contributions, and employees who are employed by a participating employer. As under prior law, participation in an MSA is conditioned upon coverage under a high-deductible health plan. The IRS has recently announced the inflation-adjusted amounts for 2001 (Rev. Proc. 2001-13, I.R.B. 2001-3). A high deductible health plan is a health insurance plan that has the following deductibles and out-of-pocket limitations for 2001:

(1) For individual coverage: The minimum deductible is $1,600, the maximum deductible is $2,400, and the maximum out-of-pocket limitation is $3,200.

(2) For family coverage: The minimum deductible is $3,200, the maximum deductible is $4,800, and the maximum out-of-pocket limitation is $5,850.

Name redesignation. The term "medical savings accounts" has been renamed "Archer MSAs" in all Internal Revenue Code references to the term (Act Sec. 202 of the 2000 Act).

PRACTICAL ANALYSIS. Ben G. Baldwin, President of Baldwin Financial Systems, Inc., Northbrook, Ill., points out that Medical Savings Accounts (MSAs) based health insurance plans have not grown as it was expected they would when the legislation that enabled them was passed. The government mandated that 750,000 be the maximum number of taxpayers that would be allowed to participate in MSA plans. The IRS reports that fewer than 100,000 have adopted such plans. Only about one-half of the people using the high-deductible MSA qualifying health plan are putting money in the Medical Savings Account that it provides.

Some of the reasons for the lack of interest in MSA qualifying medical insurance plans are:

● The law allowing medical savings accounts is federal. Health insurance plans are regulated at the state level. Some states mandate specific benefits in health insurance plans that are in conflict with the federal plan design so that plans cannot be in compliance with both state and federal regulations. As a result MSAs are not available in all states.

● The rules for medical savings accounts and the eligible medical plan have been undergoing unsettling change. Insurance companies and employers are reluctant to enter the market because of the potential for disqualification and the continuing governmental micro-management of the plan design requirements.

● MSAs have been poorly marketed to the public because few insurance companies offer qualifying plan designs and because the sale of an MSA-based health insurance policy is a more difficult and a less rewarding sale for agents.

● Few insurance companies have designed MSA qualifying health insurance plans because the cost to design and market them, as well as to train staff to administer them can run upward of one million dollars. Insurers have not been able to price the health

insurance competitively with more traditional plan designs. Insurers fear that the huge investment that would be required would be for naught should the pilot program be canceled, or if they are unable to create a sufficiently large book of business to make the ongoing administration of such plans cost-effective. Although senior citizens also were supposed to be able to buy Medicare MSAs, Mr. Baldwin is not aware of any private insurance company that has stepped up to offer them.

● Although proponents of MSAs say that the savings accounts do encourage people to become more savvy consumers and shop around for health care, critics contend that MSAs may encourage people to hoard their MSA money and to not seek health care when necessary.

● While MSAs may work well for the healthy (few medical bills) and wealthy (able to take maximum advantage of the amount they are allowed to contribute to the Medical Savings Account), they offer little advantage to the not so healthy or so wealthy.

What will it take to get MSAs off the ground? In Mr. Baldwin's opinion, it will take state and federal cooperation and agreement on basic health insurance plan design and then agreement on what benefits are to be paid from the individually controlled Medical Savings Accounts available to all. The provincialism of the states, the hammer of the federal government and the propensity for both to micro-manage are working against the best interests of the citizenry. If it continues, MSA-based health insurance is unlikely to accomplish its objective of providing lower cost health insurance and more consumer responsibility and authority of spending for personal health care.

While the MSA concept is being allowed to continue, Mr. Baldwin points out that it also is being allowed to continue to fail as a result of political micro-management. He is gratified to see that some private health insurance companies have picked up on the MSA concept with contributions to personal medical funds that are not tax-deductible, which avoids the problems of Federal regulation. In spite of this disadvantage, such health plans build on many of the other advantages of the MSA concept.

★ *Effective date.* The provisions are effective on December 21, 2000 (Act Sec. 201(c) and Act Sec. 202 of the Community Renewal Tax Relief Act of 2000).

Act Sec. 201(a) of the Community Renewal Tax Relief Act of 2000, amending Code Sec. 220(i)(2) and Code Sec. 220(i)(3)(B); Act Sec. 201(b), amending Code Sec. 220(j)(2) and Code Sec. 220(j)(4)(A), and adding Code Sec. 220(j)(2)(C). Act Sec. 201(c). Act Sec. 202, amending Code Sec. 26(b)(2)(Q), Code Sec. 62(a)(16), Code Sec. 106(b), Code Sec. 138(b), Code Sec. 138(f), Code Sec. 220, Code Sec. 848(e)(1)(B)(iv), Code Sec. 3231(e)(10), Code Sec. 4973(a)(2), Code Sec. 4973(d), Code Sec. 4975(c)(4), Code Sec. 4975(e)(1)(D), Code Sec. 4980E(a), Code Sec. 4980E(b), Code Sec. 4980E(d), Code Sec. 6051(a)(11), and Code Sec. 6693(a)(2)(B). Law at ¶ 5230. Committee Report at ¶ 10,245.

QUALIFIED PLANS

Definition of Lump-Sum Distribution

¶ 620

Background————————————————————————————————

Distributions may be made from a Code Sec. 401(k) plan upon the termination of the plan if the employer does not establish or maintain a successor plan. However, distributions made because of the termination of the plan must be made in the form of a lump-sum payment of the participant's entire interest and must be made within one year.

The Small Business Job Protection Act of 1996 (P.L. 104-188) repealed the five-year forward averaging provisions applicable to lump-sum distributions for tax years beginning after December 31, 1999. In addition, the 1996 Act moved the definition of a lump-sum distribution for other tax purposes from Code Sec. 402(d)(4)(A) to Code Sec. 402(e)(4)(D). However, the language of the provision retained after the 1996 Act did not include a sentence, which had been in the provision prior to the 1996 Act, concerning distributions from annuity contracts. Code Sec. 401(k)(10)(B) allows special tax treatment for lump-sum distributions upon the termination of a plan and contains a reference to the incomplete post-1996 definition of lump-sum distributions.

Technical Corrections Impact

Definition of lump-sum distribution includes annuity contracts.—A technical correction amends the definition of a lump-sum distribution for purposes of Code Sec. 401(k)(10) to include a distribution of an annuity contract from a qualified trust or an annuity plan (Code Sec. 401(k)(10)(B)(ii), as amended by the Community Renewal Tax Relief Act of 2000).

★ *Effective date.* The provision is effective for tax years beginning after December 31, 1999 (Act Sec. 316(e) of the Community Renewal Tax Relief Act of 2000; Act Sec. 1401 of the Small Business Job Protection Act of 1996 (P.L. 104-188)).

Act Sec. 316(c) of the Community Renewal Tax Relief Act of 2000, amending Code Sec. 401(k)(10)(B); Act Sec. 316(e). Law at ¶ 5280. Committee Report at ¶ 10,335.

Transportation Benefits Treated as Compensation

¶ 625

Background————————————————————————————————

Under Code Sec. 132(f), certain employer-provided qualified transportation fringe benefits are excluded from income up to an inflation-adjusted maximum. The amounts so provided are not included in an employee's income merely because an employer offers a choice between one or more qualified transportation fringe benefits, such as employer-provided parking and cash. The amount of cash offered is includible in income *only* if accepted by the employee. Qualified transportation fringe benefits may be provided to employees in lieu of salary under a salary reduction agreement.

Background

Salary reduction amounts are taken into account when determining compensation for purposes of the qualified plan rules. Annual limitations apply to the allowable amount of contributions that can be made to qualified plans (Code Sec. 415(c)(1)). A participant's compensation for purposes of determining whether the limitation is met includes taxable compensation and certain salary reduction contributions (Code Sec. 415(c)(3)). Salary reduction contributions include those contributions made under a qualified cash or deferred arrangement (401(k) plan), a tax-sheltered annuity (Code Sec. 403(b) annuity), a SIMPLE plan (Code Sec. 408(p)), certain deferred compensation plans for state and local government employees and employees of tax-exempt organizations (a Code Sec. 457 plan) or a cafeteria plan (Code Sec. 125) (Code Sec. 415(c)(3)(D)). Annual contributions to a tax-sheltered annuity are also limited in amount and may not exceed an exclusion allowance (Code Sec. 403(b)). The definition of includible compensation used to determine the exclusion corresponds to the Code Sec. 415 limitation rules and includes these salary reduction contributions (Code Sec. 403(b)(3)). The nondiscrimination rules under Code Sec. 410 through Code Sec. 417 generally define compensation in the same manner as the Code Sec. 415 limitation rules (Code Sec. 414(s)(1)). However, for purposes of nondiscrimination testing, an employer may elect not to include as compensation, salary reduction contributions made under a Code Sec. 401(k) plan, a tax-sheltered annuity or a cafeteria plan (Code Sec. 414(s)(2)).

Technical Corrections Impact

Qualified transportation fringe benefits.—A technical correction clarifies that salary reduction amounts used for qualified transportation fringe benefits are treated like other salary reduction amounts when determining compensation under the qualified plan rules. The definition of a participant's compensation, for purposes of determining the contribution limitation that applies to qualified plans, is expanded to take into account amounts that are not includible in gross income under a salary reduction agreement used for qualified transportation fringe benefits (Code Sec. 415(c)(3)(D)(ii), as amended by the Community Renewal Tax Relief Act of 2000 (P.L. 106-554)). Similarly, under the Code Sec. 403(b) tax-sheltered annuity rules, compensation includes elective contributions and deferrals that are not included in an employee's gross income under a salary reduction agreement used for qualified transportation fringe benefits (Code Sec. 403(b)(3)(B), as amended by the 2000 Act). For purposes of the nondiscrimination testing rules in Code Sec. 410 through Code Sec. 417, an employer may elect not to treat as compensation the amounts it contributes to such a salary reduction agreement (Code Sec. 414(s)(2), as amended by the 2000 Act).

Comment. Salary reduction agreements first became available for qualified employer-provided parking under the Taxpayer Relief Act of 1997 (P.L. 105-34). The Act excepted qualified parking from the rule that prohibited offering qualified transportation fringe benefits in lieu of compensation. Salary reduction agreements became available for all qualified transportation fringe benefits when the Transportation Equity Act for the 21st Century (P.L. 105-178) entirely eliminated the prohibition. Proposed Reg. § 1.132-9 contains rules for providing qualified transportation fringe benefits through a salary reduction agreement.

★ *Effective date.* The provision applies to tax years beginning after December 31, 1997 (Act Sec. 314(g) of the Community Renewal Tax Relief Act of 2000; Act Sec. 1072(b) of the Taxpayer Relief Act of 1997 (P.L. 105-34)).

Act Sec. 314(e)(1) of the Community Renewal Tax Relief Act of 2000, amending Code Sec. 403(b)(3)(B) and Code Sec. 415(c)(3)(D)(ii); Act Sec. 314(e)(2), amending Code Sec. 414(s)(2); Act Sec. 314(g). Law at ¶ 5290, ¶ 5310, and ¶ 5320. Committee Report at ¶ 10,325.

CODE SECTIONS ADDED, AMENDED OR REPEALED

[¶ 5000] INTRODUCTION

The law as amended by the FSC Repeal and Extraterritorial Income Exclusion Act of 2000 (P.L. 106-519), the Community Renewal Tax Relief Act of 2000 (P.L. 106-554), and the Installment Tax Correction Act of 2000 (P.L. 106-573) is shown in the following paragraphs. For your convenience, the changes made by all three laws are presented in one consolidated section. Amendments made by each act are listed under their respective P.L. numbers in the amendment notes following each subsection of the Code.

[¶ 5001] CODE SEC. 1. TAX IMPOSED.

* * *

(h) MAXIMUM CAPITAL GAINS RATE.—

* * *

(8) SECTION 1202 GAIN.—For purposes of this subsection, the term "section 1202 gain" *means the excess of—*

(A) the gain which would be excluded from gross income under section 1202 but for the percentage limitation in section 1202(a), over

(B) the gain excluded from gross income under section 1202.

* * *

[CCH Explanation at ¶ 160. Committee Reports at ¶ 10,155.]

Amendment Notes

P.L. 106-554 (Community Renewal)

Act Sec. 117(b)(1) amended Code Sec. 1(h)(8) by striking "means" and all that follows and inserting new text to read as above. Prior to amendment, Code Sec. 1(h)(8) read as follows:

(8) SECTION 1202 GAIN.—For purposes of this subsection, the term "section 1202 gain" means an amount equal to the gain excluded from gross income under section 1202(a).

The above amendment applies to stock acquired after December 21, 2000.

[¶ 5010] CODE SEC. 26. LIMITATION BASED ON TAX LIABILITY; DEFINITION OF TAX LIABILITY.

* * *

(b) REGULAR TAX LIABILITY.—For purposes of this part—

* * *

(2) EXCEPTION FOR CERTAIN TAXES.—For purposes of paragraph (1), any tax imposed by any of the following provisions shall not be treated as tax imposed by this chapter:

* * *

(Q) section 220(f)(4) (relating to additional tax on *Archer MSA* distributions not used for qualified medical expenses).

* * *

[CCH Explanation at ¶ 615. Committee Reports at ¶ 10,245.]

Amendment Notes

P.L. 106-554 (Community Renewal)

Act Sec. 202(a)(1) amended Code Sec. 26(b)(2)(Q) by striking "medical savings account" each place it appears in the text and inserting "Archer MSA".

The above amendment is effective on December 21, 2000.

[¶ 5020] CODE SEC. 30A. PUERTO RICO ECONOMIC ACTIVITY CREDIT.

* * *

(f) DENIAL OF DOUBLE BENEFIT.—*Any wages or other expenses taken into account in determining the credit under this section may not be taken into account in determining the credit under section 41.*

[CCH Explanation at ¶ 255. Committee Reports at ¶ 10,310.]

Amendment Notes

P.L. 106-554 (Community Renewal)

Act Sec. 311(a)(2) amended Code Sec. 30A by redesignating subsections (f) and (g) as subsections (g) and (h), respectively, and by inserting after subsection (e) a new subsection (f) to read as above.

The above amendment is effective as if included in the provision of the Ticket to Work and Work Incentives Improvement Act of 1999 to which it relates.

(g) DEFINITIONS.—For purposes of this section, any term used in this section which is also used in section 936 shall have the same meaning given such term by section 936.

[CCH Explanation at ¶ 255. Committee Reports at ¶ 10,310.]

Amendment Notes

P.L. 106-554 (Community Renewal)
Act Sec. 311(a)(2) amended Code Sec. 30A by redesignating subsection (f) as subsection (g).
The above amendment is effective as if included in the provision of the Ticket to Work and Work Incentives
Improvement Act of 1999 (P.L. 106-170) to which it relates [effective for amounts paid or incurred after June 30, 1999.—CCH.].

(h) APPLICATION OF SECTION.—This section shall apply to taxable years beginning after December 31, 1995, and before January 1, 2006.

[CCH Explanation at ¶ 255. Committee Reports at ¶ 10,310.]

Amendment Notes

P.L. 106-554 (Community Renewal)
Act Sec. 311(a)(2) amended Code Sec. 30A by redesignating subsection (g) as subsection (h).
The above amendment is effective as if included in the provision of the Ticket to Work and Work Incentives
Improvement Act of 1999 (P.L. 106-170) to which it relates [effective for amounts paid or incurred after June 30, 1999.—CCH.].

[¶ 5030] CODE SEC. 38. GENERAL BUSINESS CREDIT.

* * *

(b) CURRENT YEAR BUSINESS CREDIT.—For purposes of this subpart, the amount of the current year business credit is the sum of the following credits determined for the taxable year:

* * *

(11) the employer social security credit determined under section 45B(a),

(12) the orphan drug credit determined under section 45C(a), *plus*

(13) the new markets tax credit determined under section 45D(a).

* * *

[CCH Explanation at ¶ 235. Committee Reports at ¶ 10,165.]

Amendment Notes

P.L. 106-554 (Community Renewal)
Act Sec. 121(b)(1) amended Code Sec. 38(b) by striking "plus" at the end of paragraph (11), by striking the period at the end of paragraph (12) and inserting ", plus", and by adding at the end a new paragraph (13) to read as above.
The above amendment applies to investments made after December 31, 2000.

[¶ 5040] CODE SEC. 39. CARRYBACK AND CARRYFORWARD OF UNUSED CREDITS.

* * *

(d) TRANSITIONAL RULES.—

* * *

(9) NO CARRYBACK OF NEW MARKETS TAX CREDIT BEFORE JANUARY 1, 2001.—*No portion of the unused business credit for any taxable year which is attributable to the credit under section 45D may be carried back to a taxable year ending before January 1, 2001.*

[CCH Explanation at ¶ 235. Committee Reports at ¶ 10,165.]

Amendment Notes

P.L. 106-554 (Community Renewal)
Act Sec. 121(b)(2) amended Code Sec. 39(d) by adding at the end a new paragraph (9) to read as above.
The above amendment applies to investments made after December 31, 2000.

[¶ 5050] CODE SEC. 42. LOW-INCOME HOUSING CREDIT.

* * *

(d) ELIGIBLE BASIS.—For purposes of this section—

* * *

(4) SPECIAL RULES RELATING TO DETERMINATION OF ADJUSTED BASIS.—For purposes of this subsection—

(A) IN GENERAL.—Except as provided in *subparagraphs (B) and (C)*, the adjusted basis of any building shall be determined without regard to the adjusted basis of any property which is not residential rental property.

(B) BASIS OF PROPERTY IN COMMON AREAS, ETC., INCLUDED.—The adjusted basis of any building shall be determined by taking into account the adjusted basis of property (of a character subject to the allowance for depreciation) used in common areas or provided as comparable amenities to all residential rental units in such building.

(C) *INCLUSION OF BASIS OF PROPERTY USED TO PROVIDE SERVICES FOR CERTAIN NONTENANTS.*—

(i) *IN GENERAL.—The adjusted basis of any building located in a qualified census tract (as defined in paragraph (5)(C)) shall be determined by taking into account the adjusted basis of property (of a character subject to the allowance for depreciation and not otherwise taken into account) used throughout the taxable year in providing any community service facility.*

(ii) *LIMITATION.—The increase in the adjusted basis of any building which is taken into account by reason of clause (i) shall not exceed 10 percent of the eligible basis of the qualified low-income housing project of which it is a part. For purposes of the preceding sentence, all community service facilities which are part of the same qualified low-income housing project shall be treated as one facility.*

(iii) *COMMUNITY SERVICE FACILITY.—For purposes of this subparagraph, the term "community service facility" means any facility designed to serve primarily individuals whose income is 60 percent or less of area median income (within the meaning of subsection (g)(1)(B)).*

(D) NO REDUCTION FOR DEPRECIATION.—The adjusted basis of any building shall be determined without regard to paragraphs (2) and (3) of section 1016(a).

(5) SPECIAL RULES FOR DETERMINING ELIGIBLE BASIS.—

* * *

(C) INCREASE IN CREDIT FOR BUILDINGS IN HIGH COST AREAS.—

* * *

(ii) QUALIFIED CENSUS TRACT.—

(I) IN GENERAL.—The term "qualified census tract" means any census tract which is designated by the Secretary of Housing and Urban Development and, for the most recent year for which census data are available on household income in such tract, *either* in which 50 percent or more of the households have an income which is less than 60 percent of the area median gross income for such year *or which has a poverty rate of at least 25 percent.* If the Secretary of Housing and Urban Development determines that sufficient data for any period are not available to apply this clause on the basis of census tracts, such Secretary shall apply this clause for such period on the basis of enumeration districts.

* * *

[CCH Explanation at ¶ 240. Committee Reports at ¶ 10,190 and ¶ 10,195.]

Amendment Notes

P.L. 106-554 (Community Renewal)

Act Sec. 134(a)(1)-(3) amended Code Sec. 42(d)(4) by striking "subparagraph (B)" in subparagraph (A) and inserting "subparagraphs (B) and (C)", by redesignating subparagraph (C) as subparagraph (D), and by inserting after subparagraph (B) a new subparagraph (C) to read as above.

Act Sec. 135(b)(1)-(2) amended the first sentence of Code Sec. 42(d)(5)(C)(ii)(I) by inserting "either" before "in which 50 percent", and by inserting before the period "or which has a poverty rate of at least 25 percent".

For the effective date of the above amendments, see Act Sec. 137, below.

Act Sec. 137 provides:

Except as otherwise provided in this subtitle, the amendments made by this subtitle shall apply to—

(1) housing credit dollar amounts allocated after December 31, 2000; and

(2) buildings placed in service after such date to the extent paragraph (1) of section 42(h) of the Internal Revenue Code of 1986 does not apply to any building by reason of paragraph (4) thereof, but only with respect to bonds issued after such date.

(h) LIMITATION ON AGGREGATE CREDIT ALLOWABLE WITH RESPECT TO PROJECTS LOCATED IN A STATE.—

(1) CREDIT MAY NOT EXCEED CREDIT AMOUNT ALLOCATED TO BUILDING.—

* * *

(E) EXCEPTION WHERE 10 PERCENT OF COST INCURRED.—

* * *

(ii) QUALIFIED BUILDING.—For purposes of clause (i), the term "qualified building" means any building which is part of a project if the taxpayer's basis in such project *(as of* the later of the date which is 6 months after the date that the allocation was made or the close of the calendar year in which the allocation is made) is more than 10 percent of the taxpayer's reasonably expected basis in such project (as of the close of the second calendar year referred to in clause (i)). Such term does not include any existing building unless a credit is allowable under subsection (e) for rehabilitation expenditures paid or incurred by the taxpayer with respect to such building for a taxable year ending during the second calendar year referred to in clause (i) or the prior taxable year.

* * *

(3) HOUSING CREDIT DOLLAR AMOUNT FOR AGENCIES.—

* * *

(C) STATE HOUSING CREDIT CEILING.—The State housing credit ceiling applicable to any State for any calendar year shall be an amount equal to the sum of—

(i) the unused State housing credit ceiling (if any) of such State for the preceding calendar year,

(ii) the greater of—

(I) $1.75 ($1.50 for 2001) multiplied by the State population, or

(II) $2,000,000,

(iii) the amount of State housing credit ceiling returned in the calendar year, plus

(iv) the amount (if any) allocated under subparagraph (D) to such State by the Secretary.

For purposes of clause (i), the unused State housing credit ceiling for any calendar year is the excess (if any) of the sum of the amounts described in clauses (i)[(ii)] through (iv) over the aggregate housing credit dollar amount allocated for such year. For purposes of clause (iii), the amount of State housing credit ceiling returned in the calendar year equals the housing credit dollar amount previously allocated within the State to any project which fails to meet the 10 percent test under paragraph (1)(E)(ii) on a date after the close of the calendar year in which the allocation was made or which does not become a qualified low-income housing project within the period required by this section or the terms of the allocation or to any project with respect to which an allocation is cancelled by mutual consent of the housing credit agency and the allocation recipient.

(D) UNUSED HOUSING CREDIT CARRYOVERS ALLOCATED AMONG CERTAIN STATES.—

* * *

(ii) UNUSED HOUSING CREDIT CARRYOVER.—For purposes of this subparagraph, the unused housing credit carryover of a State for any calendar year is the excess (if any) of the unused State housing credit ceiling for such year (as defined in subparagraph (C)(i)) over the excess (if any) of—

(I) the unused State housing credit ceiling for the year preceding such year, over

(II) the aggregate housing credit dollar amount allocated for such year.

* * *

(H) COST-OF-LIVING ADJUSTMENT.—

(i) IN GENERAL.—In the case of a calendar year after 2002, the $2,000,000 and $1.75 amounts in subparagraph (C) shall each be increased by an amount equal to—

(I) such dollar amount, multiplied by

(II) the cost-of-living adjustment determined under section 1(f)(3) for such calendar year by substituting "calendar year 2001" for "calendar year 1992" in subparagraph (B) thereof.

(ii) ROUNDING.—

(I) In the case of the $2,000,000 amount, any increase under clause (i) which is not a multiple of $5,000 shall be rounded to the next lowest multiple of $5,000.

(II) In the case of the $1.75 amount, any increase under clause (i) which is not a multiple of 5 cents shall be rounded to the next lowest multiple of 5 cents.

* * *

[CCH Explanation at ¶ 240. Committee Reports at ¶ 10,175, ¶ 10,195 and ¶ 10,200.]

¶ 5050   Code Sec. 42(h)

Amendment Notes
P.L. 106-554 (Community Renewal)

Act Sec. 131(a) amended Code Sec. 42(h)(3)(C)(i)-(ii) to read as above. Prior to amendment, Code Sec. 42(h)(3)(C)(i)-(ii) read as follows:

(i) $1.25 multiplied by the State population,

(ii) the unused State housing credit ceiling (if any) of such State for the preceding calendar year,

Act Sec. 131(b) amended Code Sec. 42(h)(3) by adding at the end a new subparagraph (H) to read as above.

Act Sec. 131(c)(1)(A)-(B) amended Code Sec. 42(h)(3)(C) (as amended by Act Sec. 131(a)) by striking "clause (ii)" in the matter following clause (iv) and inserting "clause (i)", and by striking "clauses (i)" in the matter following clause (iv) and inserting "clauses (ii)".

Act Sec. 131(c)(2)(A)-(B) amended Code Sec. 42(h)(3)(D)(ii) by striking "subparagraph (C)(ii)" and inserting "subparagraph (C)(i)", and by striking "clauses (i)" in subclause (II) and inserting "clauses (ii)".

The above amendments apply to calendar years after 2000.

Act Sec. 135(a)(1) amended the first sentence of Code Sec. 42(h)(1)(E)(ii) by striking "(as of" the first place it appears and inserting "(as of the later of the date which is 6 months after the date that the allocation was made or".

Act Sec. 135(a)(2) amended the last sentence of Code Sec. 42(h)(3)(C) by striking "project which" and inserting "project which fails to meet the 10 percent test under paragraph (1)(E)(ii) on a date after the close of the calendar year in which the allocation was made or which".

Act Sec. 136(a) amended Code Sec. 42(h)(3)(D)(ii) by striking "the excess" and all that follows and inserting new text to read as above. Prior to amendment, Code Sec. 42(h)(3)(D)(ii) read as follows:

(ii) UNUSED HOUSING CREDIT CARRYOVER.—For purposes of this subparagraph, the unused housing credit carryover of a State for any calendar year is the excess (if any) of the unused State housing credit ceiling for such year (as defined in subparagraph (C)(i)) over the excess (if any) of—

(I) the aggregate housing credit dollar amount allocated for such year, over

(II) the sum of the amounts described in clauses (ii) and (iii) of subparagraph (C).

Act Sec. 136(b) amended the second sentence of Code Sec. 42(h)(3)(C) by striking "clauses (i)[(ii)] and (iii)" and inserting "clauses (i)[(ii)] through (iv)".

For the effective date of the above amendments, see Act Sec. 137, below.

Act Sec. 137 provides:

Except as otherwise provided in this subtitle, the amendments made by this subtitle shall apply to—

(1) housing credit dollar amounts allocated after December 31, 2000; and

(2) buildings placed in service after such date to the extent paragraph (1) of section 42(h) of the Internal Revenue Code of 1986 does not apply to any building by reason of paragraph (4) thereof, but only with respect to bonds issued after such date.

(i) DEFINITIONS AND SPECIAL RULES.—For purposes of this section—

* * *

(2) DETERMINATION OF WHETHER BUILDING IS FEDERALLY SUBSIDIZED.—

* * *

(E) BUILDINGS RECEIVING HOME ASSISTANCE *OR NATIVE AMERICAN HOUSING ASSISTANCE.*—

(i) IN GENERAL.—Assistance provided under the HOME Investment Partnerships Act (as in effect on the date of the enactment of this subparagraph) *or the Native American Housing Assistance and Self-Determination Act of 1996 (25 U.S.C. 4101 et seq.) (as in effect on October 1, 1997)* with respect to any building shall not be taken into account under subparagraph (D) if 40 percent or more of the residential units in the building are occupied by individuals whose income is 50 percent or less of area median gross income. Subsection (d)(5)(C) shall not apply to any building to which the preceding sentence applies.

* * *

[CCH Explanation at ¶ 240. Committee Reports at ¶ 10,190.]

Amendment Notes
P.L. 106-554 (Community Renewal)

Act Sec. 134(b)(1) amended Code Sec. 42(i)(2)(E)(i) by inserting "or the Native American Housing Assistance and Self-Determination Act of 1996) (25 U.S.C. 4101 et seq.) (as in effect on October 1, 1997)" after "this subparagraph)".

Act Sec. 134(b)(2) amended Code Sec. 42(i)(2)(E) by inserting "OR NATIVE AMERICAN HOUSING ASSISTANCE" after "HOME ASSISTANCE" in the subparagraph heading.

For the effective date of the above amendments, see Act Sec. 137, below.

Act Sec. 137 provides:

Except as otherwise provided in this subtitle, the amendments made by this subtitle shall apply to—

(1) housing credit dollar amounts allocated after December 31, 2000; and

(2) buildings placed in service after such date to the extent paragraph (1) of section 42(h) of the Internal Revenue Code of 1986 does not apply to any building by reason of paragraph (4) thereof, but only with respect to bonds issued after such date.

(m) RESPONSIBILITIES OF HOUSING CREDIT AGENCIES.—

(1) PLANS FOR ALLOCATION OF CREDIT AMONG PROJECTS.—

(A) IN GENERAL.—Notwithstanding any other provision of this section, the housing credit dollar amount with respect to any building shall be zero unless—

(i) such amount was allocated pursuant to a qualified allocation plan of the housing credit agency which is approved by the governmental unit (in accordance with rules similar to the rules of section 147(f)(2) (other than subparagraph (B)(ii) thereof)) of which such agency is a part,

Code Sec. 42(m)   ¶ 5050

(ii) such agency notifies the chief executive officer (or the equivalent) of the local jurisdiction within which the building is located of such project and provides such individual a reasonable opportunity to comment on the project,

(iii) a comprehensive market study of the housing needs of low-income individuals in the area to be served by the project is conducted before the credit allocation is made and at the developer's expense by a disinterested party who is approved by such agency, and

(iv) a written explanation is available to the general public for any allocation of a housing credit dollar amount which is not made in accordance with established priorities and selection criteria of the housing credit agency.

(B) QUALIFIED ALLOCATION PLAN.—For purposes of this paragraph, the term "qualified allocation plan" means any plan—

(i) which sets forth selection criteria to be used to determine housing priorities of the housing credit agency which are appropriate to local conditions,

(ii) which also gives preference in allocating housing credit dollar amounts among selected projects to—

(I) projects serving the lowest income tenants,

(II) projects obligated to serve qualified tenants for the longest periods, *and*

(III) projects which are located in qualified census tracts (as defined in subsection (d)(5)(C)) and the development of which contributes to a concerted community revitalization plan,

(iii) which provides a procedure that the agency (or an agent or other private contractor of such agency) will follow in monitoring for noncompliance with the provisions of this section and in notifying the Internal Revenue Service of such noncompliance which such agency becomes aware of *and in monitoring for noncompliance with habitability standards through regular site visits.*

(C) CERTAIN SELECTION CRITERIA MUST BE USED.—The selection criteria set forth in a qualified allocation plan must include—

(i) project location,

(ii) housing needs characteristics,

(iii) project characteristics, *including whether the project includes the use of existing housing as part of a community revitalization plan,*

(iv) sponsor characteristics,

(v) tenant populations with special housing needs,

(vi) public housing waiting lists,

(vii) tenant populations of individuals with children, and

(viii) projects intended for eventual tenant ownership.

* * *

[CCH Explanation at ¶ 240. Committee Reports at ¶ 10,180 and ¶ 10,185.]

Amendment Notes

P.L. 106-554 (Community Renewal)

Act Sec. 132(a)(1)-(2) amended Code Sec. 42(m)(1)(C) by inserting ", including whether the project includes the use of existing housing as part of a community revitalization plan" before the comma at the end of clause (iii), and by striking clauses (v), (vi), and (vii) and inserting new clauses (v)-(viii) to read as above. Prior to amendment, Code Sec. 42(m)(1)(C)(v)-(vii) read as follows:

(v) participation of local tax-exempt organizations,

(vi) tenant populations with special housing needs, and

(vii) public housing waiting lists.

Act Sec. 132(b) amended Code Sec. 42(m)(1)(B)(ii) by striking "and" at the end of subclause (I), by adding "and" at the end of subclause (II), and by inserting after subclause (II) a new subclause (III) to read as above.

Act Sec. 133(a) amended Code Sec. 42(m)(1)(A) by striking "and" at the end of clause (i), by striking the period at the end of clause (ii) and inserting a comma, and by adding at the end new clauses (iii) and (iv) to read as above.

Act Sec. 133(b) amended Code Sec. 42(m)(1)(B)(iii) by inserting before the period "and in monitoring for noncompliance with habitability standards through regular site visits".

For the effective date of the above amendments, see Act Sec. 137, below.

Act Sec. 137 provides:

Except as otherwise provided in this subtitle, the amendments made by this subtitle shall apply to—

(1) housing credit dollar amounts allocated after December 31, 2000; and

(2) buildings placed in service after such date to the extent paragraph (1) of section 42(h) of the Internal Revenue Code of 1986 does not apply to any building by reason of paragraph (4) thereof, but only with respect to bonds issued after such date.

¶ 5050   Code Sec. 42(m)

[¶ 5060] CODE SEC. 43. ENHANCED OIL RECOVERY CREDIT.

* * *

(c) QUALIFIED ENHANCED OIL RECOVERY COSTS.—For purposes of this section—

(1) IN GENERAL.—The term "qualified enhanced oil recovery costs" means any of the following:

* * *

(C) Any qualified tertiary injectant expenses *(as defined in section 193(b))* which are paid or incurred in connection with a qualified enhanced oil recovery project and for which a deduction is allowable for the taxable year.

* * *

[CCH Explanation at ¶ 250. Committee Reports at ¶ 10,340.]

Amendment Notes

P.L. 106-554 (Community Renewal)
Act Sec. 317(a)(1)-(2) amended Code Sec. 43(c)(1)(C) by inserting "(as defined in section 193(b))" after "expenses", and by striking "under section 193" following "is allowable".

The above amendment is effective as if included in section 11511 of the Revenue Reconciliation Act of 1990 (P.L. 101-508) [effective for costs paid or incurred in tax years beginning after December 31, 1990.—CCH.].

[¶ 5070] CODE SEC. 45. ELECTRICITY PRODUCED FROM CERTAIN RENEWABLE RESOURCES.

* * *

(d) DEFINITIONS AND SPECIAL RULES.—For purposes of this section—

* * *

(7) CREDIT NOT TO APPLY TO ELECTRICITY SOLD TO UTILITIES UNDER CERTAIN CONTRACTS.—

(A) IN GENERAL.—The credit determined under subsection (a) shall not apply to electricity—

(i) produced at a qualified facility described in *subsection (c)(3)(A)* which is placed in service by the taxpayer after June 30, 1999, and

(ii) sold to a utility pursuant to a contract originally entered into before January 1, 1987 (whether or not amended or restated after that date).

* * *

[CCH Explanation at ¶ 30,050.]

Amendment Notes

P.L. 106-554 (Community Renewal)
Act Sec. 319(1) amended Code Sec. 45(d)(7)(A)(i) by striking "paragraph (3)(A)" and inserting "subsection (c)(3)(A)".

The above amendment is effective on December 21, 2000.

[¶ 5080] CODE *SEC. 45D. NEW MARKETS TAX CREDIT.*

(a) ALLOWANCE OF CREDIT.—

(1) IN GENERAL.—For purposes of section 38, in the case of a taxpayer who holds a qualified equity investment on a credit allowance date of such investment which occurs during the taxable year, the new markets tax credit determined under this section for such taxable year is an amount equal to the applicable percentage of the amount paid to the qualified community development entity for such investment at its original issue.

(2) APPLICABLE PERCENTAGE.—For purposes of paragraph (1), the applicable percentage is—

(A) 5 percent with respect to the first 3 credit allowance dates, and

(B) 6 percent with respect to the remainder of the credit allowance dates.

(3) CREDIT ALLOWANCE DATE.—For purposes of paragraph (1), the term "credit allowance date" means, with respect to any qualified equity investment—

(A) the date on which such investment is initially made, and

(B) each of the 6 anniversary dates of such date thereafter.

(b) QUALIFIED EQUITY INVESTMENT.—For purposes of this section—

(1) IN GENERAL.—The term "qualified equity investment" means any equity investment in a qualified community development entity if—

(A) such investment is acquired by the taxpayer at its original issue (directly or through an underwriter) solely in exchange for cash,

(B) substantially all of such cash is used by the qualified community development entity to make qualified low-income community investments, and

(C) such investment is designated for purposes of this section by the qualified community development entity.

Such term shall not include any equity investment issued by a qualified community development entity more than 5 years after the date that such entity receives an allocation under subsection (f). Any allocation not used within such 5-year period may be reallocated by the Secretary under subsection (f).

(2) LIMITATION.—The maximum amount of equity investments issued by a qualified community development entity which may be designated under paragraph (1)(C) by such entity shall not exceed the portion of the limitation amount allocated under subsection (f) to such entity.

(3) SAFE HARBOR FOR DETERMINING USE OF CASH.—The requirement of paragraph (1)(B) shall be treated as met if at least 85 percent of the aggregate gross assets of the qualified community development entity are invested in qualified low-income community investments.

(4) TREATMENT OF SUBSEQUENT PURCHASERS.—The term "qualified equity investment" includes any equity investment which would (but for paragraph (1)(A)) be a qualified equity investment in the hands of the taxpayer if such investment was a qualified equity investment in the hands of a prior holder.

(5) REDEMPTIONS.—A rule similar to the rule of section 1202(c)(3) shall apply for purposes of this subsection.

(6) EQUITY INVESTMENT.—The term "equity investment" means—

(A) any stock (other than nonqualified preferred stock as defined in section 351(g)(2)) in an entity which is a corporation, and

(B) any capital interest in an entity which is a partnership.

(c) QUALIFIED COMMUNITY DEVELOPMENT ENTITY.—For purposes of this section—

(1) IN GENERAL.—The term "qualified community development entity" means any domestic corporation or partnership if—

(A) the primary mission of the entity is serving, or providing investment capital for, low-income communities or low-income persons,

(B) the entity maintains accountability to residents of low-income communities through their representation on any governing board of the entity or on any advisory board to the entity, and

(C) the entity is certified by the Secretary for purposes of this section as being a qualified community development entity.

(2) SPECIAL RULES FOR CERTAIN ORGANIZATIONS.—The requirements of paragraph (1) shall be treated as met by—

(A) any specialized small business investment company (as defined in section 1044(c)(3)), and

(B) any community development financial institution (as defined in section 103 of the Community Development Banking and Financial Institutions Act of 1994 (12 U.S.C. 4702)).

(d) QUALIFIED LOW-INCOME COMMUNITY INVESTMENTS.—For purposes of this section—

(1) IN GENERAL.—The term "qualified low-income community investment" means—

(A) any capital or equity investment in, or loan to, any qualified active low-income community business,

(B) the purchase from another community development entity of any loan made by such entity which is a qualified low-income community investment,

(C) financial counseling and other services specified in regulations prescribed by the Secretary to businesses located in, and residents of, low-income communities, and

(D) any equity investment in, or loan to, any qualified community development entity.

(2) QUALIFIED ACTIVE LOW-INCOME COMMUNITY BUSINESS.—

(A) IN GENERAL.—For purposes of paragraph (1), the term "qualified active low-income community business" means, with respect to any taxable year, any corporation (including a nonprofit corporation) or partnership if for such year—

(i) at least 50 percent of the total gross income of such entity is derived from the active conduct of a qualified business within any low-income community,

(ii) a substantial portion of the use of the tangible property of such entity (whether owned or leased) is within any low-income community,

(iii) a substantial portion of the services performed for such entity by its employees are performed in any low-income community,

(iv) less than 5 percent of the average of the aggregate unadjusted bases of the property of such entity is attributable to collectibles (as defined in section 408(m)(2)) other than collectibles that are held primarily for sale to customers in the ordinary course of such business, and

(v) less than 5 percent of the average of the aggregate unadjusted bases of the property of such entity is attributable to nonqualified financial property (as defined in section 1397C(e)).

(B) PROPRIETORSHIP.—Such term shall include any business carried on by an individual as a proprietor if such business would meet the requirements of subparagraph (A) were it incorporated.

(C) PORTIONS OF BUSINESS MAY BE QUALIFIED ACTIVE LOW-INCOME COMMUNITY BUSINESS.—The term "qualified active low-income community business" includes any trades or businesses which would qualify as a qualified active low-income community business if such trades or businesses were separately incorporated.

(3) QUALIFIED BUSINESS.—For purposes of this subsection, the term "qualified business" has the meaning given to such term by section 1397C(d); except that—

(A) in lieu of applying paragraph (2)(B) thereof, the rental to others of real property located in any low-income community shall be treated as a qualified business if there are substantial improvements located on such property, and

(B) paragraph (3) thereof shall not apply.

(e) LOW-INCOME COMMUNITY.—For purposes of this section—

(1) IN GENERAL.—The term "low-income community" means any population census tract if—

(A) the poverty rate for such tract is at least 20 percent, or

(B)(i) in the case of a tract not located within a metropolitan area, the median family income for such tract does not exceed 80 percent of statewide median family income, or

(ii) in the case of a tract located within a metropolitan area, the median family income for such tract does not exceed 80 percent of the greater of statewide median family income or the metropolitan area median family income.

Subparagraph (B) shall be applied using possessionwide median family income in the case of census tracts located within a possession of the United States.

(2) TARGETED AREAS.—The Secretary may designate any area within any census tract as a low-income community if—

(A) the boundary of such area is continuous,

(B) the area would satisfy the requirements of paragraph (1) if it were a census tract, and

(C) an inadequate access to investment capital exists in such area.

(3) AREAS NOT WITHIN CENSUS TRACTS.—In the case of an area which is not tracted for population census tracts, the equivalent county divisions (as defined by the Bureau of the Census for purposes of defining poverty areas) shall be used for purposes of determining poverty rates and median family income.

(f) NATIONAL LIMITATION ON AMOUNT OF INVESTMENTS DESIGNATED.—

(1) IN GENERAL.—There is a new markets tax credit limitation for each calendar year. Such limitation is—

(A) $1,000,000,000 for 2001,

(B) $1,500,000,000 for 2002 and 2003,

(C) $2,000,000,000 for 2004 and 2005, and

(D) $3,500,000,000 for 2006 and 2007.

(2) ALLOCATION OF LIMITATION.—The limitation under paragraph (1) shall be allocated by the Secretary among qualified community development entities selected by the Secretary. In making allocations under the preceding sentence, the Secretary shall give priority to any entity—

(A) with a record of having successfully provided capital or technical assistance to disadvantaged businesses or communities, or

(B) which intends to satisfy the requirement under subsection (b)(1)(B) by making qualified low-income community investments in 1 or more businesses in which persons unrelated to such entity (within the meaning of section 267(b) or 707(b)(1)) hold the majority equity interest.

(3) CARRYOVER OF UNUSED LIMITATION.—If the new markets tax credit limitation for any calendar year exceeds the aggregate amount allocated under paragraph (2) for such year, such limitation for the succeeding calendar year shall be increased by the amount of such excess. No amount may be carried under the preceding sentence to any calendar year after 2014.

(g) RECAPTURE OF CREDIT IN CERTAIN CASES.—

(1) IN GENERAL.—If, at any time during the 7-year period beginning on the date of the original issue of a qualified equity investment in a qualified community development entity, there is a recapture event with respect to such investment, then the tax imposed by this chapter for the taxable year in which such event occurs shall be increased by the credit recapture amount.

(2) CREDIT RECAPTURE AMOUNT.—For purposes of paragraph (1), the credit recapture amount is an amount equal to the sum of—

(A) the aggregate decrease in the credits allowed to the taxpayer under section 38 for all prior taxable years which would have resulted if no credit had been determined under this section with respect to such investment, plus

(B) interest at the underpayment rate established under section 6621 on the amount determined under subparagraph (A) for each prior taxable year for the period beginning on the due date for filing the return for the prior taxable year involved.

No deduction shall be allowed under this chapter for interest described in subparagraph (B).

(3) RECAPTURE EVENT.—For purposes of paragraph (1), there is a recapture event with respect to an equity investment in a qualified community development entity if—

(A) such entity ceases to be a qualified community development entity,

(B) the proceeds of the investment cease to be used as required of subsection (b)(1)(B), or

(C) such investment is redeemed by such entity.

(4) SPECIAL RULES.—

(A) TAX BENEFIT RULE.—The tax for the taxable year shall be increased under paragraph (1) only with respect to credits allowed by reason of this section which were used to reduce tax liability. In the case of credits not so used to reduce tax liability, the carryforwards and carrybacks under section 39 shall be appropriately adjusted.

(B) NO CREDITS AGAINST TAX.—Any increase in tax under this subsection shall not be treated as a tax imposed by this chapter for purposes of determining the amount of any credit under this chapter or for purposes of section 55.

(h) BASIS REDUCTION.—The basis of any qualified equity investment shall be reduced by the amount of any credit determined under this section with respect to such investment. This subsection shall not apply for purposes of sections 1202, 1400B, and 1400F.

(i) REGULATIONS.—The Secretary shall prescribe such regulations as may be appropriate to carry out this section, including regulations—

(1) which limit the credit for investments which are directly or indirectly subsidized by other Federal tax benefits (including the credit under section 42 and the exclusion from gross income under section 103),

(2) which prevent the abuse of the purposes of this section,

(3) which provide rules for determining whether the requirement of subsection (b)(1)(B) is treated as met,

(4) which impose appropriate reporting requirements, and

(5) which apply the provisions of this section to newly formed entities.

¶ 5080   Code Sec. 45D(g)

[CCH Explanation at ¶ 235. Committee Reports at ¶ 10,165.]

Amendment Notes
P.L. 106-554 (Community Renewal)
Act Sec. 121(a) amended subpart D of part IV of subchapter A of chapter 1 by adding at the end a new Code Sec. 45D to read as above.

The above amendment applies to investments made after December 31, 2000.

[¶ 5090] CODE SEC. 51. AMOUNT OF CREDIT.

* * *

(d) MEMBERS OF TARGETED GROUPS.—For purposes of this subpart—

* * *

(2) QUALIFIED IV-A RECIPIENT.—

* * *

(B) IV-A PROGRAM.—For purposes of this paragraph, the term "IV-A program" means any program providing assistance under a State *program funded* under part A of title IV of the Social Security Act and any successor of such program.

* * *

(5) HIGH-RISK YOUTH.—

(A) IN GENERAL.—The term "high-risk youth" means any individual who is certified by the designated local agency—

(i) as having attained age 18 but not age 25 on the hiring date, and

(ii) as having his principal place of abode within an *empowerment zone, enterprise community, or renewal community.*

(B) YOUTH MUST CONTINUE TO RESIDE IN ZONE *OR COMMUNITY*.—In the case of a high-risk youth, the term "qualified wages" shall not include wages paid or incurred for services performed while such youth's principal place of abode is outside an *empowerment zone, enterprise community, or renewal community.*

* * *

(7) QUALIFIED SUMMER YOUTH EMPLOYEE.—

(A) IN GENERAL.—The term "qualified summer youth employee" means any individual—

(i) who performs services for the employer between May 1 and September 15,

(ii) who is certified by the designated local agency as having attained age 16 but not 18 on the hiring date (or if later, on May 1 of the calendar year involved),

(iii) who has not been an employee of the employer during any period prior to the 90-day period described in subparagraph (B)(i), and

(iv) who is certified by the designated local agency as having his principal place of abode within an *empowerment zone, enterprise community, or renewal community.*

* * *

(C) YOUTH MUST CONTINUE TO RESIDE IN ZONE *OR COMMUNITY*.—Paragraph (5)(B) shall apply for purposes of subparagraph (A)(iv).

* * *

[CCH Explanation at ¶ 125 and ¶ 245. Committee Reports at ¶ 10,141 and ¶ 10,335.]

Amendment Notes
P.L. 106-554 (Community Renewal)
Act Sec. 102(a) amended Code Sec. 51(d)(5)(A)(ii) and (B) by striking "empowerment zone or enterprise community" and inserting "empowerment zone, enterprise community, or renewal community".
Act Sec. 102(b) amended Code Sec. 51(d)(7)(A)(iv) by striking "empowerment zone or enterprise community" and inserting "empowerment zone, enterprise community, or renewal community".
Act Sec. 102(c) amended Code Sec. 51(d)(5)(B) and (7)(C) by inserting "OR COMMUNITY" in the heading after "ZONE".

The above amendments apply to individuals who begin work for the employer after December 31, 2001.

Act Sec. 316(a)(1)-(2) amended Code Sec. 51(d)(2)(B) by striking "plan approved" and inserting "program funded", and by striking "(relating to assistance for needy families with minor children)" following "Social Security Act".

The above amendment is effective as if included in the provision of the Small Business Job Protection Act of 1996 (P.L. 104-188) to which it relates [effective for individuals who begin work for the employer after September 30, 1996.—CCH.].

[¶ 5100] CODE SEC. 56. ADJUSTMENTS IN COMPUTING ALTERNATIVE MINIMUM TAXABLE INCOME.

(a) ADJUSTMENTS APPLICABLE TO ALL TAXPAYERS.—In determining the amount of the .alternative minimum taxable income for any taxable year the following treatment shall apply (in lieu of the treatment applicable for purposes of computing the regular tax):

(1) DEPRECIATION.—

(A) IN GENERAL.—

* * *

(ii) 150-PERCENT DECLINING BALANCE METHOD FOR CERTAIN PROPERTY.—The method of depreciation used shall be—

(I) the 150 percent declining balance method,

(II) switching to the straight line method for the 1st taxable year for which using the straight line method with respect to the adjusted basis as of the beginning of the year will yield a higher allowance.

The preceding sentence shall not apply to any section 1250 property (as defined in section 1250(c)) *(and the straight line method shall be used for such 1250 property)* or to any other property if the depreciation deduction determined under section 168 with respect to such other property for purposes of the regular tax is determined by using the straight line method.

* * *

[CCH Explanation at ¶ 215. Committee Reports at ¶ 10,325.]

Amendment Notes

P.L. 106-554 (Community Renewal)

Act Sec. 314(d) amended Code Sec. 56(a)(1)(A) by inserting before "or to any other property" in the flush sentence at the end of clause (ii) the following: "(and the straight line method shall be used for such 1250 property)".

The above amendment is effective as if included in the provision of the Taxpayer Relief Act of 1997 (P.L. 105-34) to which it relates [effective August 5, 1997.—CCH.].

(g) ADJUSTMENTS BASED ON ADJUSTED CURRENT EARNINGS.—

* * *

(4) ADJUSTMENTS.—In determining adjusted current earnings, the following adjustments shall apply:

* * *

(B) INCLUSION OF ITEMS INCLUDED FOR PURPOSES OF COMPUTING EARNINGS AND PROFITS.—

(i) IN GENERAL.—In the case of any amount which is excluded from gross income for purposes of computing alternative minimum taxable income but is taken into account in determining the amount of earnings and profits—

(I) such amount shall be included in income in the same manner as if such amount were includible in gross income for purposes of computing alternative minimum taxable income, and

(II) the amount of such income shall be reduced by any deduction which would have been allowable in computing alternative minimum taxable income if such amount were includible in gross income.

The preceding sentence shall not apply in· the case of any amount excluded from gross income under section 108 (or the corresponding provisions of prior law). In the case of any insurance company taxable under section 831(b), this clause shall not apply to any amount not described in section 834(b) *or under section 114.*

* * *·

[CCH Explanation at ¶ 515. Committee Reports at ¶ 10,115.]

Amendment Notes

P.L. 106-519 (FSC Repeal)

Act Sec. 4(1) amended the second sentence of Code Sec. 56(g)(4)(B)(i) by inserting before the period "or under section 114".

The above amendment applies generally to transactions after September 30, 2000. For special rules, see Act Sec. 5(b)-(d) in the amendment notes following Code Sec. 921, below.

[¶ 5110] CODE SEC. 62. ADJUSTED GROSS INCOME DEFINED.

(a) GENERAL RULE.—For purposes of this subtitle, the term "adjusted gross income" means, in the case of an individual, gross income minus the following deductions:

* * *

(16) ARCHER MSAS.—The deduction allowed by section 220.

* * *

[CCH Explanation at ¶ 615. Committee Reports at ¶ 10,245.]

Amendment Notes

P.L. 106-554 (Community Renewal)

Act Sec. 202(b)(1) amended Code Sec. 62(a)(16) to read as above. Prior to amendment, Code Sec. 62(a)(16) read as follows:

(16) MEDICAL SAVINGS ACCOUNTS.—The deduction allowed by section 220.

The above amendment is effective on December 21, 2000.

[¶ 5120] CODE SEC. 67. 2-PERCENT FLOOR ON MISCELLANEOUS ITEMIZED DEDUCTIONS.

* * *

(f) COORDINATION WITH OTHER LIMITATION.—This section shall be applied before the application of the dollar limitation of *the second sentence* of section 162(a) (relating to trade or business expenses).

[CCH Explanation at ¶ 30,050.]

Amendment Notes

P.L. 106-554 (Community Renewal)

Act Sec. 319(2) amended Code Sec. 67(f) by striking "the last sentence" and inserting "the second sentence".

The above amendment is effective on December 21, 2000.

[¶ 5130] CODE SEC. 106. CONTRIBUTIONS BY EMPLOYER TO ACCIDENT AND HEALTH PLANS.

* * *

(b) CONTRIBUTIONS TO *ARCHER MSAS.*—

(1) IN GENERAL.—In the case of an employee who is an eligible individual, amounts contributed by such employee's employer to any *Archer MSA* of such employee shall be treated as employer-provided coverage for medical expenses under an accident or health plan to the extent such amounts do not exceed the limitation under section 220(b)(1) (determined without regard to this subsection) which is applicable to such employee for such taxable year.

(2) NO CONSTRUCTIVE RECEIPT.—No amount shall be included in the gross income of any employee solely because the employee may choose between the contributions referred to in paragraph (1) and employer contributions to another health plan of the employer.

(3) SPECIAL RULE FOR DEDUCTION OF EMPLOYER CONTRIBUTIONS.—Any employer contribution to an *Archer MSA*, if otherwise allowable as a deduction under this chapter, shall be allowed only for the taxable year in which paid.

(4) EMPLOYER MSA CONTRIBUTIONS REQUIRED TO BE SHOWN ON RETURN.—Every individual required to file a return under section 6012 for the taxable year shall include on such return the aggregate amount contributed by employers to the *Archer MSAs* of such individual or such individual's spouse for such taxable year.

(5) MSA CONTRIBUTIONS NOT PART OF COBRA COVERAGE.—Paragraph (1) shall not apply for purposes of section 4980B.

(6) DEFINITIONS.—For purposes of this subsection, the terms "eligible individual" and "*Archer MSA*" have the respective meanings given to such terms by section 220.

(7) CROSS REFERENCE.—For penalty on failure by employer to make comparable contributions to the *Archer MSAs* of comparable employees, see section 4980E.

* * *

[CCH Explanation at ¶ 615. Committee Reports at ¶ 10,245.]

Amendment Notes

P.L. 106-554 (Community Renewal)

Act Sec. 202(a)(2) amended Code Sec. 106(b) by striking "medical savings account" each place it appears in the text and inserting "Archer MSA".

Act Sec. 202(b)(2)(A) amended Code Sec. 106(b)(4) and (7) by striking "medical savings accounts" each place it appears in the text and inserting "Archer MSAs".

Act Sec. 202(b)(6) amended the heading for Code Sec. 106(b) by striking "MEDICAL SAVINGS ACCOUNTS" and inserting "ARCHER MSAs".

Act Sec. 202(b)(10) amended Code Sec. 106(b) by striking "a Archer" and inserting "an Archer".

The above amendments are effective on December 21, 2000.

[¶ 5140] CODE SEC. 114. EXTRATERRITORIAL INCOME.

(a) EXCLUSION.—Gross income does not include extraterritorial income.

(b) EXCEPTION.—Subsection (a) shall not apply to extraterritorial income which is not qualifying foreign trade income as determined under subpart E of part III of subchapter N.

(c) DISALLOWANCE OF DEDUCTIONS.—

(1) IN GENERAL.—Any deduction of a taxpayer allocated under paragraph (2) to extraterritorial income of the taxpayer excluded from gross income under subsection (a) shall not be allowed.

(2) ALLOCATION.—Any deduction of the taxpayer properly apportioned and allocated to the extraterritorial income derived by the taxpayer from any transaction shall be allocated on a proportionate basis between—

(A) the extraterritorial income derived from such transaction which is excluded from gross income under subsection (a); and

(B) the extraterritorial income derived from such transaction which is not so excluded.

(d) DENIAL OF CREDITS FOR CERTAIN FOREIGN TAXES.—Notwithstanding any other provision of this chapter, no credit shall be allowed under this chapter for any income, war profits, and excess profits taxes paid or accrued to any foreign country or possession of the United States with respect to extraterritorial income which is excluded from gross income under subsection (a).

(e) EXTRATERRITORIAL INCOME.—For purposes of this section, the term "extraterritorial income" means the gross income of the taxpayer attributable to foreign trading gross receipts (as defined in section 942) of the taxpayer.

[CCH Explanation at ¶ 515. Committee Reports at ¶ 10,115.]

<table>
<tr><td>Amendment Notes</td><td></td></tr>
<tr><td>P.L. 106-519 (FSC Repeal)</td><td></td></tr>
</table>

Amendment Notes

P.L. 106-519 (FSC Repeal)

Act Sec. 3(a) amended part III of subchapter B of chapter 1 by inserting before Code Sec. 115 a new Code Sec. 114 to read as above.

The above amendment applies generally to transactions after September 30, 2000. For special rules, see Act Sec. 5(b)-(d) in the amendment notes following Code Sec. 921, below.

[¶ 5150] CODE SEC. 138. MEDICARE+CHOICE MSA.

* * *

(b) MEDICARE+CHOICE MSA.—For purposes of this section, the term "Medicare+Choice MSA" means *an Archer MSA* (as defined in section 220(d))—

(1) which is designated as a Medicare+Choice MSA,

(2) with respect to which no contribution may be made other than—

(A) a contribution made by the Secretary of Health and Human Services pursuant to part C of title XVIII of the Social Security Act, or

(B) a trustee-to-trustee transfer described in subsection (c)(4),

(3) the governing instrument of which provides that trustee-to-trustee transfers described in subsection (c)(4) may be made to and from such account, and

(4) which is established in connection with an MSA plan described in section 1859(b)(3) of the Social Security Act.

* * *

[CCH Explanation at ¶ 615. Committee Reports at ¶ 10,245.]

Amendment Notes

P.L. 106-554 (Community Renewal)

Act Sec. 202(a)(3) amended Code Sec. 138(b) by striking "medical savings account" and inserting "Archer MSA".

Act Sec. 202(b)(10) amended Code Sec. 138(b) by striking "a Archer" and inserting "an Archer".

The above amendments are effective on December 21, 2000.

(f) COORDINATION WITH LIMITATION ON NUMBER OF TAXPAYERS HAVING *ARCHER MSAs.*—Subsection (i) of section 220 shall not apply to an individual with respect to a Medicare+Choice MSA, and Medicare+Choice MSA's shall not be taken into account in determining whether the numerical limitations under section 220(j) are exceeded.

* * *

[CCH Explanation at ¶ 615. Committee Reports at ¶ 10,245.]

Amendment Notes

P.L. 106-554 (Community Renewal)

Act Sec. 202(b)(6) amended the heading for Code Sec. 138(f) by striking "MEDICAL SAVINGS ACCOUNTS" and inserting "ARCHER MSAs".

The above amendment is effective on December 21, 2000.

[¶ 5160] CODE SEC. 146. VOLUME CAP.

* * *

(d) STATE CEILING.—For purposes of this section.—

(1) *IN GENERAL.*—*The State ceiling applicable to any State for any calendar year shall be the greater of*—

(A) *an amount equal to $75 ($62.50 in the case of calendar year 2001) multiplied by the State population, or*

(B) *$225,000,000 ($187,500,000 in the case of calendar year 2001).*

(2) *COST-OF-LIVING ADJUSTMENT.*—*In the case of a calendar year after 2002, each of the dollar amounts contained in paragraph (1) shall be increased by an amount equal to*—

(A) *such dollar amount, multiplied by*

(B) *the cost-of-living adjustment determined under section 1(f)(3) for such calendar year by substituting "calendar year 2001" for "calendar year 1992" in subparagraph (B) thereof.*

If any increase determined under the preceding sentence is not a multiple of $5 ($5,000 in the case of the dollar amount in paragraph (1)(B)), such increase shall be rounded to the nearest multiple thereof.

* * *

[CCH Explanation at ¶ 285. Committee Reports at ¶ 10,210.]

Amendment Notes

P.L. 106-554 (Community Renewal)

Act Sec. 161(a) amended Code Sec. 146(d)(1) and (2) to read as above. Prior to amendment, Code Sec. 146(d)(1) and (2) read as follows:

(1) IN GENERAL.—The State ceiling applicable to any State for any calendar year shall be the greater of—

(A) an amount equal to the per capita limit for such year multiplied by the State population, or

(B) the aggregate limit for such year.

Subparagraph (B) shall not apply to any possession of the United States.

(2) PER CAPITA LIMIT; AGGREGATE LIMIT.—For purposes of paragraph (1), the per capita limit, and the aggregate limit, for any calendar year shall be determined in accordance with the following table:

Calendar Year	Per Capita Limit	Aggregate Limit
1999 through 2002 ..	$ 50	$150,000,000
2003	55	165,000,000
2004	60	180,000,000
2005	65	195,000,000
2006	70	210,000,000
2007 and thereafter ..	75	225,000,000

The above amendment applies to calendar years after 2000.

[¶ 5170] CODE SEC. 151. ALLOWANCE OF DEDUCTIONS FOR PERSONAL EXEMPTIONS.

* * *

(c) ADDITIONAL EXEMPTION FOR DEPENDENTS.—

* * *

(6) *TREATMENT OF MISSING CHILDREN.*—

(A) *IN GENERAL.*—*Solely for the purposes referred to in subparagraph (B), a child of the taxpayer*—

(i) *who is presumed by law enforcement authorities to have been kidnapped by someone who is not a member of the family of such child or the taxpayer, and*

(ii) *who was (without regard to this paragraph) the dependent of the taxpayer for the portion of the taxable year before the date of the kidnapping,*

shall be treated as a dependent of the taxpayer for all taxable years ending during the period that the child is kidnapped.

(B) *PURPOSES.*—*Subparagraph (A) shall apply solely for purposes of determining*—

(i) *the deduction under this section,*

(ii) *the credit under section 24 (relating to child tax credit), and*

Code Sec. 151(c)   ¶ 5170

(iii) whether an individual is a surviving spouse or a head of a household (such terms are defined in section 2).

(C) COMPARABLE TREATMENT FOR EARNED INCOME CREDIT.—For purposes of section 32, an individual—

(i) who is presumed by law enforcement authorities to have been kidnapped by someone who is not a member of the family of such individual or the taxpayer, and

(ii) who had, for the taxable year in which the kidnapping occurred, the same principal place of abode as the taxpayer for more than one-half of the portion of such year before the date of the kidnapping,

shall be treated as meeting the requirement of section 32(c)(3)(A)(ii) with respect to a taxpayer for all taxable years ending during the period that the individual is kidnapped.

(D) TERMINATION OF TREATMENT.—Subparagraphs (A) and (C) shall cease to apply as of the first taxable year of the taxpayer beginning after the calendar year in which there is a determination that the child is dead (or, if earlier, in which the child would have attained age 18).

* * *

[CCH Explanation at ¶ 390. Committee Reports at ¶ 10,280.]

Amendment Notes

P.L. 106-554 (Community Renewal)

Act Sec. 306(a) amended Code Sec. 151(c) by adding at the end a new paragraph (6) to read as above.

The above amendment applies to tax years ending after December 21, 2000.

[¶ 5180] CODE SEC. 165. LOSSES.

* * *

(g) WORTHLESS SECURITIES.—

* * *

(3) SECURITIES IN AFFILIATED CORPORATION.—For purposes of paragraph (1), any security in a corporation affiliated with a taxpayer which is a domestic corporation shall not be treated as a capital asset. For purposes of the preceding sentence, a corporation shall be treated as affiliated with the taxpayer only if—

(A) the taxpayer owns directly stock in such corporation meeting the requirements of section 1504(a)(2), and

(B) more than 90 percent of the aggregate of its gross receipts for all taxable years has been from sources other than royalties, rents (except rents derived from rental of properties to employees of the corporation in the ordinary course of its operating business), dividends, interest (except interest received on deferred purchase price of operating assets sold), annuities, and gains from sales or exchanges of stocks and securities.

In computing gross receipts for purposes of the preceding sentence, gross receipts from sales or exchanges of stocks and securities shall be taken into account only to the extent of gains therefrom.

* * *

[CCH Explanation at ¶ 230. Committee Reports at ¶ 10,345.]

Amendment Notes

P.L. 106-554 (Community Renewal)

Act Sec. 318(b)(1) amended Code Sec. 165(g)(3)(A) to read as above. Prior to amendment, Code Sec. 165(g)(3)(A) read as follows:

(A) stock possessing at least 80 percent of the voting power of all classes of its stock and at least 80 percent of each class of its nonvoting stock is owned directly by the taxpayer, and

Act Sec. 318(b)(2) amended Code Sec. 165(g)(3) by striking the last sentence. Prior to amendment, the last sentence of Code Sec. 165(g)(3) read as follows:

As used in subparagraph (A), the term "stock" does not include nonvoting stock which is limited and preferred as to dividends.

The above amendments apply to tax years beginning after December 31, 1984.

[¶ 5190] CODE SEC. 170. CHARITABLE, ETC., CONTRIBUTIONS AND GIFTS.

* * *

(e) CERTAIN CONTRIBUTIONS OF ORDINARY INCOME AND CAPITAL GAIN PROPERTY.—

* * *

(6) SPECIAL RULE FOR CONTRIBUTIONS OF COMPUTER TECHNOLOGY AND EQUIPMENT FOR *EDUCATIONAL PURPOSES.*—

(A) LIMIT ON REDUCTION.—In the case of a *qualified computer contribution*, the reduction under paragraph (1)(A) shall be no greater than the amount determined under paragraph (3)(B).

(B) *QUALIFIED COMPUTER CONTRIBUTION*.—For purposes of this paragraph, the term "*qualified computer contribution*" means a charitable contribution by a corporation of any computer technology or equipment, but only if—

(i) the contribution is to—

(I) an educational organization described in subsection (b)(1)(A)(ii),

(II) an entity described in section 501(c)(3) and exempt from tax under section 501(a) (other than an entity described in subclause (I)) that is organized primarily for purposes of supporting elementary and secondary education, *or*

(III) *a public library (within the meaning of section 213(2)(A) of the Library Services and Technology Act (20 U.S.C. 9122(2)(A)), as in effect on the date of the enactment of the Community Renewal Tax Relief Act of 2000, established and maintained by an entity described in subsection (c)(1),*

(ii) the contribution is made not later than *3 years* after the date the taxpayer acquired the property (or in the case of property constructed by the taxpayer, the date the construction of the property is substantially completed),

(iii) the original use of the property is by the donor or the donee,

(iv) substantially all of the use of the property by the donee is for use within the United States for educational purposes that are related to the purpose or function of the donee,

(v) the property is not transferred by the donee in exchange for money, other property, or services, except for shipping, installation and transfer costs,

(vi) the property will fit productively into the donee's education plan,

(vii) the donee's use and disposition of the property will be in accordance with the provisions of clauses (iv) and (v), *and*

(viii) *the property meets such standards, if any, as the Secretary may prescribe by regulation to assure that the property meets minimum functionality and suitability standards for educational purposes.*

(C) CONTRIBUTION TO PRIVATE FOUNDATION.—A contribution by a corporation of any computer technology or equipment to a private foundation (as defined in section 509) shall be treated as a *qualified computer contribution* for purposes of this paragraph if—

(i) the contribution to the private foundation satisfies the requirements of clauses (ii) and (v) of subparagraph (B), and

(ii) within 30 days after such contribution, the private foundation—

(I) contributes the property to a donee described in clause (i) of subparagraph (B) that satisfies the requirements of clauses (iv) through (vii) of subparagraph (B), and

(II) notifies the donor of such contribution.

(D) *DONATIONS OF PROPERTY REACQUIRED BY MANUFACTURER*.—*In the case of property which is reacquired by the person who constructed the property*—

(i) *subparagraph (B)(ii) shall be applied to a contribution of such property by such person by taking into account the date that the original construction of the property was substantially completed, and*

(ii) *subparagraph (B)(iii) shall not apply to such contribution.*

(E) SPECIAL RULE RELATING TO CONSTRUCTION OF PROPERTY.—For the purposes of this paragraph, the rules of paragraph (4)(C) shall apply.

(F) DEFINITIONS.—For the purposes of this paragraph—

(i) COMPUTER TECHNOLOGY OR EQUIPMENT.—The term "computer technology or equipment" means computer software (as defined by section 197(e)(3)(B)), computer or peripheral equipment (as defined by section 168(i)(2)(B)), and fiber optic cable related to computer use.

(ii) CORPORATION.—The term "corporation" has the meaning given to such term by paragraph (4)(D).

* * *

(G) TERMINATION.—This paragraph shall not apply to any contribution made during any taxable year beginning after *December 31, 2003.*

* * *

Code Sec. 170(e)   ¶ 5190

[CCH Explanation at ¶ 220. Committee Reports at ¶ 10,230.]

Amendment Notes
P.L. 106-554 (Community Renewal)

Act Sec. 165(a)(1) amended Code Sec. 170(e)(6) by striking "qualified elementary or secondary educational contribution" each place it occurs in the headings and text and inserting "qualified computer contribution".

Act Sec. 165(a)(2) amended Code Sec. 170(e)(6)(B)(i) by striking "or" at the end of subclause (I), by adding "or" at the end of subclause (II), and by inserting after subclause (II) a new subclause (III) to read as above.

Act Sec. 165(a)(3) amended Code Sec. 170(e)(6)(B)(ii) by striking "2 years" and inserting "3 years".

Act Sec. 165(b)(1) amended Code Sec. 170(e)(6)(B)(iv) by striking "in any grades of the K–12" following "educational purposes".

Act Sec. 165(b)(2) amended the heading of Code Sec. 170(e)(6) by striking "ELEMENTARY OR SECONDARY SCHOOL PURPOSES" and inserting "EDUCATIONAL PURPOSES".

Act Sec. 165(c) amended Code Sec. 170(e)(6)(F) by striking "December 31, 2000" and inserting "December 31, 2003".

Act Sec. 165(d) amended Code Sec. 170(e)(6)(B) by striking "and" at the end of clause (vi), by striking the period at the end of clause (vii) and inserting ", and", and by adding at the end a new clause (viii) to read as above.

Act Sec. 165(e) amended Code Sec. 170(e)(6) by redesignating subparagraphs (D), (E), and (F) as subparagraphs (E), (F), and (G), respectively, and by inserting after subparagraph (C) a new subparagraph (D) to read as above.

The above amendments apply to contributions made after December 31, 2000.

[¶ 5200] CODE SEC. 196. DEDUCTION FOR CERTAIN UNUSED BUSINESS CREDITS.

* * *

(c) QUALIFIED BUSINESS CREDITS.—For purposes of this section, the term "qualified business credits" means—

(1) the investment credit determined under section 46 (but only to the extent attributable to property the basis of which is reduced by section 50(c)),

(2) the work opportunity credit determined under section 51(a),

(3) the alcohol fuels credit determined under section 40(a),

(4) the research credit determined under section 41(a) (other than such credit determined under section 280C(c)(3)) for taxable years beginning after December 31, 1988,

(5) the enhanced oil recovery credit determined under section 43(a),

(6) the empowerment zone employment credit determined under section 1396(a),

(7) the Indian employment credit determined under section 45A(a),

(8) the employer Social Security credit determined under section 45B(a), *and*

(9) *the new markets tax credit determined under section 45D(a).*

* * *

[CCH Explanation at ¶ 235. Committee Reports at ¶ 10,165.]

Amendment Notes
P.L. 106-554 (Community Renewal)

Act Sec. 121(c) amended Code Sec. 196(c) by striking "and" at the end of paragraph (7), by striking the period at the end of paragraph (8) and inserting ", and", and by adding at the end a new paragraph (9) to read as above.

The above amendment applies to investments made after December 31, 2000.

[¶ 5210] CODE SEC. 198. EXPENSING OF ENVIRONMENTAL REMEDIATION COSTS.

* * *

(c) *QUALIFIED CONTAMINATED SITE.—For purposes of this section—*

(1) *IN GENERAL.—The term "qualified contaminated site" means any area—*

(A) *which is held by the taxpayer for use in a trade or business or for the production of income, or which is property described in section 1221(a)(1) in the hands of the taxpayer, and*

(B) *at or on which there has been a release (or threat of release) or disposal of any hazardous substance.*

(2) *NATIONAL PRIORITIES LISTED SITES NOT INCLUDED.—Such term shall not include any site which is on, or proposed for, the national priorities list under section 105(a)(8)(B) of the Comprehensive Environmental Response, Compensation, and Liability Act of 1980 (as in effect on the date of the enactment of this section).*

(3) *TAXPAYER MUST RECEIVE STATEMENT FROM STATE ENVIRONMENTAL AGENCY.—An area shall be treated as a qualified contaminated site with respect to expenditures paid or incurred during any taxable year*

only if the taxpayer receives a statement from the appropriate agency of the State in which such area is located that such area meets the requirement of paragraph (1)(B).

(4) APPROPRIATE STATE AGENCY.—For purposes of paragraph (3), the chief executive officer of each State may, in consultation with the Administrator of the Environmental Protection Agency, designate the appropriate State environmental agency within 60 days of the date of the enactment of this section. If the chief executive officer of a State has not designated an appropriate environmental agency within such 60-day period, the appropriate environmental agency for such State shall be designated by the Administrator of the Environmental Protection Agency.

* * *

[CCH Explanation at ¶ 225. Committee Reports at ¶ 10,215.]

Amendment Notes

P.L. 106-554 (Community Renewal)

Act Sec. 162(a) amended Code Sec. 198(c) to read as above. Prior to amendment, Code Sec. 198(c) read as follows:

(c) QUALIFIED CONTAMINATED SITE.—For purposes of this section—

(1) QUALIFIED CONTAMINATED SITE.—

(A) IN GENERAL.—The term "qualified contaminated site" means any area—

(i) which is held by the taxpayer for use in a trade or business or for the production of income, or which is property described in section 1221(a)(1) in the hands of the taxpayer,

(ii) which is within a targeted area, and

(iii) at or on which there has been a release (or threat of release) or disposal of any hazardous substance.

(B) TAXPAYER MUST RECEIVE STATEMENT FROM STATE ENVIRONMENTAL AGENCY.—An area shall be treated as a qualified contaminated site with respect to expenditures paid or incurred during any taxable year only if the taxpayer receives a statement from the appropriate agency of the State in which such area is located that such area meets the requirements of clauses (ii) and (iii) of subparagraph (A).

(C) APPROPRIATE STATE AGENCY.—For purposes of subparagraph (B), the chief executive officer of each State may, in consultation with the Administrator of the Environmental Protection Agency, designate the appropriate State environmental agency within 60 days of the date of the enactment of this section. If the chief executive officer of a State has not designated an appropriate State environmental agency within such 60-day period, the appropriate environmental

agency for such State shall be designated by the Administrator of the Environmental Protection Agency.

(2) TARGETED AREA.—

(A) IN GENERAL.—The term "targeted area" means—

(i) any population census tract with a poverty rate of not less than 20 percent,

(ii) a population census tract with a population of less than 2,000 if—

(I) more than 75 percent of such tract is zoned for commercial or industrial use, and

(II) such tract is contiguous to 1 or more other population census tracts which meet the requirement of clause (i) without regard to this clause,

(iii) any empowerment zone or enterprise community (and any supplemental zone designated on December 21, 1994), and

(iv) any site announced before February 1, 1997, as being included as a brownfields pilot project of the Environmental Protection Agency.

(B) NATIONAL PRIORITIES LISTED SITES NOT INCLUDED.— Such term shall not include any site which is on, or proposed for, the national priorities list under section 105(a)(8)(B) of the Comprehensive Environmental Response, Compensation, and Liability Act of 1980 (as in effect on the date of the enactment of this section).

(C) CERTAIN RULES TO APPLY.—For purposes of this paragraph the rules of sections 1392(b)(4) and 1393(a)(9) shall apply.

The above amendment applies to expenditures paid or incurred after December 21, 2000.

(h) TERMINATION.—This section shall not apply to expenditures paid or incurred after December 31, 2003.

[CCH Explanation at ¶ 225. Committee Reports at ¶ 10,215.]

Amendment Notes

P.L. 106-554 (Community Renewal)

Act Sec. 162(b) amended Code Sec. 198(h) by striking "2001" and inserting "2003".

The above amendment applies to expenditures paid or incurred after December 21, 2000.

[¶ 5220] CODE SEC. 219. RETIREMENT SAVINGS.

* * *

(c) SPECIAL RULES FOR CERTAIN MARRIED INDIVIDUALS.—

(1) IN GENERAL.—In the case of an individual to whom this paragraph applies for the taxable year, the limitation of paragraph (1) of subsection (b) shall be equal to the lesser of—

(A) the dollar amount in effect under subsection (b)(1)(A) for the taxable year, or

(B) the sum of—

(i) the compensation includible in such individual's gross income for the taxable year, plus

(ii) the compensation includible in the gross income of such individual's spouse for the taxable year reduced by—

(I) the amount allowed as a deduction under subsection (a) to such spouse for such taxable year,

(II) the amount of any designated nondeductible contribution (as defined in section 408(o)) on behalf of such spouse for such taxable year, and

(III) the amount of any contribution on behalf of such spouse to a Roth IRA under section 408A for such taxable year.

* * *

[CCH Explanation at ¶ 605. Committee Reports at ¶ 10,335.]

Amendment Notes

P.L. 106-554 (Community Renewal)

Act Sec. 316(d) amended Code Sec. 219(c)(1)(B)(ii) by striking "and" at the end of subclause (I), by redesignating subclause (II) as subclause (III), and by inserting after subclause (I) a new subclause (II) to read as above.

The above amendment is effective as if included in the provision of the Small Business Job Protection Act of 1996 (P.L. 104-188) to which it relates [effective for tax years beginning after December 31, 1996.—CCH.].

[¶ 5230] *CODE SEC. 220. ARCHER MSAS.*

(a) DEDUCTION ALLOWED.—In the case of an individual who is an eligible individual for any month during the taxable year, there shall be allowed as a deduction for the taxable year an amount equal to the aggregate amount paid in cash during such taxable year by such individual to *an Archer MSA* of such individual.

[CCH Explanation at ¶ 615. Committee Reports at ¶ 10,245.]

Amendment Notes

P.L. 106-554 (Community Renewal)

Act Sec. 202(a)(4) amended Code Sec. 220 by striking "medical savings account" each place it appears in the text and inserting "Archer MSA".

Act Sec. 202(b)(8) amended the section heading for Code Sec. 220 to read as above. Prior to amendment, the section heading for Code Sec. 220 read as follows:

SEC. 220. MEDICAL SAVINGS ACCOUNTS.

Act Sec. 202(b)(10) amended Code Sec. 220 by striking "a Archer" each place it appears and inserting "an Archer".

The above amendments are effective on December 21, 2000.

(b) LIMITATIONS.—

* * *

(5) COORDINATION WITH EXCLUSION FOR EMPLOYER CONTRIBUTIONS.—No deduction shall be allowed under this section for any amount paid for any taxable year to *an Archer MSA* of an individual if—

(A) any amount is contributed to any *Archer MSA* of such individual for such year which is excludable from gross income under section 106(b), or

(B) if such individual's spouse is covered under the high deductible health plan covering such individual, any amount is contributed for such year to any *Archer MSA* of such spouse which is so excludable.

* * *

[CCH Explanation at ¶ 615. Committee Reports at ¶ 10,245.]

Amendment Notes

P.L. 106-554 (Community Renewal)

Act Sec. 202(a)(4) amended Code Sec. 220 by striking "medical savings account" each place it appears in the text and inserting "Archer MSA".

Act Sec. 202(b)(10) amended Code Sec. 220 by striking "a Archer" each place it appears and inserting "an Archer".

The above amendments are effective on December 21, 2000.

(c) DEFINITIONS.—For purposes of this section—

(1) ELIGIBLE INDIVIDUAL.—

* * *

(C) CONTINUED ELIGIBILITY OF EMPLOYEE AND SPOUSE ESTABLISHING *ARCHER MSAS*.—If, while an employer is a small employer—

(i) any amount is contributed to *an Archer MSA* of an individual who is an employee of such employer or the spouse of such an employee, and

(ii) such amount is excludable from gross income under section 106(b) or allowable as a deduction under this section,

such individual shall not cease to meet the requirement of subparagraph (A)(iii)(I) by reason of such employer ceasing to be a small employer so long as such employee continues to be an employee of such employer.

(D) LIMITATIONS ON ELIGIBILITY.—For limitations on number of taxpayers who are eligible to have *Archer MSAs*, see subsection (i).

* * *

(4) SMALL EMPLOYER.—

* * *

(C) CERTAIN GROWING EMPLOYERS RETAIN TREATMENT AS SMALL EMPLOYER.—The term "small employer" includes, with respect to any calendar year, any employer if—

(i) such employer met the requirement of subparagraph (A) (determined without regard to subparagraph (B)) for any preceding calendar year after 1996,

(ii) any amount was contributed to the *Archer MSA* of any employee of such employer with respect to coverage of such employee under a high deductible health plan of such employer during such preceding calendar year and such amount was excludable from gross income under section 106(b) or allowable as a deduction under this section, and

(iii) such employer employed an average of 200 or fewer employees on business days during each preceding calendar year after 1996.

* * *

[CCH Explanation at ¶ 615. Committee Reports at ¶ 10,245.]

Amendment Notes
P.L. 106-554 (Community Renewal)

Act Sec. 202(a)(4) amended Code Sec. 220 by striking "medical savings account" each place it appears in the text and inserting "Archer MSA".

Act Sec. 202(b)(2)(B) amended Code Sec. 220(c)(1)(D) by striking "medical savings accounts" and inserting "Archer MSAs".

Act Sec. 202(b)(7) amended the heading for Code Sec. 220(c)(1)(C) by striking "MEDICAL SAVINGS ACCOUNTS" and inserting "ARCHER MSAS".

Act Sec. 202(b)(10) amended Code Sec. 220 by striking "a Archer" each place it appears and inserting "an Archer".

The above amendments are effective on December 21, 2000.

(d) ARCHER MSA.—For purposes of this section—

(1) ARCHER MSA.—The term "*Archer MSA*" means a trust created or organized in the United States *as a medical savings account* exclusively for the purpose of paying the qualified medical expenses of the account holder, but only if the written governing instrument creating the trust meets the following requirements:

* * *

(2) QUALIFIED MEDICAL EXPENSES.—

* * *

(C) MEDICAL EXPENSES OF INDIVIDUALS WHO ARE NOT ELIGIBLE INDIVIDUALS.—Subparagraph (A) shall apply to an amount paid by an account holder for medical care of an individual who is not described in clauses (i) and (ii) of subsection (c)(1)(A) for the month in which the expense for such care is incurred only if no amount is contributed (other than a rollover contribution) to any *Archer MSA* of such account holder for the taxable year which includes such month. This subparagraph shall not apply to any expense for coverage described in subclause (I) or (III) of subparagraph (B)(ii).

(3) ACCOUNT HOLDER.—The term "account holder" means the individual on whose behalf the *Archer MSA* was established.

* * *

[CCH Explanation at ¶ 615. Committee Reports at ¶ 10,245.]

Amendment Notes
P.L. 106-554 (Community Renewal)

Act Sec. 202(a)(4) amended Code Sec. 220 by striking "medical savings account" each place it appears in the text and inserting "Archer MSA".

Act Sec. 202(b)(3) amended Code Sec. 220(d)(1) by inserting "as a medical savings account" after "United States".

Act Sec. 202(b)(4) amended the heading for Code Sec. 220(d) by striking "MEDICAL SAVINGS ACCOUNT" and inserting "ARCHER MSA".

Act Sec. 202(b)(5) amended the heading for Code Sec. 220(d)(1) by striking "MEDICAL SAVINGS ACCOUNT" and inserting "ARCHER MSA".

The above amendments are effective on December 21, 2000.

(e) TAX TREATMENT OF ACCOUNTS.—

(1) IN GENERAL.—*An Archer MSA* is exempt from taxation under this subtitle unless such account has ceased to be *an Archer MSA*. Notwithstanding the preceding sentence, any such account

Code Sec. 220(e)   ¶ 5230

is subject to the taxes imposed by section 511 (relating to imposition of tax on unrelated business income of charitable, etc. organizations).

(2) ACCOUNT TERMINATIONS.—Rules similar to the rules of paragraphs (2) and (4) of section 408(e) shall apply to *Archer MSAs*, and any amount treated as distributed under such rules shall be treated as not used to pay qualified medical expenses.

[CCH Explanation at ¶ 615. Committee Reports at ¶ 10,245.]

Amendment Notes

P.L. 106-554 (Community Renewal)

Act Sec. 202(a)(4) amended Code Sec. 220 by striking "medical savings account" each place it appears in the text and inserting "Archer MSA".

Act Sec. 202(b)(2)(B) amended Code Sec. 220(e)(2) by striking "medical savings accounts" and inserting "Archer MSAs".

Act Sec. 202(b)(10) amended Code Sec. 220 by striking "a Archer" and inserting "an Archer".

Act Sec. 202(b)(11) amended Code Sec. 220(e)(1) by striking "A Archer" and inserting "An Archer".

The above amendments are effective on December 21, 2000.

(f) TAX TREATMENT OF DISTRIBUTIONS.—

(1) AMOUNTS USED FOR QUALIFIED MEDICAL EXPENSES.—Any amount paid or distributed out of *an Archer MSA* which is used exclusively to pay qualified medical expenses of any account holder shall not be includible in gross income.

(2) INCLUSION OF AMOUNTS NOT USED FOR QUALIFIED MEDICAL EXPENSES.—Any amount paid or distributed out of *an Archer MSA* which is not used exclusively to pay the qualified medical expenses of the account holder shall be included in the gross income of such holder.

(3) EXCESS CONTRIBUTIONS RETURNED BEFORE DUE DATE OF RETURN.—

(A) IN GENERAL.—If any excess contribution is contributed for a taxable year to any *Archer MSA* of an individual, paragraph (2) shall not apply to distributions from the *Archer MSAs* of such individual (to the extent such distributions do not exceed the aggregate excess contributions to all such accounts of such individual for such year) if—

(i) such distribution is received by the individual on or before the last day prescribed by law (including extensions of time) for filing such individual's return for such taxable year, and

(ii) such distribution is accompanied by the amount of net income attributable to such excess contribution.

Any net income described in clause (ii) shall be included in the gross income of the individual for the taxable year in which it is received.

(B) EXCESS CONTRIBUTION.—For purposes of subparagraph (A), the term "excess contribution" means any contribution (other than a rollover contribution) which is neither excludable from gross income under section 106(b) nor deductible under this section.

(4) ADDITIONAL TAX ON DISTRIBUTIONS NOT USED FOR QUALIFIED MEDICAL EXPENSES.—

(A) IN GENERAL.—The tax imposed by this chapter on the account holder for any taxable year in which there is a payment or distribution from *an Archer MSA* of such holder which is includible in gross income under paragraph (2) shall be increased by 15 percent of the amount which is so includible.

* * *

(5) ROLLOVER CONTRIBUTION.—An amount is described in this paragraph as a rollover contribution if it meets the requirements of subparagraphs (A) and (B).

(A) IN GENERAL.—Paragraph (2) shall not apply to any amount paid or distributed from *an Archer MSA* to the account holder to the extent the amount received is paid into *an Archer MSA* for the benefit of such holder not later than the 60th day after the day on which the holder receives the payment or distribution.

(B) LIMITATION.—This paragraph shall not apply to any amount described in subparagraph (A) received by an individual from *an Archer MSA* if, at any time during the 1-year period ending on the day of such receipt, such individual received any other amount described in subparagraph (A) from *an Archer MSA* which was not includible in the individual's gross income because of the application of this paragraph.

(6) COORDINATION WITH MEDICAL EXPENSE DEDUCTION.—For purposes of determining the amount of the deduction under section 213, any payment or distribution out of *an Archer MSA* for qualified medical expenses shall not be treated as an expense paid for medical care.

(7) TRANSFER OF ACCOUNT INCIDENT TO DIVORCE.—The transfer of an individual's interest in *an Archer MSA* to an individual's spouse or former spouse under a divorce or separation instrument described in subparagraph (A) of section 71(b)(2) shall not be considered a taxable transfer made by such individual notwithstanding any other provision of this subtitle, and such interest shall, after such transfer, be treated as *an Archer MSA* with respect to which such spouse is the account holder.

(8) TREATMENT AFTER DEATH OF ACCOUNT HOLDER.—

(A) TREATMENT IF DESIGNATED BENEFICIARY IS SPOUSE.—If the account holder's surviving spouse acquires such holder's interest in *an Archer MSA* by reason of being the designated beneficiary of such account at the death of the account holder, such *Archer MSA* shall be treated as if the spouse were the account holder.

(B) OTHER CASES.—

(i) IN GENERAL.—If, by reason of the death of the account holder, any person acquires the account holder's interest in *an Archer MSA* in a case to which subparagraph (A) does not apply—

(I) such account shall cease to be *an Archer MSA* as of the date of death, and

(II) an amount equal to the fair market value of the assets in such account on such date shall be includible if such person is not the estate of such holder, in such person's gross income for the taxable year which includes such date, or if such person is the estate of such holder, in such holder's gross income for the last taxable year of such holder.

* * *

[CCH Explanation at ¶ 615. Committee Reports at ¶ 10,245.]

Amendment Notes

P.L. 106-554 (Community Renewal)

Act Sec. 202(a)(4) amended Code Sec. 220 by striking "medical savings account" each place it appears in the text and inserting "Archer MSA".

Act Sec. 202(b)(2)(B) amended Code Sec. 220(f)(3)(A) by striking "medical savings accounts" each place it appears in the text and inserting "Archer MSAs".

Act Sec. 202(b)(10) amended Code Sec. 220 by striking "a Archer" each place it appears and inserting "an Archer".

The above amendments are effective on December 21, 2000.

(h) REPORTS.—The Secretary may require the trustee of *an Archer MSA* to make such reports regarding such account to the Secretary and to the account holder with respect to contributions, distributions, and such other matters as the Secretary determines appropriate. The reports required by this subsection shall be filed at such time and in such manner and furnished to such individuals at such time and in such manner as may be required by the Secretary.

[CCH Explanation at ¶ 615. Committee Reports at ¶ 10,245.]

Amendment Notes
P.L. 106-554 (Community Renewal)
Act Sec. 202(a)(4) amended Code Sec. 220 by striking "medical savings account" each place it appears in the text and inserting "Archer MSA".

Act Sec. 202(b)(10) amended Code Sec. 220 by striking "a Archer" each place it appears and inserting "an Archer".

The above amendments are effective on December 21, 2000.

(i) LIMITATION ON NUMBER OF TAXPAYERS HAVING *ARCHER MSAs*.—

* * *

(2) CUT-OFF YEAR.—For purposes of paragraph (1), the term "cut-off year" means the earlier of—

(A) calendar year *2002*, or

(B) the first calendar year before *2002* for which the Secretary determines under subsection (j) that the numerical limitation for such year has been exceeded.

(3) ACTIVE MSA PARTICIPANT.—For purposes of this subsection—

(A) IN GENERAL.—The term "active MSA participant" means, with respect to any taxable year, any individual who is the account holder of any *Archer MSA* into which any contribution was made which was excludable from gross income under section 106(b), or allowable as a deduction under this section, for such taxable year.

(B) SPECIAL RULE FOR CUT-OFF YEARS BEFORE *2002*.—In the case of a cut-off year before *2002*—

(i) an individual shall not be treated as an eligible individual for any month of such year or an active MSA participant under paragraph (1)(A) unless such individual is, on or before the cut-off date, covered under a high deductible health plan, and

(ii) an employer shall not be treated as an MSA-participating employer unless the employer, on or before the cut-off date, offered coverage under a high deductible health plan to any employee.

* * *

(4) MSA-PARTICIPATING EMPLOYER.—For purposes of this subsection, the term "MSA-participating employer" means any small employer if—

(A) such employer made any contribution to the *Archer MSA* of any employee during the cut-off year or any preceding calendar year which was excludable from gross income under section 106(b), or

(B) at least 20 percent of the employees of such employer who are eligible individuals for any month of the cut-off year by reason of coverage under a high deductible health plan of such employer each made a contribution of at least $100 to their *Archer MSAs* for any taxable year ending with or within the cut-off year which was allowable as a deduction under this section.

* * *

[CCH Explanation at ¶ 615. Committee Reports at ¶ 10,245.]

Amendment Notes

P.L. 106-554 (Community Renewal)

Act Sec. 201(a) amended Code Sec. 220(i)(2) and (3)(B) by striking "2000" each place it appears and inserting "2002".

Act Sec. 202(a)(4) amended Code Sec. 220 by striking "medical savings account" each place it appears in the text and inserting "Archer MSA".

Act Sec. 202(b)(2)(B) amended Code Sec. 220(i)(4)(B) by striking "medical savings accounts" and inserting "Archer MSAs".

Act Sec. 202(b)(6) amended the heading for Code Sec. 220(i) by striking "MEDICAL SAVINGS ACCOUNTS" and inserting "ARCHER MSAS".

The above amendments are effective on December 21, 2000.

(j) DETERMINATION OF WHETHER NUMERICAL LIMITS ARE EXCEEDED.—

(1) DETERMINATION OF WHETHER LIMIT EXCEEDED FOR 1997.—The numerical limitation for 1997 is exceeded if, based on the reports required under paragraph (4), the number of *Archer MSAs* established as of—

(A) April 30, 1997, exceeds 375,000, or

(B) June 30, 1997, exceeds 525,000.

(2) DETERMINATION OF WHETHER LIMIT EXCEEDED FOR *1998, 1999,* OR *2001.*—

(A) IN GENERAL.—The numerical limitation for *1998, 1999, or 2001* is exceeded if the sum of—

(i) the number of MSA returns filed on or before April 15 of such calendar year for taxable years ending with or within the preceding calendar year, plus

(ii) the Secretary's estimate (determined on the basis of the returns described in clause (i)) of the number of MSA returns for such taxable years which will be filed after such date,

exceeds *750,000 (600,000 in the case of 1998).* For purposes of the preceding sentence, the term "MSA return" means any return on which any exclusion is claimed under section 106(b) or any deduction is claimed under this section.

(B) ALTERNATIVE COMPUTATION OF LIMITATION.—The numerical limitation for *1998, 1999, or 2001* is also exceeded if the sum of—

(i) 90 percent of the sum determined under subparagraph (A) for such calendar year, plus

(ii) the product of 2.5 and the number of *Archer MSAs* established during the portion of such year preceding July 1 (based on the reports required under paragraph (4)) for taxable years beginning in such year,

exceeds 750,000.

(C) NO LIMITATION FOR 2000.—*The numerical limitation shall not apply for 2000.*

(3) PREVIOUSLY UNINSURED INDIVIDUALS NOT INCLUDED IN DETERMINATION.—

(A) IN GENERAL.—The determination of whether any calendar year is a cut-off year shall be made by not counting the *Archer MSA* of any previously uninsured individual.

(B) PREVIOUSLY UNINSURED INDIVIDUAL.—For purposes of this subsection, the term "previously uninsured individual" means, with respect to any *Archer MSA*, any individual who had no health plan coverage (other than coverage referred to in subsection (c)(1)(B)) at any time during the 6-month period before the date such individual's coverage under the high deductible health plan commences.

(4) REPORTING BY MSA TRUSTEES.—

(A) IN GENERAL.—Not later than August 1 of 1997, 1998, *1999, and 2001*, each person who is the trustee of *an Archer MSA* established before July 1 of such calendar year shall make a report to the Secretary (in such form and manner as the Secretary shall specify) which specifies—

(i) the number of *Archer MSAs* established before such July 1 (for taxable years beginning in such calendar year) of which such person is the trustee,

(ii) the name and TIN of the account holder of each such account, and

(iii) the number of such accounts which are accounts of previously uninsured individuals.

(B) ADDITIONAL REPORT FOR 1997.—Not later than June 1, 1997, each person who is the trustee of *an Archer MSA* established before May 1, 1997, shall make an additional report described in subparagraph (A) but only with respect to accounts established before May 1, 1997.

(C) PENALTY FOR FAILURE TO FILE REPORT.—The penalty provided in section 6693(a) shall apply to any report required by this paragraph, except that—

(i) such section shall be applied by substituting "$25" for "$50", and

(ii) the maximum penalty imposed on any trustee shall not exceed $5,000.

(D) AGGREGATION OF ACCOUNTS.—To the extent practical, in determining the number of *Archer MSAs* on the basis of the reports under this paragraph, all *Archer MSAs* of an individual shall be treated as 1 account and all accounts of individuals who are married to each other shall be treated as 1 account.

(5) DATE OF MAKING DETERMINATIONS.—Any determination under this subsection that a calendar year is a cut-off year shall be made by the Secretary and shall be published not later than October 1 of such year.

[CCH Explanation at ¶ 615. Committee Reports at ¶ 10,245.]

Amendment Notes

P.L. 106-554 (Community Renewal)

Act Sec. 201(b)(1)(A)-(C) amended Code Sec. 220(j)(2) by striking "1998 or 1999" each place it appears and inserting "1998, 1999, or 2001", by striking "600,000 (750,000 in the case of 1999)" and inserting "750,000 (600,000 in the case of 1998)", and by inserting after subparagraph (B) a new subparagraph (C) to read as above.

Act Sec. 201(b)(2) amended Code Sec. 220(j)(4)(A) by striking "and 1999" and inserting "1999, and 2001".

Act Sec. 202(a)(4) amended Code Sec. 220 by striking "medical savings account" each place it appears in the text and inserting "Archer MSA".

Act Sec. 202(b)(2)(B) amended Code Sec. 220(j) by striking "medical savings accounts" each place it appears in the text and inserting "Archer MSAs".

Act Sec. 202(b)(10) amended Code Sec. 220 by striking "a Archer" each place it appears and inserting "an Archer".

The above amendments are effective on December 21, 2000.

[¶ 5240] CODE SEC. 275. CERTAIN TAXES.

(a) GENERAL RULE.—No deduction shall be allowed for the following taxes:

(1) Federal income taxes, including—

(A) the tax imposed by section 3101 (relating to the tax on employees under the Federal Insurance Contributions Act);

(B) the taxes imposed by sections 3201 and 3211 (relating to the taxes on railroad employees and railroad employee representatives); and

(C) the tax withheld at source on wages under section 3402.

(2) Federal war profits and excess profits taxes.

(3) Estate, inheritance, legacy, succession, and gift taxes.

(4) Income, war profits, and excess profits taxes imposed by the authority of any foreign country or possession of the United States if—

(A) the taxpayer chooses to take to any extent the benefits of section 901,

(B) such taxes are paid or accrued with respect to foreign trade income (within the meaning of section 923(b)) of a FSC, *or*

(C) such taxes are paid or accrued with respect to qualifying foreign trade income (as defined in section 941).

(5) Taxes on real property, to the extent that section 164(d) requires such taxes to be treated as imposed on another taxpayer.

(6) Taxes imposed by chapters 41, 42, 43, 44, 46, and 54.

Paragraph (1) shall not apply to any taxes to the extent such taxes are allowable as a deduction under section 164(f). Paragraph (1) shall not apply to the tax imposed by section 59A. *A rule similar to the rule of section 943(d) shall apply for purposes of paragraph (4)(C).*

* * *

[CCH Explanation at ¶ 515 and ¶ 520. Committee Reports at ¶ 10,115.]

Amendment Notes

P.L. 106-519 (FSC Repeal)

Act Sec. 4(2)(A)-(B) amended Code Sec. 275(a) by striking "or" at the end of paragraph (4)(A), by striking the period at the end of paragraph (4)(B) and inserting ", or", and by adding at the end of paragraph (4) a new subparagraph (C); and by adding at the end a new sentence to read as above.

The above amendment applies generally to transactions after September 30, 2000. For special rules, see Act Sec. 5(b)-(d) in the amendment notes following Code Sec. 921, below.

[¶ 5250] CODE SEC. 280C. CERTAIN EXPENSES FOR WHICH CREDITS ARE ALLOWABLE.

* * *

(c) CREDIT FOR INCREASING RESEARCH ACTIVITIES.—

(1) IN GENERAL.—No deduction shall be allowed for that portion of the qualified research expenses (as defined in section 41(b)) or basic research expenses (as defined in section 41(e)(2)) otherwise allowable as a deduction for the taxable year which is equal to the amount of the credit determined for such taxable year under section 41(a).

* * *

[CCH Explanation at ¶ 255. Committee Reports at ¶ 10,310.]

Amendment Notes

P.L. 106-554 (Community Renewal)

Act Sec. 311(a)(1) amended Code Sec. 280C(c)(1) by striking "or credit" after "deduction" each place it appears.

The above amendment is effective as if included in the provision of the Ticket to Work and Work Incentives

Improvement Act of 1999 (P.L. 106-170) to which it relates [effective for amounts paid or incurred after June 30, 1999.—CCH.].

[¶ 5260] CODE SEC. 357. ASSUMPTION OF LIABILITY.

* * *

(d) DETERMINATION OF AMOUNT OF LIABILITY ASSUMED.—

(1) IN GENERAL.—For purposes of this section, section 358(d), *section 358(h)*, section 362(d), section 368(a)(1)(C), and section 368(a)(2)(B), except as provided in regulations—

(A) a recourse liability (or portion thereof) shall be treated as having been assumed if, as determined on the basis of all facts and circumstances, the transferee has agreed to, and is expected to, satisfy such liability (or portion), whether or not the transferor has been relieved of such liability; and

(B) except to the extent provided in paragraph (2), a nonrecourse liability shall be treated as having been assumed by the transferee of any asset subject to such liability.

* * *

[CCH Explanation at ¶ 265. Committee Reports at ¶ 10,295.]

Amendment Notes

P.L. 106-554 (Community Renewal)

Act Sec. 309(b) amended Code Sec. 357(d)(1) by inserting "section 358(h)," after "section 358(d),".

The above amendment generally applies to assumptions of liability after October 18, 1999. For special rules, see Act Sec. 309(c)(1)-(2) and (d)(2), below.

Act Sec. 309(c)(1)-(2) and (d)(2) provide:

(c) APPLICATION OF COMPARABLE RULES TO PARTNERSHIPS AND S CORPORATIONS.—The Secretary of the Treasury or his delegate—

(1) shall prescribe rules which provide appropriate adjustments under subchapter K of chapter 1 of the Internal Revenue Code of 1986 to prevent the acceleration or duplication of losses through the assumption of (or transfer of assets subject to) liabilities described in section 358(h)(3) of such

Code (as added by subsection (a)) in transactions involving partnerships, and

(2) may prescribe rules which provide appropriate adjustments under subchapter S of chapter 1 of such Code in transactions described in paragraph (1) involving S corporations rather than partnerships.

[¶ 5270] CODE SEC. 358. BASIS TO DISTRIBUTEES.

* * *

(h) SPECIAL RULES FOR ASSUMPTION OF LIABILITIES TO WHICH SUBSECTION (d) DOES NOT APPLY.—

(1) IN GENERAL.—If, after application of the other provisions of this section to an exchange or series of exchanges, the basis of property to which subsection (a)(1) applies exceeds the fair market value of such property, then such basis shall be reduced (but not below such fair market value) by the amount (determined as of the date of the exchange) of any liability—

(A) which is assumed in exchange for such property, and

(B) with respect to which subsection (d)(1) does not apply to the assumption.

(2) EXCEPTIONS.—Except as provided by the Secretary, paragraph (1) shall not apply to any liability if—

(A) the trade or business with which the liability is associated is transferred to the person assuming the liability as part of the exchange, or

(B) substantially all of the assets with which the liability is associated are transferred to the person assuming the liability as part of the exchange.

(3) LIABILITY.—For purposes of this subsection, the term "liability" shall include any fixed or contingent obligation to make payment, without regard to whether the obligation is otherwise taken into account for purposes of this title.

[CCH Explanation at ¶ 265. Committee Reports at ¶ 10,295.]

Amendment Notes

P.L. 106-554 (Community Renewal)

Act Sec. 309(a) amended Code Sec. 358 by adding at the end a new subsection (h) to read as above.

The above amendment generally applies to assumptions of liability after October 18, 1999. For special rules, see Act Sec. 309(c)(1)-(2) and (d)(2), below.

Act Sec. 309(c)(1)-(2) and (d)(2) provide:

(c) APPLICATION OF COMPARABLE RULES TO PARTNERSHIPS AND S CORPORATIONS.—The Secretary of the Treasury or his delegate—

(1) shall prescribe rules which provide appropriate adjustments under subchapter K of chapter 1 of the Internal Revenue Code of 1986 to prevent the acceleration or duplication of losses through the assumption of (or transfer of assets subject to) liabilities described in section 358(h)(3) of such Code (as added by subsection (a)) in transactions involving partnerships, and

(2) may prescribe rules which provide appropriate adjustments under subchapter S of chapter 1 of such Code in transactions described in paragraph (1) involving S corporations rather than partnerships.

(d) EFFECTIVE DATES.—

* * *

(2) RULES.—The rules prescribed under subsection (c) shall apply to assumptions of liability after October 18, 1999, or such later date as may be prescribed in such rules.

[¶ 5280] CODE SEC. 401. QUALIFIED PENSION, PROFIT-SHARING, AND STOCK BONUS PLANS.

* * *

(k) CASH OR DEFERRED ARRANGEMENTS.—

* * *

(10) DISTRIBUTIONS UPON TERMINATION OF PLAN OR DISPOSITION OF ASSETS OR SUBSIDIARY.—

* * *

(B) DISTRIBUTIONS MUST BE LUMP SUM DISTRIBUTIONS.—

(i) IN GENERAL.—An event shall not be treated as described in subparagraph (A) with respect to any employee unless the employee receives a lump sum distribution by reason of the event.

(ii) LUMP-SUM DISTRIBUTION.—For purposes of this subparagraph, the term "lump-sum distribution" has the meaning given such term by section 402(e)(4)(D) (without regard to subclauses (I), (II), (III), and (IV) of clause (i) thereof). *Such term includes a distribution of an annuity contract from—*

(I) a trust which forms a part of a plan described in section 401(a) and which is exempt from tax under section 501(a), or

(II) an annuity plan described in section 403(a).

* * *

[CCH Explanation at ¶ 620. Committee Reports at ¶ 10,335.]

Amendment Notes

P.L. 106-554 (Community Renewal)
Act Sec. 316(c) amended Code Sec. 401(k)(10)(B)(ii) by adding at the end a new sentence to read as above.

The above amendment is effective as if included in the provision of the Small Business Job Protection Act of 1996 (P.L. 104-188) to which it relates [effective for tax years beginning after December 31, 1999.—CCH.].

[¶ 5290] CODE SEC. 403. TAXATION OF EMPLOYEE ANNUITIES.

* * *

(b) TAXABILITY OF BENEFICIARY UNDER ANNUITY PURCHASED BY SECTION 501(c)(3) ORGANIZATION OR PUBLIC SCHOOL.—

* * *

(3) INCLUDIBLE COMPENSATION.—For purposes of this subsection, the term "includible compensation" means, in the case of any employee, the amount of compensation which is received from the employer described in paragraph (1)(A), and which is includible in gross income (computed without regard to section 911) for the most recent period (ending not later than the close of the taxable year) which under paragraph (4) may be counted as one year of service. Such term does not include any amount contributed by the employer for any annuity contract to which this subsection applies. Such term includes—

(A) any elective deferral (as defined in section 402(g)(3)), and

(B) any amount which is contributed or deferred by the employer at the election of the employee and which is not includible in the gross income of the employee by reason of *section 125, 132(f)(4), or 457.*

* * *

[CCH Explanation at ¶ 625. Committee Reports at ¶ 10,325.]

Amendment Notes

P.L. 106-554 (Community Renewal)
Act Sec. 314(e)(1) amended Code Sec. 403(b)(3)(B) by striking "section 125 or" and inserting "section 125, 132(f)(4), or".

The above amendment is effective as if included in the provision of the Taxpayer Relief Act of 1997 (P.L. 105-34) to which it relates [effective for years beginning after December 31, 1997.—CCH.].

[¶ 5300] CODE SEC. 408. INDIVIDUAL RETIREMENT ACCOUNTS.

* * *

(d) TAX TREATMENT OF DISTRIBUTIONS.—

* * *

(5) DISTRIBUTIONS OF EXCESS CONTRIBUTIONS AFTER DUE DATE FOR TAXABLE YEAR AND CERTAIN EXCESS ROLLOVER CONTRIBUTIONS.—

* * *

[CCH Explanation at ¶ 30,050.]

Amendment Notes

P.L. 106-554 (Community Renewal)
Act Sec. 319(3) amended the heading for Code Sec. 408(d)(5) to read as above. Prior to amendment, the heading for Code Sec. 408(d)(5) read as follows:

(5) CERTAIN DISTRIBUTIONS OF EXCESS CONTRIBUTIONS AFTER DUE DATE FOR TAXABLE YEAR.

The above amendment is effective on December 21, 2000.

[¶ 5310] CODE SEC. 414. DEFINITIONS AND SPECIAL RULES.

* * *

(s) COMPENSATION.—For purposes of any applicable provision—

* * *

(2) EMPLOYER MAY ELECT NOT TO TREAT CERTAIN DEFERRALS AS COMPENSATION.—An employer may elect not to include as compensation any amount which is contributed by the employer pursuant to a salary reduction agreement and which is not includible in the gross income of an employee under *section 125, 132(f)(4), 402(e)(3),* 402(h) or 403(b).

* * *

[CCH Explanation at ¶ 625. Committee Reports at ¶ 10,325.]

Amendment Notes

P.L. 106-554 (Community Renewal)

Act Sec. 314(e)(2) amended Code Sec. 414(s)(2) by striking "section 125, 402(e)(3)" and inserting "section 125, 132(f)(4), 402(e)(3)".

The above amendment is effective as if included in the provisions of the Taxpayer Relief Act of 1997 (P.L. 105-34) to which it relates [effective for tax years beginning after December 31, 1997.—CCH.].

[¶ 5320] CODE SEC. 415. LIMITATIONS ON BENEFITS AND CONTRIBUTION UNDER QUALIFIED PLANS.

* * *

(c) LIMITATION FOR DEFINED CONTRIBUTION PLANS.—

* * *

(3) PARTICIPANT'S COMPENSATION.—For purposes of paragraph (1)—

* * *

(D) CERTAIN DEFERRALS INCLUDED.—The term "participant's compensation" shall include—

(i) any elective deferral (as defined in section 402(g)(3)), and

(ii) any amount which is contributed or deferred by the employer at the election of the employee and which is not includible in the gross income of the employee by reason of *section 125, 132(f)(4), or 457.*

* * *

[CCH Explanation at ¶ 625. Committee Reports at ¶ 10,325.]

Amendment Notes

P.L. 106-554 (Community Renewal)

Act Sec. 314(e)(1) amended Code Sec. 415(c)(3)(D)(ii) by striking "section 125 or" and inserting "section 125, 132(f)(4), or".

The above amendment is effective as if included in the provisions of the Taxpayer Relief Act of 1997 (P.L. 105-34) to which it relates [effective for tax years beginning after December 31, 1997.—CCH.].

[¶ 5330] CODE SEC. 453. INSTALLMENT METHOD.

(a) GENERAL RULE.—*Except as otherwise provided in this section, income from an installment sale shall be taken into account for purposes of this title under the installment method.*

* * *

[CCH Explanation at ¶ 205. Committee Reports at ¶ 10,375.]

Amendment Notes

P.L. 106-573 (Installment Tax Correction)

Act Sec. 2(a) repealed section 536(a)(1) of the Ticket to Work and Work Incentives Improvement Act of 1999 (P.L. 106-170), which amended Code Sec. 453(a). Thus, the amendment made to Code Sec. 453(a) never took effect and Code Sec. 453(a) is restored to read as above. Prior to the amendment's being stricken, Code Sec. 453(a) read as follows:

(a) USE OF INSTALLMENT METHOD.—

(1) IN GENERAL.—Except as otherwise provided in this section, income from an installment sale shall be taken into

account for purposes of this title under the installment method.

(2) ACCRUAL METHOD TAXPAYER.—The installment method shall not apply to income from an installment sale if such income would be reported under an accrual method of accounting without regard to this section. The preceding sentence shall not apply to a disposition described in subparagraph (A) or (B) of subsection (l)(2).

The above amendment is effective with respect to sales and other dispositions occurring on or after the date of the enactment of such Act (P.L. 106-170) [effective December 17, 1999.—CCH.].

(d) ELECTION OUT.—

(1) IN GENERAL.—Subsection *(a)* shall not apply to any disposition if the taxpayer elects to have subsection *(a)* not apply to such disposition.

* * *

[CCH Explanation at ¶ 205. Committee Reports at ¶ 10,375.]

Amendment Notes

P.L. 106-573 (Installment Tax Correction)

Act Sec. 2(a) repealed section 536(a)(2) of the Ticket to Work and Work Incentives Improvement Act of 1999 (P.L. 106-170), which amended Code Sec. 453(d)(1) by striking "(a)" each place it appeared and inserting "(a)(1)". Thus,

the amendment made to Code Sec. 453(d)(1) never took effect and Code Sec. 453(d)(1) is restored to read as above.

The above amendment is effective with respect to sales and other dispositions occurring on or after the date of the enactment of such Act (P.L. 106-170) [effective December 17, 1999.—CCH.].

(i) RECOGNITION OF RECAPTURE INCOME IN YEAR OF DISPOSITION.—

(1) IN GENERAL.—In the case of any installment sale of property to which subsection *(a)* applies—

(A) notwithstanding subsection *(a)*, any recapture income shall be recognized in the year of the disposition, and

(B) any gain in excess of the recapture income shall be taken into account under the installment method.

* * *

[CCH Explanation at ¶ 205. Committee Reports at ¶ 10,375.]

Amendment Notes

P.L. 106-573 (Installment Tax Correction)

Act Sec. 2(a) repealed Act Sec. 536(a)(2) of the Ticket to Work and Work Incentives Improvement Act of 1999 (P.L. 106-170), which amended Code Sec. 453(i)(1) by striking "(a)" each place it appeared and inserting "(a)(1)". Thus,

the amendment made to Code Sec. 453(i)(1) never took effect and Code Sec. 453(i)(1) is restored to read as above.

The above amendment is effective with respect to sales and other dispositions occurring on or after the date of the enactment of such Act (P.L. 106-170) [effective December 17, 1999.—CCH.].

(k) CURRENT INCLUSION IN CASE OF REVOLVING CREDIT PLANS, ETC.—In the case of—

(1) any disposition of personal property under a revolving credit plan, or

(2) any installment obligation arising out of a sale of—

(A) stock or securities which are traded on an established securities market, or

(B) to the extent provided in regulations, property (other than stock or securities) of a kind regularly traded on an established market,

subsection *(a)* shall not apply, and, for purposes of this title, all payments to be received shall be treated as received in the year of disposition. The Secretary may provide for the application of this subsection in whole or in part for transactions in which the rules of this subsection otherwise would be avoided through the use of related parties, pass-thru entities, or intermediaries.

* * *

[CCH Explanation at ¶ 205. Committee Reports at ¶ 10,375.]

Amendment Notes

P.L. 106-573 (Installment Tax Correction)

Act Sec. 2(a) repealed Act Sec. 536(a)(2) of the Ticket to Work and Work Incentives Improvement Act of 1999 (P.L. 106-170), which amended Code Sec. 453(k) by striking "(a)" and inserting "(a)(1)". Thus, the amendment made to Code

Sec. 453(k) never took effect and Code Sec. 453(k) is restored to read as above.

The above amendment is effective with respect to sales and other dispositions occurring on or after the date of the enactment of such Act (P.L. 106-170) [effective December 17, 1999.—CCH.].

[¶ 5340] CODE SEC. 469. PASSIVE ACTIVITY LOSSES AND CREDITS LIMITED.

* * *

(i) $25,000 OFFSET FOR RENTAL REAL ESTATE ACTIVITIES.—

* * *

(3) PHASE-OUT OF EXEMPTION.—

* * *

(C) *EXCEPTION FOR COMMERCIAL REVITALIZATION DEDUCTION.—Subparagraph (A) shall not apply to any portion of the passive activity loss for any taxable year which is attributable to the commercial revitalization deduction under section 1400I.*

(D) EXCEPTION FOR LOW-INCOME HOUSING CREDIT.—Subparagraph (A) shall not apply to any portion of the passive activity credit for any taxable year which is attributable to any credit determined under section 42.

(E) *ORDERING RULES TO REFLECT EXCEPTIONS AND SEPARATE PHASE-OUTS.—If subparagraph (B), (C), or (D) applies for a taxable year, paragraph (1) shall be applied—*

(i) *first to the portion of the passive activity loss to which subparagraph (C) does not apply,*

(ii) *second to the portion of the passive activity credit to which subparagraph (B) or (D) does not apply,*

(iii) *third to the portion of such credit to which subparagraph (B) applies,*

(iv) *fourth to the portion of such loss to which subparagraph (C) applies, and*

(v) *then to the portion of such credit to which subparagraph (D) applies.*

(F) ADJUSTED GROSS INCOME.—For purposes of this paragraph, adjusted gross income shall be determined without regard to—

* * *

(6) ACTIVE PARTICIPATION.—

* * *

(B) No PARTICIPATION REQUIREMENT FOR LOW-INCOME HOUSING, REHABILITATION CREDIT, OR COMMERCIAL REVITALIZATION DEDUCTION.—Paragraphs (1) and (4)(A) shall be applied without regard to the active participation requirement in the case of—

(i) any credit determined under section 42 for any taxable year,

(ii) any rehabilitation credit determined under section 47, *or*

(iii) *any deduction under section 1400I (relating to commercial revitalization deduction).*

* * *

[CCH Explanation at ¶ 115. Committee Reports at ¶ 10,140.]

Amendment Notes

P.L. 106-554 (Community Renewal)

Act Sec. 101(b)(1) amended Code Sec. 469(i)(3) by redesignating subparagraphs (C), (D), and (E) as subparagraphs (D), (E), and (F), respectively, and by inserting after subparagraph (B) a new subparagraph (C) to read as above.

Act Sec. 101(b)(2) amended Code Sec. 469(i)(3)(E), as resdesignated by Act Sec. 101(b)(1)(A) [Act Sec. 101(b)(1)], to read as above. Prior to amendment, Code Sec. 469(i)(3)(E) read as follows:

(E) ORDERING RULES TO REFLECT EXCEPTION AND SEPARATE PHASE-OUT.—If subparagraph (B) or (C) applies for any taxable year, paragraph (1) shall be applied—

(i) first to the passive activity loss,

(ii) second to the portion of the passive activity credit to which subparagraph (B) or (C) does not apply,

(iii) third to the portion of such credit to which subparagraph (B) applies, and

(iv) then to the portion of such credit to which subparagraph (C) applies.

Act Sec. 101(b)(3)(A) amended Code Sec. 469(i)(6)(B) by striking "or" at the end of clause (i), by striking the period at the end of clause (ii) and inserting ", or", and by adding at the end a new clause (iii) to read as above.

Act Sec. 101(b)(3)(B) amended the heading for Code Sec. 469(i)(6)(B) by striking "OR REHABILITATION CREDIT" and inserting ", REHABILITATION CREDIT, OR COMMERCIAL REVITALIZATION DEDUCTION".

The above amendments are effective on December 21, 2000.

[¶ 5350] CODE SEC. 475. MARK TO MARKET ACCOUNTING METHOD FOR DEALERS IN SECURITIES.

* * *

(g) REGULATORY AUTHORITY.—The Secretary shall prescribe such regulations as may be necessary or appropriate to carry out the purposes of this section, including rules—

* * *

(3) to prevent the use by taxpayers of subsection (c)(4) to avoid the application of this section to a receivable that is inventory in the hands of the taxpayer (or a person who bears a relationship to the taxpayer described in sections *267(b) or 707*(b)).

[CCH Explanation at ¶ 30,050.]

Amendment Notes

P.L. 106-554 (Community Renewal)

Act Sec. 319(4) amended Code Sec. 475(g)(3) by striking "267(b) of" and inserting "267(b) or".

The above amendment is effective on December 21, 2000.

[¶ 5360] CODE SEC. 529. QUALIFIED STATE TUITION PROGRAMS.

* * *

(e) OTHER DEFINITIONS AND SPECIAL RULES.—For purposes of this section—

* * *

(3) QUALIFIED HIGHER EDUCATION EXPENSES.—

* * *

(B) ROOM AND BOARD INCLUDED FOR STUDENTS WHO ARE AT LEAST HALF-TIME.—

* * *

[CCH Explanation at ¶ 30,050.]

Amendment Notes

P.L. 106-554 (Community Renewal)

Act Sec. 319(5) amended the heading for Code Sec. 529(e)(3)(B) by striking "UNDER GUARANTEED PLANS" after "STUDENTS".

The above amendment is effective on December 21, 2000.

[¶ 5370] CODE SEC. 530. EDUCATION INDIVIDUAL RETIREMENT ACCOUNTS.

* * *

(d) TAX TREATMENT OF DISTRIBUTIONS.—

* * *

(4) ADDITIONAL TAX FOR DISTRIBUTIONS NOT USED FOR EDUCATIONAL EXPENSES.—

* * *

(B) EXCEPTIONS.—Subparagraph (A) shall not apply if the payment or distribution is—

* * *

(iii) made on account of a scholarship, allowance, or payment described in section 25A(g)(2) received by the account holder to the extent the amount of the payment or distribution does not exceed the amount of the scholarship, allowance, or payment, *or*

* * *

[CCH Explanation at ¶ 30,050.]

<table>
<tr><td>Amendment Notes</td><td>The above amendment is effective on December 21, 2000.</td></tr>
<tr><td>P.L. 106-554 (Community Renewal)
Act Sec. 319(6) amended Code Sec. 530(d)(4)(B)(iii) by striking "; or" at the end and inserting ", or".</td><td></td></tr>
</table>

[¶ 5380] CODE SEC. 664. CHARITABLE REMAINDER TRUSTS.

* * *

(d) DEFINITIONS.—

(1) CHARITABLE REMAINDER ANNUITY TRUST.—For purposes of this section, a charitable remainder annuity trust is a trust—

(A) from which a sum certain (which is not less than 5 percent nor more than 50 percent of the initial net fair market value of all property placed in trust) is to be paid, not less often than annually, to one or more persons (at least one of which is not an organization described in section 170(c) and, in the case of individuals, only to an individual who is living at the time of the creation of the trust) for a term of years (not in excess of 20 years) or for the life or lives of such individual or individuals,

(B) from which no amount other than the payments described in subparagraph (A) and other than qualified gratuitous transfers described in subparagraph (C) may be paid to or for the use of any person other than an organization described in section 170(c),

(C) following the termination of the payments described in subparagraph (A), the remainder interest in the trust is to be transferred to, or for the use of, an organization described in section 170(c) or is to be retained by the trust for such a use or, to the extent the remainder interest is in qualified employer securities (as defined in subsection (g)(4)), all or part of such securities are to be transferred to an employee stock ownership plan (as defined in section 4975(e)(7)) in a qualified gratuitous transfer (as defined by subsection (g)), and

(D) the value (determined under section 7520) of such remainder interest is at least 10 percent of the initial net fair market value of all property placed in the trust.

(2) CHARITABLE REMAINDER UNITRUST.—For purposes of this section, a charitable remainder unitrust is a trust—

(A) from which a fixed percentage (which is not less than 5 percent nor more than 50 percent) of the net fair market value of its assets, valued annually, is to be paid, not less often than annually, to one or more persons (at least one of which is not an organization described in section 170(c) and, in the case of individuals, only to an individual who is living at the time of the creation of the trust) for a term of years (not in excess of 20 years) or for the life or lives of such individual or individuals,

(B) from which no amount other than the payments described in subparagraph (A) and other than qualified gratuitous transfers described in subparagraph (C) may be paid to or for the use of any person other than an organization described in section 170(c),

(C) following the termination of the payments described in subparagraph (A), the remainder interest in the trust is to be transferred to, or for the use of, an organization described in section 170(c) or is to be retained by the trust for such a use or, to the extent the remainder interest is in qualified employer securities (as defined in subsection (g)(4)), all or part of such securities are to be transferred to an employee stock ownership plan (as defined in section 4975(e)(7)) in a qualified gratuitous transfer (as defined by subsection (g)), and

(D) with respect to each contribution of property to the trust, the value (determined under section 7520) of such remainder interest in such property is at least 10 percent of the net fair market value of such property as of the date such property is contributed to the trust.

[CCH Explanation at ¶ 30,050.]

Amendment Notes

P.L. 106-554 (Community Renewal)

Act Sec. 319(7) amended Code Sec. 664(d)(1)(C) and (2)(C) by striking the period after "subsection (g))".

The above amendment is effective on December 21, 2000.

[¶ 5390] CODE SEC. 678. PERSON OTHER THAN GRANTOR TREATED AS SUBSTANTIAL OWNER.

* * *

(e) CROSS REFERENCE.—

For provision under which beneficiary of trust is treated as owner of the portion of the trust which consists of stock in *an S corporation*, see section 1361(d).

[CCH Explanation at ¶ 30,050.]

Amendment Notes

P.L. 106-554 (Community Renewal)

Act Sec. 319(8)(A) amended Code Sec. 678(e) by striking "an electing small business corporation" and inserting "an S corporation".

The above amendment is effective on December 21, 2000.

[¶ 5400] CODE SEC. 848. CAPITALIZATION OF CERTAIN POLICY ACQUISITION EXPENSES.

* * *

(e) CLASSIFICATION OF CONTRACTS.—For purposes of this section—

(1) SPECIFIED INSURANCE CONTRACT.—

* * *

(B) EXCEPTIONS.—The term "specified insurance contract" shall not include—

(i) any pension plan contract (as defined in section 818(a)),

(ii) any flight insurance or similar contract,

(iii) any qualified foreign contract (as defined in section 807(e)(4) without regard to paragraph (5) of this subsection), and

(iv) any contract which is *an Archer MSA* (as defined in section 220(d)).

* * *

[CCH Explanation at ¶ 615. Committee Reports at ¶ 10,245.]

Amendment Notes

P.L. 106-554 (Community Renewal)

Act Sec. 202(a)(5) amended Code Sec. 848(e)(1)(B)(iv) by srtiking "medical savings account" and inserting "Archer MSA".

Act Sec. 202(b)(10) amended Code Sec. 848(e)(1)(B)(iv) by striking "a Archer" and inserting "an Archer".

The above amendments are effective on December 21, 2000.

[¶ 5410] CODE SEC. 856. DEFINITION OF REAL ESTATE INVESTMENT TRUST.

* * *

(c) LIMITATIONS.—A corporation, trust, or association shall not be considered a real estate investment trust for any taxable year unless—

* * *

(7) STRAIGHT DEBT SAFE HARBOR IN APPLYING PARAGRAPH (4).—Securities of an issuer which are straight debt (as defined in section 1361(c)(5) without regard to subparagraph (B)(iii) thereof) shall not be taken into account in applying *paragraph (4)(B)(iii)(III)* if—

(A) the issuer is an individual, or

(B) the only securities of such issuer which are held by the trust or a taxable REIT subsidiary of the trust are straight debt (as so defined), or

Code Sec. 856(c)   ¶ 5410

(C) the issuer is a partnership and the trust holds at least a 20 percent profits interest in the partnership.

* * *

[CCH Explanation at ¶ 30,050.]

Amendment Notes

P.L. 106-554 (Community Renewal)

Act Sec. 319(9) amended Code Sec. 856(c)(7) by striking "paragraph (4)(B)(ii)(III)" and inserting "paragraph (4)(B)(iii)(III)".

The above amendment is effective on December 21, 2000.

(l) TAXABLE REIT SUBSIDIARY.—For purposes of this part—

* * *

(4) DEFINITIONS.—For purposes of paragraph (3)—

(A) LODGING FACILITY.—The term "lodging facility" has the meaning given to such term by *subsection (d)(9)(D)(ii)*.

* * *

[CCH Explanation at ¶ 30,050.]

Amendment Notes

P.L. 106-554 (Community Renewal)

Act Sec. 319(10) amended Code Sec. 856(l)(4)(A) by striking "paragraph (9)(D)(ii)" and inserting "subsection (d)(9)(D)(ii)".

The above amendment is effective on December 21, 2000.

[¶ 5420] CODE SEC. 857. TAXATION OF REAL ESTATE INVESTMENT TRUSTS AND THEIR BENEFICIARIES.

* * *

(b) METHOD OF TAXATION OF REAL ESTATE INVESTMENT TRUSTS AND HOLDERS OF SHARES OR CERTIFICATES OF BENEFICIAL INTEREST.—

* * *

(7) INCOME FROM REDETERMINED RENTS, REDETERMINED DEDUCTIONS, AND EXCESS INTEREST.—

* * *

(B) REDETERMINED RENTS.—

* * *

(ii) EXCEPTION FOR CERTAIN AMOUNTS.—Clause (i) shall not apply to amounts received directly or indirectly by a real estate investment trust—

(I) for services furnished or rendered by a taxable REIT subsidiary that are described in paragraph (1)(B) of section 856(d), or

(II) from a taxable REIT subsidiary that are described in paragraph (7)(C)(ii) of such section.

* * *

[CCH Explanation at ¶ 415. Committee Reports at ¶ 10,310.]

Amendment Notes

P.L. 106-554 (Community Renewal)

Act Sec. 311(b) amended Code Sec. 857(b)(7)(B)(ii) to read as above. Prior to amendment, Code Sec. 857(b)(7)(B)(ii) read as follows:

(ii) EXCEPTION FOR CERTAIN SERVICES.—Clause (i) shall not apply to amounts received directly or indirectly by a real

estate investment trust for services described in paragraph (1)(B) or (7)(C)(i) of section 856(d).

The above amendment is effective as if included in the provision of the Ticket to Work and Work Incentives Improvement Act of 1999 (P.L. 106-170) to which it relates [effective for tax years beginning after December 31, 2000.—CCH.].

[¶ 5430] CODE SEC. 864. DEFINITIONS AND SPECIAL RULES.

* * *

(e) RULES FOR ALLOCATING INTEREST, ETC.—For purposes of this subchapter—

* * *

(3) TAX-EXEMPT ASSETS NOT TAKEN INTO ACCOUNT.—

(A) IN GENERAL.—For purposes of allocating and apportioning any deductible expense, any tax-exempt asset (and any income from such an asset) shall not be taken into account. A similar rule shall apply in the case of the portion of any dividend (other than a qualifying dividend as

defined in section 243(b)) equal to the deduction allowable under section 243 or 245(a) with respect to such dividend and in the case of a like portion of any stock the dividends on which would be so deductible and would not be qualifying dividends (as so defined).

(B) *ASSETS PRODUCING EXEMPT EXTRATERRITORIAL INCOME.—For purposes of allocating and apportioning any interest expense, there shall not be taken into account any qualifying foreign trade property (as defined in section 943(a)) which is held by the taxpayer for lease or rental in the ordinary course of trade or business for use by the lessee outside the United States (as defined in section 943(b)(2)).*

* * *

[CCH Explanation at ¶ 530. Committee Reports at ¶ 10,115.]

Amendment Notes

P.L. 106-519 (FSC Repeal)

Act Sec. 4(3)(A)-(B) amended Code Sec. 864(e)(3) by striking "For purposes of" and inserting "(A) IN GENERAL.— For purposes of"; and by adding at the end a new subparagraph (B) to read as above.

The above amendment applies generally to transactions after September 30, 2000. For special rules, see Act Sec. 5(b)-(d) in the amendment notes following Code Sec. 921, below.

[¶ 5440] CODE SEC. 871. TAX ON NONRESIDENT ALIEN INDIVIDUALS.

* * *

(f) CERTAIN ANNUITIES RECEIVED UNDER QUALIFIED PLANS—

* * *

(2) EXCLUSION.—Income received during the taxable year which would be excluded from gross income under this subsection but for the requirement of paragraph (1)(B) shall not be included in gross income if—

(A) the recipient's country of residence grants a substantially equivalent exclusion to residents and citizens of the United States; or

(B) the recipient's country of residence is a beneficiary developing country under title V of the Trade Act of 1974 *(19 U.S.C. 2461 et seq.).*

* * *

[CCH Explanation at ¶ 30,050.]

Amendment Notes

P.L. 106-554 (Community Renewal)

Act Sec. 319(11) amended Code Sec. 871(f)(2)(B) by striking "19 U.S.C." and inserting "(19 U.S.C.".

The above amendment is effective on December 21, 2000.

[¶ 5450] CODE SEC. 903. CREDIT FOR TAXES IN LIEU OF INCOME, ETC., TAXES.

For purposes of this part and of sections *114, 164(a),* and 275(a), the term "income, war profits, and excess profits taxes" shall include a tax paid in lieu of a tax on income, war profits, or excess profits otherwise generally imposed by any foreign country or by any possession of the United States.

[CCH Explanation at ¶ 515. Committee Reports at ¶ 10,115.]

Amendment Notes

P.L. 106-519 (FSC Repeal)

Act Sec. 4(4) amended Code Sec. 903 by striking "164(a)" and inserting "114, 164(a),".

The above amendment applies generally to transactions after September 30, 2000. For special rules, see Act Sec. 5(b)-(d) in the amendment notes following Code Sec. 921, below.

[¶ 5460] CODE SEC. 921. EXEMPT FOREIGN TRADE INCOME EXCLUDED FROM GROSS INCOME. [Repealed.]

[CCH Explanation at ¶ 505–¶ 545. Committee Reports at ¶ 10,115.]

Amendment Notes

P.L. 106-519 (FSC Repeal)

Act Sec. 2 repealed subpart C of part III of subchapter N of chapter 1 (Code Secs. 921-927). Prior to repeal, Code Sec. 921 read as follows:

SEC. 921. EXEMPT FOREIGN TRADE INCOME EXCLUDED FROM GROSS INCOME.

(a) EXCLUSION.—Exempt foreign trade income of a FSC shall be treated as foreign source income which is not effectively connected with the conduct of a trade or business within the United States.

(b) PROPORTIONATE ALLOCATION OF DEDUCTIONS TO EXEMPT FOREIGN TRADE INCOME.—Any deductions of the FSC properly apportioned and allocated to the foreign trade income derived by a FSC from any transaction shall be allocated between—

(1) the exempt foreign trade income derived from such transaction, and

(2) the foreign trade income (other than exempt foreign trade income) derived from such transaction, on a proportionate basis.

(c) DENIAL OF CREDITS.—Notwithstanding any other provision of this chapter, no credit (other than a credit allowable under section 27(a), 33, or 34) shall be allowed under this chapter to any FSC.

(d) FOREIGN TRADE INCOME, INVESTMENT INCOME, AND CARRYING CHARGES TREATED AS EFFECTIVELY CONNECTED WITH UNITED STATES BUSINESS.—For purposes of this chapter—

(1) all foreign trade income of a FSC other than—

(A) exempt foreign trade income, and

(B) section 923(a)(2) non-exempt income,

(2) all interest, dividends, royalties, and other investment income received or accrued by a FSC, and

(3) all carrying charges received or accrued by a FSC,

shall be treated as income effectively connected with a trade or business conducted through a permanent establishment of such corporation within the United States. Income described in paragraph (1) shall be treated as derived from sources within the United States.

The above amendment applies generally to transactions after September 30, 2000. For special rules, see Act Sec. 5(b)-(d), below.

Act Sec. 5(b)-(d) provides:

(b) NO NEW FSCS; TERMINATION OF INACTIVE FSCS.—

(1) NO NEW FSCS.—No corporation may elect after September 30, 2000, to be a FSC (as defined in section 922 of the Internal Revenue Code of 1986, as in effect before the amendments made by this Act).

(2) TERMINATION OF INACTIVE FSCS.—If a FSC has no foreign trade income (as defined in section 923(b) of such Code, as so in effect) for any period of 5 consecutive taxable years beginning after December 31, 2001, such FSC shall cease to be treated as a FSC for purposes of such Code for any taxable year beginning after such period.

(c) TRANSITION PERIOD FOR EXISTING FOREIGN SALES CORPORATIONS.—

(1) IN GENERAL.—In the case of a FSC (as so defined) in existence on September 30, 2000, and at all times thereafter, the amendments made by this Act shall not apply to any transaction in the ordinary course of trade or business involving a FSC which occurs—

(A) before January 1, 2002; or

(B) after December 31, 2001, pursuant to a binding contract—

(i) which is between the FSC (or any related person) and any person which is not a related person; and

(ii) which is in effect on September 30, 2000, and at all times thereafter.

For purposes of this paragraph, a binding contract shall include a purchase option, renewal option, or replacement option which is included in such contract and which is enforceable against the seller or lessor.

(2) ELECTION TO HAVE AMENDMENTS APPLY EARLIER.—A taxpayer may elect to have the amendments made by this Act apply to any transaction by a FSC or any related person to which such amendments would apply but for the application of paragraph (1). Such election shall be effective for the taxable year for which made and all subsequent taxable years, and, once made, may be revoked only with the consent of the Secretary of the Treasury.

(3) EXCEPTION FOR OLD EARNINGS AND PROFITS OF CERTAIN CORPORATIONS.—

(A) IN GENERAL.—In the case of a foreign corporation to which this paragraph applies—

(i) earnings and profits of such corporation accumulated in taxable years ending before October 1, 2000, shall not be included in the gross income of the persons holding stock in such corporation by reason of section 943(e)(4)(B)(i); and

(ii) rules similar to the rules of clauses (ii), (iii), and (iv) of section 953(d)(4)(B) shall apply with respect to such earnings and profits.

The preceding sentence shall not apply to earnings and profits acquired in a transaction after September 30, 2000, to which section 381 applies unless the distributor or transferor corporation was immediately before the transaction a foreign corporation to which this paragraph applies.

(B) EXISTING FSCS.—This paragraph shall apply to any controlled foreign corporation (as defined in section 957) if—

(i) such corporation is a FSC (as so defined) in existence on September 30, 2000;

(ii) such corporation is eligible to make the election under section 943(e) by reason of being described in paragraph (2)(B) of such section; and

(iii) such corporation makes such election not later than for its first taxable year beginning after December 31, 2001.

(C) OTHER CORPORATIONS.—This paragraph shall apply to any controlled foreign corporation (as defined in section 957), and such corporation shall (notwithstanding any provision of section 943(e)) be treated as an applicable foreign corporation for purposes of section 943(e), if—

(i) such corporation is in existence on September 30, 2000;

(ii) as of such date, such corporation is wholly owned (directly or indirectly) by a domestic corporation (determined without regard to any election under section 943(e));

(iii) for each of the 3 taxable years preceding the first taxable year to which the election under section 943(e) by such controlled foreign corporation applies—

(I) all of the gross income of such corporation is subpart F income (as defined in section 952), including by reason of section 954(b)(3)(B); and

(II) in the ordinary course of such corporation's trade or business, such corporation regularly sold (or paid commissions) to a FSC which on September 30, 2000, was a related person to such corporation;

(iv) such corporation has never made an election under section 922(a)(2) (as in effect before the date of enactment of this paragraph) to be treated as a FSC; and

(v) such corporation makes the election under section 943(e) not later than for its first taxable year beginning after December 31, 2001.

The preceding sentence shall cease to apply as of the date that the domestic corporation referred to in clause (ii) ceases to wholly own (directly or indirectly) such controlled foreign corporation.

(4) RELATED PERSON.—For purposes of this subsection, the term "related person" has the meaning given to such term by section 943(b)(3).

(5) SECTION REFERENCES.—Except as otherwise expressly provided, any reference in this subsection to a section or other provision shall be considered to be a reference to a section or other provision of the Internal Revenue Code of 1986, as amended by this Act.

(d) SPECIAL RULES RELATING TO LEASING TRANSACTIONS.—

(1) SALES INCOME.—If foreign trade income in connection with the lease or rental of property described in section 927(a)(1)(B) of such Code (as in effect before the amendments made by this Act) is treated as exempt foreign trade income for purposes of section 921(a) of such Code (as so in effect), such property shall be treated as property described in section 941(c)(1)(B) of such Code (as added by this Act) for purposes of applying section 941(c)(2) of such Code (as so added) to any subsequent transaction involving such property to which the amendments made by this Act apply.

(2) LIMITATION ON USE OF GROSS RECEIPTS METHOD.—If any person computed its foreign trade income from any transaction with respect to any property on the basis of a transfer price determined under the method described in section 925(a)(1) of such Code (as in effect before the amendments made by this Act), then the qualifying foreign trade income (as defined in section 941(a) of such Code, as in effect after such amendment) of such person (or any related person) with respect to any other transaction involving such property

(and to which the amendments made by this Act apply) shall be zero.

[¶ 5470] CODE SEC. 922. FSC DEFINED. *[Repealed.]*

[CCH Explanation at ¶ 505 and ¶ 510. Committee Reports at ¶ 10,115.]

Amendment Notes

P.L. 106-519 (FSC Repeal)

Act Sec. 2 repealed subpart C of part III of subchapter N of chapter 1 (Code Secs. 921-927). Prior to repeal, Code Sec. 922 read as follows:

SEC. 922. FSC DEFINED.

(a) FSC DEFINED.—For purposes of this title, the term "FSC" means any corporation—

(1) which—

(A) was created or organized—

(i) under the laws of any foreign country which meets the requirements of section 927(e)(3), or

(ii) under the laws applicable to any possession of the United States,

(B) has no more than 25 shareholders at any time during the taxable year,

(C) does not have any preferred stock outstanding at any time during the taxable year,

(D) during the taxable year—

(i) maintains an office located outside the United States in a foreign country which meets the requirements of section 927(e)(3) or in any possession of the United States,

(ii) maintains a set of the permanent books of account (including invoices) of such corporation at such office, and

(iii) maintains at a location within the United States the records which such corporation is required to keep under section 6001,

(E) at all times during the taxable year, has a board of directors which includes at least one individual who is not a resident of the United States, and

(F) is not a member, at any time during the taxable year, of any controlled group of corporations of which a DISC is a member, and

(2) which has made an election (at the time and in the manner provided in section 927(f)(1)) which is in effect for the taxable year to be treated as a FSC.

(b) SMALL FSC DEFINED.—For purposes of this title, a FSC is a small FSC with respect to any taxable year if—

(1) such corporation has made an elecion (at the time and in the manner provided in section 927(f)(1)) which is in effect for the taxable year to be treated as a small FSC, and

(2) such corporation is not a member, at any time during the taxable year, of controlled group of corporations which includes a FSC unless such other FSC has also made an election under paragraph (1) which is in effect for such year.

The above amendment applies generally to transactions after September 30, 2000. For special rules, see Act Sec. 5(b)-(d) in the amendment notes following Code Sec. 921, above.

[¶ 5480] CODE SEC. 923. EXEMPT FOREIGN TRADE INCOME. *[Repealed.]*

[CCH Explanation at ¶ 505 and ¶ 510. Committee Reports at ¶ 10,115.]

Amendment Notes

P.L. 106-519 (FSC Repeal)

Act Sec. 2 repealed subpart C of part III of subchapter N of chapter 1 (Code Secs. 921-927). Prior to repeal, Code Sec. 923 read as follows:

SEC. 923. EXEMPT FOREIGN TRADE INCOME.

(a) EXEMPT FOREIGN TRADE INCOME.—For purposes of this subpart—

(1) IN GENERAL.—The term "exempt foreign trade income" means the aggregate amount of all foreign trade income of a FSC for the taxable year which is described in paragraph (2) or (3).

(2) INCOME DETERMINED WITHOUT REGARD TO ADMINISTRATIVE PRICING RULES.—In the case of any transaction to which paragraph (3) does not apply, 32 percent of the foreign trade income derived from such transaction shall be treated as described in this paragraph. For purposes of the preceding sentence, foreign trade income shall not include any income properly allocable to excluded property described in subparagraph (B) of section 927(a)(2) (relating to intangibles).

(3) INCOME DETERMINED WITH REGARD TO ADMINISTRATIVE PRICING RULES.—In the case of any transaction with respect to which paragraph (1) or (2) of section 925(a) (or the corresponding provisions of the regulations prescribed under section 925(b)) applies, 16/23 of the foreign trade income derived from such transaction shall be treated as described in this paragraph.

(4) SPECIAL RULE FOR FOREIGN TRADE INCOME ALLOCABLE TO A COOPERATIVE.—

(A) IN GENERAL.—In any case in which a qualified cooperative is a shareholder of a FSC, paragraph (3) shall be applied with respect to that portion of the foreign trade income of such FSC for any taxable year which is properly allocable to the marketing of agricultural or horticultural products (or the providing of related services) by such cooperative by substituting "100 percent" for "16/23".

(B) PARAGRAPH ONLY TO APPLY TO AMOUNTS FSC DISTRIBUTES.—Subparagraph (A) shall not apply for any taxable year unless the FSC distributes to the qualified cooperative the amount which (but for such subparagraph) would not be treated as exempt foreign trade income. Any distribution under this subparagraph for any taxable year—

(i) shall be made before the due date for filing the return of tax for such taxable year, but

(ii) shall be treated as made on the last day of such taxable year.

(5) SPECIAL RULE FOR MILITARY PROPERTY.—Under regulations prescribed by the Secretary, that portion of the foreign trading gross receipts of the FSC for the taxable year attributable to the disposition of, or services relating to, military property (within the meaning of section 995(b)(3)(B)) which may be treated as exempt foreign trade income shall equal 50 percent of the amount which (but for this paragraph) would be treated as exempt foreign trade income.

(6) CROSS REFERENCE.—For reduction in amount of exempt foreign trade income, see section 291(a)(4).

(b) FOREIGN TRADE INCOME DEFINED.—For purposes of this subpart, the term "foreign trade income" means the gross income of a FSC attributable to foreign trading gross receipts.

The above amendment applies generally to transactions after September 30, 2000. For special rules, see Act Sec. 5(b)-(d) in the amendment notes following Code Sec. 921, above.

[¶ 5490] CODE SEC. 924. FOREIGN TRADING GROSS RECEIPTS. *[Repealed.]*

[CCH Explanation at ¶ 505 and ¶ 510. Committee Reports at ¶ 10,115.]

Amendment Notes

P.L. 106-519 (FSC Repeal)

Act Sec. 2 repealed subpart C of part III of subchapter N of chapter 1 (Code Secs. 921-927). Prior to repeal, Code Sec. 924 read as follows:

SEC. 924. FOREIGN TRADING GROSS RECEIPTS.

(a) IN GENERAL.—Except as otherwise provided in this section, for purposes of this subpart, the term "foreign trading gross receipts" means the gross receipts of any FSC which are—

(1) from the sale, exchange, or other disposition of export property,

(2) from the lease or rental of export property for use by the lessee outside the United States,

(3) for services which are related and subsidiary to—

(A) any sale, exchange, or other disposition of export property by such corporation, or

(B) any lease or rental of export property described in paragraph (2) by such corporation,

(4) for engineering or architectural services for construction projects located (or proposed for location) outside the United States, or

(5) for the performance of managerial services for an unrelated FSC or DISC in furtherance of the production of foreign trading gross receipts described in paragraph (1), (2), or (3).

Paragraph (5) shall not apply to a FSC for any taxable year unless at least 50 percent of its gross receipts for such taxable year is derived from activities described in paragraph (1), (2), or (3).

(b) FOREIGN MANAGEMENT AND FOREIGN ECONOMIC PROCESS REQUIREMENTS.—

(1) IN GENERAL.—Except as provided in paragraph (2)—

(A) a FSC shall be treated as having foreign trading gross receipts for the taxable year only if the management of such corporation during such taxable year takes place outside the United States as required by subsection (c), and

(B) a FSC has foreign trading gross receipts from any transaction only if economic processes with respect to such transaction take place outside the United States as required by subsection (d).

(2) EXCEPTION FOR SMALL FSC.—

(A) IN GENERAL.—Paragraph (1) shall not apply with respect to any small FSC.

(B) LIMITATION ON AMOUNT OF FOREIGN TRADING GROSS RECEIPTS OF SMALL FSC TAKEN INTO ACCOUNT.—

(i) IN GENERAL.—Any foreign trading gross receipts of a small FSC for the taxable year which exceed $5,000,000 shall not be taken into account in determining the exempt foreign trade income of such corporation and shall not be taken into account under any other provision of this subpart.

(ii) ALLOCATION OF LIMITATION.—If the foreign trading gross receipts of a small FSC exceed the limitation of clause (i), the corporation may allocate such limitation among such gross receipts in such manner as it may select (at such time and in such manner as may be prescribed in regulations).

(iii) RECEIPTS OF CONTROLLED GROUP AGGREGATED.—For purposes of applying clauses (i) and (ii), all small FSC's which are members of the same controlled group of corporations shall be treated as a single corporation.

(iv) ALLOCATION OF LIMITATION AMONG MEMBERS OF CONTROLLED GROUP.—The limitation under clause (i) shall be allocated among the foreign trading gross receipts of small FSC's which are members of the same controlled group of corporations in a manner provided in regulations prescribed by the Secretary.

(c) REQUIREMENT THAT FSC BE MANAGED OUTSIDE THE UNITED STATES.—The management of a FSC meets the requirements of this subsection for the taxable year if—

(1) all meetings of the board of directors of the corporation, and all meetings of the shareholders of the corporation, are outside the United States,

(2) the principal bank account of the corporation is maintained in a foreign country which meets the requirements of section 927(e)(3) or in a possession of the United States at all times during the taxable year, and

(3) all dividends, legal and accounting fees, and salaries of officers and members of the board of directors of the corporation disbursed during the taxable year are disbursed out of bank accounts of the corporation maintained outside the United States.

(d) REQUIREMENT THAT ECONOMIC PROCESSES TAKE PLACE OUTSIDE THE UNITED STATES.—

(1) IN GENERAL.—The requirements of this subsection are met with respect to the gross receipts of a FSC derived from any transaction if—

(A) such corporation (or any person acting under a contract with such corporation) has participated outside the United States in the solicitation (other than advertising), the negotiation, or the making of the contract relating to such transaction, and

(B) the foreign direct costs incurred by the FSC attributable to the transaction equal or exceed 50 percent of the total direct costs attributable to the transaction.

(2) ALTERNATIVE 85-PERCENT TEST.—A corporation shall be treated as satisfying the requirements of paragraph (1)(B) with respect to any transaction if, with respect to each of at least 2 paragraphs of subsection (e), the foreign direct costs incurred by such corporation attributable to activities described in such paragraph equal or exceed 85 percent of the total direct costs attributable to activities described in such paragraph.

(3) DEFINITIONS.—For purposes of this subsection—

(A) TOTAL DIRECT COSTS.—The term "total direct costs" means, with respect to any transaction, the total direct costs incurred by the FSC attributable to activities described in subsection (e) performed at any location by the FSC or any person acting under a contract with such FSC.

(B) FOREIGN DIRECT COSTS.—The term "foreign direct costs" means, with respect to any transaction, the portion of the total direct costs which are attributable to activities performed outside the United States.

(4) RULES FOR COMMISSIONS, ETC.—The Secretary shall prescribe such regulations as may be necessary to carry out the purposes of this subsection and subsection (e) in the case of commissions, rentals, and furnishing of services.

(e) ACTIVITIES RELATING TO DISPOSITION OF EXPORT PROPERTY.—The activities referred to in subsection (d) are—

(1) advertising and sales promotion,

(2) the processing of customer orders and the arranging for delivery of the export property,

(3) transportation from the time of acquisition by the FSC (or, in the case of a commission relationship, from the beginning of such relationship for such transaction) to the delivery to the customer,

(4) the determination and transmittal of a final invoice or statement of account and the receipt of payment, and

(5) the assumption of credit risk.

(f) CERTAIN RECEIPTS NOT INCLUDED IN FOREIGN TRADING GROSS RECEIPTS.—

(1) CERTAIN RECEIPTS EXCLUDED ON BASIS OF USE; SUBSIDIZED RECEIPTS AND RECEIPTS FROM RELATED PARTIES EXCLUDED.—The term "foreign trading gross receipts" shall not include receipts of a FSC from a transaction if—

(A) the export property or services—

(i) are for ultimate use in the United States, or

(ii) are for use by the United States or any instrumentality thereof and such use of export property or services is required by law or regulation,

(B) such transaction is accomplished by a subsidy granted by the United States or any instrumentality thereof, or

(C) such receipts are from another FSC which is a member of the same controlled group of corporations of which such corporation is a member.

In the case of gross receipts of a FSC from a transaction involving any property, subparagraph (C) shall not apply if such FSC (and all other FSC's which are members of the same controlled group and which receive gross receipts from a transaction involving such property) do not use the pricing rules under paragraph (1) of section 925(a) (or the corresponding provisions of the regulations prescribed under sec-tion 925(b)) with respect to any transaction involving such property.

(2) INVESTMENT INCOME; CARRYING CHARGES.—The term "foreign trading gross receipts" shall not include any invest-ment income or carrying charges.

The above amendment applies generally to transac-tions after September 30, 2000. For special rules, see Act Sec. 5(b)-(d) in the amendment notes following Code Sec. 921, above.

[¶ 5500] CODE SEC. 925. TRANSFER PRICING RULES. *[Repealed.]*

[CCH Explanation at ¶ 505 and ¶ 510. Committee Reports at ¶ 10,115.]

Amendment Notes

P.L. 106-519 (FSC Repeal)

Act Sec. 2 repealed subpart C of part III of subchapter N of Chapter 1 (Code Secs. 921-927). Prior to repeal, Code Sec. 925 read as follows:

SEC. 925. TRANSFER PRICING RULES.

(a) IN GENERAL.—In the case of a sale of export property to a FSC by a person described in section 482, the taxable income of such FSC and such person shall be based upon a transfer price which would allow such FSC to derive taxable income attributable to such sale (regardless of the sales price actually charged) in an amount which does not exceed the greatest of—

(1) 1.83 percent of the foreign trading gross receipts derived from the sale of such property by such FSC,

(2) 23 percent of the combined taxable income of such FSC and such person which is attributable to the foreign trading gross receipts derived from the sale of such property by such FSC, or

(3) taxable income based upon the sale price actually charged (but subject to the rules provided in section 482).

Paragraphs (1) and (2) shall apply only if the FSC meets the requirements of subsection (c) with respect to the sale.

(b) RULES FOR COMMISSIONS, RENTALS, AND MARGINAL COSTING.—The Secretary shall prescribe regulations setting forth—

(1) rules which are consistent with the rules set forth in subsection (a) for the application of this section in the case of commissions, rentals, and other income, and

(2) rules for the allocation of expenditures in computing combined taxable income under subsection (a)(2) in those cases where a FSC is seeking to establish or maintain a market for export property.

(c) REQUIREMENTS FOR USE OF ADMINISTRATIVE PRICING RULES.—A sale by a FSC meets the requirements of this subsection if—

(1) all of the activities described in section 924(e) attribu-table to such sale, and

(2) all of the activities relating to the solicitation (other than advertising), negotiation, and making of the contract for such sale,

have been performed by such FSC (or by another person acting under a contract with such FSC).

(d) LIMITATION ON GROSS RECEIPTS PRICING RULE.—The amount determined under subsection (a)(1) with respect to any transaction shall not exceed 2 times the amount which would be determined under subsection (a)(2) with respect to such transaction.

(e) TAXABLE INCOME.—For purposes of this section, the taxable income of a FSC shall be determined without regard to section 921.

(f) SPECIAL RULE FOR COOPERATIVES.—In any case in which a qualified cooperative sells export property to a FSC, in computing the combined taxable income of such FSC and such organization for purposes of subsection (a)(2), there shall not be taken into account any deduction allowable under subsection (b) or (c) of section 1382 (relating to patronage dividends, per-unit retain allocations, and nonpa-tronage distributions).

The above amendment applies generally to transac-tions after September 30, 2000. For special rules, see Act Sec. 5(b)-(d) in the amendment notes following Code Sec. 921, above.

[¶ 5510] CODE SEC. 926. DISTRIBUTIONS TO SHAREHOLDERS. *[Repealed.]*

[CCH Explanation at ¶ 505 and ¶ 510. Committee Reports at ¶ 10,115.]

Amendment Notes

P.L. 106-519 (FSC Repeal)

Act Sec. 2 repealed subpart C of part III of subchapter N of chapter 1 (Code Secs. 921-927). Prior to repeal, Code Sec. 926 read as follows:

SEC. 926. DISTRIBUTIONS TO SHAREHOLDERS.

(a) DISTRIBUTIONS MADE FIRST OUT OF FOREIGN TRADE INCOME.—For purposes of this title, any distribution to a shareholder of a FSC by such FSC which is made out of earnings and profits shall be treated as made—

(1) first, out of earnings and profits attributable to foreign trade income, to the extent thereof, and

(2) then, out of any other earnings and profits.

(b) DISTRIBUTIONS BY FSC TO NONRESIDENT ALIENS AND FOREIGN CORPORATIONS TREATED AS UNITED STATES CON-NECTED.—For purposes of this title, any distribution by a FSC which is made out of earnings and profits attributable to foreign trade income to any shareholder of such corporation which is a foreign corporation or a nonresident alien individ-ual shall be treated as a distribution—

(1) which is effectively connected with the conduct of a trade or business conducted through a permanent establish-ment of such shareholder within the United States, and

(2) of income which is derived from sources within the United States.

(c) FSC INCLUDES FORMER FSC.—For purposes of this section, the term "FSC" includes a former FSC.

The above amendment applies generally to transac-tions after September 30, 2000. For special rules, see Act Sec. 5(b)-(d) in the amendment notes following Code Sec. 921, above.

[¶ 5520] CODE SEC. 927. OTHER DEFINITIONS AND SPECIAL RULES. *[Repealed.]*

[CCH Explanation at ¶ 505 and ¶ 510. Committee Reports at ¶ 10,115.]

Amendment Notes

P.L. 106-519 (FSC Repeal)

Act Sec. 2 repealed subpart C of part III of subchapter N of chapter 1 (Code Secs. 921-927). Prior to repeal, Code Sec. 927 read as follows:

SEC. 927. OTHER DEFINITIONS AND SPECIAL RULES.

(a) EXPORT PROPERTY.—For purposes of this subpart—

(1) IN GENERAL.—The term "export property" means property—

(A) manufactured, produced, grown, or extracted in the United States by a person other than a FSC,

(B) held primarily for sale, lease, or rental, in the ordinary course of trade or business, by, or to, a FSC, for direct use, consumption, or disposition outside the United States, and

(C) not more than 50 percent of the fair market value of which is attributable to articles imported into the United States.

For purposes of subparagraph (C), the fair market value of any article imported into the United States shall be its appraised value, as determined by the Secretary under section 402 of the Tariff Act of 1930 (19 U.S.C. 1401a) in connection with its importation.

(2) EXCLUDED PROPERTY.—The term "export property" shall not include—

(A) property leased or rented by a FSC for use by any member of a controlled group of corporations of which such FSC is a member,

(B) patents, inventions, models, designs, formulas, or processes whether or not patented, copyrights (other than films, tapes, records, or similar reproductions, and other than computer software (whether or not patented), for commercial or home use), good will, trademarks, trade brands, franchises, or other like property,

(C) oil or gas (or any primary product thereof),

(D) products the export of which is prohibited or curtailed to effectuate the policy set forth in paragraph (2)(C) of section 3 of the Export Administration Act of 1979 (relating to the protection of the domestic economy), or

(E) any unprocessed timber which is a softwood.

For purposes of subparagraph (E), the term "unprocessed timber" means any log, cant, or similar form of timber.

(3) PROPERTY IN SHORT SUPPLY.—If the President determines that the supply of any property described in paragraph (1) is insufficient to meet the requirements of the domestic economy, he may by Executive order designate the property as in short supply. Any property so designated shall not be treated as export property during the period beginning with the date specified in the Executive order and ending with the date specified in an Executive order setting forth the President's determination that the property is no longer in short supply.

(4) QUALIFIED COOPERATIVE.—The term "qualified cooperative" means any organization to which part I of subchapter T applies which is engaged in the marketing of agricultural or horticultural products.

(b) GROSS RECEIPTS.—

(1) IN GENERAL.—For purposes of this subpart, the term "gross receipts" means—

(A) the total receipts from the sale, lease, or rental of property held primarily for sale, lease, or rental in the ordinary course of trade or business, and

(B) gross income from all other sources.

(2) GROSS RECEIPTS TAKEN INTO ACCOUNT IN CASE OF COMMISSIONS.—In the case of commissions on the sale, lease, or rental of property, the amount taken into account for purposes of this subpart as gross receipts shall be the gross receipts on the sale, lease, or rental of the property on which such commissions arose.

(c) INVESTMENT INCOME.—For purposes of this subpart, the term "investment income" means—

(1) dividends,

(2) interest,

(3) royalties,

(4) annuities,

(5) rents (other than rents from the lease or rental of export property for use by the lessee outside of the United States),

(6) gains from the sale or exchange of stock or securities,

(7) gains from futures transactions in any commodity on, or subject to the rules of, a board of trade or commodity exchange (other than gains which arise out of a bona fide hedging transaction reasonably necessary to conduct the business of the FSC in the manner in which such business is customarily conducted by others),

(8) amounts includible in computing the taxable income of the corporation under part I of subchapter J, and

(9) gains from the sale or other disposition of any interest in an estate or trust.

(d) OTHER DEFINITIONS.—For purposes of this subpart—

(1) CARRYING CHARGES.—The term "carrying charges" means—

(A) carrying charges, and

(B) under regulations prescribed by the Secretary, any amount in excess of the price for an immediate cash sale and any other unstated interest.

(2) TRANSACTION.—

(A) IN GENERAL.—The term "transaction" means—

(i) any sale, exchange, or other disposition,

(ii) any lease or rental, and

(iii) any furnishing of services.

(B) GROUPING OF TRANSACTIONS.—To the extent provided in regulations, any provision of this subpart which, but for this subparagraph, would be applied on a transaction-by-transaction basis may be applied by the taxpayer on the basis of groups of transactions based on product lines or recognized industry or trade usage. Such regulations may permit different groupings for different purposes.

(3) UNITED STATES DEFINED.—The term "United States" includes the Commonwealth of Puerto Rico.

(4) CONTROLLED GROUP OF CORPORATIONS.—The term "controlled group of corporations" has the meaning given to such term by section 1563(a), except that—

(A) "more than 50 percent" shall be substituted for "at least 80 percent" each place it appears therein, and

(B) section 1563(b) shall not apply.

(5) POSSESSIONS.—The term "possession of the United States" means Guam, American Samoa, the Commonwealth of the Northern Mariana Islands, and the Virgin Islands of the United States.

(6) SECTION 923(A)(2) NON-EXEMPT INCOME.—The term "section 923(a)(2) non-exempt income" means any foreign trade income from a transaction with respect to which paragraph (1) or (2) of section 925(a) does not apply and which is not exempt foreign trade income. Such term shall not include any income which is effectively connected with the conduct of a trade or business within the United States (determined without regard to this subpart).

(e) SPECIAL RULES.—

(1) SOURCE RULES FOR RELATED PERSONS.—Under regulations, the income of a person described in section 482 from a transaction giving rise to foreign trading gross receipts of a FSC which is treated as from sources outside the United States shall not exceed the amount which would be treated as foreign source income earned by such person if the pricing rule under section 994 which corresponds to the rule used under section 925 with respect to such transaction applied to such transaction.

(2) PARTICIPATION IN INTERNATIONAL BOYCOTTS, ETC.—Under regulations prescribed by the Secretary, the exempt foreign trade income of a FSC for any taxable year shall be

limited under rules similar to the rules of clauses (ii) and (iii) of section 995(b)(1)(F).

(3) EXCHANGE OF INFORMATION REQUIREMENTS.—For purposes of this title, the term "FSC" shall not include any corporation which was created or organized under the laws of any foreign country unless there is in effect between such country and the United States—

(A) a bilateral or multilateral agreement described in section 274(h)(6)(C) (determined by treating any reference to a beneficiary country as being a reference to any foreign country and by applying such section without regard to clause (ii) thereof), or

(B) an income tax treaty which contains an exchange of information program—

(i) which the Secretary certifies (and has not revoked such certification) is satisfactory in practice for purposes of this title, and

(ii) to which the FSC is subject.

(4) DISALLOWANCE OF TREATY BENEFITS.—Any corporation electing to be treated as a FSC under subsection (f)(1) may not claim any benefits under any income tax treaty between the United States and any foreign country.

(5) COORDINATION WITH POSSESSIONS TAXATION.—

(A) EXEMPTION.—No tax shall be imposed by any possession of the United States on any foreign trade income derived before January 1, 1987. The preceding sentence shall not apply to any income attributable to the sale of property or the performance of services for ultimate use, consumption, or disposition within the possession.

(B) CLARIFICATION THAT POSSESSION MAY EXEMPT CERTAIN INCOME FROM TAX.—Nothing in any provision of law shall be construed as prohibiting any possession of the United States from exempting from tax any foreign trade income of a FSC or any other income of a FSC described in paragraph (2) or (3) of section 921(d).

(C) NO COVER OVER OF TAXES IMPOSED ON FSC.—Nothing in any provision of law shall be construed as requiring any tax imposed by this title on a FSC to be covered over (or otherwise transferred) to any possession of the United States.

(f) ELECTION OF STATUS AS FSC (AND AS SMALL FSC).—

(1) ELECTION.—

(A) TIME FOR MAKING.—An election by a corporation under section 922(a)(2) to be treated as a FSC, and an election under section 922(b)(1) to be a small FSC, shall be made by such corporation for a taxable year at any time during the 90-day period immediately preceding the beginning of the taxable year, except that the Secretary may give his consent to the making of an election at such other times as he may designate.

(B) MANNER OF ELECTION.—An election under subparagraph (A) shall be made in such manner as the Secretary shall prescribe and shall be valid only if all persons who are shareholders in such corporation on the first day of the first taxable year for which such election is effective consent to such election.

(2) EFFECT OF ELECTION.—If a corporation makes an election under paragraph (1), then the provisions of this subpart shall apply to such corporation for the taxable year of the corporation for which made and for all succeeding taxable years.

(3) TERMINATION OF ELECTION.—

(A) REVOCATION.—An election under this subsection made by any corporation may be terminated by revocation of such election for any taxable year of the corporation after the first taxable year of the corporation for which the election is effective. A termination under this paragraph shall be effective with respect to such election—

(i) for the taxable year in which made, if made at any time during the first 90 days of such taxable year, or

(ii) for the taxable year following the taxable year in which made, if made after the close of such 90 days, and

for all succeeding taxable years of the corporation. Such termination shall be made in such manner as the Secretary shall prescribe by regulations.

(B) CONTINUED FAILURE TO BE A FSC.—If a corporation is not a FSC for each of any 5 consecutive taxable years of the corporation for which an election under this subsection is effective, the election to be a FSC shall be terminated and not be in effect for any taxable year of the corporation after such 5th year.

(g) TREATMENT OF SHARED FSC'S.—

(1) IN GENERAL.—Except as provided in paragraph (2), each separate account referred to in paragraph (3) maintained by a shared FSC shall be treated as a separate corporation for purposes of this subpart.

(2) CERTAIN REQUIREMENTS APPLIED AT SHARED FSC LEVEL.— Paragraph (1) shall not apply—

(A) for purposes of—

(i) subparagraphs (A), (B), (D), and (E) of section 922(a)(1),

(ii) paragraph (2) of section 922(a),

(iii) subsections (b), (c), and (e) of section 924, and

(iv) subsection (f) of this section, and

(B) for such other purposes as the Secretary may by regulations prescribe.

(3) SHARED FSC.—For purposes of this subsection, the term "shared FSC" means any corporation if—

(A) such corporation maintains a separate account for transactions with each shareholder (and persons related to such shareholder),

(B) distributions to each shareholder are based on the amounts in the separate account maintained with respect to such shareholder, and

(C) such corporation meets such other requirements as the Secretary may by regulations prescribe.

The above amendment applies generally to transactions after September 30, 2000. For special rules, see Act Sec. 5(b)-(d) in the amendment notes following Code Sec. 921, above.

[¶ 5530] *CODE SEC. 941. QUALIFYING FOREIGN TRADE INCOME.*

(a) *QUALIFYING FOREIGN TRADE INCOME.—For purposes of this subpart and section 114—*

(1) *IN GENERAL.—The term "qualifying foreign trade income" means, with respect to any transaction, the amount of gross income which, if excluded, will result in a reduction of the taxable income of the taxpayer from such transaction equal to the greatest of—*

(A) *30 percent of the foreign sale and leasing income derived by the taxpayer from such transaction,*

(B) *1.2 percent of the foreign trading gross receipts derived by the taxpayer from the transaction, or*

(C) *15 percent of the foreign trade income derived by the taxpayer from the transaction.*

In no event shall the amount determined under subparagraph (B) exceed 200 percent of the amount determined under subparagraph (C).

(2) *ALTERNATIVE COMPUTATION.*—*A taxpayer may compute its qualifying foreign trade income under a subparagraph of paragraph (1) other than the subparagraph which results in the greatest amount of such income.*

(3) *LIMITATION ON USE OF FOREIGN TRADING GROSS RECEIPTS METHOD.*—*If any person computes its qualifying foreign trade income from any transaction with respect to any property under paragraph (1)(B), the qualifying foreign trade income of such person (or any related person) with respect to any other transaction involving such property shall be zero.*

(4) *RULES FOR MARGINAL COSTING.*—*The Secretary shall prescribe regulations setting forth rules for the allocation of expenditures in computing foreign trade income under paragraph (1)(C) in those cases where a taxpayer is seeking to establish or maintain a market for qualifying foreign trade property.*

(5) *PARTICIPATION IN INTERNATIONAL BOYCOTTS, ETC.*—*Under regulations prescribed by the Secretary, the qualifying foreign trade income of a taxpayer for any taxable year shall be reduced (but not below zero) by the sum of*—

(A) *an amount equal to such income multiplied by the international boycott factor determined under section 999, and*

(B) *any illegal bribe, kickback, or other payment (within the meaning of section 162(c)) paid by or on behalf of the taxpayer directly or indirectly to an official, employee, or agent in fact of a government.*

(b) *FOREIGN TRADE INCOME.*—*For purposes of this subpart*—

(1) *IN GENERAL.*—*The term "foreign trade income" means the taxable income of the taxpayer attributable to foreign trading gross receipts of the taxpayer.*

(2) *SPECIAL RULE FOR COOPERATIVES.*—*In any case in which an organization to which part I of subchapter T applies which is engaged in the marketing of agricultural or horticultural products sells qualifying foreign trade property, in computing the taxable income of such cooperative, there shall not be taken into account any deduction allowable under subsection (b) or (c) of section 1382 (relating to patronage dividends, per-unit retain allocations, and nonpatronage distributions).*

(c) *FOREIGN SALE AND LEASING INCOME.*—*For purposes of this section*—

(1) *IN GENERAL.*—*The term "foreign sale and leasing income" means, with respect to any transaction*—

(A) *foreign trade income properly allocable to activities which*—

(i) *are described in paragraph (2)(A)(i) or (3) of section 942(b), and*

(ii) *are performed by the taxpayer (or any person acting under a contract with such taxpayer) outside the United States, or*

(B) *foreign trade income derived by the taxpayer in connection with the lease or rental of qualifying foreign trade property for use by the lessee outside the United States.*

(2) *SPECIAL RULES FOR LEASED PROPERTY.*—

(A) *SALES INCOME.*—*The term "foreign sale and leasing income" includes any foreign trade income derived by the taxpayer from the sale of property described in paragraph (1)(B).*

(B) *LIMITATION IN CERTAIN CASES.*—*Except as provided in regulations, in the case of property which*—

(i) *was manufactured, produced, grown, or extracted by the taxpayer, or*

(ii) *was acquired by the taxpayer from a related person for a price which was not determined in accordance with the rules of section 482,*

the amount of foreign trade income which may be treated as foreign sale and leasing income under paragraph (1)(B) or subparagraph (A) of this paragraph with respect to any transaction involving such property shall not exceed the amount which would have been determined if the taxpayer had acquired such property for the price determined in accordance with the rules of section 482.

(3) *SPECIAL RULES.*—

(A) *EXCLUDED PROPERTY.*—*Foreign sale and leasing income shall not include any income properly allocable to excluded property described in subparagraph (B) of section 943(a)(3) (relating to intangibles).*

(B) *ONLY DIRECT EXPENSES TAKEN INTO ACCOUNT.*—*For purposes of this subsection, any expense other than a directly allocable expense shall not be taken into account in computing foreign trade income.*

[CCH Explanation at ¶ 515–¶ 535. Committee Reports at ¶ 10,115.]

Amendment Notes

P.L. 106-519 (FSC Repeal)

Act Sec. 3(b) amended part III of subchapter N of chapter 1 by inserting after subpart D a new subpart E (Code Secs. 941-943) to read as above.

The above amendment applies generally to transactions after September 30, 2000. For special rules, see Act Sec. 5(b)-(d) in the amendment notes following Code Sec. 921, above.

[¶ 5540] *CODE SEC. 942. FOREIGN TRADING GROSS RECEIPTS.*

(a) FOREIGN TRADING GROSS RECEIPTS.—

(1) IN GENERAL.—Except as otherwise provided in this section, for purposes of this subpart, the term "foreign trading gross receipts" means the gross receipts of the taxpayer which are—

(A) from the sale, exchange, or other disposition of qualifying foreign trade property,

(B) from the lease or rental of qualifying foreign trade property for use by the lessee outside the United States,

(C) for services which are related and subsidiary to—

(i) any sale, exchange, or other disposition of qualifying foreign trade property by such taxpayer, or

(ii) any lease or rental of qualifying foreign trade property described in subparagraph (B) by such taxpayer,

(D) for engineering or architectural services for construction projects located (or proposed for location) outside the United States, or

(E) for the performance of managerial services for a person other than a related person in furtherance of the production of foreign trading gross receipts described in subparagraph (A), (B), or (C).

Subparagraph (E) shall not apply to a taxpayer for any taxable year unless at least 50 percent of its foreign trading gross receipts (determined without regard to this sentence) for such taxable year is derived from activities described in subparagraph (A), (B), or (C).

(2) CERTAIN RECEIPTS EXCLUDED ON BASIS OF USE: SUBSIDIZED RECEIPTS EXCLUDED.—The term "foreign trading gross receipts" shall not include receipts of a taxpayer from a transaction if—

(A) the qualifying foreign trade property or services—

(i) are for ultimate use in the United States, or

(ii) are for use by the United States or any instrumentality thereof and such use of qualifying foreign trade property or services is required by law or regulation, or

(B) such transaction is accomplished by a subsidy granted by the government (or any instrumentality thereof) of the country or possession in which the property is manufactured, produced, grown, or extracted.

(3) ELECTION TO EXCLUDE CERTAIN RECEIPTS.—The term "foreign trading gross receipts" shall not include gross receipts of a taxpayer from a transaction if the taxpayer elects not to have such receipts taken into account for purposes of this subpart.

(b) FOREIGN ECONOMIC PROCESS REQUIREMENTS.—

(1) IN GENERAL.—Except as provided in subsection (c), a taxpayer shall be treated as having foreign trading gross receipts from any transaction only if economic processes with respect to such transaction take place outside the United States as required by paragraph (2).

(2) REQUIREMENT.—

(A) IN GENERAL.—The requirements of this paragraph are met with respect to the gross receipts of a taxpayer derived from any transaction if—

(i) such taxpayer (or any person acting under a contract with such taxpayer) has participated outside the United States in the solicitation (other than advertising), the negotiation, or the making of the contract relating to such transaction, and

(ii) the foreign direct costs incurred by the taxpayer attributable to the transaction equal or exceed 50 percent of the total direct costs attributable to the transaction.

(B) ALTERNATIVE 85-PERCENT TEST.—A taxpayer shall be treated as satisfying the requirements of subparagraph (A)(ii) with respect to any transaction if, with respect to each of at least 2 subparagraphs of paragraph (3), the foreign direct costs incurred by such taxpayer attributable

to activities described in such subparagraph equal or exceed 85 percent of the total direct costs attributable to activities described in such subparagraph.

(C) DEFINITIONS.—For purposes of this paragraph—

(i) TOTAL DIRECT COSTS.—The term "total direct costs" means, with respect to any transaction, the total direct costs incurred by the taxpayer attributable to activities described in paragraph (3) performed at any location by the taxpayer or any person acting under a contract with such taxpayer.

(ii) FOREIGN DIRECT COSTS.—The term "foreign direct costs" means, with respect to any transaction, the portion of the total direct costs which are attributable to activities performed outside the United States.

(3) ACTIVITIES RELATING TO QUALIFYING FOREIGN TRADE PROPERTY.—The activities described in this paragraph are any of the following with respect to qualifying foreign trade property—

(A) advertising and sales promotion,

(B) the processing of customer orders and the arranging for delivery,

(C) transportation outside the United States in connection with delivery to the customer,

(D) the determination and transmittal of a final invoice or statement of account or the receipt of payment, and

(E) the assumption of credit risk.

(4) ECONOMIC PROCESSES PERFORMED BY RELATED PERSONS.—A taxpayer shall be treated as meeting the requirements of this subsection with respect to any sales transaction involving any property if any related person has met such requirements in such transaction or any other sales transaction involving such property.

(c) EXCEPTION FROM FOREIGN ECONOMIC PROCESS REQUIREMENT.—

(1) IN GENERAL.—The requirements of subsection (b) shall be treated as met for any taxable year if the foreign trading gross receipts of the taxpayer for such year do not exceed $5,000,000.

(2) RECEIPTS OF RELATED PERSONS AGGREGATED.—All related persons shall be treated as one person for purposes of paragraph (1), and the limitation under paragraph (1) shall be allocated among such persons in a manner provided in regulations prescribed by the Secretary.

(3) SPECIAL RULE FOR PASS-THRU ENTITIES.—In the case of a partnership, S corporation, or other pass-thru entity, the limitation under paragraph (1) shall apply with respect to the partnership, S corporation, or entity and with respect to each partner, shareholder, or other owner.

[CCH Explanation at ¶ 515–¶ 535. Committee Reports at ¶ 10,115.]

Amendment Notes

P.L. 106-519 (FSC Repeal)

Act Sec. 3(b) amended part III of subchapter N of chapter 1 by inserting after subpart D a new subpart E (Code Secs. 941-943) to read as above.

The above amendment applies generally to transactions after September 30, 2000. For special rules, see Act Sec. 5(b)-(d) in the amendment notes following Code Sec. 921, above.

[¶ 5550] *CODE SEC. 943. OTHER DEFINITIONS AND SPECIAL RULES.*

(a) QUALIFYING FOREIGN TRADE PROPERTY.—For purposes of this subpart—

(1) IN GENERAL.—The term "qualifying foreign trade property" means property—

(A) manufactured, produced, grown, or extracted within or outside the United States,

(B) held primarily for sale, lease, or rental, in the ordinary course of trade or business for direct use, consumption, or disposition outside the United States, and

(C) not more than 50 percent of the fair market value of which is attributable to—

(i) articles manufactured, produced, grown, or extracted outside the United States, and

(ii) direct costs for labor (determined under the principles of section 263A) performed outside the United States.

For purposes of subparagraph (C), the fair market value of any article imported into the United States shall be its appraised value, as determined by the Secretary under section 402 of the Tariff Act of 1930 (19 U.S.C. 1401a) in connection with its importation, and the direct costs for labor under clause (ii) do not include costs that would be treated under the principles of section 263A as direct labor costs attributable to articles described in clause (i).

(2) U.S. TAXATION TO ENSURE CONSISTENT TREATMENT.—Property which (without regard to this paragraph) is qualifying foreign trade property and which is manufactured, produced, grown, or extracted

outside the United States shall be treated as qualifying foreign trade property only if it is manufactured, produced, grown, or extracted by—

(A) a domestic corporation,

(B) an individual who is a citizen or resident of the United States,

(C) a foreign corporation with respect to which an election under subsection (e) (relating to foreign corporations electing to be subject to United States taxation) is in effect, or

(D) a partnership or other pass-thru entity all of the partners or owners of which are described in subparagraph (A), (B), or (C).

Except as otherwise provided by the Secretary, tiered partnerships or pass-thru entities shall be treated as described in subparagraph (D) if each of the partnerships or entities is directly or indirectly wholly owned by persons described in subparagraph (A), (B), or (C).

(3) EXCLUDED PROPERTY.—The term "qualifying foreign trade property" shall not include—

(A) property leased or rented by the taxpayer for use by any related person,

(B) patents, inventions, models, designs, formulas, or processes whether or not patented, copyrights (other than films, tapes, records, or similar reproductions, and other than computer software (whether or not patented), for commercial or home use), goodwill, trademarks, trade brands, franchises, or other like property,

(C) oil or gas (or any primary product thereof),

(D) products the transfer of which is prohibited or curtailed to effectuate the policy set forth in paragraph (2)(C) of section 3 of Public Law 96-72, or

(E) any unprocessed timber which is a softwood.

For purposes of subparagraph (E), the term "unprocessed timber" means any log, cant, or similar form of timber.

(4) PROPERTY IN SHORT SUPPLY.—If the President determines that the supply of any property described in paragraph (1) is insufficient to meet the requirements of the domestic economy, the President may by Executive order designate the property as in short supply. Any property so designated shall not be treated as qualifying foreign trade property during the period beginning with the date specified in the Executive order and ending with the date specified in an Executive order setting forth the President's determination that the property is no longer in short supply.

(b) OTHER DEFINITIONS AND RULES.—For purposes of this subpart—

(1) TRANSACTION.—

(A) IN GENERAL.—The term "transaction" means—

(i) any sale, exchange, or other disposition,

(ii) any lease or rental, and

(iii) any furnishing of services.

(B) GROUPING OF TRANSACTIONS.—To the extent provided in regulations, any provision of this subpart which, but for this subparagraph, would be applied on a transaction-by-transaction basis may be applied by the taxpayer on the basis of groups of transactions based on product lines or recognized industry or trade usage. Such regulations may permit different groupings for different purposes.

(2) UNITED STATES DEFINED.—The term "United States" includes the Commonwealth of Puerto Rico. The preceding sentence shall not apply for purposes of determining whether a corporation is a domestic corporation.

(3) RELATED PERSON.—A person shall be related to another person if such persons are treated as a single employer under subsection (a) or (b) of section 52 or subsection (m) or (o) of section 414, except that determinations under subsections (a) and (b) of section 52 shall be made without regard to section 1563(b).

(4) GROSS AND TAXABLE INCOME.—Section 114 shall not be taken into account in determining the amount of gross income or foreign trade income from any transaction.

(c) SOURCE RULE.—Under regulations, in the case of qualifying foreign trade property manufactured, produced, grown, or extracted within the United States, the amount of income of a taxpayer from any sales transaction with respect to such property which is treated as from sources without the United States shall not exceed—

(1) in the case of a taxpayer computing its qualifying foreign trade income under section 941(a)(1)(B), the amount of the taxpayer's foreign trade income which would (but for this subsection) be treated as from sources without the United States if the foreign trade income were reduced by an amount equal to 4 percent of the foreign trading gross receipts with respect to the transaction, and

(2) in the case of a taxpayer computing its qualifying foreign trade income under section 941(a)(1)(C), 50 percent of the amount of the taxpayer's foreign trade income which would (but for this subsection) be treated as from sources without the United States.

(d) TREATMENT OF WITHHOLDING TAXES.—

(1) IN GENERAL.—For purposes of section 114(d), any withholding tax shall not be treated as paid or accrued with respect to extraterritorial income which is excluded from gross income under section 114(a). For purposes of this paragraph, the term "withholding tax" means any tax which is imposed on a basis other than residence and for which credit is allowable under section 901 or 903.

(2) EXCEPTION.—Paragraph (1) shall not apply to any taxpayer with respect to extraterritorial income from any transaction if the taxpayer computes its qualifying foreign trade income with respect to the transaction under section 941(a)(1)(A).

(e) ELECTION TO BE TREATED AS DOMESTIC CORPORATION.—

(1) IN GENERAL.—An applicable foreign corporation may elect to be treated as a domestic corporation for all purposes of this title if such corporation waives all benefits to such corporation granted by the United States under any treaty. No election under section 1362(a) may be made with respect to such corporation.

(2) APPLICABLE FOREIGN CORPORATION.—For purposes of paragraph (1), the term "applicable foreign corporation" means any foreign corporation if—

(A) such corporation manufactures, produces, grows, or extracts property in the ordinary course of such corporation's trade or business, or

(B) substantially all of the gross receipts of such corporation are foreign trading gross receipts.

(3) PERIOD OF ELECTION.—

(A) IN GENERAL.—Except as otherwise provided in this paragraph, an election under paragraph (1) shall apply to the taxable year for which made and all subsequent taxable years unless revoked by the taxpayer. Any revocation of such election shall apply to taxable years beginning after such revocation.

(B) TERMINATION.—If a corporation which made an election under paragraph (1) for any taxable year fails to meet the requirements of subparagraph (A) or (B) of paragraph (2) for any subsequent taxable year, such election shall not apply to any taxable year beginning after such subsequent taxable year.

(C) EFFECT OF REVOCATION OR TERMINATION.—If a corporation which made an election under paragraph (1) revokes such election or such election is terminated under subparagraph (B), such corporation (and any successor corporation) may not make such election for any of the 5 taxable years beginning with the first taxable year for which such election is not in effect as a result of such revocation or termination.

(4) SPECIAL RULES.—

(A) REQUIREMENTS.—This subsection shall not apply to an applicable foreign corporation if such corporation fails to meet the requirements (if any) which the Secretary may prescribe to ensure that the taxes imposed by this chapter on such corporation are paid.

(B) EFFECT OF ELECTION, REVOCATION, AND TERMINATION.—

(i) ELECTION.—For purposes of section 367, a foreign corporation making an election under this subsection shall be treated as transferring (as of the first day of the first taxable year to which the election applies) all of its assets to a domestic corporation in connection with an exchange to which section 354 applies.

(ii) REVOCATION AND TERMINATION.—For purposes of section 367, if—

(I) an election is made by a corporation under paragraph (1) for any taxable year, and

(II) such election ceases to apply for any subsequent taxable year,

such corporation shall be treated as a domestic corporation transferring (as of the 1st day of the first such subsequent taxable year to which such election ceases to apply) all of its property to a foreign corporation in connection with an exchange to which section 354 applies.

(C) ELIGIBILITY FOR ELECTION.—The Secretary may by regulation designate one or more classes of corporations which may not make the election under this subsection.

(f) RULES RELATING TO ALLOCATIONS OF QUALIFYING FOREIGN TRADE INCOME FROM SHARED PARTNERSHIPS.—

(1) IN GENERAL.—If—

(A) a partnership maintains a separate account for transactions (to which this subpart applies) with each partner,

(B) distributions to each partner with respect to such transactions are based on the amounts in the separate account maintained with respect to such partner, and

(C) such partnership meets such other requirements as the Secretary may by regulations prescribe,

then such partnership shall allocate to each partner items of income, gain, loss, and deduction (including qualifying foreign trade income) from any transaction to which this subpart applies on the basis of such separate account.

(2) SPECIAL RULES.—For purposes of this subpart, in the case of a partnership to which paragraph (1) applies—

(A) any partner's interest in the partnership shall not be taken into account in determining whether such partner is a related person with respect to any other partner, and

(B) the election under section 942(a)(3) shall be made separately by each partner with respect to any transaction for which the partnership maintains separate accounts for each partner.

(g) EXCLUSION FOR PATRONS OF AGRICULTURAL AND HORTICULTURAL COOPERATIVES.—Any amount described in paragraph (1) or (3) of section 1385(a)—

(1) which is received by a person from an organization to which part I of subchapter T applies which is engaged in the marketing of agricultural or horticultural products, and

(2) which is allocable to qualifying foreign trade income and designated as such by the organization in a written notice mailed to its patrons during the payment period described in section 1382(d),

shall be treated as qualifying foreign trade income of such person for purposes of section 114. The taxable income of the organization shall not be reduced under section 1382 by reason of any amount to which the preceding sentence applies.

(h) SPECIAL RULE FOR DISCS.—Section 114 shall not apply to any taxpayer for any taxable year if, at any time during the taxable year, the taxpayer is a member of any controlled group of corporations (as defined in section 927(d)(4), as in effect before the date of the enactment of this subsection) of which a DISC is a member.

[CCH Explanation at ¶ 515–¶ 535. Committee Reports at ¶ 10,115.]

Amendment Notes

P.L. 106-519 (FSC Repeal)

Act Sec. 3(b) amended part III of subchapter N of chapter 1 by inserting after subpart D a new subpart E (Code Secs. 941-943) to read as above.

The above amendment applies generally to transactions after September 30, 2000. For special rules, see Act Sec. 5(b)-(d) in the amendment notes following Code Sec. 921, above.

[¶ 5560] CODE SEC. 995. TAXATION OF DISC INCOME TO SHAREHOLDERS.

* * *

(b) DEEMED DISTRIBUTIONS.—

* * *

(3) TAXABLE INCOME ATTRIBUTABLE TO MILITARY PROPERTY.—

* * *

(B) MILITARY PROPERTY.—For purposes of subparagraph (A), the term "military property" means any property which is an arm, ammunition, or implement of war designated in the munitions list published pursuant to section 38 of the International Security Assistance and Arms Export Control Act of 1976 (22 U.S.C. 2778).

* * *

[CCH Explanation at ¶ 30,050.]

Amendment Notes

P.L. 106-554 (Community Renewal)

Act Sec. 319(12) amended Code Sec. 995(b)(3)(B) by striking "the Military Security Act of 1954 (22 U.S.C. 1934)" and inserting "section 38 of the International Security Assis-

tance and Arms Export Control Act of 1976 (22 U.S.C. 2778)".

The above amendment is effective on December 21, 2000.

(f) INTEREST ON DISC-RELATED DEFERRED TAX LIABILITY.—

* * *

(4) BASE PERIOD T-BILL RATE.—For purposes of this subsection, the term "base period T-bill rate" means the annual rate of interest determined by the Secretary to be equivalent to *the average of the 1-year constant maturity Treasury yields, as published by the Board of Governors of the Federal Reserve System, for the 1-year period* ending on September 30 of the calendar year ending with (or of the most recent calendar year ending before) the close of the taxable year of the shareholder.

* * *

[CCH Explanation at ¶ 375. Committee Reports at ¶ 10,285.]

Amendment Notes

P.L. 106-554 (Community Renewal)

Act Sec. 307(c) amended Code Sec. 995(f)(4) by striking "the average investment yield of United States Treasury bills with maturities of 52 weeks which were auctioned during the 1-year period" and inserting "the average of the

1-year constant maturity Treasury yields, as published by the Board of Governors of the Federal Reserve System, for the 1-year period".

The above amendment is effective on December 21, 2000.

[¶ 5570] CODE SEC. 999. REPORTS BY TAXPAYERS; DETERMINATIONS.

* * *

(c) INTERNATIONAL BOYCOTT FACTOR.—

(1) INTERNATIONAL BOYCOTT FACTOR.—For purposes of sections 908(a), *941(a)(5),* 952(a)(3), and 995(b)(1)(F)(ii), the international boycott factor is a fraction, determined under regulations prescribed by the Secretary, the numerator of which reflects the world-wide operations of a person (or, in the case of a controlled group (within the meaning of section 993(a)(3)) which includes that person, of the group) which are operations in or related to a group of countries associated in carrying out an international boycott in or with which that person or a member of that controlled group has participated or cooperated in the taxable year, and the denominator of which reflects the world-wide operations of that person or group.

* * *

[CCH Explanation at ¶ 520. Committee Reports at ¶ 10,115.]

Amendment Notes

P.L. 106-519 (FSC Repeal)

Act Sec. 4(5) amended Code Sec. 999(c)(1) by inserting "941(a)(5)," after "908(a),".

The above amendment applies generally to transactions after September 30, 2000. For special rules, see Act Sec. 5(b)-(d) in the amendment notes following Code Sec. 921, above.

[¶ 5580] CODE SEC. 1016. ADJUSTMENTS TO BASIS.

(a) GENERAL RULE.—Proper adjustment in respect of the property shall in all cases be made—

* * *

(23) in the case of property the acquisition of which resulted under section 1043, 1044, *1045, or 1397B* in the nonrecognition of any part of the gain realized on the sale of other property, to the extent provided in section 1043(c), 1044(d), *1045(b)(4), or 1397B(b)(4),* as the case may be,

* * *

[CCH Explanation at ¶ 155. Committee Reports at ¶ 10,150.]

Amendment Notes

P.L. 106-554 (Community Renewal)

Act Sec. 116(b)(1)(A)-(B) amended Code Sec. 1016(a)(23) by striking "or 1045" and inserting "1045, or 1397B", and by

striking "or 1045(b)(4)" and inserting "1045(b)(4), or 1397B(b)(4)".

The above amendment applies to qualified empowerment zone assets acquired after December 21, 2000.

[¶ 5590] CODE SEC. 1032. EXCHANGE OF STOCK FOR PROPERTY.

(a) NONRECOGNITION OF GAIN OR LOSS.—No gain or loss shall be recognized to a corporation on the receipt of money or other property in exchange for stock (including treasury stock) of such corporation. No gain or loss shall be recognized by a corporation with respect to any lapse or acquisition of an option, *or with respect to a securities futures contract (as defined in section 1234B),* to buy or sell its stock (including treasury stock).

* * *

[CCH Explanation at ¶ 260. Committee Reports at ¶ 10,355.]

Amendment Notes

P.L. 106-554 (Community Renewal)

Act Sec. 401(c) amended the second sentence of Code Sec. 1032(a) by inserting ", or with respect to a securities futures contract (as defined in section 1234B)," after "an option".

The above amendment is effective on December 21, 2000.

[¶ 5600] CODE SEC. 1091. LOSS FROM WASH SALES OF STOCK OR SECURITIES.

* * *

(f) CASH SETTLEMENT.—This section shall not fail to apply to a contract or option to acquire or sell stock or securities solely by reason of the fact that the contract or option settles in (or could be settled in) cash or property other than such stock or securities.

[CCH Explanation at ¶ 260. Committee Reports at ¶ 10,355.]

Amendment Notes

P.L. 106-554 (Community Renewal)

Act Sec. 401(d) amended Code Sec. 1091 by adding at the end a new subsection (f) to read as above.

The above amendment is effective on December 21, 2000.

[¶ 5610] CODE SEC. 1092. STRADDLES.

* * *

(d) DEFINITIONS AND SPECIAL RULES.—For purposes of this section—

* * *

(3) SPECIAL RULES FOR STOCK.—For purposes of paragraph (1)—

* * *

(B) EXCEPTIONS.—The term "personal property" includes—

(i) any stock which is part of a straddle at least 1 of the offsetting positions of which is—

(I) an option with respect to such stock or substantially identical stock or securities,

(II) a securities futures contract (as defined in section 1234B) with respect to such stock or substantially identical stock or securities, or

(III) under regulations, a position with respect to substantially similar or related property (other than stock), and

(ii) any stock of a corporation formed or availed of to take positions in personal property which offset positions taken by any shareholder.

* * *

[CCH Explanation at ¶ 260. Committee Reports at ¶ 10,355.]

Amendment Notes

P.L. 106-554 (Community Renewal)

Act Sec. 401(e) amended Code Sec. 1092(d)(3)(B)(i) by striking "or" at the end of subclause (I), by redesignating subclause (II) as subclause (III), and by inserting after subclause (I) new subclause (II) to read as above.

The above amendment is effective on December 21, 2000.

[¶ 5620] CODE SEC. 1202. *PARTIAL* EXCLUSION FOR GAIN FROM CERTAIN SMALL BUSINESS STOCK.

(a) EXCLUSION.—

(1) IN GENERAL.—In the case of a taxpayer other than a corporation, gross income shall not include 50 percent of any gain from the sale or exchange of qualified small business stock held for more than 5 years.

(2) EMPOWERMENT ZONE BUSINESSES.—

(A) IN GENERAL.—In the case of qualified small business stock acquired after the date of the enactment of this paragraph in a corporation which is a qualified business entity (as defined in section 1397C(b)) during substantially all of the taxpayer's holding period for such stock, paragraph (1) shall be applied by substituting "60 percent" for "50 percent".

(B) *CERTAIN RULES TO APPLY.*—Rules similar to the rules of paragraphs (5) and (7) of section 1400B(b) shall apply for purposes of this paragraph.

(C) *GAIN AFTER 2014 NOT QUALIFIED.*—Subparagraph (A) shall not apply to gain attributable to periods after December 31, 2014.

(D) *TREATMENT OF DC ZONE.*—The District of Columbia Enterprise Zone shall not be treated as an empowerment zone for purposes of this paragraph.

* * *

[CCH Explanation at ¶ 160. Committee Reports at ¶ 10,155.]

Amendment Notes

P.L. 106-554 (Community Renewal)

Act Sec. 117(a) amended Code Sec. 1202(a) to read as above. Prior to amendment, Code Sec. 1202(a) read as follows:

(a) 50-PERCENT EXCLUSION.—In the case of a taxpayer other than a corporation, gross income shall not include 50 percent of any gain from the sale or exchange of qualified small business stock held for more than 5 years.

Act Sec. 117(b)(2) amended the section heading for Code Sec. 1202 by striking "50-PERCENT" and inserting "PARTIAL".

The above amendments apply to stock acquired after December 21, 2000.

[¶ 5630] CODE SEC. 1223. HOLDING PERIOD OF PROPERTY.

For purposes of this subtitle—

* * *

(15) Except for purposes of sections 1202(a)(2), 1202(c)(2)(A), 1400B(b), and 1400F(b), in determining the period for which the taxpayer has held property the acquisition of which resulted under section 1045 or 1397B in the nonrecognition of any part of the gain realized on the sale of other property, there shall be included the period for which such other property has been held as of the date of such sale.

(16) If the security to which a securities futures contract (as defined in section 1234B) relates (other than a contract to which section 1256 applies) is acquired in satisfaction of such contract, in determining the period for which the taxpayer has held such security, there shall be included the period for which the taxpayer held such contract if such contract was a capital asset in the hands of the taxpayer.

(17) CROSS REFERENCE.—

For special holding period provision relating to certain partnership distributions, see section 735(b).

[CCH Explanation at ¶ 155 and ¶ 260. Committee Reports at ¶ 10,150 and ¶ 10,355.]

Amendment Notes

P.L. 106-554 (Community Renewal)

Act Sec. 116(b)(2) amended Code Sec. 1223(15) to read as above. Prior to amendment, Code Sec. 1223(15) read as follows:

(15) In determining the period for which the taxpayer has held property the acquisition of which resulted under section 1045 in the nonrecognition of any part of the gain realized on the sale of other property, there shall be included the period for which such other property has been held as of the date of such sale.

The above amendment applies to qualified empowerment zone assets acquired after December 21, 2000.

Act Sec. 401(h)(1) amended Code Sec. 1223 by redesignating paragraph (16) as paragraph (17) and by inserting after paragraph (15) a new paragraph (16) to read as above.

The above amendment is effective on December 21, 2000.

[¶ 5635] CODE SEC. 1233. GAINS AND LOSSES FROM SHORT SALES.

* * *

(e) RULES FOR APPLICATION OF SECTION.—

* * *

(2) For purposes of subsections (b) and (d)—

(A) the term "property" includes only stocks and securities (including stocks and securities dealt with on a "when issued" basis), and commodity futures, which are capital assets in the hands of the taxpayer, but does not include any position to which section 1092(b) applies;

(B) in the case of futures transactions in any commodity on or subject to the rules of a board of trade or commodity exchange, a commodity future requiring delivery in 1 calendar month shall not be considered as property substantially identical to another commodity future requiring delivery in a different calendar month;

(C) in the case of a short sale of property by an individual, the term "taxpayer", in the application of this subsection and subsections (b) and (d), shall be read as "taxpayer or his spouse"; but an individual who is legally separated from the taxpayer under a decree of divorce or of separate maintenance shall not be considered as the spouse of the taxpayer; *and*

(D) a securities futures contract (as defined in section 1234B) to acquire substantially identical property shall be treated as substantially identical property.

* * *

[CCH Explanation at ¶ 260. Committee Reports at ¶ 10,355.]

Amendment Notes

P.L. 106-554 (Community Renewal)

Act Sec. 401(f) amended Code Sec. 1233(e)(2) by striking "and" at the end of subparagraph (B), by striking the period at the end of subparagraph (C) and inserting "; and", and by adding at the end a new subparagraph (D) to read as above.

The above amendment is effective on December 21, 2000.

[¶ 5640] CODE SEC. 1234A. GAINS OR LOSSES FROM CERTAIN TERMINATIONS.

Gain or loss attributable to the cancellation, lapse, expiration, or other termination of—

(1) a right or obligation *(other than a securities contract, as defined in section 1234B)* with respect to property which is (or on acquisition would be) a capital asset in the hands of the taxpayer,

(2) a section 1256 contract (as defined in section 1256) not described in paragraph (1) which is a capital asset in the hands of the taxpayer, *or*

(3) a securities futures contract (as so defined) which is a capital asset in the hands of the taxpayer,

shall be treated as gain or loss from the sale of a capital asset. The preceding sentence shall not apply to the retirement of any debt instrument (whether or not through a trust or other participation arrangement).

[CCH Explanation at ¶ 260. Committee Reports at ¶ 10,355.]

Amendment Notes

P.L. 106-554 (Community Renewal)

Act Sec. 401(b)(1)-(4) amended Code Sec. 1234A by inserting "(other than a securities contract, as defined in section 1234B)" after "right or obligation" in paragraph (1), by striking "or" at the end of paragraph (1), by adding "or" at the end of paragraph (2), and by inserting after paragraph (2) a new paragraph (3) to read as above.

The above amendment is effective on December 21, 2000.

[¶ 5650] *CODE SEC. 1234B. GAINS OR LOSSES FROM SECURITIES FUTURES CONTRACTS.*

(a) TREATMENT OF GAIN OR LOSS.—

(1) IN GENERAL.—Gain or loss attributable to the sale or exchange of a securities futures contract shall be considered gain or loss from the sale or exchange of property which has the same character as the property to which the contract relates has in the hands of the taxpayer (or would have in the hands of the taxpayer if acquired by the taxpayer).

(2) NONAPPLICATION OF SUBSECTION.—This subsection shall not apply to—

(A) a contract which constitutes property described in paragraph (1) or (7) of section 1221(a), and

(B) any income derived in connection with a contract which, without regard to this subsection, is treated as other than gain from the sale or exchange of a capital asset.

(b) SHORT-TERM GAINS AND LOSSES.—Except as provided in the regulations under section 1092(b) or this section, if gain or loss on the sale or exchange of a securities futures contract to sell property is considered as gain or loss from the sale or exchange of a capital asset, such gain or loss shall be treated as short-term capital gain or loss.

(c) SECURITIES FUTURES CONTRACT.—For purposes of this section, the term "securities futures contract" means any security future (as defined in section 3(a)(55)(A) of the Securities Exchange Act of 1934, as in effect on the date of the enactment of this section).

(d) CONTRACTS NOT TREATED AS COMMODITY FUTURES CONTRACTS.—For purposes of this title, a securities futures contract shall not be treated as a commodity futures contract.

(e) REGULATIONS.—The Secretary shall prescribe such regulations as may be appropriate to provide for the proper treatment of securities futures contracts under this title.

[CCH Explanation at ¶ 260. Committee Reports at ¶ 10,355.]

Amendment Notes

P.L. 106-554 (Community Renewal)

Act Sec. 401(a) amended subpart IV of subchapter P of chapter 1 by inserting after Code Sec. 1234A a new Code Sec. 1234B to read as above.

The above amendment is effective on December 21, 2000.

[¶ 5660] CODE SEC. 1256. SECTION 1256 CONTRACTS MARKED TO MARKET

* * *

(b) SECTION 1256 CONTRACT DEFINED.—For purposes of this section, the term "section 1256 contract" means—

    (1) any regulated futures contract,

    (2) any foreign currency contract,

    (3) any nonequity option,

    (4) any dealer equity option, *and*

    (5) any dealer securities futures contract.

The term "section 1256 contract" shall not include any securities futures contract or option on such a contract unless such contract or option is a dealer securities futures contract.

* * *

[CCH Explanation at ¶ 260. Committee Reports at ¶ 10,355.]

Amendment Notes

P.L. 106-554 (Community Renewal)

Act Sec. 401(g)(1)(A) amended Code Sec. 1256(b) is amended by striking "and" at the end of paragraph (3), by striking the period at the end of paragraph (4) and inserting ", and", and by adding at the end new text to read as above.

The above amendment is effective on December 21, 2000.

(f) SPECIAL RULES.—

* * *

    (4) SPECIAL RULE FOR DEALER EQUITY OPTIONS *AND DEALER SECURITIES FUTURES CONTRACTS* OF LIMITED PARTNERS OR LIMITED ENTREPRENEURS.—In the case of any gain or loss with respect to dealer equity options, *or dealer securities futures contracts,* which are allocable to limited partners or limited entrepreneurs (within the meaning of subsection (e)(3))—

        (A) paragraph (3) of subsection (a) shall not apply to any such gain or loss, and

        (B) all such gains or losses shall be treated as short-term capital gains or losses, as the case may be.

[CCH Explanation at ¶ 260. Committee Reports at ¶ 10,355.]

Amendment Notes

P.L. 106-554 (Community Renewal)

Act Sec. 401(g)(2)(A)-(B) amended Code Sec. 1256(f)(4) by inserting ", or dealer securities futures contracts," after "dealer equity options" in the text, and by inserting "AND DEALER SECURITIES FUTURES CONTRACTS" after "DEALER EQUITY OPTIONS" in the heading.

The above amendment is effective on December 21, 2000.

(g) DEFINITIONS.—For purposes of this section—

* * *

    (6) EQUITY OPTION.—The term "equity option" means any option—

        (A) to buy or sell stock, or

        (B) the value of which is determined directly or indirectly by reference to any stock or any narrow-based security index (as defined in section 3(a)(55) of the Securities Exchange Act of 1934, as in effect on the date of the enactment of this paragraph).

The term "equity option" includes such an option on a group of stocks only if such group meets the requirements for a narrow-based security index (as so defined).

* * *

    (9) DEALER SECURITIES FUTURES CONTRACT.—

        (A) IN GENERAL.—The term "dealer securities futures contract" means, with respect to any dealer, any securities futures contract, and any option on such a contract, which—

            (i) is entered into by such dealer (or, in the case of an option, is purchased or granted by such dealer) in the normal course of his activity of dealing in such contracts or options, as the case may be, and

(ii) is traded on a qualified board or exchange.

(B) DEALER.—*For purposes of subparagraph (A), a person shall be treated as a dealer in securities futures contracts or options on such contracts if the Secretary determines that such person performs, with respect to such contracts or options, as the case may be, functions similar to the functions performed by persons described in paragraph (8)(A). Such determination shall be made to the extent appropriate to carry out the purposes of this section.*

(C) SECURITIES FUTURES CONTRACT.—*The term "securities futures contract" has the meaning given to such term by section 1234B.*

[CCH Explanation at ¶ 260. Committee Reports at ¶ 10,355.]

Amendment Notes

P.L. 106-554 (Community Renewal)

Act Sec. 401(g)(1)(B) amended Code Sec. 1256(g) by adding at the end a new paragraph (9) to read as above.

Act Sec. 401(g)(3) amended Code Sec. 1256(g)(6) to read as above. Prior to amendment, Code Sec. 1256(g)(6) read as follows:

(6) EQUITY OPTION.—

(A) IN GENERAL.—Except as provided in subparagraph (B), the term "equity option" means any option—

(i) to buy or sell stock, or

(ii) the value of which is determined directly or indirectly by reference to any stock (or group of stocks) or stock index.

(B) EXCEPTION FOR CERTAIN OPTIONS REGULATED BY COMMODITIES FUTURES TRADING COMMISSION.—The term "equity option" does not include any option with respect to any group of stocks or stock index if—

(i) there is in effect a designation by the Commodities Futures Trading Commission of a contract market for a contract based on such group of stocks or index, or

(ii) the Secretary determines that such option meets the requirements of law for such a designation.

The above amendments are effective on December 21, 2000.

[¶ 5670] CODE SEC. 1275. OTHER DEFINITIONS AND SPECIAL RULES.

(a) DEFINITIONS.—For purposes of this subpart—

(1) DEBT INSTRUMENT.—

* * *

(B) EXCEPTION FOR CERTAIN ANNUITY CONTRACTS.—The term "debt instrument" shall not include any annuity contract to which section 72 applies and which—

(i) depends (in whole or in substantial part) on the life expectancy of 1 or more individuals, or

(ii) *is issued by an insurance company subject to tax under subchapter L (or by an entity described in section 501(c) and exempt from tax under section 501(a) which would be subject to tax under subchapter L were it not so exempt)*—

(I) in a transaction in which there is no consideration other than cash or another annuity contract meeting the requirements of this clause,

(II) pursuant to the exercise of an election under an insurance contract by a beneficiary thereof on the death of the insured party under such contract, or

(III) in a transaction involving a qualified pension or employee benefit plan.

* * *

[CCH Explanation at ¶ 210. Committee Reports at ¶ 10,345.]

Amendment Notes

P.L. 106-554 (Community Renewal)

Act Sec. 318(c)(1) amended Code Sec. 1275(a)(1)(B)(ii) by striking "subchapter L" and inserting "subchapter L (or by an entity described in section 501(c) and exempt from tax under section 501(a) which would be subject to tax under subchapter L were it not so exempt)".

The above amendment is effective as if included in the amendments made by section 41 of the Tax Reform Act of 1984 (P.L. 98-369) [effective for tax years ending after July 18, 1984.—CCH.].

[¶ 5680] CODE SEC. 1361. S CORPORATION DEFINED.

* * *

(e) ELECTING SMALL BUSINESS TRUST DEFINED.—

(1) ELECTING SMALL BUSINESS TRUST.—For purposes of this section—

(A) IN GENERAL.—Except as provided in subparagraph (B), the term "electing small business trust" means any trust if—

(i) such trust does not have as a beneficiary any person other than (I) an individual, (II) an estate, (III) an organization described in paragraph (2), (3), (4), or (5) of section

170(c), *or (IV) an organization described in section 170(c)(1) which holds a contingent interest in such trust and is not a potential current beneficiary,*

(ii) no interest in such trust was acquired by purchase, and

(iii) an election under this subsection applies to such trust.

* * *

[CCH Explanation at ¶ 420. Committee Reports at ¶ 10,335.]

Amendment Notes

P.L. 106-554 (Community Renewal)
Act Sec. 316(b) amended Code Sec. 1361(e)(1)(A)(i) by striking "or" before "(III)" and by adding at the end new text to read as above.

The above amendment is effective as if included in the provision of the Small Business Job Protection Act of 1996 (P.L. 104-188) to which it relates [effective for tax years beginning after December 31, 1996.—CCH.].

[¶ 5690] CODE SEC. 1391. DESIGNATION PROCEDURE.

* * *

(d) PERIOD FOR WHICH DESIGNATION IS IN EFFECT.—

(1) IN GENERAL.—Any designation under this section shall remain in effect during the period beginning on the date of the designation and ending on the earliest of—

(A)(i) in the case of an empowerment zone, December 31, 2009, or

(ii) in the case of an enterprise community, the close of the 10th calendar year beginning on or after such date of designation,

(B) the termination date designated by the State and local governments as provided for in their nomination, or

(C) the date the appropriate Secretary revokes the designation.

* * *

[CCH Explanation at ¶ 135. Committee Reports at ¶ 10,146.]

Amendment Notes

P.L. 106-554 (Community Renewal)
Act Sec. 112 amended Code Sec. 1391(d)(1)(A) to read as above. Prior to amendment, Code Sec. 1391(d)(1)(A) read as follows:

(A) the close of the 10th calendar year beginning on or after such date of designation,

The above amendment is effective on December 21, 2000.

(g) ADDITIONAL DESIGNATIONS PERMITTED.—

* * *

(3) MODIFICATIONS TO ELIGIBILITY CRITERIA, ETC.—

* * *

(C) AGGREGATE POPULATION LIMITATION.—The aggregate population limitation under the last sentence of subsection (b)(2) shall not apply to a designation under *paragraph (1)*.

* * *

[CCH Explanation at ¶ 30,050.]

Amendment Notes

P.L. 106-554 (Community Renewal)
Act Sec. 319(13) amended Code Sec. 1391(g)(3)(C) by striking "paragraph (1)(B)" and inserting "paragraph (1)".

The above amendment is effective on December 21, 2000.

(h) ADDITIONAL DESIGNATIONS PERMITTED.—

(1) IN GENERAL.—In addition to the areas designated under subsections (a) and (g), the appropriate Secretaries may designate in the aggregate an additional 9 nominated areas as empowerment zones under this section, subject to the availability of eligible nominated areas. Of that number, not more than seven may be designated in urban areas and not more than 2 may be designated in rural areas.

(2) PERIOD DESIGNATIONS MAY BE MADE AND TAKE EFFECT.—A designation may be made under this subsection after the date of the enactment of this subsection and before January 1, 2002. Subject to subparagraphs (B) and (C) of subsection (d)(1), such designations shall remain in effect during the period beginning on January 1, 2002, and ending on December 31, 2009.

(3) MODIFICATIONS TO ELIGIBILITY CRITERIA, ETC.—The rules of subsection (g)(3) shall apply to designations under this subsection.

(4) EMPOWERMENT ZONES WHICH BECOME RENEWAL COMMUNITIES.—The number of areas which may be designated as empowerment zones under this subsection shall be increased by 1 for each area which ceases to be an empowerment zone by reason of section 1400E(e). Each additional area designated by reason of the preceding sentence shall have the same urban or rural character as the area it is replacing.

[CCH Explanation at ¶ 130. Committee Reports at ¶ 10,145.]

Amendment Notes

P.L. 106-554 (Community Renewal)

Act Sec. 111 amended Code Sec. 1391 by adding at the end a new subsection (h) to read as above.

The above amendment is effective on December 21, 2000.

[¶ 5700] CODE SEC. 1394. TAX-EXEMPT ENTERPRISE ZONE FACILITY BONDS.

* * *

(b) ENTERPRISE ZONE FACILITY.—For purposes of this section—

* * *

(2) QUALIFIED ZONE PROPERTY.—The term "qualified zone property" has the meaning given such term by *section 1397D* ; except that—

(A) the references to empowerment zones shall be treated as including references to enterprise communities, and

(B) *section 1397D(a)(2)* shall be applied by substituting "an amount equal to 15 percent of the adjusted basis" for "an amount equal to the adjusted basis".

(3) ENTERPRISE ZONE BUSINESS.—

(A) IN GENERAL.—Except as modified in this paragraph, the term "enterprise zone business" has the meaning given such term by *section 1397C.*

(B) MODIFICATIONS.—In applying *section 1397C* for purposes of this section—

(i) BUSINESSES IN ENTERPRISE COMMUNITIES ELIGIBLE.—References in *section 1397C* to empowerment zones shall be treated as including references to enterprise communities.

(ii) WAIVER OF REQUIREMENTS DURING STARTUP PERIOD.—A business shall not fail to be treated as an enterprise zone business during the startup period if—

(I) as of the beginning of the startup period, it is reasonably expected that such business will be an enterprise zone business (as defined in *section 1397C* as modified by this paragraph) at the end of such period, and

(II) such business makes bona fide efforts to be such a business.

(iii) REDUCED REQUIREMENTS AFTER TESTING PERIOD.—A business shall not fail to be treated as an enterprise zone business for any taxable year beginning after the testing period by reason of failing to meet any requirement of subsection (b) or (c) of *section 1397C* if at least 35 percent of the employees of such business for such year are residents of an empowerment zone or an enterprise community. The preceding sentence shall not apply to any business which is not a qualified business by reason of paragraph (1), (4), or (5) of *section 1397C(d).*

* * *

[CCH Explanation at ¶ 155. Committee Reports at ¶ 10,150.]

Amendment Notes

P.L. 106-554 (Community Renewal)

Act Sec. 116(b)(3)(A)-(B) amended Code Sec. 1394(b)(2) by striking "section 1397C" and inserting "section 1397D", and by striking "section 1397C(a)(2)" and inserting "section 1397D(a)(2)".

Act Sec. 116(b)(4)(A)-(B) amended Code Sec. 1394(b)(3) by striking "section 1397B" each place it appears and inserting "section 1397C", and by striking "section 1397B(d)" and inserting "section 1397C(d)".

The above amendments apply to qualified empowerment zone assets acquired after December 21, 2000.

(f) BONDS FOR EMPOWERMENT ZONES DESIGNATED UNDER SECTION 1391(g).—

* * *

[Caution: Code Sec. 1394(f)(3), below, as amended by Act Sec. 115(a), applies to obligations issued after December 31, 2001.—CCH.]

(3) EMPOWERMENT ZONE FACILITY BOND.—*For purposes of this subsection, the term "empowerment zone facility bond" means any bond which would be described in subsection (a) if—*

(A) *in the case of obligations issued before January 1, 2002, only empowerment zones designated under section 1391(g) were taken into account under sections 1397C and 1397D, and*

(B) *in the case of obligations issued after December 31, 2001, all empowerment zones (other than the District of Columbia Enterprise Zone) were taken into account under sections 1397C and 1397D.*

[CCH Explanation at ¶ 150. Committee Reports at ¶ 10,149.]

Amendment Notes

P.L. 106-554 (Community Renewal)

Act Sec. 115(a) amended Code Sec. 1394(f)(3) to read as above. Prior to amendment, Code Sec. 1394(f)(3) read as follows:

(3) NEW EMPOWERMENT ZONE FACILITY BOND.—For purposes of this subsection, the term "new empowerment zone facility bond" means any bond which would be described in subsection (a) if only empowerment zones designated under section 1391(g) were taken into account under sections 1397B and 1397C.

The above amendment applies to obligations issued after December 31, 2001.

[¶ 5710] CODE SEC. 1396. EMPOWERMENT ZONE EMPLOYMENT CREDIT.

* * *

[Caution: Code Sec. 1396(b), below, as amended by Act Sec. 113(a), applies to wages paid or incurred after December 31, 2001.—CCH.]

(b) APPLICABLE PERCENTAGE.—*For purposes of this section, the applicable percentage is 20 percent.*

* * *

[CCH Explanation at ¶ 140. Committee Reports at ¶ 10,147.]

Amendment Notes

P.L. 106-554 (Community Renewal)

Act Sec. 113(a) amended Code Sec. 1396(b) to read as above. Prior to amendment, Code Sec. 1396(b) read as follows:

(b) APPLICABLE PERCENTAGE.—For purposes of this section—

(1) IN GENERAL.—Except as provided in paragraph (2), the term "applicable percentage" means the percentage determined in accordance with the following table:

In the case of wages paid or incurred during calendar year:	The applicable percentage is:
1994 through 2001	20
2002	15
2003	10
2004	5

(2) SPECIAL RULE.—With respect to each empowerment zone designated pursuant to the amendments made by the Taxpayer Relief Act of 1997 to section 1391(b)(2), the following table shall apply in lieu of the table in paragraph (1):

In the case of wages paid or incurred during calendar year—	The applicable percentage is—
2000 through 2004	20
2005	15
2006	10
2007	5

The above amendment applies to wages paid or incurred after December 31, 2001.

[Caution: Code Sec. 1396(e), below, was stricken by Act Sec. 113(b), applicable to wages paid or incurred after December 31, 2001.—CCH.]

(e) *[Stricken.]*

[CCH Explanation at ¶ 140. Committee Reports at ¶ 10,147.]

Amendment Notes

P.L. 106-554 (Community Renewal)

Act Sec. 113(b) amended Code Sec. 1396 by striking subsection (e). Prior to being stricken, Code Sec. 1396(e) read as follows:

(e) CREDIT NOT TO APPLY TO EMPOWERMENT ZONES DESIGNATED UNDER SECTION 1391(g).—This section shall be applied without regard to any empowerment zone designated under section 1391(g).

The above amendment applies to wages paid or incurred after December 31, 2001.

[¶ 5720] CODE SEC. 1397A. INCREASE IN EXPENSING UNDER SECTION 179.

(a) GENERAL RULE.—In the case of an enterprise zone business, for purposes of section 179—

(1) the limitation under section 179(b)(1) shall be increased by the lesser of—

[Caution: Code Sec. 1397A(a)(1)(A), below, as amended by Act Sec. 114(a), applies to tax years beginning after December 31, 2001.—CCH.]

(A) *$35,000, or*

(B) the cost of section 179 property which is qualified zone property placed in service during the taxable year, and

(2) the amount taken into account under section 179(b)(2) with respect to any section 179 property which is qualified zone property shall be 50 percent of the cost thereof.

* * *

[CCH Explanation at ¶ 145. Committee Reports at ¶ 10,148.]

Amendment Notes

P.L. 106-554 (Community Renewal)

Act Sec. 114(a) amended Code Sec. 1397A(a)(1)(A) by striking "$20,000" and inserting "$35,000".

The above amendment applies to tax years beginning after December 31, 2001.

[Caution: Code Sec. 1397A(c), below, was stricken by Act Sec. 114(b), applicable to tax years beginning after December 31, 2001.—CCH.]

(c) *[Stricken.]*

[CCH Explanation at ¶ 145. Committee Reports at ¶ 10,148.]

Amendment Notes

P.L. 106-554 (Community Renewal)

Act Sec. 114(b) amended Code Sec. 1397A by striking subsection (c). Prior to being stricken, Code Sec. 1397A(c) read as follows:

(c) LIMITATION.—For purposes of this section, qualified zone property shall not include any property substantially all of the use of which is in any parcel described in section 1391(g)(3)(A)(iii).

The above amendment applies to tax years beginning after December 31, 2001.

[¶ 5730] CODE SEC. 1397B. NONRECOGNITION OF GAIN ON ROLLOVER OF EMPOWERMENT ZONE INVESTMENTS.

(a) NONRECOGNITION OF GAIN.—*In the case of any sale of a qualified empowerment zone asset held by the taxpayer for more than 1 year and with respect to which such taxpayer elects the application of this section, gain from such sale shall be recognized only to the extent that the amount realized on such sale exceeds—*

(1) *the cost of any qualified empowerment zone asset (with respect to the same zone as the asset sold) purchased by the taxpayer during the 60-day period beginning on the date of such sale, reduced by*

(2) *any portion of such cost previously taken into account under this section.*

(b) DEFINITIONS AND SPECIAL RULES.—*For purposes of this section—*

(1) QUALIFIED EMPOWERMENT ZONE ASSET.—

(A) IN GENERAL.—*The term "qualified empowerment zone asset" means any property which would be a qualified community asset (as defined in section 1400F) if in section 1400F—*

(i) *references to empowerment zones were substituted for references to renewal communities,*

(ii) *references to enterprise zone businesses (as defined in section 1397C) were substituted for references to renewal community businesses, and*

(iii) *the date of the enactment of this paragraph were substituted for "December 31, 2001" each place it appears.*

(B) TREATMENT OF DC ZONE.—*The District of Columbia Enterprise Zone shall not be treated as an empowerment zone for purposes of this section.*

(2) CERTAIN GAIN NOT ELIGIBLE FOR ROLLOVER.—*This section shall not apply to—*

(A) *any gain which is treated as ordinary income for purposes of this subtitle, and*

(B) *any gain which is attributable to real property, or an intangible asset, which is not an integral part of an enterprise zone business.*

(3) PURCHASE.—*A taxpayer shall be treated as having purchased any property if, but for paragraph (4), the unadjusted basis of such property in the hands of the taxpayer would be its cost (within the meaning of section 1012).*

(4) BASIS ADJUSTMENTS.—If gain from any sale is not recognized by reason of subsection (a), such gain shall be applied to reduce (in the order acquired) the basis for determining gain or loss of any qualified empowerment zone asset which is purchased by the taxpayer during the 60-day period described in subsection (a). This paragraph shall not apply for purposes of section 1202.

(5) HOLDING PERIOD.—For purposes of determining whether the nonrecognition of gain under subsection (a) applies to any qualified empowerment zone asset which is sold—

(A) the taxpayer's holding period for such asset and the asset referred to in subsection (a)(1) shall be determined without regard to section 1223, and

(B) only the first year of the taxpayer's holding period for the asset referred to in subsection (a)(1) shall be taken into account for purposes of paragraphs (2)(A)(iii), (3)(C), and (4)(A)(iii) of section 1400F(b).

[CCH Explanation at ¶ 155. Committee Reports at ¶ 10,150.]

Amendment Notes

P.L. 106-554 (Community Renewal)

Act Sec. 116(a)(2)-(3) amended part III of subchapter U of chapter 1 by redesignating subpart C as subpart D, by redesignating Code Secs. 1397B and 1397C as Code Secs.

1397C and 1397D, respectively, and by inserting after subpart B a new subpart C (Code Sec. 1397B) to read as above.

The above amendment applies to qualified empowerment zone assets acquired after December 21, 2000.

[¶ 5740] CODE SEC. *1397C*. ENTERPRISE ZONE BUSINESS DEFINED.

* * *

[CCH Explanation at ¶ 155. Committee Reports at ¶ 10,150.]

Amendment Notes

P.L. 106-554 (Community Renewal)

Act Sec. 116(a)(2) amended part III of subchapter U of chapter 1 by redesignating Code Secs. 1397B and 1397C as Code Secs. 1397C and 1397D, respectively.

The above amendment applies to qualified empowerment zone assets acquired after December 21, 2000.

[¶ 5750] CODE SEC. *1397D*. QUALIFIED ZONE PROPERTY DEFINED.

* * *

[CCH Explanation at ¶ 155. Committee Reports at ¶ 10,150.]

Amendment Notes

P.L. 106-554 (Community Renewal)

Act Sec. 116(a)(2) amended part III of subchapter U of chapter 1 by redesignating Code Secs. 1397B and 1397C as Code Secs. 1397C and 1397D, respectively.

The above amendment applies to qualified empowerment zone assets acquired after December 21, 2000.

[¶ 5760] CODE SEC. 1400. ESTABLISHMENT OF DC ZONE.

* * *

[Caution: Code Sec. 1400(d), below, as amended by Act Sec. 113(c), applies to wages paid or incurred after December 31, 2001.—CCH.]

(d) SPECIAL RULE FOR APPLICATION OF EMPLOYMENT CREDIT.—With respect to the DC Zone, section 1396(d)(1)(B) (relating to empowerment zone employment credit) shall be applied by substituting "the District of Columbia" for "such empowerment zone".

[CCH Explanation at ¶ 140. Committee Reports at ¶ 10,147.]

Amendment Notes

P.L. 106-554 (Community Renewal)

Act Sec. 113(c) amended Code Sec. 1400(d) to read as above. Prior to amendment, Code Sec. 1400(d) read as follows:

(d) SPECIAL RULES FOR APPLICATION OF EMPLOYMENT CREDIT.—

(1) EMPLOYEES WHOSE PRINCIPAL PLACE OF ABODE IS IN DISTRICT OF COLUMBIA.—With respect to the DC Zone, section 1396(d)(1)(B) (relating to empowerment zone employment credit) shall be applied by substituting "the District of Columbia" for "such empowerment zone".

(2) NO DECREASE OF PERCENTAGE IN 2002.—In the case of the DC Zone, section 1396 (relating to empowerment zone employment credit) shall be applied by substituting "20" for "15" in the table contained in section 1396(b). The preceding sentence shall apply only with respect to qualified zone employees, as defined in section 1396(d), determined by treating no area other than the DC Zone as an empowerment zone or enterprise community.

The above amendment applies to wages paid or incurred after December 31, 2001.

(e) SPECIAL RULE FOR APPLICATION OF ENTERPRISE ZONE BUSINESS DEFINITION.—For purposes of this subchapter and for purposes of applying subchapter U with respect to the DC Zone, section 1397C shall be applied without regard to subsections (b)(6) and (c)(5) thereof.

[CCH Explanation at ¶ 155. Committee Reports at ¶ 10,150.]

Amendment Notes
P.L. 106-554 (Community Renewal)
Act Sec. 116(b)(5) amended Code Sec. 1400(e) by striking "section 1397B" and inserting "section 1397C".

The above amendment applies to qualified empowerment zone assets acquired after December 21, 2000.

(f) Time For Which Designation Applicable.—

(1) In General.—The designation made by subsection (a) shall apply for the period beginning on January 1, 1998, and ending on December 31, *2003.*

(2) Coordination with DC enterprise community designated under subchapter U.—The designation under subchapter U of the census tracts referred to in subsection (b)(1) as an enterprise community shall terminate on December 31, *2003.*

[CCH Explanation at ¶ 170. Committee Reports at ¶ 10,225.]

Amendment Notes
P.L. 106-554 (Community Renewal)
Act Sec. 164(a)(1) amended Code Sec. 1400(f) by striking "2002" each place it appears and inserting "2003".

The above amendment is effective on December 21, 2000.

[¶ 5770] CODE SEC. 1400A. TAX-EXEMPT ECONOMIC DEVELOPMENT BONDS.

* * *

(b) Period of Applicability.—This section shall apply to bonds issued during the period beginning on January 1, 1998, and ending on December 31, *2003.*

[CCH Explanation at ¶ 170. Committee Reports at ¶ 10,225.]

Amendment Notes
P.L. 106-554 (Community Renewal)
Act Sec. 164(a)(2) amended Code Sec. 1400A(b) by striking "2002" and inserting "2003".

The above amendment is effective on December 21, 2000.

[¶ 5780] CODE SEC. 1400B. ZERO PERCENT CAPITAL GAINS RATE.

* * *

(b) DC Zone Asset.—For purposes of this section—

* * *

(2) DC zone business stock.—

(A) In General.—The term "DC Zone business stock" means any stock in a domestic corporation which is originally issued after December 31, 1997, if—

(i) such stock is acquired by the taxpayer, before January 1, *2004*, at its original issue (directly or through an underwriter) solely in exchange for cash,

(ii) as of the time such stock was issued, such corporation was a DC Zone business (or, in the case of a new corporation, such corporation was being organized for purposes of being a DC Zone business), and

(iii) during substantially all of the taxpayer's holding period for such stock, such corporation qualified as a DC Zone business.

(B) Redemptions.—A rule similar to the rule of section 1202(c)(3) shall apply for purposes of this paragraph.

(3) DC zone partnership interest.—The term "DC Zone partnership interest" means any capital or profits interest in a domestic partnership which is originally issued after December 31, 1997, if—

(A) such interest is acquired by the taxpayer, before January 1, *2004*, from the partnership solely in exchange for cash,

(B) as of the time such interest was acquired, such partnership was a DC Zone business (or, in the case of a new partnership, such partnership was being organized for purposes of being a DC Zone business), and

(C) during substantially all of the taxpayer's holding period for such interest, such partnership qualified as a DC Zone business.

A rule similar to the rule of paragraph (2)(B) shall apply for purposes of this paragraph.

(4) DC zone business property.—

(A) IN GENERAL.—The term "DC Zone business property" means tangible property if—

(i) such property was acquired by the taxpayer by purchase (as defined in section 179(d)(2)) after December 31, 1997, and before January 1, *2004*,

(ii) the original use of such property in the DC Zone commences with the taxpayer, and

(iii) during substantially all of the taxpayer's holding period for such property, substantially all of the use of such property was in a DC Zone business of the taxpayer.

(B) SPECIAL RULE FOR BUILDINGS WHICH ARE SUBSTANTIALLY IMPROVED.—

(i) IN GENERAL.—The requirements of clauses (i) and (ii) of subparagraph (A) shall be treated as met with respect to—

(I) property which is substantially improved by the taxpayer before January 1, *2004*, and

(II) any land on which such property is located.

(ii) SUBSTANTIAL IMPROVEMENT.—For purposes of clause (i), property shall be treated as substantially improved by the taxpayer only if, during any 24-month period beginning after December 31, 1997, additions to basis with respect to such property in the hands of the taxpayer exceed the greater of—

(I) an amount equal to the adjusted basis of such property at the beginning of such 24-month period in the hands of the taxpayer, or

(II) $5,000.

* * *

[CCH Explanation at ¶ 170. Committee Reports at ¶ 10,225.]

Amendment Notes

P.L. 106-554 (Community Renewal)

Act Sec. 164(b)(1) amended Code Sec. 1400B by striking "2003" each place it appears and inserting "2004".

The above amendment is effective on December 21, 2000.

(c) DC ZONE BUSINESS.—For purposes of this section, the term "DC Zone business" means any enterprise zone business (as defined in *section 1397C*), determined—

(1) after the application of section 1400(e),

(2) by substituting "80 percent" for "50 percent" in subsections (b)(2) and (c)(1) of *section 1397C*, and

(3) by treating no area other than the DC Zone as an empowerment zone or enterprise community.

* * *

[CCH Explanation at ¶ 155. Committee Reports at ¶ 10,150.]

Amendment Notes

P.L. 106-554 (Community Renewal)

Act Sec. 116(b)(5) amended Code Sec. 1400B(c) by striking "section 1397B" each place it appears and inserting "section 1397C".

The above amendment applies to qualified empowerment zone assets acquired after December 21, 2000.

(e) OTHER DEFINITIONS AND SPECIAL RULES.—For purposes of this section—

* * *

(2) GAIN BEFORE 1998 OR AFTER *2008* NOT QUALIFIED.—The term "qualified capital gain" shall not include any gain attributable to periods before January 1, 1998, or after December 31, *2008*.

* * *

[CCH Explanation at ¶ 170. Committee Reports at ¶ 10,225.]

Amendment Notes

P.L. 106-554 (Community Renewal)

Act Sec. 164(b)(2) amended Code Sec. 1400B by striking "2007" each place it appears and inserting "2008".

The above amendment is effective on December 21, 2000.

(g) SALES AND EXCHANGES OF INTERESTS IN PARTNERSHIPS AND S CORPORATIONS WHICH ARE DC ZONE BUSINESSES.—In the case of the sale or exchange of an interest in a partnership, or of stock in an S corporation, which was a DC Zone business during substantially all of the period the taxpayer held such interest or stock, the amount of qualified capital gain shall be determined without regard to—

¶ 5780 Code Sec. 1400B(c)

(1) any gain which is attributable to real property, or an intangible asset, which is not an integral part of a DC Zone business, and

(2) any gain attributable to periods before January 1, 1998, or after December 31, *2008.*

[CCH Explanation at ¶ 170. Committee Reports at ¶ 10,225.]

Amendment Notes

P.L. 106-554 (Community Renewal)
  Act Sec. 164(b)(2) amended Code Sec. 1400B by striking "2007" and inserting "2008".

The above amendment is effective on December 21, 2000.

[¶ 5790] CODE SEC. 1400C. FIRST-TIME HOMEBUYER CREDIT FOR DISTRICT OF COLUMBIA.

* * *

(i) APPLICATION OF SECTION.—This section shall apply to property purchased after August 4, 1997, and before January 1, *2004.*

[CCH Explanation at ¶ 165. Committee Reports at ¶ 10,220.]

Amendment Notes

P.L. 106-554 (Community Renewal)
  Act Sec. 163 amended Code Sec. 1400C(i) by striking "2002" and inserting "2004".

The above amendment is effective on December 21, 2000.

[¶ 5800] *CODE SEC. 1400E. DESIGNATION OF RENEWAL COMMUNITIES.*

(a) *DESIGNATION.—*

(1) *DEFINITIONS.—For purposes of this title, the term "renewal community" means any area—*

(A) *which is nominated by 1 or more local governments and the State or States in which it is located for designation as a renewal community (hereafter in this section referred to as a "nominated area"), and*

(B) *which the Secretary of Housing and Urban Development designates as a renewal community, after consultation with—*

(i) *the Secretaries of Agriculture, Commerce, Labor, and the Treasury; the Director of the Office of Management and Budget, and the Administrator of the Small Business Administration, and*

(ii) *in the case of an area on an Indian reservation, the Secretary of the Interior.*

(2) *NUMBER OF DESIGNATIONS.—*

(A) *IN GENERAL.—Not more than 40 nominated areas may be designated as renewal communities.*

(B) *MINIMUM DESIGNATION IN RURAL AREAS.—Of the areas designated under paragraph (1), at least 12 must be areas—*

(i) *which are within a local government jurisdiction or jurisdictions with a population of less than 50,000,*

(ii) *which are outside of a metropolitan statistical area (within the meaning of section 143(k)(2)(B)), or*

(iii) *which are determined by the Secretary of Housing and Urban Development, after consultation with the Secretary of Commerce, to be rural areas.*

(3) *AREAS DESIGNATED BASED ON DEGREE OF POVERTY, ETC.—*

(A) *IN GENERAL.—Except as otherwise provided in this section, the nominated areas designated as renewal communities under this subsection shall be those nominated areas with the highest average ranking with respect to the criteria described in subparagraphs (B), (C), and (D) of subsection (c)(3). For purposes of the preceding sentence, an area shall be ranked within each such criterion on the basis of the amount by which the area exceeds such criterion, with the area which exceeds such criterion by the greatest amount given the highest ranking.*

(B) *EXCEPTION WHERE INADEQUATE COURSE OF ACTION, ETC.—An area shall not be designated under subparagraph (A) if the Secretary of Housing and Urban Development determines that the course of action described in subsection (d)(2) with respect to such area is inadequate.*

(C) *PREFERENCE FOR ENTERPRISE COMMUNITIES AND EMPOWERMENT ZONES.—With respect to the first 20 designations made under this section, a preference shall be provided to those nominated areas* which are enterprise communities or empowerment zones (and are otherwise eligible for designation under this section).

(4) LIMITATION ON DESIGNATIONS.—

(A) PUBLICATION OF REGULATIONS.—The Secretary of Housing and Urban Development shall prescribe by regulation no later than 4 months after the date of the enactment of this section, after consultation with the officials described in paragraph (1)(B)—

(i) the procedures for nominating an area under paragraph (1)(A),

(ii) the parameters relating to the size and population characteristics of a renewal community, and

(iii) the manner in which nominated areas will be evaluated based on the criteria specified in subsection (d).

(B) TIME LIMITATIONS.—The Secretary of Housing and Urban Development may designate nominated areas as renewal communities only during the period beginning on the first day of the first month following the month in which the regulations described in subparagraph (A) are prescribed and ending on December 31, 2001.

(C) PROCEDURAL RULES.—The Secretary of Housing and Urban Development shall not make any designation of a nominated area as a renewal community under paragraph (2) unless—

(i) the local governments and the States in which the nominated area is located have the authority—

(I) to nominate such area for designation as a renewal community,

(II) to make the State and local commitments described in subsection (d), and

(III) to provide assurances satisfactory to the Secretary of Housing and Urban Development that such commitments will be fulfilled,

(ii) a nomination regarding such area is submitted in such a manner and in such form, and contains such information, as the Secretary of Housing and Urban Development shall by regulation prescribe, and

(iii) the Secretary of Housing and Urban Development determines that any information furnished is reasonably accurate.

(5) NOMINATION PROCESS FOR INDIAN RESERVATIONS.—For purposes of this subchapter, in the case of a nominated area on an Indian reservation, the reservation governing body (as determined by the Secretary of the Interior) shall be treated as being both the State and local governments with respect to such area.

(b) PERIOD FOR WHICH DESIGNATION IS IN EFFECT.—

(1) IN GENERAL.—Any designation of an area as a renewal community shall remain in effect during the period beginning on January 1, 2002, and ending on the earliest of—

(A) December 31, 2009,

(B) the termination date designated by the State and local governments in their nomination, or

(C) the date the Secretary of Housing and Urban Development revokes such designation.

(2) REVOCATION OF DESIGNATION.—The Secretary of Housing and Urban Development may revoke the designation under this section of an area if such Secretary determines that the local government or the State in which the area is located—

(A) has modified the boundaries of the area, or

(B) is not complying substantially with, or fails to make progress in achieving, the State or local commitments, respectively, described in subsection (d).

(3) EARLIER TERMINATION OF CERTAIN BENEFITS IF EARLIER TERMINATION OF DESIGNATION.—If the designation of an area as a renewal community terminates before December 31, 2009, the day after the date of such termination shall be substituted for "January 1, 2010" each place it appears in sections 1400F and 1400J with respect to such area.

(c) AREA AND ELIGIBILITY REQUIREMENTS.—

(1) IN GENERAL.—The Secretary of Housing and Urban Development may designate a nominated area as a renewal community under subsection (a) only if the area meets the requirements of paragraphs (2) and (3) of this subsection.

(2) AREA REQUIREMENTS.—A nominated area meets the requirements of this paragraph if—

(A) the area is within the jurisdiction of one or more local governments,

(B) the boundary of the area is continuous, and

(C) the area—

(i) has a population of not more than 200,000 and at least—

(I) 4,000 if any portion of such area (other than a rural area described in subsection (a)(2)(B)(i)) is located within a metropolitan statistical area (within the meaning of section 143(k)(2)(B)) which has a population of 50,000 or greater, or

(II) 1,000 in any other case, or

(ii) is entirely within an Indian reservation (as determined by the Secretary of the Interior).

(3) ELIGIBILITY REQUIREMENTS.—A nominated area meets the requirements of this paragraph if the State and the local governments in which it is located certify in writing (and the Secretary of Housing and Urban Development, after such review of supporting data as he deems appropriate, accepts such certification) that—

(A) the area is one of pervasive poverty, unemployment, and general distress,

(B) the unemployment rate in the area, as determined by the most recent available data, was at least 1 1/2 times the national unemployment rate for the period to which such data relate,

(C) the poverty rate for each population census tract within the nominated area is at least 20 percent, and

(D) in the case of an urban area, at least 70 percent of the households living in the area have incomes below 80 percent of the median income of households within the jurisdiction of the local government (determined in the same manner as under section 119(b)(2) of the Housing and Community Development Act of 1974).

(4) CONSIDERATION OF OTHER FACTORS.—The Secretary of Housing and Urban Development, in selecting any nominated area for designation as a renewal community under this section—

(A) shall take into account—

(i) the extent to which such area has a high incidence of crime, or

(ii) if such area has census tracts identified in the May 12, 1998, report of the General Accounting Office regarding the identification of economically distressed areas, and

(B) with respect to 1 of the areas to be designated under subsection (a)(2)(B), may, in lieu of any criteria described in paragraph (3), take into account the existence of outmigration from the area.

(d) REQUIRED STATE AND LOCAL COMMITMENTS.—

(1) IN GENERAL.—The Secretary of Housing and Urban Development may designate any nominated area as a renewal community under subsection (a) only if—

(A) the local government and the State in which the area is located agree in writing that, during any period during which the area is a renewal community, such governments will follow a specified course of action which meets the requirements of paragraph (2) and is designed to reduce the various burdens borne by employers or employees in such area, and

(B) the economic growth promotion requirements of paragraph (3) are met.

(2) COURSE OF ACTION.—

(A) IN GENERAL.—A course of action meets the requirements of this paragraph if such course of action is a written document, signed by a State (or local government) and neighborhood organizations, which evidences a partnership between such State or government and community-based organizations and which commits each signatory to specific and measurable goals, actions, and timetables. Such course of action shall include at least 4 of the following:

(i) A reduction of tax rates or fees applying within the renewal community.

(ii) An increase in the level of efficiency of local services within the renewal community.

(iii) Crime reduction strategies, such as crime prevention (including the provision of crime prevention services by nongovernmental entities).

(iv) Actions to reduce, remove, simplify, or streamline governmental requirements applying within the renewal community.

(v) *Involvement in the program by private entities, organizations, neighborhood organizations, and community groups, particularly those in the renewal community, including a commitment from such private entities to provide jobs and job training for, and technical, financial, or other assistance to, employers, employees, and residents from the renewal community.*

(vi) *The gift (or sale at below fair market value) of surplus real property (such as land, homes, and commercial or industrial structures) in the renewal community to neighborhood organizations, community development corporations, or private companies.*

(B) RECOGNITION OF PAST EFFORTS.—*For purposes of this section, in evaluating the course of action agreed to by any State or local government, the Secretary of Housing and Urban Development shall take into account the past efforts of such State or local government in reducing the various burdens borne by employers and employees in the area involved.*

(3) ECONOMIC GROWTH PROMOTION REQUIREMENTS.—*The economic growth promotion requirements of this paragraph are met with respect to a nominated area if the local government and the State in which such area is located certify in writing that such government and State (respectively) have repealed or reduced, will not enforce, or will reduce within the nominated area at least 4 of the following:*

(A) *Licensing requirements for occupations that do not ordinarily require a professional degree.*

(B) *Zoning restrictions on home-based businesses which do not create a public nuisance.*

(C) *Permit requirements for street vendors who do not create a public nuisance.*

(D) *Zoning or other restrictions that impede the formation of schools or child care centers.*

(E) *Franchises or other restrictions on competition for businesses providing public services, including taxicabs, jitneys, cable television, or trash hauling.*

This paragraph shall not apply to the extent that such regulation of businesses and occupations is necessary for and well-tailored to the protection of health and safety.

(e) COORDINATION WITH TREATMENT OF EMPOWERMENT ZONES AND ENTERPRISE COMMUNITIES.—*For purposes of this title, the designation under section 1391 of any area as an empowerment zone or enterprise community shall cease to be in effect as of the date that the designation of any portion of such area as a renewal community takes effect.*

(f) DEFINITIONS AND SPECIAL RULES.—*For purposes of this subchapter—*

(1) GOVERNMENTS.—*If more than one government seeks to nominate an area as a renewal community, any reference to, or requirement of, this section shall apply to all such governments.*

(2) LOCAL GOVERNMENT.—*The term "local government" means—*

(A) *any county, city, town, township, parish, village, or other general purpose political subdivision of a State, and*

(B) *any combination of political subdivisions described in subparagraph (A) recognized by the Secretary of Housing and Urban Development.*

(3) APPLICATION OF RULES RELATING TO CENSUS TRACTS.—*The rules of section 1392(b)(4) shall apply.*

(4) CENSUS DATA.—*Population and poverty rate shall be determined by using 1990 census data.*

[CCH Explanation at ¶ 105. Committee Reports at ¶ 10,135.]

Amendment Notes

P.L. 106-554 (Community Renewal)

Act Sec. 101(a) amended chapter 1 by adding at the end a new subchapter X (Code Secs. 1400E-1400J) to read as above.

The above amendment is effective on December 21, 2000. For a special rule, see Act Sec. 101(c).

Act Sec. 101(c) provides:

(c) AUDIT AND REPORT.—Not later than January 31 of 2004, 2007, and 2010, the Comptroller General of the United States shall, pursuant to an audit of the renewal community program established under section 1400E of the Internal Revenue Code of 1986 (as added by subsection (a)) and the empowerment zone and enterprise community program under subchapter U of chapter 1 of such Code, report to Congress on such program and its effect on poverty, unemployment, and economic growth within the designated renewal communities, empowerment zones, and enterprise communities.

[¶ 5810] *CODE SEC. 1400F. RENEWAL COMMUNITY CAPITAL GAIN.*

(a) GENERAL RULE.—*Gross income does not include any qualified capital gain from the sale or exchange of a qualified community asset held for more than 5 years.*

(b) QUALIFIED COMMUNITY ASSET.—*For purposes of this section—*

(1) IN GENERAL.—*The term "qualified community asset" means—*

(A) any qualified community stock,

(B) any qualified community partnership interest, and

(C) any qualified community business property.

(2) QUALIFIED COMMUNITY STOCK.—

(A) IN GENERAL.—Except as provided in subparagraph (B), the term "qualified community stock" means any stock in a domestic corporation if—

(i) such stock is acquired by the taxpayer after December 31, 2001, and before January 1, 2010, at its original issue (directly or through an underwriter) from the corporation solely in exchange for cash,

(ii) as of the time such stock was issued, such corporation was a renewal community business (or, in the case of a new corporation, such corporation was being organized for purposes of being a renewal community business), and

(iii) during substantially all of the taxpayer's holding period for such stock, such corporation qualified as a renewal community business.

(B) REDEMPTIONS.—A rule similar to the rule of section 1202(c)(3) shall apply for purposes of this paragraph.

(3) QUALIFIED COMMUNITY PARTNERSHIP INTEREST.—The term "qualified community partnership interest" means any capital or profits interest in a domestic partnership if—

(A) such interest is acquired by the taxpayer after December 31, 2001, and before January 1, 2010, from the partnership solely in exchange for cash,

(B) as of the time such interest was acquired, such partnership was a renewal community business (or, in the case of a new partnership, such partnership was being organized for purposes of being a renewal community business), and

(C) during substantially all of the taxpayer's holding period for such interest, such partnership qualified as a renewal community business.

A rule similar to the rule of paragraph (2)(B) shall apply for purposes of this paragraph.

(4) QUALIFIED COMMUNITY BUSINESS PROPERTY.—

(A) IN GENERAL.—The term "qualified community business property" means tangible property if—

(i) such property was acquired by the taxpayer by purchase (as defined in section 179(d)(2)) after December 31, 2001, and before January 1, 2010,

(ii) the original use of such property in the renewal community commences with the taxpayer, and

(iii) during substantially all of the taxpayer's holding period for such property, substantially all of the use of such property was in a renewal community business of the taxpayer.

(B) SPECIAL RULE FOR SUBSTANTIAL IMPROVEMENTS.—The requirements of clauses (i) and (ii) of subparagraph (A) shall be treated as satisfied with respect to—

(i) property which is substantially improved by the taxpayer before January 1, 2010, and

(ii) any land on which such property is located.

The determination of whether a property is substantially improved shall be made under clause (ii) of section 1400B(b)(4)(B), except that "December 31, 2001" shall be substituted for "December 31, 1997" in such clause.

(c) QUALIFIED CAPITAL GAIN.—For purposes of this section—

(1) IN GENERAL.—Except as otherwise provided in this subsection, the term "qualified capital gain" means any gain recognized on the sale or exchange of—

(A) a capital asset, or

(B) property used in the trade or business (as defined in section 1231(b)).

(2) GAIN BEFORE 2002 OR AFTER 2014 NOT QUALIFIED.—The term "qualified capital gain" shall not include any gain attributable to periods before January 1, 2002, or after December 31, 2014.

(3) CERTAIN RULES TO APPLY.—Rules similar to the rules of paragraphs (3), (4), and (5) of section 1400B(e) shall apply for purposes of this subsection.

Code Sec. 1400F(c)   ¶ 5810

(d) *CERTAIN RULES TO APPLY.*—For purposes of this section, rules similar to the rules of paragraphs (5), (6), and (7) of subsection (b), and subsections (f) and (g), of section 1400B shall apply; except that for such purposes section 1400B(g)(2) shall be applied by substituting "January 1, 2002" for "January 1, 1998" and "December 31, 2014" for "December 31, 2007".

(e) *REGULATIONS.*—The Secretary shall prescribe such regulations as may be appropriate to carry out the purposes of this section, including regulations to prevent the abuse of the purposes of this section.

[CCH Explanation at ¶ 107. Committee Reports at ¶ 10,137.]

Amendment Notes

P.L. 106-554 (Community Renewal)

Act Sec. 101(a) amended chapter 1 by adding at the end a new subchapter X (Code Secs. 1400E-1400J) to read as above.

The above amendment is effective on December 21, 2000.

[¶ 5820] CODE SEC. 1400G. RENEWAL COMMUNITY BUSINESS DEFINED.

For purposes of this subchapter, the term "renewal community business" means any entity or proprietorship which would be a qualified business entity or qualified proprietorship under section 1397C if references to renewal communities were substituted for references to empowerment zones in such section.

[CCH Explanation at ¶ 107. Committee Reports at ¶ 10,137.]

Amendment Notes

P.L. 106-554 (Community Renewal)

Act Sec. 101(a) amended chapter 1 by adding at the end a new subchapter X (Code Secs. 1400E-1400J) to read as above.

The above amendment is effective on December 21, 2000.

[¶ 5830] CODE SEC. 1400H. RENEWAL COMMUNITY EMPLOYMENT CREDIT.

(a) *IN GENERAL.*—Subject to the modification in subsection (b), a renewal community shall be treated as an empowerment zone for purposes of section 1396 with respect to wages paid or incurred after December 31, 2001.

(b) *MODIFICATION.*—In applying section 1396 with respect to renewal communities—

(1) the applicable percentage shall be 15 percent, and

(2) subsection (c) thereof shall be applied by substituting "$10,000" for "$15,000" each place it appears.

[CCH Explanation at ¶ 110. Committee Reports at ¶ 10,138.]

Amendment Notes

P.L. 106-554 (Community Renewal)

Act Sec. 101(a) amended chapter 1 by adding at the end a new subchapter X (Code Secs. 1400E-1400J) to read as above.

The above amendment is effective on December 21, 2000.

[¶ 5840] CODE SEC. 1400I. COMMERCIAL REVITALIZATION DEDUCTION.

(a) *GENERAL RULE.*—At the election of the taxpayer, either—

(1) one-half of any qualified revitalization expenditures chargeable to capital account with respect to any qualified revitalization building shall be allowable as a deduction for the taxable year in which the building is placed in service, or

(2) a deduction for all such expenditures shall be allowable ratably over the 120-month period beginning with the month in which the building is placed in service.

(b) *QUALIFIED REVITALIZATION BUILDINGS AND EXPENDITURES.*—For purposes of this section—

(1) *QUALIFIED REVITALIZATION BUILDING.*—The term "qualified revitalization building" means any building (and its structural components) if—

(A) the building is placed in service by the taxpayer in a renewal community and the original use of the building begins with the taxpayer, or

(B) in the case of such building not described in subparagraph (A), such building—

(i) is substantially rehabilitated (within the meaning of section 47(c)(1)(C)) by the taxpayer, and

(ii) is placed in service by the taxpayer after the rehabilitation in a renewal community.

(2) *QUALIFIED REVITALIZATION EXPENDITURE.*—

(A) IN GENERAL.—The term "qualified revitalization expenditure" means any amount properly chargeable to capital account for property for which depreciation is allowable under section 168 (without regard to this section) and which is—

(i) nonresidential real property (as defined in section 168(e)), or

(ii) section 1250 property (as defined in section 1250(c)) which is functionally related and subordinate to property described in clause (i).

(B) CERTAIN EXPENDITURES NOT INCLUDED.—

(i) ACQUISITION COST.—In the case of a building described in paragraph (1)(B), the cost of acquiring the building or interest therein shall be treated as a qualified revitalization expenditure only to the extent that such cost does not exceed 30 percent of the aggregate qualified revitalization expenditures (determined without regard to such cost) with respect to such building.

(ii) CREDITS.—The term "qualified revitalization expenditure" does not include any expenditure which the taxpayer may take into account in computing any credit allowable under this title unless the taxpayer elects to take the expenditure into account only for purposes of this section.

(c) DOLLAR LIMITATION.—The aggregate amount which may be treated as qualified revitalization expenditures with respect to any qualified revitalization building shall not exceed the lesser of—

(1) $10,000,000, or

(2) the commercial revitalization expenditure amount allocated to such building under this section by the commercial revitalization agency for the State in which the building is located.

(d) COMMERCIAL REVITALIZATION EXPENDITURE AMOUNT.—

(1) IN GENERAL.—The aggregate commercial revitalization expenditure amount which a commercial revitalization agency may allocate for any calendar year is the amount of the State commercial revitalization expenditure ceiling determined under this paragraph for such calendar year for such agency.

(2) STATE COMMERCIAL REVITALIZATION EXPENDITURE CEILING.—The State commercial revitalization expenditure ceiling applicable to any State—

(A) for each calendar year after 2001 and before 2010 is $12,000,000 for each renewal community in the State, and

(B) for each calendar year thereafter is zero.

(3) COMMERCIAL REVITALIZATION AGENCY.—For purposes of this section, the term "commercial revitalization agency" means any agency authorized by a State to carry out this section.

(4) TIME AND MANNER OF ALLOCATIONS.—Allocations under this section shall be made at the same time and in the same manner as under paragraphs (1) and (7) of section 42(h).

(e) RESPONSIBILITIES OF COMMERCIAL REVITALIZATION AGENCIES.—

(1) PLANS FOR ALLOCATION.—Notwithstanding any other provision of this section, the commercial revitalization expenditure amount with respect to any building shall be zero unless—

(A) such amount was allocated pursuant to a qualified allocation plan of the commercial revitalization agency which is approved (in accordance with rules similar to the rules of section 147(f)(2) (other than subparagraph (B)(ii) thereof)) by the governmental unit of which such agency is a part, and

(B) such agency notifies the chief executive officer (or its equivalent) of the local jurisdiction within which the building is located of such allocation and provides such individual a reasonable opportunity to comment on the allocation.

(2) QUALIFIED ALLOCATION PLAN.—For purposes of this subsection, the term "qualified allocation plan" means any plan—

(A) which sets forth selection criteria to be used to determine priorities of the commercial revitalization agency which are appropriate to local conditions,

(B) which considers—

(i) the degree to which a project contributes to the implementation of a strategic plan that is devised for a renewal community through a citizen participation process,

Code Sec. 1400I(e)   ¶ 5840

(ii) the amount of any increase in permanent, full-time employment by reason of any project, and

(iii) the active involvement of residents and nonprofit groups within the renewal community, and

(C) which provides a procedure that the agency (or its agent) will follow in monitoring compliance with this section.

(f) SPECIAL RULES.—

(1) DEDUCTION IN LIEU OF DEPRECIATION.—The deduction provided by this section for qualified revitalization expenditures shall—

(A) with respect to the deduction determined under subsection (a)(1), be in lieu of any depreciation deduction otherwise allowable on account of one-half of such expenditures, and

(B) with respect to the deduction determined under subsection (a)(2), be in lieu of any depreciation deduction otherwise allowable on account of all of such expenditures.

(2) BASIS ADJUSTMENT, ETC.—For purposes of sections 1016 and 1250, the deduction under this section shall be treated in the same manner as a depreciation deduction. For purposes of section 1250(b)(5), the straight line method of adjustment shall be determined without regard to this section.

(3) SUBSTANTIAL REHABILITATIONS TREATED AS SEPARATE BUILDINGS.—A substantial rehabilitation (within the meaning of section 47(c)(1)(C)) of a building shall be treated as a separate building for purposes of subsection (a).

(4) CLARIFICATION OF ALLOWANCE OF DEDUCTION UNDER MINIMUM TAX.—Notwithstanding section 56(a)(1), the deduction under this section shall be allowed in determining alternative minimum taxable income under section 55.

(g) TERMINATION.—This section shall not apply to any building placed in service after December 31, 2009.

[CCH Explanation at ¶ 115. Committee Reports at ¶ 10,139.]

<table>
<tr><td>Amendment Notes</td><td>The above amendment is effective on December 21,</td></tr>
</table>

P.L. 106-554 (Community Renewal)
Act Sec. 101(a) amended chapter 1 by adding at the end a new subchapter X (Code Secs. 1400E-1400J) to read as above.

The above amendment is effective on December 21, 2000.

[¶ 5850] CODE SEC. 1400J. INCREASE IN EXPENSING UNDER SECTION 179.

(a) IN GENERAL.—For purposes of section 1397A—

(1) a renewal community shall be treated as an empowerment zone,

(2) a renewal community business shall be treated as an enterprise zone business, and

(3) qualified renewal property shall be treated as qualified zone property.

(b) QUALIFIED RENEWAL PROPERTY.—For purposes of this section—

(1) IN GENERAL.—The term "qualified renewal property" means any property to which section 168 applies (or would apply but for section 179) if—

(A) such property was acquired by the taxpayer by purchase (as defined in section 179(d)(2)) after December 31, 2001, and before January 1, 2010, and

(B) such property would be qualified zone property (as defined in section 1397D) if references to renewal communities were substituted for references to empowerment zones in section 1397D.

(2) CERTAIN RULES TO APPLY.—The rules of subsections (a)(2) and (b) of section 1397D shall apply for purposes of this section.

[CCH Explanation at ¶ 120. Committee Reports at ¶ 10,140.]

<table>
<tr><td>Amendment Notes</td><td>The above amendment is effective on December 21,</td></tr>
</table>

P.L. 106-554 (Community Renewal)
Act Sec. 101(a) amended chapter 1 by adding at the end a new subchapter X (Code Secs. 1400E-1400J) to read as above.

The above amendment is effective on December 21, 2000.

[¶ 5860] CODE SEC. 2035. ADJUSTMENTS FOR CERTAIN GIFTS MADE WITHIN 3 YEARS OF DECEDENT'S DEATH.

* * *

(c) OTHER RULES RELATING TO TRANSFERS WITHIN 3 YEARS OF DEATH.—

* * *

(2) COORDINATION WITH SECTION 6166.—An estate shall be treated as meeting the 35 percent of adjusted gross estate requirement of section 6166(a)(1) only if the estate meets such requirement both with and without the application of *subsection (a)*.

* * *

[CCH Explanation at ¶ 30,050.]

Amendment Notes
P.L. 106-554 (Community Renewal)
  Act Sec. 319(14)(A) amended Code Sec. 2035(c)(2) by striking "paragraph (1)" and inserting "subsection (a)".

The above amendment is effective on December 21, 2000.

(d) EXCEPTION.—Subsection (a) *and paragraph (1) of subsection (c)* shall not apply to any bona fide sale for an adequate and full consideration in money or money's worth.

* * *

[CCH Explanation at ¶ 30,050.]

Amendment Notes
P.L. 106-554 (Community Renewal)
  Act Sec. 319(14)(B) amended Code Sec. 2035(d) by inserting "and paragraph (1) of subsection (c)" after "Subsection (a)".

The above amendment is effective on December 21, 2000.

[¶ 5870] CODE SEC. 3121. DEFINITIONS.

(a) WAGES.—For purposes of this chapter, the term "wages" means all remuneration for employment, including the cash value of all remuneration (including benefits) paid in any medium other than cash; except that such term shall not include—

* * *

(5) any payment made to, or on behalf of, an employee or his beneficiary—

* * *

(G) under a cafeteria plan (within the meaning of section 125) if such payment would not be treated as wages without regard to such plan and it is reasonable to believe that (if section 125 applied for purposes of this section) section 125 would not treat any wages as constructively received,

* * *

[CCH Explanation at ¶ 30,050.]

Amendment Notes
P.L. 106-554 (Community Renewal)
  Act Sec. 319(15) amended Code Sec. 3121(a)(5) by striking the semicolon at the end of subparagraph (G) and inserting a comma.

The above amendment is effective on December 21, 2000.

[¶ 5880] CODE SEC. 3231. DEFINITIONS.

* * *

(e) COMPENSATION.—For purposes of this chapter—

* * *

(10) ARCHER MSA CONTRIBUTIONS.—The term "compensation" shall not include any payment made to or for the benefit of an employee if at the time of such payment it is reasonable to believe that the employee will be able to exclude such payment from income under section 106(b).

* * *

[CCH Explanation at ¶ 615. Committee Reports at ¶ 10,245.]

Amendment Notes
P.L. 106-554 (Community Renewal)
  Act Sec. 202(b)(5) amended the heading for Code Sec. 3231(e)(10) by striking "MEDICAL SAVINGS ACCOUNT" and inserting "ARCHER MSA".

The above amendment is effective on December 21, 2000.

[¶ 5890] CODE SEC. 3306. DEFINITIONS.

* * *

(c) EMPLOYMENT.—For purposes of this chapter, the term "employment" means any service performed prior to 1955, which was employment for purposes of subchapter C of chapter 9 of the Internal Revenue Code of 1939 under the law applicable to the period in which such service was performed, and (A) any service, of whatever nature, performed after 1954 by an employee for the person employing him, irrespective of the citizenship or residence of either, (i) within the United States, or (ii) on or in connection with an American vessel or American aircraft under a contract of service which is entered into within the United States or during the performance of which and while the employee is employed on the vessel or aircraft it touches at a port in the United States, if the employee is employed on and in connection with such vessel or aircraft when outside the United States, and (B) any service, of whatever nature, performed after 1971 outside the United States (except in a contiguous country with which the United States has an agreement relating to unemployment compensation) by a citizen of the United States as an employee of an American employer (as defined in subsection (j)(3)), except—

* * *

(7) service performed in the employ of a State, or any political subdivision thereof, *or in the employ of an Indian tribe*, or any instrumentality of any one or more of the foregoing which is wholly owned by one or more States or political subdivisions *or Indian tribes*; and any service performed in the employ of any instrumentality of one or more States or political subdivisions to the extent that the instrumentality is, with respect to such service, immune under the Constitution of the United States from the tax imposed by section 3301;

* * *

[CCH Explanation at ¶ 290. Committee Reports at ¶ 10,235.]

Amendment Notes

P.L. 106-554 (Community Renewal)

Act Sec. 166(a)(1)-(2) amended Code Sec. 3306(c)(7) by inserting "or in the employ of an Indian tribe," after "service performed in the employ of a State, or any political subdivision thereof,"; and by inserting "or Indian tribes" after "wholly owned by one or more States or political subdivisions".

The above amendments apply to service performed on or after December 21, 2000. For a transition rule, see Act Sec. 166(e)(2), below.

Act Sec. 166(e)(2) provides:

(2) TRANSITION RULE.—For purposes of the Federal Unemployment Tax Act, service performed in the employ of an Indian tribe (as defined in section 3306(u) of the Internal Revenue Code of 1986 (as added by this section)) shall not be treated as employment (within the meaning of section 3306 of such Code) if—

(A) it is service which is performed before the date of the enactment of this Act and with respect to which the tax imposed under the Federal Unemployment Tax Act has not been paid, and

(B) such Indian tribe reimburses a State unemployment fund for unemployment benefits paid for service attributable to such tribe for such period.

(u) INDIAN TRIBE.—*For purposes of this chapter, the term "Indian tribe" has the meaning given to such term by section 4(e) of the Indian Self-Determination and Education Assistance Act (25 U.S.C. 450b(e)), and includes any subdivision, subsidiary, or business enterprise wholly owned by such an Indian tribe.*

[CCH Explanation at ¶ 290. Committee Reports at ¶ 10,235.]

Amendment Notes

P.L. 106-554 (Community Renewal)

Act Sec. 166(d) amended Code Sec. 3306 by adding at the end a new subsection (u) to read as above.

The above amendment applies to service performed on or after December 21, 2000. For a transition rule, see Act Sec. 166(e)(2) in the amendment notes following Code Sec. 3306(c), above.

[¶ 5900] CODE SEC. 3309. STATE LAW COVERAGE OF SERVICES PERFORMED FOR NONPROFIT ORGANIZATIONS OR GOVERNMENTAL ENTITIES.

(a) STATE LAW REQUIREMENTS.—For purposes of section 3304(a)(6)—

(1) except as otherwise provided in subsections (b) and (c), the services to which this paragraph applies are—

(A) service excluded from the term "employment" solely by reason of paragraph (8) of section 3306(c), and

(B) service excluded from the term "employment" solely by reason of paragraph (7) of section 3306(c); and

(2) the State law shall provide that a governmental entity, *including an Indian tribe*, or any other organization (or group of governmental entities or other organizations) which, but for the requirements of this paragraph, would be liable for contributions with respect to service to which

paragraph (1) applies may elect, for such minimum period and at such time as may be provided by State law, to pay (in lieu of such contributions) into the State unemployment fund amounts equal to the amounts of compensation attributable under the State law to such service. The State law may provide safeguards to ensure that governmental entities or other organizations so electing will make the payments required under such elections.

[CCH Explanation at ¶ 290. Committee Reports at ¶ 10,235.]

Amendment Notes

P.L. 106-554 (Community Renewal)

Act Sec. 166(b)(1) amended Code Sec. 3309(a)(2) by inserting ", including an Indian tribe," after " the State law shall provide that a governmental entity".

The above amendment applies to service performed on or after December 21, 2000. For a transition rule, see Act Sec. 166(e)(2) in the amendment notes following Code Sec. 3306(c), above.

(b) SECTION NOT TO APPLY TO CERTAIN SERVICE.—This section shall not apply to service performed—

* * *

(3) in the employ of a governmental entity referred to in paragraph (7) of section 3306(c), if such service is performed by an individual in the exercise of his duties—

(A) as an elected official;

(B) as a member of a legislative body, or a member of the judiciary, of a State or political subdivision thereof, *or of an Indian tribe*;

(C) as a member of the State National Guard or Air National Guard;

(D) as an employee serving on a temporary basis in case of fire, storm, snow, earthquake, flood, or similar emergency;

(E) in a position which, under or pursuant to the State *or tribal* law, is designated as (i) a major nontenured policymaking or advisory position, or (ii) a policymaking or advisory position the performance of the duties of which ordinarily does not require more than 8 hours per week; or

(F) as an election official or election worker if the amount of remuneration received by the individual during the calendar year for services as an election official or election worker is less than $1,000;

* * *

(5) as part of an unemployment work-relief or work-training program assisted or financed in whole or in part by any Federal agency or an agency of a State or political subdivision thereof *or of an Indian tribe*, by an individual receiving such work relief or work training; and

* * *

[CCH Explanation at ¶ 290. Committee Reports at ¶ 10,235.]

Amendment Notes

P.L. 106-554 (Community Renewal)

Act Sec. 166(b)(2) amended Code Sec. 3309(b)(3)(B) by inserting ", or of an Indian tribe" after "of a State or political subdivision thereof".

Act Sec. 166(b)(3) amended Code Sec. 3309(b)(3)(E) by inserting "or tribal" after "the State".

Act Sec. 166(b)(4) amended Code Sec. 3309(b)(5) by inserting "or of an Indian tribe" after "an agency of a State or political subdivision thereof".

The above amendments apply to service performed on or after December 21, 2000. For a transition rule, see Act Sec. 166(e)(2) in the amendment notes following Code Sec. 3306(c), above.

(d) *ELECTION BY INDIAN TRIBE.—The State law shall provide that an Indian tribe may make contributions for employment as if the employment is within the meaning of section 3306 or make payments in lieu of contributions under this section, and shall provide that an Indian tribe may make separate elections for itself and each subdivision, subsidiary, or business enterprise wholly owned by such Indian tribe. State law may require a tribe to post a payment bond or take other reasonable measures to assure the making of payments in lieu of contributions under this section. Notwithstanding the requirements of section 3306(a)(6), if, within 90 days of having received a notice of delinquency, a tribe fails to make contributions, payments in lieu of contributions, or payment of penalties or interest (at amounts or rates comparable to those applied to all other employers covered under the State law) assessed with respect to such failure, or if the tribe fails to post a required payment bond, then service for the tribe shall not be excepted from employment under section 3306(c)(7) until any such failure is corrected. This subsection shall apply to an Indian tribe within the meaning of section 4(e) of the Indian Self-Determination and Education Assistance Act (25 U.S.C. 450b(e)).*

[CCH Explanation at ¶ 290. Committee Reports at ¶ 10,235.]

Amendment Notes

P.L. 106-554 (Community Renewal)

Act Sec. 166(c) amended Code Sec. 3309 by adding at the end a new subsection (d) to read as above.

The above amendment applies to service performed on or after December 21, 2000. For a transition rule, see Act Sec. 166(e)(2) in the amendment notes following Code Sec. 3306(c), above.

Code Sec. 3309(d)   ¶ 5900

[¶ 5910] CODE SEC. 3405. SPECIAL RULES FOR PENSIONS, ANNUITIES, AND CERTAIN OTHER DEFERRED INCOME.

* * *

(e) DEFINITIONS AND SPECIAL RULES.—For purposes of this section—

(1) DESIGNATED DISTRIBUTION.—

* * *

(B) EXCEPTIONS.—The term "designated distribution" shall not include—

(i) any amount which is wages without regard to this section,

(ii) the portion of a distribution or payment which it is reasonable to believe is not includible in gross income,

(iii) any amount which is subject to withholding under subchapter A of chapter 3 (relating to withholding of tax on nonresident aliens and foreign corporations) by the person paying such amount or which would be so subject but for a tax treaty, or

(iv) any distribution described in section 404(k)(2).

For purposes of clause (ii), any distribution or payment from or under an individual retirement plan *(other than a Roth IRA)* shall be treated as includible in gross income.

* * *

[CCH Explanation at ¶ 610. Committee Reports at ¶ 10,325.]

Amendment Notes

P.L. 106-554 (Community Renewal)

Act Sec. 314(b) amended Code Sec. 3405(e)(1)(B) by inserting "(other than a Roth IRA)" after "individual retirement plan" in the last sentence.

The above amendment is effective as if included in the provision of the Taxpayer Relief Act of 1997 (P.L. 105-34) to which it relates [effective for tax years beginning after December 31, 1997.—CCH.].

[¶ 5920] CODE SEC. 4946. DEFINITIONS AND SPECIAL RULES.

* * *

(c) GOVERNMENT OFFICIAL.—For purposes of subsection (a)(1)(I) and section 4941, the term "government official" means, with respect to an act of self-dealing described in section 4941, an individual who, at the time of such act, holds any of the following offices or positions (other than as a "special Government employee", as defined in section 202(a) of title 18, United States Code):

* * *

(3) a position in the executive, legislative, or judicial branch of the Government of the United States—

(A) which is listed in schedule C of rule VI of the Civil Service Rules, or

(B) the compensation for which is equal to or greater than *the lowest rate of basic pay for the Senior Executive Service under section 5382* of title 5, United States Code,

* * *

[CCH Explanation at ¶ 30,050.]

Amendment Notes

P.L. 106-554 (Community Renewal)

Act Sec. 319(16) amended Code Sec. 4946(c)(3)(B) by striking "the lowest rate of compensation prescribed for GS-16 of the General Schedule under section 5332" and

inserting "the lowest rate of basic pay for the Senior Executive Service under section 5382".

The above amendment is effective on December 21, 2000.

[¶ 5930] CODE SEC. 4973. TAX ON EXCESS CONTRIBUTIONS TO CERTAIN TAX-FAVORED ACCOUNTS AND ANNUITIES.

(a) TAX IMPOSED.—In the case of—

(1) an individual retirement account (within the meaning of section 408(a)),

(2) *an Archer MSA* (within the meaning of section 220(d)),

(3) an individual retirement annuity (within the meaning of section 408(b)), a custodial account treated as an annuity contract under section 403(b)(7)(A) (relating to custodial accounts for regulated investment company stock), or

(4) an education individual retirement account (as defined in section 530),

there is imposed for each taxable year a tax in an amount equal to 6 percent of the amount of the excess contributions to such individual's accounts or annuities (determined as of the close of the taxable year).

The amount of such tax for any taxable year shall not exceed 6 percent of the value of the account or annuity (determined as of the close of the taxable year). In the case of an endowment contract described in section 408(b), the tax imposed by this section does not apply to any amount allocable to life, health, accident, or other insurance under such contract. The tax imposed by this subsection shall be paid by such individual.

* * *

[CCH Explanation at ¶ 615. Committee Reports at ¶ 10,245.]

Amendment Notes

P.L. 106-554 (Community Renewal)

Act Sec. 202(a)(6) amended Code Sec. 4973(a)(2) by striking "medical savings account" and inserting "Archer MSA".

Act Sec. 202(b)(10) amended Code Sec. 4973(a)(2) by striking "a Archer" and inserting "an Archer".

The above amendments are effective on December 21, 2000.

(d) EXCESS CONTRIBUTIONS TO *ARCHER MSAs.*—For purposes of this section, in the case of *Archer MSAs* (within the meaning of section 220(d)), the term "excess contributions" means the sum of—

(1) the aggregate amount contributed for the taxable year to the accounts (other than rollover contributions described in section 220(f)(5)) which is neither excludable from gross income under section 106(b) nor allowable as a deduction under section 220 for such year, and

(2) the amount determined under this subsection for the preceding taxable year, reduced by the sum of—

(A) the distributions out of the accounts which were included in gross income under section 220(f)(2), and

(B) the excess (if any) of—

(i) the maximum amount allowable as a deduction under section 220(b)(1) (determined without regard to section 106(b)) for the taxable year, over

(ii) the amount contributed to the accounts for the taxable year.

For purposes of this subsection, any contribution which is distributed out of the *Archer MSA* in a distribution to which section 220(f)(3) or section 138(c)(3) applies shall be treated as an amount not contributed.

* * *

[CCH Explanation at ¶ 615. Committee Reports at ¶ 10,245.]

Amendment Notes

P.L. 106-554 (Community Renewal)

Act Sec. 202(a)(6) amended Code Sec. 4973(d) by striking "medical savings account" and inserting "Archer MSA".

Act Sec. 202(b)(2)(C) amended Code Sec. 4973(d) by striking "medical savings accounts" and inserting "Archer MSAs".

Act Sec. 202(b)(6) amended the heading for Code Sec. 4973(d) by striking "MEDICAL SAVINGS ACCOUNTS" and inserting "ARCHER MSAs".

The above amendments are effective on December 21, 2000.

[¶ 5940] CODE SEC. 4975. TAX ON PROHIBITED TRANSACTIONS.

* * *

(c) PROHIBITED TRANSACTION.—

* * *

(4) SPECIAL RULE FOR *ARCHER MSAS.*—An individual for whose benefit *an Archer MSA* (within the meaning of section 220(d)) is established shall be exempt from the tax imposed by this section with respect to any transaction concerning such account (which would otherwise be taxable under this section) if section 220(e)(2) applies to such transaction.

* * *

[CCH Explanation at ¶ 615. Committee Reports at ¶ 10,245.]

Amendment Notes

P.L. 106-554 (Community Renewal)

Act Sec. 202(a)(7) amended Code Sec. 4975(c)(4) by striking "medical savings account" and inserting "Archer MSA".

Act Sec. 202(b)(7) amended the heading for Code Sec. 4975(c)(4) by striking "MEDICAL SAVINGS ACCOUNTS" and inserting "ARCHER MSAs".

Act Sec. 202(b)(10) amended Code Sec. 4975(c)(4) by striking "a Archer" and inserting "an Archer".

The above amendments are effective on December 21, 2000.

(e) DEFINITIONS.—

(1) PLAN.—For purposes of this section, the term "plan" means—

(A) a trust described in section 401(a) which forms a part of a plan, or a plan described in section 403(a), which trust or plan is exempt from tax under section 501(a),

(B) an individual retirement account described in section 408(a),

(C) an individual retirement annuity described in section 408(b),

(D) *an Archer MSA* described in section 220(d),

(E) an education individual retirement account described in section 530, or

(F) a trust, plan, account, or annuity which, at any time, has been determined by the Secretary to be described in any preceding subparagraph of this paragraph.

* * *

[CCH Explanation at ¶ 615. Committee Reports at ¶ 10,245.]

Amendment Notes

P.L. 106-554 (Community Renewal)

Act Sec. 202(a)(7) amended Code Sec. 4975(e)(1)(D) by striking "medical savings account" and inserting "Archer MSA".

Act Sec. 202(b)(10) amended Code Sec. 4975(e)(1)(D) by striking "a Archer" and inserting "an Archer".

The above amendments are effective on December 21, 2000.

[¶ 5950] CODE SEC. 4980E. FAILURE OF EMPLOYER TO MAKE COMPARABLE MEDICAL SAVINGS ACCOUNT CONTRIBUTIONS.

(a) GENERAL RULE.—In the case of an employer who makes a contribution to the *Archer MSA* of any employee with respect to coverage under a high deductible health plan of the employer during a calendar year, there is hereby imposed a tax on the failure of such employer to meet the requirements of subsection (d) for such calendar year.

[CCH Explanation at ¶ 615. Committee Reports at ¶ 10,245.]

Amendment Notes

P.L. 106-554 (Community Renewal)

Act Sec. 202(a)(8) amended Code Sec. 4980E(a) by striking "medical savings account" and inserting "Archer MSA".

The above amendment is effective on December 21, 2000.

(b) AMOUNT OF TAX.—The amount of the tax imposed by subsection (a) on any failure for any calendar year is the amount equal to 35 percent of the aggregate amount contributed by the employer to *Archer MSAs* of employees for taxable years of such employees ending with or within such calendar year.

* * *

[CCH Explanation at ¶ 615. Committee Reports at ¶ 10,245.]

Amendment Notes

P.L. 106-554 (Community Renewal)

Act Sec. 202(b)(2)(D) amended Code Sec. 4980E(b) by striking "medical savings accounts" and inserting "Archer MSAs".

The above amendment is effective on December 21, 2000.

(d) EMPLOYER REQUIRED TO MAKE COMPARABLE MSA CONTRIBUTIONS FOR ALL PARTICIPATING EMPLOYEES.—

(1) IN GENERAL.—An employer meets the requirements of this subsection for any calendar year if the employer makes available comparable contributions to the *Archer MSAs* of all comparable participating employees for each coverage period during such calendar year.

(2) COMPARABLE CONTRIBUTIONS.—

(A) IN GENERAL.—For purposes of paragraph (1), the term "comparable contributions" means contributions—

(i) which are the same amount, or

(ii) which are the same percentage of the annual deductible limit under the high deductible health plan covering the employees.

(B) PART-YEAR EMPLOYEES.—In the case of an employee who is employed by the employer for only a portion of the calendar year, a contribution to the *Archer MSA* of such employee shall be treated as comparable if it is an amount which bears the same ratio to the comparable amount (determined without regard to this subparagraph) as such portion bears to the entire calendar year.

* * *

[CCH Explanation at ¶ 615. Committee Reports at ¶ 10,245.]

¶ 5950   Code Sec. 4980E(a)

Amendment Notes

P.L. 106-554 (Community Renewal)

Act Sec. 202(a)(8) amended Code Sec. 4980E(d)(2)(B) by striking "medical savings account" and inserting "Archer MSA".

Act Sec. 202(b)(2)(D) amended Code Sec. 4980E(d)(1) by striking "medical savings accounts" and inserting "Archer MSAs".

The above amendments are effective on December 21, 2000.

[¶ 5960] CODE SEC. 5702. DEFINITIONS.

When used in this chapter—

* * *

(f) *[Stricken.]*

[CCH Explanation at ¶ 293. Committee Reports at ¶ 10,330.]

Amendment Notes

P.L. 106-554 (Community Renewal)

Act Sec. 315(a)(2)(B) amended Code Sec. 5702, as amended by Act Sec. 315(a)(2)(A), by striking subsection (f) and by redesignating subsections (g) through (p) as subsections (f) through (o), respectively. Prior to being stricken, Code Sec. 5702(f) read as follows:

(f) CIGARETTE PAPERS.—"Cigarette papers" means taxable books or sets of cigarette papers.

The above amendment is effective as if included in section 9302 of the Balanced Budget Act of 1997 (P.L. 105-33) [effective August 5, 1997.—CCH.].

(f) CIGARETTE TUBE.—"Cigarette tube" means cigarette paper made into a hollow cylinder for use in making cigarettes.

[CCH Explanation at ¶ 293. Committee Reports at ¶ 10,330.]

Amendment Notes

P.L. 106-554 (Community Renewal)

Act Sec. 315(a)(2)(B) amended Code Sec. 5702 by redesignating subsection (g) as subsection (f).

The above amendment is effective as if included in section 9302 of the Balanced Budget Act of 1997 (P.L. 105-33) [effective August 5, 1997.—CCH.].

(g) MANUFACTURER OF CIGARETTE PAPERS AND TUBES.—"Manufacturer of cigarette papers and tubes" means any person who manufactures cigarette paper, or makes up cigarette paper into tubes, except for his own personal use or consumption.

[CCH Explanation at ¶ 293. Committee Reports at ¶ 10,330.]

Amendment Notes

P.L. 106-554 (Community Renewal)

Act Sec. 315(a)(2)(A) amended Code Sec. 5702(h), prior to redesignation by Act Sec. 315(a)(2)(B), to read as above. Prior to amendment, Code Sec. 5702(h) read as follows:

(h) MANUFACTURER OF CIGARETTE PAPERS AND TUBES.— "Manufacturer of cigarette papers and tubes" means any person who makes up cigarette paper into books or sets

containing more than 25 papers each, or into tubes, except for his own personal use or consumption.

Act Sec. 315(a)(2)(B) amended Code Sec. 5702, as amended by Act Sec. 315(a)(2)(A), by redesignating subsection (h) as subsection (g).

The above amendments are effective as if included in section 9302 of the Balanced Budget Act of 1997 (P.L. 105-33) [effective August 5, 1997.—CCH.].

(h) EXPORT WAREHOUSE.—"Export warehouse" means a bonded internal revenue warehouse for the storage of tobacco products and cigarette papers and tubes, upon which the internal revenue tax has not been paid, for subsequent shipment to a foreign country, Puerto Rico, the Virgin Islands, or a possession of the United States, or for consumption beyond the jurisdiction of the internal revenue laws of the United States.

[CCH Explanation at ¶ 293. Committee Reports at ¶ 10,330.]

Amendment Notes

P.L. 106-554 (Community Renewal)

Act Sec. 315(a)(2)(B) amended Code Sec. 5702 by redesignating subsection (i) as subsection (h).

The above amendment is effective as if included in section 9302 of the Balanced Budget Act of 1997 (P.L. 105-33) [effective August 5, 1997.—CCH.].

(i) EXPORT WAREHOUSE PROPRIETOR.—"Export warehouse proprietor" means any person who operates an export warehouse.

[CCH Explanation at ¶ 293. Committee Reports at ¶ 10,330.]

Amendment Notes

P.L. 106-554 (Community Renewal)

Act Sec. 315(a)(2)(B) amended Code Sec. 5702 by redesignating subsection (j) as subsection (i).

The above amendment is effective as if included in section 9302 of the Balanced Budget Act of 1997 (P.L. 105-33) [effective August 5, 1997.—CCH.].

(j) REMOVAL OR REMOVE.—"Removal" or "remove" means the removal of tobacco products or cigarette papers or tubes from the factory or from internal revenue bond under section 5704, as the

Secretary shall by regulation prescribe, or release from customs custody, and shall also include the smuggling or other unlawful importation of such articles into the United States.

[CCH Explanation at ¶ 293. Committee Reports at ¶ 10,330.]

Amendment Notes   The above amendment is effective as if included in
                                            section 9302 of the Balanced Budget Act of 1997 (P.L.
P.L. 106-554 (Community Renewal)   105-33) [effective August 5, 1997.—CCH.].
   Act Sec. 315(a)(2)(B) amended Code Sec. 5702 by redesig-
nating subsection (k) as subsection (j).

(k) IMPORTER.—"Importer" means any person in the United States to whom nontaxpaid tobacco products or cigarette papers or tubes manufactured in a foreign country, Puerto Rico, the Virgin Islands, or a possession of the United States are shipped or consigned; any person who removes cigars or cigarettes for sale or consumption in the United States from a customs bonded manufacturing warehouse; and any person who smuggles or otherwise unlawfully brings tobacco products or cigarette papers or tubes into the United States.

[CCH Explanation at ¶ 293. Committee Reports at ¶ 10,330.]

Amendment Notes   The above amendment is effective as if included in
                                            section 9302 of the Balanced Budget Act of 1997 (P.L.
P.L. 106-554 (Community Renewal)   105-33) [effective August 5, 1997.—CCH.].
   Act Sec. 315(a)(2)(B) amended Code Sec. 5702 by redesig-
nating subsection (l) as subsection (k).

(l) DETERMINATION OF PRICE ON CIGARS.—In determining price for purposes of section 5701(a)(2)—

   (1) there shall be included any charge incident to placing the article in condition ready for use,

   (2) there shall be excluded—

      (A) the amount of the tax imposed by this chapter or section 7652, and

      (B) if stated as a separate charge, the amount of any retail sales tax imposed by any State or political subdivision thereof or the District of Columbia, whether the liability for such tax is imposed on the vendor or vendee, and

   (3) rules similar to the rules of section 4216(b) shall apply.

[CCH Explanation at ¶ 293. Committee Reports at ¶ 10,330.]

Amendment Notes   The above amendment is effective as if included in
                                            section 9302 of the Balanced Budget Act of 1997 (P.L.
P.L. 106-554 (Community Renewal)   105-33) [effective August 5, 1997.—CCH.].
   Act Sec. 315(a)(2)(B) amended Code Sec. 5702 by redesig-
nating subsection (m) as subsection (l).

(m) DEFINITIONS RELATING TO SMOKELESS TOBACCO.—

   (1) SMOKELESS TOBACCO.—The term "smokeless tobacco" means any snuff or chewing tobacco.

   (2) SNUFF.—The term "snuff" means any finely cut, ground, or powdered tobacco that is not intended to be smoked.

   (3) CHEWING TOBACCO.—The term "chewing tobacco" means any leaf tobacco that is not intended to be smoked.

[CCH Explanation at ¶ 293. Committee Reports at ¶ 10,330.]

Amendment Notes   The above amendment is effective as if included in
                                            section 9302 of the Balanced Budget Act of 1997 (P.L.
P.L. 106-554 (Community Renewal)   105-33) [effective August 5, 1997.—CCH.].
   Act Sec. 315(a)(2)(B) amended Code Sec. 5702 by redesig-
nating subsection (n) as subsection (m).

(n) PIPE TOBACCO.—The term "pipe tobacco" means any tobacco which, because of its appearance, type, packaging, or labeling, is suitable for use and likely to be offered to, or purchased by, consumers as tobacco to be smoked in a pipe.

[CCH Explanation at ¶ 293. Committee Reports at ¶ 10,330.]

Amendment Notes   The above amendment is effective as if included in
                                            section 9302 of the Balanced Budget Act of 1997 (P.L.
P.L. 106-554 (Community Renewal)   105-33) [effective August 5, 1997.—CCH.].
   Act Sec. 315(a)(2)(B) amended Code Sec. 5702 by redesig-
nating subsection (o) as subsection (n).

(o) ROLL-YOUR-OWN TOBACCO.—The term "roll-your-own tobacco" means any tobacco which, because of its appearance, type, packaging, or labeling, is suitable for use and likely to be offered to, or purchased by, consumers as tobacco for making cigarettes.

[CCH Explanation at ¶ 293. Committee Reports at ¶ 10,330.]

Amendment Notes

P.L. 106-554 (Community Renewal)

Act Sec. 315(a)(2)(B) amended Code Sec. 5702 by redesignating subsection (p) as subsection (o).

The above amendment is effective as if included in section 9302 of the Balanced Budget Act of 1997 (P.L. 105-33) [effective August 5, 1997.—CCH.].

[¶ 5970] CODE SEC. 5761. CIVIL PENALTIES.

* * *

(c) SALE OF TOBACCO PRODUCTS AND CIGARETTE PAPERS AND TUBES FOR EXPORT.—Except as provided in subsections (b) and (d) of section 5704—

(1) every person who sells, relands, or receives within the jurisdiction of the United States any tobacco products or cigarette papers or tubes which have been labeled or shipped for exportation under this chapter,

(2) every person who sells or receives such relanded tobacco products or cigarette papers or tubes, and

(3) every person who aids or abets in such selling, relanding, or receiving,

shall, in addition to the tax and any other penalty provided in this title, be liable for a penalty equal to the greater of $1,000 or 5 times the amount of the tax imposed by this chapter. All tobacco products and cigarette papers and tubes relanded within the jurisdiction of the United States, and all vessels, vehicles, and aircraft used in such relanding or in removing such products, papers, and tubes from the place where relanded, shall be forfeited to the United States. *This subsection and section 5754 shall not apply to any person who relands or receives tobacco products in the quantity allowed entry free of tax and duty under chapter 98 of the Harmonized Tariff Schedule of the United States, and such person may voluntarily relinquish to the Secretary at the time of entry any excess of such quantity without incurring the penalty under this subsection. No quantity of tobacco products other than the quantity referred to in the preceding sentence may be relanded or received as a personal use quantity.*

* * *

[CCH Explanation at ¶ 293. Committee Reports at ¶ 10,330.]

Amendment Notes

P.L. 106-554 (Community Renewal)

Act Sec. 315(a)(3) amended Code Sec. 5761(c) by adding at the end the last two sentences to read as above.

The above amendment is effective as if included in section 9302 of the Balanced Budget Act of 1997 (P.L. 105-33) [effective August 5, 1997.—CCH.].

[¶ 5980] CODE SEC. 6015. RELIEF FROM JOINT AND SEVERAL LIABILITY ON JOINT RETURN.

* * *

(c) PROCEDURES TO LIMIT LIABILITY FOR TAXPAYERS NO LONGER MARRIED OR TAXPAYERS LEGALLY SEPARATED OR NOT LIVING TOGETHER.—

* * *

(3) ELECTION.—

* * *

(B) TIME FOR ELECTION.—An election under this subsection for any taxable year *may be made at any time after a deficiency for such year is asserted but* not later than 2 years after the date on which the Secretary has begun collection activities with respect to the individual making the election.

* * *

[CCH Explanation at ¶ 335. Committee Reports at ¶ 10,320.]

Amendment Notes

P.L. 106-554 (Community Renewal)

Act Sec. 313(a)(1) amended Code Sec. 6015(c)(3)(B) by striking "shall be made" and inserting "may be made at any time after a deficiency for such year is asserted but".

The above amendment is effective on December 21, 2000.

(e) PETITION FOR REVIEW BY TAX COURT.—

(1) IN GENERAL.—In the case of an individual *against whom a deficiency has been asserted and* who elects to have subsection (b) or (c) apply—

(A) IN GENERAL.—*In addition to any other remedy provided by law, the individual may petition the Tax Court (and the Tax Court shall have jurisdiction) to determine the appropriate relief available to the individual under this section if such petition is filed—*

(i) at any time after the earlier of—

(I) the date the Secretary mails, by certified or registered mail to the taxpayer's last known address, notice of the Secretary's final determination of relief available to the individual, or

(II) the date which is 6 months after the date such election is filed with the Secretary, and

(ii) not later than the close of the 90th day after the date described in clause (i)(I).

(B) RESTRICTIONS APPLICABLE TO COLLECTION OF ASSESSMENT.—

(i) IN GENERAL.—Except as otherwise provided in section 6851 or 6861, no levy or proceeding in court shall be made, begun, or prosecuted against the individual making an election under subsection (b) or (c) for collection of any assessment to which such election relates *until the close of the 90th day referred to in subparagraph (A)(ii)*, or, if a petition has been filed with the Tax Court *under subparagraph (A)*, until the decision of the Tax Court has become final. Rules similar to the rules of section 7485 shall apply with respect to the collection of such assessment.

(ii) AUTHORITY TO ENJOIN COLLECTION ACTIONS.—Notwithstanding the provisions of section 7421(a), the beginning of such levy or proceeding during the time the prohibition under clause (i) is in force may be enjoined by a proceeding in the proper court, including the Tax Court. The Tax Court shall have no jurisdiction under this subparagraph to enjoin any action or proceeding unless a timely petition has been filed under subparagraph (A) and then only in respect of the amount of the assessment to which the election under subsection (b) or (c) relates.

(2) SUSPENSION OF RUNNING OF PERIOD OF LIMITATIONS.—The running of the period of limitations in section 6502 on the collection of the assessment to which the petition under paragraph (1)(A) relates shall be suspended—

(A) for the period during which the Secretary is prohibited by paragraph (1)(B) from collecting by levy or a proceeding in court and for 60 days thereafter, and

(B) if a waiver under paragraph (5) is made, from the date the claim for relief was filed until 60 days after the waiver is filed with the Secretary.

(3) LIMITATION ON TAX COURT JURISDICTION.—If a suit for refund is begun by either individual filing the joint return pursuant to section 6532—

(A) the Tax Court shall lose jurisdiction of the individual's action under this section to whatever extent jurisdiction is acquired by the district court or the United States Court of Federal Claims over the taxable years that are the subject of the suit for refund, and

(B) the court acquiring jurisdiction shall have jurisdiction over the petition filed under this subsection.

(4) NOTICE TO OTHER SPOUSE.—The Tax Court shall establish rules which provide the individual filing a joint return but not making the election under subsection (b) or (c) with adequate notice and an opportunity to become a party to a proceeding under either such subsection.

(5) WAIVER.—An individual who elects the application of subsection (b) or (c) (and who agrees with the Secretary's determination of relief) may waive in writing at any time the restrictions in paragraph (1)(B) with respect to collection of the outstanding assessment (whether or not a notice of the Secretary's final determination of relief has been mailed).

* * *

[CCH Explanation at ¶ 335. Committee Reports at ¶ 10,320.]

Amendment Notes

P.L. 106-554 (Community Renewal)

Act Sec. 313(a)(2)(B) amended Code Sec. 6015(e)(3) to read as above. Prior to amendment, Code Sec. 6015(e)(3) read as follows:

(3) APPLICABLE RULES.—

(A) ALLOWANCE OF CREDIT OR REFUND.—Except as provided in subparagraph (B), notwithstanding any other law or rule of law (other than section 6512(b), 7121, or 7122), credit or refund shall be allowed or made to the extent attributable to the application of subsection (b) or (f).

(B) RES JUDICATA.—In the case of any election under subsection (b) or (c), if a decision of the Tax Court in any

prior proceeding for the same taxable year has become final, such decision shall be conclusive except with respect to the qualification of the individual for relief which was not an issue in such proceeding. The exception contained in the preceding sentence shall not apply if the Tax Court determines that the individual participated meaningfully in such prior proceeding.

(C) LIMITATION ON TAX COURT JURISDICTION.—If a suit for refund is begun by either individual filing the joint return pursuant to section 6532—

(i) the Tax Court shall lose jurisdiction of the individual's action under this section to whatever extent jurisdiction is acquired by the district court or the United States Court of

Federal Claims over the taxable years that are the subject of the suit for refund; and

(ii) the court acquiring jurisdiction shall have jurisdiction over the petition filed under this subsection.

Act Sec. 313(a)(3)(A) amended Code Sec. 6015(e)(1) in the matter preceding subparagraph (A) by inserting "against whom a deficiency has been asserted and" after "individual".

Act Sec. 313(a)(3)(B) amended Code Sec. 6015(e)(1)(A) to read as above. Prior to amendment, Code Sec. 6015(e)(1)(A) read as follows:

(A) IN GENERAL.—The individual may petition the Tax Court (and the Tax Court shall have jurisdiction) to determine the appropriate relief available to the individual under this section if such petition is filed during the 90-day period beginning on the date on which the Secretary mails by certified or registered mail a notice to such individual of the Secretary's determination of relief available to the individual. Notwithstanding the preceding sentence, an individual may file such petition at any time after the date which is 6 months after the date such election is filed with the Secretary and before the close of such 90-day period.

Act Sec. 313(a)(3)(C)(i)-(ii) amended Code Sec. 6015(e)(1)(B)(i) by striking "until the expiration of the 90-day period described in subparagraph (A)" and inserting "until the close of the 90th day referred to in subparagraph (A)(ii)", and by inserting "under subparagraph (A)" after "filed with the Tax Court".

Act Sec. 313(a)(3)(D)(i) amended Code Sec. 6015(e) by adding at the end a new paragraph (5) to read as above.

Act Sec. 313(a)(3)(D)(ii) amended Code Sec. 6015(e)(2) to read as above. Prior to amendment, Code Sec. 6015(e)(2) read as follows:

(2) SUSPENSION OF RUNNING OF PERIOD OF LIMITATIONS.—The running of the period of limitations in section 6502 on the collection of the assessment to which the petition under paragraph (1)(A) relates shall be suspended for the period during which the Secretary is prohibited by paragraph (1)(B) from collecting by levy or a proceeding in court and for 60 days thereafter.

The above amendments are effective on December 21, 2000.

(g) CREDITS AND REFUNDS.—

(1) IN GENERAL.—Except as provided in paragraphs (2) and (3), notwithstanding any other law or rule of law (other than section 6511, 6512(b), 7121, or 7122), credit or refund shall be allowed or made to the extent attributable to the application of this section.

(2) RES JUDICATA.—In the case of any election under subsection (b) or (c), if a decision of a court in any prior proceeding for the same taxable year has become final, such decision shall be conclusive except with respect to the qualification of the individual for relief which was not an issue in such proceeding. The exception contained in the preceding sentence shall not apply if the court determines that the individual participated meaningfully in such prior proceeding.

(3) CREDIT AND REFUND NOT ALLOWED UNDER SUBSECTION (c).—No credit or refund shall be allowed as a result of an election under subsection (c).

[CCH Explanation at ¶ 335. Committee Reports at ¶ 10,320.]

Amendment Notes
P.L. 106-554 (Community Renewal)
Act Sec. 313(a)(2)(A) amended Code Sec. 6015 by redesignating subsection (g) as subsection (h) and by inserting after subsection (f) a new subsection (g) to read as above.

The above amendment is effective on December 21, 2000.

(h) REGULATIONS.—The Secretary shall prescribe such regulations as are necessary to carry out the provisions of this section, including—

(1) regulations providing methods for allocation of items other than the methods under subsection (d)(3); and

(2) regulations providing the opportunity for an individual to have notice of, and an opportunity to participate in, any administrative proceeding with respect to an election made under subsection (b) or (c) by the other individual filing the joint return.

[CCH Explanation at ¶ 330. Committee Reports at ¶ 10,315.]

Amendment Notes
P.L. 106-554 (Community Renewal)
Act Sec. 312(a)(2)(A) amended Code Sec. 6015 by redesignating subsection (g) as subsection (h).

The above amendment is effective on December 21, 2000.

[¶ 5990] CODE SEC. 6051. RECEIPTS FOR EMPLOYEES.

(a) REQUIREMENT.—Every person required to deduct and withhold from an employee a tax under section 3101 or 3402, or who would have been required to deduct and withhold a tax under section 3402 (determined without regard to subsection (n)) if the employee had claimed no more than one withholding exemption, or every employer engaged in a trade or business who pays remuneration for services performed by an employee, including the cash value of such remuneration paid in any medium other than cash, shall furnish to each such employee in respect of the remuneration paid by such person to such employee during the calendar year, on or before January 31 of the succeeding year, or, if his employment is terminated before the close of such calendar year, within 30 days after the date of receipt of a written request from the employee if such 30-day period ends before January 31, a written statement showing the following:

(1) the name of such person,

(2) the name of the employee (and his social security account number if wages as defined in section 3121(a) have been paid),

(3) the total amount of wages as defined in section 3401(a),

(4) the total amount deducted and withheld as tax under section 3402,

(5) the total amount of wages as defined in section 3121(a),

(6) the total amount deducted and withheld as tax under section 3101,

(7) the total amount paid to the employee under section 3507 (relating to advance payment of earned income credit),

(8) the total amount of elective deferrals (within the meaning of section 402(g)(3)) and compensation deferred under section 457,

(9) the total amount incurred for dependent care assistance with respect to such employee under a dependent care assistance program described in section 129(d),

(10) in the case of an employee who is a member of the Armed Forces of the United States, such employee's earned income as determined for purposes of section 32 (relating to earned income credit), and

(11) the amount contributed to any *Archer MSA* (as defined in section 220(d)) of such employee or such employee's spouse.

* * *

[CCH Explanation at ¶ 615. Committee Reports at ¶ 10,245.]

Amendment Notes

P.L. 106-554 (Community Renewal)
Act Sec. 202(a)(9) amended Code Sec. 6051(a)(11) by striking "medical savings account" and inserting "Archer MSA".

The above amendment is effective on December 21, 2000.

[¶ 6000] CODE SEC. 6103. CONFIDENTIALITY AND DISCLOSURE OF RETURNS AND RETURN INFORMATION.

* * *

(b) DEFINITIONS.—For purposes of this section—

* * *

(2) RETURN INFORMATION.—The term "return information" means—

(A) a taxpayer's identity, the nature, source, or amount of his income, payments, receipts, deductions, exemptions, credits, assets, liabilities, net worth, tax liability, tax withheld, deficiencies, overassessments, or tax payments, whether the taxpayer's return was, is being, or will be examined or subject to other investigation or processing, or any other data, received by, recorded by, prepared by, furnished to, or collected by the Secretary with respect to a return or with respect to the determination of the existence, or possible existence, of liability (or the amount thereof) of any person under this title for any tax, penalty, interest, fine, forfeiture, or other imposition, or offense,

(B) any part of any written determination or any background file document relating to such written determination (as such terms are defined in section 6110(b)) which is not open to public inspection under section 6110,

(C) any advance pricing agreement entered into by a taxpayer and the Secretary and any background information related to such agreement or any application for an advance pricing agreement, *and*

(D) *any agreement under section 7121, and any similar agreement, and any background information related to such an agreement or request for such an agreement,*

but such term does not include data in a form which cannot be associated with, or otherwise identify, directly or indirectly, a particular taxpayer. Nothing in the preceding sentence, or in any other provision of law, shall be construed to require the disclosure of standards used or to be used for the selection of returns for examination, or data used or to be used for determining such standards, if the

Secretary determines that such disclosure will seriously impair assessment, collection, or enforcement under the internal revenue laws.

* * *

[CCH Explanation at ¶ 305. Committee Reports at ¶ 10,270.]

Amendment Notes

P.L. 106-554 (Community Renewal)

Act Sec. 304(a) amended Code Sec. 6103(b)(2) by striking "and" at the end of subparagraph (B), by inserting "and" at the end of subparagraph (C), and by inserting after subparagraph (C) a new subparagraph (D) to read as above.

The above amendment is effective on December 21, 2000.

(e) DISCLOSURE TO PERSONS HAVING MATERIAL INTEREST.—

(1) IN GENERAL.—The return of a person shall, upon written request, be open to inspection by or disclosure to—

(A) in the case of the return of an individual—

(i) that individual,

(ii) the spouse of that individual if the individual and such spouse have signified their consent to consider a gift reported on such return as made one-half by him and one-half by the spouse pursuant to the provisions of section 2513, or

(iii) the child of that individual (or such child's legal representative) to the extent necessary to comply with the provisions of section (1)(g);

(B) in the case of an income tax return filed jointly, either of the individuals with respect to whom the return is filed;

(C) in the case of the return of a partnership, any person who was a member of such partnership during any part of the period covered by the return;

(D) in the case of the return of a corporation or a subsidiary thereof—

(i) any person designated by resolution of its board of directors or other similar governing body,

(ii) any officer or employee of such corporation upon written request signed by any principal officer and attested to by the secretary or other officer,

(iii) any bona fide shareholder of record owning 1 percent or more of the outstanding stock of such corporation,

(iv) if the corporation was a foreign personal holding company, as defined by section 552, any person who was a shareholder during any part of a period covered by such return if with respect to that period, or any part thereof, such shareholder was required under section 551 to include in his gross income undistributed foreign personal holding company income of such company,

(v) if the corporation was an S corporation, any person who was a shareholder during any part of the period covered by such return during which an election under section 1362(a) was in effect, or

(vi) if the corporation has been dissolved, any person authorized by applicable State law to act for the corporation or any person who the Secretary finds to have a material interest which will be affected by information contained therein;

(E) in the case of the return of an estate—

(i) the administrator, executor, or trustee of such estate, and

(ii) any heir at law, next of kin, or beneficiary under the will, of the decedent, but only if the Secretary finds that such heir at law, next of kin, or beneficiary has a material interest which will be affected by information contained therein; and

(F) in the case of the return of a trust—

(i) the trustee or trustees, jointly or separately, and

(ii) any beneficiary of such trust, but only if the Secretary finds that such beneficiary has a material interest which will be affected by information contained therein.

* * *

[CCH Explanation at ¶ 30,050.]

Code Sec. 6103(e)   ¶ 6000

Amendment Notes

P.L. 106-554 (Community Renewal)

Act Sec. 319(8)(B) amended Code Sec. 6103(e)(1)(D)(v) to read as above. Prior to amendment, Code Sec. 6103(e)(1)(D)(v) read as follows:

(v) if the corporation was an electing small business corporation under subchapter S of chapter 1, any person who

was a shareholder during any part of the period covered by such return during which an election was in effect, or

The above amendment is effective on December 21, 2000.

(j) STATISTICAL USE.—

* * *

(6) *CONGRESSIONAL BUDGET OFFICE.*—*Upon written request by the Director of the Congressional Budget Office, the Secretary shall furnish to officers and employees of the Congressional Budget Office return information for the purpose of, but only to the extent necessary for, long-term models of the social security and medicare programs.*

[CCH Explanation at ¶ 307. Committee Reports at ¶ 10,300.]

Amendment Notes

P.L. 106-554 (Community Renewal)

Act Sec. 310(a)(1) amended Code Sec. 6103(j) by adding at the end a new paragraph (6) to read as above.

The above amendment is effective on December 21, 2000.

(k) DISCLOSURE OF CERTAIN RETURNS AND RETURN INFORMATION FOR TAX ADMINISTRATION PURPOSES.—

* * *

(6) DISCLOSURE BY *CERTAIN* OFFICERS AND EMPLOYEES FOR INVESTIGATIVE PURPOSES.—An internal revenue officer or employee *and an officer or employee of the Office of Treasury Inspector General for Tax Administration* may, in connection with his official duties relating to any audit, collection activity, or civil or criminal tax investigation or any other offense under the internal revenue laws, disclose return information to the extent that such disclosure is necessary in obtaining information, which is not otherwise reasonably available, with respect to the correct determination of tax, liability for tax, or the amount to be collected or with respect to the enforcement of any other provision of this title. Such disclosures shall be made only in such situations and under such conditions as the Secretary may prescribe by regulation.

* * *

[CCH Explanation at ¶ 310. Committee Reports at ¶ 10,320.]

Amendment Notes

P.L. 106-554 (Community Renewal)

Act Sec. 313(c)(1)-(2) amended Code Sec. 6103(k)(6) by inserting "and an officer or employee of the Office of Treasury Inspector General for Tax Administration" after "internal revenue officer or employee", and by striking "INTERNAL REVENUE" in the heading and inserting "CERTAIN".

The above amendment is effective as if included in the provision of the Internal Revenue Service Restructuring and Reform Act of 1998 (P.L. 105-206) to which it relates [effective July 22, 1998.—CCH.].

(p) PROCEDURE AND RECORDKEEPING.—

* * *

(4) SAFEGUARDS.—Any Federal agency described in subsection (h)(2), (h)(5), (i)(1), (2), (3), or (5), (j)(1), (2), or (5), (k)(8), (l)(1), (2), (3), (5), (10), (11), (13), (14), or (17), or (o)(1), the General Accounting Office, *the Congressional Budget Office,* or any agency, body, or commission described in subsection (d), (i)(3)(B)(i), or (l)(6), *(7), (8), (9), (12), (15), or (16) or any other person described in subsection (l)(16) shall, as a condition* for receiving returns or return information—

(A) establish and maintain, to the satisfaction of the Secretary, a permanent system of standardized records with respect to any request, the reason for such request, and the date of such request made by or of it and any disclosure of return or return information made by or to it;

(B) establish and maintain, to the satisfaction of the Secretary, a secure area or place in which such returns or return information shall be stored;

(C) restrict, to the satisfaction of the Secretary, access to the returns or return information only to persons whose duties or responsibilities require access and to whom disclosure may be made under the provisions of this title;

(D) provide such other safeguards which the Secretary determines (and which he prescribes in regulations) to be necessary or appropriate to protect the confidentiality of the returns or return information;

(E) furnish a report to the Secretary, at such time and containing such information as the Secretary may prescribe, which describes the procedures established and utilized by such agency, body, or *commission, the General Accounting Office, or the Congressional Budget Office* for ensuring the confidentiality of returns and return information required by this paragraph; and

(F) upon completion of use of such returns or return information—

(i) in the case of an agency, body, or commission described in subsection (d), (i)(3)(B)(i), or (l)(6), (7), (8), (9), or (16), or any other person described in subsection (l)(16) return to the Secretary such returns or return information (along with any copies made therefrom) or make such returns or return information undisclosable in any manner and furnish a written report to the Secretary describing such manner,

(ii) in the case of an agency described in subsections (h)(2), (h)(5), (i)(1), (2), (3), or (5), (j)(1), (2), or (5), (k)(8), (l)(1), (2), (3), (5), (10), (11), (12), (13), (14), (15), or (17) or (o)(1), *the General Accounting Office, or the Congressional Budget Office,* either—

(I) return to the Secretary such returns or return information (along with any copies made therefrom),

(II) otherwise make such returns or return information undisclosable, or

(III) to the extent not so returned or made undisclosable, ensure that the conditions of subparagraphs (A), (B), (C), (D), and (E) of this paragraph continue to be met with respect to such returns or return information, and

(iii) in the case of the Department of Health and Human Services for purposes of subsection (m)(6), destroy all such return information upon completion of its use in providing the notification for which the information was obtained, so as to make such information undisclosable;

except that the conditions of subparagraphs (A), (B), (C), (D), and (E) shall cease to apply with respect to any return or return information if, and to the extent that, such return or return information is disclosed in the course of any judicial or administrative proceeding and made a part of the public record thereof. If the Secretary determines that any such agency, body, or commission, including an agency or any other person described in subsection (l)(16), or the General Accounting Office *or the Congressional Budget Office* has failed to, or does not, meet the requirements of this paragraph, he may, after any proceedings for review established under paragraph (7), take such actions as are necessary to ensure such requirements are met, including refusing to disclose returns or return information to such agency, body, or commission, including an agency or any other person described in subsection (l)(16), or the General Accounting Office *or the Congressional Budget Office* until he determines that such requirements have been or will be met. In the case of any agency which receives any mailing address under paragraph (2), (4), (6), or (7) of subsection (m) and which discloses any such mailing address to any agent or which receives any information under paragraph (6)(A), (12)(B), or (16) of subsection (l) and which discloses any such information to any agent, or any person including an agent described in subsection (l)(16), this paragraph shall apply to such agency and each such agent or other person (except that, in the case of an agent, or any person including an agent described in subsection (l)(16), any report to the Secretary or other action with respect to the Secretary shall be made or taken through such agency). For purposes of applying this paragraph in any case to which subsection (m)(6) applies, the term "return information" includes related blood donor records (as defined in section 1141(h)(2) of the Social Security Act).

(5) REPORT ON PROCEDURES AND SAFEGUARDS.—After the close of each calendar year, the Secretary shall furnish to each committee described in subsection (f)(1) a report which describes the procedures and safeguards established and utilized by such agencies, bodies, or *commissions, the General Accounting Office, and the Congressional Budget Office* for ensuring the confidentiality of returns and return information as required by this subsection. Such report shall also describe instances of deficiencies in, and failure to establish or utilize, such procedures.

(6) AUDIT OF PROCEDURES AND SAFEGUARDS.—

(A) AUDIT BY COMPTROLLER GENERAL.—The Comptroller General may audit the procedures and safeguards established by such agencies, bodies, or commissions *and the Congressional Budget Office* pursuant to this subsection to determine whether such safeguards and procedures meet the requirements of this subsection and ensure the confidentiality of returns and return information. The Comptroller General shall notify the Secretary before any such audit is conducted.

* * *

[CCH Explanation at ¶ 307 and ¶ 30,050. Committee Reports at ¶ 10,300.]

Amendment Notes
P.L. 106-554 (Community Renewal)

Act Sec. 310(a)(2)(A)(i)-(iv) amended Code Sec. 6103(p)(4) by inserting "the Congressional Budget Office," after "General Accounting Office," in the matter preceding subparagraph (A), by striking "commission or the General Accounting Office" and inserting "commission, the General Accounting Office, or the Congressional Budget Office" in subparagraph (E), by striking "or the General Accounting Office," and inserting "the General Accounting Office, or the Congressional Budget Office," in subparagraph (F)(ii), and by inserting "or the Congressional Budget Office" after "General Accounting Office" both places it appears in the matter following subparagraph (F).

Act Sec. 310(a)(2)(B) amended Code Sec. 6103(p)(5) by striking "commissions and the General Accounting Office" and inserting "commissions, the General Accounting Office, and the Congressional Budget Office".

Act Sec. 310(a)(2)(C) amended Code Sec. 6103(p)(6)(A) by inserting "and the Congressional Budget Office" after "commissions".

Act Sec. 319(17)(A) amended Code Sec. 6103(p) by striking the second comma after "(13)", and by striking "(7)" and all that follows through "shall, as a condition" and inserting "(7), (8), (9), (12), (15), or (16) or any other person described in subsection (l)(16) shall, as a condition" in the matter preceding subparagraph (4)(A). Prior to amendment, the matter preceding subparagraph (A) of Code Sec. 6103(p)(4) read as follows:

(4) SAFEGUARDS.—Any Federal agency described in subsection (h)(2), (h)(5), (i)(1), (2), (3), or (5), (j)(1), (2), or (5), (k)(8), (l)(1), (2), (3), (5), (10), (11), (13), (14), or (17), or (o)(1), the General Accounting Office, or any agency, body, or commission described in subsection (d), (i)(3)(B)(i), or (l)(6), (7), (8), (9), (12), or[sic] (15), or (16), or any other person described in subsection (l)(16) shall, as a condition for receiving returns or return information—

Act Sec. 319(17)(B) amended Code Sec. 6103(p)(4)(F)(ii) by striking the second comma after "(14)".

The above amendments are effective on December 21, 2000.

[¶ 6010] CODE SEC. 6104. PUBLICITY OF INFORMATION REQUIRED FROM CERTAIN EXEMPT ORGANIZATIONS AND CERTAIN TRUSTS.

* * *

(d) PUBLIC INSPECTION OF CERTAIN ANNUAL RETURNS, REPORTS, APPLICATIONS FOR EXEMPTION, AND NOTICES OF STATUS.—

(1) IN GENERAL.—In the case of an organization described in subsection (c) or (d) of section 501 and exempt from taxation under section 501(a) or an organization exempt from taxation under section 527(a)—

(A) a copy of—

(i) the annual return filed under section 6033 (relating to returns by exempt organizations) or section 6012(a)(6) (relating to returns by political organizations) by such organization,

(ii) if the organization filed an application for recognition of exemption under section 501 or notice of status under section 527(i), the exempt status application materials or any notice materials of such organization, and

(iii) the reports filed under section 527(j) (relating to required disclosure of expenditures and contributions) by such organization,

shall be made available by such organization for inspection during regular business hours by any individual at the principal office of such organization and, if such organization regularly maintains 1 or more regional or district offices having 3 or more employees, at each such regional or district office, and

(B) upon request of an individual made at such principal office or such a regional or district office, a copy of such annual return, reports, and exempt status application materials or such notice materials shall be provided to such individual without charge other than a reasonable fee for any reproduction and mailing costs.

The request described in subparagraph (B) must be made in person or in writing. If such request is made in person, such copy shall be provided immediately and, if made in writing, shall be provided within 30 days.

(2) 3-YEAR LIMITATION ON INSPECTION OF RETURNS.—Paragraph (1) shall apply to an annual return filed under section 6033 or section 6012(a)(6) only during the 3-year period beginning on the last day prescribed for filing such return (determined with regard to any extension of time for filing).

(3) EXCEPTIONS FROM DISCLOSURE REQUIREMENT.—

(A) NONDISCLOSURE OF CONTRIBUTORS, ETC.—In the case of an organization which is not a private foundation (within the meaning of section 509(a)) or a political organization exempt from taxation under section 527, paragraph (1) shall not require the disclosure of the name or address of any contributor to the organization. In the case of an organization described in section 501(d), paragraph (1) shall not require the disclosure of the copies referred to in section 6031(b) with respect to such organization.

¶ 6010   Code Sec. 6104(d)

(B) NONDISCLOSURE OF CERTAIN OTHER INFORMATION.—Paragraph (1) shall not require the disclosure of any information if the Secretary withheld such information from public inspection under subsection (a)(1)(D).

(4) LIMITATION ON PROVIDING COPIES.—Paragraph (1)(B) shall not apply to any request if, in accordance with regulations promulgated by the Secretary, the organization has made the requested documents widely available, or the Secretary determines, upon application by an organization, that such request is part of a harassment campaign and that compliance with such request is not in the public interest.

(5) EXEMPT STATUS APPLICATION MATERIALS.—For purposes of paragraph (1), the term "exempt status application materials" means the application for recognition of exemption under section 501 and any papers submitted in support of such application and any letter or other document issued by the Internal Revenue Service with respect to such application.

(6) NOTICE MATERIALS.—For purposes of paragraph (1), the term "notice materials" means the notice of status filed under section 527(i) and any papers submitted in support of such notice and any letter or other document issued by the Internal Revenue Service with respect to such notice.

(6)[(7)] DISCLOSURE OF REPORTS BY INTERNAL REVENUE SERVICE.—Any report filed by an organization under section 527(j) (relating to required disclosure of expenditures and contributions) shall be made available to the public at such times and in such places as the Secretary may prescribe.

(6)[(8)] APPLICATION TO NONEXEMPT CHARITABLE TRUSTS AND NONEXEMPT PRIVATE FOUNDATIONS.—The organizations referred to in paragraphs (1) and (2) of section 6033(d) shall comply with the requirements of this subsection relating to annual returns filed under section 6033 in the same manner as the organizations referred to in paragraph (1).

[CCH Explanation at ¶ 330. Committee Reports at ¶ 10,315.]

Amendment Notes

P.L. 106-554 (Community Renewal)

Act Sec. 312(a) amended Code Sec. 6104(d) by adding at the end a new paragraph (6)[(8)] to read as above.

The above amendment is effective as if included in the provision of the Tax and Trade Relief Extension Act of

1998 (P.L. 105-277) to which it relates [effective for requests made after the later of December 31, 1998, or the 60th day after the Treasury first issues the regulations referred to in Code Sec. 6104(d)(4).—CCH.].

[¶ 6020] *CODE SEC. 6105. CONFIDENTIALITY OF INFORMATION ARISING UNDER TREATY OBLIGATIONS.*

(a) IN GENERAL.—Tax convention information shall not be disclosed.

(b) EXCEPTIONS.—Subsection (a) shall not apply—

(1) to the disclosure of tax convention information to persons or authorities (including courts and administrative bodies) which are entitled to such disclosure pursuant to a tax convention,

(2) to any generally applicable procedural rules regarding applications for relief under a tax convention, or

(3) in any case not described in paragraphs (1) or (2), to the disclosure of any tax convention information not relating to a particular taxpayer if the Secretary determines, after consultation with each other party to the tax convention, that such disclosure would not impair tax administration.

(c) DEFINITIONS.—For purposes of this section—

(1) TAX CONVENTION INFORMATION.—The term "tax convention information" means any—

(A) agreement entered into with the competent authority of one or more foreign governments pursuant to a tax convention,

(B) application for relief under a tax convention,

(C) any background information related to such agreement or application,

(D) document implementing such agreement, and

(E) any other information exchanged pursuant to a tax convention which is treated as confidential or secret under the tax convention.

(2) TAX CONVENTION.—The term "tax convention" means—

(A) any income tax or gift and estate tax convention, or

(B) any other convention or bilateral agreement (including multilateral conventions and agreements and any agreement with a possession of the United States) providing for the avoidance of double taxation, the prevention of fiscal evasion, nondiscrimination with respect to

Code Sec. 6105(c)   ¶6020

taxes, the exchange of tax relevant information with the United States, or mutual assistance in tax matters.

(d) Cross References.—

For penalties for the unauthorized disclosure of tax convention information which is return or return information, see sections 7213, 7213A, and 7431.

[CCH Explanation at ¶ 305. Committee Reports at ¶ 10,271.]

Amendment Notes

P.L. 106-554 (Community Renewal)

Act Sec. 304(b)(1) amended subchapter B of chapter 61 by inserting after Code Sec. 6104 a new Code Sec. 6105 to read as above.

The above amendment is effective on December 21, 2000.

[¶ 6030] CODE SEC. 6110. PUBLIC INSPECTION OF WRITTEN DETERMINATIONS.

* * *

(b) DEFINITIONS.—For purposes of this section—

(1) WRITTEN DETERMINATION.—

(A) IN GENERAL.—The term "written determination" means a ruling, determination letter, technical advice memorandum, or Chief Counsel advice.

(B) EXCEPTIONS.—Such term shall not include any matter referred to in subparagraph (C) or (D) of section 6103(b)(2).

* * *

[CCH Explanation at ¶ 305. Committee Reports at ¶ 10,272.]

Amendment Notes

P.L. 106-554 (Community Renewal)

Act Sec. 304(c)(1) amended Code Sec. 6110(b)(1) to read as above. Prior to amendment, Code Sec. 6110(b)(1) read as follows:

(1) WRITTEN DETERMINATION.—The term "written determination" means a ruling, determination letter, technical

advice memorandum, or Chief Counsel advice. Such term shall not include any advance pricing agreement entered into by a taxpayer and the Secretary and any background information related to such agreement or any application for an advance pricing agreement.

The above amendment is effective on December 21, 2000.

(g) TIME FOR DISCLOSURE.—

* * *

(5) SPECIAL RULES FOR CERTAIN WRITTEN DETERMINATIONS, ETC.—Notwithstanding the provisions of paragraph (1), the Secretary shall not be required to make available to the public—

(A) any technical advice memorandum, *any Chief Counsel advice,* and any related background file document involving any matter which is the subject of a civil fraud or criminal investigation or jeopardy or termination assessment until after any action relating to such investigation or assessment is completed, or

(B) any general written determination and any related background file document that relates solely to approval of the Secretary of any adoption or change of—

(i) the funding method or plan year of a plan under section 412,

(ii) a taxpayer's annual accounting period under section 442,

(iii) a taxpayer's method of accounting under section 446(e), or

(iv) a partnership's or partner's taxable year under section 706,

but the Secretary shall make any such written determination and related background file document available upon the written request of any person after the date on which (except for this subparagraph) such determination would be open to public inspection.

* * *

[CCH Explanation at ¶ 315. Committee Reports at ¶ 10,320.]

Amendment Notes

P.L. 106-554 (Community Renewal)

Act Sec. 313(e) amended Code Sec. 6110(g)(5)(A) by inserting ", any Chief Counsel advice," after "technical advice memorandum".

The above amendment is effective as if included in the provision of the Internal Revenue Service Restructuring and Reform Act of 1998 (P.L. 105-206) to which it relates [effective for Chief Counsel advice issued after October 20, 1998, generally.—CCH].

(l) SECTION NOT TO APPLY.—This section shall not apply to—

(1) any matter to which section 6104 *or 6105* applies, or

(2) any—

(A) written determination issued pursuant to a request made before November 1, 1976, with respect to the exempt status under section 501(a) of an organization described in section 501(c) or (d), the status of an organization as a private foundation under section 509(a), or the status of an organization as an operating foundation under section 4942(j)(3),

(B) written determination described in subsection (g)(5)(B) issued pursuant to a request made before November 1, 1976,

(C) determination letter not otherwise described in subparagraph (A), (B), or (E) issued pursuant to a request made before November 1, 1976,

(D) background file document relating to any general written determination issued before July 5, 1967, or

(E) letter or other document described in section 6104(a)(1)(B)(iv) issued before September 2, 1974.

* * *

[CCH Explanation at ¶ 305. Committee Reports at ¶ 10,272.]

Amendment Notes

P.L. 106-554 (Community Renewal)
Act Sec. 304(c)(2) amended Code Sec. 6110(l)(1) by inserting "or 6105" after "6104".

The above amendment is effective on December 21, 2000.

[¶ 6040] CODE SEC. 6166. EXTENSION OF TIME FOR PAYMENT OF ESTATE TAX WHERE ESTATE CONSISTS LARGELY OF INTEREST IN CLOSELY HELD BUSINESS.

* * *

(k) CROSS REFERENCES.—

* * *

(5) Transfers within 3 years of death.—For special rule for qualifying an estate under this section where property has been transferred within 3 years of decedent's death, see section *2035(c)(2)*.

[CCH Explanation at ¶ 30,050.]

Amendment Notes

P.L. 106-554 (Community Renewal)
Act Sec. 319(18) amended Code Sec. 6166(k)(5) by striking "2035(d)(4)" and inserting "2035(c)(2)".

The above amendment is effective on December 21, 2000.

[¶ 6050] CODE SEC. 6211. DEFINITION OF A DEFICIENCY.

* * *

(b) RULES FOR APPLICATION OF SUBSECTION (a).—For purposes of this section—

* * *

(4) For purposes of subsection (a)—

(A) any excess of the sum of the credits allowable under *sections 24(d), 32, and 34* over the tax imposed by subtitle A (determined without regard to such credits), and

(B) any excess of the sum of such credits as shown by the taxpayer on his return over the amount shown as the tax by the taxpayer on such return (determined without regard to such credits),

shall be taken into account as negative amounts of tax.

* * *

[CCH Explanation at ¶ 360. Committee Reports at ¶ 10,325.]

Amendment Notes

P.L. 106-554 (Community Renewal)
Act Sec. 314(a) amended Code Sec. 6211(b)(4) by striking "sections 32 and 34" and inserting "sections 24(d), 32, and 34".

The above amendment is effective as if included in the provision of the Taxpayer Relief Act of 1997 (P.L. 105-34) to which it relates [effective for tax years beginning after December 31, 1997.—CCH.].

[¶ 6060] CODE SEC. 6330. NOTICE AND OPPORTUNITY FOR HEARING BEFORE LEVY.

* * *

(d) PROCEEDING AFTER HEARING.—

(1) JUDICIAL REVIEW OF DETERMINATION.—The person may, within 30 days of a determination under this section, appeal such determination—

(A) to the Tax Court (and the Tax Court shall have jurisdiction *with respect to* such matter); or

(B) if the Tax Court does not have jurisdiction of the underlying tax liability, to a district court of the United States.

If a court determines that the appeal was to an incorrect court, a person shall have 30 days after the court determination to file such appeal with the correct court.

* * *

[CCH Explanation at ¶ 355. Committee Reports at ¶ 10,320.]

Amendment Notes

P.L. 106-554 (Community Renewal)

Act Sec. 313(d) amended Code Sec. 6330(d)(1)(A) by striking "to hear" and inserting "with respect to".

The above amendment is effective as if included in the provision of the Internal Revenue Service Restructuring and Reform Act of 1998 (P.L. 105-206) to which it relates [effective for collection actions initiated after January 18, 1999.—CCH.].

(e) SUSPENSION OF COLLECTIONS AND STATUTE OF LIMITATIONS.—

(1) IN GENERAL.—Except as provided in paragraph (2), if a hearing is requested under subsection (a)(3)(B), the levy actions which are the subject of the requested hearing and the running of any period of limitations under section 6502 (relating to collection after assessment), section 6531 (relating to criminal prosecutions), or section 6532 (relating to other suits) shall be suspended for the period during which such hearing, and appeals therein, are pending. In no event shall any such period expire before the 90th day after the day on which there is a final determination in such hearing. *Notwithstanding the provisions of section 7421(a), the beginning of a levy or proceeding during the time the suspension under this paragraph is in force may be enjoined by a proceeding in the proper court, including the Tax Court. The Tax Court shall have no jurisdiction under this paragraph to enjoin any action or proceeding unless a timely appeal has been filed under subsection (d)(1) and then only in respect of the unpaid tax or proposed levy to which the determination being appealed relates.*

* * *

[CCH Explanation at ¶ 345. Committee Reports at ¶ 10,320.]

Amendment Notes

P.L. 106-554 (Community Renewal)

Act Sec. 313(b)(2)(A) amended Code Sec. 6330(e)(1) by adding at the end the last two sentences to read as above.

The above amendment is effective on December 21, 2000.

[¶ 6070] CODE SEC. 6331. LEVY AND DISTRAINT.

* * *

(k) NO LEVY WHILE CERTAIN OFFERS PENDING OR INSTALLMENT AGREEMENT PENDING OR IN EFFECT.—

* * *

(3) CERTAIN RULES TO APPLY.—Rules similar to the rules of paragraphs *(3) and (4)* of subsection (i) shall apply for purposes of this subsection.

* * *

[CCH Explanation at ¶ 365. Committee Reports at ¶ 10,320.]

Amendment Notes

P.L. 106-554 (Community Renewal)

Act Sec. 313(b)(3) amended Code Sec. 6331(k)(3) by striking "(3), (4), and (5)" and inserting "(3) and (4)".

The above amendment is effective on December 21, 2000.

[¶ 6080] CODE SEC. 6405. REPORTS OF REFUNDS AND CREDITS.

(a) BY TREASURY TO JOINT COMMITTEE.—No refund or credit of any income, war profits, excess profits, estate, or gift tax, or any tax imposed with respect to public charities, private foundations, operators' trust funds, pension plans, or real estate investment trusts under chapter 41, 42, 43, or 44, in excess of *$2,000,000* shall be made until after the expiration of 30 days from the date upon which a report giving the name of the person to whom the refund or credit is to be made, the amount of such refund or credit, and a summary of the facts and the decision of the Secretary, is submitted to the Joint Committee on Taxation.

[CCH Explanation at ¶ 370. Committee Reports at ¶ 10,275.]

Amendment Notes

P.L. 106-554 (Community Renewal)
Act Sec. 305(a) amended Code Sec. 6405(a) by striking "$1,000,000" and inserting "$2,000,000".
The above amendment is effective on December 21, 2000, except that such amendment shall not apply with respect to any refund or credit with respect to a report that has been made before such date under Code Sec. 6405.

(b) TENTATIVE ADJUSTMENTS.—Any credit or refund allowed or made under section 6411 shall be made without regard to the provisions of subsection (a) of this section. In any such case, if the credit or refund, reduced by any deficiency in such tax thereafter assessed and by deficiencies in any other tax resulting from adjustments reflected in the determination of the credit or refund, is in excess of *$2,000,000*, there shall be submitted to such committee a report containing the matter specified in subsection (a) at such time after the making of the credit or refund as the Secretary shall determine the correct amount of the tax.

* * *

[CCH Explanation at ¶ 370. Committee Reports at ¶ 10,275.]

Amendment Notes

P.L. 106-554 (Community Renewal)
Act Sec. 305(a) amended Code Sec. 6405(b) by striking "$1,000,000" and inserting "$2,000,000".
The above amendment is effective on December 21, 2000, except that such amendment shall not apply with respect to any refund or credit with respect to a report that has been made before such date under Code Sec. 6405.

[¶ 6090] CODE SEC. 6411. TENATIVE CARRYBACK AND REFUND ADJUSTMENTS.

(a) APPLICATION FOR ADJUSTMENT.—A taxpayer may file an application for a tentative carryback adjustment of the tax for the prior taxable year affected by a net operating loss carryback provided in section 172(b), by a business credit carryback provided in section 39, or by a capital loss carryback provided in *subsection (a)(1) or (c) of section 1212*, from any taxable year. The application shall be verified in the manner prescribed by section 6065 in the case of a return of such taxpayer and shall be filed, on or after the date of filing for the return for the taxable year of the net operating loss, net capital loss, or unused business credit from which the carryback results and within a period of 12 months after such taxable year or, with respect to any portion of a business credit carryback attributable to a net operating loss carryback or a net capital loss carryback from a subsequent taxable year, within a period of 12 months from the end of such subsequent taxable year, in the manner and form required by regulations prescribed by the Secretary. The applications shall set forth in such detail and with such supporting data and explanation as such regulations shall require—

(1) The amount of the net operating loss, net capital loss, or unused business credit;

(2) The amount of the tax previously determined for the prior taxable year affected by such carryback, the tax previously determined being ascertained in accordance with the method prescribed in section 1314(a);

(3) The amount of decrease in such tax, attributable to such carryback, such decrease being determined by applying the carryback in the manner provided by law to the items on the basis of which such tax was determined;

(4) The unpaid amount of such tax, not including any amount required to be shown under paragraph (5);

(5) The amount, with respect to the tax for the taxable year immediately preceding the taxable year from which the carryback is made, as to which an extension of time for payment under section 6164 is in effect; and

(6) Such other information for purposes of carrying out the provisions of this section as may be required by such regulations.

Except for purposes of applying section 6611(f)(3)(B), an application under this subsection shall not constitute a claim for credit or refund.

* * *

Code Sec. 6411(a)   ¶ 6090

[CCH Explanation at ¶ 280. Committee Reports at ¶ 10,345.]

Amendment Notes

P.L. 106-554 (Community Renewal)
    Act Sec. 318(d)(1) amended Code Sec. 6411(a) by striking "section 1212(a)(1)" and inserting "subsection (a)(1) or (c) of section 1212".

The above amendment is effective as if included in the amendments made by section 504 of the Economic Recovery Tax Act of 1981 (P.L. 97-34) [effective for property acquired and positions established after June 23, 1981.—CCH.].

[¶ 6100] CODE SEC. 6512. LIMITATIONS IN CASE OF PETITION TO TAX COURT.

(a) EFFECT OF PETITION TO TAX COURT.—If the Secretary has mailed to the taxpayer a notice of deficiency under section 6212(a) (relating to deficiencies of income, estate, gift, and certain excise taxes) and if the taxpayer files a petition with the Tax Court within the time prescribed in section 6213(a) (or 7481(c) with respect to a determination of statutory interest or section 7481(d) solely with respect to a determination of estate tax by the Tax Court), no credit or refund of income tax for the same taxable year, of gift tax for the same calendar year or calendar quarter, of estate tax in respect of the taxable estate of the same decedent, or of tax imposed by chapter 41, 42, 43, or 44 with respect to any act (or failure to act) to which such petition relates, in respect of which the Secretary has determined the deficiency shall be allowed or made and no suit by the taxpayer for the recovery of any part of the tax shall be instituted in any court except—

(1) As to overpayments determined by a decision of the Tax Court which has become final, *and*

(2) As to any amount collected in excess of an amount computed in accordance with the decision of the Tax Court which has become final, *and*

(3) As to any amount collected after the period of limitation upon the making of levy or beginning a proceeding in court for collection has expired; but in any such claim for credit or refund or in any such suit for refund the decision of the Tax Court which has become final, as to whether such period has expired before the notice of deficiency was mailed, shall be conclusive, and

(4) As to overpayments attributable to partnership items, in accordance with subchapter C of chapter 63, and

(5) As to any amount collected within the period during which the Secretary is prohibited from making the assessment or from collecting by levy or through a proceeding in court under the provisions of section 6213(a), *and*

(6) As to overpayments the Secretary is authorized to refund or credit pending appeal as provided in subsection (b).

* * *

[CCH Explanation at ¶ 30,050.]

Amendment Notes

P.L. 106-554 (Community Renewal)
    Act Sec. 319(19) amended Code Sec. 6512(a) by striking "; and" at the end of paragraphs (1), (2), and (5) and inserting ", and".

The above amendment is effective on December 21, 2000.

[¶ 6110] CODE SEC. 6611. INTEREST ON OVERPAYMENTS.

* * *

(g) NO INTEREST UNTIL RETURN IN PROCESSIBLE FORM.—

(1) For purposes of subsections (b)(3) and (e) a return shall not be treated as filed until it is filed in processible form.

* * *

[CCH Explanation at ¶ 30,050.]

Amendment Notes

P.L. 106-554 (Community Renewal)
    Act Sec. 319(20) amended Code Sec. 6611(g)(1) by striking the comma after "(b)(3)".

The above amendment is effective on December 21, 2000.

[¶ 6120] CODE SEC. 6655. FAILURE BY CORPORATION TO PAY ESTIMATED INCOME TAX.

* * *

(e) LOWER REQUIRED INSTALLMENT WHERE ANNUALIZED INCOME INSTALLMENT OR ADJUSTED SEASONAL INSTALLMENT IS LESS THAN AMOUNT DETERMINED UNDER SUBSECTION (d).—

* * *

(5) TREATMENT OF CERTAIN REIT DIVIDENDS.—

(A) IN GENERAL.—Any dividend received from a closely held real estate investment trust by any person which owns (after application of *subsection (d)(5)* of section 856) 10 percent or more (by vote or value) of the stock or beneficial interests in the trust shall be taken into account in computing annualized income installments under paragraph (2) in a manner similar to the manner under which partnership income inclusions are taken into account.

(B) CLOSELY HELD REIT.—For purposes of subparagraph (A), the term "closely held real estate investment trust" means a real estate investment trust with respect to which 5 or fewer persons own (after application of *subsection (d)(5)* of section 856) 50 percent or more (by vote or value) of the stock or beneficial interests in the trust.

* * *

[CCH Explanation at ¶ 30,050.]

Amendment Notes
P.L. 106-554 (Community Renewal)
Act Sec. 319(21) amended Code Sec. 6655(e)(5)(A) and (B) by striking "subsections (d)(5) and (l)(3)(B)" and inserting "subsection (d)(5)".

The above amendment is effective on December 21, 2000.

[¶ 6130] CODE SEC. 6693. FAILURE TO PROVIDE REPORTS ON CERTAIN TAX-FAVORED ACCOUNTS OR ANNUITIES; PENALTIES RELATING TO DESIGNATED NONDEDUCTIBLE CONTRIBUTIONS.

(a) REPORTS.—

* * *

(2) PROVISIONS.—The provisions referred to in this paragraph are—

(A) subsections (i) and (l) of section 408 (relating to individual retirement plans),

(B) section 220(h) (relating to *Archer MSAs*),

(C) section 529(d) (relating to qualified State tuition programs), and

(D) section 530(h) (relating to education individual retirement accounts).

This subsection shall not apply to any report which is an information return described in section 6724(d)(1)(C)(i) or a payee statement described in section 6724(d)(2)(X).

* * *

[CCH Explanation at ¶ 615. Committee Reports at ¶ 10,245.]

Amendment Notes
P.L. 106-554 (Community Renewal)
Act Sec. 202(b)(2)(E) amended Code Sec. 6693(a)(2)(B) by striking "medical savings accounts" each place it appears in the text and inserting "Archer MSAs".

The above amendment is effective on December 21, 2000.

[¶ 6140] CODE SEC. 6724. WAIVER; DEFINITIONS AND SPECIAL RULES.

* * *

(d) DEFINITIONS.—For purposes of this part—

(1) INFORMATION RETURN.—The term "information return" means—

(A) any statement of the amount of payments to another person required by—

(i) section 6041(a) or (b) (relating to certain information at source),

(ii) section 6042(a)(1) (relating to payments of dividends),

(iii) section 6044(a)(1) (relating to payments of patronage dividends),

(iv) section 6049(a) (relating to payments of interest),

(v) section 6050A(a) (relating to reporting requirements of certain fishing boat operators),

(vi) section 6050N(a) (relating to payments of royalties),

(vii) section 6051(d) (relating to information returns with respect to income tax withheld),

(viii) section 6050R (relating to returns relating to certain purchases of fish), or

(ix) section 110(d) (relating to qualified lessee construction allowances for short-term leases),

(B) any return required by—

(i) section 6041A(a) or (b) (relating to returns of direct sellers),

(ii) section 6045(a) or (d) (relating to returns of brokers),

(iii) section 6050H(a) (relating to mortgage interest received in trade or business from individuals),

(iv) section 6050I(a) or (g)(1) (relating to cash received in trade or business, etc.),

(v) section 6050J(a) (relating to foreclosures and abandonments of security),

(vi) section 6050K(a) (relating to exchanges of certain partnership interests),

(vii) section 6050L(a) (relating to returns relating to certain dispositions of donated property),

(viii) section 6050P (relating to returns relating to the cancellation of indebtedness by certain financial entities),

(ix) section 6050Q (relating to certain long-term care benefits),

(x) section 6050S (relating to returns relating to payments for qualified tuition and related expenses),

(xi) section 6052(a) (relating to reporting payment of wages in the form of group-life insurance),

(xii) section 6053(c)(1) (relating to reporting with respect to certain tips),

(xiii) subsection (b) or (e) of section 1060 (relating to reporting requirements of transferors and transferees in certain asset acquisitions),

(xiv) subparagraph (A) or (C) of subsection (c)(4) of section 4093 (relating to information reporting with respect to tax on diesel and aviation fuels),

(xv) section 4101(d) (relating to information reporting with respect to fuels taxes),

(xvi) subparagraph (C) of section 338(h)(10) (relating to information required to be furnished to the Secretary in case of elective recognition of gain or loss), or

(xvii) section 264(f)(5)(A)(iv) (relating to reporting with respect to certain life insurance and annuity contracts), and

(C) any statement of the amount of payments to another person required to be made to the Secretary under—

(i) section 408(i) (relating to reports with respect to individual retirement accounts or annuities), or

(ii) section 6047(d) (relating to reports by employers, plan administrators, etc.).

Such term also includes any form, statement, or schedule required to be filed with the Secretary with respect to any amount from which tax was required to be deducted and withheld under chapter 3 (or from which tax would be required to be so deducted and withheld but for an exemption under this title or any treaty obligation of the United States).

* * *

(2) PAYEE STATEMENT.—The term "payee statement" means any statement required to be furnished under—

* * *

(Z) section 6050S(d) (relating to returns relating to qualified tuition and related expenses),

or

* * *

[CCH Explanation at ¶ 30,050.]
Amendment Notes

P.L. 106-554 (Community Renewal)

Act Sec. 319(23)(A) amended Code Sec. 6724(d)(1)(B) by striking clauses (xiv) through (xvii) and inserting new clauses (xiv) through (xvii) to read as above. Prior to amendment, Code Sec. 6724(d)(1)(B)(xiv)-(xvii) read as follows:

(xiv) subparagraph (A) or (C) of subsection (c)(4) of section 4093 (relating to information reporting with respect to tax on diesel and aviation fuels), or

(xv) section 4101(d) (relating to information reporting with respect to fuels taxes)[,]

(xvi) subparagraph (C) of section 338(h)(10) (relating to information required to be furnished to the Secretary in case of elective recognition of gain or loss); or

(xvii) section 264(f)(5)(A)(iv) (relating to reporting with respect to certain life insurance and annuity contracts).

Act Sec. 319(23)(B) amended section 6010(o)(4)(C) of the Internal Revenue Restructuring and Reform Act of 1998 (P.L. 105-206) by striking "inserting 'or', and by adding at the end" and inserting "inserting ', or', and by adding after

subparagraph (Z)". The effect of this amendment is to amend Code Sec. 6724(d)(2)(Z) by striking "or" and inserting ", or".

The above amendments are effective on December 21, 2000.

[¶ 6150] CODE SEC. 7421. PROHIBITION OF SUITS TO RESTRAIN ASSESSMENT OR COLLECTION.

(a) TAX.—Except as provided in sections 6015(e), 6212(a) and (c), 6213(a), 6225(b), 6246(b), *6330(e)(1)*, 6331(i), *6672(c)*, 6694(c), 7426(a) and (b)(1), 7429(b), and 7436, no suit for the purpose of restraining the assessment or collection of any tax shall be maintained in any court by any person, whether or not such person is the person against whom such tax was assessed.

* * *

[CCH Explanation at ¶ 345 and ¶ 30,050. Committee Reports at ¶ 10,320.]

Amendment Notes
P.L. 106-554 (Community Renewal)
Act Sec. 313(b)(2)(B) amended Code Sec. 7421(a) by inserting "6330(e)(1)," after "6246(b),".

Act Sec. 319(24) amended Code Sec. 7421(a) by striking "6672(b)" and inserting "6672(c)".

The above amendments are effective on December 21, 2000.

[¶ 6160] CODE SEC. 7430. AWARDING OF COSTS AND CERTAIN FEES.

* * *

(c) DEFINITIONS.—For purposes of this section—

* * *

(3) *ATTORNEYS' FEES.—*

* * *

(B) PRO BONO SERVICES.—The court may award reasonable *attorneys' fees* under subsection (a) in excess of the *attorneys' fees* paid or incurred if such fees are less than the reasonable *attorneys' fees* because an individual is representing the prevailing party for no fee or for a fee which (taking into account all the facts and circumstances) is no more than a nominal fee. This subparagraph shall apply only if such award is paid to such individual or such individual's employer.

* * *

[CCH Explanation at ¶ 30,050.]

Amendment Notes
P.L. 106-554 (Community Renewal)
Act Sec. 319(25)(A)-(B) amended Code Sec. 7430(c)(3) by striking "ATTORNEYS" and inserting "ATTORNEYS' " in the paragraph heading, and by striking "attorneys fees" each

place it appears in subparagraph (B) and inserting "attorneys' fees".

The above amendment is effective on December 21, 2000.

[¶ 6170] CODE SEC. 7436. PROCEEDINGS FOR DETERMINATION OF EMPLOYMENT STATUS.

(a) CREATION OF REMEDY.—If, in connection with an audit of any person, there is an actual controversy involving a determination by the Secretary as part of an examination that—

(1) one or more individuals performing services for such person are employees of such person for purposes of subtitle C, or

(2) such person is not entitled to the treatment under subsection (a) of section 530 of the Revenue Act of 1978 with respect to such an individual,

upon the filing of an appropriate pleading, the Tax Court may determine whether such a determination by the Secretary is correct *and the proper amount of employment tax under such determination.* Any such redetermination by the Tax Court shall have the force and effect of a decision of the Tax Court and shall be reviewable as such.

* * *

[CCH Explanation at ¶ 350. Committee Reports at ¶ 10,325.]

Amendment Notes

P.L. 106-554 (Community Renewal)

Act Sec. 314(f) amended Code Sec. 7436(a) by inserting before the period at the end of the first sentence "and the

proper amount of employment tax under such determination".

The above amendment is effective as if included in the provision of the Taxpayer Relief Act of 1997 (P.L. 105-34) to which it relates [effective August 5, 1997.— CCH.].

[¶ 6180] CODE SEC. 7463. DISPUTES INVOLVING $50,000 OR LESS.

* * *

(f) *Additional Cases in Which Proceedings May Be Conducted Under This Section.*—At the option of the taxpayer concurred in by the Tax Court or a division thereof before the hearing of the case, proceedings may be conducted under this section (in the same manner as a case described in subsection (a)) in the case of—

(1) a petition to the Tax Court under section 6015(e) in which the amount of relief sought does not exceed $50,000, and

(2) an appeal under section 6330(d)(1)(A) to the Tax Court of a determination in which the unpaid tax does not exceed $50,000.

[CCH Explanation at ¶ 340. Committee Reports at ¶ 10,320.]

Amendment Notes

P.L. 106-554 (Community Renewal)
Act Sec. 313(b)(1) amended Code Sec. 7463 by adding at the end a new subsection (f) to read as above.

The above amendment is effective on December 21, 2000.

[¶ 6190] CODE SEC. 7603. SERVICE OF SUMMONS.

* * *

(b) Service by Mail to Third-Party Recordkeepers.—

* * *

(2) Third-party recordkeeper.—For purposes of paragraph (1), the term "third-party recordkeeper" means—

(A) any mutual savings bank, cooperative bank, domestic building and loan association, or other savings institution chartered and supervised as a savings and loan or similar association under Federal or State law, any bank (as defined in section 581), or any credit union (within the meaning of section 501(c)(14)(A)),

(B) any consumer reporting agency (as defined under section 603(f) of the Fair Credit Reporting Act (15 U.S.C. 1681a(f))),

(C) any person extending credit through the use of credit cards or similar devices,

(D) any broker (as defined in section 3(a)(4) of the Securities Exchange Act of 1934 (15 U.S.C. 78c(a)(4))),

(E) any attorney,

(F) any accountant,

(G) any barter exchange (as defined in section 6045(c)(3)),

(H) any regulated investment company (as defined in section 851) and any agent of such regulated investment company when acting as an agent thereof,

(I) any enrolled agent, and

(J) any owner or developer of a computer software source code (as defined in section 7612(d)(2)).

Subparagraph (J) shall apply only with respect to a summons requiring the production of the source code referred to in subparagraph (J) or the program and data described in section 7612(b)(1)(A)(ii) to which such source code relates.

[CCH Explanation at ¶ 30,050.]

Amendment Notes

P.L. 106-554 (Community Renewal)
Act Sec. 319(26) amended Code Sec. 7603(b)(2) by striking the semicolon at the end of subparagraphs (A), (B), (C), (D), (E), (F), and (G) and inserting a comma.

The above amendment is effective on December 21, 2000.

[¶ 6200] CODE SEC. 7608. AUTHORITY OF INTERNAL REVENUE ENFORCEMENT OFFICERS.

* * *

(c) Rules Relating to Undercover Operations.—

* * *

(6) Application of Section.—The provisions of this subsection—

(A) shall apply after November 17, 1988, and before January 1, 1990, and

(B) shall apply after the date of the enactment of this paragraph and before *January 1, 2006.*

All amounts expended pursuant to this subsection during the period described in subparagraph (B) shall be recovered to the extent possible, and deposited in the Treasury of the United States as miscellaneous receipts, before *January 1, 2006.*

[CCH Explanation at ¶ 385. Committee Reports at ¶ 10,265.]

Amendment Notes
P.L. 106-554 (Community Renewal)
    Act Sec. 303 amended Code Sec. 7608(c)(6) and the last sentence of Code Sec. 7608 by striking "January 1, 2001" and inserting "January 1, 2006".

The above amendment is effective on December 21, 2000.

[¶ 6210] CODE SEC. 7701. DEFINITIONS.

* * *

(m) DESIGNATION OF CONTRACT MARKETS.—*Any designation by the Commodity Futures Trading Commission of a contract market which could not have been made under the law in effect on the day before the date of the enactment of the Commodity Futures Modernization Act of 2000 shall apply for purposes of this title except to the extent provided in regulations prescribed by the Secretary.*

[CCH Explanation at ¶ 260. Committee Reports at ¶ 10,355.]

Amendment Notes
P.L. 106-554 (Community Renewal)
    Act Sec. 401(i) amended Code Sec. 7701 by redesignating subsection (m) as subsection (n) and by inserting after subsection (l) a new subsection (m) to read as above.

The above amendment is effective on December 21, 2000.

(n) CROSS REFERENCES.—

   (1) OTHER DEFINITIONS.—

      For other definitions, see the following sections of Title 1 of the United States Code:

      (1) Singular as including plural, section 1.

      (2) Plural as including singular, section 1.

      (3) Masculine as including feminine, section 1.

      (4) Officer, section 1.

      (5) Oath as including affirmation, section 1.

      (6) County as including parish, section 2.

      (7) Vessel as including all means of water transportation, section 3.

      (8) Vehicle as including all means of land transportation, section 4.

      (9) Company or association as including successors and assigns, section 5.

   (2) EFFECT OF CROSS REFERENCES.—

      For effect of cross references in this title, see section 7806(a).

[CCH Explanation at ¶ 260. Committee Reports at ¶ 10,355.]

Amendment Notes
P.L. 106-554 (Community Renewal)
    Act Sec. 401(i) amended Code Sec. 7701 by redesignating subsection (m) as subsection (n).

The above amendment is effective on December 21, 2000.

[¶ 6220] CODE SEC. 7702A. MODIFIED ENDOWMENT CONTRACT DEFINED.

(a) GENERAL RULE.—For purposes of section 72, the term "modified endowment contract" means any contract meeting the requirements of section 7702—

   (1) which—

      (A) is entered into on or after June 21, 1988, and

      (B) fails to meet the 7-pay test of subsection (b), or

   (2) which is received in exchange for a contract described in paragraph (1) *or this paragraph.*

* * *

[CCH Explanation at ¶ 405. Committee Reports at ¶ 10,345.]

Act Sec. 7702A(a)   ¶ 6220

Amendment Notes

P.L. 106-554 (Community Renewal)

Act Sec. 318(a)(1) amended Code Sec. 7702A(a)(2) by inserting "or this paragraph" before the period.

The above amendment is effective as if included in the amendments made by section 5012 of the Technical and

Miscellaneous Revenue Act of 1988 (P.L. 100-647) [effective for contracts entered into or materially changed on or after June 21, 1988.—CCH.].

(c) COMPUTATIONAL RULES.—

* * *

(3) TREATMENT OF MATERIAL CHANGES.—

(A) IN GENERAL.—If there is a material change in the benefits under (or in other terms of) the contract which was not reflected in any previous determination under this section, for purposes of this section—

(i) such contract shall be treated as a new contract entered into on the day on which such material change takes effect, and

(ii) appropriate adjustments shall be made in determining whether such contract meets the 7-pay test of subsection (b) to take into account the cash surrender value *under the old contract.*

* * *

[CCH Explanation at ¶ 405. Committee Reports at ¶ 10,345.]

Amendment Notes

P.L. 106-554 (Community Renewal)

Act Sec. 318(a)(2) amended Code Sec. 7702A(c)(3)(A)(ii) by striking "under the contract" and inserting "under the old contract".

The above amendment is effective as if included in the amendments made by section 5012 of the Technical and Miscellaneous Revenue Act of 1988 (P.L. 100-647) [effective for contracts entered into or materially changed on or after June 21, 1988.—CCH.].

[¶ 6230] CODE SEC. 7802. INTERNAL REVENUE SERVICE OVERSIGHT BOARD.

* * *

(b) MEMBERSHIP.—

* * *

(2) QUALIFICATIONS AND TERMS.—

* * *

(B) TERMS.—Each member who is described in subparagraph (A) or (D) of paragraph (1) shall be appointed for a term of 5 years, except that of the members first appointed under paragraph (1)(A)—

(i) two members shall be appointed for a term of 3 years,

(ii) two members shall be appointed for a term of 4 years, *and*

(iii) two members shall be appointed for a term of 5 years.

* * *

[CCH Explanation at ¶ 30,050.]

Amendment Notes

P.L. 106-554 (Community Renewal)

Act Sec. 319(27) amended Code Sec. 7802(b)(2)(B)(ii) by striking "; and" at the end and inserting ", and".

The above amendment is effective on December 21, 2000.

[¶ 6240] CODE SEC. 7811. TAXPAYER ASSISTANCE ORDERS.

(a) AUTHORITY TO ISSUE.—

* * *

(3) STANDARD WHERE ADMINISTRATIVE GUIDANCE NOT FOLLOWED.—In cases where any Internal Revenue Service employee is not following applicable published administrative guidance (including the Internal Revenue Manual), the National Taxpayer Advocate shall construe the factors taken into account in determining whether to issue a *Taxpayer Assistance Order* in the manner most favorable to the taxpayer.

* * *

[CCH Explanation at ¶ 30,050.]

Amendment Notes

P.L. 106-554 (Community Renewal)

Act Sec. 319(28) amended Code Sec. 7811(a)(3) by striking "taxpayer assistance order" and inserting "Taxpayer Assistance Order".

The above amendment is effective on December 21, 2000.

(d) SUSPENSION OF RUNNING OF PERIOD OF LIMITATION.—The running of any period of limitation with respect to any action described in subsection (b) shall be suspended for—

(1) the period beginning on the date of the taxpayer's application under subsection (a) and ending on the date of the *National Taxpayer Advocate's* decision with respect to such application, and

(2) any period specified by the National Taxpayer Advocate in a Taxpayer Assistance Order issued pursuant to such application.

* * *

[CCH Explanation at ¶ 30,050.]

Amendment Notes

P.L. 106-554 (Community Renewal)

Act Sec. 319(29) amended Code Sec. 7811(d)(1) by striking "Ombudsman's" and inserting "National Taxpayer Advocate's". [Note: This amendment was previously enacted by

Act Sec. 1102(d)(2) of the IRS Restructuring and Reform Act of 1998 (P.L. 105-206).—CCH.]

The above amendment is effective on December 21, 2000.

[¶ 6250] CODE SEC. 7872. TREATMENT OF LOANS WITH BELOW-MARKET INTEREST RATES.

* * *

(f) OTHER DEFINITIONS AND SPECIAL RULES.—For purposes of this section—

* * *

(3) GIFT LOAN.—The term "gift loan" means any below-market loan where the *forgoing* of interest is in the nature of a gift.

* * *

[CCH Explanation at ¶ 30,050.]

Amendment Notes

P.L. 106-554 (Community Renewal)

Act Sec. 319(30) amended Code Sec. 7872(f)(3) by striking "foregoing" and inserting "forgoing".

The above amendment is effective on December 21, 2000.

[¶ 6260] CODE SEC. 9503. HIGHWAY TRUST FUND.

* * *

(b) TRANSFER TO HIGHWAY TRUST FUND OF AMOUNTS EQUIVALENT TO CERTAIN TAXES.—

* * *

(5) LIMITATION ON TRANSFERS TO HIGHWAY TRUST FUND.—

(A) IN GENERAL.—Except as provided in subparagraph (B), no amount may be appropriated to the Highway Trust Fund on and after the date of any expenditure from the Highway Trust Fund which is not permitted by this section. The determination of whether an expenditure is so permitted shall be made without regard to—

(i) any provision of law which is not contained or referenced in this title or in a revenue Act, and

(ii) whether such provision of law is a subsequently enacted provision or directly or indirectly seeks to waive the application of this paragraph.

(B) EXCEPTION FOR PRIOR OBLIGATIONS.—Subparagraph (A) shall not apply to any expenditure to liquidate any contract entered into (or for any amount otherwise obligated) before October 1, 2003, in accordance with the provisions of this section.

* * *

[CCH Explanation at ¶ 295. Committee Reports at ¶ 10,345.]

Code Sec. 9503(b)   ¶ 6260

Amendment Notes

P.L. 106-554 (Community Renewal)

Act Sec. 318(e)(1) amended Code Sec. 9503(b) by striking paragraph (5) and redesignating paragraph (6) as paragraph (5). Prior to being stricken, Code Sec. 9503(b)(5) read as follows:

(5) GENERAL REVENUE DEPOSITS OF CERTAIN TAXES ON ALCOHOL MIXTURES.—For purposes of this section, the amounts which would (but for this paragraph) be required to be appropriated under subparagraphs (A) and (E) of paragraph (1) shall be reduced by—

(A) 0.6 cent per gallon in the case of taxes imposed on any mixture at least 10 percent of which is alcohol (as defined in section 4081(c)(3)) if any portion of such alcohol is ethanol, and

(B) 0.67 cent per gallon in the case of gasoline, diesel fuel, or kerosene used in producing a mixture described in subparagraph (A).

The above amendment applies with respect to taxes received in the Treasury after December 21, 2000.

[¶ 6270] CODE SEC. 9510. VACCINE INJURY COMPENSATION TRUST FUND.

* * *

(c) EXPENDITURES FROM TRUST FUND.—

(1) IN GENERAL.—Amounts in the Vaccine Injury Compensation Trust Fund shall be available, as provided in appropriation Acts, only for—

(A) the payment of compensation under subtitle 2 of title XXI of the Public Health Service Act (as in effect on *October 18, 2000*) for vaccine-related injury or death with respect to any vaccine—

(i) which is administered after September 30, 1988, and

(ii) which is a taxable vaccine (as defined in section 4132(a)(1)) at the time compensation is paid under such subtitle 2, or

(B) the payment of all expenses of administration (but not in excess of $9,500,000 for any fiscal year) incurred by the Federal Government in administering such subtitle.

* * *

[CCH Explanation at ¶ 297. Committee Reports at ¶ 10,345.]

Amendment Notes

P.L. 106-554 (Community Renewal)

Act Sec. 318(f) amended Code Sec. 9510(c)(1)(A) by striking "December 31, 1999" and inserting "October 18, 2000".

The above amendment is effective on December 21, 2000.

ACT SECTIONS NOT AMENDING CODE SECTIONS

COMMUNITY RENEWAL TAX RELIEF ACT OF 2000

[¶ 7001] ACT SEC. 1. SHORT TITLE; AMENDMENT OF 1986 CODE.

(a) SHORT TITLE.—This Act may be cited as the "Community Renewal Tax Relief Act of 2000".

(b) AMENDMENT OF 1986 CODE.—Except as otherwise expressly provided, whenever in this Act an amendment or repeal is expressed in terms of an amendment to, or repeal of, a section or other provision, the reference shall be considered to be made to a section or other provision of the Internal Revenue Code of 1986.

* * *

TITLE I—COMMUNITY RENEWAL AND NEW MARKETS

Subtitle A—Tax Incentives for Renewal Communities

[¶ 7060] ACT SEC. 101. DESIGNATION OF AND TAX INCENTIVES FOR RENEWAL COMMUNITIES.

* * *

(c) AUDIT AND REPORT.—Not later than January 31 of 2004, 2007, and 2010, the Comptroller General of the United States shall, pursuant to an audit of the renewal community program established under section 1400E of the Internal Revenue Code of 1986 (as added by subsection (a)) and the empowerment zone and enterprise community program under subchapter U of chapter 1 of such Code, report to Congress on such program and its effect on poverty, unemployment, and economic growth within the designated renewal communities, empowerment zones, and enterprise communities.

* * *

[CCH Explanation at ¶ 105. Committee Reports at ¶ 10,135.]

Subtitle C—New Markets Tax Credit

[¶ 7065] ACT SEC. 121. NEW MARKETS TAX CREDIT.

* * *

(f) GUIDANCE ON ALLOCATION OF NATIONAL LIMITATION.—Not later than 120 days after the date of the enactment of this Act, the Secretary of the Treasury or the Secretary's delegate shall issue guidance which specifies—

(1) how entities shall apply for an allocation under section 45D(f)(2) of the Internal Revenue Code of 1986, as added by this section;

(2) the competitive procedure through which such allocations are made; and

(3) the actions that such Secretary or delegate shall take to ensure that such allocations are properly made to appropriate entities.

(g) AUDIT AND REPORT.—Not later than January 31 of 2004, 2007, and 2010, the Comptroller General of the United States shall, pursuant to an audit of the new markets tax credit program established under section 45D of the Internal Revenue Code of 1986 (as added by subsection (a)), report to Congress on such program, including all qualified community development entities that receive an allocation under the new markets credit under such section.

* * *

[CCH Explanation at ¶ 235. Committee Reports at ¶ 10,165.]

Subtitle E—Other Community Renewal and New Markets Assistance

PART I—PROVISIONS RELATING TO HOUSING AND SUBSTANCE ABUSE PREVENTION AND TREATMENT

[¶ 7070] ACT SEC. 141. TRANSFER OF UNOCCUPIED AND SUBSTANDARD HUD-HELD HOUSING TO LOCAL GOVERNMENTS AND COMMUNITY DEVELOPMENT CORPORATIONS.

Section 204 of the Departments of Veterans Affairs and Housing and Urban Development, and Independent Agencies Appropriations Act, 1997 (12 U.S.C. 1715z-11a) is amended—

(1) by striking "FLEXIBLE AUTHORITY.—" and inserting "DISPOSITION OF HUD-OWNED PROPERTIES. (a) FLEXIBLE AUTHORITY FOR MULTIFAMILY PROJECTS.—"; and

(2) by adding at the end the following new subsection:

"(b) TRANSFER OF UNOCCUPIED AND SUBSTANDARD HOUSING TO LOCAL GOVERNMENTS AND COMMUNITY DEVELOPMENT CORPORATIONS.—

"(1) TRANSFER AUTHORITY.—Notwithstanding the authority under subsection (a) and the last sentence of section 204(g) of the National Housing Act (12 U.S.C. 1710(g)), the Secretary of Housing and Urban Development shall transfer ownership of any qualified HUD property, subject to the requirements of this section, to a unit of general local government having jurisdiction for the area in which the property is located or to a community development corporation which operates within such a unit of general local government in accordance with this subsection, but only to the extent that units of general local government and community development corporations consent to transfer and the Secretary determines that such transfer is practicable.

"(2) QUALIFIED HUD PROPERTIES.—For purposes of this subsection, the term 'qualified HUD property' means any property for which, as of the date that notification of the property is first made under paragraph (3)(B), not less than 6 months have elapsed since the later of the date that the property was acquired by the Secretary or the date that the property was determined to be unoccupied or substandard, that is owned by the Secretary and is—

"(A) an unoccupied multifamily housing project;

"(B) a substandard multifamily housing project; or

"(C) an unoccupied single family property that—

"(i) has been determined by the Secretary not to be an eligible asset under section 204(h) of the National Housing Act (12 U.S.C. 1710(h)); or

"(ii) is an eligible asset under such section 204(h), but—

"(I) is not subject to a specific sale agreement under such section; and

"(II) has been determined by the Secretary to be inappropriate for continued inclusion in the program under such section 204(h) pursuant to paragraph (10) of such section.

"(3) TIMING.—The Secretary shall establish procedures that provide for—

"(A) time deadlines for transfers under this subsection;

"(B) notification to units of general local government and community development corporations of qualified HUD properties in their jurisdictions;

"(C) such units and corporations to express interest in the transfer under this subsection of such properties;

"(D) a right of first refusal for transfer of qualified HUD properties to units of general local government and community development corporations, under which—

"(i) the Secretary shall establish a period during which the Secretary may not transfer such properties except to such units and corporations;

"(ii) the Secretary shall offer qualified HUD properties that are single family properties for purchase by units of general local government at a cost of $1 for each property, but only to the extent that the costs to the Federal Government of disposal at such price do not exceed the costs to the Federal Government of disposing of property subject to the procedures for single family property established by the Secretary pursuant to the authority under the last sentence of section 204(g) of the National Housing Act (12 U.S.C. 1710(g));

"(iii) the Secretary may accept an offer to purchase a property made by a community development corporation only if the offer provides for purchase on a cost recovery basis; and

"(iv) the Secretary shall accept an offer to purchase such a property that is made during such period by such a unit or corporation and that complies with the requirements of this paragraph; and

"(E) a written explanation, to any unit of general local government or community development corporation making an offer to purchase a qualified HUD property under this subsection that is not accepted, of the reason that such offer was not acceptable.

"(4) OTHER DISPOSITION.—With respect to any qualified HUD property, if the Secretary does not receive an acceptable offer to purchase the property pursuant to the procedure established under paragraph (3), the Secretary shall dispose of the property to the unit of general local government in which property is located or to community development corporations located in such unit of general local government on a negotiated, competitive bid, or other basis, on such terms as the Secretary deems appropriate.

"(5) SATISFACTION OF INDEBTEDNESS.—Before transferring ownership of any qualified HUD property pursuant to this subsection, the Secretary shall satisfy any indebtedness incurred in connection with the property to be transferred, by canceling the indebtedness.

"(6) DETERMINATION OF STATUS OF PROPERTIES.—To ensure compliance with the requirements of this subsection, the Secretary shall take the following actions:

"(A) UPON ENACTMENT.—Upon the enactment of this subsection, the Secretary shall promptly assess each residential property owned by the Secretary to determine whether such property is a qualified HUD property.

"(B) UPON ACQUISITION.—Upon acquiring any residential property, the Secretary shall promptly determine whether the property is a qualified HUD property.

"(C) UPDATES.—The Secretary shall periodically reassess the residential properties owned by the Secretary to determine whether any such properties have become qualified HUD properties.

"(7) TENANT LEASES.—This subsection shall not affect the terms or the enforceability of any contract or lease entered into with respect to any residential property before the date that such property becomes a qualified HUD property.

"(8) USE OF PROPERTY.—Property transferred under this subsection shall be used only for appropriate neighborhood revitalization efforts, including homeownership, rental units, commercial space, and parks, consistent with local zoning regulations, local building codes, and subdivision regulations and restrictions of record.

"(9) INAPPLICABILITY TO PROPERTIES MADE AVAILABLE FOR HOMELESS.—Notwithstanding any other provision of this subsection, this subsection shall not apply to any properties that the Secretary determines are to be made available for use by the homeless pursuant to subpart E of part 291 of title 24, Code of Federal Regulations, during the period that the properties are so available.

"(10) PROTECTION OF EXISTING CONTRACTS.—This subsection may not be construed to alter, affect, or annul any legally binding obligations entered into with respect to a qualified HUD property before the property becomes a qualified HUD property.

"(11) DEFINITIONS.—For purposes of this subsection, the following definitions shall apply:

"(A) COMMUNITY DEVELOPMENT CORPORATION.—The term 'community development corporation' means a nonprofit organization whose primary purpose is to promote community development by providing housing opportunities for low-income families.

"(B) COST RECOVERY BASIS.—The term 'cost recovery basis' means, with respect to any sale of a residential property by the Secretary, that the purchase price paid by the purchaser is equal to or greater than the sum of: (i) the appraised value of the property, as determined in accordance with such requirements as the Secretary shall establish; and (ii) the costs incurred by the Secretary in connection with such property during the period beginning on the date on which the Secretary acquires title to the property and ending on the date on which the sale is consummated.

"(C) MULTIFAMILY HOUSING PROJECT.—The term 'multifamily housing project' has the meaning given the term in section 203 of the Housing and Community Development Amendments of 1978.

"(D) RESIDENTIAL PROPERTY.—The term 'residential property' means a property that is a multifamily housing project or a single family property.

"(E) SECRETARY.—The term 'Secretary' means the Secretary of Housing and Urban Development.

"(F) SEVERE PHYSICAL PROBLEMS.—The term 'severe physical problems' means, with respect to a dwelling unit, that the unit—

"(i) lacks hot or cold piped water, a flush toilet, or both a bathtub and a shower in the unit, for the exclusive use of that unit;

"(ii) on not less than three separate occasions during the preceding winter months, was uncomfortably cold for a period of more than 6 consecutive hours due to a malfunction of the heating system for the unit;

"(iii) has no functioning electrical service, exposed wiring, any room in which there is not a functioning electrical outlet, or has experienced three or more blown fuses or tripped circuit breakers during the preceding 90-day period;

"(iv) is accessible through a public hallway in which there are no working light fixtures, loose or missing steps or railings, and no elevator; or

"(v) has severe maintenance problems, including water leaks involving the roof, windows, doors, basement, or pipes or plumbing fixtures, holes or open cracks in walls or ceilings, severe paint peeling or broken plaster, and signs of rodent infestation.

"(G) SINGLE FAMILY PROPERTY.—The term 'single family property' means a 1- to 4- family residence.

"(H) SUBSTANDARD.—The term 'substandard' means, with respect to a multifamily housing project, that 25 percent or more of the dwelling units in the project have severe physical problems.

"(I) UNIT OF GENERAL LOCAL GOVERNMENT.—The term 'unit of general local government' has the meaning given such term in section 102(a) of the Housing and Community Development Act of 1974.

"(J) UNOCCUPIED.—The term 'unoccupied' means, with respect to a residential property, that the unit of general local government having jurisdiction over the area in which the project is located has certified in writing that the property is not inhabited.

"(12) REGULATIONS.—

"(A) INTERIM.—Not later than 30 days after the date of the enactment of this subsection, the Secretary shall issue such interim regulations as are necessary to carry out this subsection.

"(B) FINAL.—Not later than 60 days after the date of the enactment of this subsection, the Secretary shall issue such final regulations as are necessary to carry out this subsection.".

[¶ 7075] ACT SEC. 142. TRANSFER OF HUD ASSETS IN REVITALIZATION AREAS.

In carrying out the program under section 204(h) of the National Housing Act (12 U.S.C. 1710(h)), upon the request of the chief executive officer of a county or the government of appropriate jurisdiction and not later than 60 days after such request is made, the Secretary of Housing and Urban Development shall designate as a revitalization area all portions of such county that meet the criteria for such designation under paragraph (3) of such section.

[¶ 7080] ACT SEC. 143. RISK-SHARING DEMONSTRATION.

Section 249 of the National Housing Act (12 U.S.C. 1715z-14) is amended—

(1) by striking the section heading and inserting the following:

"RISK-SHARING DEMONSTRATION";

(2) by striking "reinsurance" each place such term appears and insert "risk-sharing";

(3) in subsection (a)—

(A) in the first sentence, by inserting "and with insured community development financial institutions" after "private mortgage insurers";

(B) in the second sentence—

(i) by striking "two" and inserting "four"; and

(ii) by striking "March 15, 1988" and inserting "the expiration of the 5-year period beginning on the date of the enactment of the Community Renewal Tax Relief Act of 2000"; and

(C) in the third sentence—

(i) by striking "insured" and inserting "for which risk of nonpayment is shared"; and

(ii) by striking "10 percent" and inserting "20 percent";

(4) in subsection (b)—

(A) in the first sentence—

(i) by striking "to provide" and inserting ", in providing";

(ii) by striking "through" and inserting ", to enter into"; and

(iii) by inserting "and with insured community development financial institutions" before the period at the end;

(B) in the second sentence, by inserting "and insured community development financial institutions" after "private mortgage insurance companies";

(C) by striking paragraph (1) and inserting the following new paragraph:

"(1) assume a secondary percentage of loss on any mortgage insured pursuant to section 203(b), 234, or 245 covering a one- to four-family dwelling, which percentage of loss shall be set forth in the risk-sharing contract, with the first percentage of loss to be borne by the Secretary;"; and

(D) in paragraph (2)—

(i) by striking "carry out (under appropriate delegation) such" and inserting "perform or delegate underwriting,";

(ii) by striking "function as the Secretary pursuant to regulations," and inserting "functions as the Secretary"; and

(iii) by inserting before the period at the end the following: "and shall set forth in the risk-sharing contract";

(5) in subsection (c)—

(A) in the first sentence—

(i) by striking "of" the first place it appears and inserting "for";

(ii) by inserting "received by the Secretary with a private mortgage insurer or insured community development financial institution" after "sharing of premiums";

(iii) by striking "insurance reserves" and inserting "loss reserves";

(iv) by striking "such insurance" and inserting "such risk-sharing contract"; and

(v) by striking "right" and inserting "rights"; and

(B) in the second sentence—

(i) by inserting "or insured community development financial institution" after "private mortgage insurance company"; and

(ii) by striking "for insurance" and inserting "for risk-sharing";

(6) in subsection (d), by inserting "or insured community development financial institution" after "private mortgage insurance company"; and

(7) by adding at the end the following new subsection:

"(e) INSURED COMMUNITY DEVELOPMENT FINANCIAL INSTITUTION.—For purposes of this section, the term 'insured community development financial institution' means a community development financial institution, as such term is defined in section 103 of Reigle Community Development and Regulatory Improvement Act of 1994 (12 U.S.C. 4702) that is an insured depository institution (as such term is defined in section 3 of the Federal Deposit Insurance Act (12 U.S.C. 1813)) or an insured credit union (as such term is defined in section 101 of the Federal Credit Union Act (12 U.S.C. 1752)).".

[¶ 7085] ACT SEC. 144. PREVENTION AND TREATMENT OF SUBSTANCE ABUSE; SERVICES PROVIDED THROUGH RELIGIOUS ORGANIZATIONS.

Title V of the Public Health Service Act (42 U.S.C. 290aa et seq.) is amended by adding at the end the following part:

"PART G—SERVICES PROVIDED THROUGH RELIGIOUS ORGANIZATIONS

"SEC. 581. APPLICABILITY TO DESIGNATED PROGRAMS.

"(a) DESIGNATED PROGRAMS.—Subject to subsection (b), this part applies to discretionary and formula grant programs administered by the Substance Abuse and Mental Health Services Administration that make awards of financial assistance to public or private entities for the purpose of carrying out activities to prevent or treat substance abuse (in this part referred to as a 'designated program'). Designated programs include the program under subpart II of part B of title XIX (relating to formula grants to the States).

"(b) LIMITATION.—This part does not apply to any award of financial assistance under a designated program for a purpose other than the purpose specified in subsection (a).

"(c) DEFINITIONS.—For purposes of this part (and subject to subsection (b)):

"(1) The term 'designated program' has the meaning given such term in subsection (a).

"(2) The term 'financial assistance' means a grant, cooperative agreement, or contract.

"(3) The term 'program beneficiary' means an individual who receives program services.

"(4) The term 'program participant' means a public or private entity that has received financial assistance under a designated program.

"(5) The term 'program services' means treatment for substance abuse, or preventive services regarding such abuse, provided pursuant to an award of financial assistance under a designated program.

"(6) The term 'religious organization' means a nonprofit religious organization.

"SEC. 582. RELIGIOUS ORGANIZATIONS AS PROGRAM PARTICIPANTS.

"(a) IN GENERAL.—Notwithstanding any other provision of law, a religious organization, on the same basis as any other nonprofit private provider—

"(1) may receive financial assistance under a designated program; and

"(2) may be a provider of services under a designated program.

"(b) RELIGIOUS ORGANIZATIONS.—The purpose of this section is to allow religious organizations to be program participants on the same basis as any other nonprofit private provider without impairing the religious character of such organizations, and without diminishing the religious freedom of program beneficiaries.

"(c) NONDISCRIMINATION AGAINST RELIGIOUS ORGANIZATIONS.—

"(1) ELIGIBILITY AS PROGRAM PARTICIPANTS.—Religious organizations are eligible to be program participants on the same basis as any other nonprofit private organization as long as the programs are implemented consistent with the Establishment Clause and Free Exercise Clause of the First Amendment to the United States Constitution. Nothing in this Act shall be construed to restrict the ability of the Federal Government, or a State or local government receiving funds under such programs, to apply to religious organizations the same eligibility conditions in designated programs as are applied to any other nonprofit private organization.

"(2) NONDISCRIMINATION.—Neither the Federal Government nor a State or local government receiving funds under designated programs shall discriminate against an organization that is or applies to be a program participant on the basis that the organization has a religious character.

"(d) RELIGIOUS CHARACTER AND FREEDOM.—

"(1) RELIGIOUS ORGANIZATIONS.—Except as provided in this section, any religious organization that is a program participant shall retain its independence from Federal, State, and local government, including such organization's control over the definition, development, practice, and expression of its religious beliefs.

¶ 7085 Act Sec. 144

"(2) ADDITIONAL SAFEGUARDS.—Neither the Federal Government nor a State shall require a religious organization to—

"(A) alter its form of internal governance; or

"(B) remove religious art, icons, scripture, or other symbols,

in order to be a program participant.

"(e) EMPLOYMENT PRACTICES.—Nothing in this section shall be construed to modify or affect the provisions of any other Federal or State law or regulation that relates to discrimination in employment. A religious organization's exemption provided under section 702 of the Civil Rights Act of 1964 regarding employment practices shall not be affected by its participation in, or receipt of funds from, a designated program.

"(f) RIGHTS OF PROGRAM BENEFICIARIES.—

"(1) IN GENERAL.—If an individual who is a program beneficiary or a prospective program beneficiary objects to the religious character of a program participant, within a reasonable period of time after the date of such objection such program participant shall refer such individual to, and the appropriate Federal, State, or local government that administers a designated program or is a program participant shall provide to such individual (if otherwise eligible for such services), program services that—

"(A) are from an alternative provider that is accessible to, and has the capacity to provide such services to, such individual; and

"(B) have a value that is not less than the value of the services that the individual would have received from the program participant to which the individual had such objection.

Upon referring a program beneficiary to an alternative provider, the program participant shall notify the appropriate Federal, State, or local government agency that administers the program of such referral.

"(2) NOTICES.—Program participants, public agencies that refer individuals to designated programs, and the appropriate Federal, State, or local governments that administer designated programs or are program participants shall ensure that notice is provided to program beneficiaries or prospective program beneficiaries of their rights under this section.

"(3) ADDITIONAL REQUIREMENTS.—A program participant making a referral pursuant to paragraph (1) shall—

"(A) prior to making such referral, consider any list that the State or local government makes available of entities in the geographic area that provide program services; and

"(B) ensure that the individual makes contact with the alternative provider to which the individual is referred.

"(4) NONDISCRIMINATION.—A religious organization that is a program participant shall not in providing program services or engaging in outreach activities under designated programs discriminate against a program beneficiary or prospective program beneficiary on the basis of religion or religious belief.

"(g) FISCAL ACCOUNTABILITY.—

"(1) IN GENERAL.—Except as provided in paragraph (2), any religious organization that is a program participant shall be subject to the same regulations as other recipients of awards of Federal financial assistance to account, in accordance with generally accepted auditing principles, for the use of the funds provided under such awards.

"(2) LIMITED AUDIT.—With respect to the award involved, a religious organization that is a program participant shall segregate Federal amounts provided under award into a separate account from non-Federal funds. Only the award funds shall be subject to audit by the government.

"(h) COMPLIANCE.—With respect to compliance with this section by an agency, a religious organization may obtain judicial review of agency action in accordance with chapter 7 of title 5, United States Code.

"SEC. 583. LIMITATIONS ON USE OF FUNDS FOR CERTAIN PURPOSES.

"No funds provided under a designated program shall be expended for sectarian worship, instruction, or proselytization.

Act Sec. 144 ¶ 7085

"SEC. 584. EDUCATIONAL REQUIREMENTS FOR PERSONNEL IN DRUG TREATMENT PROGRAMS.

"(a) FINDINGS.—The Congress finds that—

"(1) establishing unduly rigid or uniform educational qualification for counselors and other personnel in drug treatment programs may undermine the effectiveness of such programs; and

"(2) such educational requirements for counselors and other personnel may hinder or prevent the provision of needed drug treatment services.

"(b) NONDISCRIMINATION.—In determining whether personnel of a program participant that has a record of successful drug treatment for the preceding three years have satisfied State or local requirements for education and training, a State or local government shall not discriminate against education and training provided to such personnel by a religious organization, so long as such education and training includes basic content substantially equivalent to the content provided by nonreligious organizations that the State or local government would credit for purposes of determining whether the relevant requirements have been satisfied.".

PART II—ADVISORY COUNCIL ON COMMUNITY RENEWAL

[¶ 7090] ACT SEC. 151. SHORT TITLE.

This part may be cited as the "Advisory Council on Community Renewal Act".

[¶ 7095] ACT SEC. 152. ESTABLISHMENT.

There is established an advisory council to be known as the "Advisory Council on Community Renewal" (in this part referred to as the "Advisory Council").

[¶ 7100] ACT SEC. 153. DUTIES OF ADVISORY COUNCIL.

The Advisory Council shall advise the Secretary of Housing and Urban Development (in this part referred to as the "Secretary") on the designation of renewal communities pursuant to the amendment made by section 101 and on the exercise of any other authority granted to the Secretary pursuant to the amendments made by this title.

[¶ 7105] ACT SEC. 154. MEMBERSHIP.

(a) NUMBER AND APPOINTMENT.—The Advisory Council shall be composed of 7 members appointed by the Secretary.

(b) CHAIRPERSON.—The Chairperson of the Advisory Council (in this part referred to as the "Chairperson") shall be designated by the Secretary at the time of the appointment.

(c) TERMS.—Each member shall be appointed for the life of the Advisory Council.

(d) BASIC PAY.—

(1) CHAIRPERSON.—The Chairperson shall be paid at a rate equal to the daily rate of basic pay for level III of the Executive Schedule for each day (including travel time) during which the Chairperson is engaged in the actual performance of duties vested in the Advisory Council.

(2) OTHER MEMBERS.—Members other than the Chairperson shall each be paid at a rate equal to the daily rate of basic pay for level IV of the Executive Schedule for each day (including travel time) during which they are engaged in the actual performance of duties vested in the Advisory Council.

(e) TRAVEL EXPENSES.—Each member shall receive travel expenses, including per diem in lieu of subsistence, in accordance with applicable provisions under subchapter I of chapter 57 of title 5, United States Code.

(f) QUORUM.—Four members of the Advisory Council shall constitute a quorum but a lesser number may hold hearings.

(g) MEETINGS.—The Advisory Council shall meet at the call of the Secretary or the Chairperson.

[¶ 7110] ACT SEC. 155. POWERS OF ADVISORY COUNCIL.

(a) HEARINGS AND SESSIONS.—The Advisory Council may, for the purpose of carrying out this part, hold hearings, sit and act at times and places, take testimony, and receive evidence as the Advisory Council considers appropriate. The Advisory Council may administer oaths or affirmations to witnesses appearing before it.

(b) POWERS OF MEMBERS AND AGENTS.—Any member or agent of the Advisory Council may, if authorized by the Advisory Council, take any action which the Advisory Council is authorized to take by this section.

(c) OBTAINING OFFICIAL DATA.—The Advisory Council may secure directly from any department or agency of the United States information necessary to enable it to carry out this part. Upon request of the Chairperson of the Advisory Council, the head of that department or agency shall furnish that information to the Advisory Council.

[¶ 7115] ACT SEC. 156. REPORTS.

(a) ANNUAL REPORTS.—The Advisory Council shall submit to the Secretary an annual report for each fiscal year.

(b) INTERIM REPORTS.—The Advisory Council may submit to the Secretary such interim reports as the Advisory Council considers appropriate.

(c) FINAL REPORT.—The Advisory Council shall transmit a final report to the Secretary not later September 30, 2003. The final report shall contain a detailed statement of the findings and conclusions of the Advisory Council, together with any recommendations for legislative or administrative action that the Advisory Council considers appropriate.

[¶ 7120] ACT SEC. 157. TERMINATION.

(a) IN GENERAL.—The Advisory Council shall terminate 30 days after submitting its final report under section 156(c).

(b) EXTENSION.—Notwithstanding subsection (a), the Secretary may postpone the termination of the Advisory Council for a period not to exceed 3 years after the Advisory Council submits its final report under section 156(c).

[¶ 7125] ACT SEC. 158. APPLICABILITY OF FEDERAL ADVISORY COMMITTEE ACT.

The Federal Advisory Committee Act (5 U.S.C. App.) shall not apply to the Advisory Council.

[¶ 7130] ACT SEC. 159. RESOURCES.

The Secretary shall provide to the Advisory Council appropriate resources so that the Advisory Council may carry out its duties and fuctions under this part.

[¶ 7135] ACT SEC. 160. EFFECTIVE DATE.

This part shall be effective 30 days after the date of its enactment.

* * *

TITLE III—ADMINISTRATIVE AND TECHNICAL PROVISIONS

Subtitle A—Administrative Provisions

[¶ 7140] ACT SEC. 301. EXEMPTION OF CERTAIN REPORTING REQUIREMENTS.

Section 3003(a)(1) of the Federal Reports Elimination and Sunset Act of 1995 (31 U.S.C. 1113 note) shall not apply to any report required to be submitted under any of the following provisions of law:

(1) Section 13031(f) of the Consolidated Omnibus Budget Reconciliation Act of 1985 (19 U.S.C. 58c(f)).

(2) Section 16(c) of the Foreign Trade Zones Act (19 U.S.C. 81p(c)).

(3) The following provisions of the Tariff Act of 1930:

(A) Section 330(c)(1) (19 U.S.C. 1330(c)(1)).

(B) Section 607(c) (19 U.S.C. 1607(c)).

(4) Section 5 of the International Coffee Agreement Act of 1980 (19 U.S.C. 1356n).

(5) Section 351(a)(2) of the Trade Expansion Act of 1962 (19 U.S.C. 1981(a)(2)).

(6) Section 502 of the Automotive Products Trade Act of 1965 (19 U.S.C. 2032).

(7) Section 3131 of the Customs Enforcement Act of 1986 (19 U.S.C. 2081).

(8) The following provisions of the Trade Act of 1974 (19 U.S.C. 2101 et seq.):

(A) Section 102(b)(4)(A)(ii)(I) (19 U.S.C. 2112(b)(4)(A)(ii)(I)).

(B) Section 102(e)(1) (19 U.S.C. 2112(e)(1)).

(C) Section 102(e)(2) (19 U.S.C. 2112(e)(2)).

(D) Section 104(d) (19 U.S.C. 2114(d)).

(E) Section 125(e) (19 U.S.C. 2135(e)).

(F) Section 135(e)(1) (19 U.S.C. 2155(e)(1)).

(G) Section 141(c) (19 U.S.C. 2171(c)).

(H) Section 162 (19 U.S.C. 2212).

(I) Section 163(b) (19 U.S.C. 2213(b)).

(J) Section 163(c) (19 U.S.C. 2213(c)).

(K) Section 203(b) (19 U.S.C. 2253(b)).

(L) Section 302(b)(2)(C) (19 U.S.C. 2412(b)(2)(C)).

(M) Section 303 (19 U.S.C. 2413).

(N) Section 309 (19 U.S.C. 2419).

(O) Section 407(a) (19 U.S.C. 2437(a)).

(P) Section 502(f) (19 U.S.C. 2462(f)).

(Q) Section 504 (19 U.S.C. 2464).

(9) The following provisions of the Trade Agreements Act of 1979 (19 U.S.C. 2501 et seq.):

(A) Section 2(b) (19 U.S.C. 2503(b)).

(B) Section 3(c) (19 U.S.C. 2504(c)).

(C) Section 305(c) (19 U.S.C. 2515(c)).

(10) Section 303(g)(1) of the Convention on Cultural Property Implementation Act (19 U.S.C. 2602(g)(1)).

(11) The following provisions of the Caribbean Basin Economic Recovery Act (19 U.S.C. 2701 et seq.):

(A) Section 212(a)(1)(A) (19 U.S.C. 2702(a)(1)(A)).

(B) Section 212(a)(2) (19 U.S.C. 2702(a)(2)).

(12) The following provisions of the Omnibus Trade and Competitiveness Act of 1988 (19 U.S.C. 2901 et seq.):

(A) Section 1102 (19 U.S.C. 2902).

(B) Section 1103 (19 U.S.C. 2903).

(C) Section 1206(b) (19 U.S.C. 3006(b)).

(13) Section 123(a) of the Customs and Trade Act of 1990 (Public Law 101-382) (19 U.S.C. 2083).

(14) Section 243(b)(2) of the Caribbean Basin Economic Recovery Expansion Act of 1990 (Public Law 101-382).

(15) The following provisions of the Internal Revenue Code of 1986:

(A) Section 6103(p)(5).

(B) Section 7608.

(C) Section 7802(f)(3).

(D) Section 8022(3).

(E) Section 9602(a).

(16) The following provisions relating to the revenue laws of the United States:

(A) Section 1552(c) of the Tax Reform Act of 1986 (100 Stat. 2753).

(B) Section 231 of the Deficit Reduction Act of 1984 (26 U.S.C. 801 note).

(C) Section 208 of the Tax Treatment Extension Act of 1977 (26 U.S.C. 911 note).

(D) Section 7105 of the Technical and Miscellaneous Revenue Act of 1988 (45 U.S.C. 369).

(17) Section 4008 of the Employee Retirement Income Security Act of 1974 (29 U.S.C. 1308).

(18) Section 426 of the Black Lung Benefits Act (30 U.S.C. 936(b)).

(19) Section 7502(g) of title 31, United States Code.

(20) The following provisions of the Social Security Act:

    (A) Section 215(i)(2)(C)(i) (42 U.S.C. 415(i)(2)(C)(i)).

    (B) Section 221(i)(2) (42 U.S.C. 421(i)(2)).

    (C) Section 221(i)(3) (42 U.S.C. 421(i)(3)).

    (D) Section 233(e)(1) (42 U.S.C. 433(e)(1)).

    (E) Section 452(a)(10) (42 U.S.C. 652(a)(10)).

    (F) Section 452(g)(3)(B) (42 U.S.C. 652(g)(3)(B)).

    (G) Section 506(a)(1) (42 U.S.C. 706(a)).

    (H) Section 908 (42 U.S.C. 1108).

    (I) Section 1114(f) (42 U.S.C. 1314(f)).

    (J) Section 1120 (42 U.S.C. 1320).

    (K) Section 1161 (42 U.S.C. 1320c-10).

    (L) Section 1875(b) (42 U.S.C. 1395ll(b)).

    (M) Section 1881 (42 U.S.C. 1395rr).

    (N) Section 1882 (42 U.S.C. 1395ss(f)(2)).

(21) Section 104(b) of the Social Security Independence and Program Improvements Act of 1994 (42 USC 904 note).

(22) Section 10 of the Railroad Retirement Act of 1937 (45 U.S.C. 231f).

(23) The following provisions of the Railroad Retirement Act of 1974:

    (A) Section 22(a)(1) (45 U.S.C. 231u(a)(1)).

    (B) Section 22(b)(1) (45 U.S.C. 231u(b)(1)).

(24) Section 502 of the Railroad Retirement Solvency Act of 1983 (45 U.S.C. 231f-1).

(25) Section 47121(c) of title 49, United States Code.

(26) The following provisions of the Omnibus Budget Reconciliation Act of 1987 (Public Law 100-203; 101 Stat. 1330-182):

    (A) Section 4007(c)(4) (42 U.S.C. 1395ww note).

    (B) Section 4079 (42 U.S.C. 1395mm note).

    (C) Section 4205 (42 U.S.C. 1395i-3 note).

    (D) Section 4215 (42 U.S.C. 1396r note).

(27) The following provisions of the Inspector General Act of 1978 (Public Law 95-452).

    (A) Section 5(b).

    (B) Section 5(d).

(28) The following provisions of the Public Health Service Act:

    (A) In section 308(a) (42 U.S.C. 242m(a)), subparagraphs (A), (B), (C), and (D) of paragraph (1).

    (B) Section 403 (42 U.S.C. 283).

(29) Section 404 of the Health Services and Centers Amendments of 1978 (42 U.S.C. 242p) (Public Law 95-626).

(30) The following provisions of the Older Americans Act of 1965:

    (A) Section 206(d) (42 U.S.C. 3017(d)).

    (B) Section 207 (42 U.S.C. 3018).

(31) Section 308 of the Age Discrimination Act of 1975 (42 U.S.C. 6106a(b)).

(32) Section 509(c)(3) of the Americans with Disabilities Act Of 1990 (42 U.S.C. 12209(c)(3)).

(33) Section 4207(f) of the Omnibus Budget Reconciliation Act of 1990 (42 U.S.C. 1395b-1 note).

[CCH Explanation at ¶ 320. Committee Reports at ¶ 10,255.]

[¶ 7145] ACT SEC. 302. EXTENSION OF DEADLINES FOR IRS COMPLIANCE WITH CERTAIN NOTICE REQUIREMENTS.

(a) ANNUAL INSTALLMENT AGREEMENT NOTICE.—Section 3506 of the Internal Revenue Service Restructuring and Reform Act of 1998 is amended by striking "July 1, 2000" and inserting "September 1, 2001".

● ● *IRS RESTRUCTURING ACT OF 1998 ACT SEC. 3506 AS AMENDED* ———————

ACT SEC. 3506. STATEMENTS REGARDING INSTALLMENT AGREEMENTS.

The Secretary of the Treasury or the Secretary's delegate shall, beginning not later than *September 1, 2001*, provide each taxpayer who has an installment agreement in effect under section 6159 of the Internal Revenue Code of 1986 an annual statement setting forth the initial balance at the beginning of the year, the payments made during the year, and the remaining balance as of the end of the year.

(b) NOTICE REQUIREMENTS RELATING TO COMPUTATION OF PENALTY.—Subsection (c) of section 3306 of the Internal Revenue Service Restructuring and Reform Act of 1998 is amended—

(1) by striking "December 31, 2000" and inserting "June 30, 2001", and

(2) by adding at the end the following: "In the case of any notice of penalty issued after June 30, 2001, and before July 1, 2003, the requirements of section 6751(a) of the Internal Revenue Code of 1986 shall be treated as met if such notice contains a telephone number at which the taxpayer can request a copy of the taxpayer's assessment and payment history with respect to such penalty.".

● ● *IRS RESTRUCTURING ACT OF 1998 ACT SEC. 3306(c) AS AMENDED* ———————

ACT SEC. 3306. PROCEDURAL REQUIREMENTS FOR IMPOSITION OF PENALTIES AND ADDITIONAL TAX.

* * *

(c) EFFECTIVE DATE.—*The amendments made by this section shall apply to notices issued, and penalties assessed, after June 30, 2000. In the case of any notice of penalty issued after June 30, 2001, and before July 1, 2003, the requirements of section 6751(a) of the Internal Revenue Code of 1986 shall be treated as met if such notice contains a telephone number at which the taxpayer can request a copy of the taxpayer's assessment and payment history with respect to such penalty.*

(c) NOTICE REQUIREMENTS RELATING TO INTEREST IMPOSED.—Subsection (c) of section 3308 of the Internal Revenue Service Restructuring and Reform Act of 1998 is amended—

(1) by striking "December 31, 2000" and inserting "June 30, 2001", and

(2) by adding at the end the following: "In the case of any notice issued after June 30, 2001, and before July 1, 2003, to which section 6631 of the Internal Revenue Code of 1986 applies, the requirements of section 6631 of such Code shall be treated as met if such notice contains a telephone number at which the taxpayer can request a copy of the taxpayer's payment history relating to interest amounts included in such notice.".

● ● *IRS RESTRUCTURING ACT OF 1998 ACT SEC. 3308(c) AS AMENDED* ———————

ACT SEC. 3308. NOTICE OF INTEREST CHARGES.

* * *

(c) EFFECTIVE DATE.—*The amendments made by this section shall apply to notices issued after June 30, 2001. In the case of any notice issued after June 30, 2001, and before July 1, 2003, to which section 6631 of the Internal Revenue Code of 1986 applies, the requirements of section 6631 of such Code shall be treated as met if such notice contains a telephone number at which the taxpayer can request a copy of the taxpayer's payment history relating to interest amounts included in such notice.*

---

* * *

[CCH Explanation at ¶ 325. Committee Reports at ¶ 10,260.]

[¶ 7150] ACT SEC. 307. AMENDMENTS TO STATUTES REFERENCING YIELD ON 52-WEEK TREASURY BILLS.

(a) AMENDMENT TO THE ACT OF FEBRUARY 26, 1931.—Section 6 of the Act of February 26, 1931 (40 U.S.C. 258e-1) (relating to the interest rate on compensation owed for takings of property) is amended—

(1) in paragraph (1), by striking "the coupon issue yield equivalent (as determined by the Secretary of the Treasury) of the average accepted auction price for the last auction of 52 week United States Treasury bills settled immediately before" and inserting "the weekly average 1-year constant maturity Treasury yield, as published by the Board of Governors of the Federal Reserve System, for the calendar week preceding"; and

(2) in paragraph (2), by striking "the coupon issue yield equivalent (as determined by the Secretary of the Treasury) of the average accepted auction price for the last auction of 52 week United States Treasury bills settled immediately before" and inserting "the weekly average 1-year constant maturity Treasury yield, as published by the Board of Governors of the Federal Reserve System, for the calendar week preceding".

(b) AMENDMENT TO TITLE 18, UNITED STATES CODE.—Section 3612(f)(2)(B) of title 18, United States Code (relating to the interest rate on unpaid criminal fines and penalties of more than $2,500) is amended by striking "the coupon issue yield equivalent (as determined by the Secretary of the Treasury) of the average accepted auction price for the last auction of fifty-two week United States Treasury bills settled before" and inserting 'the weekly average 1-year constant maturity Treasury yield, as published by the Board of Governors of the Federal Reserve System, for the calendar week preceding.".

* * *

(d) AMENDMENTS TO TITLE 28, UNITED STATES CODE.—

(1) AMENDMENT TO SECTION 1961.—Section 1961(a) of title 28, United States Code (relating to the interest rate on money judgments in civil cases recovered in Federal district court) is amended by striking "the coupon issue yield equivalent (as determined by the Secretary of the Treasury) of the average accepted auction price for the last auction of fifty-two week United States Treasury bills settled immediately prior to" and inserting "the weekly average 1-year constant maturity Treasury yield, as published by the Board of Governors of the Federal Reserve System, for the calendar week preceding.".

(2) AMENDMENT TO SECTION 2516.—Section 2516(b) of title 28, United States Code (relating to the interest rate on a judgment against the United States affirmed by the Supreme Court after review on petition of the United States) is amended by striking "the coupon issue yield equivalent (as determined by the Secretary of the Treasury) of the average accepted auction price for the last auction of fifty-two week United States Treasury bills settled immediately before" and inserting "the weekly average 1-year constant maturity Treasury yield, as published by the Board of Governors of the Federal Reserve System, for the calendar week preceding".

[CCH Explanation at ¶ 375. Committee Reports at ¶ 10,285.]

[¶ 7155] ACT SEC. 308. ADJUSTMENTS FOR CONSUMER PRICE INDEX ERROR.

(a) DETERMINATIONS BY OMB.—As soon as practicable after the date of the enactment of this Act, the Director of the Office of Management and Budget shall determine with respect to each applicable Federal benefit program whether the CPI computation error for 1999 has or will result in a shortfall in payments to beneficiaries under such program (as compared to payments that would have been made if the error had not occurred). As soon as practicable after the date of the enactment of this Act, but not later than 60 days after such date, the Director shall direct the head of the Federal agency which administers such program to make a payment or payments that, insofar as the Director finds practicable and feasible—

(1) are targeted to the amount of the shortfall experienced by individual beneficiaries, and

(2) compensate for the shortfall.

(b) COORDINATION WITH FEDERAL AGENCIES.—As soon as practicable after the date of the enactment of this Act, each Federal agency that administers an applicable Federal benefit program shall, in accordance with such guidelines as are issued by the Director pursuant to this section, make an initial determination of whether, and the extent to which, the CPI computation error for 1999 has or will result in a shortfall in payments to beneficiaries of an applicable Federal benefit program administered by such agency. Not later than 30 days after such date, the head of such agency shall submit a report to the Director and to each House of the Congress of such determination, together with a complete description of the nature of the shortfall.

(c) IMPLEMENTATION PURSUANT TO AGENCY REPORTS.—Upon receipt of the report submitted by a Federal agency pursuant to subsection (b), the Director shall review the initial determination of the agency, the agency's description of the nature of the shortfall, and the compensation payments proposed by the agency. Prior to directing payment of such payments pursuant to subsection (a), the Director shall make appropriate adjustments (if any) in the compensation payments proposed by the agency that the Director determines are necessary to comply with the requirements of subsection (a) and transmit to the agency a summary report of the review, indicating any adjustments made by the Director. The agency shall make the compensation payments as directed by the Director pursuant to subsection (a) in accordance with the Director's summary report.

(d) INCOME DISREGARD UNDER FEDERAL MEANS-TESTED BENEFIT PROGRAMS.—A payment made under this section to compensate for a shortfall in benefits shall, in accordance with guidelines issued by the Director pursuant to this section, be disregarded in determining income under title VIII of the Social Security Act or any applicable Federal benefit program that is means-tested.

(e) FUNDING.—Funds otherwise available under each applicable Federal benefit program for making benefit payments under such program are hereby made available for making compensation payments under this section in connection with such program.

(f) NO JUDICIAL REVIEW.—No action taken pursuant to this section shall be subject to judicial review.

(g) DIRECTOR'S REPORT.—Not later than April 1, 2001, the Director shall submit to each House of the Congress a report on the activities performed by the Director pursuant to this section.

(h) DEFINITIONS.—For purposes of this section:

(1) APPLICABLE FEDERAL BENEFIT PROGRAM.—The term "applicable Federal benefit program" means any program of the Government of the United States providing for regular or periodic payments or cash assistance paid directly to individual beneficiaries, as determined by the Director of the Office of Management and Budget.

(2) FEDERAL AGENCY.—The term "Federal agency" means a department, agency, or instrumentality of the Government of the United States.

(3) CPI COMPUTATION ERROR FOR 1999.—The term "CPI computation error for 1999" means the error in the computation of the Consumer Price Index announced by the Bureau of Labor Statistics on September 28, 2000.

(i) TAX PROVISIONS.—In the case of taxable years (and other periods) beginning after December 31, 2000, if any Consumer Price Index (as defined in section 1(f)(5) of the Internal Revenue Code of 1986) reflects the CPI computation error for 1999—

(1) the correct amount of such Index shall (in such manner and to such extent as the Secretary of the Treasury determines to be appropriate) be taken into account for purposes of such Code, and

(2) tables prescribed under section 1(f) of such Code to reflect such correct amount shall apply in lieu of any tables that were prescribed based on the erroneous amount.

[CCH Explanation at ¶ 380. Committee Reports at ¶ 10,290.]

[¶ 7160] ACT SEC. 309. PREVENTION OF DUPLICATION OF LOSS THROUGH ASSUMPTION OF LIABILITIES GIVING RISE TO A DEDUCTION.

* * *

(c) APPLICATION OF COMPARABLE RULES TO PARTNERSHIPS AND S CORPORATIONS.—The Secretary of the Treasury or his delegate—

(1) shall prescribe rules which provide appropriate adjustments under subchapter K of chapter 1 of the Internal Revenue Code of 1986 to prevent the acceleration or duplication of losses through the assumption of (or transfer of assets subject to) liabilities described in section 358(h)(3) of such Code (as added by subsection (a)) in transactions involving partnerships, and

(2) may prescribe rules which provide appropriate adjustments under subchapter S of chapter 1 of such Code in transactions described in paragraph (1) involving S corporations rather than partnerships.

* * *

[CCH Explanation at ¶ 265. Committee Reports at ¶ 10,295.]

[¶ 7165] CODE SEC. 310. DISCLOSURE OF CERTAIN INFORMATION TO CONGRESSIONAL BUDGET OFFICE.

* * *

(b) CONFIDENTIALITY OF RECORDS.—

(1) IN GENERAL.—Section 203 of the Congressional Budget Act of 1974 (2 U.S.C. 603) is amended by adding at the end the following:

"(e) LEVEL OF CONFIDENTIALITY.—With respect to information, data, estimates, and statistics obtained under sections 201(d) and 201(e), the Director shall maintain the same level of confidentiality as is required by law of the department, agency, establishment, or regulatory agency or commission from which it is obtained. Officers and employees of the Congressional Budget Office shall be subject to the same statutory penalties for unauthorized disclosure or use as officers or employees of the department, agency, establishment, or regulatory agency or commission from which it is obtained.".

(2) CONFORMING AMENDMENT.—Subsection (a) of section 203 of such Act is amended by striking "subsections (c) and (d)" and inserting "subsections (c), (d), and (e)".

[CCH Explanation at ¶ 307. Committee Reports at ¶ 10,300.]

Subtitle B—Technical Corrections

[¶ 7170] ACT SEC. 311. AMENDMENTS RELATED TO TICKET TO WORK AND WORK INCENTIVES IMPROVEMENT ACT OF 1999.

* * *

(c) CLARIFICATION RELATED TO SECTION 538 OF THE ACT.—The reference to section 332(b)(1) of the Internal Revenue Code of 1986 in Treasury Regulation section 1.1502-34 shall be deemed to include a reference to section 732(f) of such Code.

* * *

[CCH Explanation at ¶ 410. Committee Reports at ¶ 10,310.]

[¶ 7175] CODE SEC. 312. AMENDMENTS RELATED TO TAX AND TRADE RELIEF EXTENSION ACT OF 1998.

* * *

(b) AMENDMENT RELATED TO SECTION 4003 OF THE ACT.—Subsection (b) of section 4003 of the Tax and Trade Relief Extension Act of 1998 is amended by inserting "(7)(A)(i)(II)," after "(5)(A)(ii)(I),".

● ● *TAX AND TRADE RELIEF ACT OF 1998 ACT SEC. 4003(b) AS AMENDED* ———

ACT SEC. 4003. AMENDMENTS RELATED TO TAXPAYER RELIEF ACT OF 1997.

* * *

(b) PROVISION RELATED TO SECTION 311 OF 1997 ACT.—In the case of any capital gain distribution made after 1997 by a trust to which section 664 of the 1986 Code applies with respect to amounts properly taken into account by such trust during 1997, paragraphs (5)(A)(i)(I), (5)(A)(ii)(I), *(7)(A)(i)(II)*, and (13)(A) of section 1(h) of the 1986 Code (as in effect for taxable years ending on December 31, 1997) shall not apply.

---

* * *

[CCH Explanation at ¶ 270. Committee Reports at ¶ 10,315.]

[¶ 7180] ACT SEC. 314. AMENDMENTS RELATED TO TAXPAYER RELIEF ACT OF 1997.

* * *

(c) AMENDMENT TO SECTION 311 OF THE ACT.—Paragraph (3) of section 311(e) of the Taxpayer Relief Act of 1997 (relating to election to recognize gain on assets held on January 1, 2001) is amended by adding at the end the following new sentence: "Such an election shall not apply to any asset which is disposed of (in a transaction in which gain or loss is recognized in whole or in part) before the close of the 1-year period beginning on the date that the asset would have been treated as sold under such election."

Act Sec. 314(c)   ¶ 7180

● ● *TAXPAYER RELIEF ACT OF 1997 ACT SEC. 311(e)(3) AS AMENDED* ─────

ACT SEC. 311. MAXIMUM CAPITAL GAINS RATE FOR INDIVIDUALS.

* * *

(e) Election To Recognize Gain on Assets Held on January 1, 2001.

* * *

(3) Election.—An election under paragraph (1) shall be made in such manner as the Secretary of the Treasury or his delegate may prescribe and shall specify the assets for which such election is made. Such an election, once made with respect to any asset, shall be irrevocable. *Such an election shall not apply to any asset which is disposed of (in a transaction in which gain or loss is recognized in whole or in part) before the close of the 1-year period beginning on the date that the asset would have been treated as sold under such election.*

* * *

[CCH Explanation at ¶ 275. Committee Reports at ¶ 10,325.]

[¶ 7185] ACT SEC. 315. AMENDMENTS RELATED TO BALANCED BUDGET ACT OF 1997.

(a) Amendments Related to Section 9302 of the Act.—

(1) Paragraph (1) of section 9302(j) of the Balanced Budget Act of 1997 is amended by striking "tobacco products and cigarette papers and tubes" and inserting "cigarettes".

● ● *BALANCED BUDGET ACT OF 1997 ACT SEC. 9302(j)(1) AS AMENDED* ─────

ACT SEC. 9302. INCREASE IN EXCISE TAXES ON TOBACCO PRODUCTS.

* * *

(j) Floor Stocks Taxes.—

(1) Imposition of Tax.—On *cigarettes* manufactured in or imported into the United States which are removed before any tax increase date, and held on such date for sale by any person, there is hereby imposed a tax in an amount equal to the excess of—

(A) the tax which would be imposed under section 5701 of the Internal Revenue Code of 1986 on the article if the article had been removed on such date, over

(B) the prior tax (if any) imposed under section 5701 of such Code on such article.

* * *

[CCH Explanation at ¶ 293. Committee Reports at ¶ 10,330.]

[¶ 7190] ACT SEC. 319. CLERICAL CHANGES.

* * *

(23) * * *

(B) Section 6010(o)(4)(C) of the Internal Revenue Service Restructuring and Reform Act of 1998 is amended by striking "inserting 'or', and by adding at the end" and inserting "inserting ', or', and by adding after subparagraph (Z)".

● ● *IRS RESTRUCTURING ACT OF 1998 ACT SEC. 6010(o)(4)(C) AS AMENDED* ——
ACT SEC. 6010. AMENDMENTS RELATED TO TITLE X OF 1997 ACT.

* * *

(o) Amendments Related to Section 1084 of 1997 Act.—

* * *

(4) * * *

* * *

(C) Paragraph (2) of section 6724(d) of the 1986 Code is amended by striking "or" at the end of subparagraph (Y), by striking the period at the end of subparagraph (Z) and *inserting ", or", and by adding after subparagraph (Z)* the following new subparagraph:

"(AA) section 264(f)(5)(A)(iv) (relating to reporting with respect to certain life insurance and annuity contracts).".

* * *

TITLE IV—TAX TREATMENT OF SECURITIES FUTURES CONTRACTS

[¶ 7195] ACT SEC. 401. TAX TREATMENT OF SECURITIES FUTURES CONTRACTS.

* * *

(g) Treatment Under Section 1256.—

* * *

(4) The Secretary of the Treasury or his delegate shall make the determinations under section 1256(g)(9)(B) of the Internal Revenue Code of 1986, as added by this Act, not later than July 1, 2001.

* * *

[CCH Explanation at ¶ 260. Committee Reports at ¶ 10,355.]

Committee Reports

FSC Repeal and Extraterritorial Income Exclusion Act of 2000

Introduction

[¶ 10,001]

The FSC Repeal and Extraterritorial Income Exclusion Act of 2000 (P.L. 106-519) was introduced in the House on July 27, 2000, as H.R. 4986. The bill was favorably reported by the House Ways and Means Committee on September 13, 2000 (H.R. REP. NO. 106-845). H.R. 4986 was then passed by the House under suspension of rules by a 2/3 vote on September 13, 2000.

An amendment in the nature of a substitute for H.R. 4986 was favorably reported by the Senate Finance Committee on September 20, 2000 (S. REP. NO. 106-416). H.R. 4986 was then incorporated as Title I of the Taxpayer Relief Act of 2000 (H.R. 5542) by the House Ways and Means Committee. H.R. 5542 was one of five bills introduced on October 25, 2000, and incorporated by reference in the conference agreement for H.R. 2614, the Certified Development Company Program Improvements Bill of 2000. A conference report on H.R. 2614 was filed in the House on October 26, 2000 (H.R. CONF. REP. NO. 106-1004), and the House agreed to the conference report on October 26, 2000.

On November 1, 2000, the Senate approved H.R. 4986 as a stand-alone bill. The provisions of this bill, as amended on the Senate floor, were incorporated in the Senate-passed version on November 1, 2000. The House agreed to the Senate-passed version on November 14, 2000. H.R. 4986 was signed by the President on November 15, 2000.

H.R. 4986 was passed with a House Committee Report (H.R. REP. NO. 106-845), but without a controlling conference committee report. However, the provisions of H.R. 4986 are substantially identical to provisions included in H.R. 2614. Consequently, excerpts from the committee reports relating to H.R. 2614 are reproduced below to provide the reader with more legislative background on the newly enacted provisions.

This section includes the pertinent texts of the committee reports that explain the changes enacted in the FSC Repeal and Extraterritorial Income Exclusion Act of 2000. The following material is the official wording of the relevant House and Conference Committee Reports. Headings have been added for convenience in locating the committee reports. Any omission of text is indicated by asterisks (* * *). References are to the following official reports:

● The FSC Repeal and Extraterritorial Income Exclusion Act of 2000 (H.R. 4986) House Ways and Means Committee Report, reported on September 13, 2000, is referred to as **House Committee Report (H.R. REP. NO. 106-845).**

● The Conference Committee Report on the Taxpayer Relief Act of 2000, as released on October 26, 2000, and issued as CCH Special 1, STANDARD FEDERAL TAX REPORTS, Issue No. 50 (Part 2), November 30, 2000, is referred to as **Conference Committee Report (H.R. CONF. REP. NO. 106-1004).**

¶ 10,001

[¶ 10,115]   Act Sec. 1 2 3 4 and 5 [Act Sec. 101 102 103 and 104 of H.R. 2614]. Repeal of FSC provisions and exclusion for extraterritorial income

House Committee Report (H.R. REP. NO. 106-845)

[Code Secs. 114, 921, 922, 923, 924, 925, 926, 927, 941, 942 and 943]

Present Law

Summary of U.S. income taxation of foreign persons

Income earned by a foreign corporation from its foreign operations generally is subject to U.S. tax only when such income is distributed to any U.S. persons that hold stock in such corporation. Accordingly, a U.S. person that conducts foreign operations through a foreign corporation generally is subject to U.S. tax on the income from those operations when the income is repatriated to the United States through a dividend distribution to the U.S. person.[5] The income is reported on the U.S. person's tax return for the year the distribution is received, and the United States imposes tax on such income at that time. An indirect foreign tax credit may reduce the U.S. tax imposed on such income.

Foreign sales corporations

The income of an eligible FSC is partially subject to U.S. income tax and partially exempt from U.S. income tax. In addition, a U.S. corporation generally is not subject to U.S. tax on dividends distributed from the FSC out of certain earnings.

A FSC must be located and managed outside the United States, and must perform certain economic processes outside the United States. A FSC is often owned by a U.S. corporation that produces goods in the United States. The U.S. corporation either supplies goods to the FSC for resale abroad or pays the FSC a commission in connection with such sales. The income of the FSC, a portion of which is exempt from U.S. tax under the FSC rules, equals the FSC's gross markup or gross commission income, less the expenses incurred by the FSC. The gross markup or the gross commission is determined according to specified pricing rules.

A FSC generally is not subject to U.S. tax on its exempt foreign trade income. The exempt foreign trade income of a FSC is treated as foreign-source income that is not effectively connected with the conduct of a trade or business within the United States.

Foreign trade income other than exempt foreign trade income generally is treated as U.S.-source income effectively connected with the conduct of a trade or business conducted through a permanent establishment within the United States. Thus, a FSC's income other than exempt foreign trade income generally is subject to U.S. tax currently and is treated as U.S.-source income for purposes of the foreign tax credit limitation.

Foreign trade income of a FSC is defined as the FSC's gross income attributable to foreign trading gross receipts. Foreign trading gross receipts generally are the gross receipts attributable to the following types of transactions: the sale of export property; the lease or rental of export property; services related and subsidiary to such a sale or lease of export property; engineering and architectural services for projects outside the United States; and export management services. Investment income and carrying charges are excluded from the definition of foreign trading gross receipts.

The term "export property" generally means property (1) which is manufactured, produced, grown or extracted in the United States by a person other than a FSC, (2) which is held primarily for sale, lease, or rental in the ordinary course of a trade or business for direct use or consumption outside the United States, and (3) not more than 50 percent of the fair market value of which is attributable to articles imported into the United States. The term "export property" does not include property leased or rented by a FSC for use by any member of a controlled group of which the FSC is a member; patents, copyrights (other than films, tapes, records, similar reproductions, and other than computer software, whether or not patented), and other intangibles; oil or gas (or any primary product thereof); unprocessed softwood timber; or products the export of which is prohibited or curtailed. Export property also excludes property designated by the President as being in short supply.

If export property is sold to a FSC by a related person (or a commission is paid by a related person to a FSC with respect to export property), the income with respect to the export transactions must be allocated between the FSC and the re-

---

[5] A variety of anti-deferral regimes impose current U.S. tax on income earned by a U.S. person through a foreign corporation. The Code sets forth the following anti-deferral regimes: the controlled foreign corporation rules of subpart F (secs. 951-954), the passive foreign investment company rules (secs. 1291-1298), the foreign personal holding company rules (secs. 551-558), the personal holding company rules (secs. 541-547), the accumulated earnings tax rules (secs. 531-537), and the foreign investment company rules (sec. 1246). Detailed rules for coordination among the anti-deferral regimes are provided to prevent a U.S. person from being subject to U.S. tax on the same item of income under multiple regimes.

lated person. The taxable income of the FSC and the taxable income of the related person are computed based upon a transfer price determined under section 482 or under one of two formulas.

The portion of a FSC's foreign trade income that is treated as exempt foreign trade income depends on the pricing rule used to determine the income of the FSC. If the amount of income earned by the FSC is based on section 482 pricing, the exempt foreign trade income generally is 30 percent of the foreign trade income the FSC derives from a transaction. If the income earned by the FSC is determined under one of the two formulas specified in the FSC provisions, the exempt foreign trade income generally is 15/23 of the foreign trade income the FSC derives from the transaction.

A FSC is not required or deemed to make distributions to its shareholders. Actual distributions are treated as being made first out of earnings and profits attributable to foreign trade income, and then out of any other earnings and profits. Any distribution made by a FSC out of earnings and profits attributable to foreign trade income to a foreign shareholder is treated as U.S.-source income that is effectively connected with a business conducted through a permanent establishment of the shareholder within the United States. Thus, the foreign shareholder is subject to U.S. tax on such a distribution.

A U.S. corporation generally is allowed a 100 percent dividends-received deduction for amounts distributed from a FSC out of earnings and profits attributable to foreign trade income. The 100 percent dividends-received deduction is not allowed for nonexempt foreign trade income determined under section 482 pricing.

Reasons for Change

In general

On February 24, 2000, the Appellate Body, over the objections of the United States, upheld the finding of the Panel that had found that the FSC provisions of sections 921 through 927 of the Code constitute a prohibited export subsidy under the WTO Agreement on Subsidies and Countervailing Measures and under the Agreement on Agriculture. The Panel specified that "FSC subsidies must be withdrawn at the latest with effect from 1 October 2000."[6]

The purpose of this legislation is to comply with the recommendations and rulings of the Panel and the Appellate Body, as adopted by the WTO Dispute Settlement Body, in the dispute before the World Trade Organization entitled United States—Tax Treatment for "Foreign Sales Corporations," WT/DS108/R, WT/DS108/AB/R, Report of the Panel, as modified by the Appellate Body, adopted March 20, 2000.

The legislation complies with the Panel and Appellate Body Decisions by repealing the FSC provisions of the Code, thereby eliminating the measures which the Panel and Appellate Body found to be prohibited export subsidies. The legislation makes fundamental adjustments to the Code that move the U.S. tax system in the direction of many European tax systems by incorporating certain of the territorial features of those systems.

Before turning to the details of this legislation, however, the Committee feels compelled to make certain observations regarding the history of the FSC dispute, the actions of the European Union in initiating the dispute, and the decision of the Appellate Body. The origins of this dispute go back many years, and arise, in part, out of certain fundamental differences between tax systems. There are two basic types of income tax systems: (1) a residence-based (or "worldwide") system; and (2) a territorial system. Under a worldwide system, such as that of the United States, all of the income earned by a resident (e.g., a corporation incorporated in one of the fifty states or the District of Columbia) is subject to tax, regardless of where that income is earned. Under a territorial system, such as those of a number of European countries, only income earned within the borders of the taxing jurisdiction is subject to tax. In practice, neither the United States nor the member states of the European Union employ a "pure" territorial system or a "pure" worldwide system, as most countries employ some combination of the two concepts.

It is important to note that each type of system generally uses a different method to avoid double taxation of foreign-source income. Although this is an oversimplification, in a worldwide system, the "credit method" typically is used; that is, a tax credit is provided for taxes paid to foreign governments on income earned abroad. In a territorial system, the "exemption method" is used; that is, income earned abroad is simply not subject to tax. While tax policy arguments can be used to justify the superiority of one method over the other, both methods are accepted internationally, and it also is accepted internationally that a country is free to use either method or both. However, it also is recognized internationally—and, as the Committee understands it, was acknowledged by the European Union in the course of the FSC dispute—that the exemption method tends to result in exports being taxed more favorably than comparable domestic transactions.

Turning to the history of the FSC dispute, in 1971, the United States enacted the Domestic International Sales Corporation ("DISC") legislation, which provided a special tax exemption for exports. The European Communities challenged

---

[6] Report of the Panel at 334.

the DISC in the General Agreement on Tariffs and Trade ("GATT"), alleging that it constituted an export subsidy because it resulted in exports being taxed more favorably than comparable domestic transactions. In response, the United States challenged the tax regimes of Belgium, France and the Netherlands, alleging that the use of the exemption method by those countries constituted an export subsidy because it also resulted in exports being taxed more favorably than comparable domestic transactions. In 1976, a GATT panel ruled against the DISC provisions, but also ruled against the European regimes, finding, as a factual matter, that those regimes did tax exports more favorably than comparable domestic transactions.

Following the issuance of the panel rulings, those rulings languished unadopted as the European Communities refused to accept that their regimes provided export subsidies. The European Communities' criticisms of the panel rulings, however, focused on the panel's legal reasoning, not on the panel's factual findings that the European regimes taxed exports more favorably than comparable domestic transactions. Eventually, the disputes were resolved based on the negotiation of an "Understanding" which was adopted by the GATT Council in 1981. Essentially, this Understanding—elements of which already had been incorporated into the Tokyo Round Subsidies Code—provided that countries did not provide an export subsidy when they refrained from taxing foreign-source income, even if this resulted in exports being taxed more favorably than comparable domestic transactions. The European countries in question interpreted the Understanding as overruling the panel and sanctioning their use of the exemption method. Subsequently, using the principles set forth in the Understanding as a guide, the United States enacted the FSC legislation, the objective being to reap the export-enhancing benefits of the exemption method.

Many years later, the European Union abruptly challenged the FSC provisions in the WTO. Notwithstanding the fact that the FSC provisions were intended to emulate certain elements of a territorial tax system—namely, the use of the exemption method—the Panel and the Appellate Body ruled that the manner in which the United States sought to achieve this objective conflicted with the rules of the WTO Agreement on Subsidies and Countervailing Measures ("SCM Agreement") and the Agreement on Agriculture. However, neither body said that the use of the exemption method itself was an impermissible one, nor did either body rule that a WTO member may not maintain a tax regime that includes features of both worldwide and territorial tax systems. What the Committee is intending to do with this legislation is once again to incorporate elements of a territorial tax system into the U.S.

system of worldwide taxation, this time in a manner which does not conflict with WTO rules.

Turning to the actions of the European Union in this dispute, it is the Committee's understanding that this dispute did not arise out of private sector complaints, but instead was initiated by the European Union primarily as a response to its losses in the so-called "bananas" and "beef" disputes. Indeed, it is the Committee's understanding that during the course of this dispute, European Union officials failed, when asked, to provide a single example of actual commercial harm suffered by a European firm as a result of the FSC provisions. In light of this, the Committee finds the European Union's decision to walk away from the 1981 Understanding deeply troubling and provocative as well as threatening to the international trading system.

Notwithstanding these concerns, the United States has moved quickly to comply with the decisions of the Panel and Appellate Body. With the adoption of this legislation, the United States will have met the short deadline set by the Panel under the pressures and constraints of an election year. More significantly, in order to comply with a decision that significantly affects issues of national tax policy, the United States has made fundamental modifications to its tax structure, including features that are common to many European tax systems. The Committee hopes and expects that the European Union will regard this legislation as a faithful and responsible implementation of the WTO rulings in this dispute, understanding that each WTO member enjoys a sovereign right to decide its own system of taxation within the parameters of its international obligations. The Committee also hopes and expects that the European Union will appreciate the extremely detrimental consequences which a prolongation of this dispute would bring both to our bilateral relations and the successful functioning of the multilateral trading system. The Committee expects the United States to strongly pursue its rights under the WTO, including, as appropriate, the initiation of cases challenging tax systems that exclude certain income from taxation.

The Committee strongly believes that the substantial modification to U.S. tax law provided in this bill is WTO compliant. While the Committee believes it is important for all nations to honor their trade agreements and the obligations those agreements may impart, the Committee also believes it is important that U.S. business interests not be foreclosed from opportunities abroad because of differences in the tax laws in the United States compared to tax laws in other countries. Indeed, the Committee believes that the WTO was not established to conform and restructure tax systems of contracting parties.

Compliance with WTO rulings

In its ruling, the Panel raised the following objections to the FSC provisions of the Code. First, the Panel found that "but for" the existence of the FSC provisions, revenue that otherwise would be fully taxable under the Code enjoyed a lower rate of taxation. Thus, the Panel found the FSC provisions to be a subsidy because partial tax exemptions accorded by the FSC provisions represented, in its view, a forgoing of "government revenue that is otherwise due." Second, the Panel found that the FSC provisions constituted a prohibited export subsidy because only exports receive preferential tax treatment.

The Administration has informed the Committee that the European Union has expressed additional concerns regarding the FSC provisions, even though they were not addressed in the Appellate Body Decision or Panel Decision. Among the European Union's many allegations are that the FSC administrative pricing rules violated the arm's-length pricing provisions of the Subsidies Agreement and that the FSC structure encouraged the use of tax havens.

The Committee believes the approach of H.R. 4986 complies with the Appellate Body and Panel Decisions and modifies the U.S. tax system in a WTO-consistent manner. In addition, the legislation addresses other concerns raised by the European Union that were not decided by the Panel or Appellate Body. The legislation complies with the WTO decisions by repealing the FSC provisions of the Code, thereby eliminating the FSC subsidies issue. Furthermore, the replacement regime achieves WTO-consistency. The legislation responds to both of the determinative findings in the Panel and Appellate Body Decisions—(1) the conclusion that the FSC constitutes a "subsidy," and (2) the conclusion that it constitutes an "export contingent subsidy." The legislation also goes further than the decisions and addresses additional concerns raised by the European Union by eliminating the use of administrative pricing rules to establish transfer prices and by eliminating the arguable encouragement for the use of tax haven entities.

FSC repeal

The Committee believes that H.R. 4986 complies with the deadline set by the Panel, upheld by the Appellate Body, that "FSC subsidies must be withdrawn at the latest with effect from 1 October 2000." The legislation repeals the FSC provisions thereby eliminating the subsidy at issue in the Panel Decision. By repealing the FSC provisions, the United States has withdrawn what the WTO has found to be a subsidy.

H.R. 4986 confers no "subsidy"

The Panel and Appellate Body ruled that the FSC provisions constitute a "subsidy" because "government revenue that is otherwise due" is forgone. The Appellate Body has acknowledged that a WTO member has the sovereign right to not tax certain categories of income, whether foreign or domestic. Indeed, pure territorial tax systems exclude all foreign source income, including export income, from tax. WTO rules do not compel members to adopt pure territorial tax regimes. Accordingly, the United States, like European Union countries with territorial tax systems (whether pure territorial systems or partial territorial systems) must be free to elect not to tax certain categories of income.

In determining whether revenue forgone is "otherwise due," the Panel, in an analysis upheld by the Appellate Body, examined "the fiscal treatment that would be applicable 'but for' the measures in question."[7] The Appellate Body, in reviewing the Panel Decision, stated that "[t]here must * * * be some defined, normative benchmark against which a comparison can be made between the revenue actually raised and the revenue that would have been raised 'otherwise.' " Thus, the appropriate analysis requires the identification of a prevailing standard of taxation for a particular category of income and a determination of whether this standard is applied consistently to income falling within that category.

The Panel ruled that the FSC provisions excepted certain types of income from the Code's general rule that worldwide income is taxable and, thus, from the taxes that would be due in the absence of the FSC provisions. The Appellate Body, however, confirmed that a WTO member is free to determine how broadly to assert its general taxing authority and "has the sovereign authority to tax any particular categories of revenue it wishes." The Appellate Body Decision also specifically stated that a WTO member is "free not to tax any particular categories of revenues."

H.R. 4986 modifies the general rule of U.S. taxation by fundamentally amending the definition of gross income. Under the Code, the definition of "gross income" defines the outer boundaries of U.S. income taxation. The bill excludes income derived from certain activities performed outside the United States, referred to as "extraterritorial income," from the definition of gross income and, thus, modifies the extent to which the United States seeks to tax such income.

---

[7] The Appellate Body considered the "but for" test a "sound basis for comparison because it is not difficult to establish in what way the foreign-source income of a FSC would be taxed 'but for' the contested measure." However, the Appellate Body cautioned that "we have certain abiding reservations about applying any legal standard, such as this 'but for' test, in the place of the actual treaty language." The Appellate Body observed that the application of a "but for" test is most effective when there is a general rule that applies formally to the revenues in question, absent the contested measures.

This new general rule thus becomes the normative benchmark for taxing income derived in connection with certain activities performed outside the United States. This general rule applies to foreign trade income, whether the goods are manufactured in the United States or abroad—a substantially broader category of income than that which was exempted from tax under the FSC provisions. The Committee believes that it is important that the activities giving rise to excludable extraterritorial income involve real economic activity, or "economic processes," performed outside the United States. The Committee also believes that it is appropriate to except certain forms of extraterritorial income from the exclusion; however, the Committee emphasizes that the taxation of certain forms of extraterritorial income are exceptions to the general rule of not taxing extraterritorial income.

The Committee emphasizes that, consistent with the Appellate Body Decision, the United States is exercising its sovereign authority not to tax a category of revenue. Because of this substantive change in U.S. income taxation, the exclusion of extraterritorial income becomes the United States' general rule with respect to this category of income. Therefore, the exclusion of such income from taxation does not constitute revenue forgone that is otherwise due and, accordingly, does not give rise to a "subsidy" within the meaning of the WTO rules.

H.R. 4986 does not provide "export-contingent" benefits

In addition to ensuring that the FSC replacement regime is not a "subsidy," the Committee believes that, in order to ensure WTO compatibility, it is important that the new regime not confer export-contingent benefits.[8] To achieve this goal, the Committee has relied on the WTO Appellate Body's interpretation of the meaning of "contingent" for purposes of the Agreement on Subsidies and Countervailing Measures in crafting this legislation.[9] It is the Committee's intent and belief that the exclusion of extraterritorial income from U.S. gross income is not dependent on such income arising from export activities. Accordingly, the Committee has determined that it is appropriate to treat all foreign sales alike, whether the goods were manufactured in the United States or abroad. A taxpayer would receive the same U.S. tax treatment with respect to its foreign sales regardless of whether it exports. As a result, the exclusion for certain extraterritorial income is not

"conditional" or "dependent" on whether an entity exports; therefore, it clearly is not export contingent.

The Committee emphasizes that the extraterritorial income excluded by this legislation from the scope of U.S. income taxation is parallel to the foreign-source income excluded from tax under most territorial tax systems. Under neither the U.S. tax system as modified by this legislation nor many European tax systems is the income excluded from taxation limited to income earned through exporting. At the same time, under both systems, exporting is one way to earn foreign source income that is excluded from taxation, and exporters under both systems are among those who can avail themselves of the limitations on the taxing authority of both systems. While exporters may be among those who are eligible for the exclusion, this fact does not make that exclusion "export contingent." If it did, every general exclusion from tax applicable to, among others, exporters would become a prohibited export subsidy.

Addressing other European Union concerns

The Administration has informed the Committee that during the course of the WTO litigation and subsequent consultations with European Union officials, the European Union also raised certain issues relating to the FSC rules that the Panel and Appellate Body did not consider. In this regard, the European Union argued that the administrative pricing rules used to determine the amount of exempt income generated by FSCs were in violation of the arm's-length transfer price provisions in the SCM Agreement. In addition, the European Union alleged that the companies established as FSCs were essentially "sham" corporations and that the FSCs were often located in tax haven countries.

The Committee wants to be clear that because neither the Panel nor the Appellate Body made recommendations with respect to these complaints, the United States is under no obligation to address these issues. Nonetheless, the Committee believes that there is some benefit to be achieved by removing these issues as a source of contention. In addition, the Committee believes that addressing these issues provides an opportunity to simplify the administration of the tax law as well as corporate record keeping.

First, unlike the FSC regime, the bill does not require the use of a separate foreign entity such as the FSC. Therefore, it cannot be argued that the

---

[8] Under Article 3.1(a) of the Agreement on Subsidies and Countervailing Measures, subsidies contingent, in law or in fact, whether solely or as one of several other conditions, upon export performance, are prohibited. This standard is met when the facts demonstrate that the granting of a subsidy, without having been made legally contingent upon export performance, is in fact tied to actual or anticipated exportation or export earnings. However, the mere fact that a subsidy is granted to enterprises which export shall not for

that reason alone be considered to be an export subsidy within the meaning of this provision.

[9] See Canada—Measures Affecting the Export of Civilian Aircraft; see also Canada—Certain Measures Affecting the Automotive Industry. In these cases, the WTO Appellate Body has found the term "contingent" to have its ordinary meaning of "conditional" or "dependent for its existence on something else."

¶ 10,115   Act Sec. 1

new legislation encourages the formation of "sham" corporations in tax-haven jurisdictions. Second, because there is no separate entity required, there are no transfers required between related domestic and foreign companies. The administrative pricing rules are therefore eliminated as transfer pricing mechanisms. If there are transfers between related parties, general arm's-length principles apply. Further, the Committee notes that the elimination of the need for a separate foreign entity simplifies the administration of the tax law from the perspective of both the IRS and the taxpayer.

Conclusion

The Committee believes that this legislation complies with the WTO decisions and honors U.S. obligations under the WTO. The Committee is of the view that repealing the FSC provisions provides an opportunity to revise the Code in a manner that rationalizes tax treatment for extraterritorial income. The Committee is confident that, should the bill be challenged in WTO dispute settlement proceedings, the legislation would withstand scrutiny under the trade agreements. The Committee contrasts the timely and thorough action by the United States represented by this legislation with the response of certain foreign nations to findings of other WTO dispute settlement panels in recent cases involving trade in beef and bananas—findings dealing with pure trade issues and not with the fundamental nature of a country's tax regime.

It is the Committee's sincere hope that through this legislation the United States will be able to resolve this dispute.

Explanation of Provisions

Repeal of the FSC rules

The bill repeals the present-law FSC rules found in sections 921 through 927 of the Code.

Exclusion of extraterritorial income

The bill provides that gross income for U.S. tax purposes does not include extraterritorial income. Because the exclusion of such extraterritorial income is a means of avoiding double taxation, no foreign tax credit is allowed for income taxes paid with respect to such excluded income. Extraterritorial income is eligible for the exclusion to the extent that it is "qualifying foreign trade income." Because U.S. income tax principles generally deny deductions for expenses related to exempt income, otherwise deductible expenses that are allocated to qualifying foreign trade income generally are disallowed.

The bill applies in the same manner with respect to both individuals and corporations who are U.S. taxpayers. In addition, the exclusion from gross income applies for individual and corporate alternative minimum tax purposes.

Qualifying foreign trade income

Under the bill, qualifying foreign trade income is the amount of gross income that, if excluded, would result in a reduction of taxable income by the greatest of (1) 1.2 percent of the "foreign trading gross receipts" derived by the taxpayer from the transaction,[10] (2) 15 percent of the "foreign trade income" derived by the taxpayer from the transaction, or (3) 30 percent of the "foreign sale and leasing income" derived by the taxpayer from the transaction. The amount of qualifying foreign trade income determined using 1.2 percent of the foreign trading gross receipts is limited to 200 percent of the qualifying foreign trade income that would result using 15 percent of the foreign trade income. Notwithstanding the general rule that qualifying foreign trade income is based on one of the three calculations that results in the greatest reduction in taxable income, a taxpayer may choose instead to use one of the other two calculations that does not result in the greatest reduction in taxable income. Although these calculations are determined by reference to a reduction of taxable income (a net income concept), qualifying foreign trade income is an exclusion from gross income. Hence, once a taxpayer determines the appropriate reduction of taxable income, that amount must be "grossed up" for related expenses in order to determine the amount of gross income excluded.[11]

If a taxpayer uses 1.2 percent of foreign trading gross receipts to determine the amount of qualifying foreign trade income with respect to a transaction, the taxpayer or any other related persons will be treated as having no qualifying foreign trade income with respect to any other transaction involving the same property.[12] For example, assume that a manufacturer and a distributor of the same product are related persons. The manufacturer sells the product to the distributor at an arm's-length price of $80 (generating $30 of profit) and the distributor sells the product to an unrelated customer outside of the United States for $100 (generating $20 of profit). If the distributor chooses to calculate its qualifying foreign trade income on the basis of 1.2 percent of foreign trading gross receipts, then the manufacturer will be considered to have no qualifying foreign trade income and, thus, would have no excluded income. The distributor's qualifying foreign trade income would be 1.2 percent of $100, and the manufac-

---

[10] The term "transaction" means (1) any sale, exchange, or other disposition; (2) any lease or rental, and (3) any furnishing of services.

[11] For an example of these calculations, see the General Example, below.

[12] Persons are considered to be related if they are treated as a single employer under section 52(a) or (b) (determined without taking into account section 1563(b), thus including foreign corporations) or section 414(m) or (o).

turer's qualifying foreign trade income would be zero. This limitation is intended to prevent a duplication of exclusions from gross income because the distributor's $100 of gross receipts includes the $80 of gross receipts of the manufacturer. Absent this limitation, $80 of gross receipts would have been double counted for purposes of the exclusion. If both persons were permitted to use 1.2 percent of their foreign trading gross receipts in this example, then the related-person group would have an exclusion based on $180 of foreign trading gross receipts notwithstanding that the related-person group really only generated $100 of gross receipts from the transaction. However, if the distributor chooses to calculate its qualifying foreign trade income on the basis of 15 percent of foreign trade income (15 percent of $20 of profit), then the manufacturer would also be eligible to calculate its qualifying foreign trade income in the same manner (15 percent of $30 of profit).[13] Thus, in the second case, each related person may exclude an amount of income based on their respective profits. The total foreign trade income of the related-person group is $50. Accordingly, allowing each person to calculate the exclusion based on their respective foreign trade income does not result in duplication of exclusions.

Under the bill, a taxpayer may determine the amount of qualifying foreign trade income either on a transaction-by-transaction basis or on an aggregate basis for groups of transactions, so long as the groups are based on product lines or recognized industry or trade usage. Under the grouping method, the Committee intends that taxpayers be given reasonable flexibility to identify product lines or groups on the basis of recognized industry or trade usage. In general, provided that the taxpayer's grouping is not unreasonable, it will not be rejected merely because the grouped products fall within more than one of the two-digit Standard Industrial Classification codes.[14] The Secretary of the Treasury is granted authority to prescribe rules for grouping transactions in determining qualifying foreign trade income.

Qualifying foreign trade income must be reduced by illegal bribes, kickbacks and similar payments, and by a factor for operations in or related to a country associated in carrying out an international boycott, or participating or cooperating with an international boycott.

In addition, the bill directs the Secretary of the Treasury to prescribe rules for marginal costing in those cases in which a taxpayer is seeking to establish or maintain a market for qualifying foreign trade property.

Foreign trading gross receipts

Under the bill, "foreign trading gross receipts" are gross receipts derived from certain activities in connection with "qualifying foreign trade property" with respect to which certain "economic processes" take place outside of the United States. Specifically, the gross receipts must be (1) from the sale, exchange, or other disposition of qualifying foreign trade property; (2) from the lease or rental of qualifying foreign trade property for use by the lessee outside of the United States; (3) for services which are related and subsidiary to the sale, exchange, disposition, lease, or rental of qualifying foreign trade property (as described above); (4) for engineering or architectural services for construction projects located outside of the United States; or (5) for the performance of certain managerial services for unrelated persons. Gross receipts from the lease or rental of qualifying foreign trade property include gross receipts from the license of qualifying foreign trade property. Consistent with the policy adopted in the Taxpayer Relief Act of 1997,[15] this includes the license of computer software for reproduction abroad.

Foreign trading gross receipts do not include gross receipts from a transaction if the qualifying foreign trade property or services are for ultimate use in the United States, or for use by the United States (or an instrumentality thereof) and such use is required by law or regulation. Foreign trading gross receipts also do not include gross receipts from a transaction that is accomplished by a subsidy granted by the government (or any instrumentality thereof) of the country or possession in which the property is manufactured.

A taxpayer may elect to treat gross receipts from a transaction as not foreign trading gross receipts. As a consequence of such an election, the taxpayer could utilize any related foreign tax credits in lieu of the exclusion as a means of avoiding double taxation. It is intended that this election be accomplished by the taxpayer's treatment of such items on its tax return for the taxable year. Provided that the taxpayer's taxable year is still open under the statute of limitations for making claims for refund under section 6511, a taxpayer can make redeterminations as to whether the gross receipts from a transaction constitute foreign trading gross receipts.

Foreign economic processes

Under the bill, gross receipts from a transaction are foreign trading gross receipts only if certain economic processes take place outside of the United States. The foreign economic processes requirement is satisfied if the taxpayer (or any

---

[13] The manufacturer also could compute qualifying foreign trade income based on 30 percent of foreign sale and leasing income.

[14] By reference to Standard Industrial Classification codes, the Committee intends to include industries as defined in the North American Industrial Classification System.

[15] The Taxpayer Relief Act of 1997, Public Law 105-34.

person acting under a contract with the taxpayer) participates outside of the United States in the solicitation (other than advertising), negotiation, or making of the contract relating to such transaction and incurs a specified amount of foreign direct costs attributable to the transaction.[16] For this purpose, foreign direct costs include only those costs incurred in the following categories of activities: (1) advertising and sales promotion; (2) the processing of customer orders and the arranging for delivery; (3) transportation outside of the United States in connection with delivery to the customer; (4) the determination and transmittal of a final invoice or statement of account or the receipt of payment; and (5) the assumption of credit risk. An exception from the foreign economic processes requirement is provided for taxpayers with foreign trading gross receipts for the year of $5 million or less.[17]

The foreign economic processes requirement must be satisfied with respect to each transaction and, if so, any gross receipts from such transaction could be considered as foreign trading gross receipts. For example, all of the lease payments received with respect to a multi-year lease contract, which contract met the foreign economic processes requirement at the time it was entered into, would be considered as foreign trading gross receipts. On the other hand, a sale of property that was formerly a leased asset, which was not sold pursuant to the original lease agreement, generally would be considered a new transaction that must independently satisfy the foreign economic processes requirement.

A taxpayer's foreign economic processes requirement is treated as satisfied with respect to a sales transaction (solely for the purpose of determining whether gross receipts are foreign trading gross receipts) if any related person has satisfied the foreign economic processes requirement in connection with another sales transaction involving the same qualifying foreign trade property.

Qualifying foreign trade property

Under the bill, the threshold for determining if gross receipts will be treated as foreign trading gross receipts is whether the gross receipts are derived from a transaction involving "qualifying foreign trade property." Qualifying foreign trade property is property manufactured, produced, grown, or extracted ("manufactured") within or outside of the United States that is held primarily for sale, lease, or rental,[18] in the ordinary course of a trade or business, for direct use, consumption, or disposition outside of the United States.[19] In addition, not more than 50 percent of the fair market value of such property can be attributable to the sum of (1) the fair market value of articles manufactured outside of the United States plus (2) direct costs of labor performed outside of the United States.[20]

The Committee understands that under current industry practice, the purchaser of an aircraft contracts separately for the aircraft engine and the airframe, albeit contracting with the airframe manufacturer to attach the separately purchased engine. The Committee intends that an aircraft engine be qualifying foreign trade property (assuming that all other requirements are satisfied) if (1) it is specifically designed to be separated from the airframe to which it is incorporated without significant damage to either the engine or the airframe, (2) it is reasonably expected to be separated from the airframe in the ordinary course of business (other than by reason of temporary separation for servicing, maintenance, or repair) before the end of the useful life of either the engine or the airframe, whichever is shorter, and (3) the terms under which the aircraft engine was sold were directly and separately negotiated between the manufacturer of the aircraft engine and the person to whom the aircraft will be ultimately delivered. By articulating this application of the foreign destination test in the case of certain separable aircraft engines, the Committee intends no inference with respect to the application of any destination test under present law or with respect to any other rule of law outside this bill.[21]

The bill excludes certain property from the definition of qualifying foreign trade property. The excluded property is (1) property leased or rented by the taxpayer for use by a related person, (2) certain intangibles,[22] (3) oil and gas (or any primary product thereof), (4) unprocessed softwood timber, (5) certain products the transfer of which are prohibited or curtailed to effectuate

---

[16] The foreign direct costs attributable to the transaction generally must exceed 50 percent of the total direct costs attributable to the transaction, but the requirement also will be satisfied if, with respect to at least two categories of direct costs, the foreign direct costs equal or exceed 85 percent of the total direct costs attributable to each category.

[17] For this purpose, the receipts of related persons are aggregated and, in the case of pass-through entities, the determination of whether the foreign trading gross receipts exceed $5 million is made both at the entity and at the partner/shareholder level.

[18] In addition, consistent with the policy adopted in the Taxpayer Relief Act of 1997, computer software licensed for reproduction is considered as property held primarily for sale, lease, or rental.

[19] "United States" includes Puerto Rico for these purposes because Puerto Rico is included in the customs territory of the United States.

[20] For this purpose, the fair market value of any article imported into the United States is its appraised value as determined under the Tariff Act of 1930. In addition, direct labor costs are determined under the principles of section 263A and do not include costs that would be treated as direct labor costs attributable to "articles," again applying principles of section 263A.

[21] See, e.g., sections 927(a)(1)(B) and 993(c)(1)(B).

[22] The intangibles that are treated as excluded property under the bill are: patents, inventions, models, designs, formulas, or processes whether or not patented, copyrights (other than films, tapes, records, or similar reproductions, and other than computer software (whether or not pat-

the policy set forth in Public Law 9672, and (6) property designated by Executive order as in short supply. In addition, it is the intention of the Committee that property that is leased or licensed to a related person who is the lessor, licensor, or seller of the same property in a sublease, sublicense, or sale to an unrelated person for the ultimate and predominate use by the unrelated person outside of the United States is not excluded property by reason of such lease or license to a related person.

With respect to property that is manufactured outside of the United States, rules are provided to ensure consistent U.S. tax treatment with respect to manufacturers. The bill requires that property manufactured outside of the United States be manufactured by (1) a domestic corporation, (2) an individual who is a citizen or resident of the United States, (3) a foreign corporation that elects to be subject to U.S. taxation in the same manner as a U.S. corporation, or (4) a partnership or other pass-through entity all of the partners or owners of which are described in (1), (2), or (3) above.[23]

Foreign trade income

Under the bill, "foreign trade income" is the taxable income of the taxpayer (determined without regard to the exclusion of qualifying foreign trade income) attributable to foreign trading gross receipts. Certain dividends-paid deductions of cooperatives are disregarded in determining foreign trade income for this purpose.

Foreign sale and leasing income

Under the bill, "foreign sale and leasing income" is the amount of the taxpayer's foreign trade income (with respect to a transaction) that is properly allocable to activities that constitute foreign economic processes (as described above). For example, a distribution company's profit from the sale of qualifying foreign trade property that is associated with sales activities, such as solicitation or negotiation of the sale, advertising, processing customer orders and arranging for delivery, transportation outside of the United States, and other enumerated activities, would constitute foreign sale and leasing income.

Foreign sale and leasing income also includes foreign trade income derived by the taxpayer in connection with the lease or rental of qualifying foreign trade property for use by the lessee outside of the United States. Income from the sale, exchange, or other disposition of qualifying foreign trade property that is or was subject to such a lease[24] (i.e., the sale of the residual interest

in the leased property) gives rise to foreign sale and leasing income. Except as provided in regulations, a special limitation applies to leased property that (1) is manufactured by the taxpayer or (2) is acquired by the taxpayer from a related person for a price that was other than arm's length. In such cases, foreign sale and leasing income may not exceed the amount of foreign sale and leasing income that would have resulted if the taxpayer had acquired the leased property in a hypothetical arm's-length purchase and then engaged in the actual sale or lease of such property. For example, if a manufacturer leases qualifying foreign trade property that it manufactured, the foreign sale and leasing income derived from that lease may not exceed the amount of foreign sale and leasing income that the manufacturer would have earned with respect to that lease had it purchased the property for an arm's-length price on the day that the manufacturer entered into the lease. For purposes of calculating the limit on foreign sale and leasing income, the manufacturer's basis and, thus, depreciation would be based on this hypothetical arm's-length price. This limitation is intended to prevent foreign sale and leasing income from including profit associated with manufacturing activities.

For purposes of determining foreign sale and leasing income, only directly allocable expenses is taken into account in calculating the amount of foreign trade income. In addition, income properly allocable to certain intangibles is excluded for this purpose.

General example

The following is an example of the calculation of qualifying foreign trade income.

XYZ Corporation, a U.S. corporation, manufactures property that is sold to unrelated customers for use outside of the United States. XYZ Corporation satisfies the foreign economic processes requirement through conducting activities such as solicitation, negotiation, transportation, and other salesrelated activities outside of the United States with respect to its transactions. During the year, qualifying foreign trade property was sold for gross proceeds totaling $1,000. The cost of this qualifying foreign trade property was $600. XYZ Corporation incurred $275 of costs that are directly related to the sale and distribution of qualifying foreign trade property. XYZ Corporation paid $40 of income tax to a foreign jurisdiction related to the sale and distribution of the qualifying foreign trade property. XYZ Corporation also

---

(Footnote Continued)

ented), for commercial or home use), goodwill, trademarks, trade brands, franchises, or other like property. Computer software that is licensed for reproduction outside of the United States is not excluded from the definition of qualifying foreign trade property.

[23] Except as provided by the Secretary of the Treasury, tiered partnerships or pass-through entities will be consid-

ered as partnerships or pass-through entities for purposes of this rule if each of the partnerships or entities is directly or indirectly wholly-owned by persons described in (1), (2), or (3) above.

[24] For this purpose, such a lease includes a lease that gave rise to exempt foreign trade income under the FSC provisions.

generated gross income of $7,600 (gross receipts of $24,000 and cost of goods sold of $16,400) and direct expenses of $4,225 that relate to the manufacture and sale of products other than qualifying foreign trade property. XYZ Corporation also incurred $500 of overhead expenses. XYZ Corporation's financial information for the year is summarized as follows:

	Total	Other property	QFTP [25]
Gross receipts	$25,000.00	$24,000.00	$1,000.00
Cost of goods sold	17,000.00	16,400.00	600.00
Gross income	8,000.00	7,600.00	400.00
Direct expenses	4,500.00	4,225.00	275.00
Overhead expenses	500.00	....	....
Net income	3,000.00	....	....

Illustrated below is the computation of the amount of qualifying foreign trade income that is excluded from XYZ Corporation's gross income and the amount of related expenses that are disallowed. In order to calculate qualifying foreign trade income, the amount of foreign trade income first must be determined. Foreign trade income is the taxable income (determined without regard to the exclusion of qualifying foreign trade income) attributable to foreign trading gross receipts. In this example, XYZ Corporation's foreign trading gross receipts equal $1,000. This amount of gross receipts is reduced by the related cost of goods sold, the related direct expenses, and a portion of the overhead expenses in order to arrive at the related taxable income[26] Thus, XYZ Corporation's foreign trade income equals $100, calculated as follows:

Foreign trading gross receipts	$1,000.00
Cost of goods sold	600.00
Gross income	400.00
Direct expenses	275.00
Apportioned overhead expenses	25.00
Foreign trade income	100.00

Foreign sale and leasing income is defined as an amount of foreign trade income (calculated taking into account only directly-related expenses) that is properly allocable to certain specified foreign activities. Assume for purposes of this example that of the $125 of foreign trade income ($400 of

gross income from the sale of qualifying foreign trade property less only the direct expenses of $275), $35 is properly allocable to such foreign activities (e.g., solicitation, negotiation, advertising, foreign transportation, and other enumerated sales-like activities) and, therefore, is considered to be foreign sale and leasing income.

Qualifying foreign trade income is the amount of gross income that, if excluded, will result in a reduction of taxable income equal to the greatest of (1) 30 percent of foreign sale and leasing income, (2) 1.2 percent of foreign trading gross receipts, or (3) 15 percent of foreign trade income. Thus, in order to calculate the amount that is excluded from gross income, taxable income must be determined and then "grossed up" for allocable expenses in order to arrive at the appropriate gross income figure. First, for each method of calculating qualifying foreign trade income, the reduction in taxable income is determined. Then, the $275 of direct and $25 of overhead expenses, totaling $300, attributable to foreign trading gross receipts is apportioned to the reduction in taxable income based on the proportion of the reduction in taxable income to foreign trade income. This apportionment is done for each method of calculating qualifying foreign trade income. The sum of the taxable income reduction and the apportioned expenses the respective qualifying foreign trade income (i.e., the amount of gross income excluded) under each method, as follows:

	1.2% FTGR [27]	15% FTI [28]	30% FS&LI [29]
Reduction of taxable income:			
1.2% of FTGR (1.2% * $1,000)	12.00	.....	......
15% of FTI (15% * $100)	.....	15.00	....

---

[25] "QFTP" refers to qualifying foreign trade property.
[26] Overhead expenses must be apportioned in a reasonable manner that does not result in a material distortion of income. In this example, the apportionment of the $500 of overhead expenses on the basis of gross income is assumed not to result in a material distortion of income and is assumed to be a reasonable method of apportionment. Thus, $25 ($500 of total overhead expenses multiplied by 5 percent, i.e., $400 of gross income from the sale of qualifying

foreign trade property divided by $8,000 of total gross income) is apportioned to qualifying foreign trading gross receipts. The remaining $475 ($500 of total overhead expenses less the $25 apportioned to qualifying income) is apportioned to XYZ Corporation's other income.

[27] "FTGR" refers to foreign trading gross receipts.
[28] "FTI" refers to foreign trade income.
[29] "FS&LI" refers to foreign sale and leasing income.

30% of FS&LI (30% * $35)	.....	.....	10.50

Gross-up for disallowed expenses:

$300 * ($12/$100)	36.00	.....	....
$300 * ($15/$100)	.....	45.00	....
$275 * ($10.50/$100) [30]	.....	.....	28.88
Qualifying foreign trade income	48.00	60.00	39.38

In the example, the $60 of qualifying foreign trade income is excluded from XYZ Corporation's gross income (determined based on 15 percent of foreign trade income).[31] In connection with excluding $60 of gross income, certain expenses that are allocable to this income are not deductible for U.S. Federal income tax purposes. Thus, $45 ($300 of related expenses multiplied by 15 percent, i.e., $60 of qualifying foreign trade income divided by $400 of gross income from the sale of qualifying foreign trade property) of expenses are disallowed.[32]

	Other Property	QFTP	Excluded/ Disallowed	Total
Gross receipts	$24,000.00	$1,000.00	......	....
Cost of goods sold	16,400.00	600.00	......	....
Gross income	7,600.00	400.00	(60.00)	7,940.00
Direct expenses	4,225.00	275.00	(41.25)	4,458.75
Overhead expenses	475.00	25.00	(3.75)	496.25
Taxable income		....	......	2,985.00

XYZ Corporation paid $40 of income tax to a foreign jurisdiction related to the sale and distribution of the qualifying foreign trade property. A portion of this $40 of foreign income tax is treated as paid with respect to the qualifying foreign trade income and, therefore, is not creditable for U.S. foreign tax credit purposes. In this case, $6 of such taxes paid ($40 of foreign taxes multiplied by 15 percent, i.e., $60 of qualifying foreign trade income divided by $400 of gross income from the sale of qualifying foreign trade property) is treated as paid with respect to the qualifying foreign trade income and, thus, is not creditable.

The results in this example are the same regardless of whether XYZ Corporation manufactures the property within the United States or outside of the United States through a foreign branch. If XYZ Corporation were an S corporation or limited liability company, the results also would be the same, and the exclusion would pass through to the S corporation owners or limited liability company owners as the case may be.

Other rules

Foreign-source income limitation

The bill provides a limitation with respect to the sourcing of taxable income applicable to certain sale transactions giving rise to foreign trading gross receipts. This limitation only applies with respect to sale transactions involving property that is manufactured within the United States. The special source limitation does not apply when qualifying foreign trade income is determined using 30 percent of the foreign sale and leasing income from the transaction.

This foreign-source income limitation is determined in one of two ways depending on whether the qualifying foreign trade income is calculated based on 1.2 percent of foreign trading gross receipts or on 15 percent of foreign trade income. If the qualifying foreign trade income is calculated based on 1.2 percent of foreign trading gross receipts, the related amount of foreign-source income may not exceed the amount of foreign trade income that (without taking into account this special foreign-source income limitation) would be treated as foreignsource income if such foreign trade income were reduced by 4 percent of the related foreign trading gross receipts.

For example, assume that foreign trading gross receipts are $2,000 and foreign trade income is $100. Assume also that the taxpayer chooses to determine qualifying foreign trade income based on 1.2 percent of foreign trading gross receipts. Taxable income after taking into account the exclusion of the qualifying foreign trade income and

---

[30] Because foreign sale and leasing income only takes into account direct expenses, it is appropriate to take into account only such expenses for purposes of this calculation.

[31] Note that XYZ Corporation could choose to use one of the other two methods notwithstanding that they would result in a smaller exclusion.

[32] The $300 of allocable expenses includes both the $275 of direct expenses and the $25 of overhead expenses. Thus, the $45 of disallowed expenses represents the sum of $41.25 of direct expenses plus $3.75 of overhead expenses. If qualifying foreign trade income was determined using 30 percent of foreign sale and leasing income, the disallowed expenses would include only the appropriate portion of the direct expenses.

the disallowance of related deductions is $76. Assume that the taxpayer manufactured its qualifying foreign trade property in the United States and that title to such property passed outside of the United States. Absent a special sourcing rule, under section 863(b) (and the regulations thereunder) the $76 of taxable income would be sourced as $38 U.S. source and $38 foreign source. Under the special sourcing rule, the amount of foreign-source income may not exceed the amount of the foreign trade income that otherwise would be treated as foreign source if the foreign trade income were reduced by 4 percent of the related foreign trading gross receipts. Reducing foreign trade income by 4 percent of the foreign trading gross receipts (4 percent of $2,000, or $80) would result in $20 ($100 foreign trade income less $80). Applying section 863(b) to the $20 of reduced foreign trade income would result in $10 of foreign-source income and $10 of U.S.-source income. Accordingly, the limitation equals $10. Thus, although under the general sourcing rule $38 of the $76 taxable income would be treated as foreign source, the special sourcing rule limits foreign-source income in this example to $10 (with the remaining $66 being treated as U.S.-source income).

If the qualifying foreign trade income is calculated based on 15 percent of foreign trade income, the amount of related foreign-source income may not exceed 50 percent of the foreign trade income that (without taking into account this special foreign-source income limitation) would be treated as foreign-source income.

For example, assume that foreign trade income is $100 and the taxpayer chooses to determine its qualifying foreign trade income based on 15 percent of foreign trade income. Taxable income after taking into account the exclusion of the qualifying foreign trade income and the disallowance of related deductions is $85. Assume that the taxpayer manufactured its qualifying foreign trade property in the United States and that title to such property passed outside of the United States. Absent a special sourcing rule, under section 863(b) the $85 of taxable income would be sourced as $42.50 U.S. source and $42.50 foreign source. Under the special sourcing rule, the amount of foreign-source income may not exceed 50 percent of the foreign trade income that otherwise would be treated as foreign source. Applying section 863(b) to the $100 of foreign trade income would result in $50 of foreign-source income and $50 of U.S.-source income. Accordingly, the limitation

equals $25, which is 50 percent of the $50 foreign-source income. Thus, although under the general sourcing rule $42.50 of the $85 taxable income would be treated as foreign source, the special sourcing rule limits foreign-source income in this example to $25 (with the remaining $60 being treated as U.S.source income).[33]

Treatment of withholding taxes

The bill generally provides that no foreign tax credit is allowed for foreign taxes paid or accrued with respect to qualifying foreign trade income (i.e., excluded extraterritorial income). In determining whether foreign taxes are paid or accrued with respect to qualifying foreign trade income, foreign withholding taxes generally are treated as not paid or accrued with respect to qualifying foreign trade income.[34] Accordingly, the bill's denial of foreign tax credits would not apply to such taxes. For this purpose, the term "withholding tax" refers to any foreign tax that is imposed on a basis other than residence and that is otherwise a creditable foreign tax under sections 901 or 903.[35] It is intended that such taxes would be similar in nature to the gross-basis taxes described in sections 871 and 881.

If, however, qualifying foreign trade income is determined based on 30 percent of foreign sale and leasing income, the special rule for withholding taxes is not applicable. Thus, in such cases foreign withholding taxes may be treated as paid or accrued with respect to qualifying foreign trade income and, accordingly, are not creditable under the bill.

Election to be treated as a U.S. corporation

The bill provides that certain foreign corporations may elect, on an original return, to be treated as domestic corporations. The election applies to the taxable year when made and all subsequent taxable years unless revoked by the taxpayer or terminated for failure to qualify for the election. Such election is available for a foreign corporation (1) that manufactures property in the ordinary course of such corporation's trade or business, or (2) if substantially all of the gross receipts of such corporation reasonably may be expected to be foreign trading gross receipts. For this purpose, "substantially all" is based on the relevant facts and circumstances.

In order to be eligible to make this election, the foreign corporation must waive all benefits granted to such corporation by the United States

---

[33] The foreign-source income limitation provisions also apply when source is determined solely in accordance with section 862 (e.g., a distributor of qualifying foreign trade property that is manufactured in the United States by an unrelated person and sold for use outside of the United States).

[34] With respect to the withholding taxes that are paid or accrued (a prerequisite to the taxes being otherwise credita-

ble), the provision in the bill treats such taxes as not being paid or accrued with respect to qualifying foreign trade income.

[35] This also would apply to any withholding tax that is creditable for U.S. foreign tax credit purposes under an applicable treaty.

pursuant to a treaty.[36] Absent such a waiver, it would be unclear, for example, whether the permanent establishment article of a relevant tax treaty would override the electing corporation's treatment as a domestic corporation under this provision. A foreign corporation that elects to be treated as a domestic corporation is not permitted to make an S corporation election. The Secretary is granted authority to prescribe rules to ensure that the electing foreign corporation pays its U.S. income tax liabilities and to designate one or more classes of corporations that may not make such an election.[37] If such an election is made, for purposes of section 367 the foreign corporation is treated as transferring (as of the first day of the first taxable year to which the election applies) all of its assets to a domestic corporation in connection with an exchange to which section 354 applies.

If a corporation fails to meet the applicable requirements, described above, for making the election to be treated as a domestic corporation for any taxable year beginning after the year of the election, the election will terminate. In addition, a taxpayer, at its option and at any time, may revoke the election to be treated as a domestic corporation. In the case of either a termination or a revocation, the electing foreign corporation will not be considered as a domestic corporation effective beginning on the first day of the taxable year following the year of such termination or revocation. For purposes of section 367, if the election to be treated as a domestic corporation is terminated or revoked, such corporation is treated as a domestic corporation transferring (as of the first day of the first taxable year to which the election ceases to apply) all of its property to a foreign corporation in connection with an exchange to which section 354 applies. Moreover, once a termination occurs or a revocation is made, the former electing corporation may not again elect to be taxed as a domestic corporation under the provisions of the bill for a period of five tax years beginning with the first taxable year that begins after the termination or revocation.

For example, assume a U.S. corporation owns 100 percent of a foreign corporation. The foreign corporation manufactures outside of the United States and sells what would be qualifying foreign trade property were it manufactured by a person subject to U.S. taxation. Such foreign corporation could make the election under this provision to be treated as a domestic corporation. As a result, its earnings no longer would be deferred from U.S. taxation. However, by electing to be subject to U.S. taxation, a portion of its income would be qualifying foreign trade income.[38] The requirement that the foreign corporation be treated as a domestic corporation (and, therefore, subject to U.S. taxation) is intended to provide parity between U.S. corporations that manufacture abroad in branch form and U.S. corporations that manufacture abroad through foreign subsidiaries. The election, however, is not limited to U.S.-owned foreign corporations. A foreign-owned foreign corporation that wishes to qualify for the treatment provided under the bill could avail itself of such election (unless otherwise precluded from doing so by Treasury regulations).

Shared partnerships

The bill provides rules relating to allocations of qualifying foreign trade income by certain shared partnerships. To the extent that such a partnership (1) maintains a separate account for transactions involving foreign trading gross receipts with each partner, (2) makes distributions to each partner based on the amounts in the separate account, and (3) meets such other requirements as the Treasury Secretary may prescribe by regulations, such partnership then would allocate to each partner items of income, gain, loss, and deduction (including qualifying foreign trade income) from such transactions on the basis of the separate accounts. It is intended that with respect to, and only with respect to, such allocations and distributions (i.e., allocations and distributions related to transactions between the partner and the shared partnership generating foreign trading gross receipts), these rules would apply in lieu of the otherwise applicable partnership allocation rules such as those in section 704(b). For this purpose, a partnership is a foreign or domestic entity that is considered to be a partnership for U.S. Federal income tax purposes.

Under the bill, any partner's interest in the shared partnership is not taken into account in determining whether such partner is a "related person" with respect to any other partner for purposes of the bill's provisions. Also, the election to exclude certain gross receipts from foreign trading gross receipts must be made separately by each partner with respect to any transaction for which the shared partnership maintains a separate account.

Certain assets not taken into account for purposes of interest expense allocation

The bill also provides that qualifying foreign trade property that is held for lease or rental, in the ordinary course of a trade or business, for use by the lessee outside of the United States is not

---

[36] The waiver of treaty benefits applies to the corporation itself and not, for example, to employees of or independent contractors associated with the corporation.

[37] For example, the Secretary of the Treasury may prescribe rules to prevent "per se" corporations under the entity-classification rules from making such an election.

[38] The sourcing limitation described above would not apply to this example because the property is manufactured outside of the United States.

taken into account for interest allocation purposes.

Distributions of qualifying foreign trade income by cooperatives

Agricultural and horticultural producers often market their products through cooperatives, which are member-owned corporations formed under Subchapter T of the Code. At the cooperative level, the bill provides the same treatment of foreign trading gross receipts derived from products marketed through cooperatives as it provides for foreign trading gross receipts of other taxpayers. That is, the qualifying foreign trade income attributable to those foreign trading gross receipts is excluded from the gross income of the cooperative. Absent a special rule, however, patronage dividends or per-unit retain allocations attributable to qualifying foreign trade income paid to members of cooperatives would be taxable in the hands of those members. The Committee believes that this would disadvantage agricultural and horticultural producers who choose to market their products through cooperatives relative to those individuals who market their products directly or through pass-through entities such as partnerships, limited liability companies, or S corporations. Accordingly, the bill provides that the amount of any patronage dividends or per-unit retain allocations paid to a member of an agricultural or horticultural cooperative (to which Part I of Subchapter T applies), which is allocable to qualifying foreign trade income of the cooperative, is treated as qualifying foreign trade income of the member (and, thus, excludable from such member's gross income). In order to qualify, such amount must be designated by the organization as allocable to qualifying foreign trade income in a written notice mailed to its patrons not later than the payment period described in section 1382(d). The cooperative cannot reduce its income (e.g., cannot claim a "dividends-paid deduction") under section 1382 for such amounts.

Certain dividends allocable to qualifying foreign trade income

Under the bill, a U.S. corporation may claim a 100 percent dividends-received deduction with respect to any dividend that is distributed out of earnings and profits of a controlled foreign corporation (as defined in section 957), but only if such dividend is attributable to qualifying foreign trade income. Only U.S. corporations that are also U.S. shareholders (as defined in section 951(b)) are eligible for this 100 percent dividends-received deduction.

Gap period before administrative guidance is issued

The Committee recognizes that there may be a gap in time between the enactment of the bill and the issuance of detailed administrative guidance. It is intended that during this gap period before administrative guidance is issued, taxpayers and the Internal Revenue Service may apply the principles of present-law regulations and other administrative guidance under sections 921 through 927 to analogous concepts under the bill. Some examples of the application of the principles of present-law regulations to the bill are described below. These limited examples are intended to be merely illustrative and are not intended to imply any limitation regarding the application of the principles of other analogous rules or concepts under present law.

Marginal costing and grouping

Under the bill, the Secretary of the Treasury is provided authority to prescribe rules for using marginal costing and for grouping transactions in determining qualifying foreign trade income. It is intended that similar principles under present-law regulations apply for these purposes.[39]

Excluded property

The bill provides that qualifying foreign trade property does not include property leased or rented by the taxpayer for use by a related person. It is intended that similar principles under present-law regulations apply for this purpose. Thus, excluded property does not apply, for example, to property leased by the taxpayer to a related person if the property is held for sublease, or is subleased, by the related person to an unrelated person and the property is ultimately used by such unrelated person predominantly outside of the United States.[40] In addition, consistent with the policy adopted in the Taxpayer Relief Act of 1997, computer software that is licensed for reproduction outside of the United States is not excluded property. Accordingly, the license of computer software to a related person for reproduction outside of the United States for sale, sublicense, lease, or rental to an unrelated person for use outside of the United States is not treated as excluded property by reason of the license to the related person.

Foreign trading gross receipts

Under the bill, foreign trading gross receipts are gross receipts from, among other things, the sale, exchange, or other disposition of qualifying foreign trade property, and from the lease of qualifying foreign trade property for use by the lessee

---

[39] See, e.g., Treas. Reg. sec. 1.924(d)-1(c)(5) and (e); Treas. Reg. sec. 1.925(a)-1T(c)(8); Treas. Reg. sec. 1.925(b)-1T.

[40] See Treas. Reg. sec. 1.927(a)-1T(f)(2)(i). The bill also provides that oil or gas or primary products from oil or gas are excluded from the definition of qualifying foreign trade

property. It is intended that similar principles under present-law regulations apply for these purposes. Thus, for this purpose, petrochemicals, medicinal products, insecticides, and alcohols are not considered primary products from oil or gas and, thus, are not treated as excluded property. See Treas. Reg. sec. 1.927(a)-1T(g)(2)(iv).

outside of the United States. It is intended that the principles of present-law regulations that define foreign trading gross receipts apply for this purpose. For example, a sale includes an exchange or other disposition and a lease includes a rental or sublease and a license or a sublicense.[41]

Foreign use requirement

Under the bill, property constitutes qualifying foreign trade property if, among other things, the property is held primarily for lease, sale, or rental, in the ordinary course of business, for direct use, consumption, or disposition outside of the United States.[42] It is intended that the principles of the present-law regulations apply for purposes of this foreign use requirement. For example, for purposes of determining whether property is sold for use outside of the United States, property that is sold to an unrelated person as a component to be incorporated into a second product which is produced, manufactured, or assembled outside of the United States will not be considered to be used in the United States (even if the second product ultimately is used in the United States), provided that the fair market value of such seller's components at the time of delivery to the purchaser constitutes less than 20 percent of the fair market value of the second product into which the components are incorporated (determined at the time of completion of the production, manufacture, or assembly of the second product).[43]

In addition, for purposes of the foreign use requirement, property is considered to be used by a lessee outside of the United States during a taxable year if it is used predominantly outside of the United States.[44] For this purpose, property is considered to be used predominantly outside of the United States for any period if, during that period, the property is located outside of the United States more than 50 percent of the time.[45] An aircraft or other property used for transportation purposes (e.g., railroad rolling stock, a vessel, a motor vehicle, or a container) is considered to be used outside of the United States for any period if, for the period, either the property is located outside of the United States more than 50 percent of the time or more than 50 percent of the miles traveled in the use of the property are traveled outside of the United States.[46] An orbiting satellite is considered to be located outside of the United States for these purposes.[47]

Foreign economic processes

Under the bill, gross receipts from a transaction are foreign trading gross receipts eligible for exclusion from the tax base only if certain economic processes take place outside of the United States. The foreign economic processes requirement compares foreign direct costs to total direct costs. It is intended that the principles of the present-law regulations apply during the gap period for purposes of the foreign economic processes requirement including the measurement of direct costs. The Committee recognizes that the measurement of foreign direct costs under the present-law regulations often depend on activities conducted by the FSC, which is a separate entity. The Committee is aware that some of these concepts will have to be modified when new guidance is promulgated as a result of the bill's elimination of the requirement for a separate entity.

Effective Date

In general

The bill is effective for transactions entered into after September 30, 2000. In addition, no corporation may elect to be a FSC after September 30, 2000.

The bill also provides a rule requiring the termination of a dormant FSC when the FSC has been inactive for a specified period of time. Under this rule, a FSC that generates no foreign trade income for any five consecutive years beginning after December 31, 2001, will cease to be treated as a FSC.

Transition rules

The bill provides a transition period for existing FSCs and for binding contractual agreements. The new rules do not apply to transactions in the ordinary course of business[48] involving a FSC before January 1, 2002. Furthermore, the new rules do not apply to transactions in the ordinary course of business after December 31, 2001, if such transactions are pursuant to a binding contract between a FSC (or a person related to the FSC on September 30, 2000) and any other person (that is not a related person) and such contract is in effect on September 30, 2000, and all times thereafter. For this purpose, binding contracts include purchase options, renewal options, and replacement options that are enforceable against a lessor or seller (provided that the options are a part of a contract that is binding and in effect on September 30, 2000).

Similar to the limitation on use of the gross receipts method under the bill's operative provisions, the bill provides a rule that limits the use of the gross receipts method for transactions after the effective date of the bill if that same property generated foreign trade income to a FSC using the

---

[41] See Treas. Reg. sec. 1.924(a)-1T(a)(2).

[42] Foreign trading gross receipts eligible for exclusion from the tax base do not include gross receipts from a transaction if the qualifying foreign trade property is for ultimate use in the United States.

[43] See Treas. Reg. sec. 1.927(a)-1T(d)(4)(ii).

[44] See Treas. Reg. sec. 1.927(a)-1T(d)(4)(v).

[45] See Treas. Reg. sec. 1.927(a)-1T(d)(4)(vi).

[46] Id.

[47] Id.

[48] The mere entering into of a single transaction, such as a lease, would not, in and of itself, prevent the transaction from being in the ordinary course of business.

gross receipts method. Under the rule, if any person used the gross receipts method under the FSC regime, neither that person nor any related person will have qualifying foreign trade income with respect to any other transaction involving the same item of property.

Notwithstanding the transition period, FSCs (or related persons) may elect to have the rules of the bill apply in lieu of the rules applicable to FSCs. Thus, for transactions to which the transition rules apply, taxpayers may choose to apply either the FSC rules or the amendments made by this bill, but not both.

Conference Committee Report (H.R. Conf. Rep. No. 106-1004)

* * *

House Bill

No provision. However, H.R. 4986, as passed by the House, repeals the present-law FSC rules and replaces them with an exclusion for extraterritorial income.

Senate Amendment

No provision. However, the Senate Finance Committee reported favorably an amended version of H.R. 4986 to the Senate (the "Senate Finance Committee amendment"). The Senate has taken no action with respect to the Senate Finance Committee amendment. The Senate Finance Committee amendment generally follows H.R. 4986, as passed by the House, with one amendment to strike a provision providing for a dividends-received deduction for certain dividends allocable to qualifying foreign trade income. Like H.R. 4986, the Senate Finance Committee amendment repeals the present-law FSC rules and replaces them with an exclusion for extraterritorial income.

Conference Agreement

The conference agreement generally follows H.R. 4986, as passed by the House, and the Senate Finance Committee amendment, with some modifications. The conference agreement, like the Senate Finance Committee amendment, does not include the provision in the House bill that provides a dividends-received deduction for certain dividends allocable to qualifying foreign trade income.

Repeal of the FSC rules

The conference agreement repeals the present-law FSC rules found in sections 921 through 927 of the Code.

Exclusion of extraterritorial income

The conference agreement provides that gross income for U.S. tax purposes does not include extraterritorial income. Because the exclusion of such extraterritorial income is a means of avoiding double taxation, no foreign tax credit is allowed for income taxes paid with respect to such excluded income. Extraterritorial income is eligible for the exclusion to the extent that it is "qualifying foreign trade income." Because U.S. income tax principles generally deny deductions for expenses related to exempt income, otherwise deductible expenses that are allocated to qualifying foreign trade income generally are disallowed.

The conference agreement applies in the same manner with respect to both individuals and corporations who are U.S. taxpayers. In addition, the exclusion from gross income applies for individual and corporate alternative minimum tax purposes.

Qualifying foreign trade income

Under the conference agreement, qualifying foreign trade income is the amount of gross income that, if excluded, would result in a reduction of taxable income by the greatest of (1) 1.2 percent of the "foreign trading gross receipts" derived by the taxpayer from the transaction,[2] (2) 15 percent of the "foreign trade income" derived by the taxpayer from the transaction, or (3) 30 percent of the "foreign sale and leasing income" derived by the taxpayer from the transaction. The amount of qualifying foreign trade income determined using 1.2 percent of the foreign trading gross receipts is limited to 200 percent of the qualifying foreign trade income that would result using 15 percent of the foreign trade income. Notwithstanding the general rule that qualifying foreign trade income is based on one of the three calculations that results in the greatest reduction in taxable income, a taxpayer may choose instead to use one of the other two calculations that does not result in the greatest reduction in taxable income. Although these calculations are determined by reference to a reduction of *taxable* income (a net income concept), qualifying foreign trade income is an exclusion from *gross* income. Hence, once a taxpayer determines the appropriate reduction of taxable income, that amount must be "grossed up" for related expenses in order to determine the amount of gross income excluded.[3]

If a taxpayer uses 1.2 percent of foreign trading gross receipts to determine the amount of qualifying foreign trade income with respect to a transaction, the taxpayer or any other related persons will be treated as having no qualifying foreign

---

[2] The term "transaction" means (1) any sale, exchange, or other disposition; (2) any lease or rental; and (3) any furnishing of services.

[3] For an example of these calculations, see the General Example, below.

trade income with respect to any other transaction involving the same property.[4] For example, assume that a manufacturer and a distributor of the same product are related persons. The manufacturer sells the product to the distributor at an arm's-length price of $80 (generating $30 of profit) and the distributor sells the product to an unrelated customer outside of the United States for $100 (generating $20 of profit). If the distributor chooses to calculate its qualifying foreign trade income on the basis of 1.2 percent of foreign trading gross receipts, then the manufacturer will be considered to have no qualifying foreign trade income and, thus, would have no excluded income. The distributor's qualifying foreign trade income would be 1.2 percent of $100, and the manufacturer's qualifying foreign trade income would be zero. This limitation is intended to prevent a duplication of exclusions from gross income because the distributor's $100 of gross receipts includes the $80 of gross receipts of the manufacturer. Absent this limitation, $80 of gross receipts would have been double counted for purposes of the exclusion. If both persons were permitted to use 1.2 percent of their foreign trading gross receipts in this example, then the related-person group would have an exclusion based on $180 of foreign trading gross receipts notwithstanding that the related-person group really only generated $100 of gross receipts from the transaction. However, if the distributor chooses to calculate its qualifying foreign trade income on the basis of 15 percent of foreign trade income (15 percent of $20 of profit), then the manufacturer would also be eligible to calculate its qualifying foreign trade income in the same manner (15 per cent of $30 of profit).[5] Thus, in the second case, each related person may exclude an amount of income based on their respective profits. The total foreign trade income of the related-person group is $50. Accordingly, allowing each person to calculate the exclusion based on their respective foreign trade income does not result in duplication of exclusions.

Under the conference agreement, a taxpayer may determine the amount of qualifying foreign trade income either on a transaction-by-transaction basis or on an aggregate basis for groups of transactions, so long as the groups are based on product lines or recognized industry or trade usage. Under the grouping method, the conferees intend that taxpayers be given reasonable flexibility to identify product lines or groups on the basis of recognized industry or trade usage. In general, provided that the taxpayer's grouping is not un-reasonable, it will not be rejected merely because the grouped products fall within more than one of the two-digit Standard Industrial Classification codes.[6] The Secretary of the Treasury is granted authority to prescribe rules for grouping transactions in determining qualifying foreign trade income.

Qualifying foreign trade income must be reduced by illegal bribes, kickbacks and similar payments, and by a factor for operations in or related to a country associated in carrying out an international boycott, or participating or cooperating with an international boycott.

In addition, the conference agreement directs the Secretary of the Treasury to prescribe rules for marginal costing in those cases in which a taxpayer is seeking to establish or maintain a market for qualifying foreign trade property.

Foreign trading gross receipts

Under the conference agreement, "foreign trading gross receipts" are gross receipts derived from certain activities in connection with "qualifying foreign trade property" with respect to which certain "economic processes" take place outside of the United States. Specifically, the gross receipts must be (1) from the sale, exchange, or other disposition of qualifying foreign trade property; (2) from the lease or rental of qualifying foreign trade property for use by the lessee outside of the United States; (3) for services which are related and subsidiary to the sale, exchange, disposition, lease, or rental of qualifying foreign trade property (as described above); (4) for engineering or architectural services for construction projects located outside of the United States; or (5) for the performance of certain managerial services for unrelated persons. Gross receipts from the lease or rental of qualifying foreign trade property include gross receipts from the license of qualifying foreign trade property. Consistent with the policy adopted in the Taxpayer Relief Act of 1997,[7] this includes the license of computer software for reproduction abroad.

Foreign trading gross receipts do not include gross receipts from a transaction if the qualifying foreign trade property or services are for ultimate use in the United States, or for use by the United States (or an instrumentality thereof) and such use is required by law or regulation. Foreign trading gross receipts also do not include gross receipts from a transaction that is accomplished by a subsidy granted by the government (or any instrumentality thereof) of the country or possession in which the property is manufactured.

---

[4] Persons are considered to be related if they are treated as a single employer under section 52(a) or (b) (determined without taking into account section 1563(b), thus including foreign corporations) or section 414(m) or (o).

[5] The manufacturer also could compute qualifying foreign trade income based on 30 percent of foreign sale and leasing income.

[6] By reference to Standard Industrial Classification codes, the conferees intend to include industries as defined in the North American Industrial Classification System.

[7] The Taxpayer Relief Act of 1997, Public Law 105-34.

A taxpayer may elect to treat gross receipts from a transaction as not foreign trading gross receipts. As a consequence of such an election, the taxpayer could utilize any related foreign tax credits in lieu of the exclusion as a means of avoiding double taxation. It is intended that this election be accomplished by the taxpayer's treatment of such items on its tax return for the taxable year. Provided that the taxpayer's taxable year is still open under the statute of limitations for making claims for refund under section 6511, a taxpayer can make redeterminations as to whether the gross receipts from a transaction constitute foreign trading gross receipts.

Foreign economic processes

Under the conference agreement, gross receipts from a transaction are foreign trading gross receipts only if certain economic processes take place outside of the United States. The foreign economic processes requirement is satisfied if the taxpayer (or any person acting under a contract with the taxpayer) participates outside of the United States in the solicitation (other than advertising), negotiation, or making of the contract relating to such transaction and incurs a specified amount of foreign direct costs attributable to the transaction.[8] For this purpose, foreign direct costs include only those costs incurred in the following categories of activities: (1) advertising and sales promotion; (2) the processing of customer orders and the arranging for delivery; (3) transportation outside of the United States in connection with delivery to the customer; (4) the determination and transmittal of a final invoice or statement of account or the receipt of payment; and (5) the assumption of credit risk. An exception from the foreign economic processes requirement is provided for taxpayers with foreign trading gross receipts for the year of $5 million or less.[9]

The foreign economic processes requirement must be satisfied with respect to each transaction and, if so, any gross receipts from such transaction could be considered as foreign trading gross receipts. For example, all of the lease payments received with respect to a multi-year lease contract, which contract met the foreign economic processes requirement at the time it was entered into, would be considered as foreign trading gross receipts. On the other hand, a sale of property that was formerly a leased asset, which was not sold pursuant to the original lease agreement, generally would be considered a new transaction that must independently satisfy the foreign economic processes requirement.

A taxpayer's foreign economic processes requirement is treated as satisfied with respect to a sales transaction (solely for the purpose of determining whether gross receipts are foreign trading gross receipts) if any related person has satisfied the foreign economic processes requirement in connection with another sales transaction involving the same qualifying foreign trade property.

Qualifying foreign trade property

Under the conference agreement, the threshold for determining if gross receipts will be treated as foreign trading gross receipts is whether the gross receipts are derived from a transaction involving "qualifying foreign trade property." Qualifying foreign trade property is property manufactured, produced, grown, or extracted ("manufactured") within or outside of the United States that is held primarily for sale, lease, or rental,[10] in the ordinary course of a trade or business, for direct use, consumption, or disposition outside of the United States.[11] In addition, not more than 50 percent of the fair market value of such property can be attributable to the sum of (1) the fair market value of articles manufactured outside of the United States plus (2) the direct costs of labor performed outside of the United States.[12]

The conferees understand that under current industry practice, the purchaser of an aircraft contracts separately for the aircraft engine and the airframe, albeit contracting with the airframe manufacturer to attach the separately purchased engine. The conferees intend that an aircraft engine be qualifying foreign trade property (assuming that all other requirements are satisfied) if (1) it is specifically designed to be separated from the airframe to which it is attached without significant damage to either the engine or the airframe, (2) it is reasonably expected to be separated from the airframe in the ordinary course of business (other than by reason of temporary separation for servicing, maintenance, or repair) before the end of the useful life of either the engine or the airframe, whichever is shorter, and (3) the terms under which the aircraft engine was sold were

---

[8] The foreign direct costs attributable to the transaction generally must exceed 50 percent of the total direct costs attributable to the transaction, but the requirement also will be satisfied if, with respect to at least two categories of direct costs, the foreign direct costs equal or exceed 85 percent of the total direct costs attributable to each category.

[9] For this purpose, the receipts of related persons are aggregated and, in the case of pass-through entities, the determination of whether the foreign trading gross receipts exceed $5 million is made both at the entity and at the partner/shareholder level.

[10] In addition, consistent with the policy adopted in the Taxpayer Relief Act of 1997, computer software licensed for reproduction is considered as property held primarily for sale, lease, or rental.

[11] "United States" includes Puerto Rico for these purposes because Puerto Rico is included in the customs territory of the United States.

[12] For this purpose, the fair market value of any article imported into the United States is its appraised value as determined under the Tariff Act of 1930. In addition, direct labor costs are determined under the principles of section 263A and do not include costs that would be treated as direct labor costs attributable to "articles," again applying principles of section 263A.

directly and separately negotiated between the manufacturer of the aircraft engine and the person to whom the aircraft will be ultimately delivered. By articulating this application of the foreign destination test in the case of certain separable aircraft engines, the conferees intend no inference with respect to the application of any destination test under present law or with respect to any other rule of law outside the conference agreement.[13]

The conference agreement excludes certain property from the definition of qualifying foreign trade property. The excluded property is (1) property leased or rented by the taxpayer for use by a related person, (2) certain intangibles,[14] (3) oil and gas (or any primary product thereof), (4) unprocessed softwood timber, (5) certain products the transfer of which are prohibited or curtailed to effectuate the policy set forth in Public Law 96-72, and (6) property designated by Executive order as in short supply. In addition, it is the intention of the conferees that property that is leased or licensed to a related person who is the lessor, licensor, or seller of the same property in a sublease, sublicense, sale, or rental to an unrelated person for the ultimate and predominate use by the unrelated person outside of the United States is not excluded property by reason of such lease or license to a related person.

With respect to property that is manufactured outside of the United States, rules are provided to ensure consistent U.S. tax treatment with respect to manufacturers. The conference agreement requires that property manufactured outside of the United States be manufactured by (1) a domestic corporation, (2) an individual who is a citizen or resident of the United States, (3) a foreign corporation that elects to be subject to U.S. taxation in the same manner as a U.S. corporation, or (4) a partnership or other pass-through entity all of the partners or owners of which are described in (1), (2), or (3) above.[15]

Foreign trade income

Under the conference agreement, "foreign trade income" is the taxable income of the taxpayer (determined without regard to the exclusion of qualifying foreign trade income) attributable to foreign trading gross receipts. Certain dividends-paid deductions of cooperatives are disregarded in determining foreign trade income for this purpose.

Foreign sale and leasing income

Under the conference agreement, "foreign sale and leasing income" is the amount of the taxpayer's foreign trade income (with respect to a transaction) that is properly allocable to activities that constitute foreign economic processes (as described above). For example, a distribution company's profit from the sale of qualifying foreign trade property that is associated with sales activities, such as solicitation or negotiation of the sale, advertising, processing customer orders and arranging for delivery, transportation outside of the United States, and other enumerated activities, would constitute foreign sale and leasing income.

Foreign sale and leasing income also includes foreign trade income derived by the taxpayer in connection with the lease or rental of qualifying foreign trade property for use by the lessee outside of the United States. Income from the sale, exchange, or other disposition of qualifying foreign trade property that is or was subject to such a lease[16] (i.e., the sale of the residual interest in the leased property) gives rise to foreign sale and leasing income. Except as provided in regulations, a special limitation applies to leased property that (1) is manufactured by the taxpayer or (2) is acquired by the taxpayer from a related person for a price that was other than arm's length. In such cases, foreign sale and leasing income may not exceed the amount of foreign sale and leasing income that would have resulted if the taxpayer had acquired the leased property in a hypothetical arm's-length purchase and then engaged in the actual sale or lease of such property. For example, if a manufacturer leases qualifying foreign trade property that it manufactured, the foreign sale and leasing income derived from that lease may not exceed the amount of foreign sale and leasing income that the manufacturer would have earned with respect to that lease had it purchased the property for an arm's-length price on the day that the manufacturer entered into the lease. For purposes of calculating the limit on foreign sale and leasing income, the manufacturer's basis and, thus, depreciation would be based on this hypothetical arm's-length price. This limitation is intended to prevent foreign sale and leasing income from including profit associated with manufacturing activities.

For purposes of determining foreign sale and leasing income, only directly allocable expenses

---

[13] See, e.g., sections 927(a)(1)(B) and 993(c)(1)(B).

[14] The intangibles that are treated as excluded property under the bill are: patents, inventions, models, designs, formulas, or processes whether or not patented, copyrights (other than films, tapes, records, or similar reproductions, and other than computer software (whether or not patented), for commercial or home use), goodwill, trademarks, trade brands, franchises, or other like property. Computer software that is licensed for reproduction outside of the United States is not excluded from the definition of qualifying foreign trade property.

[15] Except as provided by the Secretary of the Treasury, tiered partnerships or pass-through entities will be considered as partnerships or pass-through entities for purposes of this rule if each of the partnerships or entities is directly or indirectly wholly-owned by persons described in (1), (2), or (3) above.

[16] For this purpose, such a lease includes a lease that gave rise to exempt foreign trade income under the FSC provisions.

are taken into account in calculating the amount of foreign trade income. In addition, income properly allocable to certain intangibles is excluded for this purpose.

General example

The following is an example of the calculation of qualifying foreign trade income.

XYZ Corporation, a U.S. corporation, manufactures property that is sold to unrelated customers for use outside of the United States. XYZ Corporation satisfies the foreign economic processes requirement through conducting activities such as solicitation, negotiation, transportation, and other sales-related activities outside of the United States with respect to its transactions. During the year, qualifying foreign trade property was sold for gross proceeds totaling $1,000. The cost of this qualifying foreign trade property was $600. XYZ Corporation incurred $275 of costs that are directly related to the sale and distribution of qualifying foreign trade property. XYZ Corporation paid $40 of income tax to a foreign jurisdiction related to the sale and distribution of the qualifying foreign trade property. XYZ Corporation also generated gross income of $7,600 (gross receipts of $24,000 and cost of goods sold of $16,400) and direct expenses of $4,225 that relate to the manufacture and sale of products other than qualifying foreign trade property. XYZ Corporation also incurred $500 of overhead expenses. XYZ Corporation's financial information for the year is summarized as follows:

	Total	Other Property	OFTP [17]
Gross receipts	$25,000.00	$24,000.00	$1,000.00
Cost of goods sold	17,000.00	16,400.00	600.00
Gross income	8,000.00	7,600.00	400.00
Direct expenses	4,500.00	4,225.00	275.00
Overhead expenses	500.00		
Net income	3,000.00		

Illustrated below is the computation of the amount of qualifying foreign trade income that is excluded from XYZ Corporation's gross income and the amount of related expenses that are disallowed. In order to calculate qualifying foreign trade income, the amount of foreign trade income first must be determined. Foreign trade income is the taxable income (determined without regard to the exclusion of qualifying foreign trade income) attributable to foreign trading gross receipts. In this example, XYZ Corporation's foreign trading gross receipts equal $1,000. This amount of gross receipts is reduced by the related cost of goods sold, the related direct expenses, and a portion of the overhead expenses in order to arrive at the related taxable income.[18] Thus, XYZ Corporation's foreign trade income equals $100, calculated as follows:

Foreign trading gross receipts	$1,000.00
Cost of goods sold	600.00
Gross income	400.00
Direct expenses	275.00
Apportioned overhead expenses	25.00
Foreign trade income	100.00

Foreign sale and leasing income is defined as an amount of foreign trade income (calculated taking into account only directly-related expenses) that is properly allocable to certain specified foreign activities. Assume for purposes of this example that of the $125 of foreign trade income ($400 of gross income from the sale of qualifying foreign trade property less only the direct expenses of $275), $35 is properly allocable to such foreign activities (e.g., solicitation, negotiation, advertising, foreign transportation, and other enumerated sales-like activities) and, therefore, is considered to be foreign sale and leasing income.

Qualifying foreign trade income is the amount of *gross income* that, if excluded, will result in a reduction of *taxable income* equal to the greatest of (1) 30 percent of foreign sale and leasing income, (2) 1.2 percent of foreign trading gross receipts, or (3) 15 percent of foreign trade income. Thus, in order to calculate the amount that is excluded from gross income, taxable income must be determined and then "grossed up" for allocable expenses in order to arrive at the appropriate gross income figure. First, for each method of calculating qualifying foreign trade income, the reduction in taxable income is determined. Then, the $275 of direct and $25 of overhead expenses, totaling $300, attributable to foreign trading gross receipts is apportioned to the reduction in taxable income based on the proportion of the reduction in taxable income to foreign trade income. This apportionment is done for each method of calculating qualifying foreign trade

---

[17] "QFTP" refers to qualifying foreign trade property.

[18] Overhead expenses must be apportioned in a reasonable manner that does not result in a material distortion of income. In this example, the apportionment of the $500 of overhead expenses on the basis of gross income is assumed not to result in a material distortion of income and is assumed to be a reasonable method of apportionment. Thus,

$25 ($500 of total overhead expenses multiplied by 5 percent, i.e., $400 of gross income from the sale of qualifying foreign trade property divided by $8,000 of total gross income) is apportioned to qualifying foreign trading gross receipts. The remaining $475 ($500 of total overhead expenses less the $25 apportioned to qualifying foreign trade income) is apportioned to XYZ Corporation's other income.

income. The sum of the taxable income reduction and the apportioned expenses equals the respective qualifying foreign trade income (i.e., the amount of gross income excluded) under each method, as follows:

	1.2% FTGR [1]	15% FTI [2]	30% FS&LI [3]
Reduction of taxable income			
1.2% of FTGR (1.2% * $1,000)	12.00		
15% of FTI (15% * $100)..............................		15.00	
30% of FS&LI (30% * $35)			10.50
Gross-up for disallowed expenses			
$300 * ($12/$100)	36.00		
$300 * ($15/$100)		45.00	
$275 * ($10.50/$100) [4]			28.88
Qualifying foreign trade income	48.00	60.00	39.38

[1] "FTGR" refers to foreign trading gross receipts.
[2] "FTT" refers to foreign trade income.
[3] "FS&LI" refers to foreign sale and leasing income.
[4] Because foreign sale and leasing income only takes into account direct expenses, it is appropriate to take into account only such expenses for purposes of this calculation.

In the example, the $60 of qualifying foreign trade income is excluded from XYZ Corporation's gross income (determined based on 15 percent of foreign trade income).[19] In connection with excluding $60 of gross income, certain expenses that are allocable to this income are not deductible for U.S. Federal income tax purposes. Thus, $45 ($300 of related expenses multiplied by 15 percent, i.e., $60 of qualifying foreign trade income divided by $400 of gross income from the sale of qualifying foreign trade property) of expenses are disallowed.[20]

	Other Property	QFTP	Excluded/ Disallowed	Total
Gross receipts	$24,000.00	$1,000.00		
Cost of goods sold	16,400.00	600.00		
Gross income	7,600.00	400.00	(60.00)	7,940.00
Direct expenses.................	4,225.00	275.00	(41.25)	4,458.75
Overhead expenses	475.00	25.00	(3.75)	496.25
Taxable income.................				2,985.00

XYZ Corporation paid $40 of income tax to a foreign jurisdiction related to the sale and distribution of the qualifying foreign trade property. A portion of this $40 of foreign income tax is treated as paid with respect to the qualifying foreign trade income and, therefore, is not creditable for U.S. foreign tax credit purposes. In this case, $6 of such taxes paid ($40 of foreign taxes multiplied by 15 percent, i.e., $60 of qualifying foreign trade income divided by $400 of gross income from the sale of qualifying foreign trade property) is treated as paid with respect to the qualifying foreign trade income and, thus, is not creditable.

The results in this example are the same regardless of whether XYZ Corporation manufactures the property within the United States or outside of the United States through a foreign branch. If XYZ Corporation were an S corporation or limited liability company, the results also would be the same, and the exclusion would pass

[19] Note that XYZ Corporation could choose to use one of the other two methods notwithstanding that they would result in a smaller exclusion.
[20] The $300 of allocable expenses includes both the $275 of direct expenses and the $25 of overhead expenses. Thus, the $45 of disallowed expenses represents the sum of $41.25 of direct expenses plus $3.75 of overhead expenses. If qualifying foreign trade income were determined using 30 percent of foreign sale and leasing income, the disallowed expenses would include only the appropriate portion of the direct expenses.

through to the S corporation owners or limited liability company owners as the case may be.

Other rules

Foreign-source income limitation

The conference agreement provides a limitation with respect to the sourcing of taxable income applicable to certain sale transactions giving rise to foreign trading gross receipts. This limitation only applies with respect to sale transactions involving property that is manufactured within the United States. The special source limitation does not apply when qualifying foreign trade income is determined using 30 percent of the foreign sale and leasing income from the transaction.

This foreign-source income limitation is determined in one of two ways depending on whether the qualifying foreign trade income is calculated based on 1.2 percent of foreign trading gross receipts or on 15 percent of foreign trade income. If the qualifying foreign trade income is calculated based on 1.2 percent of foreign trading gross receipts, the related amount of foreign-source income may not exceed the amount of foreign trade income that (without taking into account this special foreign-source income limitation) would be treated as foreign-source income if such foreign trade income were reduced by 4 percent of the related foreign trading gross receipts.

For example, assume that foreign trading gross receipts are $2,000 and foreign trade income is $100. Assume also that the taxpayer chooses to determine qualifying foreign trade income based on 1.2 percent of foreign trading gross receipts. Taxable income after taking into account the exclusion of the qualifying foreign trade income and the disallowance of related deductions is $76. Assume that the taxpayer manufactured its qualifying foreign trade property in the United States and that title to such property passed outside of the United States. Absent a special sourcing rule, under section 863(b) (and the regulations thereunder) the $76 of taxable income would be sourced as $38 U.S. source and $38 foreign source. Under the special sourcing rule, the amount of foreign-source income may not exceed the amount of the foreign trade income that otherwise would be treated as foreign source if the foreign trade income were reduced by 4 percent of the related foreign trading gross receipts. Reducing foreign trade income by 4 percent of the foreign trading gross receipts (4 percent of $2,000, or $80) would result in $20 ($100 foreign trade income less $80). Applying section 863(b) to the $20 of reduced foreign trade income would result in $10 of foreign-source income and $10 of U.S.-source income.

Accordingly, the limitation equals $10. Thus, although under the general sourcing rule $38 of the $76 taxable income would be treated as foreign source, the special sourcing rule limits foreign-source income in this example to $10 (with the remaining $66 being treated as U.S.-source income).

If the qualifying foreign trade income is calculated based on 15 percent of foreign trade income, the amount of related foreign-source income may not exceed 50 percent of the foreign trade income that (without taking into account this special foreign-source income limitation) would be treated as foreign-source income.

For example, assume that foreign trade income is $100 and the taxpayer chooses to determine its qualifying foreign trade income based on 15 percent of foreign trade income. Taxable income after taking into account the exclusion of the qualifying foreign trade income and the disallowance of related deductions is $85. Assume that the taxpayer manufactured its qualifying foreign trade property in the United States and that title to such property passed outside of the United States. Absent a special sourcing rule, under section 863(b) the $85 of taxable income would be sourced as $42.50 U.S. source and $42.50 foreign source. Under the special sourcing rule, the amount of foreign-source income may not exceed 50 percent of the foreign trade income that otherwise would be treated as foreign source. Applying section 863(b) to the $100 of foreign trade income would result in $50 of foreign-source income and $50 of U.S.-source income. Accordingly, the limitation equals $25, which is 50 percent of the $50 foreign-source income. Thus, although under the general sourcing rule $42.50 of the $85 taxable income would be treated as foreign source, the special sourcing rule limits foreign-source income in this example to $25 (with the remaining $60 being treated as U.S.-source income).[21]

Treatment of withholding taxes

The conference agreement generally provides that no foreign tax credit is allowed for foreign taxes paid or accrued with respect to qualifying foreign trade income (i.e., excluded extraterritorial income). In determining whether foreign taxes are paid or accrued with respect to qualifying foreign trade income, foreign withholding taxes generally are treated as not paid or accrued with respect to qualifying foreign trade income.[22] Accordingly, the conference agreement's denial of foreign tax credits would not apply to such taxes. For this purpose, the term "withholding tax" refers to any foreign tax that is imposed on a basis

---

[21] The foreign-source income limitation provisions also apply when source is determined solely in accordance with section 862 (e.g., a distributor of qualifying foreign trade property that is manufactured in the United States by an unrelated person and sold for use outside of the United States).

[22] With respect to the withholding taxes that are paid or accrued (a prerequisite to the taxes being otherwise creditable), the provision in the bill treats such taxes as not being paid or accrued *with respect to* qualifying foreign trade income.

other than residence and that is otherwise a creditable foreign tax under sections 901 or 903.[23] It is intended that such taxes would be similar in nature to the gross-basis taxes described in sections 871 and 881.

If, however, qualifying foreign trade income is determined based on 30 percent of foreign sale and leasing income, the special rule for withholding taxes is not applicable. Thus, in such cases foreign withholding taxes may be treated as paid or accrued with respect to qualifying foreign trade income and, accordingly, are not creditable under the conference agreement.

Election to be treated as a U.S. corporation

The conference agreement provides that certain foreign corporations may elect, on an original return, to be treated as domestic corporations. The election applies to the taxable year when made and all subsequent taxable years unless revoked by the taxpayer or terminated for failure to qualify for the election. Such election is available for a foreign corporation (1) that manufactures property in the ordinary course of such corporation's trade or business, or (2) if substantially all of the gross receipts of such corporation are foreign trading gross receipts. For this purpose, "substantially all" is based on the relevant facts and circumstances.

In order to be eligible to make this election, the foreign corporation must waive all benefits granted to such corporation by the United States pursuant to a treaty.[24] Absent such a waiver, it would be unclear, for example, whether the permanent establishment article of a relevant tax treaty would override the electing corporation's treatment as a domestic corporation under this provision. A foreign corporation that elects to be treated as a domestic corporation is not permitted to make an S corporation election. The Secretary is granted authority to prescribe rules to ensure that the electing foreign corporation pays its U.S. income tax liabilities and to designate one or more classes of corporations that may not make such an election.[25] If such an election is made, for purposes of section 367 the foreign corporation is treated as transferring (as of the first day of the first taxable year to which the election applies) all of its assets to a domestic corporation in connection with an exchange to which section 354 applies.

If a corporation fails to meet the applicable requirements, described above, for making the election to be treated as a domestic corporation for any taxable year beginning after the year of the election, the election will terminate. In addition, a taxpayer, at its option and at any time, may revoke the election to be treated as a domestic corporation. In the case of either a termination or a revocation, the electing foreign corporation will not be considered as a domestic corporation effective beginning on the first day of the taxable year following the year of such termination or revocation. For purposes of section 367, if the election to be treated as a domestic corporation is terminated or revoked, such corporation is treated as a domestic corporation transferring (as of the first day of the first taxable year to which the election ceases to apply) all of its property to a foreign corporation in connection with an exchange to which section 354 applies. Moreover, once a termination occurs or a revocation is made, the former electing corporation may not again elect to be taxed as a domestic corporation under the provisions of the conference agreement for a period of five tax years beginning with the first taxable year that begins after the termination or revocation.

For example, assume a U.S. corporation owns 100 percent of a foreign corporation. The foreign corporation manufactures outside of the United States and sells what would be qualifying foreign trade property were it manufactured by a person subject to U.S. taxation. Such foreign corporation could make the election under this provision to be treated as a domestic corporation. As a result, its earnings no longer would be deferred from U.S. taxation. However, by electing to be subject to U.S. taxation, a portion of its income would be qualifying foreign trade income.[26] The requirement that the foreign corporation be treated as a domestic corporation (and, therefore, subject to U.S. taxation) is intended to provide parity between U.S. corporations that manufacture abroad in branch form and U.S. corporations that manufacture abroad through foreign subsidiaries. The election, however, is not limited to U.S.-owned foreign corporations. A foreign-owned foreign corporation that wishes to qualify for the treatment provided under the conference agreement could avail itself of such election (unless otherwise precluded from doing so by Treasury regulations).

Shared partnerships

The conference agreement provides rules relating to allocations of qualifying foreign trade income by certain shared partnerships. To the extent that such a partnership (1) maintains a separate account for transactions involving foreign trading gross receipts with each partner, (2) makes distributions to each partner based on the amounts in the separate account, and (3) meets

---

[23] This also would apply to any withholding tax that is creditable for U.S. foreign tax credit purposes under an applicable treaty.
[24] The waiver of treaty benefits applies to the corporation itself and not, for example, to employees of or independent contractors associated with the corporation.

[25] For example, the Secretary of the Treasury may prescribe rules to prevent "per se" corporations under the entity-classification rules from making such an election.
[26] The sourcing limitation described above would not apply to this example because the property is manufactured outside of the United States.

such other requirements as the Treasury Secretary may prescribe by regulations, such partnership then would allocate to each partner items of income, gain, loss, and deduction (including qualifying foreign trade income) from such transactions on the basis of the separate accounts. It is intended that with respect to, and only with respect to, such allocations and distributions (i.e., allocations and distributions related to transactions between the partner and the shared partnership generating foreign trading gross receipts), these rules would apply in lieu of the otherwise applicable partnership allocation rules such as those in section 704(b). For this purpose, a partnership is a foreign or domestic entity that is considered to be a partnership for U.S. Federal income tax purposes.

Under the conference agreement, any partner's interest in the shared partnership is not taken into account in determining whether such partner is a "related person" with respect to any other partner for purposes of the conference agreement's provisions. Also, the election to exclude certain gross receipts from foreign trading gross receipts must be made separately by each partner with respect to any transaction for which the shared partnership maintains a separate account.

Certain assets not taken into account for purposes of interest expense allocation

The conference agreement also provides that qualifying foreign trade property that is held for lease or rental, in the ordinary course of a trade or business, for use by the lessee outside of the United States is not taken into account for interest allocation purposes.

Distributions of qualifying foreign trade income by cooperatives

Agricultural and horticultural producers often market their products through cooperatives, which are member-owned corporations formed under Subchapter T of the Code. At the cooperative level, the conference agreement provides the same treatment of foreign trading gross receipts derived from products marketed through cooperatives as it provides for foreign trading gross receipts of other taxpayers. That is, the qualifying foreign trade income attributable to those foreign trading gross receipts is excluded from the gross income of the cooperative. Absent a special rule, however, patronage dividends or per-unit retain allocations attributable to qualifying foreign trade income paid to members of cooperatives would be taxable in the hands of those members. The conferees believe that this would disadvantage agricultural and horticultural producers who choose to market their products through cooperatives relative to those individuals who market

their products directly or through pass-through entities such as partnerships, limited liability companies, or S corporations. Accordingly, the conference agreement provides that the amount of any patronage dividends or per-unit retain allocations paid to a member of an agricultural or horticultural cooperative (to which Part I of Subchapter T applies), which is allocable to qualifying foreign trade income of the cooperative, is treated as qualifying foreign trade income of the member (and, thus, excludable from such member's gross income). In order to qualify, such amount must be designated by the organization as allocable to qualifying foreign trade income in a written notice mailed to its patrons not later than the payment period described in section 1382(d). The cooperative cannot reduce its income (e.g., cannot claim a "dividends-paid deduction") under section 1382 for such amounts.

Gap period before administrative guidance is issued

The conferees recognize that there may be a gap in time between the enactment of the bill and the issuance of detailed administrative guidance. It is intended that during this gap period before administrative guidance is issued, taxpayers and the Internal Revenue Service may apply the principles of present-law regulations and other administrative guidance under sections 921 through 927 to analogous concepts under the conference agreement. Some examples of the application of the principles of present-law regulations to the conference agreement are described below. These limited examples are intended to be merely illustrative and are not intended to imply any limitation regarding the application of the principles of other analogous rules or concepts under present law.

Marginal costing and grouping

Under the conference agreement, the Secretary of the Treasury is provided authority to prescribe rules for using marginal costing and for grouping transactions in determining qualifying foreign trade income. It is intended that similar principles under present-law regulations apply for these purposes.[27]

Excluded property

The conference agreement provides that qualifying foreign trade property does not include property leased or rented by the taxpayer for use by a related person. It is intended that similar principles under present-law regulations apply for this purpose. Thus, excluded property does not apply, for example, to property leased by the taxpayer to a related person if the property is held for sublease, or is subleased, by the related person to an unrelated person and the property is

---

[27] See, e.g., Treas. Reg. sec. 1.924(d)-1(c)(5) and (e); Temp. Treas. Reg. sec. 1.925(a)-1T(c)(8); Temp. Treas. Reg. sec. 1.925(b)-1T.

ultimately used by such unrelated person predominantly outside of the United States.[28] In addition, consistent with the policy adopted in the Taxpayer Relief Act of 1997, computer software that is licensed for reproduction outside of the United States is not excluded property. Accordingly, the license of computer software to a related person for reproduction outside of the United States for sale, sublicense, lease, or rental to an unrelated person for use outside of the United States is not treated as excluded property by reason of the license to the related person.

Foreign trading gross receipts

Under the conference agreement, foreign trading gross receipts are gross receipts from, among other things, the sale, exchange, or other disposition of qualifying foreign trade property, and from the lease of qualifying foreign trade property for use by the lessee outside of the United States. It is intended that the principles of present-law regulations that define foreign trading gross receipts apply for this purpose. For example, a sale includes an exchange or other disposition and a lease includes a rental or sublease and a license or a sublicense.[29]

Foreign use requirement

Under the conference agreement, property constitutes qualifying foreign trade property if, among other things, the property is held primarily for lease, sale, or rental, in the ordinary course of business, for direct use, consumption, or disposition outside of the United States.[30] It is intended that the principles of the present-law regulations apply for purposes of this foreign use requirement. For example, for purposes of determining whether property is sold for use outside of the United States, property that is sold to an unrelated person as a component to be incorporated into a second product which is produced, manufactured, or assembled outside of the United States will not be considered to be used in the United States (even if the second product ultimately is used in the United States), provided that the fair market value of such seller's components at the time of delivery to the purchaser constitutes less than 20 percent of the fair market value of the second product into which the components are incorporated (determined at the time of completion of the production, manufacture, or assembly of the second product).[31]

In addition, for purposes of the foreign use requirement, property is considered to be used by a purchaser or lessee outside of the United States during a taxable year if it is used predominantly outside of the United States.[32] For this purpose, property is considered to be used predominantly outside of the United States for any period if, during that period, the property is located outside of the United States more than 50 percent of the time.[33] An aircraft or other property used for transportation purposes (e.g., railroad rolling stock, a vessel, a motor vehicle, or a container) is considered to be used outside of the United States for any period if, for the period, either the property is located outside of the United States more than 50 percent of the time or more than 50 percent of the miles traveled in the use of the property are traveled outside of the United States.[34] An orbiting satellite is considered to be located outside of the United States for these purposes.[35]

Foreign economic processes

Under the conference agreement, gross receipts from a transaction are foreign trading gross receipts eligible for exclusion from the tax base only if certain economic processes take place outside of the United States. The foreign economic processes requirement compares foreign direct costs to total direct costs. It is intended that the principles of the present-law regulations apply during the gap period for purposes of the foreign economic processes requirement including the measurement of direct costs. The conferees recognize that the measurement of foreign direct costs under the present-law regulations often depend on activities conducted by the FSC, which is a separate entity. The conferees are aware that some of these concepts will have to be modified when new guidance is promulgated as a result of the conference agreement's elimination of the requirement for a separate entity.

Effective Date

In general

The conference agreement is effective for transactions entered into after September 30, 2000. In addition, no corporation may elect to be a FSC after September 30, 2000.

The conference agreement also provides a rule requiring the termination of a dormant FSC when the FSC has been inactive for a specified period of time. Under this rule, a FSC that generates no foreign trade income for any five consecutive

---

[28] See Temp. Treas. Reg. sec. 1.927(a)-1T(f)(2)(i). The bill also provides that oil or gas or primary products from oil or gas are excluded from the definition of qualifying foreign trade property. It is intended that similar principles under present-law regulations apply for these purposes. Thus, for this purpose, petrochemicals, medicinal products, insecticides, and alcohols are not considered primary products from oil or gas and, thus, are not treated as excluded property. See Temp. Treas. Reg. sec. 1.927(a)-1T(g)(2)(iv).

[29] See Temp. Treas. Reg. sec. 1.924(a)-1T(a)(2).

[30] Foreign trading gross receipts eligible for exclusion from the tax base do not include gross receipts from a transaction if the qualifying foreign trade property is for ultimate use in the United States.

[31] See Temp. Treas. Reg. sec. 1.927(a)-1T(d)(4)(ii).

[32] See Temp. Treas. Reg. sec. 1.927(a)-1T(d)(4)(iii), (iv), and (v).

[33] See Temp. Treas. Reg. sec. 1.927(a)-1T(d)(4)(vi).

[34] Id.

[35] Id.

years beginning after December 31, 2001, will cease to be treated as a FSC.

Transition rules

Winding down existing FSCs and binding contract relief

The conference agreement provides a transition period for existing FSCs and for binding contractual agreements. The new rules do not apply to transactions in the ordinary course of business[36] involving a FSC before January 1, 2002. Furthermore, the new rules do not apply to transactions in the ordinary course of business after December 31, 2001, if such transactions are pursuant to a binding contract between a FSC (or a person related to the FSC on September 30, 2000) and any other person (that is not a related person) and such contract is in effect on September 30, 2000, and all times thereafter. For this purpose, binding contracts include purchase options, renewal options, and replacement options that are enforceable against a lessor or seller (provided that the options are a part of a contract that is binding and in effect on September 30, 2000).

Old earnings and profits of corporations electing to be treated as domestic corporations

A transition rule also is provided for certain corporations electing to be treated as a domestic corporation under the bill. In the case of a corporation to which this transition rule applies, the corporation's earnings and profits accumulated in taxable years ending before October 1, 2000 are not included in the gross income of the shareholder by reason of the deemed asset transfer for section 367 purposes that the bill provides. Thus, although the electing corporation may be treated as transferring all of its assets to a domestic corporation in a reorganization described in section 368(a)(1)(F), the earnings and profits amount that would otherwise be treated as a deemed dividend to the U.S. shareholder under the regulations under section 367(b) will not include the earnings and profits accumulated in taxable years ending before October 1, 2000. This treatment is similar to the treatment of earnings and profits of a foreign insurance company that makes the election to be treated as a domestic corporation under section 953(d), which election was a model for the election to be treated as a domestic corporation under the bill. Under section 953(d), earnings and profits accumulated in taxable years beginning before January 1, 1988 were not included in the earnings and profits amount that would be a deemed dividend for section 367(b) purposes.

Like the pre-1988 earnings and profits of a domesticating foreign insurance company under section 953(d), the earnings and profits to which this transition rule applies would continue to be treated as earnings and profits of a foreign corporation even after the corporation elects to be treated as a domestic corporation. Thus, a distribution out of earnings and profits of an electing corporation accumulated in taxable years ending before October 1, 2000 would be treated as a distribution made by a foreign corporation.[37] Rules similar to those applicable to corporations making the section 953(d) election that prevent the repatriation of pre-election period earnings and profits without current U.S. taxation apply for this purpose. Thus, for example, the earnings and profits accumulated in taxable years beginning before October 1, 2000 would continue to be taken into account for section 1248 purposes.[38]

The earnings and profits to which the transition rule applies are the earnings and profits accumulated by the electing corporation in taxable years ending before October 1, 2000. The transition rule will not apply to earnings and profits accumulated before that date that are succeeded to after that date by the electing corporation in a transaction to which section 381 applies unless, like the electing corporation, the distributor or transferor (from whom the electing corporation acquired the earnings and profits) could have itself made the election under the bill to be treated as a domestic corporation and would have been eligible for the transition relief.

The transition rule for old earnings and profits applies to two classes of taxpayers. The first class is FSCs in existence on September 30, 2000 that make an election to be treated as a domestic corporation because they satisfy the requirement that substantially all of their gross receipts are foreign trading gross receipts. To be eligible for the transition relief, the election must be made not later than for the FSC's first taxable year beginning after December 31, 2001.

The second class of corporations to which this transition relief applies is certain controlled foreign corporations (as defined in section 957). Notwithstanding other requirements for making the election to be treated as a domestic corporation provided under the bill's general provisions, such controlled foreign corporations are eligible under the transition rule to make the election to be treated as a domestic corporation and will not have the resulting deemed asset transfer cause a deemed inclusion of earnings and profits for earnings and profits accumulated in taxable years ending before October 1, 2000. To be eligible for

---

[36] The mere entering into of a single transaction, such as a lease, would not, in and of itself, prevent the transaction from being in the ordinary course of business.

[37] It is anticipated that ordering rules similar to those that have been applied in guidance under section 953(d)

would apply to distributions from the electing corporation. See Notice 89-79, 1989-2 C.B. 392.

[38] See the rules of section 953(d)(4)(ii), (iii) and (iv).

the transition relief, such a controlled foreign corporation must be in existence on September 30, 2000. The controlled foreign corporation must be wholly owned, directly or indirectly, by a domestic corporation.[39] The controlled foreign corporation must never have made an election to be treated as a FSC and must make the election to be treated as a domestic corporation not later than for its first taxable year beginning after December 31, 2001. In addition, the controlled foreign corporation must satisfy certain tests with respect to its income and activities. For administrative convenience, these tests are limited to the three taxable years preceding the first taxable year for which the election to be treated as a domestic corporation applies. First, during that three-year period, all of the controlled foreign corporation's gross income must be subpart F income. Thus, the income was subject to full inclusion to the U.S. shareholder and, accordingly, subject to current U.S. taxation. Second, during that three-year period, the controlled foreign corporation must have, in the ordinary course of its trade or business, entered into transactions in which it regularly sold or paid commissions to a related FSC (which also was in existence on September 30, 2000).[40] If an electing corporation in this second class ceases to be (directly or indirectly) wholly owned by the domestic corporation that owns it on September 30, 2000, the election to be treated as a domestic corporation is terminated.

Limitation on use of the gross receipts method

Similar to the limitation on use of the gross receipts method under the conference agreement's operative provisions, the conference agreement provides a rule that limits the use of the gross receipts method for transactions after the effective date of the conference agreement if that same property generated foreign trade income to a FSC using the gross receipts method. Under the rule, if any person used the gross receipts method under the FSC regime, neither that person nor any related person will have qualifying foreign trade income with respect to any other transaction involving the same item of property.

Coordination of new regime with prior law

Notwithstanding the transition period, FSCs (or related persons) may elect to have the rules of the conference agreement apply in lieu of the rules applicable to FSCs. Thus, for transactions to which the transition rules apply (i.e., transactions *after* September 30, 2000 that occur (1) before January 1, 2002 or (2) after December 31, 2001 pursuant to a binding contract which is in effect on September 30, 2000), taxpayers may choose to apply either the FSC rules or the amendments made by this bill, but not both. In addition, a taxpayer would not be able to avail itself of the rules of the conference agreement in addition to the rules applicable to domestic international sales corporations because the conference agreement provides that the exclusion of extraterritorial income will not apply if a taxpayer is a member of any controlled group of which a domestic international sales corporation is a member.

[Law at ¶ 5100, ¶ 5140, ¶ 5240, ¶ 5430, ¶ 5450, ¶ 5460, ¶ 5470, ¶ 5480, ¶ 5490, ¶ 5500, ¶ 5510, ¶ 5520, ¶ 5530, ¶ 5540, ¶ 5550 and ¶ 5570. CCH Explanation at ¶ 505, ¶ 510, ¶ 515, ¶ 520, ¶ 525, ¶ 530, ¶ 535, ¶ 540 and ¶ 545.]

---

[39] The ultimate owner must be an actual domestic corporation, not a corporation that elects to be treated as a domestic corporation under the bill. In addition, although the controlled foreign corporation must be wholly owned for this purpose, it is intended that the mere nominal ownership of an insignificant number of shares of insignificant value (which may, for example, be required by foreign law) by someone unrelated to the domestic parent would not cause the controlled foreign corporation to fail to be wholly owned for these purposes.

[40] It is intended that, if the controlled foreign corporation's and related FSC's taxable years are still open under the statute of limitations for claims for refund under section 6511, redeterminations with respect to sales or commissions paid to the FSC are permitted for this purpose. See Temp. Treas. Reg. sec. 1.925(a)-1T(d)(4).

Committee Reports
Community Renewal Tax Relief Act of 2000
Introduction

[¶ 10,131]

The Community Renewal Tax Relief Act of 2000 (P.L. 106-554) was introduced in the House on December 14, 2000, as H.R. 5662. H.R. 5662 was then incorporated by reference into the Consolidated Appropriations Act, 2001 (H.R. 4577), on December 15, 2000. A conference report on H.R. 4577 was filed in the House on December 15, 2000 (H.R. CONF. REP. NO. 106-1033) and the House favorably passed the conference bill. The Senate agreed to the conference bill by voice vote on December 15, 2000. H.R. 4577 was signed by the President on December 21, 2000.

The provisions of H.R. 5662 are substantially similar to the community renewal tax provisions contained in the Tax Relief Act of 2000 (H.R. 5542). H.R. 5542 was one of five bills introduced on October 25, 2000, and incorporated by reference in the conference agreement for H.R. 2614, the Certified Development Company Program Improvements Bill of 2000. A conference report on H.R. 2614 was filed in the House on October 26, 2000 (H.R. CONF. REP. NO. 106-1004), and the House agreed to the conference bill on October 26, 2000. For purposes of clarity, only the conference committee report for H.R. 4577, which incorporates H.R. 5662, is reproduced herein (H.R. CONF. REP. NO. 106-1033).

This section includes the pertinent texts of the controlling committee report that explain the changes enacted in the Community Renewal Tax Relief Act of 2000. The following material is the official wording of the relevant Conference Committee Report in Act Sec. order. Headings have been added for convenience in locating the committee reports. Any omission of text is indicated by asterisks (* * *). References are to the following official report:

● The Conference Committee Explanation of the Tax-Related Portions of the Consolidated Appropriations Act, 2001 (H.R. 4577), reported on December 15, 2000, and issued as CCH Special 1, STANDARD FEDERAL TAX REPORTS, Issue No. 3 (extra issue), Janaury 10, 2001, is referred to as **Conference Committee Report** (H.R. CONF. REP. NO. 106-1033).

[¶ 10,135]   Act Sec. 101(a) and 101(c).   Designation and treatment of renewal communities

Conference Committee Report (H.R. CONF. REP. NO. 106-1033)

[Code Sec. 1400E]

Present Law

In recent years, provisions have been added to the Internal Revenue Code that target specific geographic areas for special Federal income tax treatment. For example, empowerment zones and enterprise communities generally provide tax incentives for businesses that locate within certain geographic areas designated by the Secretaries of Housing and Urban Development ("HUD") and Agriculture.

House Bill

No provision. However, H.R. 5542[1] authorizes the designation of 40 "renewal communities" within which special tax incentives would be

---

[1] H.R. 5542 was incorporated by reference into the conference agreement that accompanied H.R. 2614 (H. Rpt. 106-1004), which was passed by the House of Representatives on October 26, 2000.

available. The following is a description of the designation process * * *

Designation process

Designation of 40 renewal communities

The Secretary of HUD,[2] is authorized to designate up to 40 "renewal communities" from areas nominated by States and local governments. At least 12 of the designated communities must be in rural areas. Of the 12 rural renewal communities, one shall be an area within Mississippi, designated by the State of Mississippi, that includes at least one census tract within Madison County, Mississippi.

The Secretary of HUD is required to publish (within four months after enactment) regulations describing the nomination and selection process. Designations of renewal communities are to be made during the period beginning on the first day of the first month after the regulations are published and ending on December 31, 2001. The designation of an area as a renewal community generally will be effective on January 1, 2002, and will terminate after December 31, 2009.[3]

Eligibility criteria

To be designated as a renewal community, a nominated area must meet the following criteria: (1) each census tract must have a poverty rate of at least 20 percent;[4] (2) in the case of an urban area, at least 70 percent of the households have incomes below 80 percent of the median income of households within the local government jurisdiction; (3) the unemployment rate is at least 1.5 times the national unemployment rate; and (4) the area is one of pervasive poverty, unemployment, and general distress. Those areas with the highest average ranking of eligibility factors (1), (2), and (3) above would be designated as renewal communities. One nominated area within the District of Columbia becomes a renewal community (without regard to its ranking of eligibility factors) provided that it satisfies the area and eligibility requirements and the required State and local commitments described below.[5] The Secretary of HUD shall take into account in selecting areas for designation the extent to which such areas have a high incidence of crime, as well as whether the area has census tracts identified in the May 12, 1998, report of the General Accounting Office regarding the identification of economically distressed areas. In lieu of the poverty, income, and unemployment criteria, outmigration may be taken into account in the designation of one rural renewal community.

There are no geographic size limitations placed on renewal communities. Instead, the boundary of a renewal community must be continuous. In addition, the renewal community must have a minimum population of 4,000 if the community is located within a metropolitan statistical area (at least 1,000 in all other cases), and a maximum population of not more than 200,000. The population limitations do not apply to any renewal community that is entirely within an Indian reservation.

Required State and local commitments

In order for an area to be designated as a renewal community, State and local governments are required to submit a written course of action in which the State and local governments promise to take at least four of the following governmental actions within the nominated area: (1) a reduction of tax rates or fees; (2) an increase in the level of efficiency of local services; (3) crime reduction strategies; (4) actions to remove or streamline governmental requirements; (5) involvement by private entities and community groups, such as to provide jobs and job training and financial assistance; and (6) the gift (or sale at below fair market value) of surplus realty by the State or local government to community organizations or private companies.

In addition, the nominating State and local governments must promise to promote economic growth in the nominated area by repealing or not enforcing four of the following: (1) licensing requirements for occupations that do not ordinarily require a professional degree; (2) zoning restrictions on home-based businesses that do not create a public nuisance; (3) permit requirements for street vendors who do not create a public nuisance; (4) zoning or other restrictions that impede the formation of schools or child care centers; and (5) franchises or other restrictions on competition for businesses providing public services, including but not limited to taxicabs, jitneys, cable television, or trash hauling, unless such regulations are necessary for and well-tailored to the protection of health and safety.

Empowerment zones and enterprise communities seeking designation as renewal communities

With respect to the first 20 designations of nominated areas as renewal communities, preference will be given to nominated areas that are enterprise communities and empowerment zones under present law that otherwise meet the requirements for designation as a renewal community. An empowerment zone or enterprise

---

[2] In making the designations, the Secretary of HUD must consult with the Secretaries of Agriculture, Commerce, Labor, Treasury, the Director of the Office of Management and Budget; and the Administrator of the Small Business Administration (and the Secretary of the Interior in the case of an area within an Indian reservation).

[3] The designation would terminate earlier than December 31, 2009, if (1) an earlier termination date is designated by the State or local government in their designation, or (2) the Secretary of HUD revokes the designation as of an earlier date.

[4] Determined using 1990 census data.

[5] The designation of a nominated area within the District of Columbia as a renewal community becomes effective on January 1, 2003 (upon the expiration of the designation of the District of Columbia Enterprise Zone).

community can apply for designation as a renewal community. If a renewal community designation is granted, then an area's designation as an empowerment zone or enterprise community ceases as of the date the area's designation as a renewal community takes effect.

* * *

GAO report

The General Accounting Office will audit and report to Congress on January 31, 2004, and again in 2007 and 2010, on the renewal community program and its effect on poverty, unemployment, and economic growth within the designated renewal communities.

Effective Date

Renewal communities must be designated during the period beginning on the first day of the first month after the publication of regulations by HUD and ending on December 31, 2001. * * *

Senate Amendment

No provision. However, S. 3152[8] authorizes the Secretaries of HUD and Agriculture to designate up to 30 renewal zones from areas nominated by States and local governments. At least six of the designated renewal zones must be in rural areas. The Secretary of HUD is required to publish (within four months after enactment) regulations describing the nomination and selection process. Designations of renewal zones must be made before January 1, 2002, and the designations are effective for the period beginning on January 1, 2002 through December 31, 2009.

The eligibility criteria (as well as the population and geographic limitations) are similar to those for renewal communities in the House bill, except that S. 3152 provides that any State without any empowerment zone would be given priority in the designation process. Also, the designations of renewal zones must result in (after taking into account existing empowerment zones) each State having at least one zone designation

(empowerment or renewal zone). In addition, S. 3152 provides that, in lieu of the poverty, income, and unemployment criteria, outmigration may be taken into account in the designation of one rural renewal zone. Under a separate provision in S. 3152, the designation of the District of Columbia Enterprise Zone is extended through December 31, 2006.

In order for an area to be designated as a renewal zone, State and local governments are required to submit a written course of action in which the State and local governments promise to take at least four of the governmental actions described in the House bill with respect to renewal communities. However, S. 3152 does not contain any of the economic growth provision requirements described in the House bill.

* * *

GAO report

The General Accounting Office will audit and report to Congress every three years (beginning on January 31, 2004) on the renewal zone program and its effect on poverty, unemployment, and economic growth within the designated renewal zones.

Effective Date

The 30 renewal zones must be designated by January 1, 2002 * * *

Conference Agreement

The conference agreement follows H.R. 5542 with the following modifications. The conference agreement does not include the rural renewal community designation with respect to an area within the State of Mississippi. The conference agreement does not include the special rule that provides that one nominated area within the District of Columbia becomes a renewal community (without regard to its ranking of eligibility factors).

[Law at ¶ 5800 and ¶ 7060. CCH Explanation at ¶ 105.]

[¶ 10,137] Act Sec. 101(a). Renewal community capital gain

Conference Committee Report (H.R. Conf. Rep. No. 106-1033)

[Code Secs. 1400F and 1400G]

Present Law

In recent years, provisions have been added to the Internal Revenue Code that target specific geographic areas for special Federal income tax treatment. For example, empowerment zones and enterprise communities generally provide tax incentives for businesses that locate within certain geographic areas designated by the Secretaries of Housing and Urban Development ("HUD") and Agriculture.

House Bill

No provision. However, H.R. 5542[1] authorizes the designation of 40 "renewal communities" within which special tax incentives would be available. The following is a description of * * * the tax incentives that would be available within the renewal communities.

* * *

---

[8] S. 3152 was introduced by Senator Roth and others on October 3, 2000.
[1] H.R. 5542 was incorporated by reference into the conference agreement that accompanied H.R. 2614 (H. Rpt.

106-1004), which was passed by the House of Representatives on October 26, 2000.

Tax incentives for renewal communities

The following tax incentives generally are available during the period beginning January 1, 2002, and ending December 31, 2009.[6]

Zero-percent capital gain rate

A zero-percent capital gains rate applies with respect to gain from the sale of a qualified community asset acquired after December 31, 2001, and before January 1, 2010, and held for more than five years. A "qualified community asset" includes: (1) qualified community stock (meaning original-issue stock purchased for cash in a renewal community business); (2) a qualified community partnership interest (meaning a partnership interest acquired for cash in a renewal community business); and (3) qualified community business property (meaning tangible property originally used in a renewal community business by the taxpayer) that is purchased or substantially improved after December 31, 2001.

A "renewal community business" is similar to the present-law definition of an enterprise zone business.[7] Property will continue to be a qualified community asset if sold (or otherwise transferred) to a subsequent purchaser, provided that the property continues to represent an interest in (or tangible property used in) a renewal community business. The termination of an area's status as a renewal community will not affect whether property is a qualified community asset, but any gain

attributable to the period before January 1, 2002, or after December 31, 2014, will not be eligible for the zero-percent rate.

* * *

Effective Date

* * * The tax benefits available in renewal communities are effective for the period beginning January 1, 2002, and ending December 31, 2009.

Senate Amendment
* * *

No provision. However, * * * Under S. 3152, businesses in renewal zones would be eligible for the following tax incentives during the period beginning January 1, 2002 and ending December 31, 2009: (1) a zero-percent capital gains rate for qualifying assets limited to an aggregate amount not to exceed $25 million of gain per taxpayer;[9] * * *

Effective Date

* * * the tax benefits are available for the period beginning January 1, 2002, and ending December 31, 2009.

Conference Agreement

The conference agreement follows H.R. 5542 * * *

[Law at ¶ 5810 and ¶ 5820. CCH Explanation at ¶ 107.]

[¶ 10,138]   Act Sec. 101(a).   Renewal community employment credit

Conference Committee Report (H.R. CONF. REP. NO. 106-1033)

[Code Sec. 1400H]

Present Law

In recent years, provisions have been added to the Internal Revenue Code that target specific geographic areas for special Federal income tax treatment. For example, empowerment zones and enterprise communities generally provide tax incentives for businesses that locate within certain geographic areas designated by the Secretaries of Housing and Urban Development ("HUD") and Agriculture.

House Bill

No provision. However, H.R. 5542[1] authorizes the designation of 40 "renewal communities" within which special tax incentives would be available. The following is a description of * * * the tax incentives that would be available within the renewal communities.

* * *

Tax incentives for renewal communities

The following tax incentives generally are available during the period beginning January 1, 2002, and ending December 31, 2009.[6]

* * *

Renewal community employment credit

A 15-percent wage credit is available to employers for the first $10,000 of qualified wages paid to each employee who (1) is a resident of the renewal community, and (2) performs substantially all employment services within the renewal community in a trade or business of the employer.

The wage credit rate applies to qualifying wages paid after December 31, 2001, and before January 1, 2010. Wages that qualify for the credit are wages that are considered "qualified zone wages" for purposes of the empowerment zone wage credit (including coordination with the Work Opportunity Tax Credit). In general, any

---

[6] If a renewal community designation is terminated prior to December 31, 2009, the tax incentives would cease to be available as of the termination date.

[7] An "enterprise zone business" is defined in section 1397B.

[9] Any gain attributable to the period before January 1, 2002, or after December 31, 2014, would not be eligible for the zero-percent capital gains rate.

[1] H.R. 5542 was incorporated by reference into the conference agreement that accompanied H.R. 2614 (H. Rpt. 106-1004), which was passed by the House of Representatives on October 26, 2000.

[6] If a renewal community designation is terminated prior to December 31, 2009, the tax incentives would cease to be available as of the termination date.

taxable business carrying out activities in the renewal community may claim the wage credit.
* * *

Effective Date

* * * The tax benefits available in renewal communities are effective for the period beginning January 1, 2002, and ending December 31, 2009.

Senate Amendment
* * *

No provision. However, * * * Under S. 3152, businesses in renewal zones would be eligible for the following tax incentives during the period

beginning January 1, 2002 and ending December 31, 2009: * * * (2) a 15-percent wage credit for the first $15,000 of qualifying wages; * * *

Effective Date

* * * the tax benefits are available for the period beginning January 1, 2002, and ending December 31, 2009.

Conference Agreement

The conference agreement follows H.R. 5542 * * *

[Law at ¶ 5830. CCH Explanation at ¶ 110.]

[¶ 10,139]   Act Sec. 101(a).   Commercial revitalization deduction

Conference Committee Report (H.R. CONF. REP. NO. 106-1033)

[Code Secs. 469 and 1400I]

Present Law

In recent years, provisions have been added to the Internal Revenue Code that target specific geographic areas for special Federal income tax treatment. For example, empowerment zones and enterprise communities generally provide tax incentives for businesses that locate within certain geographic areas designated by the Secretaries of Housing and Urban Development ("HUD") and Agriculture.

House Bill

No provision. However, H.R. 5542[1] authorizes the designation of 40 "renewal communities" within which special tax incentives would be available. The following is a description of * * * the tax incentives that would be available within the renewal communities.
* * *

Tax incentives for renewal communities

The following tax incentives generally are available during the period beginning January 1, 2002, and ending December 31, 2009.[6]
* * *

Commercial revitalization deduction

Each State is permitted to allocate up to $12 million of "commercial revitalization expenditures" to each renewal community located within the State for each calendar year after 2001 and before 2010. The appropriate State agency will make the allocations pursuant to a qualified allocation plan.

A "commercial revitalization expenditure" means the cost of a new building or the cost of substantially rehabilitating an existing building. The building must be used for commercial purposes and be located in a renewal community. In the case of the rehabilitation of an existing build-

ing, the cost of acquiring the building will be treated as qualifying expenditures only to the extent that such costs do not exceed 30 percent of the other rehabilitation expenditures. The qualifying expenditures for any building cannot exceed $10 million.

A taxpayer can elect either to (a) deduct one-half of the commercial revitalization expenditures for the taxable year the building is placed in service or (b) amortize all the expenditures ratably over the 120-month period beginning with the month the building is placed in service. No depreciation is allowed for amounts deducted under this provision. The adjusted basis is reduced by the amount of the commercial revitalization deduction, and the deduction is treated as a depreciation deduction in applying the depreciation recapture rules (e.g., sec. 1250). The commercial revitalization deduction is treated in the same manner as the low-income housing credit in applying the passive loss rules (sec. 469). Thus, up to $25,000 of deductions (together with the other deductions and credits not subject to the passive loss limitation by reason of section 469(i)) are allowed to an individual taxpayer regardless of the taxpayer's adjusted gross income. The commercial revitalization deduction is allowed in computing a taxpayer's alternative minimum taxable income.

* * *

Effective Date

* * * The tax benefits available in renewal communities are effective for the period beginning January 1, 2002, and ending December 31, 2009.

Senate Amendment

No provision. * * *

---

[1] H.R. 5542 was incorporated by reference into the conference agreement that accompanied H.R. 2614 (H. Rpt. 106-1004), which was passed by the House of Representatives on October 26, 2000.

[6] If a renewal community designation is terminated prior to December 31, 2009, the tax incentives would cease to be available as of the termination date.

Conference Agreement

The conference agreement follows H.R. 5542 * * *

[Law at ¶ 5340 and ¶ 5840. CCH Explanation at ¶ 115.]

[¶ 10,140] Act Sec. 101(a) and 101(b). Increase in expensing under section 179

Conference Committee Report (H.R. CONF. REP. NO. 106-1033)

[Code Sec. 1400J]

Present Law

In recent years, provisions have been added to the Internal Revenue Code that target specific geographic areas for special Federal income tax treatment. For example, empowerment zones and enterprise communities generally provide tax incentives for businesses that locate within certain geographic areas designated by the Secretaries of Housing and Urban Development ("HUD") and Agriculture.

House Bill

No provision. However, H.R. 5542[1] authorizes the designation of 40 "renewal communities" within which special tax incentives would be available. The following is a description of * * * the tax incentives that would be available within the renewal communities.

* * *

Tax incentives for renewal communities

The following tax incentives generally are available during the period beginning January 1, 2002, and ending December 31, 2009.[6]

* * *

Additional section 179 expensing

A renewal community business is allowed an additional $35,000 of section 179 expensing for qualified renewal property placed in service after December 31, 2001, and before January 1, 2010. The section 179 expensing allowed to a taxpayer

is phased out by the amount by which 50 percent of the cost of qualified renewal property placed in service during the year by the taxpayer exceeds $200,000. The term "qualified renewal property" is similar to the definition of "qualified zone property" used in connection with empowerment zones.

* * *

Effective Date

* * * The tax benefits available in renewal communities are effective for the period beginning January 1, 2002, and ending December 31, 2009.

Senate Amendment

No provision. However, * * * Under S. 3152, businesses in renewal zones would be eligible for the following tax incentives during the period beginning January 1, 2002 and ending December 31, 2009: * * * (3) $35,000 in additional 179 expensing for qualifying property; * * *

Effective Date

* * * the tax benefits are available for the period beginning January 1, 2002, and ending December 31, 2009.

Conference Agreement

The conference agreement follows H.R. 5542 * * *

[Law at ¶ 5850. CCH Explanation at ¶ 120.]

[¶ 10,141] Act Sec. 102. Work opportunity credit for hiring youth residing in renewal communities

Conference Committee Report (H.R. CONF. REP. NO. 106-1033)

[Code Sec. 51]

Present Law

In recent years, provisions have been added to the Internal Revenue Code that target specific geographic areas for special Federal income tax treatment. For example, empowerment zones and enterprise communities generally provide tax incentives for businesses that locate within certain

geographic areas designated by the Secretaries of Housing and Urban Development ("HUD") and Agriculture.

House Bill

No provision. However, H.R. 5542[1] authorizes the designation of 40 "renewal communities" within which special tax incentives would be available. The following is a description

---

[1] H.R. 5542 was incorporated by reference into the conference agreement that accompanied H.R. 2614 (H. Rpt. 106-1004), which was passed by the House of Representatives on October 26, 2000.

[6] If a renewal community designation is terminated prior to December 31, 2009, the tax incentives would cease to be available as of the termination date.

[1] H.R. 5542 was incorporated by reference into the conference agreement that accompanied H.R. 2614 (H. Rpt. 106-1004), which was passed by the House of Representatives on October 26, 2000.

of * * * the tax incentives that would be available within the renewal communities.

* * *

Tax incentives for renewal communities

The following tax incentives generally are available during the period beginning January 1, 2002, and ending December 31, 2009.[6]

* * *

Extension of work opportunity tax credit ("WOTC")

The bill expands the high-risk youth and qualified summer youth categories in the WOTC to include qualified individuals who live in a renewal community.

* * *

Effective Date

* * * The tax benefits available in renewal communities are effective for the period beginning January 1, 2002, and ending December 31, 2009.

Senate Amendment

No provision. * * *

Conference Agreement

The conference agreement follows H.R. 5542 * * *

[Law at ¶ 5090. CCH Explanation at ¶ 125.]

[¶ 10,145] Act Sec. 111 and 101(c). Authority to designate nine additional empowerment zones

Conference Committee Report (H.R. CONF. REP. NO. 106-1033)

[Code Sec. 1391]

Present Law

Round I empowerment zones

The Omnibus Budget Reconciliation Act of 1993 ("OBRA 1993") authorized the designation of nine empowerment zones ("Round I empowerment zones") to provide tax incentives for businesses to locate within targeted areas designated by the Secretaries to HUD and Agriculture. The Taxpayer Relief Act of 1997 ("1997 Act") authorized the designation of two additional Round I urban empowerment zones.

* * *

Round II empowerment zones

The 1997 Act also authorized the designation of 20 additional empowerment zones ("Round II empowerment zones"), of which 15 are located in urban areas and five are located in rural areas. * * *

House Bill

No provision. However, H.R. 5542 * * * authorizes the designation of nine new empowerment zones ("Round III empowerment zones").

* * *

Nine new empowerment zones

The Secretaries of HUD and Agriculture are authorized to designate nine additional empowerment zones ("Round III empowerment zones"). Seven of the Round III empowerment zones will be located in urban areas, and two will be located in rural areas.

The eligibility and selection criteria for the Round III empowerment zones are the same as the criteria that applied to the Round II empowerment zones. The Round III empowerment zones must be designated by January 1, 2002, and the

tax incentives with respect to the Round III empowerment zones generally are available during the period beginning on January 1, 2002, and ending on December 31, 2009.

Business in the Round III empowerment zones are eligible for the same tax incentives that, under the bill, are available to Round I and Round II empowerment zones (i.e., a 20-percent wage credit, an additional $35,000 of section 179 expensing, and the enhanced tax-exempt financing benefits presently available to Round II empowerment zones).

GAO report

The bill provides that the GAO will audit and report to Congress on January 31, 2004, and again in 2007 and 2010, on the empowerment zone and enterprise community program and its effect on poverty, unemployment, and economic growth within the designated areas.

Effective Date

* * * The new Round III empowerment zones must be designated by January 1, 2002, and the tax incentives with respect to the Round III empowerment zones generally are available during the period beginning on January 1, 2002, and ending on December 31, 2009.

Senate Amendment

No provision. * * *

Conference Agreement

The conference agreement follows H.R. 5542. The conference agreement also provides that the Secretaries of HUD and Agriculture are authorized to designate a replacement empowerment zone for each empowerment zone that becomes a renewal community. The replacement empowerment zone will have the same urban or rural

---

[6] If a renewal community designation is terminated prior to December 31, 2009, the tax incentives would cease to be available as of the termination date.

character as the empowerment zone that it is replacing.

[Law at ¶ 5690. CCH Explanation at ¶ 130.]

[¶ 10,146]   Act Sec. 112.   Extension of empowerment zone treatment through 2009

Conference Committee Report (H.R. CONF. REP. NO. 106-1033)

[Code Sec. 1391]

Present Law

Round I empowerment zones

The Omnibus Budget Reconciliation Act of 1993 ("OBRA 1993") authorized the designation of nine empowerment zones ("Round I empowerment zones") to provide tax incentives for businesses to locate within targeted areas designated by the Secretaries to HUD and Agriculture. The Taxpayer Relief Act of 1997 ("1997 Act") authorized the designation of two additional Round I urban empowerment zones.

* * *

Round II empowerment zones

The 1997 Act also authorized the designation of 20 additional empowerment zones ("Round II empowerment zones"), of which 15 are located in urban areas and five are located in rural areas. * * *

House Bill

No provision. However, H.R. 5542 conforms and enhances the tax incentives for the Round I and Round II empowerment zones and extends their designations through December 31, 2009. * * *

Extension of tax incentives for Round I and Round II empowerment zones

The designation of empowerment zone status for Round I and II empowerment zones (other than the District of Columbia Enterprise Zone) is extended through December 31, 2009. * * *

Effective Date

The extension of the existing empowerment zone designations is effective after the date of enactment. * * *

Senate Amendment

No provision. However, S. 3152 contains a provision that conforms and enhances incentives for existing empowerment zones. Specifically, the provision extends the designation of empowerment zone status for Round I and II empowerment zones through December 31, 2009. * * *

Effective Date

The extension of the existing empowerment zone designations is effective after the date of enactment. * * *

Conference Agreement

The conference agreement follows H.R. 5542. * * *

[Law at ¶ 5690. CCH Explanation at ¶ 135.]

[¶ 10,147]   Act Sec. 113.   20 percent employment credit for all empowerment zones

Conference Committee Report (H.R. CONF. REP. NO. 106-1033)

[Code Secs. 1396 and 1400]

Present Law

Round I empowerment zones

The Omnibus Budget Reconciliation Act of 1993 ("OBRA 1993") authorized the designation of nine empowerment zones ("Round I empowerment zones") to provide tax incentives for businesses to locate within targeted areas designated by the Secretaries to HUD and Agriculture. The Taxpayer Relief Act of 1997 ("1997 Act") authorized the designation of two additional Round I urban empowerment zones.

Businesses in the 11 Round I empowerment zones qualify for the following tax incentives: (1)

a 20-percent wage credit for the first $15,000 of wages paid to a zone resident who works in the empowerment zone,[10] * * * The tax incentives with respect to the empowerment zones designated by OBRA 1993 generally are available during the 10-year period of 1995 through 2004. The tax incentives with respect to the two additional Round I empowerment zones generally are available during the 10-year period of 2000 through 2009.[11]

Round II empowerment zones

* * * Businesses in the Round II empowerment zones are not eligible for the wage credit, * * *

---

[10] For wages paid in calendar years during the period 1994 through 2001, the credit rate is 20 percent. The credit rate is reduced to 15 percent for calendar year 2002, 10 percent for calendar year 2003, and 5 percent for calendar year 2004. No wage credit is available after 2004 in the original nine empowerment zones.

[11] Except for the wage credit, which is reduced to 15 percent for calendar year 2005, and then reduced by five percentage points in each year in 2006 and 2007, with no wage credit available after 2007.

House Bill

No provision. However, H.R. 5542 conforms and enhances the tax incentives for the Round I and Round II empowerment zones * * *

Extension of tax incentives for Round I and Round II empowerment zones

* * * the 20-percent wage credit is made available in all Round I and II empowerment zones for qualifying wages paid or incurred after December 31, 2001. The credit rate remains at 20 percent (rather than being phased down) through December 31, 2009, in Round I and Round II empowerment zones.

* * *

Effective Date

* * * The extension of the tax benefits to existing empowerment zones (i.e., the expanded wage credit, * * *) generally is effective after December 31, 2001. * * *

Senate Amendment

No provision. However, S. 3152 contains a provision that conforms and enhances incentives for existing empowerment zones. Specifically, * * * a 15-percent wage credit is made available in all Round I and II empowerment zones, effective in 2002 (except in the case of the two additional Round I empowerment zones added by the 1997 Act, for which the 15-percent wage credit takes effect in 2005 as scheduled under present law). For all the empowerment zones, the 15-percent wage credit expires on December 31, 2009.

* * *

Effective Date

* * * The 15-percent wage credit generally is effective for qualifying wages paid after December 31, 2001 (December 31, 2004 for the two additional Round I empowerment zones).

Conference Agreement

The conference agreement follows H.R. 5542. * * *

[Law at ¶ 5710 and ¶ 5760. CCH Explanation at ¶ 140.]

[¶ 10,148]   Act Sec. 114.   Increased expensing under section 179

Conference Committee Report (H.R. CONF. REP. NO. 106-1033)

[Code Sec. 1397A]

Present Law

Round I empowerment zones

The Omnibus Budget Reconciliation Act of 1993 ("OBRA 1993") authorized the designation of nine empowerment zones ("Round I empowerment zones") to provide tax incentives for businesses to locate within targeted areas designated by the Secretaries to HUD and Agriculture. The Taxpayer Relief Act of 1997 ("1997 Act") authorized the designation of two additional Round I urban empowerment zones.

Businesses in the 11 Round I empowerment zones qualify for the following tax incentives: * * * (2) an additional $20,000 of section 179 expensing for qualifying zone property, * * * The tax incentives with respect to the empowerment zones designated by OBRA 1993 generally are available during the 10-year period of 1995 through 2004. The tax incentives with respect to the two additional Round I empowerment zones generally are available during the 10-year period of 2000 through 2009.[11]

Round II empowerment zones

* * * Businesses in the Round II empowerment zones are * * * eligible to receive up to $20,000 of additional section 179 expensing. * * * The tax incentives with respect to the Round II empowerment zones generally are available during the 10-year period of 1999 through 2008.

House Bill

No provision. However, H.R. 5542 conforms and enhances the tax incentives for the Round I and Round II empowerment zones * * *

Extension of tax incentives for Round I and Round II empowerment zones

* * *

In addition, $35,000 (rather than $20,000) of additional section 179 expensing is available for qualified zone property placed in service in taxable years beginning after December 31, 2001, by a qualified business in any of the empowerment zones.[12] Businesses in the D.C. Enterprise Zone are entitled to the additional section 179 expensing until the termination of the D.C. Enterprise zone designation.

* * *

Effective Date

* * * The extension of the tax benefits to existing empowerment zones (i.e., * * * the additional section 179 expensing * * *) generally is effective after December 31, 2001. * * *

---

[11] Except for the wage credit, which is reduced to 15 percent for calendar year 2005, and then reduced by five percentage points in each year in 2006 and 2007, with no wage credit available after 2007.

[12] The additional $35,000 of section 179 expensing is available throughout all areas that are part of a designated empowerment zone, including the non-contiguous "developable sites" that were allowed to be part of the designated Round II empowerment zones under the 1997 Act.

Senate Amendment

No provision. However, S. 3152 contains a provision that conforms and enhances incentives for existing empowerment zones. * * * As in the House bill, $35,000 (rather than $20,000) in additional section 179 expensing is made available for qualified zone property placed in service in taxable years beginning after December 31, 2001, by a qualified business in any of the empowerment zones. * * *

Effective Date

* * * The additional section 179 expensing and the more generous tax-exempt bond rules for the existing empowerment zones is effective after December 31, 2001. * * *

Conference Agreement

The conference agreement follows H.R. 5542. * * *

[Law at ¶ 5720. CCH Explanation at ¶ 145.]

[¶ 10,149]   Act Sec. 115.   Higher limits on tax-exempt empowerment zone facility bonds

Conference Committee Report (H.R. CONF. REP. NO. 106-1033)

[Code Sec. 1394]

Present Law

Round I empowerment zones

The Omnibus Budget Reconciliation Act of 1993 ("OBRA 1993") authorized the designation of nine empowerment zones ("Round I empowerment zones") to provide tax incentives for businesses to locate within targeted areas designated by the Secretaries to HUD and Agriculture. The Taxpayer Relief Act of 1997 ("1997 Act") authorized the designation of two additional Round I urban empowerment zones.

Businesses in the 11 Round I empowerment zones qualify for the following tax incentives: * * * (3) tax-exempt financing for certain qualifying zone facilities. The tax incentives with respect to the empowerment zones designated by OBRA 1993 generally are available during the 10-year period of 1995 through 2004. The tax incentives with respect to the two additional Round I empowerment zones generally are available during the 10-year period of 2000 through 2009.[11]

Round II empowerment zones

* * * Businesses in the Round II empowerment zones also are eligible for more generous tax-exempt financing benefits than those available in the Round I empowerment zones. Specifically, the tax-exempt financing benefits for the Round II empowerment zones are not subject to the State private activity bond volume caps (but are subject to separate per-zone volume limitations), and the per-business size limitations that apply to the Round I empowerment zones and enterprise communities (i.e., $3 million for each qualified enterprise zone business with a maximum of $20 million for each principal user for all zones and communities) do not apply to qualifying bonds issued for Round II empowerment zones. The tax incentives with respect to the Round II empowerment zones generally are available during the 10-year period of 1999 through 2008.

House Bill

No provision. However, H.R. 5542 conforms and enhances the tax incentives for the Round I and Round II empowerment zones * * *

Extension of tax incentives for Round I and Round II empowerment zones
* * *

Businesses located in Round I empowerment zones (other than the D.C. Enterprise Zone)[13] also are eligible for the more generous tax-exempt bond rules that apply under present law to businesses in the Round II empowerment zones (sec. 1394(f)). The bill applies to tax-exempt bonds issued after December 31, 2001. Bonds that have been issued by businesses in Round I zones before January 1, 2002, are not taken into account in applying the limitations on the amount of new empowerment zone facility bonds that can be issued under the bill.
* * *

Effective Date

* * * The extension of the tax benefits to existing empowerment zones (i.e., * * * the more generous tax-exempt bond rules) generally is effective after December 31, 2001. * * *

Senate Amendment

No provision. However, S. 3152 contains a provision that conforms and enhances incentives for existing empowerment zones. * * * Similarly, S. 3152 extends to businesses located in Round I empowerment zones the more generous tax-exempt bond rules that apply under present law to businesses in the Round II empowerment zones (sec. 1394(f) for bonds issued after December 31, 2001. * * *

---

[11] Except for the wage credit, which is reduced to 15 percent for calendar year 2005, and then reduced by five percentage points in each year in 2006 and 2007, with no wage credit available after 2007.

[13] The present-law rules of sections 1394 and 1400A continue to apply with respect to the D.C. Enterprise Zone.

Effective Date

* * * The additional section 179 expensing and the more generous tax-exempt bond rules for the existing empowerment zones is effective after December 31, 2001. * * *

Conference Agreement

The conference agreement follows H.R. 5542. * * *

[Law at ¶ 5700. CCH Explanation at ¶ 150.]

[¶ 10,150] Act Sec. 116. Rollover of gain from the sale of qualified empowerment zone investments

Conference Committee Report (H.R. Conf. Rep. No. 106-1033)

[Code Sec. 1397B]

Present Law

In general, gain or loss is recognized on any sale, exchange, or other disposition of property. A taxpayer (other than a corporation) may elect to roll over without payment of tax any capital gain realized upon the sale of qualified small business stock held for more than six months where the taxpayer uses the proceeds to purchase other qualified small business stock within 60 days of the sale of the original stock.

House Bill

No provision. However, H.R. 5542 provides that a taxpayer can elect to roll over capital gain from the sale or exchange of any qualified empowerment zone asset purchased after the date of enactment and held for more than one year ("original zone asset") where the taxpayer uses the proceeds to purchase other qualifying empowerment zone assets in the same zone ("replacement zone asset") within 60 days of the sale of the original zone asset. The holding period of the replacement zone asset includes the holding period of the original zone asset, except that the replacement asset must actually be held for more

than one year to qualify for another tax-free rollover. The basis of the replacement zone asset is reduced by the gain not recognized on the rollover. However, if the replacement zone asset is qualified small business stock (as defined in sec. 1202), the exclusion under section 1202 would not apply to gain accrued on the original zone asset.[14] A "qualified empowerment zone asset" means an asset that would be a qualified community asset if the empowerment zone were a renewal community (and the asset is acquired after the date of enactment of the bill). Assets in the D.C. Enterprise Zone are not eligible for the tax-free rollover treatment.[15]

Effective Date

The provision is effective for qualifying assets purchased after the date of enactment.

Senate Amendment

No provision.

Conference Agreement

The conference agreement follows H.R. 5542.

[Law at ¶ 5580, ¶ 5630, ¶ 5700, ¶ 5730, ¶ 5740, ¶ 5750, ¶ 5760 and ¶ 5780. CCH Explanation at ¶ 155.]

[¶ 10,155] Act Sec. 117. Increased exclusion of gain from the sale of qualifying empowerment zone stock

Conference Committee Report (H.R. Conf. Rep. No. 106-1033)

[Code Sec. 1202]

Present Law

Under present law, an individual, subject to limitations, may exclude 50 percent of the gain[16] from the sale of qualifying small business stock held more than five years (sec. 1202).

House Bill

No provision. However, H.R. 5542 increases the exclusion for small business stock to 60 percent for stock purchased after the date of enactment in a corporation that is a qualified business entity and that is held for more than five years. A "qualified business entity" means a corporation that satis-

fies the requirements of a qualifying business under the empowerment zone rules during substantially all the taxpayer's holding period.

Effective Date

The provision is effective for qualified stock purchased after the date of enactment.

Senate Amendment

No provision.

Conference Agreement

The conference agreement follows H.R. 5542.

[Law at ¶ 5001 and 5620. CCH Explanation at ¶ 160.]

---

[14] See section 1045 for rollover of qualified small business stock to other small business stock.

[15] However, a qualifying D.C. Zone asset held for more than five years is eligible for a 100-percent capital gains exclusion (sec. 1400B).

[16] The portion of the capital gain included in income is subject to a maximum regular tax rate of 28 percent, and 42 percent of the excluded gain is a minimum tax preference.

Act Sec. 117   ¶ 10,155

[¶ 10,165]　Act Sec. 121.　New markets tax credit

Conference Committee Report (H.R. CONF. REP. NO. 106-1033)

[Code Sec. 45D]

Present Law

Tax incentives are available to taxpayers making investments and loans in low-income communities. For example, tax incentives are available to taxpayers that invest in specialized small business investment companies licensed by the SBA to make loans to, or equity investments in, small businesses owned by persons who are socially or economically disadvantaged.

House Bill

No provision. However, H.R. 5542 includes a provision that creates a new tax credit for qualified equity investments made to acquire stock in a selected community development entity ("CDE"). The maximum annual amount of qualifying equity investments is capped as follows:

Calendar Year	Maximum Qualifying Equity Investment
2001	$1.0 billion
2002-2003	$1.5 billion per year
2004-2005	$2.0 billion per year
2006-2007	$3.5 billion per year

The amount of the new tax credit to the investor (either the original purchaser or a subsequent holder) is (1) a five-percent credit for the year in which the equity interest is purchased from the CDE and the first two anniversary dates after the interest is purchased from the CDE, and (2) a six percent credit on each anniversary date thereafter for the following four years.[17] The taxpayer's basis in the investment is reduced by the amount of the credit (other than for purposes of calculating the capital gain exclusion under sections 1202, 1400B, and 1400F). The credit is subject to the general business credit rules.

A CDE is any domestic corporation or partnership (1) whose primary mission is serving or providing investment capital for low-income communities or low-income persons, (2) that maintains accountability to residents of low-income communities by their representation on any governing board or on any advisory board of the CDE, and (3) is certified by the Treasury Department as an eligible CDE.[18] No later than 120 days after enactment, the Treasury Department shall issue regulations that specify objective criteria to be used by the Treasury to allocate the credits among eligible CDEs. In allocating the credits, the Treasury Department will give priority to entities with records of having successfully provided capital or technical assistance to disadvantaged businesses or communities,[19] as well as to entities that intend to invest substantially all of the proceeds from their investors in businesses in which persons unrelated to the CDE hold the majority of the equity interest.

If a CDE fails to sell equity interests to investors up to the amount authorized within five years of the authorization, then the remaining authorization is canceled. The Treasury Department can authorize another CDE to issue equity interests for the unused portion. No authorization can be made after 2014.

A "qualified equity investment" is defined as stock or a similar equity interest acquired directly from a CDE in exchange for cash. Substantially all of the investment proceeds must be used by the CDE to make "qualified low-income community investments." Qualified low-income community investments include: (1) capital or equity investments in, or loans to, qualified active businesses located in low-income communities,[20] (2) certain financial counseling and other services specified in regulations to businesses and residents in low-income communities, (3) the purchase from another CDE of any loan made by such entity that is a qualified low income community investment, or (4) an equity investment in, or loans to, another CDE.[21] Treasury Department regulations will provide guidance with respect to the "substantially all" standard.

The stock or equity interest cannot be redeemed (or otherwise cashed out) by the CDE for at least seven years. If an entity fails to be a CDE during the seven-year period following the taxpayer's investment, or if the equity interest is

---

[17] Thus, a credit would be available on the date on which the investment is made and for each of the six anniversary dates thereafter.

[18] A specialized small business investment company and a community development financial institution are treated as satisfying the requirements for a CDE.

[19] A record of having successfully provided capital or technical assistance to disadvantaged businesses or communities could be demonstrated by the past actions of the CDE itself or an affiliate (e.g., in the case where a new CDE is established by a nonprofit organization with a history of providing assistance to disadvantaged communities).

[20] Thus, a qualified low-income community investment may include an investment in a qualifying business in which the CDE (or a related party) holds a significant

interest. However, as previously mentioned, in allocating the credits among eligible CDEs, the Treasury Department will give priority to CDEs that intend to invest substantially all of the proceeds from their investors in businesses in which persons unrelated to the CDE hold the majority of the equity interest. Persons are related to each other if they are described in sections 267(b) or 707(b)(1).

[21] If at least 85 percent of the aggregate gross assets of the CDE are invested (directly or indirectly) in equity interests in, or loans to, qualified active businesses located in low-income communities, then there would be no need to trace the use of the proceeds from the particular stock (or other equity ownership) issuance with respect to which the credit is claimed.

redeemed by the issuing CDE during that seven-year period, then any credits claimed with respect to the equity interest are recaptured (with interest) and no further credits are allowed.

A "low-income community" is defined as census tracts with either (1) poverty rates of at least 20 percent (based on the most recent census data), or (2) median family income which does not exceed 80 percent of the greater of metropolitan area income or statewide median family income (for a non-metropolitan census tract, 80 percent of non-metropolitan statewide median family income). In addition, the Secretary may designate any area within any census tract as a "low income community" provided that (1) the boundary of the area is continuous,[22] (2) the area (if it were a census tract) would satisfy the poverty rate or median income requirements within the targeted area, and (3) an inadequate access to investment capital exists in the area.

A "qualified active business" is defined as a business which satisfies the following requirements: (1) at least 50 percent of the total gross income of the business is derived from the active conduct of trade or business activities in low-income communities; (2) a substantial portion of the use of the tangible property of such business is used in low-income communities; (3) a substantial portion of the services performed for such business by its employees is performed in low-income communities; and (4) less than 5 percent of the average aggregate of unadjusted bases of the property of such business is attributable to certain financial property or to collectibles (other than collectibles held for sale to customers). There is no requirement that employees of the business be residents of the low-income community.

Rental of improved commercial real estate located in a low-income community is a qualified active business, regardless of the characteristics of the commercial tenants of the property. The purchase and holding of unimproved real estate is not a qualified active business. In addition, a qualified active business does not include (a) any business consisting predominantly of the development or holding of intangibles for sale or license;

or (b) operation of any facility described in sec. 144(c)(6)(B). A qualified active business can include an organization that is organized on a non-profit basis.

The GAO will audit and report to Congress by January 31, 2004, and again in 2007 and 2010, on the new markets tax credit program, including on all qualified community development entities that receive an allocation under the new markets tax credit program.

Effective Date

The provision is effective for qualified investments made after December 31, 2000.

Senate Amendment

No provision. However, S. 3152 includes a provision that creates a new markets tax credit that is similar to the provision in H.R. 5542. However, under S. 3152, the maximum annual amount of qualifying equity investments is capped as follows:

Calendar Year	Maximum Qualifying Equity Investment
2002	$1.0 billion
2003-2006	$1.5 billion per year

Under S. 3152, if a CDE fails to sell equity interests to investors up to the amount authorized within five years of the authorization, then the remaining authorization is canceled. The Treasury Department can authorize another CDE to issue equity interests for the unused portion. No authorization can be made after 2013.

Effective Date

The provision is effective for qualified investments made after December 31, 2001.

Conference Agreement

The conference agreement follows H.R. 5542. The conference agreement also clarifies that a low-income community can include a possession of the United States[23] (and thus investments in a U.S. possession may qualify for the new markets tax credit).

[Law at ¶ 5030, ¶ 5040, ¶ 5080, ¶ 5200 and ¶ 7065. CCH Explanation at ¶ 235.]

---

[22] It is intended that the continuous boundary that delineates the portion of the census tract as a "low-income community" should be a pre-existing boundary (such as an established neighborhood, political, or geographic boundary).

[23] For this purpose, a U.S. possession means Puerto Rico, the Virgin Islands, Guam, the Northern Mariana Islands, and American Samoa.

[¶ 10,175]   Act Sec. 131.   Modification of State ceiling on low-income housing credit

Conference Committee Report (H.R. Conf. Rep. No. 106-1033)

[Code Sec. 42]

Present Law

In general

The low-income housing tax credit may be claimed over a 10-year period for the cost of rental housing occupied by tenants having incomes below specified levels. The credit percentage for newly constructed or substantially rehabilitated housing that is not Federally subsidized is adjusted monthly by the Internal Revenue Service so that the 10 annual installments have a present value of 70 percent of the total qualified expenditures. The credit percentage for new substantially rehabilitated housing that is Federally subsidized and for existing housing that is substantially rehabilitated is calculated to have a present value of 30 percent qualified expenditures.

Credit cap

The aggregate credit authority provided annually to each State is $1.25 per resident, except in the case of projects that also receive financing with proceeds of tax-exempt bonds issued subject to the private activity bond volume limit and certain carry-over amounts.

* * *

House Bill

No provision. However, H.R. 5542 * * * increases the per-capita low-income housing credit cap from $1.25 per capita to $1.50 per capita in calendar year 2001 and to $1.75 per capita in calendar year 2002. Beginning in calendar year 2003, the per-capita portion of the credit cap will be adjusted annually for inflation. For small States, a minimum annual cap of $2 million is provided for calendar years 2001 and 2002. Beginning in calendar year 2003, the small State minimum is adjusted for inflation.

* * *

Effective Date

The provision is generally effective for calendar years beginning after December 31, 2000, and buildings placed-in-service after such date in the case of projects that also receive financing with proceeds of tax-exempt bonds subject to the private activity bond volume limit which are issued after such date.

Senate Amendment

* * *

No provision. However, S. 3152 increases the annual State credit caps from $1.25 to $1.75 per resident beginning in 2001. Also, beginning in 2001 the per capita cap for each State is modified so that small population State are given a minimum of $2 million of annual credit cap. The $1.75 per capita cap and the $2 million amount are indexed for inflation beginning in calendar 2002.

* * *

Effective Date

The provisions are effective for calendar years beginning after December 31, 2000 and buildings placed-in-service after such date in the case of projects that also receive financing with proceeds of tax-exempt bonds which are issued after such date subject to the private activity bond volume limit.

Conference Agreement

The conference agreement follows H.R. 5542.

[Law at ¶ 5050. CCH Explanation at ¶ 240.]

[¶ 10,180]   Act Sec. 132.   Modification of criteria for allocating housing credits among projects

Conference Committee Report (H.R. Conf. Rep. No. 106-1033)

[Code Sec. 42]

Present Law

In general

The low-income housing tax credit may be claimed over a 10-year period for the cost of rental housing occupied by tenants having incomes below specified levels. The credit percentage for newly constructed or substantially rehabilitated housing that is not Federally subsidized is adjusted monthly by the Internal Revenue Service so that the 10 annual installments have a present value of 70 percent of the total qualified expenditures. The credit percentage for new substantially rehabilitated housing that is Federally subsidized and for existing housing that is substantially rehabilitated is calculated to have a present value of 30 percent qualified expenditures.

* * *

State allocation plans

Each State must develop a plan for allocating credits and such plan must include certain allocation criteria including: (1) project location; (2) housing needs characteristics; (3) project characteristics; (4) sponsor characteristics; (5) participation of local tax-exempts; (6) tenant populations with special needs; and (7) public housing waiting lists. The State allocation plan must also give preference to housing projects: (1) that serve the lowest income tenants; and (2) that are obligated to serve qualified tenants for the longest periods.

* * *

House Bill

No provision. However, H.R. 5542 * * * strikes the plan criteria relating to participation of local tax-exempts, replacing it with two other criteria: tenant populations of individuals with children and projects intended for eventual tenant ownership. It also provides that the present-law criteria relating to sponsor characteristics include whether the project involves the use of existing housing as part of a community revitalization plan. The bill adds a third category of housing projects to the preferential list, for projects located in qualified census tracts which contribute to a concerted community revitalization plan.

* * *

Effective Date

The provision is generally effective for calendar years beginning after December 31, 2000, and buildings placed-in-service after such date in the case of projects that also receive financing with proceeds of tax-exempt bonds subject to the private activity bond volume limit which are issued after such date.

Senate Amendment

* * *

No provision.

* * *

Conference Agreement

The conference agreement follows H.R. 5542.

[Law at ¶ 5050. CCH Explanation at ¶ 240.]

[¶ 10,185]   Act Sec. 133.   Additional responsibilities of housing credit agencies

Conference Committee Report (H.R. Conf. Rep. No. 106-1033)

[Code Sec. 42]

Present Law

In general

The low-income housing tax credit may be claimed over a 10-year period for the cost of rental housing occupied by tenants having incomes below specified levels. The credit percentage for newly constructed or substantially rehabilitated housing that is not Federally subsidized is adjusted monthly by the Internal Revenue Service so that the 10 annual installments have a present value of 70 percent of the total qualified expenditures. The credit percentage for new substantially rehabilitated housing that is Federally subsidized and for existing housing that is substantially rehabilitated is calculated to have a present value of 30 percent qualified expenditures.

* * *

Credit administration

There are no explicit requirements that housing credit agencies perform a comprehensive market study of the housing needs of the low-income individuals in the area to be served by the project, nor that such agency conduct site visits to monitor for compliance with habitability standards.

* * *

House Bill

No provision. However, H.R. 5542 * * * requires a comprehensive market study of the housing needs of the low-income individuals in the area to be served by the project and a written explanation available to the general public for any allocation not made in accordance with the established priorities and selection criteria of the housing credit agency. They also require site inspections by the housing credit agency to monitor compliance with habitability standards applicable to the project.

* * *

Effective Date

The provision is generally effective for calendar years beginning after December 31, 2000, and buildings placed-in-service after such date in the case of projects that also receive financing with proceeds of tax-exempt bonds subject to the private activity bond volume limit which are issued after such date.

Senate Amendment

* * *

No provision.

* * *

Conference Agreement

The conference agreement follows H.R. 5542.

[Law at ¶ 5050. CCH Explanation at ¶ 240.]

[¶ 10,190]   Act Sec. 134.   Modifications to rules relating to basis of building which is eligible for credit

Conference Committee Report (H.R. CONF. REP. NO. 106-1033)

[Code Sec. 42]

Present Law

In general

The low-income housing tax credit may be claimed over a 10-year period for the cost of rental housing occupied by tenants having incomes below specified levels. The credit percentage for newly constructed or substantially rehabilitated housing that is not Federally subsidized is adjusted monthly by the Internal Revenue Service so that the 10 annual installments have a present value of 70 percent of the total qualified expenditures. The credit percentage for new substantially rehabilitated housing that is Federally subsidized and for existing housing that is substantially rehabilitated is calculated to have a present value of 30 percent qualified expenditures.

* * *

Basis of building eligible for the credit

Buildings receiving assistance under the HOME investment partnerships act ("HOME") are not eligible for the enhanced credit for buildings located in high cost areas (i.e., qualified census tracts and difficult development areas). Under the enhanced credit, the 70-percent and 30-percent credit are increased to a 91-percent and 39-percent credit, respectfully.

Eligible basis is generally limited to the portion of the building used by qualified low-income tenants for residential living and some common areas.

* * *

House Bill

No provision. However, H.R. 5542 * * * makes three changes to the basis rules of the credit. First, the definition of qualified census tracts for purposes of the enhanced credit is expanded to include any census tracts with a poverty rate of 25 percent or more. Second, the bill extends the credit to a portion of the building used as a community service facility not in excess of 10

percent of the total eligible basis in the building. A community service facility is defined as any facility designed to serve primarily individuals whose income is 60 percent or less of area median income. Third, the bill provides that assistance received under the Native American Housing Assistance and Self-Determination Act of 1996 is not taken into account in determining whether a building is Federally subsidized for purposes of the credit. This allows such buildings to qualify for something other than the 30-percent credit generally applicable to Federally subsidized buildings.

* * *

Effective Date

The provision is generally effective for calendar years beginning after December 31, 2000, and buildings placed-in-service after such date in the case of projects that also receive financing with proceeds of tax-exempt bonds subject to the private activity bond volume limit which are issued after such date.

Senate Amendment

* * *

The provision in S. 3152 relating to the treatment of building receiving assistance under the Native American Housing Assistance and Self-Determination Act of 1996 is the same as one of the provisions in H.R. 5542.

* * *

Effective Date

The provisions are effective for calendar years beginning after December 31, 2000 and buildings placed-in-service after such date in the case of projects that also receive financing with proceeds of tax-exempt bonds which are issued after such date subject to the private activity bond volume limit.

Conference Agreement

The conference agreement follows H.R. 5542.

[Law at ¶ 5050. CCH Explanation at ¶ 240.]

[¶ 10,195]   Act Sec. 135.   Other modifications

Conference Committee Report (H.R. CONF. REP. NO. 106-1033)

[Code Sec. 42]

Present Law

In general

The low-income housing tax credit may be claimed over a 10-year period for the cost of rental housing occupied by tenants having incomes below specified levels. The credit percent-

age for newly constructed or substantially rehabilitated housing that is not Federally subsidized is adjusted monthly by the Internal Revenue Service so that the 10 annual installments have a present value of 70 percent of the total qualified expenditures. The credit percentage for new substantially rehabilitated housing that is Federally subsidized and for existing housing that is substantially rehabilitated is calculated to have a present value of 30 percent qualified expenditures.

* * *

Expenditure test

Generally, the building must be placed in service in the year in which it receives an allocation to qualify for the credit. An exception is provided in the case where the taxpayer has expended an amount equal to 10-percent or more of the taxpayer's reasonably expected basis in the building by the end of the calendar year in which the allocation is received and certain other requirements are met.

* * *

House Bill

No provision. However, H.R. 5542 * * * allows a building which receives an allocation in the second half of a calendar to qualify under the 10-percent test if the taxpayer expends an amount equal to 10-percent or more of the tax-payer's reasonably expected basis in the building within six months of receiving the allocation regardless of whether the 10-percent test is met by the end of the calendar year.

* * *

Effective Date

The provision is generally effective for calendar years beginning after December 31, 2000, and buildings placed-in-service after such date in the case of projects that also receive financing with proceeds of tax-exempt bonds subject to the private activity bond volume limit which are issued after such date.

Senate Amendment
* * *

No provision.

* * *

Conference Agreement

The conference agreement follows H.R. 5542.

[Law at ¶ 5050. CCH Explanation at ¶ 240.]

[¶ 10,200]   Act Sec. 136.   Carryforward rules

Conference Committee Report (H.R. CONF. REP. NO. 106-1033)

[Code Sec. 42]

Present Law

In general

The low-income housing tax credit may be claimed over a 10-year period for the cost of rental housing occupied by tenants having incomes below specified levels. The credit percentage for newly constructed or substantially rehabilitated housing that is not Federally subsidized is adjusted monthly by the Internal Revenue Service so that the 10 annual installments have a present value of 70 percent of the total qualified expenditures. The credit percentage for new substantially rehabilitated housing that is Federally subsidized and for existing housing that is substantially rehabilitated is calculated to have a present value of 30 percent qualified expenditures.

* * *

Stacking rule

Authority to allocate credits remains at the State (as opposed to local) government level unless State law provides otherwise.[24] Generally, credits may be allocated only from volume author-ity arising during the calendar year in which the building is placed in service, except in the case of: (1) credits claimed on additions to qualified basis; (2) credits allocated in a later year pursuant to an earlier binding commitment made no later than the year in which the building is placed in service; and (3) carryover allocations.

Each State annually receives low-income housing credit authority equal to $1.25 per State resident for allocation to qualified low-income projects.[25] In addition to this $1.25 per resident amount, each State's "housing credit ceiling" includes the following amounts: (1) the unused State housing credit ceiling (if any) of such State for the preceding calendar year;[26] (2) the amount of the State housing credit ceiling (if any) returned in the calendar year;[27] and (3) the amount of the national pool (if any) allocated to such State by the Treasury Department.

The national pool consists of States' unused housing credit carryovers. For each State, the unused housing credit carryover for a calendar year consists of the excess (if any) of the unused State housing credit ceiling for such year over the excess (if any) of the aggregate housing credit

---

[24] For example, constitutional home rule cities in Illinois are guaranteed their proportionate share of the $1.25 amount, based on their population relative to that of the State as a whole.

[25] A State's population, for these purposes, is the most recent estimate of the State as population released by the Bureau of the Census before the beginning of the year to which the limitation applies. Also, for these purposes, the District of Columbia and the U.S. possessions (i.e., Puerto Rico, the Virgin Islands, Guam, the Northern Marianas and American Samoa) are treated as States.

[26] The unused State housing credit ceiling is the amount (if positive) of the previous year's annual credit limitation plus credit returns less the credit actually allocated in that year.

[27] Credit returns are the sum of any amounts allocated to projects within a State which fail to become a qualified low-income housing project within the allowable time period plus any amounts allocated to a project within a State under an allocation which is canceled by mutual consent of the housing credit agency and the allocation recipient.

dollar amount allocated for such year over the sum of $1.25 per resident and the credit returns for such year. The amounts in the national pool are allocated only to a State which allocated its entire housing credit ceiling for the preceding calendar year, and requested a share in the national pool not later than May 1 of the calendar year. The national pool allocation to qualified States is made on a pro rata basis equivalent to the fraction that a State's population enjoys relative to the total population of all qualified States for that year.

The present-law stacking rule provides that a State is treated as using its annual allocation of credit authority ($1.25 per State resident) and any returns during the calendar year followed by any unused credits carried forward from the preceding year's credit ceiling and finally any applicable allocations from the National pool.

House Bill

No provision. However, H.R. 5542 * * * modifies the stacking rule so that each State is treated as using its allocation of the unused State housing credit ceiling (if any) from the preceding calendar before the current year's allocation of credit (including any credits returned to the State) and then finally any National pool allocations.

Effective Date

The provision is generally effective for calendar years beginning after December 31, 2000, and buildings placed-in-service after such date in the case of projects that also receive financing with proceeds of tax-exempt bonds subject to the private activity bond volume limit which are issued after such date.

Senate Amendment
* * *

Same as the H.R. 5542.

Effective Date

The provisions are effective for calendar years beginning after December 31, 2000 and buildings placed-in-service after such date in the case of projects that also receive financing with proceeds of tax-exempt bonds which are issued after such date subject to the private activity bond volume limit.

Conference Agreement

The conference agreement follows H.R. 5542.

[Law at ¶ 5050. CCH Explanation at ¶ 240.]

[¶ 10,210] Act Sec. 151 [161]. Accelerate scheduled increase in state volume limits on tax-exempt private activity bonds

Conference Committee Report (H.R. CONF. REP. NO. 106-1033)

[Code Sec. 146]
Present Law

Interest on bonds issued by States and local governments is excluded from income if the proceeds of the bonds are used to finance activities conducted and paid for by the governmental units (sec. 103). Interest on bonds issued by these governmental units to finance activities carried out and paid for by private persons ("private activity bonds") is taxable unless the activities are specified in the Internal Revenue Code. Private activity bonds on which interest may be tax-exempt include bonds for privately operated transportation facilities (airports, docks and wharves, mass transit, and high speed rail facilities), privately owned and/or provided municipal services (water, sewer, solid waste disposal, and certain electric and heating facilities), economic development (small manufacturing facilities and redevelopment in economically depressed areas), and certain social programs (low-income rental housing, qualified mortgage bonds, student loan bonds, and exempt activities of charitable organizations described in sec. 501(c)(3)).

The volume of tax-exempt private activity bonds that States and local governments may issue for most of these purposes in each calendar

year is limited by State-wide volume limits. The current annual volume limits are $50 per resident of the State or $150 million if greater. The volume limits do not apply to private activity bonds to finance airports, docks and wharves, certain governmentally owned, but privately operated solid waste disposal facilities, certain high speed rail facilities, and to certain types of private activity tax-exempt bonds that are subject to other limits on their volume (qualified veterans' mortgage bonds and certain "new" empowerment zone and enterprise community bonds).

The current annual volume limits that apply to private activity tax-exempt bonds increase to $75 per resident of each State or $225 million, if greater, beginning in calendar year 2007. The increase is, ratably phased in, beginning with $55 per capita or $165 million, if greater, in calendar year 2003.

House Bill

No provision. However, H.R. 5542 increases the State volume limits from the greater of $50 per resident or $150 million to the greater of $62.50 per resident or $187.5 million in calendar year 2001. The volume limit will increase further, to the greater of $75 per resident or $225 million in calendar year 2002. Beginning in calendar year

2003, the volume limit will be adjusted annually for inflation.

Effective Date

The provision is effective beginning in calendar year 2001.

Senate Amendment

No provision. However, S. 3152 increases the present-law annual State private activity bond volume limits to $75 per resident of each State or $225 million (if greater) beginning in calendar

year 2001. In addition, the $75 per resident and the $225 million State limit will be indexed for inflation beginning in calendar year 2002.

Effective Date

The provisions are effective beginning in calendar year 2001.

Conference Agreement

The conference agreement follows H.R. 5542.

[Law at ¶ 5160. CCH Explanation at ¶ 285.]

[¶ 10,215] Act Sec. 152 [162]. Extension and modification to expensing of environmental remediation costs

Conference Committee Report (H.R. Conf. Rep. No. 106-1033)

[Code Sec. 198]

Present Law

Taxpayers can elect to treat certain environmental remediation expenditures that would otherwise be chargeable to capital account as deductible in the year paid or incurred (sec. 198). The deduction applies for both regular and alternative minimum tax purposes. The expenditure must be incurred in connection with the abatement or control of hazardous substances at a qualified contaminated site.

A "qualified contaminated site" generally is any property that (1) is held for use in a trade or business, for the production of income, or as inventory; (2) is certified by the appropriate State environmental agency to be located within a targeted area; and (3) contains (or potentially contains) a hazardous substance (so-called "brownfields"). Targeted areas are defined as: (1) empowerment zones and enterprise communities as designated under present law; (2) sites announced before February 1997, as being subject to one of the 76 Environmental Protection Agency ("EPA") Brownfields Pilots; (3) any population census tract with a poverty rate of 20 percent or more; and (4) certain industrial and commercial areas that are adjacent to tracts described in (3) above. However, sites that are identified on the national priorities list under the Comprehensive Environmental Response, Compensation, and Liability Act of 1980 cannot qualify as targeted areas.

Eligible expenditures are those paid or incurred before January 1, 2002.

House Bill

No provision. However, H.R. 5542 extends the expiration date for eligible expenditures to include those paid or incurred before January 1, 2004.

In addition, the bill eliminates the targeted area requirement, thereby, expanding eligible sites to include any site containing (or potentially containing) a hazardous substances that is certified by the appropriate State environmental agency. However, expenditures undertaken at sites that are identified on the national priorities list under the Comprehensive Environmental Response, Compensation, and Liability Act of 1980 would continue to not qualify as eligible expenditures.

By extending and expanding section 198, the bill is not intended to displace the general tax law principle regarding expensing versus capitalization of expenditures which continues to apply to environmental remediation efforts not specifically covered under section 198.

Effective Date

The provision to extend the expiration date is effective upon the date of enactment. The provision to expand the class of eligible sites is effective for expenditures paid or incurred after the date of enactment.

Senate Amendment

No provision. However, S. 3152 includes a provision identical to that of the House bill provision.

Conference Agreement

The conference agreement follows H.R. 5542.

[Law at ¶ 5210. CCH Explanation at ¶ 225.]

[¶ 10,220]   Act Sec. 153 [163].   Expansion of District of Columbia homebuyer tax credit

Conference Committee Report (H.R. CONF. REP. NO. 106-1033)

[Code Sec. 1400C]

Present Law

First-time homebuyers of a principal residence in the District of Columbia are eligible for a nonrefundable tax credit of up to $5,000 of the amount of the purchase price. The $5,000 maximum credit applies both to individuals and married couples. Married individuals filing separately can claim a maximum credit of $2,500 each. The credit phases out for individual taxpayers with adjusted gross income between $70,000 and $90,000 ($110,000-$130,000 for joint filers). For purposes of eligibility, "first-time homebuyer" means any individual if such individual did not have a present ownership interest in a principal residence in the District of Columbia in the one year period ending on the date of the purchase of the residence to which the credit applies. The credit is scheduled to expire for residences purchased after December 31, 2001.

House Bill

No provision. However, H.R. 5542 extends the first-time homebuyer credit for two years (through December 31, 2003).

Effective Date

The provision is effective on the date of enactment.

Senate Amendment

No provision. However, S. 3152 includes a provision that extends the first-time homebuyer credit for two years, through December 31, 2003. The provision also extends the phase-out range for married individuals filing a joint return so that it is twice that of individuals. Thus, under the provision, the District of Columbia homebuyer credit is phased out for joint filers with adjusted gross income between $140,000 and $180,000.

Effective Date

The provision is effective for taxable years beginning after December 31, 2000.

Conference Agreement

The conference agreement follows H.R. 5542.

[Law at ¶ 5790. CCH Explanation at ¶ 165.]

[¶ 10,225]   Act Sec. 154 [164].   Extension of D.C. Enterprise Zone

Conference Committee Report (H.R. CONF. REP. NO. 106-1033)

[Code Secs. 1400, 1400A and 1400B]

Present Law

The Taxpayer Relief Act of 1997 designated certain economically depressed census tracts within the District of Columbia as the District of Columbia Enterprise Zone (the "D.C. Zone"), within which businesses and individual residents are eligible for special tax incentives. The D.C. Zone designation remains in effect for the period from January 1, 1998, through December 31, 2002. In addition to the tax incentives available with respect to a Round I empowerment zone (including a 20-percent wage credit), the D.C. Zone also has a zero-percent capital gains rate that applies to gain from the sale of certain qualified D.C. Zone assets acquired after December 31, 1997 and held for more than five years.

With respect to the tax-exempt financing incentives, the D.C. Zone generally is treated like a Round I empowerment zone; therefore, the issuance of such bonds is subject to the District of Columbia's annual private activity bond volume limitation. However, the aggregate face amount of all outstanding qualified enterprise zone facility bonds per qualified D.C. Zone business may not exceed $15 million (rather than $3 million, as is the case for Round I empowerment zones).[28]

House Bill

No provision.

Senate Amendment

No provision. However, S. 3152 includes a provision that extends the D.C. Zone designation through December 31, 2006.

Conference Agreement

The conference agreement follows S. 3152, except that the D.C. Zone designation is extended for one year (through December 31, 2003).

[Law at ¶ 5760, ¶ 5770 and ¶ 5780. CCH Explanation at ¶ 170.]

---

[28] Section 1400A(a).

[¶ 10,230]   Act Sec. 155 [165].   Extension and modification of enhanced deduction for corporate donations of computer technology

Conference Committee Report (H.R. Conf. Rep. No. 106-1033)

[Code Sec. 170(e)(6)]

Present Law

The maximum charitable contribution deduction that may be claimed by a corporation for any one taxable year is limited to 10 percent of the corporation's taxable income for that year (disregarding charitable contributions and with certain other modifications) (sec. 170(b)(2)). Corporations also are subject to certain limitations based on the type of property contributed. In the case of a charitable contribution of short-term gain property, inventory, or other ordinary income property, the amount of the deduction generally is limited to the taxpayer's basis (generally, cost) in the property. However, special rules in the Code provide an augmented deduction for certain corporate contributions. Under these special rules, the amount of the augmented deduction is equal to the lesser of (1) the basis of the donated property plus one-half of the amount of ordinary income that would have been realized if the property had been sold, or (2) twice the basis of the donated property.

Section 170(e)(6) allows corporate taxpayers an augmented deduction for qualified contributions of computer technology and equipment (i.e., computer software, computer or peripheral equipment, and fiber optic cable related to computer use) to be used within the United States for educational purposes in grades K-12. Eligible donees are: (1) any educational organization that normally maintains a regular faculty and curriculum and has a regularly enrolled body of pupils in attendance at the place where its educational activities are regularly carried on; and (2) tax-exempt charitable organizations that are organized primarily for purposes of supporting elementary and secondary education. A private foundation also is an eligible donee, provided that, within 30 days after receipt of the contribution, the private foundation contributes the property to an eligible donee described above.

Qualified contributions are limited to gifts made no later than two years after the date the taxpayer acquired or substantially completed the construction of the donated property. In addition, the original use of the donated property must commence with the donor or the donee. Accordingly, qualified contributions generally are limited to property that is no more than two years old. Such donated property could be computer technology or equipment that is inventory or depreciable trade or business property in the hands of the donor.

Donee organizations are not permitted to transfer the donated property for money or services (e.g., a donee organization cannot sell the computers). However, a donee organization may transfer the donated property in furtherance of its exempt purposes and be reimbursed for shipping, installation, and transfer costs. For example, if a corporation contributes computers to a charity that subsequently distributes the computers to several elementary schools in a given area, the charity could be reimbursed by the elementary schools for shipping, transfer, and installation costs.

The special treatment applies only to donations made by C corporations. S corporations, personal holding companies, and service organizations are not eligible donors.

The provision is scheduled to expire for contributions made in taxable years beginning after December 31, 2000.

House Bill

No provision. However, H.R. 5542 includes a provision that extends the current enhanced deduction for donations of computer technology and equipment through December 31, 2003, and expands the enhanced deduction to include donations to public libraries. H.R. 5542 provides that qualified contributions include gifts made no later than three years after the date the taxpayer acquired or substantially completed the construction of the donated property.

Effective Date

The provision is effective for contributions made after December 31, 2000.

Senate Amendment

No provision. However, S. 3152 includes a provision that extends the current enhanced deduction for donations of computer technology and equipment through December 31, 2003. In addition, S. 3152 expands the enhanced deduction to include donations to public libraries.

Effective Date

The provision is effective upon the date of enactment.

Conference Agreement

The conference agreement follows H.R. 5542 with a modification that contributions may be made by a person that has reacquired the property (i.e., if a computer manufacturer reacquires the computer from the original user and then contributes it). Such reacquired property must be contributed within 3 years of the date the original construction of the property was substantially completed The conferees anticipate that for purposes of computing the enhanced deduction for a reacquirer, the Secretary will provide guidance in determining the retail value of donated computers (or other computer technology) in situations in which the number of actual retail sales of used computers similar to those donated is small in relation to the number of such computers that are donated.

In addition, the conference agreement provides that the Secretary may prescribe by regulation standards to ensure that the donations meet minimum functionality and suitability standards for educational purposes.

[Law at ¶ 5190. CCH Explanation at ¶ 220.]

[¶ 10,235]   Act Sec. 156 [166].   Treatment of Indian tribes as non-profit organizations and state or local governments for purposes of the Federal Unemployment Tax ("FUTA")

Conference Committee Report (H.R. CONF. REP. NO. 106-1033)

[Code Sec. 3306]

Present Law

Present law imposes a net tax on employers equal to 0.8 percent of the first $7,000 paid annually to each employee. The current gross FUTA tax is 6.2 percent, but employers in States meeting certain requirements and having no delinquent loans are eligible for a 5.4 percent credit making the net Federal tax rate 0.8 percent. Both non-profit organizations and State and local governments are not required to pay FUTA taxes. Instead they may elect to reimburse the unemployment compensation system for unemployment compensation benefits actually paid to their former employees. Generally, Indian tribes are not eligible for the reimbursement treatment allowable to non-profit organizations and State and local governments.

House Bill

No provision. However, H.R. 5542 provides that an Indian tribe (in including any subdivision, subsidiary, or business enterprise chartered and wholly owned by an Indian tribe) is treated like a non-profit organization or State or local government for FUTA purposes (i.e., given an election to choose the reimbursement treatment).

Effective Date

The provision generally is effective with respect to service performed beginning on or after the date of enactment. Under a transition rule, service performed in the employ of an Indian tribe is not treated as employment for FUTA purposes if: (1) it is service which is performed before the date of enactment and with respect to which FUTA tax has not been paid; and (2) such Indian tribe reimburses a State unemployment fund for unemployment benefits paid for service attributable to such tribe for such period.

Senate Amendment

No provision. However, S. 3152 is the same as H.R. 5542.

Conference Agreement

The conference agreement follows H.R. 5542 and S. 3152.

[Law at ¶ 5890 and ¶ 5900. CCH Explanation at ¶ 290.]

[¶ 10,245]   Act Sec. 201.   Medical Savings Accounts ("MSAs")

Conference Committee Report (H.R. CONF. REP. NO. 106-1033)

[Code Sec. 220]

Present Law

Within limits, contributions to a medical savings account ("MSA")[29] are deductible in determining adjusted gross income ("AGI") if made by an eligible individual and are excludable from gross income and wages for employment tax purposes if made by the employer of an eligible individual. Earnings on amounts in an MSA are not currently taxable. Distributions from an MSA for medical expenses are not taxable. Distributions not used for medical expenses are taxable. In addition, distributions not used for medical expenses are subject to an additional 15-percent tax unless the distribution is made after age 65, death, or disability.

MSAs are available to self-employed individuals[30] and to employees covered under an employer-sponsored high deductible plan of a small

---

[29] In general, an MSA is a trust or custodial account created exclusively for the benefit of the account holder and is subject to rules similar to those applicable to individual retirement arrangements. The trustee of an MSA can be a bank, insurance company, or other person who demonstrates to the satisfaction of the Secretary that the manner in which such person will administer the trust will be consistent with applicable requirements.

[30] Self-employed individuals include more than 2-percent shareholders of S corporations who are treated as partners for purposes of fringe benefit rules pursuant to section 1372. Self-employed individuals are eligible for an MSA regardless

employer. An employer is a small employer if it employed, on average, no more than 50 employees on business days during either the preceding or the second preceding year.

In order for an employee of a small employer to be eligible to make MSA contributions (or to have employer contributions made on his or her behalf), the employee must be covered under an employer-sponsored high deductible health plan (see the definition below) and must not be covered under any other health plan (other than a plan that provides certain permitted coverage).

Similarly, in order to be eligible to make contributions to an MSA, a self-employed individual must be covered under a high deductible health plan and no other health plan (other than a plan that provides certain permitted coverage). A self-employed individual is not an eligible individual (by reason of being self-employed) if the high deductible plan under which the individual is covered is established or maintained by an employer of the individual (or the individual's spouse).

The maximum annual contribution that can be made to an MSA for a year is 65 percent of the deductible under the high deductible plan in the case of individual coverage and 75 percent of the deductible in the case of family coverage.

A high deductible plan is a health plan with an annual deductible of at least $1,550 and no more than $2,350 in the case of individual coverage and at least $3,100 and no more than $4,650 in the case of family coverage. In addition, the maximum out-of-pocket expenses with respect to allowed costs (including the deductible) must be no more than $3,100 in the case of individual coverage and no more than $5,700 in the case of family coverage.[31] A plan does not fail to qualify as a high deductible plan merely because it does not have a deductible for preventive care as required by State law. A plan does not qualify as a high deductible health plan if substantially all of the coverage under the plan is for permitted coverage. In the case of a self-insured plan, the plan must in fact be insurance (e.g., there must be appropriate risk shifting) and not merely a reimbursement arrangement.

The number of taxpayers benefiting annually from an MSA contribution is limited to a threshold level (generally 750,000 taxpayers). If it is determined in a year that the threshold level has been exceeded (called a "cut-off" year) then, in general, for succeeding years during the 4-year pilot period 1997-2000, only those individuals who (1) made an MSA contribution or had an employer MSA contribution for the year or a preced-ing year (i.e., are active MSA participants) or (2) are employed by a participating employer, is eligible for an MSA contribution. In determining whether the threshold for any year has been exceeded, MSAs of individuals who were not covered under a health insurance plan for the six month period ending on the date on which coverage under a high deductible plan commences would not be taken into account.[32] However, if the threshold level is exceeded in a year, previously uninsured individuals are subject to the same restriction on contributions in succeeding years as other individuals. That is, they would not be eligible for an MSA contribution for a year following a cut-off year unless they are an active MSA participant (i.e., had an MSA contribution for the year or a preceding year) or are employed by a participating employer.

The number of MSAs established has not exceeded the threshold level.

After December 31, 2000, no new contributions may be made to MSAs except by or on behalf of individuals who previously had MSA contributions and employees who are employed by a participating employer. An employer is a participating employer if (1) the employer made any MSA contributions for any year to an MSA on behalf of employees or (2) at least 20 percent of the employees covered under a high deductible plan made MSA contributions of at least $100 in the year 2000.

Self-employed individuals who made contributions to an MSA during the period 1997-2000 also may continue to make contributions after 2000.

House Bill

No provision. However, H.R. 5542 extends the MSA program through 2002. The same rules that apply to the limit on MSAs for 1999 apply to 2000 and 2001. Thus, for example, the threshold level in those years is 750,000 taxpayers.

Effective Date

The provision is effective on the date of enactment.

Senate Amendment

No provision.

Conference Agreement

The conference report follows H.R. 5542, except that MSAs are renamed as Archer MSAs. The conference agreement clarifies that, as under present law, the cap and reporting requirements do not apply for 2000.

[Law at ¶ 5230. CCH Explanation at ¶ 615.]

(Footnote Continued)

of the size of the entity for which the individual performs services.

[31] These dollar amounts are for 2000. These amounts are indexed for inflation in $50 increments.

[32] Permitted coverage does not constitute coverage under a health insurance plan for this purpose.

[¶ 10,255] Act Sec. 301. Exempt certain reports from elimination under the Federal Reports Elimination and Sunset Act of 1995

Conference Committee Report (H.R. CONF. REP. NO. 106-1033)

[Act Sec. 301]

Present Law

Section 303 of the Federal Reports Elimination and Sunset Act of 1995 eliminates many periodic Federal reporting requirements, effective May 15, 2000.

House Bill

No provision. However, H.R. 5542 exempts certain reports from elimination and sunset pursuant to the Federal Reports Elimination and Sunset Act of 1995.

Senate Amendment

No provision.

Conference Agreement

The conference agreement follows H.R. 5542.

[Law at ¶ 7140. CCH Explanation at ¶ 320.]

[¶ 10,260] Act Sec. 302. Extension of deadlines for IRS compliance with certain notice requirements

Conference Committee Report (H.R. CONF. REP. NO. 106-1033)

[Code Secs. 6631 and 6751(a)]

Present Law

The Internal Revenue Service Restructuring and Reform Act of 1998 ("IRS Restructuring Act of 1998") imposed several notice requirements relating to penalties, interest and installment agreements. Section 6715 of the Code, added by section 3306 of the IRS Restructuring Act of 1998, requires that each notice imposing a penalty include the name of the penalty, the Code section under which the penalty is imposed, and a computation of the penalty.[33] This requirement applies to notices issued, and penalties assessed, after December 31, 2000.[34]

Section 6631 of the Code, added by section 3308 of the IRS Restructuring Act of 1998, requires that every IRS notice sent to an individual taxpayer that includes an amount of interest required to be paid by the taxpayer also include a detailed computation of the interest charged and a citation to the Code section under which such interest is imposed. The provision is effective for notices issued after December 31, 2000.

Section 3506 of the IRS Restructuring Act of 1998 requires the IRS to send every taxpayer in an installment agreement an annual statement of the initial balance owed, the payments made during the year, and the remaining balance. The provision became effective on July 1, 2000.

House Bill

No provision. However, H.R. 5542 extends the deadlines for complying with the penalty, interest, and installment agreement notice requirements. Specifically, the annual installment agreement notice requirement is extended from July 1, 2000, to September 1, 2001. The deadlines for complying with the notice requirements relating to the computation of penalties and interest[35] are both extended to June 30, 2001. In addition, for penalty notices issued after June 30, 2001, and before July 1, 2003, the notice requirements will be treated as met if the notice contains a telephone number at which the taxpayer can request a copy of the taxpayer's assessment and payment history with respect to such penalty. Similarly, for interest notices issued after June 30, 2001, and before July 1, 2003, the notice requirements will be treated as met if such notice contains a telephone number at which the taxpayer can request a copy of the taxpayer's payment history relating to interest amounts included in such notice.

Effective Date

The provision is effective on the date of enactment.

Senate Amendment

No provision.

Conference Agreement

The conference agreement follows H.R. 5542.

[Law at ¶ 7145. CCH Explanation at ¶ 325.]

---

[33] Sec. 6715(a).
[34] P.L. 105-206, sec. 3306.

[35] Secs. 6715(a) and 6631.

[¶ 10,265] Act Sec. 303. Extension of authority for undercover operations

Conference Committee Report (H.R. Conf. Rep. No. 106-1033)

[Code Sec. 7608]

Present Law

The Anti-Drug Abuse Act of 1988 exempted IRS undercover operations from the otherwise applicable statutory restrictions controlling the use of Government funds (which generally provide that all receipts must be deposited in the general fund of the Treasury and all expenses be paid out of appropriated funds). In general, the exemption permits the IRS to "churn" the income earned by an undercover operation to pay additional expenses incurred in the undercover operation. The IRS is required to conduct a detailed financial audit of large undercover operations in which the IRS is churning funds and to provide an annual audit report to the Congress on all such large undercover operations. The exemption originally expired on December 31, 1989, and was extended by the Comprehensive Crime Control Act of 1990 to December 31, 1991. In the Taxpayer Bill of Rights II (Public Law 104-168), the authority to churn funds from undercover operations was extended for five years, through 2000.

House Bill

No provision. However, H.R. 5542 extends the authority of the IRS to "churn" the income earned from undercover operations for an additional five years, through 2005.

Effective Date

The provision is effective on the date of enactment.

Senate Amendment

No provision.

Conference Agreement

The conference agreement follows H.R. 5542.

[Law at ¶ 6200. CCH Explanation at ¶ 385.]

[¶ 10,270] Act Sec. 304(a). Confidentiality of certain documents relating to closing and similar agreements

Conference Committee Report (H.R. Conf. Rep. No. 106-1033)

[Code Sec. 6103]

Present Law

Section 6103

Section 6103 of the Code sets forth the general rule that returns and return information are confidential. A return is any tax return, information return, declaration of estimated tax, or claim for refund filed under the Code on behalf of or with respect to any person. The term return also includes any amendment or supplement, including supporting schedules or attachments or lists, which are supplemental to or are part of a filed return. Return information is defined broadly. It includes the following information:

● a taxpayer's identity, the nature, source or amount of income, payments, receipts, deductions, exemptions, credits, assets, liabilities, net worth, tax liability, tax withheld, deficiencies, overassessments, or tax payments;

● whether the taxpayer's return was, is being, or will be examined or subject to other investigation or processing;

● any other data, received by, recorded by, prepared by, furnished to, or collected by the Secretary with respect to a return or with respect to the determination of the existence, or possible existence, of liability (or the amount thereof) of any person under this title for any tax, penalty, interest, fine, forfeiture, or other imposition, or offense;[36]

● any part of any written determination or any background file document relating to such written determination which is not open to public inspection under section 6110;[37] and

● any advance pricing agreement entered into by a taxpayer and the Secretary and any background information related to the agreement or any application for an advance pricing agreement.

The term "return information" does not include data in a form that cannot be associated with or otherwise identify, directly or indirectly, a particular taxpayer.

* * *

House Bill

No provision. However, H.R. 5542 affirms that closing and similar agreements, and information exchanged and agreements reached pursuant to a tax treaty, are confidential. Further, the provision clarifies that such protected documents are not to be disclosed under the FOIA or section 6110.

---

[36] Sec. 6103(b)(2)(A).

[37] Sec. 6103(b)(2)(B).

Clarification that return information includes closing agreements and similar dispute resolution agreements

Protection for closing agreements, pre-filing agreements and similar agreements not containing an exposition of the tax law

The bill provides that agreements entered into under section 7121 or similar agreements are confidential return information. Similar agreements are intended to include negotiated agreements that (1) are the result of an alternative dispute resolution or dispute avoidance process relating to liability of any person under the Code for any tax, penalty, interest, fine or forfeiture or other imposition or offense and (2) do not establish, set forth, or resolve the government's interpretation of the relevant tax law. This is not meant to preclude citation, or repetition of, the Code, Treasury regulations, or other published rules.

It is intended that pre-filing agreements be covered by this provision. It is the understanding of the conferees that pre-filing agreements do not explain the applicable provisions of law or otherwise contain any exposition of the tax law or the position of the IRS. In addition, it is not intended that the closing and similar agreement exception be used as a means of avoiding public disclosure of determinations that, under present law, would be issued in a form that would be open to public inspection. Thus, technical advice memoranda, chief counsel advice or other material clearly available to the public under present law section 6110, would not be exempt from disclosure by virtue of the fact that such material is contained in a background file for a closing agreement. For example, if a revenue agent seeks technical advice in connection with a pre-filing agreement, such technical advice would remain subject to the requirements of section 6110. Since the pre-filing agreement program involves only settled issues of law, it is the understanding of the conferees that documents of this nature generally would not be generated in the pre-filing agreement process.

The provision is not intended to foreclose the disclosure of tax-exempt organization closing agreements to the extent such disclosure is authorized under section 6104.[48] Since section 6103 permits the disclosure of return information as authorized by Title 26, a disclosure authorized by section 6104 is permissible, notwithstanding the fact that a closing agreement is return information.

Report on pre-filing agreement program

It is intended that the Secretary make publicly available an annual report relating to the pe-filing agreement program operations for the preceding calendar year. The annual reporting requirement is for five years, or the duration of the program, whichever is shorter. The report is to include (1) the number of pre-filing agreements completed, (2) the number of applications received, (3) the number of applications withdrawn, (4) the types of issues which are resolved by completed agreements, (5) whether the program is being utilized by taxpayers who were previously subject to audit by the IRS, (6) the average length of time required to complete an agreement, (7) the number, if any, and subject of technical advice and chief counsel advice memoranda issued to address issues arising in connection with any pre-filing agreement, (8) any model agreements,[49] any (9) any other information the Secretary deems appropriate. The first report, covering the calendar year 2000, is to be issued no later than March 30, 2001. The information required for the annual report is subject to the restrictions of section 6103. Therefore, the Secretary will disclose information only in a form that cannot be associated with or otherwise identify, directly or indirectly, a particular taxpayer. The Joint Committee on Taxation periodically may review pre-filing agreements to determine whether they contain legal interpretations that should be disclosed to the public.

* * *

Effective Date

The provision applies to disclosures on, or after, the date of enactment, and thus, applies to all documents in existence on, or created after, the date of enactment.

Senate Amendment

No provision.

Conference Agreement

The conference agreement follows H.R. 5542.

[Law at ¶ 6000. CCH Explanation at ¶ 305.]

---

[48] The D.C. Circuit recently remanded to the district court for factual development the issue of whether the closing agreement in that case was submitted in support of an exemption application, and therefore, subject to disclosure under section 6104. *Tax Analysts v. IRS*, 214 F.3d 179 (D.C. Cir 2000), *vacating and remanding* 99-2 U.S.T.C. (CCH) 794 (D.D.C. 1999).

[49] *See e.g.*, Appendix A of Rev. Proc. 2000-38 which is a model "Closing Agreement on Final Determination Covering Specific Matters" regarding method of accounting for distributor commissions. Rev. Proc. 2000-38, 2000-40 I.R.B. 314-315 (October 2, 2000). That model agreement does not identify any particular taxpayer but sets forth the substance of the agreement.

[¶ 10,271]   Act Sec. 304(b).   Agreements with foreign governments

Conference Committee Report (H.R. CONF. REP. NO. 106-1033)

[Code Sec. 6105]

Present Law
* * *

Secrecy of information exchanged under tax treaties

U.S. tax treaties typically contain articles governing the exchange of information. These articles generally provide for the exchange of information between the tax authorities of the two countries when such information is necessary for carrying out provisions of the treaty or of the countries' domestic tax laws. Individuals referred to as "competent authorities" are designated by each country to make written requests for information and to receive information.[38]

The exchange of information articles typically cover information relating to taxes to which the treaty applies, but can also apply to other taxes (e.g., excise taxes) not covered by the treaty. Many of the treaties permit the exchange of information even if the taxpayer involved is not a resident of one of the treaty countries. The exchange of information articles may be similar to, or represent a variation on, Article 26 of the 1996 U.S. model income tax treaty.

Information that is received under the exchange of information articles is subject to secrecy clauses contained in the treaties. In this regard, the country requesting information under the treaties typically is required to treat any information received as secret in the same manner as information obtained under its domestic laws. In general, disclosure is not permitted other than to persons or authorities involved in the administration, assessment, collection or enforcement of taxes to which the treaty applies. For example, disclosure generally can be made to legislative bodies, such as the tax-writing committees of the Congress, and the General Accounting Office for purposes of overseeing the administration of U.S. tax laws.

In addition to the exchange of information articles in U.S. tax treaties, exchange of information provisions are contained in tax information exchange agreements entered into between the United States and another country.[39] In addition, information may be exchanged pursuant to the Convention on Mutual Administrative Assistance in Tax Matters developed by the Council of Europe and the Organization for Economic Cooperation and Development (the "Multilateral Mutual Assistance Convention"), which limits the use of exchanged information and permits disclosure of such information only with the prior authorization of the competent authority of the country providing the information.[40] The United States has also entered into a number of implementation and coordination agreements with possessions that provide for the exchange of tax information. Moreover, the United States has entered into various mutual legal assistance treaties with other countries, some of which can be used to obtain tax information in criminal investigations.

Both the confidentiality provisions of section 6103, as well as treaty secrecy provisions can cover return information.
* * *

House Bill

No provision. However, H.R. 5542 affirms that closing and similar agreements, and information exchanged and agreements reached pursuant to a tax treaty, are confidential. Further, the provision clarifies that such protected documents are not to be disclosed under the FOIA or section 6110.
* * *

Clarification that information protected by treaty is confidential

Protection for agreements and information exchanged pursuant to tax treaty

The provision adds a new Code section 6105, which provides that tax convention information, with limited exceptions, cannot be disclosed. Thus, the provision confirms that agreements concluded under, and information received pursuant to, a tax convention are confidential and can only be disclosed as provided in such tax convention.

Under the provision, a tax convention is defined to include any income tax or gift and estate tax

---

[38] The U.S. competent authority is the Secretary of the Treasury or his delegate. The U.S. competent authority function has been delegated to the Commissioner of Internal Revenue, who has redelegated the authority to the Director, International. On interpretive issues, the latter acts with the concurrence of the Associate Chief Counsel (International) of the IRS.

[39] Sections 274(h)(6)(C) and 927(e)(3) specifically provide the Secretary of the Treasury the authority to enter into tax information exchange agreements. This eliminates the need for Senate ratification, which is required for a tax treaty. In addition, all tax information exchange agreements are required to include specific non-disclosure provisions which provide that information received by either country will be disclosed only to persons or authorities (including courts and administrative bodies) involved in the administration or oversight of, or in the determination of appeals in respect of, taxes of the United States, or the beneficiary country and will be used by such persons or authorities only for such purposes. Sec. 274(h)(6)(C)(i).

[40] The U.S. Senate ratified the Multilateral Mutual Assistance Convention, subject to certain reservations, in September 1990. The Multilateral Mutual Assistance Convention entered into force on April 1, 1995, and has been signed by the following countries: Denmark, Finland, Iceland, the Netherlands, Norway, Sweden, and the United States.

convention, or any other convention or bilateral agreement (including multilateral conventions and agreements and any agreement with a possession of the United States) providing for the avoidance of double taxation, the prevention of fiscal evasion, nondiscrimination with respect to taxes, the exchange of tax relevant information with the United States, or mutual assistance in tax matters.

It is the understanding of the conferees that competent authority agreements (also referred to as mutual agreements) generally do not contain an explanation of the law or application of law to facts. Instead, such agreements are negotiated arrangements to resolve issues of double taxation. Thus, the term tax convention information for purposes of the provision includes: (1) any agreement entered into with the competent authority of one or more foreign governments pursuant to a tax convention; (2) an application for relief under a tax convention (sought by either a taxpayer or another competent authority); (3) any background information related to such agreement or application; (4) documents implementing such agreement; and (5) any other information exchanged pursuant to a tax convention that is treated as confidential or secret under such tax convention. The conferees intend that tax convention information would include documents and any other information that reflects tax convention information, including the association of a particular treaty partner with a specific issue or matter.

The general rule that tax convention information cannot be disclosed does not apply to the disclosure of tax convention information to persons or authorities (including courts and administrative bodies) that are entitled to disclosure under the tax convention. It also does not apply to any generally applicable procedural rules regarding applications for relief under a tax convention. This exception is intended to ensure that there is no restriction on the release by the Secretary of publicly available procedural rules concerning matters such as how or when to make a request for competent authority assistance. Thus, certain material generated by IRS, i.e., its Competent Authority procedures (primarily reflected in Rev. Proc. 96-13), or similar material produced by a treaty partner (for example, an Information Circular produced and published by the Canadian tax authority) may be made available to the public. The general rule does not apply to the disclo-

sure of information not relating to a particular taxpayer if, after consultation with the parties to a tax convention, the Secretary determines that such disclosure would not impair tax administration. This is consistent with current practice. An example of a general agreement that could be disclosed under this provision is the agreement between the competent authorities of Mexico and the United States regarding the maquiladora industry. That agreement, which was not taxpayer specific, was publicized by press release IR-INT-1999-13. The conferees intend that the "impairment of tax administration" for purposes of this provision include, but not be limited to, the release of documents that would adversely affect the working relationship of the treaty partners. Under the provision, except as otherwise provided, taxpayer-specific tax convention information could not be publicly disclosed, even if it would not impair tax administration.

A taxpayer-specific competent authority agreement that relates to the existence or possible existence of liability (or amount thereof) of any person for any tax, penalty, interest, fine, forfeiture, or other imposition or offense under the Code is return information under section 6103. It is also an agreement pursuant to a tax convention under section 6105. Return information, including taxpayer-specific competent authority agreements, remains subject to the confidentiality provisions of section 6103. Thus, civil and criminal penalties for the unauthorized disclosure of returns and return information continue to apply to return information that is also covered by section 6105. However, tax convention information that is return information may only be disclosed to the extent provided in, and subject to the terms and conditions of, the relevant tax convention.

* * *

Effective Date

The provision applies to disclosures on, or after, the date of enactment, and thus, applies to all documents in existence on, or created after, the date of enactment.

Senate Amendment

No provision.

Conference Agreement

The conference agreement follows H.R. 5542.

[Law at ¶ 6020. CCH Explanation at ¶ 305.]

[¶ 10,272] Act Sec. 304(c). Exemption from public inspection as written determination

Conference Committee Report (H.R. Conf. Rep. No. 106-1033)

[Code Sec. 6110]

Present Law
* * *

Section 6110 and section 7121

Section 6110 of the Code provides for disclosure of written determinations. With certain exceptions, section 6110 makes the text of any written determination the Internal Revenue Service ("IRS") issues available for public inspection. A written determination is any ruling, determination letter, technical advice memorandum, or Chief Counsel advice. The IRS is required to redact certain material before making these documents publicly available.[41] Among the information to be redacted is information specifically exempted from disclosure by any statute (other than Title 26) that is applicable to the IRS. Once the IRS makes the written determination publicly available, the background file documents associated with such written determination are available for public inspection upon written request. Section 6110 defines "background file documents" as any written material submitted by the taxpayer or other requester in support of the request. Background file documents also include any communications between the IRS and persons outside the IRS concerning such written determination that occur before the IRS issues the determination.

Section 6110 was added to the Code in 1976. The legislative history provided that a written determination would not be considered a ruling, technical advice memorandum, or determination letter, unless the document satisfies three criteria:

(1) The document recites the relevant facts;

(2) The document explains the applicable provisions of law; and

(3) The document shows the application of law to the facts.[42]

The legislative history further provided that section 6110 "does not require public disclosure of a closing agreement entered into between the IRS and a taxpayer which finally determines the taxpayer's tax liability with respect to a taxable year... Your committee understands that a closing agreement is generally the result of a negotiated settlement and, as such, does not necessarily represent the IRS view of the law. Your committee intends, however, that the closing agreement exception is not to be used as a means of avoiding public disclosure of determinations which, under present practice, would be issued in a form which would be open to public inspection [under the bill]."[43]

Closing agreements are entered into under the authority of section 7121. Closing agreements finally and conclusively settle a tax issue between the IRS and a taxpayer. Closing agreements may: (1) determine a taxpayer's entire tax liability for a previous tax period; or (2) fix the tax treatment of one or more specific items affecting tax liability for any tax period. Thus, closing agreements may settle the treatment of a specific item for periods ending after the execution of the agreement. A single closing agreement may cover both the determination of a taxpayer's entire tax liability for a previous tax period and fix the tax treatment of specific items for any tax period.

Freedom of Information Act

The Freedom of Information Act ("FOIA"), enacted in 1966, established a statutory right to access government information. While the purpose of section 6103 is to restrict access to returns and return information, the basic purpose of the FOIA is to ensure that the public has access to government documents. In general, the FOIA provides that any person has a right of access to Federal agency records, except to the extent that such records (or portions thereof) are protected from disclosure by one of nine exemptions or by

---

[41] For rulings, determination letters and technical advice memoranda, section 6110(c) provides the following exemptions from disclosure:

(1) the names, addresses, and other identifying details of the person to whom the written determination pertains and of any other person, other than a person with respect to whom a notation is made under subsection (d)(1) (relating to third party contacts), identified in the written determination or any background file document;

(2) information specifically authorized under criteria established by an Executive order to be kept secret in the interest of national defense or foreign policy, and which is in fact properly classified pursuant to such Executive order;

(3) information specifically exempted from disclosure by any statute (other than [Title 26]) which is applicable to the Internal Revenue Service;

(4) trade secrets and commercial or financial information obtained from a person and privileged or confidential;

(5) information the disclosure of which would constitute a clearly unwarranted invasion of personal privacy;

(6) information contained in or related to examination, operating, or condition reports prepared by, or on behalf of, or for use of an agency responsible for the regulation or supervision of financial institutions; and

(7) geological and geophysical information and data, including maps, concerning wells.

For Chief Counsel Advice, paragraphs 2 through 7 do not apply, however, material may be deleted in accordance with subsections (b) and (c) of the FOIA (except that in applying Exemption 3 of the FOIA, no statutory provision of the Code is to be taken into account.) *See* sec. 6110(i)(3).

[42] H.R. Rep. 94-658, at 315 (1976).

[43] *Id.* at 316.

one of three special law enforcement record exclusions. Exemption 3 of the FOIA allows the withholding of information prohibited from disclosure by another statute if certain requirements are met.[44] The right of access is enforceable in court.

Pending FOIA requests and litigation involving IRS records

Records covered by treaty secrecy clauses

A publisher of tax related material and commentary has made a FOIA request for the disclosure of competent authority agreements. The request has been pending since March 14, 2000.[45] The IRS has not denied the request, nor has it produced any documents responsive to the request. At this time, no suit has been filed to compel disclosure of these documents, although such a suit may be brought in the future.

In connection with a separate request, the IRS was used under the FOIA to compel disclosure of Field Service Advice memoranda ("FSAs").[46] FSAs are prepared by attorneys in the IRS National Office of the Office of Chief Counsel. They are prepared in response to requests from IRS field personnel for legal guidance, usually with respect to issues relating to a particular taxpayer. FSAs usually contain a statement of issues, facts, legal analysis and conclusions. The primary purpose of FSAs is to ensure that IRS field personnel apply the law correctly and uniformly. The D.C. Circuit determined that FSAs are subject to disclosure. However, the court remanded the case to district court to address assertions of privilege, including those based on treaty secrecy. A decision on this issue by the district court is still pending.[47]

Pre-filing agreements

On February 11, 2000, the IRS issued Notice 2000-12, in which the IRS established a pilot program for "Pre-filing Agreements." Under this program, large businesses may request a review and resolution of specific issues relating to tax returns they expect to file between September and December of 2000. The purpose of the program is to enable taxpayers and the IRS to resolve issues that are likely to be disputed in post-filing audits. Examples of such issues include: (1) asset valuation and the allocation of a business's purchase or sale price among the assets acquired or sold; (2) the identification and documentation of hedging transactions; and (3) the determination of "market" for taxpayers using the lower of cost or market method of inventory valuation in situations involving inactive markets. The program is intended to address issues for which the law is settled.

In Notice 2000-12, the IRS stated that pre-filing agreements are closing agreements entered into pursuant to section 7121. As such, the notice provides that the information generated or received by the IRS during the pe-filing agreement process constitutes return information. The notice further provides that pre-filing agreements are not written determinations as defined in section 6110, nor are they subject to disclosure under the FOIA.

Several pre-filing agreements have been completed. A FOIA request for these agreements has not been made.

House Bill

No provision. However, H.R. 5542 affirms that closing and similar agreements, and information exchanged and agreements reached pursuant to a tax treaty, are confidential. Further, the provision clarifies that such protected documents are not to be disclosed under the FOIA or section 6110.

* * *

Interaction with FOIA and section 6110

Under the provision, closing agreements and similar agreements would not be considered written determinations for purposes of section 6110 and, thus, would not be subject to public disclosure. Such agreements would be defined as return information under section 6103 and, therefore, such documents would be protected from disclosure pursuant to Exemption 3 of the FOIA in conjunction with section 6103.

In addition, under the provision, section 6110 would not apply to material covered by section 6105. In the litigation over FSAs, there has been some dispute as to whether treaties qualify as statutes for purposes of withholding information pursuant to Exemption 3 of the FOIA. The conferees believe that treaties are the equivalent of statutes for purposes of Exemption 3 of the FOIA. Section 6105 satisfies Exemption 3 of the FOIA. Taxpayer-specific tax convention information concerning a taxpayer's tax liability, such as taxpayer-specific competent authority agreements, would be exempt from the FOIA as both return information under section 6103 and information protected from disclosure by tax convention under section 6105. Agreements not relating to a particular taxpayer, and other tax convention information related to such agreements, could be disclosed under FOIA if it is determined that the disclosure would not impair tax administration.

Effective Date

The provision applies to disclosures on, or after, the date of enactment, and thus, applies to all

---

[44] 5 U.S.C. sec. 552(b)(3).

[45] The initial FOIA request of March 14, 2000, covered all competent authority agreements executed for the United States from January 1, 1990, to date. In response to a request from the Department of Treasury, by letter dated April 17, 2000, the FOIA request was narrowed to cover competent authority agreements executed between 1997 and 1999. The right to pursue the 1990 through 1996 agreements, however, was reserved.

[46] *Tax Analysts v. IRS*, 117 F.3d 607 (D.C. Cir. 1997).

[47] *Tax Analysts v. IRS*, No. 94-CV-923 (GK) (D.D.C.).

documents in existence on, or created after, the date of enactment.

Senate Amendment

No provision.

Conference Agreement

The conference agreement follows H.R. 5542.

[Law at ¶ 6030. CCH Explanation at ¶ 305.]

[¶ 10,275] Act Sec. 305. Increase Joint Committee on Taxation refund review threshold to $2 million

Conference Committee Report (H.R. Conf. Rep. No. 106-1033)

[Code Sec. 6405]

Present Law

No refund or credit in excess of $1,000,000 of any income tax, estate or gift tax, or certain other specified taxes, may be made until 30 days after the date a report on the refund is provided to the Joint Committee on Taxation (sec. 6405). A report is also required in the case of certain tentative refunds. Additionally, the staff of the Joint Committee on Taxation conducts post-audit reviews of large deficiency cases and other select issues.

House Bill

No provision. However, H.R. 5542 increases the threshold above which refunds must be submitted to the Joint Committee on Taxation for review from $1,000,000 to $2,000,000. The staff of the Joint Committee on Taxation would continue to exercise its existing statutory authority to conduct a program of expanded post-audit reviews of large deficiency cases and other select issues, and the IRS is expected to cooperate fully in this expanded program.

Effective Date

The provision is effective on the date of enactment, except that the higher threshold does not apply to a refund or credit with respect to which a report was made before the date of enactment.

Senate Amendment

No provision.

Conference Agreement

The conference agreement follows H.R. 5542.

[Law at ¶ 6080. CCH Explanation at ¶ 370.]

[¶ 10,280] Act Sec. 306. Clarifying the allowance of certain tax benefits with respect to kidnapped children

Conference Committee Report (H.R. Conf. Rep. No. 106-1033)

[Code Sec. 151]

Present Law

The Code generally requires that a taxpayer provide over one-half of the support for each individual claimed as that taxpayer's dependent. Similarly, the child credit, the surviving spouse filing status, and the head of household filing status require that a taxpayer satisfy certain requirements with regard to individuals that qualify as the taxpayer's dependent(s). Finally, the earned income credit for taxpayers with qualifying children generally is available only if the taxpayer has the same principal place of abode for more than one-half the taxable year with an otherwise qualifying child.

Recently published IRS guidance first denied a dependency exemption to certain taxpayers with kidnapped children (TAM 200034029), then allowed such tax benefits to such taxpayers (TAM 200038059).

House Bill

No provision. However, H.R. 5542 clarifies that the dependency exemption, the child credit, the surviving spouse filing status, the head of household filing status, and the earned income credit are available to an otherwise qualifying taxpayer with respect to a child who is presumed by law enforcement authorities to have been kidnapped by someone who is not a member of the family of such child or the taxpayer. Generally, this treatment continues for all taxable years ending during the period that the child is kidnapped. However, this treatment ends for the taxable year ending after the calender year in which it is determined that the child is dead (or, if earlier, in which the child would have attained age 18).

Effective Date

The provision is effective for taxable years ending after the date of enactment.

Senate Amendment

No provision.

Conference Agreement

The conference agreement follows H.R. 5542.

[Law at ¶ 5170. CCH Explanation at ¶ 390.]

[¶ 10,285] Act Sec. 307. Conforming changes to accommodate reduced issuances of certain treasury securities

Conference Committee Report (H.R. CONF. REP. NO. 106-1033)

[Code Sec. 995(f)(4)]

Present Law

Code section 995(f)(4) dealing with the interest charge on the deferred tax liability of the shareholders of a domestic international sales corporation provides that the interest rate be determined by reference to the average investment yield on United States Treasury bills with maturities of 52 weeks. In addition, provisions of Federal law relating to interest on monetary judgments in civil cases recovered in Federal district court and on a judgment against the United States affirmed by the Supreme Court (Title 28), interest on certain unpaid criminal fines and penalties (Title 18), and interest on compensation for certain takings of property (Title 40) determine the applicable interest rate by reference to 52-week Treasury bills.

As a result of prior Congressional efforts at budgetary control, current and projected Federal budget surpluses are reducing the need of the Treasury Department to issue certain securities. The Treasury Department has informed the Congress that on grounds of efficient debt management, and predictability and liquidity for the financial markets, the Treasury Department has announced it is likely to cease issuing 52-week Treasury bills.

House Bill

No provision. However, H.R. 5542 modifies the Code (sec. 995(f)(4)) and certain other parts of Federal law relating to interest on monetary judgments in civil cases recovered in Federal district court and on a judgment against the United States affirmed by the Supreme Court (Title 28), interest on certain unpaid criminal fines and penalties (Title 18), and interest on compensation for certain takings of property (Title 40) that make specific reference to yields on 52-week Treasury bills. H.R. 5542 generally replaces the reference to 52-week Treasury bills with a reference to the weekly average one-year constant maturity Treasury yield, as published by the Board of Governors of the Federal Reserve System.

Effective Date

The provision is effective upon the date of enactment.

Senate Amendment

No provision.

Conference Agreement

The conference agreement follows H.R. 5542.

[Law at ¶ 5560 and ¶ 7150. CCH Explanation at ¶ 375.]

[¶ 10,290] Act Sec. 308. Authorization of agencies to use corrected Consumer Price Index

Conference Committee Report (H.R. CONF. REP. NO. 106-1033)

[Act Sec. 308]

Present Law

Code section 1(f) provides for adjustments in the tax tables so that inflation will not result in tax increases. Numerous other provisions of the Code are indexed as well. Section 1(f) provides that inflation is measured by changes in the consumer price index ("CPI") for the preceding year as published by the Department of Labor compared to the CPI for the calendar year 1992. Section 1(f) directs the Secretary to publish tables with applicable tax rates based upon calculated inflation adjustments by December 15 of the year before the year to which the tables are to apply.

In addition, payments made under Social Security, certain Federal employee retirement programs, and certain payments to individuals under various welfare and income support programs are adjusted annually by changes in the CPI.

On September 28, 2000, the Bureau of Labor Statistics ("BLS") announced that the agency had discovered a computational error in quality adjustments of air conditioning as a part of the cost of housing resulting in errors in the reported CPI between January 1999 and August 2000. The BLS reported that the CPI levels starting in January 1999 have been either 0.0, 0.1, or 0.2 index points lower than the levels that would have been published without the error. Consistent with agency guidelines and past practice, the BLS announced that it is revising the reported CPI back to January 2000 to the fully correct levels. The BLS will make no change to reported levels for January through December 1999. However, the BLS will make the corrected levels of the CPI for 1999 available upon request.

House Bill

No provision. However, H.R. 5542 authorizes the Secretary of the Treasury to use the corrected levels of the CPI for 1999 and 2000 for all purposes of the Code to which they might apply. H.R. 5542 directs the Secretary to prescribe new tables reflecting the correct levels of the 1999 CPI for the 2000 tax year.

In addition, H.R. 5542 provides that the Director of the Office of Management and Budget ("OMB") shall assess Federal benefit programs to ascertain the extent to which the CPI error has or will result in a shortfall in program payments to individuals for 2000 and future years. The Director is directed to issue guidelines to agency administrators to determine the extent, if any, of such shortfalls in payments to individuals. The agency administrators are to report their findings to the Director and to Congress within 30 days. H.R. 5542 provides that, within 60 days of the date of enactment, the Director instruct the head of any Federal agency which administers an affected program to make a payment or payments to compensate for the shortfall and that such payments are targeted to the amount of the shortfall experienced by individual beneficiaries. Applicable Federal benefit programs include the old-age and survivors insurance program, the disability insurance program and the supplemental security income program under the Social Security Act and other programs as determined by the Director. H.R. 5542 directs the Director to report to the Congress on the activities performed pursuant to this provision by April 1, 2001.

Effective Date

The provision is effective on the date of enactment.

Senate Bill

No provision.

Conference Agreement

The conference agreement follows H.R. 5542, except that the conference agreement directs the Secretary to prescribe new tables reflecting the correct levels of the CPI for the 2001 tax year.

The conferees note that error in the CPI was computational in nature. The conferees support the BLS's policy to incorporate methodological changes only on a prospective basis. The conferees also understand that BLS policy provides that published indices generally not be revised except for those found to be in error for the year in which the error was discovered or within the past twelve months. The conferees recognize that the errors in the CPI date to as long as 20 months prior to the announcement of the error. The conferees recognize that the BLS's policy of not publishing corrected index numbers, beyond those provided as described above, has been applied in those rare cases where an error has been discovered in the past. However, the conferees understand that in the past 25 years the few errors that have been discovered have involved sub-indices and have not affected the level of the CPI itself. The last time the U.S. City Average All Items CPI was revised was in December 1974, when the values for the months of April through October 1974 were recalculated and released with issuance of the November CPI. Therefore, past precedent does not strictly apply to the present situation.

The conferees believe that integrity of official government data is vital to policymakers and private individuals and businesses throughout the country. The conferees emphasize that the CPI plays an important role in economic planning. For this reason the conferees are concerned that, while the BLS has published corrected CPI numbers for 2000, the BLS does not intend to publish corrected CPI numbers for 1999 as part of the official CPI series. To its credit, the BLS announced the error publicly. The national press reported the error.[50] In the absence of a correction to the official CPI series, the Federal government will be left in the position of maintaining, as an official data series, index numbers that the Federal government has admitted are incorrect. The conferees believe that the public's trust in the integrity of official government data is a paramount goal and the conferees strongly encourage the Commissioner of the Bureau of Labor Statistics to review carefully the agency's current policy with respect to publishing as part of an official series corrections to data found to be in error for reasons of computational error. The conferees believe such a review should be made both with respect to the error announced on September 28, 2000, and as a matter for the future for those rare circumstances when such a similar computational error might once again arise.

[Law at ¶ 7155. CCH Explanation at ¶ 380.]

---

[50] For example, John M. Berry, "Inflation Higher Than Reported," *The Washington Post,* September 27, 2000, p. E-1, John M. Berry, "Rent Error Leads to Revision Of the CPI," *The Washington Post,* September 29, 2000, p. E-3, Nicholas Kulish, "Major Price Index Is Revised Upward As Result of Error," *The Wall Street Journal,* September 28, 2000, p. A2, and Nicholas Kulish, "Second-Period GDP Rose at 5.6% Annual Rate," *The Wall Street Journal,* September 29, 2000, p. A2. The conferees observe that these press reports highlight the potential confusion for the public regarding these data. *The Washington Post* reported that "the CPI figures for 1999 were not revised" (September 29, 2000 story) while *The Wall Street Journal* reported that "[t]he BLS said a complete revision of all the data sets would be released" (September 28, 2000 story) and "it [BLS] announced that it would revise the index" (September 29, 2000 story).

[¶ 10,295]   Act Sec. 309.   Prevent duplication or acceleration of loss through assumption of certain liabilities

Conference Committee Report (H.R. CONF. REP. NO. 106-1033)

[Code Sec. 358]

Present Law

Generally, no gain or loss is recognized when one or more persons transfer property to a corporation in exchange for stock and immediately after the exchange such person or persons control the corporation. However, a transferor recognizes gain to the extent it receives money or other property ("boot") as part of the exchange (sec. 351).

The assumption of liabilities by the controlled corporation generally is not treated as boot received by the transferor,[51] except that the transferor recognizes gain to the extent that the liabilities assumed exceed the total of the adjusted basis of the property transferred to the controlled corporation pursuant to the exchange (sec. 357(c)).

The assumption of liabilities by the controlled corporation generally reduces the transferor's basis in the stock of the controlled corporation that assumed the liabilities. The transferor's basis in the stock of the controlled corporation is the same as the basis of the property contributed to the controlled corporation, increased by the amount of any gain (or dividend) recognized by the transferor on the exchange, and reduced by the amount of any money or property received, and by the amount of any loss recognized by the transferor (sec. 358). For this purpose, the assumption of a liability is treated as money received by the transferor.

An exception to the general treatment of assumptions of liabilities applies to assumptions of liabilities that would give rise to a deduction, provided the incurrence of such liabilities did not result in the creation or increase of basis of any property. The assumption of such liabilities is not treated as money received by the transferor in determining whether the transferor has gain on the exchange. Similarly, the transferor's basis in the stock of the controlled corporation is not reduced by the assumption of such liabilities. The Internal Revenue Service has ruled that the assumption by an accrual basis corporation of certain contingent liabilities for soil and groundwater remediation would be covered by this exception.[52]

House Bill

No provision. However, H.R. 5542 contains a provisions [sic] to limit the acceleration or duplication of losses through assumptions of liabilities.

Under H.R. 5542, if the basis of stock (determined without regard to this provision) received by a transferor as part of a tax-free exchange with a controlled corporation exceeds the fair market value of the stock, then the basis of the stock received is reduced (but not below the fair market value) by the amount (determined as of the date of the exchange) of any liability that (1) is assumed in exchange for such stock, and (2) did not otherwise reduce the transferor's basis of the stock by reason of the assumption. Except as provided by the Secretary of the Treasury, this provision does not apply where the trade or business with which the liability is associated is transferred to the corporation as part of the exchange, or where substantially all the assets with which the liability is associated are transferred to the corporation as part of the exchange.

The exceptions for transfers of a trade or business, or of substantially all the assets, with which a liability is associated, are intended to obviate the need for valuation or basis reduction in such cases. The exceptions are not intended to apply to situations involving the selective transfer of assets that may bear some relationship to the liability, but that do not represent the full scope of the trade or business, (or substantially all the assets) with which the liability is associated.

For purposes of the provision, the term "liability" includes any fixed or contingent obligation to make payment, without regard to whether such obligation or potential obligation is otherwise taken into account under the Code. The determination whether a liability (as more broadly defined for purposes of this provision) has been assumed is made in accordance with the provisions of section 357(d)(1) of the Code. Under the standard of 357(d)(1), a recourse liability is treated as assumed if, based on all the facts and circumstances, the transferee has agreed to and is expected to satisfy such liability (or portion thereof), whether or not the transferor has been relieved of the liability. For example, if a trans-

---

[51] The assumption of liabilities is treated as boot if it can be shown that "the principal purpose" of the assumption is tax avoidance on the exchange, or is a non-bona fide business purpose (sec. 357(b)).

[52] Rev. Rul. 95-74, 1995-2 C.B. 36. The ruling addressed a parent corporation's transfer to a subsidiary of substantially all the assets of a manufacturing business, in exchange for stock and the assumption of liabilities associated with the business, including certain contingent environmental

remediation liabilities. These liabilities arose due to contamination of land during the parent corporation's operation of the manufacturing business. The transferor had no plan or intention to dispose of (or to have the subsidiary issue) any subsidiary stock. The IRS ruled that the contingent liabilities would not reduce the transferor's basis in the stock of the subsidiary because the liabilities had not been taken into account by the transferor prior to the transfer and had not given rise to deductions or basis for the transferor.

feree corporation does not formally assume a recourse obligation or potential obligation of the transferor, but instead agrees and is expected to indemnify the transferor with respect to all or a portion of a such an obligation, then the amount that is agreed to be indemnified is treated as assumed for purposes of the provision, whether or not the transferor has been relieved of such liability. Similarly, a nonrecourse liability is treated as assumed by the transferee of any asset subject to such liability.[53]

The application of the provision is illustrated in the following example: Assume a taxpayer transfers assets with an adjusted basis and fair market value of $100 to its wholly-owned corporation and the corporation assumes $40 of liabilities (the payment of which would give rise to a deduction). Thus, the value of the stock received by the transferor is $60. Under present law, the basis of the stock would be $100. The provision requires that the basis of the stock be reduced to $60 (i.e., a reduction of $40). Except as provided by the Secretary, no basis reduction is required if the transferred assets consisted of the trade or business, or substantially all the assets, with which the liability is associated.

The provision does not change the tax treatment with respect to the transferee corporation.

The Secretary of the Treasury is directed to prescribe rules providing appropriate adjustments to prevent the acceleration or duplication of losses through the assumption of liabilities (as defined in the provision) in transactions involving partnerships. The Secretary may also provide appropriate adjustments in the case of transactions involving S corporations. In the case of S corporations, such rules may be applied instead of the otherwise applicable basis reduction rules.

Effective Date

The provision is effective for assumptions of liabilities on or after October 19, 1999. Except as provided by the Secretary, the rules addressing transactions involving partnerships are effective with the same effective date. Any rules addressing transactions involving S corporations may likewise be effective for assumptions of liabilities on or after October 19, 1999, or such later date as may be prescribed in such rules.

Senate Amendment

No provision. On April 4, 2000, Senators Roth and Moynihan introduced a bill (S. 2354) that is the same as the provision in H.R. 5542.

Conference Agreement

The conference agreement follows H.R. 5542.

[Law at ¶ 5260, ¶ 5270 and ¶ 7160. CCH Explanation at ¶ 265.]

[¶ 10,300]   Act Sec. 310.   Disclosure of return information to the Congressional Budget Office

Conference Committee Report (H.R. CONF. REP. NO. 106-1033)

[Code Sec. 6103(j)(6)]

Present Law

Federal tax returns and return information are confidential and cannot be disclosed unless authorized by the Code. Section 6103 authorizes certain agencies to receive tax returns and return information for statistical use and for other specified purposes.[54] Section 6103 also permits the Secretary of the Treasury ("the Secretary") to provide return information to any person authorized to receive it by any mode or means that the Secretary determines necessary or appropriate.[55] Persons making unauthorized disclosures or inspections of tax returns and return information are subject to criminal and civil penalties.[56]

House Bill

No provision.

Senate Amendment

No provision.

Conference Agreement

Disclosure of return information

The Congressional Budget Office ("CBO") is in the process of developing the capability to make projections of the Social Security and Medicare programs over long periods of time. To facilitate the development and operation of long-term models of Social Security and Medicare, CBO needs continuing access to records from the IRS. Specifically, CBO seeks two SSA files that contain return information—the Social Security Earnings Record and the Master Beneficiary Record. These files contain individual earnings data compiled from tax returns (Forms W-2), which are protected from disclosure by section 6103. In addition, CBO may request other records, including those matched with survey data.

The conference agreement amends section 6103 to permit the Secretary to furnish to CBO return information to the extent such information is necessary for purposes of CBO's long-term models of

---

[53] Section 357(d)(2) contains a limitation in the case of certain nonrecourse liabilities. Also, under section 357, regulations, if issued, may provide for different results.

[54] E.g., sec. 6103(j), and 6103(l)(1) and (5).
[55] Sec. 6103(p)(2)(B).
[56] Sec. secs. 7431, 7213, and 7213A.

Social Security and Medicare. This authority extends to the development, operation, and maintenance by CBO of its long-term models of Social Security and Medicare. It is the intent of Congress that all requests for information made by CBO under this provision be made to the Secretary and that the Secretary use his authority under section 6103(p)(2) such that the SSA or other agency can furnish directly to CBO, for purposes of CBO's long-term models of Social Security and Medicare, the files they possess that incorporate return information. It is also the intent of Congress that the Secretary furnish such other return information under this provision as is necessary for purposes of CBO's Social Security and Medicare long-term models.

Under the provision, CBO is subject to the present-law safeguard requirements for tax returns and return information.[57] Further, CBO is prohibited from disclosing any tax returns and return information received under this provision except in a form that cannot be associated with, or otherwise identify, directly or indirectly a particular taxpayer. Present-law civil and criminal penalties apply to the unauthorized disclosure or inspection of tax returns or return information.[58]

Addition of general CBO confidentiality provisions

The conference agreement adds to the Congressional Budget Act of 1974[59] additional confidentiality provisions which would require CBO to provide the same level of confidentiality to data it obtains from other agencies as that to which the agencies themselves are subject. Officials and employees of CBO would be subject to the same statutory penalties for unauthorized disclosure as the employees of the agencies from which CBO obtain the data.

[Law at ¶ 6000 and ¶ 7165. CCH Explanation at ¶ 307.]

[¶ 10,310]   Act Sec. 311.   Amendments relating to the Ticket to Work and Work Incentives Improvement Act of 1999

Conference Committee Report (H.R. Conf. Rep. No. 106-1033)

[Code Secs. 30A, 280C and 857(b)(7)]

House Bill

No provision. However, H.R. 5542 includes tax technical corrections.[60] Except as otherwise provided, the technical corrections contained in the bill generally are effective as if included in the originally enacted related legislation. * * *

Amendments relating to the Ticket to Work and Work Incentives Improvement Act of 1999

Research credit

The provision clarifies the anti-double dip rule coordinating the research credit (sec. 41) and the Puerto Rico economic activity credit (sec. 30A). It is arguable that the present-law provisions could be construed so that the amount of wages on which a taxpayer could claim the section 30A credit is reduced only by the amount of credit claimed under section 41, rather than by the amount of wages upon which the section 41 credit is based. This result is inconsistent with the legislative history of the original provisions. The provision deletes the words "or credit" after "deduction" in section 280C(c)(1), and adds a new subsection in section 30A specifying that wages or other expenses taken into account for section 30A may not be taken into account for section 41.

Taxable REIT subsidiaries

The provision clarifies that a REIT's redetermined rents (described in sec. 857(b)(7)(B)) that are subject to tax under section 857(b)(7)(A) do not include amounts received from a taxable REIT subsidiary that would be excluded from unrelated business taxable income (under sec. 512(b)(3), relating to certain rents, if received by certain types of organizations described in sec. 511(a)(2)).

Partnership basis adjustments

The provision provides that the rule in the consolidated return regulations (Treas. Reg. sec. 1.1502-34) aggregating stock ownership for purposes of section 332 (relating to complete liquidation of a subsidiary that is a controlled corporation) also applies for purposes of section 732(f) (relating to basis adjustments to assets of a

---

[57] Sec. 6103(p)(4).
[58] See secs. 7431, 7213, and 7213A.
[59] 2 U.S.C. sec. 601(d).
[60] In addition to other tax technical corrections, the bill contains the technical corrections contained in H.R. 2488, the Financial Freedom Act of 1999 (106th Cong., 1st Sess., reported by the House Committee on Ways and Means, H. Rept. 106-238, July 16, 1999, 393—397), as passed by the House, and S. 1429, the Taxpayer Refund Act of 1999 (reported by the Senate Committee on Finance, S. Rept. 106-120, July 23, 1999, 221—225), as passed by the Senate.

(The technical corrections were not included in the conference agreement to H.R. 2488, the Taxpayer Refund and Relief Act of 1999 (106th Cong., 1st Sess., H. Rept. 106-289, Aug. 4, 1999, 542—543). The Taxpayer Refund and Relief Act of 1999 was vetoed by President Clinton.) However, the bill does not include the following provisions enacted in other legislation: sections 1601(b)(2) and (c) of H.R. 2488 (and section 504(c) of S. 1429), relating to the Vaccine Trust Fund, which were enacted in the "Ticket to Work and Work Incentives Improvement Act of 1999" (P.L. 106-170, sec. 523(b)).

controlled corporation received in a partnership distribution).

* * *

Senate Amendment

No provision.

[¶ 10,315] Act Sec. 312. Amendments related to Tax and Trade Relief Extension Act of 1998

Conference Committee Report (H.R. CONF. REP. NO. 106-1033)

[Code Sec. 6104(d)(6)]

House Bill

No provision. However, H.R. 5542 includes tax technical corrections.[60] Except as otherwise provided, the technical corrections contained in the bill generally are effective as if included in the originally enacted related legislation. * * *

Amendments related to the Tax and Trade Relief Extension Act of 1998

Exempt organizations.-The provision clarifies that nonexempt charitable trusts and nonexempt private foundations are subject to the public disclosure requirements of section 6104(d).

Capital gains.-The provision clarifies that if(1) a charitable remainder trust sold section 1250 property after July 28, 1997, and before January

Conference Agreement

The conference agreement follows H.R. 5542.

[Law at ¶ 5020, ¶ 5250, ¶ 5420 and ¶ 7170. CCH Explanation at ¶ 255, ¶ 410 and ¶ 415.]

1, 1998, (2) the property was held more than one year but not more than 18 months, and (3) the capital gain is distributed after December 31, 1997, then any capital gain attributable to depreciation will be taxed at 25 percent (rather than 28 percent). Treasury has published a notice (Notice 99-17, 1999-14 I.R.B., April 5, 1999) providing that the gain is taxed at 25 percent.

* * *

Senate Amendment

No provision.

Conference Agreement

The conference agreement follows H.R. 5542.

[Law at ¶ 6010 and ¶ 7175. CCH Explanation at ¶ 270 and ¶ 330.]

[¶ 10,320] Act Sec. 313. Amendments related to Internal Revenue Service Restructuring and Reform Act of 1998

Conference Committee Report (H.R. CONF. REP. NO. 106-1033)

[Code Secs. 6015, 6103, 6110, 6330, 6331, 7421 and 7463]

House Bill

No provision. However, H.R. 5542 includes tax technical corrections.[60] Except as otherwise provided, the technical corrections contained in the bill generally are effective as if included in the originally enacted related legislation. The provisions under the IRS Restructuring Act of 1998 relating to innocent spouse and to procedural and administrative issues (other than the provision

relating to clarification of Tax Court authority to issue appealable decisions) are effective upon the date of enactment of the bill.

* * *

Amendments related to the Internal Revenue Service Restructuring and Reform Act of 1998

Innocent spouse

Timing of request for relief.—Confusion currently exists as to the appropriate point at which a request for innocent spouse relief should be

---

[60] In addition to other tax technical corrections, the bill contains the technical corrections contained in H.R. 2488, the Financial Freedom Act of 1999 (106th Cong., 1st Sess., reported by the House Committee on Ways and Means, H. Rept. 106-238, July 16, 1999, 393—397), as passed by the House, and S. 1429, the Taxpayer Refund Act of 1999 (reported by the Senate Committee on Finance, S. Rept. 106-120, July 23, 1999, 221—225), as passed by the Senate. (The technical corrections were not included in the conference agreement to H.R. 2488, the Taxpayer Refund and Relief Act of 1999 (106th Cong., 1st Sess., H. Rept. 106-289, Aug. 4, 1999, 542—543). The Taxpayer Refund and Relief Act of 1999 was vetoed by President Clinton.) However, the bill does not include the following provisions enacted in other legislation: sections 1601(b)(2) and (c) of H.R. 2488 (and section 504(c) of S. 1429), relating to the Vaccine Trust Fund, which were enacted in the "Ticket to Work and Work Incentives Improvement Act of 1999" (P.L. 106-170, sec. 523(b)).

[60] In addition to other tax technical corrections, the bill contains the technical corrections contained in H.R. 2488, the Financial Freedom Act of 1999 (106th Cong., 1st Sess., reported by the House Committee on Ways and Means, H. Rept. 106-238, July 16, 1999, 393—397), as passed by the House, and S. 1429, the Taxpayer Refund Act of 1999 (reported by the Senate Committee on Finance, S. Rept. 106-120, July 23, 1999, 221—225), as passed by the Senate. (The technical corrections were not included in the conference agreement to H.R. 2488, the Taxpayer Refund and Relief Act of 1999 (106th Cong., 1st Sess., H. Rept. 106-289, Aug. 4, 1999, 542—543). The Taxpayer Refund and Relief Act of 1999 was vetoed by President Clinton.) However, the bill does not include the following provisions enacted in other legislation: sections 1601(b)(2) and (c) of H.R. 2488 (and section 504(c) of S. 1429), relating to the Vaccine Trust Fund, which were enacted in the "Ticket to Work and Work Incentives Improvement Act of 1999" (P.L. 106-170, sec. 523(b)).

made by the taxpayer and considered by the IRS. Some have read the statute to prohibit consideration by the IRS of requests for relief until after an assessment has been made, i.e., after the examination has been concluded, and if challenged, judicially determined. Others have read the statute to permit claims for relief from deficiencies to be made upon the filing of the return before any preliminary determination as to whether a deficiency exists or whether the return will be examined. The consideration of innocent spouse relief requires that the IRS focus on the particular items causing a deficiency; until such items are identified, the IRS cannot consider these claims. Congress did not intend that taxpayers be prohibited from seeking innocent spouse relief until after an assessment has been made; Congress intended the proper time to raise and have the IRS consider a claim to be at the same point where a deficiency is being considered and asserted by the IRS. This is the least disruptive for both the taxpayer and the IRS since it allows both to focus on the innocent spouse issue while also focusing on the items that might cause a deficiency. It also permits every issue, including the innocent spouse issue, to be resolved in single administrative and judicial process. The bill clarifies the intended time by permitting the election under (b) and (c) to be made at any point after a deficiency has been asserted by the IRS. A deficiency is considered to have been asserted by the IRS at the time the IRS states that additional taxes may be owed. Most commonly, this occurs during the Examination process. It does not require an assessment to have been made, nor does it require the exhaustion of administrative remedies in order for a taxpayer to be permitted to request innocent spouse relief.

Allowance of refunds.—The current placement in the statute of the provision for allowance of refunds may inappropriately suggest that the provision applies only to the United States Tax Court, whereas it was intended to apply administratively and in all courts. The bill clarifies this by moving the provision to its own subsection.

Non-exclusivity of judicial remedy.—Some have suggested that the IRS Restructuring Act administrative and judicial process for innocent spouse relief was intended to be the exclusive avenue by which relief could be sought. The bill clarifies Congressional intent that the procedures of section 6015(e) were intended to be additional, non-exclusive avenues by which innocent spouse relief could be considered.

Time for filing a petition with the Tax Court.— As enacted, the time period for seeking a redetermination in the Tax Court of innocent spouse relief begins on the date of the determination as opposed to the day after the determination. This period is one day shorter than that generally applicable to petition the Tax Court with respect to a deficiency notice (sec. 6213) and the period during which collection activities are prohibited and the limitations period is suspended. The bill clarifies the computation of this period and conforms it to the generally applicable 90-day period for petitioning the Tax Court. Conforming amendments are made as to the period for which collection activities are prohibited and collection limitations suspended.

Waiver of final determination upon agreement as to relief.—Congress intended in enacting section 6015 to provide a simple and efficient procedure by which the IRS could consider relief, and if relief was denied (in whole or in part) and the spouse requesting such relief did not agree with such denial, such issue could be considered by the Tax Court. Congress did not intend to require a rigid formal process when the IRS and the spouse requesting relief agreed on the extent of relief to be granted. However, the provisions of section 6015(e) have been interpreted as requiring the issuance in all circumstances of a formal "Notice of Determination," which contains a statement of the time period within which a petition may be filed with the Tax Court and which delays final resolution of the request for relief until the expiration of the period for filing a petition with the Tax Court. The issuance of the Notice of Determination is confusing to the taxpayer when the requested relief was fully granted or when the IRS and the taxpayer otherwise agreed on the application of the innocent spouse provisions to the taxpayer's case. It also may cause unnecessary filings with the Tax Court and delay the closing of the case until the time for filing with the Tax Court expires.

Congress has addressed the analogous situation in the deficiency context in section 6213(d). In such situations, upon written agreement, the IRS may adjust the taxpayer's liability as agreed, and no additional formal notice is necessary. The bill reflects that an analogous waiver was intended to apply in the innocent spouse context. The bill consequently permits taxpayers and the IRS to enter into a similar written agreement in innocent spouse cases, which allows for the taxpayer's liability to be immediately adjusted as agreed, and makes unnecessary a formal Notice of Determination or Tax Court review. This written agreement is to specify the details of the agreement between the IRS and the taxpayer as to the nature and extent of innocent spouse relief that will be provided. Conforming amendments are made as to the period for which collection activities are prohibited and collection limitations suspended.

Procedural and administrative issues

Disputes involving $50,000 or less.—The provision clarifies that the small case procedures of the Tax Court are available with respect to innocent spouse disputes and disputes continuing from the pre-levy administrative due process hearing. The small case procedures provide an accessible forum for taxpayers who have small claims with less formal rules of evidence and procedure. Use of the procedure is optional to the taxpayer, with the concurrence of the Tax Court. In view of the recent enactment of the innocent spouse and pre-levy administrative due process hearing provisions, it is anticipated that the Tax Court will give careful consideration to (1) a motion by the Commissioner of Internal Revenue to remove the small case designation (as authorized by Rules 172 and 173 of the Tax Court Rules) when the orderly conduct of the work of the Court or the administration of the tax laws would be better served by a regular trial of the case, as well as (2) the financial impact upon the taxpayer, including additional legal fees and costs, of not utilizing small case treatment. For example, removing the small case designation may be appropriate when a decision in the case will provide a precedent for the disposition of a substantial number of other cases. It is anticipated that motions by the Commissioner to remove the small case designation will be made infrequently.

Authority to enjoin collection actions.—While a dispute is pending under the pre-levy administrative due process hearing procedures, levy action is statutorily suspended for that period. The Tax Court and district courts are expressly granted authority to enjoin improper levy action in general, but that authority does not explicitly extend to improper levy action that occurs during the period when levy action is statutorily suspended under the administrative due process provisions. The provision clarifies the ability of the courts (including the Tax Court) to enjoin levy during the period that levy is required to be suspended with respect to a dispute under the pre-levy administrative due process hearing procedures.

Clarification of permissible extension of limitations period for installment agreements.—Uncertainty exists as to whether the permissible extension of the period of limitations in the context of installment agreements is governed by reference to an agreement of the parties pursuant to section 6502 or by reference to the period of time during which the installment agreement is in effect pursuant to sections 6331(k)(3) and (i)(5). The provision clarifies that the permissible extension of the period of limitations in the context of installment agreements is governed by the pertinent provisions of section 6502.

Clarification of Tax Court authority to issue appealable decisions.—The statutory provision for judicial review of a dispute concerning the pre-levy administrative due process hearing may be unclear as to whether a determination of the Tax Court is an appealable decision. The provision clarifies that the determination of the Tax Court (other than under the small case procedures) in a dispute concerning the pre-levy administrative due process hearing is a decision of the Tax Court and would be reviewable as such.

Other issues

IRS restructuring.—When the Office of the Chief Inspector was replaced by the Treasury Inspector General for Tax Administration (TIGTA) under the IRS Restructuring and Reform Act of 1998, Inspection's responsibilities were assigned to the TIGTA. TIGTA personnel are Treasury, rather than IRS, personnel. TIGTA personnel still need to make investigative disclosures to carry out the duties they took over from Inspection and their additional tax administration responsibilities. However, section 6103(k)(6) refers only to "internal revenue" personnel. The provision clarifies that section 6103(k)(6) permits TIGTA personnel to make investigative disclosures.

Compliance.—Section 3509 of the IRS Restructuring and Reform Act of 1998 expanded the disclosure rules of section 6110 to also cover Chief Counsel advice (sec. 6110(i)). This is a conforming change related to ongoing investigations. The provision adds to section 6110(g)(5)(A), after the words technical advice memorandum, "or Chief Counsel advice."

* * *

Senate Amendment
No provision.

Conference Agreement
The conference agreement follows H.R. 5542.

[Law at ¶ 5980, ¶ 6000, ¶ 6030, ¶ 6060, ¶ 6070, ¶ 6150, and ¶ 6180. CCH Explanation at ¶ 310, ¶ 315, ¶ 335, ¶ 340, ¶ 345, ¶ 355 and ¶ 365.]

[¶ 10,325]   Act Sec. 314.   Amendments relating to Taxpayer Relief Act of 1997

Conference Committee Report (H.R. CONF. REP. No. 106-1033)

[Code Secs. 56, 403, 414, 415, 3405, 6211 and 7436]

House Bill

No provision. However, H.R. 5542 includes tax technical corrections.[60] Except as otherwise provided, the technical corrections contained in the bill generally are effective as if included in the originally enacted related legislation. * * *

Amendments related to the Taxpayer Relief Act of 1997

Deficiency created by overstatement of refundable child credit.—The provision treats the refundable portion of the child credit under section 24(d) as part of a "deficiency." Thus, the usual assessment procedures applicable to income taxes will apply to both the nonrefundable and the refundable portions of the child credit. (This will reverse the conclusion reached by Internal Revenue Service Chief Counsel Memorandum 199948027 interpreting present law.)

Roth IRAs.—Code section 3405 provides for withholding with respect to designated distributions from certain tax-favored arrangements, including IRAs. In general, section 3405(e)(1)(B)(ii) excludes from the definition of a designated distribution the portion of any distribution which it is reasonable to believe is excludable from gross income. However, all distributions from IRAs are treated as includible in income. The exception was consistent with prior law when all IRA distributions were taxable, but does not account for the tax-free nature of certain Roth IRA distributions. The provision extends the exception to Roth IRAs.

Capital gain election.—The provision provides that an election to recognize gain or loss made pursuant to section 311(e) of the Taxpayer Relief Act of 1997 does not apply to assets disposed of in a recognition transaction within one year of the date the election would otherwise have been effective. Thus, for example, if an asset is sold in 2001, no election may be made with respect to that asset. In addition, it is clarified that the deemed sale and repurchase by reason of the election is not taken into account in applying the wash sale rules of section 1091.

Straight-line depreciation under AMT.—The provision clarifies that the Taxpayer Relief Act of 1997 did not change the requirement that the straight-line method of depreciation be used in computing the alternative minimum tax ("AMT") depreciation allowance for section 1250 property. It is arguable that the changes made by that Act could be read as inadvertently allowing accelerated depreciation under the AMT for section 1250 property which is allowed accelerated depreciation under the regular tax.

Transportation benefits.—Under present law, salary reduction amounts are generally treated as compensation for purposes of the limits on contributions and benefits under qualified plans. In addition, an employer can elect whether or not to include such amounts for nondiscrimination testing purposes. The IRS Reform Act permitted employers to offer a cash option in lieu of qualified transportation benefits. The provision treats salary reduction amounts used for qualified transportation benefits the same as other salary reduction amounts for purposes of defining compensation under the qualified plan rules.

Tax Court jurisdiction.—The Tax Court recently held that its jurisdiction pursuant to section 7436 extends only to employment status, not to the amount of employment tax in dispute (*Henry Randolph Consulting v. Comm'r*, 112 T.C. #1, Jan. 6, 1999). The provision provides that the Tax Court also has jurisdiction over the amount.

* * *

Senate Amendment

No provision.

Conference Agreement

The conference agreement follows H.R. 5542.

[Law at ¶ 5100, ¶ 5290, ¶ 5310, ¶ 5320, ¶ 5910, ¶ 6050, ¶ 6170 and ¶ 7180. CCH Explanation at ¶ 215, ¶ 275, ¶ 350, ¶ 360, ¶ 610 and ¶ 625.]

---

[60] In addition to other tax technical corrections, the bill contains the technical corrections contained in H.R. 2488, the Financial Freedom Act of 1999 (106th Cong., 1st Sess., reported by the House Committee on Ways and Means, H. Rept. 106-238, July 16, 1999, 393—397), as passed by the House, and S. 1429, the Taxpayer Refund Act of 1999 (reported by the Senate Committee on Finance, S. Rept. 106-120, July 23, 1999, 221—225), as passed by the Senate. (The technical corrections were not included in the conference agreement to H.R. 2488, the Taxpayer Refund and Relief Act of 1999 (106th Cong., 1st Sess., H. Rept. 106-289, Aug. 4, 1999, 542—543). The Taxpayer Refund and Relief Act of 1999 was vetoed by President Clinton.) However, the bill does not include the following provisions enacted in other legislation: sections 1601(b)(2) and (c) of H.R. 2488 (and section 504(c) of S. 1429), relating to the Vaccine Trust Fund, which were enacted in the "Ticket to Work and Work Incentives Improvement Act of 1999" (P.L. 106-170, sec. 523(b)).

[¶ 10,330] Act Sec. 315. Amendments related to Balanced Budget Act of 1997

Conference Committee Report (H.R. CONF. REP. NO. 106-1033)

[Code Secs. 5702 and 5761]

House Bill

No provision. However, H.R. 5542 includes tax technical corrections.[60] Except as otherwise provided, the technical corrections contained in the bill generally are effective as if included in the originally enacted related legislation. * * *

Amendments related to the Balanced Budget Act of 1997

Tobacco floor stocks tax.-The provision clarifies that the floor stocks taxes imposed on January 1, 2000, and January 1, 2002, apply only to cigarettes rather than to all tobacco products. As enacted, the law could be construed as ambiguous, referring to imposition on all tobacco products but imposing liability only with respect to cigarettes.

Tobacco excise tax.-Conforming amendments are provided to two provisions to reflect the fact that the tax on cigarette papers is not imposed on "books" of papers since January 1, 2000.

Coordination of trade rules and tobacco excise tax.-Clarification is provided that the penalty on reimporting cigarettes other than for return to a manufacturer (effective January 1, 2000) does not apply to cigarettes re-imported by individuals to the extent those cigarettes can be entered into the U.S. without duty or tax under the Harmonized Tariff Schedule.

* * *

Senate Amendment

No provision.

Conference Agreement

The conference agreement follows H.R. 5542.

[Law at ¶ 5960, ¶ 5970, and ¶ 7185. CCH Explanation at ¶ 293.]

[¶ 10,335] Act Sec. 316. Amendments related to Small Business Job Protection Act of 1996

Conference Committee Report (H.R. CONF. REP. NO. 106-1033)

[Code Secs. 51, 219, 401 and 1361]

House Bill

No provision. However, H.R. 5542 includes tax technical corrections.[60] Except as otherwise provided, the technical corrections contained in the bill generally are effective as if included in the originally enacted related legislation. * * *

Amendment related to the Small Business Job Protection Act of 1996

Work opportunity tax credit.-Section 51(d)(2) refers to eligibility for the work opportunity tax credit with respect to certain welfare recipients without taking into account the enactment of the temporary assistance for needy families

("TANF") program. The provisions conform references in the work opportunity tax credit to the operation of TANF.

Electing small business trusts holding S corporation stock.-The provision allows an electing small business trust (sec. 1361(e)) to have an organization described in section 170(c)(1) (relating to State and local governments) as a beneficiary if the organization holds a contingent interest and is not a potential current beneficiary.

Definition of lump-sum distribution.—Section 1401(b) of the Small Business Job Protection Act of 1996 Act repealed 5-year averaging for lump-sum distributions. The definition of lump-sum distribution was preserved for other provisions, pri-

---

[60] In addition to other tax technical corrections, the bill contains the technical corrections contained in H.R. 2488, the Financial Freedom Act of 1999 (106th Cong., 1st Sess., reported by the House Committee on Ways and Means, H. Rept. 106-238, July 16, 1999, 393—397), as passed by the House, and S. 1429, the Taxpayer Refund Act of 1999 (reported by the Senate Committee on Finance, S. Rept. 106-120, July 23, 1999, 221—225), as passed by the Senate. (The technical corrections were not included in the conference agreement to H.R. 2488, the Taxpayer Refund and Relief Act of 1999 (106th Cong., 1st Sess., H. Rept. 106-289, Aug. 4, 1999, 542—543). The Taxpayer Refund and Relief Act of 1999 was vetoed by President Clinton.) However, the bill does not include the following provisions enacted in other legislation: sections 1601(b)(2) and (c) of H.R. 2488 (and section 504(c) of S. 1429), relating to the Vaccine Trust Fund, which were enacted in the "Ticket to Work and Work Incentives Improvement Act of 1999" (P.L. 106-170, sec. 523(b)).

[60] In addition to other tax technical corrections, the bill contains the technical corrections contained in H.R. 2488, the Financial Freedom Act of 1999 (106th Cong., 1st Sess., reported by the House Committee on Ways and Means, H. Rept. 106-238, July 16, 1999, 393—397), as passed by the House, and S. 1429, the Taxpayer Refund Act of 1999 (reported by the Senate Committee on Finance, S. Rept. 106-120, July 23, 1999, 221—225), as passed by the Senate. (The technical corrections were not included in the conference agreement to H.R. 2488, the Taxpayer Refund and Relief Act of 1999 (106th Cong., 1st Sess., H. Rept. 106-289, Aug. 4, 1999, 542—543). The Taxpayer Refund and Relief Act of 1999 was vetoed by President Clinton.) However, the bill does not include the following provisions enacted in other legislation: sections 1601(b)(2) and (c) of H.R. 2488 (and section 504(c) of S. 1429), relating to the Vaccine Trust Fund, which were enacted in the "Ticket to Work and Work Incentives Improvement Act of 1999" (P.L. 106-170, sec. 523(b)).

marily those relating to NUA in employer securities. The definition was moved from section 402(d)(4)(A) to section 402(e)(4)(D)(i). This definition included the following sentence: "A distribution of an annuity contract from a trust or annuity plan referred to in the first sentence of this subparagraph shall be treated as a lump sum distribution." The provision adds this language back into the definition of lump-sum distribution. The sentence is relevant to section 401(k)(10)(B), which permits certain distributions if made as a "lump-sum distribution."

IRAs for nonworking spouses.—Section 1427 of the Small Business Job Protection Act of 1996 expanded the IRA deduction for nonworking spouses. The maximum permitted IRA contributions is generally limited by the individual's earned income. However, under present law, it is possible for a nonworking (or lesser earning) spouse to make IRA contributions in excess of the couple's combined earned income. The following example illustrates present law.

> *Example*: Suppose H and W retire in the middle of January, 1999. In that year, H earns $1,000 and W earns $500. Both are active participants in an employer-sponsored retirement plan. Their modified AGI is $60,000. They make no Roth IRA contributions. Before application of the income phase-out rules, the maximum deductible IRA contribution that H can make is $1,000 (sec. 219(b)(1)). After application of the income

phase-out rule in section 219(g), H's maximum contribution is $200, and H contributes that amount to an IRA. Under 408(o)(2)(B), H can make nondeductible contributions of $800 ($1,000—$200).

W's maximum permitted deductible contribution under section 219(c)(1)(B), before the income phase-out, is $1,300 (the sum of H and W's earned income ($1,500), less H's deductible IRA contribution ($200)). Under the income phase-out, W's deductible contribution is limited to $200, and she can make a nondeductible contribution of $1,000 ($1,300—$200).

The total permitted contributions for H and W are $2,300 ($1,000 for H plus $1,300 for W). The combined contribution should be limited to $1,500, their combined earned income.

The provision provides that the contributions for the spouse with the lesser income cannot exceed the combined earned income of the spouses.

* * *

Senate Amendment

No provision.

Conference Agreement

The conference agreement follows H.R. 5542.

[Law at ¶ 5090, ¶ 5220, ¶ 5280 and ¶ 5680. CCH Explanation at ¶ 245, ¶ 420, ¶ 605 and ¶ 620.]

[¶ 10,340] Act Sec. 317. Amendment related to the Revenue Reconciliation Act of 1990

Conference Committee Report (H.R. CONF. REP. NO. 106-1033)

[Code Sec. 43]

House Bill

No provision. However, H.R. 5542 includes tax technical corrections.[60] Except as otherwise provided, the technical corrections contained in the bill generally are effective as if included in the originally enacted related legislation. * * *

Amendment related to the Revenue Reconciliation Act of 1990

Qualified tertiary injectant expenses.—The provision clarifies that the enhanced oil recovery credit (sec. 43) applies with respect to qualified tertiary injectant expenses described in section

193(b) that are paid or incurred in connection with a qualified enhanced oil recovery project, and that are deductible for the taxable year (regardless of the provision allowing the deduction). Purchased and self-produced injectants are treated the same for purposes of the section 43 credit.

* * *

Senate Amendment

No provision.

Conference Agreement

The conference agreement follows H.R. 5542.

[Law at ¶ 5060. CCH Explanation at ¶ 250.]

---

[60] In addition to other tax technical corrections, the bill contains the technical corrections contained in H.R. 2488, the Financial Freedom Act of 1999 (106th Cong., 1st Sess., reported by the House Committee on Ways and Means, H. Rept. 106-238, July 16, 1999, 393—397), as passed by the House, and S. 1429, the Taxpayer Refund Act of 1999 (reported by the Senate Committee on Finance, S. Rept. 106-120, July 23, 1999, 221—225), as passed by the Senate. (The technical corrections were not included in the conference agreement to H.R. 2488, the Taxpayer Refund and

Relief Act of 1999 (106th Cong., 1st Sess., H. Rept. 106-289, Aug. 4, 1999, 542—543). The Taxpayer Refund and Relief Act of 1999 was vetoed by President Clinton.) However, the bill does not include the following provisions enacted in other legislation: sections 1601(b)(2) and (c) of H.R. 2488 (and section 504(c) of S. 1429), relating to the Vaccine Trust Fund, which were enacted in the "Ticket to Work and Work Incentives Improvement Act of 1999" (P.L. 106-170, sec. 523(b)).

[¶ 10,345]   Act Sec. 318.   Amendments to other Acts

Conference Committee Report (H.R. CONF. REP. NO. 106-1033)

[Code Secs. 165, 1275, 6411, 7702A, 9503 and 9510]

House Bill

No provision. However, H.R. 5542 includes tax technical corrections.[60] Except as otherwise provided, the technical corrections contained in the bill generally are effective as if included in the originally enacted related legislation. * * *

Amendments to other Acts (sec. 318 of the bill)

Insurance.—The legislative history of section 7702A(a) (enacted in the Technical and Miscellaneous Revenue Act of 1988) indicated that if a life insurance contract became a modified endowment contract ("MEC"), then the MEC status could not be eliminated by exchanging the MEC for another contract. Section 7702A(a)((2), however, arguably might be read to allow a policyholder to exchange a MEC for a contract that does not fail the 7-pay test of section 7702A(b), then exchange the second contract for a third contract, which would not literally have been received in exchange for a contract that failed to meet the 7-pay test. The provision clarifies section 7702A(a)(2) to correspond to the legislative history, effective as if enacted with the Technical and Miscellaneous Revenue Act of 1988 (generally, for contracts entered into on or after June 21, 1988).

Insurance.—Under section 7702A, if a life insurance contract that is not a modified endowment contract is actually or deemed exchanged for a new life insurance contract, then the 7-pay limit under the new contract is first be computed without reference to the premium paid using the cash surrender value of the old contract, and then would be reduced by 1/7 of the premium paid taking into account the cash surrender value of the old contract. For example, if the old contract had a cash surrender value of $14,000 and the 7-pay premium on the new contract would equal $10,000 per year but for the fact that there was an exchange, the 7-pay premium on the new contract would equal $8,000 ($10,000 − $14,000/7). However, section 7702A(c)(3)(A) arguably might be read to suggest that if the cash surrender value on the new contract was $0 in the first two years (due to surrender charges), then the 7-pay premium might be $10,000 in this example, uninten-

tionally permitting policyholders to engage in a series of "material changes" to circumvent the premium limitations in section 7702A. The provision clarifies section 7702A(c)(3)(A) to refer to the cash surrender value of the old contract, effective as if enacted with the Technical and Miscellaneous Revenue Act of 1988 (generally, for contracts entered into on or after June 21, 1988).

Worthless securities.—Section 165(g)(3) provides a special rule for worthless securities of an affiliated corporation. The test for affiliation in section 165(g)(3)(A) is the 80-percent vote test for affiliated groups under section 1504(a) that was in effect prior to 1984. When section 1504(a) was amended in the Deficit Reduction Act of 1984 to adopt the vote and value test of present law, no corresponding change was made to section 165(g)(3)(A), even though the tests had been identical until then. The provision conforms the affiliation test of section 165(g)(3)(A) to the test in section 1504(a)(2), effective for taxable years beginning after December 31, 1984.

Exception for certain annuities under OID rules.—The Deficit Reduction Act of 1984 expanded the prior-law rules for inclusion in income of original issue discount ("OID") on debt instruments. That Act provided an exception from the definition of a debt instrument for certain annuity contracts, including any annuity contract to which section 72 applies and that is issued by an insurance company subject to tax under subchapter L of the Code (and meets certain other requirements) (sec. 1275(a)(1)(B)(ii)). The provision clarifies that an annuity contract otherwise meeting the applicable requirements also comes within the exception of section 1275(a)(1)(B)(ii) if it is issued by an entity described in section 501(c) and exempt from tax under section 501(a), that would be subject to tax as an insurance company under subchapter L if it were not exempt under section 501(a). For example, the provision clarifies that an annuity contract otherwise meeting the requirements that is issued by a fraternal beneficiary society which is exempt from Federal income tax under section 501(a), and which is described in section 501(c)(8), comes within the exception under section 1275(a)(1)(B)(ii). It is understood that charitable

---

[60] In addition to other tax technical corrections, the bill contains the technical corrections contained in H.R. 2488, the Financial Freedom Act of 1999 (106th Cong., 1st Sess., reported by the House Committee on Ways and Means, H. Rept. 106-238, July 16, 1999, 393—397), as passed by the House, and S. 1429, the Taxpayer Refund Act of 1999 (reported by the Senate Committee on Finance, S. Rept. 106-120, July 23, 1999, 221—225), as passed by the Senate. (The technical corrections were not included in the conference agreement to H.R. 2488, the Taxpayer Refund and

Relief Act of 1999 (106th Cong., 1st Sess., H. Rept. 106-289, Aug. 4, 1999, 542—543). The Taxpayer Refund and Relief Act of 1999 was vetoed by President Clinton.) However, the bill does not include the following provisions enacted in other legislation: sections 1601(b)(2) and (c) of H.R. 2488 (and section 504(c) of S. 1429), relating to the Vaccine Trust Fund, which were enacted in the "Ticket to Work and Work Incentives Improvement Act of 1999" (P.L. 106-170, sec. 523(b)).

gift annuities (as defined in sec. 501(m)) depend (in whole or in substantial part) on the life expectancy of one or more individuals, and thus come within the exception under section 1275(a)(1)(B)(i). The provision is effective as if included with section 41 of the Deficit Reduction Act of 1984 (i.e., for taxable years ending after July 18, 1984).

Losses from section 1256 contracts.—Section 6411 allows tentative refunds for NOL carrybacks, business credit carrybacks and, for corporations only, capital loss carrybacks. Individuals normally cannot carry back a capital loss. However, section 1212(c) does allow a carryback of section 1256 losses, if elected by the taxpayer. The provision amends section 6411(a) by including a reference to section 1212(c), effective as if included with section 504 of the Economic Recovery Tax Act of 1981.

Highway Trust Fund.—The provision modifies administrative procedures of the Highway Trust Fund to conform to the 1993 repeal of the special tax rate applicable to ethanol prior to 1994. The provision is effective for taxes received after the date of enactment. This ensures that retroactive adjustments, if any, are not made to the Highway Trust Fund.

Conforming amendment for expenditures from Vaccine Injury Compensation Trust Fund.—The provision makes a conforming amendment to the expenditure purposes of the Vaccine Injury Compensation Trust Fund to enable certain payments to be made from the Trust Fund.

Clerical changes

The bill makes a number of clerical and typographical amendments to the Code.

Senate Amendment

No provision.

Conference Agreement

The conference agreement follows H.R. 5542.

[Law at ¶ 5180, ¶ 5670, ¶ 6090, ¶ 6220, ¶ 6260 and ¶ 6270. CCH Explanation at ¶ 210, ¶ 230, ¶ 280, ¶ 295, ¶ 297 and ¶ 405.]

[¶ 10,355]   Act Sec. 401.   Tax treatment of securities futures contracts

Conference Committee Report (H.R. Conf. Rep. No. 106-1033)

[Code Secs. 1234B and 1256]

Present Law

In general

Generally, gain or loss from the sale of property, including stock, is recognized at the time of sale or other disposition of the property, unless there is a specific statutory provision for nonrecognition (sec. 1001).

Gains and losses from the sale or exchange of capital assets are subject to special rules. In the case of individuals, net capital gain is generally subject to a maximum tax rate of 20 percent (sec. 1(h)). Net capital gain is the excess of net long-term capital gains over net short-term capital losses. Also, capital losses are allowed only to the extent of capital gains plus, in the case of individuals, $3,000 (sec. 1211). Capital losses of individuals may be carried forward indefinitely and capital losses of corporations may be carried back three years and forward five years (sec. 1212).

Generally, in order for gains or losses on a sale or exchange of a capital asset to be long-term capital gains or losses, the asset must be held for more than one year (sec. 1222).[61] A capital asset generally includes all property held by the taxpayer except certain enumerated types of property such as inventory (sec. 1221).

Section 1256 contracts

Special rules apply to "section 1256 contracts," which include regulated futures contracts, certain foreign currency contracts, nonequity options, and dealer equity options. Each section 1256 contract is treated as if it were sold (and repurchased) for its fair market value on the last business day of the year (i.e., "marked to market"). Any gain or loss with respect to a section 1256 contract which is subject to the mark-to-market rule is treated as if 40 percent of the gain or loss were short-term capital gain or loss and 60 percent were long-term capital gain or loss. This results in a maximum rate of 27.84 percent on any gain for taxpayers other than corporations. The mark-to-market rule (and the special 60/40 capital treatment) is inapplicable to hedging transactions.

A "regulated futures contract" is a contract (1) which is traded on or subject to the rules of a national securities exchange registered with the Securities Exchange Commission, a domestic board of trade designated a contract market by the Commodities Futures Trading Commission, or similar exchange, board of trade, or market, and (2) with respect to which the amount required to be deposited and which may be withdrawn depends on a system of marking to market.

A "dealer equity option" means, with respect to an options dealer, an equity option purchased in

---

[61] The holding period for futures transactions in a commodity is 6 months. The 6-month holding period does not apply to futures which are subject to the mark-to-market rules of section 1256, discussed below.

the normal course of the activity of dealing in options and listed on the qualified board or exchange on which the options dealer is registered. An equity option is an option to buy or sell stock or an option the value of which is determined by reference to any stock, group or stocks, or stock index, other than an option on certain broad-based groups of stock or stock index[62]. An options dealer is any person who is registered with an appropriate national securities exchange as a market maker or specialist in listed options, or who the Secretary of the Treasury determines performs functions similar to market makers and specialists.[63]

Mark to market accounting for dealers in securities

Under present law, a dealer in securities must compute its income from dealing in securities pursuant to the mark-to-market method of accounting (sec. 475). Gains and losses are treated as ordinary income and loss. Traders in securities, and dealers and traders in commodities may elect to use this method of accounting, including the ordinary income treatment. Section 1256 contracts are not treated as securities for purposes of section 475.[64]

Short sales

In the case of a "short sale" (i.e., where the taxpayer sells borrowed property and later closes the sale by repaying the lender with substantially identical property), any gain or loss on the closing transaction is considered gain or loss from the sale or exchange of a capital asset if the property used to close the short sale is a capital asset in the hands of the taxpayer, but the gain is ordinarily treated as short-term gain (sec. 1233(a)).

The Internal Revenue Code (the "Code") also contains several rules intended to prevent the transformation of short-term capital gain into long-term capital gain or long-term capital loss into short-term capital loss by simultaneously holding property and selling short substantially identical property (sec. 1233(b) and (d)). Under these rules, if a taxpayer holds property for less than the long-term holding period and sells short substantially identical property, any gain or loss upon the closing of the short sale is considered short-term capital gain, and the holding period of the substantially identical property is generally considered to begin on the date of the closing of the short sale. Also, if a taxpayer has held property for more than the long-term holding period

and sells short substantially identical property, any loss on the closing of the short sale is considered a long-term capital loss.

For purposes of these short sale rules, property includes stock, securities, and commodity futures, but commodity futures are not considered substantially identical if they call for delivery in different months.

For purposes of the short-sale rules relating to short-term gains, the acquisition of an option to sell at a fixed price is treated as a short sale, and the exercise or failure to exercise the option is considered a closing of the short sale.[65]

The Code also treats a taxpayer as recognizing gain where the taxpayer holds appreciated property and enters into a short sale of the same or substantially identical property, or enters into a contract to sell the same or substantially identical property (sec. 1259).

Wash sales

The wash-sale rule (sec. 1091) disallows certain losses from the disposition of stock or securities if substantially identical stock or securities (or an option or contract to acquire such property) are acquired by the taxpayer during the period beginning 30 days before the date of sale and ending 30 days after such date of sale. Commodity futures are not treated as stock or securities for purposes of this rule. The basis of the substantially identical stock or securities is adjusted to include the disallowed loss.

Similar rules apply to disallow any loss realized on the closing of a short sale of stock or securities where substantially identical stock or securities are sold (or a short sale, option or contract to sell is entered into) during the applicable period before and after the closing of the short sale.

Straddle rules

If a taxpayer realizes a loss with respect to a position in a straddle, the taxpayer may recognize that loss for the taxable year only to the extent that the loss exceeds the unrecognized gain (if any) with respect to offsetting positions in the straddle (sec. 1092). Disallowed losses are carried forward to the succeeding taxable year and are subject to the same limitation in that taxable year.

A "straddle" generally refers to offsetting positions with respect to actively traded personal property. Positions are offsetting if there is a substantial diminution of risk of loss from holding

---

[62] Rev. Rul. 94-63, 1994-2 C.B. 188, provides that the determination made by the Securities and Exchange Commission will determine whether or not an option is "broad based".

[63] A special rule provides that any gain or loss with respect to dealer equity options which are allocable to limited partners or limited entrepreneurs are treated as short-term capital gain or loss and do not qualify for the 60 percent long-term, 40 percent short-term capital gain or loss treatment of section 1256(a)(3).

[64] As discussed above, dealers in equity options are subject to mark-to-market accounting and the special capital gain rules of section 1256.

[65] An exception applies to an option to sell acquired on the same day as the property identified as intended to be used (and is so used) in exercising the option is acquired (sec. 1233(c)).

one position by reason of holding one or more other positions in personal property. A "position" in personal property is an interest (including a futures or forward contract or option) in personal property.

The straddle rules provide that the Secretary of the Treasury may issue regulations applying the short sale holding period rules to positions in a straddle. Temporary regulations have been issued setting forth the holding period rules applicable to positions in a straddle.[66] To the extent these rules apply to a position, the rules in section 1233(b) and (d) do not apply.

The straddle rules generally do not apply to positions in stock. However the straddle rules apply if one of the positions is stock and at least one of the offsetting positions is either (1) an option with respect to stock or (2) a position with respect to substantially similar or related property (other than stock) as defined in Treasury regulations. Under proposed Treasury regulations, a position with respect to substantially similar or related property does not include stock or a short sale of stock, but includes any other position with respect to substantially similar or related property.[67]

If a straddle consists of both positions that are section 1256 contracts and positions that are not such contracts, the taxpayer may designate the positions as a mixed straddle. Positions in a mixed straddle are not subject to the mark-to-market rule of section 1256, but instead are subject to rules written under regulations to prevent the deferral of tax or the conversion of short-term capital gain to long-term capital gain or long-term capital loss into short-term capital loss.

Transactions by a corporation in its own stock

A corporation does not recognize gain or loss on the receipt of money or other property in exchange for its own stock. Likewise, a corporation does not recognize gain or loss when it redeems its stock with cash, for less or more than it received when the stock was issued. In addition, a corporation does not recognize gain or loss on any lapse or acquisition of an option to buy or sell its stock (sec. 1032).

House Bill

No provision. However, section 124(c) and (d) of H.R. 4541[68] contained the following provisions:

In general

Except in the case of dealer securities futures contracts described below, securities futures contracts are not treated as section 1256 contracts. Thus, holders of these contracts are not subject to

the mark-to-market rules of section 1256 and are not eligible for 60-percent long-term capital gain treatment under section 1256. Instead, gain or loss on these contracts will be recognized under the general rules relating to the disposition of property.[69]

A securities futures contract is defined in section 3(a)(55)(A) of the Securities Exchange Act of 1934, as added by the bill. In general, that definition provides that a securities futures contract means a contract of sale for future delivery of a single security or a narrow-based security index. A securities futures contract will not be treated as a commodities futures contract for purposes of the Code.

Treatment of gains and losses

The bill provides that any gain or loss from the sale or exchange of a securities futures contract (other than a dealer securities futures contract) will be considered as gain or loss from the sale or exchange of property which has the same character as the property to which the contract relates has (or would have) in the hands of the taxpayer. Thus, if the underlying security would be a capital asset in the taxpayer's hands, then gain or loss from the sale or exchange of the securities futures contract would be capital gain or loss. The bill also provides that the termination of a securities futures contract which is a capital asset will be treated as a sale or exchange of the contract.

Capital gain treatment will not apply to contracts which themselves are not capital assets because of the exceptions to the definition of a capital asset relating to inventory (sec. 1221(a)(1)) or hedging (sec. 1221(a)(7)), or to any income derived in connection with a contract which would otherwise be treated as ordinary income.

Except as otherwise provided in regulations under section 1092(b) (which treats certain losses from a straddle as long-term capital losses) and section 1234B, as added by the bill, any capital gain or loss from the sale or exchange of a securities futures contract to sell property (i.e., the short side of a securities futures contract) will be short-term capital gain or loss. In other words, a securities futures contract to sell property is treated as equivalent to a short sale of the underlying property.

Wash sale rules

The bill clarifies that, under the wash sale rules, a contract or option to acquire or sell stock or securities shall include options and contracts that are (or may be) settled in cash or property

---

[66] Reg. sec. 1.1092(b)-2T.
[67] Prop. Reg. sec. 1.1092(d)-2(c).
[68] H.R. 4541 passed the House of Representatives on October 19, 2000.
[69] Any securities futures contract which is not a section 1256 contract will be treated a "security" for purposes of

section 475. Thus, for example, traders in securities futures contracts which are not section 1256 contracts could elect to have section 475 apply.

other than the stock or securities to which the contract relates. Thus, for example, the acquisition, within the period set forth in section 1091, of a securities futures contract to acquire stock of a corporation could cause the taxpayer's loss on the sale of stock in that corporation to be disallowed, notwithstanding that the contract may be settled in cash.

Short sale rules

In applying the short sale rules, a securities futures contract to acquire property will be treated in manner similar to the property itself. Thus, for example, the holding of a securities futures contract to acquire property and the short sale of property which is substantially identical to the property under the contract will result in the application of the rules of section 1233(b).[70] In addition, as stated above, a securities futures contract to sell is treated in a manner similar to a short sale of the property.

Straddle rules

Stock which is part of a straddle at least one of the offsetting positions of which is a securities futures contract with respect to the stock or substantially identical stock will be subject to the straddle rules of section 1092. Treasury regulations under section 1092 applying the principles of the section 1233(b) and (d) short sale rules to positions in a straddle will also apply.

For example, assume a taxpayer holds a long-term position in actively traded stock (which is a capital asset in the taxpayer's hands) and enters into a securities futures contract to sell substantially identical stock (at a time when the position in the stock has not appreciated in value so that the constructive sale rules of section 1259 do not apply). The taxpayer has a straddle. Treasury regulations prescribed under section 1092(b) applying the principles of section 1233(d) will apply, so that any loss on closing the securities futures contract will be a long-term capital loss.

Section 1032

A corporation will not recognize gain or loss on transactions in securities futures contracts with respect to its own stock.

Holding period

If property is delivered in satisfaction of a securities futures contract to acquire property (other than a contract to which section 1256 applies), the holding period for the property will include the period the taxpayer held the contract, provided that the contract was a capital asset in the hands of the taxpayer.

Regulations

The Secretary of the Treasury or his delegate has the authority to prescribe regulations to provide for the proper treatment of securities futures contracts under provisions of the Internal Revenue Code.

Dealers in securities futures contracts

In general, the bill provides that securities futures contracts and options on such contracts are not section 1256 contracts. The bill provides, however, that "dealer securities futures contracts" will be treated as section 1256 contracts.

The term "dealer securities futures contract" means a securities futures contract which is entered into by a dealer in the normal course of his or her trade or business activity of dealing in such contracts, and is traded on a qualified board of trade or exchange. The term also includes any option to enter into securities futures contracts purchased or granted by a dealer in the normal course of his or her trade or business activity of dealing in such options. The determination of who is to be treated as a dealer in securities futures contracts is to be made by the Secretary of the Treasury or his delegate not later than July 1, 2001. Accordingly, the bill authorizes the Secretary to treat a person as a dealer in securities futures contracts or options on such contracts if the Secretary determines that the person performs, with respect to such contracts or options, functions similar to an equity options dealer, as defined under present law.

The determination of who is a dealer in securities futures contracts is to be made in a manner that is appropriate to carry out the purposes of the provision, which generally is to provide comparable tax treatment between dealers in securities futures contracts, on the one hand, and dealers in equity options, on the other. Although traders in securities futures contracts (and options on such contracts) may not have the same market-making obligations as market makers or specialists in equity options, many traders are expected to perform analogous functions to such market makers or specialists by providing market liquidity for securities futures contracts (and options) even in the absence of a legal obligation to do so. Accordingly, the absence of market-making obligations is not inconsistent with a determination that a class of traders are dealers in securities futures contracts (and options), if the relevant factors, including providing market liquidity for such contracts (and options), indicate that the market functions of the traders is comparable to that of equity options dealers.

As in the case of dealer equity options, gains and losses allocated to any limited partner or

---

[70] Because securities futures contracts are not treated as futures contracts with respect to commodities, the rule providing that commodity futures are not substantially identical if they call for delivery in different months does not apply.

limited entrepreneur with respect to a dealer securities futures contract will be treated as short-term capital gain or loss.

Treatment of options under section 1256

The bill modifies the definition of "equity option" for purposes of section 1256 to take into account changes made by the non-tax provisions of the bill. Only options dealers are eligible for section 1256 with respect to equity options. The term "equity option" is modified to include an option to buy or sell stock, or an option the value of which is determined, directly or indirectly, by reference to any stock, or any "narrow-based security index," as defined in section 3(a)(55) of the Securities Exchange Act of 1934 (as modified by the bill). An equity option includes an option with respect to a group of stocks only if the group meets the requirements for a narrow-based security index.

As under present law, listed options that are not "equity options" are considered "nonequity options" to which section 1256 applies for all taxpayers. For example, options relating to broad-based groups of stocks and broad based stock indexes will continue to be treated as nonequity options under section 1256.

Definition of contract markets

The non-tax provisions of the bill designate certain new contract markets. The new contract markets will be contract markets for purposes of the Code, except to the extent provided in Treasury regulations.

Effective Date

These provisions will take effect on the date of enactment of the bill.

Senate Amendment

No provision.

Conference Agreement

The conference agreement follows the tax provisions contained in H.R. 4541.

[Law at ¶ 5590, ¶ 5600, ¶ 5610, ¶ 5630, ¶ 5635, ¶ 5640, ¶ 5650, ¶ 5660 and ¶ 6210. CCH Explanation at ¶ 260.]

Committee Reports
Installment Tax Correction Act of 2000
Introduction

[¶ 10,371]

The Installment Tax Correction Act of 2000 (P.L. 106-573) was introduced in the House on February 8, 2000, as H.R. 3594. The bill was referred to the House Ways and Means Committee on February 8, 2000. H.R. 3594 was passed by the House under suspension of rules by ⅔ vote and by the Senate on December 15, 2000. The bill was signed by the President on December 28, 2000.

No committee report was issued with H.R. 3594. However, the substance of the provisions of H.R. 3594 are substantially identical to provisions included in H.R. 2614, the Certified Development Company Program Improvements Bill of 2000, which incorporated the Taxpayer Relief Act of 2000 (H.R. 5542). Consequently, excerpts from the committee reports relating to H.R. 2614 are reproduced below to provide the reader with some legislative background on the newly enacted provision, despite the fact there are no official committee reports for H.R. 3594. The conference report on H.R. 2614 was filed in and agreed to by the House on October 26, 2000 (H.R. CONF. REP. NO. 106-1004).

The following material is the official wording relating to the repeal of the modification of the installment method contained in the Conference Committee Report to the Taxpayer Relief Act of 2000, a portion of which was passed as a separate bill, the Installment Tax Correction Act of 2000. Headings have been added for convenience in locating the committee report. Any omission of text is indicated by asterisks (* * *). References are to the following official report:

● The Conference Committee Report on the Taxpayer Relief Act of 2000, as released on October 26, 2000, and issued as CCH Special 1, STANDARD FEDERAL TAX REPORTS, Issue No. 50 (Part 2), November 30, 2000, is referred to as **Conference Committee Report (H.R. CONF. REP. NO. 106-1004)**.

[¶ 10,375]   Act Sec. 1 and 2 [Act Sec. 206 of H.R. 2614].   Repeal of modification of installment method

Conference Committee Report (H.R. CONF. REP. NO. 106-1004)

[Code Secs. 453 and 453A]

Present Law

The installment method of accounting allows a taxpayer to defer the recognition of income from the disposition of certain property until payment is received. Sales to customers in the ordinary course of business are not eligible for the installment method, except for sales of property that is used or produced in the trade or business of farming and sales of timeshares and residential lots if an election to pay interest under section 453(1)(2)(B) is made. Section 536(a) of the Ticket to Work and Work Incentives Improvement Act of 1999 prohibited the use of the installment method for a transaction that would otherwise be required to be reported using the accrual method of accounting, effective for dispositions occurring on or after December 17, 1999.

A pledge rule provides that if an installment obligation is pledged as security for any indebtedness, the net proceeds[45] of such indebtedness are treated as a payment on the obligation, triggering

---

[45] The net proceeds equal the gross loan proceeds less the direct expenses of obtaining the loan.

the recognition of income. Actual payments received on the installment obligation subsequent to the receipt of the loan proceeds are not taken into account until such subsequent payments exceed the loan proceeds that were treated as payments. The pledge rule does not apply to sales of property used or produced in the trade or business of farming, to sales of timeshares and residential lots where the taxpayer elects to pay interest under section 453(1)(2)(B), or to dispositions where the sales price does not exceed $150,000. The Ticket to Work and Work Incentives Improvement Act of 1999 provided that the right to satisfy a loan with an installment obligation will be treated as a pledge of the installment obligation, effective for dispositions occurring on or after December 17, 1999.

House Bill

No provision. However, H.R. 3081, as passed by the House, repeals the prohibition on the use of the installment method of accounting for dispositions of property that would otherwise be reported for Federal income tax purposes using the accrual method of accounting. Accordingly, any disposition of property that otherwise qualifies to be reported using the installment method of account-ing may be reported using that method without regard to whether the disposition would otherwise be reported using the accrual method of accounting.

The provision leaves unchanged the rule added by section 536(b) of the Ticket to Work and Work Incentives Improvement Act of 1999 that modified the installment method pledge rule.

Effective Date

The provision is effective for sales or other dispositions on or after December 17, 1999.

Senate Amendment

No provision. However, H.R. 833, as passed by the Senate, contains the provisions enacted in the Ticket to Work and Work Incentives Improvement Act of 1999 prohibiting the use of the installment method for a transaction that would otherwise be required to be reported using the accrual method of accounting and expanding the pledge rule.

Conference Agreement

The conference agreement includes the provision in H.R. 3081.

[Law at ¶ 5330. CCH Explanation at ¶ 205.]

Effective Dates

FSC Repeal and Extraterritorial Income Exclusion Act of 2000

¶ 20,001

This CCH-prepared table presents the general effective dates for major law provisions added, amended or repealed by the FSC Repeal and Extraterritorial Income Exclusion Act of 2000 (P.L. 106-519), enacted November 15, 2000. Entries are listed in Code Section order.

Code Sec.	Act Sec.	Act Provision Subject	Effective Date
56(g)(4)(B)	4(1)	Treatment of extraterritorial income—conforming amendment	Transactions after September 30, 2000
114	3(a)	Treatment of extraterritorial income	Transactions after September 30, 2000
275(a)(4)(A)-(C)	4(2)(A)	Treatment of extraterritorial income—conforming amendment	Transactions after September 30, 2000
275(a)	4(2)(B)	Treatment of extraterritorial income—conforming amendment	Transactions after September 30, 2000
864(e)(3)(B)	4(3)(B)	Treatment of extraterritorial income—conforming amendment	Transactions after September 30, 2000
864(e)(3)	4(3)(A)	Treatment of extraterritorial income—conforming amendment	Transactions after September 30, 2000
903	4(4)	Treatment of extraterritorial income—conforming amendment	Transactions after September 30, 2000
921	2	Repeal of foreign sales corporation rules	Transactions after September 30, 2000
922	2	Repeal of foreign sales corporation rules	Transactions after September 30, 2000
923	2	Repeal of foreign sales corporation rules	Transactions after September 30, 2000
924	2	Repeal of foreign sales corporation rules	Transactions after September 30, 2000
925	2	Repeal of foreign sales corporation rules	Transactions after September 30, 2000
926	2	Repeal of foreign sales corporation rules	Transactions after September 30, 2000
927	2	Repeal of foreign sales corporation rules	Transactions after September 30, 2000
941	3(b)	Qualifying foreign trade income	Transactions after September 30, 2000
942	3(b)	Foreign trading gross receipts	Transactions after September 30, 2000
943	3(b)	Qualifying foreign trade income—definitions and special rules	Transactions after September 30, 2000
999(c)(1)	4(5)	Treatment of extraterritorial income—conforming amendment	Transactions after September 30, 2000

Code Sec.	Act Sec.	Act Provision Subject	Effective Date
	4(6)	Treatment of extraterritorial income—clerical amendment	Transactions after September 30, 2000
	4(7)	Treatment of extraterritorial income—clerical amendment	Transactions after September 30, 2000
	4(8)	Treatment of extraterritorial income—clerical amendment	Transactions after September 30, 2000

Effective Dates
Community Renewal Tax Relief Act of 2000
¶ 20,005

This CCH-prepared table presents the general effective dates for major law provisions added, amended or repealed by the Community Renewal Tax Relief Act of 2000 (P.L. 106-554), enacted December 21, 2000. Entries are listed in Code Section order.

Code Sec.	Act Sec.	Act Provision Subject	Effective Date
1(h)(8)	117(b)(1)	Increased exclusion of gain on sale of empowerment zone stock—conforming amendment	Stock acquired after December 21, 2000
1(h)	312(b)	Amendment related to Section 4003 of the Tax and Trade Relief Extension Act of 1998—technical correction	Tax years ending after May 6, 1997, generally
26(b)(2)(Q)	202(a)(1)	Medical savings accounts renamed as Archer MSAs	December 21, 2000
30A(f)-(h)	311(a)(2)	Amendment related to Section 502 of the Ticket to Work and Work Incentives Improvement Act of 1999—technical correction	Amounts paid or incurred after June 30, 1999
38(b)(11)-(13)	121(b)(1)	New markets tax credit—credit made part of general business credit	Investments made after December 31, 2000
39(d)(9)	121(b)(2)	New markets tax credit—credit made part of general business credit—limitation on carryback	Investments made after December 31, 2000
42(d)(4)(A)	134(a)(1)	Modifications to rules relating to basis of building which is eligible for credit—adjusted basis to include portion of certain buildings used by low-income individuals who are not tenants and by project employees	Housing credit dollar amounts allocated after December 31, 2000, and buildings placed in service after such date to the extent Code Sec. 42(h)(1) does not apply by reason of Code Sec. 42(h)(4), but only with respect to bonds issued after that date
42(d)(4)(C)-(D)	134(a)(2)	Modifications to rules relating to basis of building which is eligible for credit—adjusted basis to include portion of certain buildings used by low-income individuals who are not tenants and by project employees	Housing credit dollar amounts allocated after December 31, 2000, and buildings placed in service after such date to the extent Code Sec. 42(h)(1) does not apply by reason of Code Sec. 42(h)(4),

Code Sec.	Act Sec.	Act Provision Subject	Effective Date
			but only with respect to bonds issued after that date
42(d)(4)(C)	134(a)(3)	Modifications to rules relating to basis of building which is eligible for credit—adjusted basis to include portion of certain buildings used by low-income individuals who are not tenants and by project employees	Housing credit dollar amounts allocated after December 31, 2000, and buildings placed in service after such date to the extent Code Sec. 42(h)(1) does not apply by reason of Code Sec. 42(h)(4), but only with respect to bonds issued after that date
42(d)(5)(C)	135(b)	Determination of whether buildings are located in high cost areas	Housing credit dollar amounts allocated after December 31, 2000, and buildings placed in service after such date to the extent Code Sec. 42(h)(1) does not apply by reason of Code Sec. 42(h)(4), but only with respect to bonds issued after that date
42(h)(1)(E)	135(a)(1)	Allocation of credit limit to certain buildings	Housing credit dollar amounts allocated after December 31, 2000, and buildings placed in service after such date to the extent Code Sec. 42(h)(1) does not apply by reason of Code Sec. 42(h)(4), but only with respect to bonds issued after that date
42(h)(3)(C)	131(a)	Modification of state ceiling on low-income housing credit	Calendar years after 2000
42(h)(3)(C)	131(c)(1)	Modification of state ceiling on low-income housing credit—conforming amendment	Calendar years after 2000
42(h)(3)(C)	135(a)(2)	Allocation of credit limit to certain buildings	Housing credit dollar amounts allocated after December 31, 2000, and buildings placed in service after such date to the

Code Sec.	Act Sec.	Act Provision Subject	Effective Date
			extent Code Sec. 42(h)(1) does not apply by reason of Code Sec. 42(h)(4), but only with respect to bonds issued after that date
42(h)(3)(C)	136(b)	Carryfoward rules—conforming amendment	Housing credit dollar amounts allocated after December 31, 2000, and buildings placed in service after such date to the extent Code Sec. 42(h)(1) does not apply by reason of Code Sec. 42(h)(4), but only with respect to bonds issued after that date
42(h)(3)(D)	131(c)(2)	Modification of state ceiling on low-income housing credit—conforming amendment	Calendar years after 2000
42(h)(3)(D)	136(a)	Carryfoward rules	Housing credit dollar amounts allocated after December 31, 2000, and buildings placed in service after such date to the extent Code Sec. 42(h)(1) does not apply by reason of Code Sec. 42(h)(4), but only with respect to bonds issued after that date
42(h)(3)(H)	131(b)	Modification of state ceiling on low-income housing credit—cost-of-living adjustment	Calendar years after 2000
42(i)(2)(E)	134(b)	Modifications to rules relating to basis of building which is eligible for credit—certain Native American housing assistance disregarded in determining whether building is federally subsidized for purposes of the low-income housing credit	Housing credit dollar amounts allocated after December 31, 2000, and buildings placed in service after such date to the extent Code Sec. 42(h)(1) does not apply by reason of Code Sec. 42(h)(4), but only with respect to bonds issued after that date

Code Sec.	Act Sec.	Act Provision Subject	Effective Date
42(m)(1)(A)	133(a)	Additional responsibilities of housing credit agencies—market study, public disclosure of rationale for not following credit allocation priorities	Housing credit dollar amounts allocated after December 31, 2000, and buildings placed in service after such date to the extent Code Sec. 42(h)(1) does not apply by reason of Code Sec. 42(h)(4), but only with respect to bonds issued after that date
42(m)(1)(B)	132(b)	Modification of criteria for allocating housing credits among projects—preference for community revitalization projects located in qualified census tracts	Housing credit dollar amounts allocated after December 31, 2000, and buildings placed in service after such date to the extent Code Sec. 42(h)(1) does not apply by reason of Code Sec. 42(h)(4), but only with respect to bonds issued after that date
42(m)(1)(B)	133(b)	Additional responsibilities of housing credit agencies—site visits	Housing credit dollar amounts allocated after December 31, 2000, and buildings placed in service after such date to the extent Code Sec. 42(h)(1) does not apply by reason of Code Sec. 42(h)(4), but only with respect to bonds issued after that date
42(m)(1)(C)	132(a)	Modification of criteria for allocating housing credits among projects—selection criteria	Housing credit dollar amounts allocated after December 31, 2000, and buildings placed in service after such date to the extent Code Sec. 42(h)(1) does not apply by reason of Code Sec. 42(h)(4), but only with respect to bonds issued after that date

Code Sec.	Act Sec.	Act Provision Subject	Effective Date
43(c)(1)(C)	317(a)	Amendment related to Section 11511 of the Revenue Reconcilation Act of 1990—technical correction	Costs paid or incurred in tax years beginning after December 31, 1990
45(d)(7)(A)	319(1)	Clerical amendment	December 21, 2000
45D	121(a)	New markets tax credit	Investments made after December 31, 2000
51(d)(2)(B)	316(a)	Amendment related to Section 1201 of the Small Business Job Protection Act of 1996—technical correction	Individuals who begin work for the employer after September 30, 1996
51(d)(5)(A)-(B)	102(a)	Work opportunity credit for hiring youth residing in renewal communities—high risk youth	Individuals who begin work for the employer after December 31, 2001.
51(d)(5)(B)	102(c)	Work opportunity credit for hiring youth residing in renewal communities—headings	Individuals who begin work for the employer after December 31, 2001.
51(d)(7)(A)	102(b)	Work opportunity credit for hiring youth residing in renewal communities—qualified summer youth employee	Individuals who begin work for the employer after December 31, 2001.
51(d)(7)(C)	102(c)	Work opportunity credit for hiring youth residing in renewal communities—headings	Individuals who begin work for the employer after December 31, 2001.
56(a)(1)(A)	314(d)	Amendment related to Section 402 of the Taxpayer Relief Act of 1997—technical correction	August 5, 1997
62(a)(16)	202(b)(1)	Medical savings accounts renamed as Archer MSAs—conforming amendment	December 21, 2000
67(f)	319(2)	Clerical amendment	December 21, 2000
106(b)(4)	202(b)(2)(A)	Medical savings accounts renamed as Archer MSAs—conforming amendment	December 21, 2000
106(b)(7)	202(b)(2)(A)	Medical savings accounts renamed as Archer MSAs—conforming amendment	December 21, 2000
106(b)	202(a)(2)	Medical savings accounts renamed as Archer MSAs	December 21, 2000
106(b)	202(b)(6)	Medical savings accounts renamed as Archer MSAs—conforming amendment	December 21, 2000
138(b)	202(a)(3)	Medical savings accounts renamed as Archer MSAs	December 21, 2000
138(f)	202(b)(6)	Medical savings accounts renamed as Archer MSAs—conforming amendment	December 21, 2000

Code Sec.	Act Sec.	Act Provision Subject	Effective Date
146(d)(1)-(2)	161(a)	Acceleration of phase-in of increase in volume cap on private activity bonds	Calendar years after 2000
151(c)(6)	306	Treatment of missing children with respect to certain tax benefits	Tax years ending after December 21, 2000
165(g)(3)(A)	318(b)(1)	Affiliated corporations in context of worthless securities—technical correction	Tax years beginning after December 31, 1984
165(g)(3)	318(b)(2)	Affiliated corporations in context of worthless securities—technical correction	Tax years beginning after December 31, 1984
170(e)(6)(B)	165(a)(2)	Extension of enhanced deduction for corporate donations of computer technology—expansion of eligible donees	Contributions made after December 31, 2000
170(e)(6)(B)	165(a)(3)	Extension of enhanced deduction for corporate donations of computer technology—extension of donation period	Contributions made after December 31, 2000
170(e)(6)(B)	165(b)(1)	Extension of enhanced deduction for corporate donations of computer technology—conforming amendment	Contributions made after December 31, 2000
170(e)(6)(B)	165(d)	Extension of enhanced deduction for corporate donations of computer technology—standards as to functionality and suitability	Contributions made after December 31, 2000
170(e)(6)(D)-(G)	165(e)	Extension of enhanced deduction for corporate donations of computer technology—donations of computers reacquired by manufacturer	Contributions made after December 31, 2000
170(e)(6)(F)	165(c)	Extension of enhanced deduction for corporate donations of computer technology—extension of deduction	Contributions made after December 31, 2000
170(e)(6)	165(a)(1)	Extension of enhanced deduction for corporate donations of computer technology—expansion of computer technology donations to public libraries	Contributions made after December 31, 2000
170(e)(6)	165(b)(2)	Extension of enhanced deduction for corporate donations of computer technology—conforming amendment	Contributions made after December 31, 2000
196(c)(7)-(9)	121(c)	New markets tax credit—deduction for unused credit	Investments made after December 31, 2000
198(c)	162(a)	Modifications to expensing of environmental remediation costs—expensing not limited to sites in targeted areas	Expenditures paid or incurred after December 21, 2000

Code Sec.	Act Sec.	Act Provision Subject	Effective Date
198(h)	162(b)	Modifications to expensing of environmental remediation costs—extension of termination date	Expenditures paid or incurred after December 21, 2000
219(c)(1)(B)	316(d)	Amendment related to Section 1427 of the Small Business Job Protection Act of 1996—technical correction	Tax years beginning after December 31, 1996
220(c)(1)(C)	202(b)(7)	Medical savings accounts renamed as Archer MSAs—conforming amendment	December 21, 2000
220(c)(1)(D)	202(b)(2)(B)	Medical savings accounts renamed as Archer MSAs—conforming amendment	December 21, 2000
220(d)(1)	202(b)(3)	Medical savings accounts renamed as Archer MSAs—conforming amendment	December 21, 2000
220(d)(1)	202(b)(5)	Medical savings accounts renamed as Archer MSAs—conforming amendment	December 21, 2000
220(d)	202(b)(4)	Medical savings accounts renamed as Archer MSAs—conforming amendment	December 21, 2000
220(e)(2)	202(b)(2)(B)	Medical savings accounts renamed as Archer MSAs—conforming amendment	December 21, 2000
220(f)(3)(A)	202(b)(2)(B)	Medical savings accounts renamed as Archer MSAs—conforming amendment	December 21, 2000
220(i)(2)	201(a)	Two-year extension of availability of medical savings accounts	December 21, 2000
220(i)(3)(B)	201(a)	Two-year extension of availability of medical savings accounts	December 21, 2000
220(i)(4)(B)	202(b)(2)(B)	Medical savings accounts renamed as Archer MSAs—conforming amendment	December 21, 2000
220(i)	202(b)(6)	Medical savings accounts renamed as Archer MSAs—conforming amendment	December 21, 2000
220(j)(2)(C)	201(b)(1)(C)	Two-year extension of availability of medical savings accounts—conforming amendment	December 21, 2000
220(j)(2)	201(b)(1)(A)-(B)	Two-year extension of availability of medical savings accounts—conforming amendment	December 21, 2000
220(j)(4)(A)	201(b)(2)	Two-year extension of availability of medical savings accounts—conforming amendment	December 21, 2000
220(j)	202(b)(2)(B)	Medical savings accounts renamed as Archer MSAs—conforming amendment	December 21, 2000

Code Sec.	Act Sec.	Act Provision Subject	Effective Date
220	202(a)(4)	Medical savings accounts renamed as Archer MSAs	December 21, 2000
220	202(b)(8)	Medical savings accounts renamed as Archer MSAs—clerical amendment	December 21, 2000
280C(c)(1)	311(a)(1)	Amendment related to Section 502 of the Ticket to Work and Work Incentives Improvement Act of 1999—technical correction	Amounts paid or incurred after June 30, 1999
357(d)(1)	309(b)	Prevention of duplication of loss through assumption of liabilities giving rise to a deduction—determination of amount of liability assumed	Assumptions of liability after October 18, 1999
358(h)	309(a)	Prevention of duplication of loss through assumption of liabilities giving rise to a deduction	Assumptions of liability after October 18, 1999
401(k)(10)(B)	316(c)	Amendment related to Section 1401 of the Small Business Job Protection Act of 1996—technical correction	Tax years beginning after December 31, 1999
403(b)(3)(B)	314(e)(1)	Amendment related to Section 1072 of the Taxpayer Relief Act of 1997—technical correction	Tax years beginning after December 31, 1997
408(d)(5)	319(3)	Clerical amendment	December 21, 2000
414(s)(2)	314(e)(2)	Amendment related to Section 1072 of the Taxpayer Relief Act of 1997—technical correction	Tax years beginning after December 31, 1997
415(c)(3)(D)	314(e)(1)	Amendment related to Section 1072 of the Taxpayer Relief Act of 1997—technical correction	Tax years beginning after December 31, 1997
469(i)(3)(C)-(F)	101(b)(1)	Designation of and tax incentives for renewal communities—exception for commercial revitalization deduction from passive loss rules	December 21, 2000
469(i)(3)(E)	101(b)(2)	Designation of and tax incentives for renewal communities—exception for commercial revitalization deduction from passive loss rules	December 21, 2000
469(i)(6)(B)	101(b)(3)(A)	Designation of and tax incentives for renewal communities—exception for commercial revitalization deduction from passive loss rules	December 21, 2000
469(i)(6)(B)	101(b)(3)(B)	Designation of and tax incentives for renewal communities—exception for commercial revitalization deduction from passive loss rules	December 21, 2000
475(g)(3)	319(4)	Clerical amendment	December 21, 2000
529(e)(3)(B)	319(5)	Clerical amendment	December 21, 2000
530(d)(4)(B)	319(6)	Clerical amendment	December 21, 2000
664(d)(1)(C)	319(7)	Clerical amendment	December 21, 2000

¶ **20,005**

Code Sec.	Act Sec.	Act Provision Subject	Effective Date
664(d)(2)(C)	319(7)	Clerical amendment	December 21, 2000
678(e)	319(8)(A)	Clerical amendment	December 21, 2000
848(e)(1)(B)	202(a)(5)	Medical savings accounts renamed as Archer MSAs	December 21, 2000
856(c)(7)	319(9)	Clerical amendment	December 21, 2000
856(l)(4)(A)	319(10)	Clerical amendment	December 21, 2000
857(b)(7)(B)	311(b)	Amendment related to Section 545 of the Ticket to Work and Work Incentives Improvement Act of 1999—technical correction	Tax years beginning after December 31, 2000
871(f)(2)(B)	319(11)	Clerical amendment	December 21, 2000
995(b)(3)(B)	319(12)	Clerical amendment	December 21, 2000
995(f)(4)	307(c)	Amendments to statutes referencing yield on 52-week treasury bills—interest rate on tax-deferred liability of shareholders of domestic international sales corporations	December 21, 2000
1016(a)(23)	116(b)(1)	Nonrecognition of gain on rollover of empowerment zone investments—conforming amendment	Qualified empowerment zone assets acquired after December 21, 2000
1032(a)	401(c)	Tax treatment of securities futures contracts—nonrecognition under Code Sec. 1032	December 21, 2000
1091(f)	401(d)	Tax treatment of securities futures contracts—treatment under wash sales rules	December 21, 2000
1092(d)(3)(B)	401(e)	Tax treatment of securities futures contracts—treatment under straddle rules	December 21, 2000
1202(a)	117(a)	Increased exclusion of gain on sale of empowerment zone stock	Stock acquired after December 21, 2000
1202	117(b)(2)	Increased exclusion of gain on sale of empowerment zone stock—clerical amendment	Stock acquired after December 21, 2000
1223(15)	116(b)(2)	Nonrecognition of gain on rollover of empowerment zone investments—conforming amendment	Qualified empowerment zone assets acquired after December 21, 2000
1223(16)-(17)	401(h)(1)	Tax treatment of securities futures contracts—conforming amendment	December 21, 2000
1233(e)(2)(D)	401(f)	Tax treatment of securities futures contracts—treatment under short sales rules	December 21, 2000
1234A(1)	401(b)(1)	Tax treatment of securities futures contracts—terminations	December 21, 2000
1234A(3)	401(b)(4)	Tax treatment of securities futures contracts—terminations	December 21, 2000
1234A	401(b)(2)-(3)	Tax treatment of securities futures contracts—terminations	December 21, 2000

Code Sec.	Act Sec.	Act Provision Subject	Effective Date
1234B	401(a)	Tax treatment of securities futures contracts—gains or losses from securities futures contracts	December 21, 2000
1256(b)(5)	401(g)(1)(A)	Tax treatment of securities futures contracts—treatment under Code Sec. 1256	December 21, 2000
1256(f)(4)	401(g)(2)(A)-(B)	Tax treatment of securities futures contracts—treatment under Code Sec. 1256	December 21, 2000
1256(g)(6)	401(g)(3)	Tax treatment of securities futures contracts—treatment under Code Sec. 1256	December 21, 2000
1256(g)(9)	401(g)(1)(B)	Tax treatment of securities futures contracts—treatment under Code Sec. 1256	December 21, 2000
1275(a)(1)(B)	318(c)(1)	Certain annuities issued by tax-exempt organizations not treated as debt instruments under original issue discount rules—technical correction	Tax years ending after July 18, 1984
1361(e)(1)(A)	316(b)	Amendment related to Section 1302 of the Small Business Job Protection Act of 1996—technical correction	Tax years beginning after December 31, 1996
1391(d)(1)(A)	112	Extension of empowerment zone treatment through 2009	December 21, 2000
1391(g)(3)(C)	319(13)	Clerical amendment	December 21, 2000
1391(h)	111	Authority to designate 9 additional empowerment zones	December 21, 2000
1394(b)(2)	116(b)(3)	Nonrecognition of gain on rollover of empowerment zone investments—conforming amendment	Qualified empowerment zone assets acquired after December 21, 2000
1394(b)(3)	116(b)(4)	Nonrecognition of gain on rollover of empowerment zone investments—conforming amendment	Qualified empowerment zone assets acquired after December 21, 2000
1394(f)(3)	115	Higher limits on tax-exempt empowerment zone facility bonds	Obligations issued after December 31, 2001
1396(b)	113(a)	20-percent employment credit for all empowerment zones	Wages paid or incurred after December 31, 2001
1396(e)	113(b)	20-percent employment credit for all empowerment zones	Wages paid or incurred after December 31, 2001
1397A(a)(1)(A)	114(a)	Increased expensing under Code Sec. 179	Tax years beginning after December 31, 2001
1397A(c)	114(b)	Increased expensing under Code Sec. 179—expensing for property used in developable sites	Tax years beginning after December 31, 2001

¶ 20,005

Code Sec.	Act Sec.	Act Provision Subject	Effective Date
1397B	116(a)	Nonrecognition of gain on rollover of empowerment zone investments	Qualified empowerment zone assets acquired after December 21, 2000
1397C	116(a)	Nonrecognition of gain on rollover of empowerment zone investments	Qualified empowerment zone assets acquired after December 21, 2000
1397D	116(a)	Nonrecognition of gain on rollover of empowerment zone investments	Qualified empowerment zone assets acquired after December 21, 2000
1400(d)	113(c)	20-percent employment credit for all empowerment zones—conforming amendment	Wages paid or incurred after December 31, 2001
1400(e)	116(b)(5)	Nonrecognition of gain on rollover of empowerment zone investments—conforming amendment	Qualified empowerment zone assets acquired after December 21, 2000
1400(f)	164(a)(1)	Extension of DC zone through 2003	December 21, 2000
1400A(b)	164(a)(2)	Extension of DC zone through 2003	December 21, 2000
1400B(c)	116(b)(5)	Nonrecognition of gain on rollover of empowerment zone investments—conforming amendment	Qualified empowerment zone assets acquired after December 21, 2000
1400B	164(b)	Extension of DC zone through 2003—zero capital gains rate	December 21, 2000
1400C(i)	163	Extension of DC homebuyer tax credit	December 21, 2000
1400E	101(a)	Designation of and tax incentives for renewal communities—designation	December 21, 2000
1400F	101(a)	Designation of and tax incentives for renewal communities—renewal community capital gain	December 21, 2000
1400G	101(a)	Designation of and tax incentives for renewal communities—renewal community business defined	December 21, 2000
1400H	101(a)	Designation of and tax incentives for renewal communities—renewal community employment credit	December 21, 2000
1400I	101(a)	Designation of and tax incentives for renewal communities—commercial revitalization deduction	December 21, 2000
1400J	101(a)	Designation of and tax incentives for renewal communities—increase in expensing under Code Sec. 179	December 21, 2000
2035(c)(2)	319(14)(A)	Clerical amendment	December 21, 2000
2035(d)	319(14)(B)	Clerical amendment	December 21, 2000
3121(a)(5)	319(15)	Clerical amendment	December 21, 2000

Code Sec.	Act Sec.	Act Provision Subject	Effective Date
3231(e)(10)	202(b)(5)	Medical savings accounts renamed as Archer MSAs—conforming amendment	December 21, 2000
3306(c)(7)	166(a)	Treatment of Indian tribal governments under FUTA	Services performed on or after December 21, 2000
3306(u)	166(d)	Treatment of Indian tribal governments under FUTA—definitions	Services performed on or after December 21, 2000
3309(a)(2)	166(b)(1)	Treatment of Indian tribal governments under FUTA—payments in lieu of contributions	Services performed on or after December 21, 2000
3309(b)(3)(B)	166(b)(2)	Treatment of Indian tribal governments under FUTA—payments in lieu of contributions	Services performed on or after December 21, 2000
3309(b)(3)(E)	166(b)(3)	Treatment of Indian tribal governments under FUTA—payments in lieu of contributions	Services performed on or after December 21, 2000
3309(b)(5)	166(b)(4)	Treatment of Indian tribal governments under FUTA—payments in lieu of contributions	Services performed on or after December 21, 2000
3309(d)	166(c)	Treatment of Indian tribal governments under FUTA—state law coverage	Services performed on or after December 21, 2000
3405(e)(1)(B)	314(b)	Amendment related to Section 302 of the Taxpayer Relief Act of 1997—technical correction	Tax years beginning after December 31, 1997
4946(c)(3)(B)	319(16)	Clerical amendment	December 21, 2000
4973(a)(2)	202(a)(6)	Medical savings accounts renamed as Archer MSAs	December 21, 2000
4973(d)	202(a)(6)	Medical savings accounts renamed as Archer MSAs	December 21, 2000
4973(d)	202(b)(2)(C)	Medical savings accounts renamed as Archer MSAs—conforming amendment	December 21, 2000
4973(d)	202(b)(6)	Medical savings accounts renamed as Archer MSAs—conforming amendment	December 21, 2000
4975(c)(4)	202(a)(7)	Medical savings accounts renamed as Archer MSAs	December 21, 2000
4975(c)(4)	202(b)(7)	Medical savings accounts renamed as Archer MSAs—conforming amendment	December 21, 2000
4975(e)(1)(D)	202(a)(7)	Medical savings accounts renamed as Archer MSAs	December 21, 2000
4980E(a)	202(a)(8)	Medical savings accounts renamed as Archer MSAs	December 21, 2000
4980E(b)	202(b)(2)(D)	Medical savings accounts renamed as Archer MSAs—conforming amendment	December 21, 2000

Code Sec.	Act Sec.	Act Provision Subject	Effective Date
4980E(d)(1)	202(b)(2)(D)	Medical savings accounts renamed as Archer MSAs—conforming amendment	December 21, 2000
4980E(d)(2)(B)	202(a)(8)	Medical savings accounts renamed as Archer MSAs	December 21, 2000
5702(f)-(p)	315(a)(2)(B)	Amendment related to Section 9302 of the Balanced Budget Act of 1997—technical correction	Articles removed from the factory or from internal revenue bond or released from customs after December 31, 1999
5702(h)	315(a)(2)(A)	Amendment related to Section 9302 of the Balanced Budget Act of 1997—technical correction	Articles removed from the factory or from internal revenue bond or released from customs after December 31, 1999
5761(c)	315(a)(3)	Amendment related to Section 9302 of the Balanced Budget Act of 1997—technical correction	Articles removed from the factory or from internal revenue bond or released from customs after December 31, 1999
6015(c)(3)(B)	313(a)(1)	Amendment related to IRS Restructuring and Reform Act of 1998—innocent spouse relief—election made any time after deficiency asserted—technical correction	December 21, 2000
6015(e)(1)(A)	313(a)(3)(B)	Amendment related to IRS Restructuring and Reform Act of 1998—innocent spouse relief—clarification regarding Tax Court review—technical correction	December 21, 2000
6015(e)(1)(B)	313(a)(3)(C)	Amendment related to IRS Restructuring and Reform Act of 1998—innocent spouse relief—clarification regarding Tax Court review—technical correction	December 21, 2000
6015(e)(1)	313(a)(3)(A)	Amendment related to IRS Restructuring and Reform Act of 1998—innocent spouse relief—clarification regarding Tax Court review—technical correction	December 21, 2000
6015(e)(2)	313(a)(3)(D)	Amendment related to IRS Restructuring and Reform Act of 1998—innocent spouse relief—clarification regarding Tax Court review—technical correction	December 21, 2000
6015(e)(3)	313(a)(2)(B)	Amendment related to IRS Restructuring and Reform Act of 1998—innocent spouse relief—clarification regarding disallowance of re-	December 21, 2000

Code Sec.	Act Sec.	Act Provision Subject	Effective Date
		funds and credits—technical correction	
6015(e)(5)	313(a)(3)(D)	Amendment related to IRS Restructuring and Reform Act of 1998—innocent spouse relief—clarification regarding Tax Court review—technical correction	December 21, 2000
6015(g)-(h)	313(a)(2)(A)	Amendment related to IRS Restructuring and Reform Act of 1998—innocent spouse relief—clarification regarding disallowance of refunds and credits—technical correction	December 21, 2000
6051(a)(11)	202(a)(9)	Medical savings accounts renamed as Archer MSAs	December 21, 2000
6103(b)(2)	304(a)	Confidentiality of certain documents relating to closing and similar agreements and to agreements with foreign governments—closing and similar agreements treated as return information	December 21, 2000
6103(e)(1)(D)	319(8)(B)	Clerical amendment	December 21, 2000
6103(j)(6)	310(a)(1)	Disclosure of certain tax information to congressional budget office	December 21, 2000
6103(k)(6)	313(c)	Amendment related to IRS Restructuring and Reform Act of 1998—procedure and administration—technical correction	July 22, 1998
6103(p)(4)(E)-(F)	310(a)(2)(A)	Disclosure of certain tax information—recordkeeping safeguards	December 21, 2000
6103(p)(4)(F)	319(17)(B)	Clerical amendment	December 21, 2000
6103(p)(4)	310(a)(2)(A)	Disclosure of certain tax information—recordkeeping safeguards	December 21, 2000
6103(p)(4)	319(17)(A)	Clerical amendment	December 21, 2000
6103(p)(5)	310(a)(2)(B)	Disclosure of certain tax information—recordkeeping safeguards	December 21, 2000
6103(p)(6)(A)	310(a)(2)(C)	Disclosure of certain tax information—recordkeeping safeguards	December 21, 2000
6104(d)(6)	312(a)	Amendment related to Section 1004(b) of the Tax and Trade Relief Extension Act of 1998—technical correction	Requests made after June 8, 1999
6105	304(b)(1)	Confidentiality of certain documents relating to closing and similar agreements and to agreements with foreign governments—agreements with foreign governments	December 21, 2000
6110(b)(1)	304(c)(1)	Confidentiality of certain documents relating to closing and similar agreements—exception from public inspection as written determinations	December 21, 2000

¶ 20,005

Code Sec.	Act Sec.	Act Provision Subject	Effective Date
6110(g)(5)(A)	313(e)	Amendment related to IRS Restructuring and Reform Act of 1998—procedure and administration—technical correction	Chief Counsel advice issued after October 20, 1998, generally
6110(l)(1)	304(c)(2)	Confidentiality of certain documents relating to agreements with foreign governments—exception from public inspection as written determinations	December 21, 2000
6166(k)(5)	319(18)	Clerical amendment	December 21, 2000
6211(b)(4)	314(a)	Amendment related to Section 101 of the Taxpayer Relief Act of 1997—technical correction	Tax years beginning after December 31, 1997
6330(d)(1)(A)	313(d)	Amendment related to IRS Restructuring and Reform Act of 1998—procedure and administration—technical correction	Collection actions initiated after January 18, 1999
6330(e)(1)	313(b)(2)(A)	Amendment related to IRS Restructuring and Reform Act of 1998—procedure and administration—authority to enjoin collection actions—technical correction	December 21, 2000
6331(k)(3)	313(b)(3)	Amendment related to IRS Restructuring and Reform Act of 1998—procedure and administration—technical correction	December 21, 2000
6405(a)-(b)	305	Increase in threshold for joint committee reports on refunds and credits	December 21, 2000, except the amendment does not apply with respect to a report made before such date
6411(a)	318(d)(1)	Tentative carryback adjustments of losses from Code Sec. 1256 contract—technical correction	Property acquired and positions established after June 23, 1981
6512(a)	319(19)	Clerical amendment	December 21, 2000
6611(g)(1)	319(20)	Clerical amendment	December 21, 2000
6655(e)(5)(A)-(B)	319(21)	Clerical amendment	December 21, 2000
6693(a)(2)(B)	202(b)(2)(E)	Medical savings accounts renamed as Archer MSAs—conforming amendment	December 21, 2000
6724(d)(1)(B)	319(23)(A)	Clerical amendment	December 21, 2000
6724(d)(2)(Z)	319(23)(B)	Clerical amendment	December 21, 2000
7421(a)	313(b)(2)(B)	Amendment related to IRS Restructuring and Reform Act of 1998—procedure and administration—authority to enjoin collection actions—technical correction	December 21, 2000
7421(a)	319(24)	Clerical amendment	December 21, 2000
7430(c)(3)	319(25)	Clerical amendment	December 21, 2000

¶ 20,005

Code Sec.	Act Sec.	Act Provision Subject	Effective Date
7436(a)	314(f)	Amendment related to Section 1454 of the Taxpayer Relief Act of 1997—technical correction	August 5, 1997
7463(f)	313(b)(1)	Amendment related to IRS Restructuring and Reform Act of 1998—procedure and administration—disputes involving $50,000 or less—technical correction	December 21, 2000
7603(b)(2)	319(26)	Clerical amendments	December 21, 2000
7608(c)(6)	303	Extension of authority for undercover operations	December 21, 2000
7701(m)-(n)	401(i)	Tax treatment of securities futures contracts—designation of contract markets	December 21, 2000
7702A(a)(2)	318(a)(1)	Modified endowment contracts—technical correction	Contracts entered into or materially changed on or after June 21, 1988
7702A(c)(3)(A)	318(a)(2)	Modified endowment contracts—technical correction	Contracts entered into or materially changed on or after June 21, 1988
7802(b)(2)(B)	319(27)	Clerical amendment	December 21, 2000
7811(a)(3)	319(28)	Clerical amendment	December 21, 2000
7811(d)(1)	319(29)	Clerical amendment	December 21, 2000
7872(f)(3)	319(30)	Clerical amendment	December 21, 2000
9503(b)(5)-(6)	318(e)(1)	Correction of calculation of amounts to be deposited in highway trust fund—technical correction	Taxes received in the Treasury after December 21, 2000
9510(c)(1)(A)	318(f)	Expenditures from vaccine injury compensation trust fund—technical correction	December 21, 2000
	101(c)	Designation of and tax incentives for renewal communities—audit and report	December 21, 2000
	101(d)	Designation of and tax incentives for renewal communities—clerical amendment	December 21, 2000
	116(b)(6)	Nonrecognition of gain on rollover of empowerment zone investments—clerical amendment	Qualified empowerment zone assets acquired after December 21, 2000
	116(b)(7)	Nonrecognition of gain on rollover of empowerment zone investments—clerical amendment	Qualified empowerment zone assets acquired after December 21, 2000
	117(b)(3)	Increased exclusion of gain on sale of empowerment zone stock—clerical amendment	Stock acquired after December 21, 2000

Code Sec.	Act Sec.	Act Provision Subject	Effective Date
	121(d)	New markets tax credit—clerical amendment	Investments made after December 31, 2000
	121(f)	New markets tax credit—guidance on allocation of national limitation	Investments made after December 31, 2000
	121(g)	New markets tax credit—audit and report	Investments made after December 31, 2000
	141	Transfer of unoccupied and substandard HUD-held housing to local governments and community development corporations	December 21, 2000
	142	Transfer of HUD assets in revitalization areas	December 21, 2000
	143	Risk-sharing demonstration	December 21, 2000
	144	Prevention and treatment of substance abuse; services provided through religious organizations	December 21, 2000
	151	Advisory Council on Community Renewal Act—short title	January 20, 2001
	152	Advisory Council on Community Renewal—establishment	January 20, 2001
	153	Advisory Council on Community Renewal—duties	January 20, 2001
	154	Advisory Council on Community Renewal—membership	January 20, 2001
	155	Advisory Council on Community Renewal—powers	January 20, 2001
	156	Advisory Council on Community Renewal—reports	January 20, 2001
	157	Advisory Council on Community Renewal—termination	January 20, 2001
	158	Applicability of Federal Advisory Committee Act	January 20, 2001
	159	Advisory Council on Community Renewal—resources	January 20, 2001
	202(b)(9)	Medical savings accounts renamed as Archer MSAs—clerical amendment	December 21, 2000
	301	Exemption of certain reporting requirements—Federal Reports Elimination and Sunset Act of 1995, Section 3003(a)(1) not to apply to certain provisions of various Federal statutes	December 21, 2000
	302(a)	Extension of deadlines for IRS compliance with certain notice re-	December 21, 2000

¶ 20,005

Code Sec.	Act Sec.	Act Provision Subject	Effective Date
		quirements—annual installment agreement notice	
	302(b)	Extension of deadlines for IRS compliance with certain notice requirements—notice requirements relating to computation of penalty	December 21, 2000
	302(c)	Extension of deadlines for IRS compliance with certain notice requirements—notice requirements relating to interest imposed	December 21, 2000
	304(b)(2)	Confidentiality of certain documents relating to closing and similar agreements and to agreements with foreign governments—agreements with foreign governments—clerical amendment	December 21, 2000
	307(a)	Amendments to statutes referencing yield on 52-week treasury bills—Act of February 26, 1931	December 21, 2000
	307(b)	Amendments to statutes referencing yield on 52-week treasury bills—USC Title 18, relating to unpaid criminal fines and certain penalties	December 21, 2000
	307(d)(1)	Amendments to statutes referencing yield on 52-week treasury bills—Title 28, Section 1961, relating to interest rate on money judgments recovered in civil suits	December 21, 2000
	307(d)(2)	Amendments to statutes referencing yield on 52-week treasury bills—Title 28, Section 2516, relating to interest rate on judgments against the United States affirmed by Supreme Court	December 21, 2000
	308(a)	Adjustments for consumer price index error—determinations by OMB	December 21, 2000
	308(b)	Adjustments for consumer price index error—coordination with federal agencies	December 21, 2000
	308(c)	Adjustments for consumer price index error—implementation pursuant to agency reports	December 21, 2000
	308(d)	Adjustments for consumer price index error—income disregard under federal means-tested benefit programs	December 21, 2000
	308(e)	Adjustments for consumer price index error—funding	December 21, 2000

¶ 20,005

Code Sec.	Act Sec.	Act Provision Subject	Effective Date
	308(f)	Adjustments for consumer price index error—no judicial review	December 21, 2000
	308(g)	Adjustments for consumer price index error—Director's report	December 21, 2000
	308(h)	Adjustments for consumer price index error—definitions	December 21, 2000
	308(i)	Adjustments for consumer price index error—tax provisions	December 21, 2000
	309(c)	Prevention of duplication of loss through assumption of liabilities giving rise to a deduction—application of comparable rules to partnerships and S corporations	Assumptions of liability after October 18, 1999, or such later date as may be prescribed in regulations
	310(b)(1)	Disclosure of certain tax information—confidentiality of records	December 21, 2000
	310(b)(2)	Disclosure of certain tax information—confidentiality of records—conforming amendment	December 21, 2000
	311(c)	Clarification related to Section 538 of Ticket to Work and Work Incentives Improvement Act of 1999—technical correction	Distributions made after July 14, 1999, generally
	314(c)	Amendment related to Section 311 of the Taxpayer Relief Act of 1997—technical correction	Tax years ending after May 6, 1997
	315(a)(1)	Amendment related to Section 9302 of the Balanced Budget Act of 1997—technical correction	Articles removed from the factory or from internal revenue bond or released from customs after December 31, 1999
	319(22)	Clerical amendment	December 21, 2000
	401(g)(4)	Tax treatment of securities futures contracts—IRS determinations under Code Sec. 1256(g)(9)(B)	December 21, 2000
	401(h)(2)	Tax treatment of securities futures contracts—clerical amendment	December 21, 2000

Effective Dates

Installment Tax Correction Act of 2000

¶ 20,010

This CCH-prepared table presents the general effective dates for major law provisions added, amended or repealed by the Installment Tax Correction Act of 2000 (P.L. 106-573), enacted December 28, 2000. Entries are listed in Code Section order.

Code Sec.	Act Sec.	Act Provision Subject	Effective Date
453(a)	2(a)	Repeal of modification of install-ment method	Sales and other disposi-tions occurring on or after December 17, 1999
453(d)(1)	2(a)	Repeal of modification of install-ment method—conforming amendment	Sales and other disposi-tions occurring on or after December 17, 1999
453(i)(1)	2(a)	Repeal of modification of install-ment method—conforming amendment	Sales and other disposi-tions occurring on or after December 17, 1999
453(k)	2(a)	Repeal of modification of install-ment method—conforming amendment	Sales and other disposi-tions occurring on or after December 17, 1999
	2(b)	Repeal of modification of install-ment method—applicability	Sales and other disposi-tions occurring on or after December 17, 1999

Code Section to Explanation Table

¶ 25,001

Code Sec.	Par.
1(h)(8)	160
26(b)(2)(Q)	615
30A(f)	255
30A(g)	255
30A(h)	255
38(b)	235
39(d)	235
42(d)(4)	240
42(d)(5)(C)(ii)(I) ...	240
42(h)(3)	240
42(h)	240
42(i)(2)(E)	240
42(m)(1)	240
43(c)(1)(C)	250
45(d)(7)(A)(i)	30,050
45D	235
51(d)(2)(B)	245
51(d)(5)(A)(ii)	125
51(d)(5)(B)	125
51(d)(7)(A)(iv)	125
51(d)(7)(C)	125
56(a)(1)(A)(ii)	215
56(g)(4)(B)(i)	515
62(a)(16)	615
67(f)	30,050
106(b)	615
114	515
138(b)	615
138(f)	615
146(d)(1)	285
146(d)(2)	285
151(c)(6)	390
165(g)(3)(A)	230
165(g)(3)	230
170(e)(6)(B)(viii) ...	220
170(e)(6)(D)	220
170(e)(6)(E)	220
170(e)(6)(F)	220
170(e)(6)(G)	220
170(e)(6)	220
196(c)	235
198(c)	225
198(h)	225
219(c)(1)(B)(ii)(II) ..	605
219(c)(1)(B)(ii)(III) .	605
220(i)(2)	615
220(i)(3)(B)	615
220(j)(2)(C)	615
220(j)(2)	615
220(j)(4)(A)	615
220	615
275(a)	515, 520
280C(c)(1)	255

Code Sec.	Par.
357(d)(1)	265
358(h)	265
401(k)(10)(B)	620
403(b)(3)(B)	625
408(d)(5)	30,050
414(s)(2)	625
415(c)(3)(D)(ii)	625
453(a)	205
453(d)	205
453(i)	205
453(k)	205
469(i)(3)(C)	115
469(i)(3)(D)	115
469(i)(3)(E)	115
469(i)(3)(F)	115
469(i)(6)(B)(iii)	115
469(i)(6)(B)	115
475(g)	30,050
529(e)(3)(B)	30,050
530(d)(4)(B)(iii)	30,050
664(d)(1)(C)	30,050
664(d)(2)(C)	30,050
678(e)	30,050
848(e)(1)(B)(iv)	615
856(c)(7)	30,050
856(l)(4)(A)	30,050
857(b)(7)(B)(ii)	415
864(e)(3)	530
871(f)(2)(B)	30,050
903	515
921-927	510
941	515, 520, 535
942	525, 535
943	515, 520, 525, 530
995(b)(3)(B)	30,050
995(f)(4)	375
999(c)(1)	520
1016(a)(23)	155
1032(a)	260
1091(f)	260
1092(d)(3)(B)(i)	260
1202(a)	160
1202	160
1223(15)	155
1223(16)	260
1233(e)(2)	260
1234A	260
1234B	260
1256	260
1275(a)(1)(B)(ii)	210
1361(e)(1)(A)(i)	420
1391(d)(1)(A)	135
1391(g)(3)(C)	30,050

Code Sections Added, Amended or Repealed

The list below notes all the Code Sections or subsections of the Internal Revenue Code that were added, amended or repealed by the FSC Repeal and Extraterritorial Income Exclusion Act of 2000 (P.L. 106-519), the Community Renewal Tax Relief Act of 2000 (P.L. 106-554), and the Installment Tax Correction Act of 2000 (P.L. 106-573). The first column indicates the Code Section added, amended or repealed and the second column indicates the Act Section. The Code Sections are listed under the pertinent Acts.

¶ 25,005

FSC Repeal and Extraterritorial Income Exclusion Act of 2000

Code Sec.	Act Sec.	Code Sec.	Act Sec.
56(g)(4)(B)(i)	4(1)	925	2
114	3(a)	926	2
275(a)	4(2)	927	2
864(e)(3)	4(3)	941	3(b)
903	4(4)	942	3(b)
921	2	943	3(b)
922	2	999(c)(1)	4(5)
923	2		
924	2		

Community Renewal Tax Relief Act of 2000

Code Sec.	Act Sec.	Code Sec.	Act Sec.
1(h)(8)	117(b)(1)	67(f)	319(2)
26(b)(2)(Q)	202(a)(1)	106(b)	202(a)(2)
30A(f)-(h)	311(a)(2)	106(b)	202(b)(6)
38(b)(11)-(13)	121(b)(1)	106(b)(4)	202(b)(2)(A)
39(d)(9)	121(b)(2)	106(b)(7)	202(b)(2)(A)
42(d)(4)	134(a)(1)-(3)	138(b)	202(a)(3)
42(d)(5)(C)(ii)(I)	135(b)(1)-(2)	138(f)	202(b)(6)
42(h)(1)(E)(ii)	135(a)(1)	146(d)(1)-(2)	161(a)
42(h)(3)(C)	131(c)(1)(A)-(B)	151(c)(6)	306(a)
42(h)(3)(C)	135(a)(2)	165(g)(3)	318(b)(2)
42(h)(3)(C)	136(b)	165(g)(3)(A)	318(b)(1)
42(h)(3)(C)(i)-(ii)	131(a)	170(e)(6)	165(a)(1)
42(h)(3)(D)(ii)	131(c)(2)(A)-(B)	170(e)(6)	165(b)(2)
42(h)(3)(D)(ii)	136(a)	170(e)(6)(B)(i)(I)-	
42(h)(3)(H)	131(b)	(III)	165(a)(2)
42(i)(2)(E)(i)	134(b)(1)-(2)	170(e)(6)(B)(ii)	165(a)(3)
42(m)(1)(A)(i)-(iv)	133(a)	170(e)(6)(B)(iv)	165(b)(1)
42(m)(1)(B)(ii)(I)-		170(e)(6)(B)(vi)-(viii)	165(d)
(III)	132(b)	170(e)(6)(D)-(G)	165(e)
42(m)(1)(B)(iii)	133(b)	170(e)(6)(F)	165(c)
42(m)(1)(C)	132(a)(1)-(2)	196(c)(7)-(9)	121(c)
43(c)(1)(C)	317(a)(1)-(2)	198(c)	162(a)
45(d)(7)(A)(i)	319(1)	198(h)	162(b)
45D	121(a)	219(c)(1)(B)(ii)(I)-	
51(d)(2)(B)	316(a)(1)-(2)	(III)	316(d)
51(d)(5)(A)(ii)	102(a)	220	202(a)(4)
51(d)(5)(B)	102(a)	220	202(b)(8)
51(d)(5)(B)	102(c)	220(c)(1)(C)	202(b)(7)
51(d)(7)(A)(iv)	102(b)	220(c)(1)(D)	202(b)(2)(B)
51(d)(7)(C)	102(c)	220(d)	202(b)(4)
56(a)(1)(A)(ii)	314(d)	220(d)(1)	202(b)(3)
62(a)(16)	202(b)(1)	220(d)(1)	202(b)(5)

Code Sec.	Act Sec.	Code Sec.	Act Sec.
220(e)(1)	202(b)(11)	1397A(a)(1)(A)	114(a)
220(e)(2)	202(b)(2)(B)	1397A(c)	114(b)
220(f)(3)(A)	202(b)(2)(B)	1397B	116(a)(2)
220(i)	202(b)(6)	1397B	116(a)(3)
220(i)(2)	201(a)	1397C	116(a)(2)
220(i)(3)(B)	201(a)	1397D	116(a)(2)
220(i)(4)(B)	202(b)(2)(B)	1400(d)	113(c)
220(j)	202(b)(2)(B)	1400(e)	116(b)(5)
220(j)(2)	201(b)(1)(A)-(C)	1400(f)	164(a)
220(j)(4)(A)	201(b)(2)	1400A(b)	164(a)
280C(c)(1)	311(a)(1)	1400B	164(b)(1)-(2)
357(d)(1)	309(b)	1400B(c)	116(b)(5)
358(h)	309(a)	1400C(i)	163
401(k)(10)(B)(ii)	316(c)	1400E	101(a)
403(b)(3)(B)	314(e)(1)	1400F	101(a)
408(d)(5)	319(3)	1400G	101(a)
414(s)(2)	314(e)(2)	1400H	101(a)
415(c)(3)(D)(ii)	314(e)(1)	1400I	101(a)
469(i)(3)(C)-(F)	101(b)(1)	1400J	101(a)
469(i)(3)(E)	101(b)(2)	2035(c)(2)	319(14)(A)
469(i)(6)(B)	101(b)(3)(B)	2035(d)	319(14)(B)
469(i)(6)(B)(i)-(iii)	101(b)(3)(A)	3121(a)(5)(G)	319(15)
475(g)(3)	319(4)	3231(e)(10)	202(b)(5)
529(e)(3)(B)	319(5)	3306(c)(7)	166(a)(1)-(2)
530(d)(4)(B)(iii)	319(6)	3306(u)	166(d)
664(d)(1)(C)	319(7)	3309(a)(2)	166(b)(1)
664(d)(2)(C)	319(7)	3309(b)(3)(B)	166(b)(2)
678(e)	319(8)(A)	3309(b)(3)(E)	166(b)(3)
848(e)(1)(B)(iv)	202(a)(5)	3309(b)(5)	166(b)(4)
856(c)(7)	319(9)	3309(d)	166(c)
856(l)(4)(A)	319(10)	3405(e)(1)(B)	314(b)
857(b)(7)(B)(ii)	311(b)	4946(c)(3)(B)	319(16)
871(f)(2)(B)	319(11)	4973(a)(2)	202(a)(6)
995(b)(3)(B)	319(12)	4973(d)	202(a)(6)
995(f)(4)	307(c)	4973(d)	202(b)(2)(C)
1016(a)(23)	116(b)(1)(A)-(B)	4973(d)	202(b)(6)
1032(a)	401(c)	4975(c)(4)	202(a)(7)
1091(f)	401(d)	4975(c)(4)	202(b)(7)
1092(d)(3)(B)(i)(I)-(III)	401(e)	4975(e)(1)(D)	202(a)(7)
1202	117(b)(2)	4980E(a)	202(a)(8)
1202(a)	117(a)	4980E(b)	202(b)(2)(D)
1223(15)	116(b)(2)	4980E(d)(1)	202(b)(2)(D)
1223(16)-(17)	401(h)(1)	4980E(d)(2)(B)	202(a)(8)
1233(e)(2)(B)-(D)	401(f)	5702(f)-(o)	315(a)(2)(B)
1234A	401(b)(1)-(4)	5702(h)	315(a)(2)(A)
1234B	401(a)	5761(c)	315(a)(3)
1256(b)	401(g)(1)(A)	6015(c)(3)(B)	313(a)(1)
1256(f)(4)	401(g)(2)(A)-(B)	6015(e)(1)	313(a)(3)(A)
1256(g)(6)	401(g)(3)	6015(e)(1)(A)	313(a)(3)(B)
1256(g)(9)	401(g)(1)(B)	6015(e)(1)(B)(i)	313(a)(3)(C)(i)-(ii)
1275(a)(1)(B)(ii)	318(c)(1)	6015(e)(2)	313(a)(3)(D)(ii)
1361(e)(1)(A)(i)	316(b)	6015(e)(3)	313(a)(2)(B)
1391(d)(1)(A)	112	6015(e)(5)	313(a)(3)(D)(i)
1391(g)(3)(C)	319(13)	6015(g)-(h)	313(a)(2)(A)
1391(h)	111	6051(a)(11)	202(a)(9)
1394(b)(2)	116(b)(3)(A)-(B)	6103(b)(2)(B)-(D)	304(a)
1394(b)(3)	116(b)(4)(A)-(B)	6103(e)(1)(D)(v)	319(8)(B)
1394(f)(3)	115(a)	6103(j)(6)	310(a)(1)
1396(b)	113(a)	6103(k)(6)	313(c)(1)-(2)
1396(e)	113(b)	6103(p)(4)	310(a)(2)(A)(i)-(iv)
		6103(p)(4)(A)	319(17)(A)(i)-(ii)

Code Sec.	Act Sec.	Code Sec.	Act Sec.
6103(p)(4)(F)(ii)	319(17)(B)	6724(d)(1)(B)(xiv)-(xvii)	319(23)(A)
6103(p)(5)	310(a)(2)(B)	6724(d)(2)(Z)	319(23)(B)
6103(p)(6)(A)	310(a)(2)(C)	7421(a)	313(b)(2)(B)
6104(d)(6)[(8)]	312(a)	7421(a)	319(24)
6105	304(b)(1)	7430(c)(3)	319(25)(A)-(B)
6110(b)(1)	304(c)(1)	7436(a)	314(f)
6110(g)(5)(A)	313(e)	7463(f)	313(b)(1)
6110(l)(1)	304(c)(2)	7603(b)(2)(A)-(G)	319(26)
6166(k)(5)	319(18)	7608(c)	303
6211(b)(4)	314(a)	7701(m)-(n)	401(i)
6330(d)(1)(A)	313(d)	7702A(a)(2)	318(a)(1)
6330(e)(1)	313(b)(2)(A)	7702A(c)(3)(A)(ii)	318(a)(2)
6331(k)(3)	313(b)(3)	7802(b)(2)(B)(ii)	319(27)
6405(a)-(b)	305(a)	7811(a)(3)	319(28)
6411(a)	318(d)(1)	7811(d)(1)	319(29)
6512(a)	319(19)	7872(f)(3)	319(30)
6611(g)(1)	319(20)	9503(b)(5)-(6)	318(e)(1)
6655(e)(5)(A)-(B)	319(21)	9510(c)(1)(A)	318(f)
6693(a)(2)(B)	202(b)(2)(E)		

Installment Tax Correction Act of 2000

Code Sec.	Act Sec.	Code Sec.	Act Sec.
453(a)	2(a)	453(i)(1)	2(a)
453(d)(1)	2(a)	453(k)	2(a)

Table of Amendments to Other Acts

¶ 25,010

Community Renewal Tax Relief Act of 2000

Amended Act Sec.	P.L. 106-554 Sec.	Par. (¶)	Amended Act Sec.	P.L. 106-554 Sec.	Par. (¶)
TAX AND TRADE RELIEF EXTENSION ACT OF 1998			**PUBLIC HEALTH SERVICE ACT**		
			581—584	144	7085
4003(b)	312(b)	7175	**DEPARTMENTS OF VETERANS AFFAIRS AND HOUSING AND URBAN DEVELOPMENT, AND INDEPENDENT AGENCIES APPROPRIATIONS ACT, 1997**		
IRS RESTRUCTURING AND REFORM ACT OF 1998					
			204	141(1)-(2)	7070
3306(c)	302(b)(1)-(2)	7145			
3308(c)	302(c)(1)-(2)	7145	**NATIONAL HOUSING ACT**		
3506	302(a)	7145	249	143(1)-(7)	7080
6010(o)(4)(C)	319(23)(B)	7190			
TAXPAYER RELIEF ACT OF 1997			**TITLE 18, UNITED STATES CODE**		
311(e)(3)	314(c)	7180	3612(f)(2)(B)	307(b)	7150
BALANCED BUDGET ACT OF 1997			**TITLE 28, UNITED STATES CODE**		
9302(j)(1)	315(a)(1)	7185	1961(a)	307(d)(1)	7150
			2516(b)	307(d)(2)	7150
CONGRESSIONAL BUDGET ACT OF 1974			**ACT OF FEBRUARY 26, 1931**		
203(a)	310(b)(2)	7165	6(1)-(2)	307(a)(1)-(2)	7150
203(e)	310(b)(1)	7165			

Table of Act Sections Not Amending Internal Revenue Code Sections

¶ 25,015

Community Renewal Tax Relief Act of 2000

Act Sections Amending Code Sections

¶ 25,020

FSC Repeal and Extraterritorial Income Exclusion Act of 2000

Act Sec.	Code Sec.	Act Sec.	Code Sec.
2	921	3(b)	942
2	922	3(b)	943
2	923	4(1)	56(g)(4)(B)(i)
2	924	4(2)	275(a)
2	925	4(3)	864(e)(3)
2	926	4(4)	903
2	927	4(5)	999(c)(1)
3(a)	114		
3(b)	941		

Community Renewal Tax Relief Act of 2000

Act Sec.	Code Sec.	Act Sec.	Code Sec.
101(a)	1400E	131(b)	42(h)(3)(H)
101(a)	1400F	131(c)(1)(A)-(B)	42(h)(3)(C)
101(a)	1400G	131(c)(2)(A)-(B)	42(h)(3)(D)(ii)
101(a)	1400H	132(a)(1)-(2)	42(m)(1)(C)
101(a)	1400I	132(b)	42(m)(1)(B)(ii)(I)-(III)
101(a)	1400J	133(a)	42(m)(1)(A)(i)-(iv)
101(b)(1)	469(i)(3)(C)-(F)	133(b)	42(m)(1)(B)(iii)
101(b)(2)	469(i)(3)(E)	134(a)(1)-(3)	42(d)(4)
101(b)(3)(A)	469(i)(6)(B)(i)-(iii)	134(b)(1)-(2)	42(i)(2)(E)(i)
101(b)(3)(B)	469(i)(6)(B)	135(a)(1)	42(h)(1)(E)(ii)
102(a)	51(d)(5)(A)(ii)	135(a)(2)	42(h)(3)(C)
102(a)	51(d)(5)(B)	135(b)(1)-(2)	42(d)(5)(C)(ii)(I)
102(b)	51(d)(7)(A)(iv)	136(a)	42(h)(3)(D)(ii)
102(c)	51(d)(5)(B)	136(b)	42(h)(3)(C)
102(c)	51(d)(7)(C)	161(a)	146(d)(1)-(2)
111	1391(h)	162(a)	198(c)
112	1391(d)(1)(A)	162(b)	198(h)
113(a)	1396(b)	163	1400C(i)
113(b)	1396(e)	164(a)	1400(f)
113(c)	1400(d)	164(a)	1400A(b)
114(a)	1397A(a)(1)(A)	164(b)(1)-(2)	1400B
114(b)	1397A(c)	165(a)(1)	170(e)(6)
115(a)	1394(f)(3)	165(a)(2)	170(e)(6)(B)(i)(I)-(III)
116(a)(2)	1397B	165(a)(3)	170(e)(6)(B)(ii)
116(a)(2)	1397C	165(b)(1)	170(e)(6)(B)(iv)
116(a)(2)	1397D	165(b)(2)	170(e)(6)
116(a)(3)	1397B	165(c)	170(e)(6)(F)
116(b)(1)(A)-(B)	1016(a)(23)	165(d)	170(e)(6)(B)(vi)-(viii)
116(b)(2)	1223(15)	165(e)	170(e)(6)(D)-(G)
116(b)(3)(A)-(B)	1394(b)(2)	166(a)(1)-(2)	3306(c)(7)
116(b)(4)(A)-(B)	1394(b)(3)	166(b)(1)	3309(a)(2)
116(b)(5)	1400(e)	166(b)(2)	3309(b)(3)(B)
116(b)(5)	1400B(c)	166(b)(3)	3309(b)(3)(E)
117(a)	1202(a)	166(b)(4)	3309(b)(5)
117(b)(1)	1(h)(8)	166(c)	3309(d)
117(b)(2)	1202	166(d)	3306(u)
121(a)	45D	201(a)	220(i)(2)
121(b)(1)	38(b)(11)-(13)	201(a)	220(i)(3)(B)
121(b)(2)	39(d)(9)	201(b)(1)(A)-(C)	220(j)(2)
121(c)	196(c)(7)-(9)	201(b)(2)	220(j)(4)(A)
131(a)	42(h)(3)(C)(i)-(ii)	202(a)(1)	26(b)(2)(Q)

Act Sec.	Code Sec.	Act Sec.	Code Sec.
202(a)(2)	106(b)	313(b)(1)	7463(f)
202(a)(3)	138(b)	313(b)(2)(A)	6330(e)(1)
202(a)(4)	220	313(b)(2)(B)	7421(a)
202(a)(5)	848(e)(1)(B)(iv)	313(b)(3)	6331(k)(3)
202(a)(6)	4973(a)(2)	313(c)(1)-(2)	6103(k)(6)
202(a)(6)	4973(d)	313(d)	6330(d)(1)(A)
202(a)(7)	4975(c)(4)	313(e)	6110(g)(5)(A)
202(a)(7)	4975(e)(1)(D)	314(a)	6211(b)(4)
202(a)(8)	4980E(a)	314(b)	3405(e)(1)(B)
202(a)(8)	4980E(d)(2)(B)	314(d)	56(a)(1)(A)(ii)
202(a)(9)	6051(a)(11)	314(e)(1)	403(b)(3)(B)
202(b)(1)	62(a)(16)	314(e)(1)	415(c)(3)(D)(ii)
202(b)(2)(A)	106(b)(4)	314(e)(2)	414(s)(2)
202(b)(2)(A)	106(b)(7)	314(f)	7436(a)
202(b)(2)(B)	220(c)(1)(D)	315(a)(2)(A)	5702(h)
202(b)(2)(B)	220(e)(2)	315(a)(2)(B)	5702(f)-(o)
202(b)(2)(B)	220(f)(3)(A)	315(a)(3)	5761(c)
202(b)(2)(B)	220(i)(4)(B)	316(a)(1)-(2)	51(d)(2)(B)
202(b)(2)(B)	220(j)	316(b)	1361(e)(1)(A)(i)
202(b)(2)(C)	4973(d)	316(c)	401(k)(10)(B)(ii)
202(b)(2)(D)	4980E(b)	316(d)	219(c)(1)(B)(ii)(I)-(III)
202(b)(2)(D)	4980E(d)(1)		
202(b)(2)(E)	6693(a)(2)(B)	317(a)(1)-(2)	43(c)(1)(C)
202(b)(3)	220(d)(1)	318(a)(1)	7702A(a)(2)
202(b)(4)	220(d)	318(a)(2)	7702A(c)(3)(A)(ii)
202(b)(5)	220(d)(1)	318(b)(1)	165(g)(3)(A)
202(b)(5)	3231(e)(10)	318(b)(2)	165(g)(3)
202(b)(6)	106(b)	318(c)(1)	1275(a)(1)(B)(ii)
202(b)(6)	138(f)	318(d)(1)	6411(a)
202(b)(6)	220(i)	318(e)(1)	9503(b)(5)-(6)
202(b)(6)	4973(d)	318(f)	9510(c)(1)(A)
202(b)(7)	220(c)(1)(C)	319(1)	45(d)(7)(A)(i)
202(b)(7)	4975(c)(4)	319(2)	67(f)
202(b)(8)	220	319(3)	408(d)(5)
202(b)(11)	220(e)(1)	319(4)	475(g)(3)
303	7608(c)	319(5)	529(e)(3)(B)
304(a)	6103(b)(2)(B)-(D)	319(6)	530(d)(4)(B)(iii)
304(b)(1)	6105	319(7)	664(d)(1)(C)
304(c)(1)	6110(b)(1)	319(7)	664(d)(2)(C)
304(c)(2)	6110(l)(1)	319(8)(A)	678(e)
305(a)	6405(a)-(b)	319(8)(B)	6103(e)(1)(D)(v)
306(a)	151(c)(6)	319(9)	856(c)(7)
307(c)	995(f)(4)	319(10)	856(l)(4)(A)
309(a)	358(h)	319(11)	871(f)(2)(B)
309(b)	357(d)(1)	319(12)	995(b)(3)(B)
310(a)(1)	6103(j)(6)	319(13)	1391(g)(3)(C)
310(a)(2)(A)(i)-(iv)	6103(p)(4)	319(14)(A)	2035(c)(2)
310(a)(2)(B)	6103(p)(5)	319(14)(B)	2035(d)
310(a)(2)(C)	6103(p)(6)(A)	319(15)	3121(a)(5)(G)
311(a)(1)	280C(c)(1)	319(16)	4946(c)(3)(B)
311(a)(2)	30A(f)-(h)	319(17)(A)(i)-(ii)	6103(p)(4)(A)
311(b)	857(b)(7)(B)(ii)	319(17)(B)	6103(p)(4)(F)(ii)
312(a)	6104(d)(6)[(8)]	319(18)	6166(k)(5)
313(a)(1)	6015(c)(3)(B)	319(19)	6512(a)
313(a)(2)(A)	6015(g)-(h)	319(20)	6611(g)(1)
313(a)(2)(B)	6015(e)(3)	319(21)	6655(e)(5)(A)-(B)
313(a)(3)(A)	6015(e)(1)	319(23)(A)	6724(d)(1)(B)(xiv)-(xvii)
313(a)(3)(B)	6015(e)(1)(A)		
313(a)(3)(C)(i)-(ii)	6015(e)(1)(B)(i)	319(23)(B)	6724(d)(2)(Z)
313(a)(3)(D)(i)	6015(e)(5)	319(24)	7421(a)
313(a)(3)(D)(ii)	6015(e)(2)	319(25)(A)-(B)	7430(c)(3)

Act Sec.	Code Sec.	Act Sec.	Code Sec.
319(26)	7603(b)(2)(A)-(G)	401(e)	1092(d)(3)(B)(i)(I)-(III)
319(27)	7802(b)(2)(B)(ii)		
319(28)	7811(a)(3)	401(f)	1233(e)(2)(B)-(D)
319(29)	7811(d)(1)	401(g)(1)(A)	1256(b)
319(30)	7872(f)(3)	401(g)(1)(B)	1256(g)(9)
401(a)	1234B	401(g)(2)(A)-(B)	1256(f)(4)
401(b)(1)-(4)	1234A	401(g)(3)	1256(g)(6)
401(c)	1032(a)	401(h)(1)	1223(16)-(17)
401(d)	1091(f)	401(i)	7701(m)-(n)

Installment Tax Correction Act of 2000

Act Sec.	Code Sec.	Act Sec.	Code Sec.
2(a)	453(a)	2(a)	453(i)(1)
2(a)	453(d)(1)	2(a)	453(k)

Clerical Amendments

¶ 30,050

The Community Renewal Tax Relief Act of 2000 makes numerous clerical amendments to the Internal Revenue Code (Act Sec. 319 of the 2000 Act). There are no committee reports for these provisions.

The following Code Sections are amended to reflect these changes:

(1) Code Sec. 45(d)(7)(A)(i) relating to the renewable electricity production credit;

(2) Code Sec. 67(f) relating to the two percent floor on miscellaneous itemized deductions;

(3) Code Sec. 408(d)(5) relating to individual retirement account excess contribution distributions;

(4) Code Sec. 475(g) relating to the mark to market accounting method for dealers in securities;

(5) Code Sec. 529(e)(3)(B) relating to qualified state tuition programs;

(6) Code Sec. 530(d)(4)(B)(iii) relating to the tax on education individual retirement accounts not used for educational expenses;

(7) Code Sec. 664(d)(1)(C) and (2)(C) relating to charitable remainder trusts;

(8) Code Sec. 678(e) and Code Sec. 6103(e)(1)(D)(v) relating to a person other than the grantor being treated as a substantial owner of S corporation stock in a trust and return disclosure requirements;

(9) Code Sec. 856(c)(7) relating to limitations on real estate investment trusts;

(10) Code Sec. 856(l)(4)(A) relating to taxable real estate investment trust subsidiaries;

(11) Code Sec. 871(f)(2)(B) relating to the exclusion for annuities received under a qualified plan by nonresident aliens;

(12) Code Sec. 995(b)(3)(B) relating to domestic international sales corporation (DISC) income attributable to military property;

(13) Code Sec. 1391(g)(3)(C) relating to the inapplicability of the population requirement to additional empowerment zone designations;

(14) Code Sec. 2035(c)(2) and (d) relating to gifts in contemplation of death and the exception applicable to bona fide sales for adequate and full consideration;

(15) Code Sec. 3121(a)(5) relating to the definition of FICA wages;

(16) Code Sec. 4946(c)(3)(B) relating to the definition of a government official for purposes of the excise tax on self-dealing where a private foundation is involved;

(17) Code Sec. 6103(p)(4) relating to safeguards on disclosure of return information to federal officers and employees;

(18) Code Sec. 6166(k)(5) relating to an extension of time for payment of estate tax when a significant estate asset is an interest in a closely held business and the estate also has a gift in contemplation of death asset;

(19) Code Sec. 6512(a)(1), (2) and (5) relating to limitations in case of a petition to the Tax Court;

(20) Code Sec. 6611(g)(1) relating to the payment of interest on overpayments;

(21) Code Sec. 6655(e)(5)(A) and (B) relating to the underpayment of estimated tax by corporations and the election to use the annualized income or adjusted seasonal installment method;

(22) the heading of subchapter D of chapter 67 relating to capitalization of the second word "requirements";

(23) Code Sec. 6724(d)(1)(B) and Act Sec. 6010(o)(4)(C) of the Internal Revenue Service Restructuring and Reform Act of 1998 relating to the definition of an information return for purposes of fuels taxes, elective recognition of gain or loss, and certain life insurance and annuity contracts;

(24) Code Sec. 7421(a) relating to the prohibition against maintaining suits to restrain assessment or collection of tax;

(25) Code Sec. 7430(c)(3) relating to the awarding of attorneys' fees in administrative or court proceedings in connection with taxes;

(26) Code Sec. 7603(b)(2) relating to service of summons for the production of books and records from third-party recordkeepers;

(27) Code Sec. 7802(b)(2)(B)(ii) relating to the term of Internal Revenue Service Oversight Board members;

(28) Code Sec. 7811(a)(3) relating to taxpayer assistance orders;

(29) Code Sec. 7811(d)(1) relating to the suspension of the running of any period of limitation while application for a taxpayer assistance order is pending or during any period specified in the order; and

(30) Code Sec. 7872(f)(3) relating to below-market interest rate loans where the foregoing of interest is in the nature of a gift.

★ *Effective date.* No specific effective date is provided by the Act. These provisions are, therefore, considered effective on December 21, 2000, the date of enactment.

INDEX

References are to explanation paragraph (¶) numbers.